D1551665

# LANDMARK CASES IN CRIMINAL LAW

Criminal cases raise difficult normative and legal questions, and are often a consequence of compelling human drama. In this collection, expert authors place leading cases in criminal law in their historical and legal contexts, highlighting their significance both in the past and for the present.

The cases in this volume range from the fifteenth to the twenty-first century. Many of them are well known to modern criminal lawyers and students; others are overlooked landmarks that deserve reconsideration. The essays, often based on extensive and original archival research, range over a wide spectrum of criminal law, covering procedure and doctrine, statute and common law, individual offences and general principles. Together, the essays explore common themes, including the scope of criminal law and criminalisation, the role of the jury, and the causes of change in criminal law.

# Landmark Cases in Criminal Law

Edited by
Philip Handler, Henry Mares and Ian Williams

·HART·
OXFORD · LONDON · NEW YORK · NEW DELHI · SYDNEY

HART PUBLISHING
Bloomsbury Publishing Plc
Kemp House, Chawley Park, Cumnor Hill, Oxford, OX2 9PH, UK

HART PUBLISHING, the Hart/Stag logo, BLOOMSBURY and the Diana logo are
trademarks of Bloomsbury Publishing Plc

First published in hardback, 2017
Paperback edition, 2019

A catalogue record for this book is available from the British Library.

Library of Congress Cataloging-in-Publication data

Names: Handler, Phil (Philip), editor. | Mares, Henry, editor. |
Williams, Ian (Lecturer in law), editor.
Title: Landmark cases in criminal law / edited by Philip Handler, Henry Mares, and Ian Williams.
Description: Oxford [UK] ; Portland, Oregon : Hart Publishing, 2017. | Series: Landmark
cases series | Includes bibliographical references and index.
Identifiers: LCCN 2016057785 (print) | LCCN 2016058884 (ebook) | ISBN 9781849466899
(hardback ) | ISBN 9781509909315 (Epub)
Subjects: LCSH: Criminal law—Great Britain—Cases.
Classification: LCC KD7869 .L36 2017 (print) | LCC KD7869 (ebook) | DDC 345.42—dc23
LC record available at https://lccn.loc.gov/2016057785

ISBN: HB: 978-1-84946-689-9
PB: 978-1-50993-215-3
ePDF: 978-1-50990-932-2
ePub: 978-1-50990-931-5

Typeset by Compuscript Ltd, Shannon

# Acknowledgements

Writing a volume such as this invariably causes debts to accrue. Happily a very welcome grant from the Cambridge Humanities Research Grants Scheme ensured that these debts were moral, not financial. We are extremely grateful to the Scheme for its support of the workshop at which the contributors to the volume were able to discuss their works in progress, and the fruits of those discussions are evident to the editors in many of the chapters. The Faculty of Law at the University of Cambridge was a helpful and supportive host for the workshop. Naturally we wish to thank Richard Hart and the staff at Hart Publishing who have assisted the production of this volume, Bill Asquith, Tom Adams, Anne Flegel, Jon Lloyd, Annie Mirza, Emma Platt and Rachel Turner, and our helpful research assistant, Christopher Sargeant. We are grateful to the contributors to the volume, especially for the good grace with which they have borne our editorial communications.

# Contents

# Notes on Contributors

**Sir John Baker** QC, LLB, PhD (London); LLD (Cambridge), FBA is Downing Professor Emeritus of the Laws of England, University of Cambridge. He is the author of *An Introduction to English Legal History* (4th ed, 2002, Butterworths) and his three volume *Collected Papers on English Legal History* was published in 2013 by Cambridge University Press.

**Kevin Crosby** LLB, LLM, PhD is a Lecturer in Law, Newcastle University. He has a particular interest in the history of the criminal justice system.

**Matthew Dyson** MA, PhD (Cantab) is an Associate Professor at the Faculty of Law, University of Oxford and Tutorial Fellow at Corpus Christi College, Oxford. He was previously a Fellow of Trinity College, Cambridge. He researches in both private and criminal law, with a particular interest in the relationship between tort and crime. He is the editor of *Comparing Tort and Crime* (2015, Cambridge University Press).

**Lindsay Farmer** LLB (Hons), MPhil in Criminology, PhD is Professor of Law, University of Glasgow. He is the author of various books, most recently *Making the Modern Criminal Law: Criminalization and Civil Order* (2016, Oxford University Press).

**Philip Handler** LLB, PhD is a Senior Lecturer in the School of Law at the University of Manchester. His research focuses on the history of criminal law.

**Jonathan Herring** is a fellow in law at Exeter College, Oxford University and Professor of Law at the Law Faculty, Oxford University. He has written on family law, medical law, criminal law and legal issues surrounding old age and care. His books including: *Vulnerable Adults and the Law* (2016, Oxford University Press); *Caring and the Law* (2013, Hart); *Altruism, Welfare and the Law* (2015, Springer) (with Charles Foster); *Medical Law and Ethics* (6th ed, 2016, Oxford University Press); *Criminal Law* (7th ed, 2016, Oxford University Press); and *Great Debates in Criminal Law* (3rd ed, 2015, Palgrave Macmillan).

**Jeremy Horder** LLD, FBA, is a Professor of Criminal Law at the London School of Economics, where he is Head of Department. He is a Fellow of the British Academy and an Honorary Bencher of the Middle Temple. He was formerly Porjes Foundation Fellow and Tutor at Worcester College, Oxford, and Edmund Davies Professor of Criminal Law, King's College London.

**David Ibbetson** MA, PhD (Cantab) is Regius Professor of Civil Law, University of Cambridge and President of Clare Hall, Cambridge. He has published widely on Roman law, English legal history and comparative legal history, most recently co-authoring *European Legal Development: The Case of Tort* (2012, Cambridge University Press)—with John Bell.

**Arlie Loughnan** BA (Hons 1) (USyd), LLB (Hons 1) (USyd), LLM (NYU), PhD (Lond) is Associate Professor and Australian Research Council (ARC) Postdoctoral Fellow in the Faculty of Law, University of Sydney. Her research interests include criminal responsibility, the interaction of expert medical and legal knowledges, and the historical development of criminal law. She is the author of *Manifest Madness: Mental Incapacity in Criminal Law* (2012, Oxford University Press).

**Henry Mares** MSc (Sydney); LLB (ANU); LLM (Cambridge) is a Fellow of Sidney Sussex College, Cambridge.

**J R Spencer** QC (Hon), LLD (Cantab) is Professor Emeritus, University of Cambridge, a Bye Fellow of Murray Edwards College and a Life Fellow, Selwyn College. His most recent book is *Hearsay Evidence in Criminal Proceedings* (2nd ed, 2014, Hart).

**Findlay Stark** LLB (Hons), LLM (Aberd), PhD (Edin) is University Lecturer in Criminal Law, Faculty of Law, University of Cambridge and Fellow, Jesus College, Cambridge. He is the Deputy Director of the Cambridge Centre for Criminal Justice.

**Simon Stern** is Associate Professor of Law and English at the University of Toronto. His recent publications include articles and book chapters on various aspects of Anglo-American legal history in the eighteenth and nineteenth centuries. He has also edited the second volume of Blackstone's *Commentaries* for the Oxford Edition of Blackstone.

**Ian Williams** MA, LLM, PhD (Cantab) is a Senior Lecturer in the Faculty of Laws, University College London. He has a particular interest in English legal history.

**Rebecca Williams** is an Associate Professor at Pembroke College and in the Faculty of Law, University of Oxford, where she teaches Criminal Law and Administrative Law. She did her undergraduate degree and BCL at Worcester College, Oxford, before completing a PhD at the University of Birmingham, later published as *Unjust Enrichment and Public Law* (2010, Hart).

# 1

# *Landmark Cases and Wider Themes in Criminal Law*

PHILIP HANDLER, HENRY MARES AND IAN WILLIAMS

MAKING THE SELECTION for a volume of landmark cases in criminal law was not an easy task. Many of the cases in this volume will be familiar to modern students of criminal law, but continuing presence in syllabi does not itself identify a case as a landmark. We suspect that many of our students would agree that selecting landmark cases on the basis that students are expected to know of a case would also hardly narrow the field.

Some cases in the volume are landmarks in the sense that they have changed the landscape of criminal law in some way. As Matthew Dyson observes in his chapter on *Hancock and Shankland*, for example, whatever the case's individual importance, it was an essential part of the process of developing the current law of intention. Rebecca Williams's chapter on *Flattery* identifies the case as a landmark in two ways: both as a signpost to current challenges and as a floodgate, the opening of which had the potential to overwhelm law and practice.

Several of the cases in the volume are landmarks at the start of journeys in the criminal law. Ian Williams identifies *The Carrier's Case* as the fifteenth-century beginning of a process of confusion in the law of larceny. That process ultimately led to calls for reform from the nineteenth century and culminated in statutory reforms to the law of theft in various parts of the common law world in the second half of the twentieth century. *Saunders and Archer*, a case well known for its poignant and unusual facts, is identified by John Baker as of particular significance in being the first detailed and thorough criminal law report, an essential step for the development of the common law of crime.

The *Landmark Cases* series focuses on placing important cases into context, seeking to understand why they were, or became, landmarks in their field. This has led to many chapters using untouched sources in investigating their cases, ranging from governmental and judicial archives through to contemporary newspapers and personal correspondence. Such sources lead to a richer understanding of the cases and decisions.

All of the cases in this volume have affected the development of criminal law, for better or worse, even if the cases themselves are no longer good law, at least in England and Wales. We aimed to include cases where a contextual understanding illuminates the case in new ways or provides perspective on the law more generally.[1] As a consequence, many of the chapters are historical, focusing on understanding a particular case in its particular context. But other chapters use their investigation of particular landmarks as gateways to the consideration of current issues in criminal law. Jonathan Herring's chapter on *Brown*, for example, suggests that the particular context of that case has shaped (and perhaps even distorted) subsequent discussion of the role of consent in criminal law.

The historical approach adopted here benefits from a certain timelessness in the problems addressed by the criminal law. This volume features the oldest case yet included in one of the *Landmark Cases* volumes, *The Carrier's Case* from 1473. One case considered for the volume, but ultimately not included, is even older.[2] The sixteenth-century Inns of Court used Roman-derived material in discussions of causation in criminal law, an issue considered in this volume in the twentieth-century case of *Jordan*.[3] Issues, even fact patterns, do recur over long temporal spans. Jeremy Horder, in his discussion of *Bembridge* and the exploitation of public office for private gain in the eighteenth century, draws parallels with controversies earlier this century concerning Members of Parliament. In his wide-ranging discussion of late medieval and early modern English criminal law learning, Baker identifies a hypothetical discussion in the early sixteenth century: if one person asks another to shoot him in order to test whether recently purchased armour is effective, and the test makes it fatally apparent that the armour is not, is this criminal? Just such facts were tried, seemingly for the first time, in 2015.[4] The technology involved has changed, but human nature, it seems, has not.

Some issues may in fact become more significant over time. Kevin Crosby's discussion of *The Dean of St Asaph's Case* is concerned with justifications

---

[1] One case excluded from this volume on this basis is *R v Dudley and Stephens* (1884) 14 QBD 273 (QB). The editors took the view that it was highly unlikely that Brian Simpson's masterful elaborations of the case and its context would be improved upon (AWB Simpson, *Cannibalism and the Common Law* (Chicago, University of Chicago Press, 1984)).

[2] *Sir Hugh's Case* (1293–94) on the long-standing common law rule that defendants had no right to counsel in felony cases. The case, and its aftermath, is discussed by TP Gallanis, 'Making Sense of Blackstone's Puzzle: Why Forbid Defence Counsel?' (2010) 53 *Studies in Law, Politics, and Society* 35.

[3] J Baker, 'Roman Law at the Third University of England' in J Baker, *Collected Papers on English Legal History*, vol 1 (Cambridge, Cambridge University Press, 2013) 369 fn 10.

[4] J Baker, '*Saunders and Archer* (1573)' in this volume, nn 19–20.

for, and understanding of, jury trial. As Crosby notes, these issues are once again important. In fact, they may be more significant than ever, in an age when it is possible that a European court might question whether such untrained lay people can ensure that defendants are provided with a fair trial. The endorsements and justifications for jury trial which appeared in the eighteenth century would serve well today in explaining how jury trial is not simply the exercise of power unrestrained by law.

It is apparent from many of the chapters, however, that while issues may have a timelessness to them, individual cases clearly do not. Cases may be shaped by the surrounding historical context, whether factual or legal. The appeal in *Jordan*, for example, can be linked to wider issues about expert evidence in English law at the time, as well as the status of the defendant as an African-American serviceman based in the UK. In *Beard*, the court's discussion of insanity, intoxication and criminal responsibility was intertwined with wider public concerns at the time: the plight of recently demobilised servicemen following the end of the First World War and the dangers of alcohol. It is these chapters which identify a particular niche that the *Landmark Cases* series fills; as David Ibbetson observes at the end of his discussion of *Jordan*, 'understanding of law as a dynamic system ... requires that we see individual cases in terms of the interrelationship between formal law and context'.[5] Such a focus on a wider context informs Herring's discussion, and reappraisal, of consent and *Brown*.

## I. WIDER THEMES

During the workshop preceding the volume, the editors were trying to identify shared issues and features across the cases in the volume, several of which are highlighted below. But one of the pleasures of editing this collection has been the welcome surprises the process has generated. Two features which were unexpectedly prominent in the papers presented were the popular awareness of many of these cases at the time they were decided and the political context of many of them.

## A. Popular Interest

Popular interest in crime and trials is to be expected. Press coverage of the salacious facts of *Lemon* and *Brown* cases fits into this mould, but

---

[5] D Ibbetson, '*R v Jordan* (1956)' in this volume, n 120.

press interest was not simply directed towards sex and violence. *Jordan* even featured in the international media and American political discourse, with concerns raised about the capital trial of an American serviceman by a foreign court. *M'Naghten's Case* went even further. While popular interest in the murder of the Prime Minister's Private Secretary by a man who believed himself to be persecuted by the Tories would be expected, what was more surprising was the nature of the public discussion. Rather than simply lurid headlines, Arlie Loughnan shows that the case generated considerable public debate and disquiet in both national and local newspapers about the wider issues of law and psychiatry which the case posed.

## B.  Political Context

Other cases feature underlying political contexts. *Hancock and Shankland* arose in the highly charged atmosphere of the miners' strike. It is only because the Crown rejected a plea of manslaughter and insisted upon a charge of murder for the activities of the miners that the question of intention in murder reached the House of Lords at all. Horder's discussion of *Bembridge* similarly occurs against a backdrop of politics. Modern readers will probably be unsurprised by the decision that Bembridge's actions were criminal, but it appears that Bembridge certainly was. It was only in a changed political context in which corruption and venality were unacceptable (at least when practised by the 'other side') that Bembridge would be prosecuted.

In most of these cases there is no direct evidence that the political context led to appeals or the development of the law directly.[6] However, there are hints (for example, in *Jordan*) that the political context may have been relevant.

## C.  Criminal Law as Constitutional Law

A thread running through several of the cases in this volume is the judicial role, both from the perspective of the separation of powers and the rule of

---

[6] *Bembridge* is an obvious exception and *M'Naghten's Case* may be too. As Loughnan observes in her chapter (A Loughnan, '*M'Naghten's Case* (1843)' in this volume, nn 77–79), the public disquiet about the decision led to the debate in the House of Lords in which the judges stated the law of insanity.

law. *M'Naghten* is a peculiar example of something very close to 'judicial legislation', such that Loughnan suggests it may not be possible to alter the *M'Naghten Rules* simply through a judicial decision.[7] By contrast, in *Hancock and Shankland*, the House of Lords appeared reluctant to engage in something close to rule-making, declining to provide a model direction for the question of intention.

Two other cases in the volume, *Shaw* and *Lemon*, were concerned with the question of how far judges ought to create or expand common law criminal offences. Both cases take a generous approach to common law crimes, an approach which, as John Spencer notes, has more recently been rejected in *Rimmington and Goldstein*.[8] To some extent, this change for offences was prefigured in relation to defences in *Howe*, where the judges were unwilling to change the law of duress. Findlay Stark argues in his chapter that this constitutional aspect to *Howe* should be given much greater prominence in the current understanding of the case. While other arguments for the conclusion reached in *Howe* are questionable, the constitutional argument is intellectually robust. If *Howe* is placed together with *Shaw*, *Lemon* and *Rimmington*, this position becomes even stronger—*Howe* occurred between *Lemon* and *Rimmington*, and may help pinpoint the time at which judicial attitudes were changing.

## D. The Role of Individual Judges

When considering the judicial role, a natural question is the role of individual judges. Lord Templeman's remarks in *Brown* have become notorious, but Spencer also suggests that Lord Scarman's views about the desirability of an offence of blasphemy in the *Lemon* case were informed by Scarman's beliefs about the role of law in a racially and religiously pluralist society, views perhaps informed by his extra-judicial experiences. However, a focus on individual judges' attitudes should not be pushed too far. The 'heroism argument' in *Howe* that duress should not be a defence to murder because people should heroically resist threats to themselves or others does not seem to have been particularly informed by judges' own experiences. As Stark observes, Lord Hailsham accepted the heroism argument following his own experiences in the Second World War. However, Lord Brandon (whose own

---

[7] Loughnan, '*M'Naghten's Case*' nn 122–25.
[8] *R v Rimmington and Goldstein* [2005] UKHL 63, [2006] 1 AC 459.

wartime activities led to the award of the Military Cross) rejected the heroism argument.

## E. The Relationship between Legal Scholarship and Legal Practice

Several of the chapters in this volume consider the links between legal scholarship and legal practice. The usual assumption is that legal scholars comment upon what judges have decided, with practice in this sense driving scholarship. Such a position is evident in some chapters. For example, scholarly consideration of causation seems to have been spurred by *Jordan* rather than influencing the case.

Other chapters point in the opposite direction. Ian Williams's examination of *The Carrier's Case* argues for influence from the civil law tradition, probably from the book known as *Bracton*, in developing the law of larceny in the late fifteenth century and through the early modern period. Simon Stern draws out that the decision in *Jones* was influential principally through the interpretation of it in William Hawkins's *Treatise of the Pleas of the Crown*. More recently, Dyson places the decision in *Hancock and Shankland* into a larger process of development of principles of mens rea, one in which judges and legal scholars interacted. In relation to *Morgan*, Lindsay Farmer describes this as a 'kind of extended dialogue'. The concern of judges for the opinion of the jurists is also evident in the discussions of *Shaw* and *Morgan* by Henry Mares and Farmer. Both cases engaged with contemporary scholarly concerns, while the House of Lords in *Morgan* was clearly concerned about academic criticisms of its activities in criminal law.

Such interaction was not always the same as cooperation. As Spencer observes of the *Lemon* decision, an important fault line between the majority and dissenting members of the House of Lords related to the acceptability of strict liability in the criminal law. While the widely accepted academic view was that criminal liability required mens rea, that view was not held by at least three members of the House of Lords. Tellingly, but perhaps in a stereotypically British anti-intellectualism, Lord Russell described this rejection of mens rea simply as 'sense'. It is interesting to observe the difference between this attitude and that visible in *Morgan*, in which Lord Fraser took the need for mens rea as axiomatic, at least for most offences. The cases occurred within a few years of one another, but in *Morgan* the House of Lords was concerned about academic views, while in *Lemon* the House was dismissive.

Finally, in an academic world in which one is increasingly expected to demonstrate the fairly short-term 'impact' of one's work, it is notable that legal scholarship did not always have rapid effects. Sometimes it did, as in Hawkins's discussion of *Jones*, but *Bracton* was written around two centuries before *The Carrier's Case*, and the interaction between scholars and judges visible in *Morgan* and *Hancock and Shankland* related to views about criminal law shaped by scholarship over the course of decades.

# 2

# *The Carrier's Case* (1473)

IAN WILLIAMS[*]

T
HE CARRIER'S CASE[1] remains an authority in certain parts of
the common law world, the oldest authority cited in a recent work
on Anglo-American theft law.[2] James Fitzjames Stephen described
the case as 'the most curious case relating to theft' in medieval law.[3] It
remains, in the words of one writer, an 'enigma', indeed the first enigma, in
the common law of larceny.[4]

The medieval law of larceny was a criminal law counterpart to trespass
to goods. Like its private law counterpart, it required a trespassory taking of possession of a chattel. For the taking to be trespassory, it had to
be performed with force and arms, which necessarily meant that the taker
obtained possession without the consent of the prior holder.[5] This position was clear in the late twelfth century in the book known as *Glanvill*.[6]
In private law, the limitations on trespass to goods were remedied by the
availability of the action of detinue. For larceny, non-trespassory takings of
possession were simply not criminal.[7]

---

[*] My thanks to John Baker, Guido Rossi and David Seipp for advice and assistance in the
research for this chapter. The year is taken as beginning in January.
  [1] *The Carrier's Case; Anon v Sheriff of London* (1473) YB Pasch 13 Edw IV, fo 9, pl 5;
SS vol 64, 30–34. Citations will be taken from the Selden Society report, based on British
Library Additional MS 37493, a manuscript associated with the early sixteenth-century lawyer
Robert Chaloner. This report contains more detail than the vulgate Yearbook report.
  [2] S Green, *Thirteen Ways to Steal a Bicycle: Theft Law in the Information Age* (Cambridge
MA, Harvard University Press, 2012) 11. New South Wales, for example, retains the common
law of larceny, while several states in the US have not adopted the Model Penal Code and retain
a law of larceny which is at least partly common law.
  [3] J Fitzjames Stephen, *A History of the Criminal Law of England*, vol 3 (London, Macmillan
& Co, 1883) 139.
  [4] GP Fletcher, 'The Metamorphosis of Larceny' (1975–76) 89 *Harvard Law Review* 469,
481.
  [5] In practice, 'force and arms' seems to have been a very low threshold; see DJ Ibbetson,
*A Historical Introduction to the Law of Obligations* (Oxford, Oxford University Press, 1999) 41.
  [6] GDG Hall (ed), *The Treatise on the Laws and Customs of the Realm of England
Commonly Called Glanvill* (London, Thomas Nelson and Sons, 1965) 128.
  [7] See JH Baker, *Introduction to English Legal History*, 4th edn (London, Butterworths
LexisNexis, 2002) 533–34.

*The Carrier's Case* is the first known case in which the limitations of larceny were an issue, a mere three centuries after the writing of *Glanvill*. It was well established in medieval law that if a person obtained possession of goods from the owner lawfully, but subsequently took those goods for himself, this could not be larceny. As *Glanvill* notes, 'Clearly he is not guilty of theft, because he initially had possession from the owner',[8] a position echoed into the fifteenth century.[9] In 1473, this changed. A bailee of a package, who had legitimately obtained possession of it from the owner, opened the package and removed the contents, taking them for himself. The judges held that this amounted to larceny, departing from the well-established common law rule.

The extension of larceny in *The Carrier's Case* was the start of a very long trend: the attempt to use larceny as a wider theft offence. This trend continued into the 1950s, but was subject to considerable criticism from the nineteenth century onwards.[10] *The Carrier's Case* was consequently one of the cases on which reformers focused their attention when advocating reform of the law of theft away from the technicalities and distinctions of the law of larceny.[11] From that perspective, *The Carrier's Case* was the first landmark on the journey to the Canadian Criminal Code, the Theft Act 1968 and the US Model Penal Code.

*The Carrier's Case* was clearly important. It was the first of a series of cases and debates in the late medieval and early modern periods 'related to the concept of theft' itself.[12] Did English law criminalise only physical violations of possession or a wider range of interferences with property? After the decision, we see the courts grappling with other arguable exceptions to the basic law of larceny, such as servants entrusted with goods.[13] The case itself was frequently cited, although for some writers, the report of *The Carrier's Case* was useful as much for the discussions it contained as the decision itself.[14]

But *The Carrier's Case* itself remains problematic. Fitzjames Stephen described the reasoning as an 'obscure distinction resting on no definite principle'.[15] For George Fletcher in the 1970s, it remained an 'enigma'. But the legal enigma is wrapped in factual mystery and itself conceals a riddle.

---

[8] Hall, *Glanvill* 128.
[9] eg (1429) YB Trin 7 Hen VI, fo 42, pl 8.
[10] JE Hall Williams, 'Reform of the Law of Larceny: An Urgent Task' (1958) 21 *MLR* 43, 44, referring to *Russell v Smith* [1957] 3 WLR 515 (QB).
[11] Green, *Thirteen Ways* 16–18, noting 'breaking bulk' from *The Carrier's Case* as a particular issue at 17.
[12] JH Baker, *The Oxford History of the Laws of England, vol VI, 1483–1558* (Oxford, Oxford University Press, 2003) (hereinafter *OHLE*) 566–67.
[13] ibid 566–70.
[14] The case is cited in seven of the eight paragraphs discussing various circumstances in which larceny can be committed by F Pulton, *De Pace Regis et Regni* (London, Companie of Stationers, 1609) fos 129–32.
[15] Stephen, *History* 140.

## I. THE MYSTERY: THE FACTS

Like many medieval cases, the facts outlined in the reports of the case are sparse. A carrier agreed to carry a bale of woad to Southampton for a foreign merchant. The carrier took the bale elsewhere and opened it, taking the woad. That woad was ultimately seized by the Sheriff of London as 'waif'. Waif was goods which had been stolen, but were abandoned by the thief, and could then be seized for the Crown.[16] Woad was essential to the English wool and cloth industries, a valuable product second in value only to wine in the imports to Southampton,[17] and one which sometimes constituted almost the entire cargo of ships.[18] The merchant, unsurprisingly, sought to have this property restored.

That summary leaves plenty of gaps, and reconstructing the case is difficult due to an absence of evidence. First, it is not clear how the case came into being. No records of the London sheriffs survive from the relevant period. The first stage of proceedings reported occurred in the Star Chamber, which in 1473 was not a court distinct from the King's Council.[19] The report in fact describes the case as being 'Before the King's Council in the Star Chamber', probably indicating that the case started not as litigation, but as a petition directly to the monarch that was then referred to the Council.[20] Such a suspicion is corroborated by the brief mention in the report of the lawfulness of proceedings before the Council in relation to the merchandise of aliens.[21] No records survive of any petition. After the initial proceedings in Council sitting in the Star Chamber, a second stage of discussion occurred between the common law judges in the Exchequer Chamber. In the fifteenth century, the Exchequer Chamber was simply a venue for informal discussions between the judges rather than the statutory court it

[16] J Rastell, *An exposition of certaine difficult and obscure words, and termes of the lawes of this realme* (London, Richard Tottel, 1579) fos 195–96.
[17] S Thrupp, 'The Grocers of London, A Study of Distributive Trade' in E Power and MM Postan (eds), *Studies in English Trade in the Fifteenth Century* (London, George Routledge & Sons, 1933) 290.
[18] A Ruddock, *Italian Merchants and Shipping in Southampton, 1270–1600* (Southampton, University College, 1951) 214, referring to a Genoese carrack which arrived in December 1470.
[19] Baker, *Introduction* 118.
[20] *The Carrier's Case* (n 1) 30.
[21] ibid 32. There are hints in the report that the Lord Chancellor, Robert Stillington, the Bishop of Bath and Wells, regarded the case as a Chancery one (ibid 32), perhaps associated with his promotion of Chancery as a court for merchants (M Beilby, 'The Profits of Expertise: The Rise of the Civil Lawyers and Chancery Equity' in M Hicks (ed), *Profit, Piety and the Professions in Later Medieval England* (Gloucester, Alan Sutton, 1990) 78–83). There is no bill surviving in the relevant Chancery records (the C1 files), although these records are not entirely reliable for the early 1470s (P Tucker, 'The Early History of the Court of Chancery: A Comparative Study' (2000) 115 *English Historical Review* 791, 798). The discussion of the lawfulness of proceedings in the Council is the best evidence that the case was seen not as one for a distinct Court of Chancery, but for the Council more generally.

subsequently became.[22] Consequently, the latter stage of the case left no trace in the records of the common law courts.

John Scurlock seems to have assumed that the carrier in the case was a 'sea captain'.[23] None of the reports make this clear, but it is highly probable. Woad was imported to Southampton from the Mediterranean, evidently by ship, and then circulated around the country either by coastal vessels or by road.[24] English woad production was virtually non-existent until the late sixteenth century, so any carriage of woad to Southampton, as the reports describe, would have been from overseas. The carrier being a ship's captain raises some interesting speculation about why the woad was not delivered in Southampton as agreed, but was found in London. Did the ship put in at an alternative port or was the relevant bale simply not offloaded in South-ampton as it should have been? The latter seems more likely, simply as I have found nothing to suggest that an entire ship and its cargo went miss-ing. The case was, in other words, one of barratry: fraud by the master of the ship.[25] Such fraudulent activity was not unknown in the affairs of Italian merchants in Southampton. A Venetian notary recorded an investigation into such fraud in 1472, in a case in which the entire cargo of a Venetian vessel was unloaded contrary to the ship's charter party.[26]

The merchant who sought restitution of his goods was probably the intended recipient of the woad rather than the original shipper. The report refers to the merchant as an alien who has 'come here under a safe conduct', indicating that he was present in England.[27] It was not usual for export-ers to England to accompany their goods. Surviving fifteenth-century mate-rial shows that London importers of woad via Southampton authorised a local agent to collect the goods and then handle the local arrangements and onward travel to the final destination in England.[28]

The woad probably arrived in England on a vessel managed by Geno-ese merchants,[29] who imported large quantities of woad via Southampton.

[22] Baker, *Introduction* 140.

[23] J Scurlock, 'The Element of Trespass in Larceny at Common Law' (1948–49) 22 *Temple Law Quarterly* 12, 15.

[24] An example of the use of coastal vessels is in Ruddock, *Italian Merchants* 103. The Over-land Trade Project at the University of Winchester has produced an excellent resource for the export of commodities from Southampton by land: see www.overlandtrade.org.

[25] For an early example of the language of barratry, which refers to the idea of breaking bulk, see G Malynes, *Consuetudo, vel Lex Mercatoria, or the Ancient Law-Merchant* (London, Adam Islip, 1622) 155.

[26] Ruddock, *Italian Merchants* 113.

[27] *The Carrier's Case* (n 1) 32.

[28] Ruddock, *Italian Merchants* 103.

[29] The ships themselves were not necessarily Genoese. London records show goods being imported and exported in the names of Genoese merchants on ships from Spain and Portu-gal (HS Cobb (ed), *The Overseas Trade of London: Exchequer Customs Accounts*, London Record Society 27 (London, London Record Society, 1990) xli–xlii). Florentine merchants also imported woad to England, but the Florentine fleet to England in 1472–73 did not have any woad on board (ME Mallett, 'Anglo-Florentine Commercial Relations 1465–91' (1962) 15 *Economic History Review (NS)* 250, 256).

In 1460 alone, the Genoese imported over 1,100 bales and more than 15,000 balets of woad into Southampton, while in 1470, a single Genoese carrack arrived carrying 5,721 balets.[30] Southampton also had a Genoese population, who acted as agents for the larger community in London.[31] That London colony was under consular control, a Genoese government official who adjudicated disputes between members of the Genoese community and also acted as a spokesman and representative of the Genoese in their dealings with the English authorities.[32] It may have been easier for an aggrieved merchant to petition the king through such a figure than as an individual. It seems likely that the merchant in *The Carrier's Case* was a Genoese merchant in London.

The mercantile transaction here would have been problematic for the common law courts. The carrier would have entered into a contract with the woad exporter to ship his goods and the exporter would have entered into a separate arrangement with the merchant in London to transfer title to the woad. An agent of the London merchant would then have been authorised to collect the woad in Southampton.

The carrier therefore had no contractual relationship with the merchant claiming the woad in England. The carriage contract would have been made overseas. Any contract between the exporting and importing merchants was also probably not made in England. Any contract made overseas would have been, at best, a matter for the Admiralty, not the common law courts.[33] The absence of a contractual relationship between the merchant claiming the goods and the carrier would also prevent the merchant bringing contractual claims for the carrier's actions. Such an absence of contractual remedies may well be important in explaining the decision in the case.

## II. THE RIDDLE: WHY DECIDE THE CASE IN THIS WAY?

Difficulties in identifying a clear legal basis for the finding of felony in *The Carrier's Case* have led writers to suggest that the decision was ultimately one of policy. Plucknett attributed the decision in *The Carrier's Case* to it being 'politically expedient to punish the carrier for larceny', despite the prosecution of the carrier not being in issue in the case.[34] Fitzjames Stephen

---

[30] Ruddock, *Italian Merchants* 81–82 and 214.

[31] ibid 103 and 214.

[32] ibid 133.

[33] The fifteenth-century history of the Admiralty remains obscure and there are very limited records (MJ Prichard and DEC Yale, *Hale and Fleetwood on Admiralty Jurisdiction*, Selden Society 103 (London, Selden Society, 1993) xxxiii). It is not clear whether the Admiralty did exercise jurisdiction over such contracts in the 1470s.

[34] TFT Plucknett, *A Concise History of the Common Law*, 5th edn (London, Butterworths, 1956) 449.

linked the finding of felony with a policy objective of favouring merchants.[35] As Fletcher observed, such arguments fail on the simple basis that the finding of felony in *The Carrier's Case* was not in the merchants' favour.[36] By holding that the carrier had committed larceny, the judges justified the sheriff's seizure of the merchant's goods as waif, hardly something merchants would have wanted.

Nevertheless, according to the report, the judges then asserted that 'the goods cannot be claimed as waif'. Because the merchant had been granted safe conduct by the King, the King could not then claim the goods on the basis that one of the King's subjects had breached that safe conduct. This would contradict the King's promise.[37] Had the judges simply wished to protect merchants, the easiest solution would have been to find that there was no felony on the facts, a position which several of them argued strongly during argument. Merchants would have been left with limited private law remedies, but would at least not have risked the seizure of their goods under the royal prerogative. Instead, the judges took a convoluted route to reach a position which had the same effect. Any explanation for the judges' position has to take account of the tortuous course taken to reach the final outcome in the case; not just the finding of felony, but also the immediate amelioration of the consequences of that finding.

Fifteenth-century judges do seem to have regarded the King's safe conduct as legally relevant on several occasions, perhaps explaining its role in the case.[38] A related concern may have arisen from a note at the end of the reports of *The Carrier's Case*, where it is observed that the Sheriff of London who had claimed the woad as waif was also claiming a prescriptive right for London to retain that property for itself rather than on behalf of the King. It was this claim that the judges denied due to the safe conduct granted by the King.[39] Given that the London sheriffs were chosen by senior members of London's commercial community[40] and that anti-Italian violence in the 1450s may have been deliberately orchestrated by London merchants against competitors, it is less surprising to see the claim to waif being blocked.[41] However, it would again have been more direct simply to have denied the existence of the felony.

[35] Stephen, *History* 139.

[36] Fletcher, 'Metamorphosis' 484.

[37] *The Carrier's Case* (n 1) 34. Safe conduct was routinely granted to merchants and was a special guarantee of the King's personal protection of the person and property of merchants. For examples of such grants, see K Kim, *Aliens in Medieval Law: The Origins of Modern Citizenship* (Cambridge, Cambridge University Press, 2000) 25–29.

[38] eg (1486) YB Hil 1 Hen VII, fo 10, pl 10.

[39] *The Carrier's Case* (n 1) 34.

[40] P Tucker, *Law Courts and Lawyers in the City of London, 1300–1550* (Cambridge, Cambridge University Press, 2007) 44.

[41] JL Bolton, 'The City and the Crown, 1456–61' (1986) 12 *London Journal* 11.

A final possibility lies in jurisdictional concerns. It was claimed in the Star Chamber that the case should be heard before the common law courts.[42] The Lord Chancellor's response was clear: a felony had been committed (contrary to the views of some of the judges), but the Chancery could provide some relief from the consequences of that for the victim's property.[43] The Chancellor was not a common lawyer. In fact, Bishop Robert Stillington was a trained civilian, graduating as Doctor of Civil Law (DCL) in June 1443.[44] Stillington's position raised the possibility of a non-common lawyer adjudicating on the commission of common law felonies. The common law courts began to resist such decisions just before *The Carrier's Case*. The common law judges saw the civilian courts as encroaching upon their exclusive jurisdiction and the first known prohibition to the civilian-staffed church courts on this point was issued in 1472.[45] Concern over the non-common law adjudication of common law felonies could explain the finding of felony in *The Carrier's Case*. By showing the Chancellor that they agreed with his view of the facts as amounting to a felony, but then explaining that the sheriff was not entitled to the merchant's goods, the judges may have made it more difficult for the Chancellor to assert a need for intervention by the Chancery.[46]

The Chancellor may still have been able to assert a need for equitable intervention. He raised a traditional justification for merchants proceeding outside the normal legal system: merchants needed speedy justice and could not be expected to know the nuances of the English legal system, using this as a justification for Chancery jurisdiction.[47] Such a concern was an accepted basis for an alternative to common law process.[48] According to the report, the judges in *The Carrier's Case* observed that a foreign merchant should 'sue to the King' in the event of goods being taken as waif, thereby also removing this basis for Chancery jurisdiction.[49]

Nevertheless, this jurisdictional explanation seems unlikely to have been determinative. The problem of jurisdiction would have been obvious in the

---

[42] *The Carrier's Case* (n 1) 32.

[43] ibid 31 and 32.

[44] M Hicks, 'Stillington, Robert' in HCG Matthews and B Harrison (eds), *The Oxford Dictionary of National Biography*, vol 52 (Oxford, Oxford University Press, 2004).

[45] *Tanner v Cornyssh* (1472), an unreported prohibition related to an accusation of theft cited in Baker, *Introduction* 438 fn 15.

[46] Unlike the church courts, it is not clear whether the common law courts had any mechanism easily to restrain the Chancery, a point which became clear in the early seventeenth century, when the common law courts and the Chancery clashed. The common law courts used prohibitions, praemunire and habeas corpus, all with questionable efficacy (JH Baker, 'The Common Lawyers and the Chancery: 1616' in J Baker, *Collected Papers on English Legal History*, vol 1 (Cambridge, Cambridge University Press, 2013)).

[47] *The Carrier's Case* (n 1) 32.

[48] See Kim, *Aliens in Medieval Law* 29–31 and 37–38 for various medieval English examples.

[49] *The Carrier's Case* (n 1) 34.

initial hearing in the Star Chamber, but the majority of the judges were still opposed to the finding of felony at the outset of the Exchequer Chamber proceedings. Had the judges been especially concerned about jurisdiction, they would have been more receptive to treating the case as felony from the outset. The sensible conclusion is that the case was actually decided on the basis of the judges' views of the law.

## III. THE ENIGMA: THE LEGAL BASIS FOR THE DECISION

It is difficult to identify any clear legal basis for the decision in *The Carrier's Case*. Various positions were presented by judges and barristers. The matter is further complicated by the nature of the proceedings in *The Carrier's Case*, which were in two distinct stages. The first was a hearing in the Star Chamber, before the King's Council, where the Lord Chancellor, some judges and even apprentices spoke.[50] The second stage was a set of discussions in the Exchequer Chamber. It was only after this second debate that the judges described the facts as amounting to larceny. This difficulty perhaps explains the analyses of *The Carrier's Case* in the sixteenth and seventeenth-century printed books of the common law. Edward Coke and Matthew Hale, for example, do not even try to explain the outcome of the case at all. They note the facts as amounting to larceny, but, unlike other unusual fact patterns, go no further.[51]

What justifications for finding a felony were presented in *The Carrier's Case*? The most fully developed set of arguments related to the bailee's possession, but another strand stressed the absence of any relevant bailment at all.

### A. Possession and the Bailee

The dominant argument presented in favour of felony was based upon the bailee's possession being either unlawful or having come to an end. This approach was crucially dependent upon the private law rules of bailment and possession, and consequently became somewhat technical.

In the Exchequer Chamber, Nedeham J argued that 'where a man has possession and it is determined, it may be felony'.[52] This position does address the possession issue, but Nedeham never explains whether the possession of the carrier actually was determined at any point. Finally, Nedeham presented

---

[50] Huse was Attorney-General at the time; Molyneux and Vavasour were apprentices.

[51] 3 Co Inst 107; 1 Hale PC 504–5.

[52] *The Carrier's Case* (n 1) 33. Stephen seems to accept the approach of determining the bailment as the ratio of the case (Stephen, *History* 139).

two scenarios in which someone appears to have possession of property, but actually does not, and hence could be convicted of larceny for taking the goods: a tavern patron taking his drinking cup away and a servant taking his owner's goods with which he had been entrusted. Presumably the purpose of these last two examples was to show the effect of an absence of possession in the bailee.

Laken J built upon Nedeham's arguments, distinguishing 'between a bailment of goods and a bargain to take and to carry'.[53] According to Laken, in a mere bailment situation, a bailee obtains possession simply from taking physical control, but in the situation of a bargain to carry, the carrier only obtains lawful possession 'if he takes them to carry ... but if he takes them with other intent than to carry them, so that he does not carry out the purpose, it seems that it shall quite well be said to be felony'. The element of contract in the context of *The Carrier's Case* is made central here. It is only if possession is taken with intention to perform the contract that the possession is lawful possession. If the possession was not lawful, then the carrier would be in the position of a servant or tavern patron as set out by Nedeham—someone with physical control but no possession. Any inappropriate taking of the goods, such as the delivery to somewhere other than specified in *The Carrier's Case*, would then amount to felony.

The same approach had been suggested by the barristers Molyneux and Vavasour in the Star Chamber. Vavasour expressly distinguished between a bailment and a bargain, describing the case here as 'better than a bailment' due to the bargain.[54] Molyneux, perhaps revealing the underlying basis of the arguments of both Nedeham and Laken, argued generally that something 'done lawfully may be said to be felony or trespass according to the intent and the circumstances, to wit, if he who committed the act does not carry out the purpose for which he took the goods'.[55] For Molyneux, this was a general principle which explained the case about tavern patrons and a rule that if a person distrained another's goods (a lawful seizure of goods, typically for rent arrears), but then acted in a manner not authorised in the law of distraint, 'this is now wrong, and yet at the start the taking was good'.[56] As Molyneux put it, once an individual acted unlawfully with the property, 'then everything is wrong'. A subsequent unlawful act rendered the initial taking wrongful *ab initio*. This may explain Nedeham's point about possession being determined. From Molyneux's perspective, once an unlawful act was performed, the bailee's possession came to an end.

For Laken, and perhaps also Nedeham, the crime of larceny in *The Carrier's Case* required analysis of two distinct moments. The first was the taking

---

[53] *The Carrier's Case* (n 1) 33.
[54] ibid 31.
[55] ibid.
[56] ibid.

of physical control—the carrier needed to have the intention not to perform the contract in order for the possession not to be lawful. The second was the time when the carrier actually took the goods for himself. At that point, the carrier would need to satisfy all the requirements for larceny. Molyneux and Vavasour in the Star Chamber were less concerned with this temporal distinction. For Molyneux, later unlawful actions rendered the earlier possession unlawful, while Vavasour explained that the carrier's subsequent taking of the property for himself 'proves that he took them as a felon and with other intent than to carry them'.[57]

This approach also had some support in the subsequent literature. In his *Plees del Coron*, William Staunford observed that if the initial taking of possession is lawful, then a subsequent taking is not felonious, citing *The Carrier's Case*. A little later, Staunford then gives the facts of the case, without citation, observing that in such a situation there is felony, '(tr) because he had more than a bailment, that is a bargain, so that he took them by the bargain, and not by the delivery', taking them by his own wrong.[58] Staunford seems to have taken Laken's position, an approach which was also adopted by Ferdinando Pulton in 1609, although Pulton specified that any 'evil intent' had to arise only after the initial taking of possession.[59]

However, despite the approach focusing on the bailee either never having had possession, or that possession coming to end, being numerically dominant in both the Star Chamber and Exchequer Chamber proceedings, it was not widely accepted. Bryan CJ rejected the distinction between bailment and bargain as 'all one' and stated several times in the proceedings that receiving by bailment precluded the possession subsequently becoming unlawful.[60] In the Star Chamber, Choke J also rejected the idea that a bailee could be said to take possession unlawfully.[61] Furthermore, in the immediate aftermath of *The Carrier's Case*, an anonymous reader in the Inns of Court in the 1470s referred to the case for the proposition that an initially lawful act, such as taking possession, cannot subsequently become unlawful.[62] While not a direct response to Laken's remarks, the view echoes that of Bryan CJ.

---

[57] ibid.

[58] W Staunford, *Les Plees del Coron* (London, Richard Tottel, 1557) fo 25.

[59] Pulton, *De Pace* fos 129–129v. Pulton also provided a further rationale for the decision, based upon the fact that 'the propertie of these goods did always remaine in the first owner', a point taken from Huse AG in the Star Chamber proceedings (*The Carrier's Case* (n 1) 31, on which see below, text at n 76). The use of two different explanations for the case suggests that Pulton was not certain what the ratio was.

[60] *The Carrier's Case* (n 1) 33, 30 and 31.

[61] ibid 31–32. The presence of the bailment must have been decisive for Choke, as he himself made Molyneux's point about distraint in a case the previous year ((1472) YB Pasch 12 Edw IV, fo 8, pl 20).

[62] Cambridge University Library MS Ee.5.22, fo 148. Readings were one of the main forms of education in the medieval and early modern Inns of Court and provide some of the best evidence of sustained doctrinal exposition and discussion for the period, especially for criminal law (JH Baker, 'The Inns of Court and Legal Doctrine' in Baker, *Collected Papers* vol 1, 359–61).

Thomas Marow's widely circulated and influential 1503 reading was more explicit on this point. According to Marow, if a defendant were given someone's goods to look after, '(tr) and he took them as a felon with felonious intent, yet this intent in this case does not make it felony', outright rejecting the views of Molyneux and Vavasour.[63]

## B. No Bailment of the Stolen Goods

The alternative explanation for a finding of felony in *The Carrier's Case* was that presented by Choke J. Choke's approach largely disregarded the nuances of private law, accepting that a bailee cannot be said to take the bailed goods feloniously. Instead, Choke explained in the Star Chamber that the carrier committed felony in this case:

> [F]or here the things which were in the bale were not given to him, but the bales as chose entire were delivered ... in which case if he had given away the bales or sold them, it would not be felony, but when he broke open and took out of it what was inside, he did this without warrant.[64]

The carrier had been given only the bale, and the bailment therefore covered the receptacle. But the felony here was only in relation to the contents, which had not expressly been bailed to the carrier. Such a position was adopted by William Lambarde in his handbook for Justices of the Peace, *Eirenarcha*, in 1581. Lambarde, referring both to woad and an example of a barrel of wine which Choke had used, notes that 'it may be saide, that neyther the verie Woad, nor the Wine were delivered hym in that kinde'.[65]

Choke's position has the advantage of simplicity and consequently concision. The position taken by Nedeham and Laken required a criminal trial judge to explain the nuances of the law of possession to a jury. Choke's approach more or less removed any need for such explanations to be presented to the jury, while still respecting the rules of private law. As all the judges were potentially criminal trial judges in the assize system, and consequently might need to explain possession to the jury, given the brevity of criminal trials, those were considerable benefits.[66] However, while this

---

[63] BH Putnam, *Early Treatises on the Practice of the Justices of the Peace in the Fifteenth and Sixteenth Centuries* (New York, Octagon Books, 1974) 375. For subsequent references to Marow's reading, see JH Baker, *Readers and Readings in the Inns of Court and Chancery*, Selden Society Supplementary Series 13 (London, Selden Society, 2000) 73; and Putnam, *Early Treatises* 209–20.

[64] *The Carrier's Case* (n 1) 32.

[65] W Lambarde, *Eirenarcha* (London, Richard Tottel, 1581) 225–26.

[66] It has been estimated that trials at the assizes typically lasted no more than 30 minutes in the late sixteenth and seventeenth centuries (JS Cockburn, *Calendar of Assize Records: Home Circuit Indictments Elizabeth I and James I, Introduction* (London, HMSO, 1985) 110), although Cockburn notes that the assize system came under considerable pressure in the Elizabethan period, so medieval trials may have been longer.

explains the attractions of Choke's position, it does not in itself explain why Choke considered there to be a felony at all. Bryan CJ's position similarly avoided this problem simply by denying any possibility of a felony, thereby keeping the case from any jury.


## C. The Enigma

None of the arguments presented in the case come close to being identified as being decisive for the majority of the judges. There is also what appears to be a textual difficulty with the surviving reports of the debate in the Exchequer Chamber and its aftermath, just at the point which appears to be decisive in the discussion. The report begins with an acknowledgement that 'all except Nedeham held that where goods are given to a man he cannot take them feloniously'. There are then speeches by Nedeham J and Laken J which seem to support a finding a felony on the facts, before Bryan CJ distinguishes Laken's argument and reaffirms his consistently held position that there must be a felonious taking of possession, which was not so on the facts. This is followed by the word 'vide' and a mention of a case described as from 1311 or 1312, but whose facts match those of *Rattlesdene v Grunestone* from 1317.[67] This case concerned a sale of a barrel of wine, where the vendor retained possession of the barrel after the sale. The vendor was subsequently sued for trespass to goods, for breaking open the barrel, taking out part of the wine and replacing it with water.[68] It is noted in *The Carrier's Case* that 'because' the vendor had possession of the barrel, the claim was challenged, but the writ was held to be good. This case seems to contradict the position taken by Bryan CJ.[69] After this, the report states that 'then the justices made report to the Chancellor that it was felony', with no further explanation.

The reference to *Rattlesdene v Grunestone* appears decisive. This case shows that someone in lawful possession could commit trespass to goods, overcoming the key difficulty in *The Carrier's Case*, and the report then shows the judges deciding that the facts of that case amounted to felony. The difficulty lies in the role that *Rattlesdene v Grunestone* actually played in the judges' decision. Given that *Rattlesdene* contradicted the point which Bryan CJ had just been making, and had consistently made throughout the proceedings in *The Carrier's Case*, it seems improbable that Bryan himself mentioned the case, but no other speaker is identified. There seem to be two possible explanations.

---

[67] *Rattlesdene v Grunestone* (1317) YB 10 Edw II, SS vol 55, 140–41.

[68] Ibbetson notes, plausibly, that the presented facts conceal a shipping accident (Ibbetson, *Historical Introduction* 44).

[69] *The Carrier's Case* (n 1) 33–34.

The first is simply that the surviving reports omit the name of the person who referred to *Rattlesdene*. The case was cited by someone in the Exchequer Chamber, perhaps as a deliberate response to Bryan's immediately preceding citation of cases, and this convinced the judges that trespass could be so committed and therefore larceny. On this interpretation, the reference to *Rattlesdene* was the determining intervention in the debate. However, this analysis suffers from two weaknesses. First, it gives the appearance of a strong adherence to precedent, something which is not a common feature of reasoning in the fifteenth century.[70] Second, the language of 'vide' preceding the reference to the case looks more like an authorial insertion than simply an alternative to the name of a speaker. The second explanation for the inclusion of *Rattlesdene* is that it was added to the report of the case by the author of the report or even by a subsequent reader. If this latter explanation is correct, then *Rattlesdene* could not have been decisive in the case.

This leaves the enigma of the case intact and the basis of the decision unknown. It is clear that the report includes a large gap. If the insertion of *Rattlesdene v Grunestone* is removed, what remains is two judges arguing for a felony having been committed, Bryan CJ's denial of a felony, and the judges then reporting to the Chancellor that a felony had been committed. The report of the Exchequer Chamber proceedings itself makes clear that it is incomplete, referring to the case as argued 'before the justices', but no arguments other than those of (some) of the judges are reported.[71] It is clear that the report of the Exchequer Chamber proceedings, at least, is not a complete record of the case.

Explaining the decision in *The Carrier's Case* consequently requires an exercise of historical imagination, suggesting plausible explanations to fill the significant gap in the sources. The remainder of this section of the chapter considers possible explanations for the finding in *The Carrier's Case* that the facts constituted larceny.

## D. Developments in Criminal law

### i. *Larceny and Packages*

The approach of Choke may have been influenced by the case of William Wody from 1470.[72] Wody was indicted for larceny of six sealed boxes containing charters of title to land. It was ultimately held that Wody had committed no felony. Most of the discussion concerns the charters, arguing that they had the character of land, which could not be stolen. None of

---

[70] Baker, *OHLE* 488.
[71] *The Carrier's Case* (n 1) 32–33.
[72] *R v Wody* (1470) YB Mich 49 Hen VI, fo 14, pl 9 (King's Bench) and 10 (Exchequer Chamber); SS vol 47, 124–26.

the judges discuss the boxes themselves. Nedeham J made it clear that the discussion concerned the 'charters within the boxes', although a barrister, Sulyard, argued that the boxes could not be stolen as they were of the same nature as the charters. Arguably, the case shows that the judges, including Choke, distinguished between a package and its contents before *The Carrier's Case*, albeit that in *Wody*, the peculiar nature of the contents affected the nature of the package too. Alternatively, *Wody* may have encouraged a certain pragmatism, as a thief of documents of title to medieval England's most valuable asset could not be prosecuted. The position taken by Choke in *The Carrier's Case* would have provided a means to prosecute Wody successfully. Instead of prosecuting for theft of the box and contents, Wody could have been indicted for theft of the boxes, to which a value could have been attached.[73]

### ii. A Different Conceptual Framework[74]

The discussion so far has been focused on *The Carrier's Case* within the confines of the law of larceny, and it is this approach which has been the basis of most of the criticism of the case. However, there is some evidence in the case of analysis from an alternative perspective, a different conceptual framework, one which regarded the case not as one of larceny, but as theft. This shifted the focus in the case away from the technical requirements of larceny and trespass. While larceny indictments used the language of theft, they also required a taking of the goods with force and arms.[75] The idea of theft advanced in *The Carrier's Case* and subsequent discussions did not.

The alternative is most obvious in Huse AG's remarks in the Star Chamber. According to Huse: 'It is felony to claim the goods feloniously without cause from the party with intent to defraud him to whom the property belongs, *animo furandi*. And here, notwithstanding the bailment as above, the property remains in him who made the bailment.'[76]

There are a few key elements to Huse's argument. The first is the absence of any discussion of the technical requirements of the offence of larceny, most notably possession and taking of possession. Instead, there is a broader focus on whether someone has any 'property' in the woad and simply a 'claiming' of the goods as criminal. Huse seems to think that the offence is about interfering with another's property, and so the rights that remain in a

---

[73] The report is not clear, but it seems likely that the indictment against Wody would not have included the relevant information to enable such a case to proceed.

[74] The language of 'frameworks' comes from DJ Ibbetson, 'What is Legal History a History of?' in A Lewis and M Lobban (eds), *Law and History*, Current Legal Issues 6 (Oxford, Oxford University Press, 2004).

[75] 1 Hale PC 504.

[76] *The Carrier's Case* (n 1) 31.

bailor will be sufficient for inappropriate acts by a bailee to be criminal. The second is the focus on the wrongdoer's intention, particularly the 'animo furandi'.[77]

The Latin phrase suggests a probable source for Huse's views: the civil law.[78] The likely route for this influence is the definition of theft (*furtum*) in the thirteenth-century book known as *Bracton*, which was drawn from civilian sources. Although *Bracton* was little cited in the medieval period, there is evidence that it was used in legal education in the Inns of Court in relation to criminal law.[79] *Bracton* does not discuss larceny, but only theft, which it defined as 'the fraudulent mishandling of another's property without the owner's consent, with the intention of stealing, for without the *animus furandi*, it is not committed'.[80] This definition contains both of the key elements in Huse's argument: the importance of intention and the focus on another's 'property' rather than possession. The definition in *Bracton* also addresses an issue to which Huse does not refer—that the carrier in *The Carrier's Case* did not take possession illegitimately. As *Bracton*'s definition refers merely to handling, it encompasses such inappropriate actions by the bailee.

The competing frameworks for analysing the case, as one of larceny or of theft, may explain other lawyers' attitudes towards it. The anonymous reader of the 1470s and Thomas Marow both focused on the general requirements of larceny.[81] The reader referred to *The Carrier's Case* to express views like those of Bryan CJ, while Marow did not even refer to it. By contrast, lawyers in the sixteenth century seem to have been more content to incorporate breaking bulk into their discussion of larceny. A shift in the predominant framework for analysing larceny may well be behind this. An approach based on *Bracton* became popular in the sixteenth century, just as *Bracton* seems to have become a more common reference in matters of criminal law.[82] In the 1520s, the reader Francis Mountford not only expressly cited *Bracton*'s definition of theft, but also described the offence

---

[77] It is tempting to see this as the explanation for the focus on intention in the views of various other common lawyers in the case too.

[78] This explains the similarity between Huse's views and those of the civilian-trained Lord Chancellor, although it is notable that the Chancellor expressed himself in a manner that would not have been alien to a common lawyer. The Chancellor is reported as saying that 'Felony is according to the intent', similar to the statement by Fairfax Sjt in (1466) YB Mich 6 Edw IV, fo 7, pl 18 that '(tr) felony is malice aforethought'.

[79] JH Baker, 'Roman Law at the Third University of England' in Baker, *Collected Papers* vol 1, 368–69.

[80] SE Thorne (ed and trans), *Bracton on the Laws and Customs of England*, vol 2 (Cambridge MA, Harvard University Press, 1968) 425.

[81] See above, nn 62–63.

[82] For the importance of *Bracton* to early modern lawyers in relation to criminal law more generally, see I Williams, 'A Medieval Book and Early Modern Law: *Bracton*'s Authority and Application in the Common Law c.1550–1640' (2011) 79 *Tijdschrift voor Rechtsgeschiedenis* 47, 62, 64–65 and 70–77.

as one of 'furtum', never using the language of larceny.[83] William Staunford took the definition of theft in *Bracton* as his definition of larceny in his influential *Plees del Coron*, the starting point for the printed canon on criminal law.[84] The surviving sources suggest that, echoing Staunford, the theft framework was dominant throughout the sixteenth and seventeenth centuries, featuring in the influential works of Coke and Hale.[85]

## E. Developments in Private Law

Theft law is widely considered to be about protecting private property rights, with such rights being creations of positive law.[86] The dominant medieval position, exemplified in the work of Thomas Aquinas, similarly linked theft to the private law of property.[87] The private law of personal property in England changed in the second half of the fifteenth century. In relation to *The Carrier's Case*, these changes suggest some degree of cross-fertilisation between the law of theft and private law actions in relation to personal property.

Most significant is the development of the action which came to be known as conversion, a form of trespass on the case writ. As a trespass on the case writ (otherwise known as an action on the case), conversion writs did not have a prescribed form. Trespass on the case writs had to include an allegation of a wrong (a 'trespass'), and plaintiffs could then elaborate on the precise facts of their case. No allegation of the use of force and arms was required. This meant that trespass on the case claims could redress non-forcible wrongdoing such as defamation or deceit.[88] In the personal property context, the absence of any requirement to allege force and arms meant that an initial taking of possession by consent would not preclude a claim in conversion. The early history of conversion has not yet been fully explored, particularly in the records of the common law courts, but there is enough evidence to indicate the possibility of influence on the judges in *The Carrier's Case* from private law actions.

It seems clear that some lawyers, at least, did relate conversion and larceny to one another. Most obviously, the report of *The Carrier's Case* summarises

---

[83] British Library Hargrave MS 87, fo 177v.

[84] Staunford, *Plees* fo 24.

[85] 3 Co Inst 107 and 1 Hale PC 504, both using *Bracton*.

[86] Theft as protecting private law rights underlies much of the criticism of *R v Hinks* [2001] 2 AC 241 (HL), such as AP Simester and J Beatson, 'Stealing One's Own Property' (1999) 115 *LQR* 372. Not all modern writers agree. Green suggests that while the law of theft is related to private property law, it is also related to an extra-legal (or 'pre-legal') concept of property (Green, *Thirteen Ways* 93–95).

[87] T Aquinas, *Summa Theologiae*, vol 38 (Marcus Lefébure ed, Cambridge, Cambridge University Press, 2006) 69 (2a2ae. 66, 2) and 75 (2a2ae. 66, 5).

[88] Baker, *Introduction* 61–63.

the facts as the carrier having 'broke open the bales and took the goods contained in the same feloniously *and converted them to his own use*, and concealed them' (emphasis added).[89] While the language of converting property to one's use is not unusual in the fifteenth-century yearbooks,[90] given the developments in conversion and the association with larceny to be discussed below, it should not be ignored.

Thomas Marow seems to have been influenced in his exposition of the law of larceny by the tort of conversion. In his 1503 reading, he discussed a set of facts which look like *specificatio*, the making of a new thing from property belonging to another:

> (tr) if a man delivers goods to another to look after safely, and the bailee changes the fashion of the goods, as he may with plate or similar, in this case if the bailor afterwards takes them with felonious intent, this is felony, and yet the goods were his property, but the property was changed.[91]

In the context of a reading, an educational exercise, this could just be seen as a teacher using an example to make a point. However, *specificatio* was a topic which was being discussed in private law cases of conversion in the later fifteenth century, and it seems plausible to suggest that Marow was influenced by the questions being raised in that context.[92]

The same sort of influence may also be visible on the facts of *The Carrier's Case* itself. While the case is the first example of breaking bulk known in the law of larceny, there is a report of a claim in conversion in relation to breaking bulk two decades earlier.[93] Furthermore, in around 1500, claims for breaking bulk seem to have been the most common claim in conversion, albeit not frequently reported.[94] Breaking bulk was not adequately remedied by detinue, as in detinue a defendant could return the damaged receptacle and avoid any liability in damages. Nor was it remedied by trespass to the goods with the force and arms. As the receptacle had been given to the tortfeasor as a bailee, this consent contradicted any claim based upon force and arms. An action on the case for conversion was therefore clearly appropriate.

---

[89] *The Carrier's Case* (n 1) 30. The association between conversion and theft remains in Canada, in language like that in *The Carrier's Case*, where the actus reus of theft is defined in terms of conversion to the thief's own use (Canadian Criminal Code, RSC 1985, c C-46, s 322(1)).

[90] eg (1431) YB Mich 10 Hen VI, fo 5b, pl 19.

[91] Putnam, *Early Treatises* 376.

[92] See (1479) YB Hil 18 Edw IV, fo 23, pl 5 and (1490) YB Hil 5 Hen VII, fo 15, pl 6, both discussed in AWB Simpson, 'The Introduction of the Action on the Case for Conversion' (1959) 75 *LQR* 364, 372–75.

[93] *Anon* (1453) Harvard Law School MS 156 (unfoliated, under Mich 32 Hen VI), cited by Baker, *OHLE* 801 fn 1 and Baker, *Introduction* 396 fn 98. This case has never been printed or reproduced on film and seems to have been unknown to Simpson.

[94] Baker, *OHLE* 802.

The availability of conversion may have highlighted that an approach to larceny focused on the availability of trespass with force and arms was inadequate. There were clear gaps in the law, and these gaps were being remedied in private law, but not in criminal law. The question then would be whether the extension of remedies in private law should be mirrored in criminal law. From this perspective, one motivation in *The Carrier's Case* may in fact have been to try and maintain alignment between criminal law and private law without entering into sustained discussion of possession, with all the difficulties that this might cause in a criminal trial. This may have been especially pertinent given that the claim was really one for restoration of property from the sheriff.

Some corroboration of the influence of contemporary debates in private law is found in the competing approaches of different judges. In *The Carrier's Case*, Bryan CJ stated that the merchant should use the writ of detinue.[95] From then on, Bryan stressed the requirement of a taking *vi et armis*, which was also a requirement of claims in trespass to goods. For Bryan, *The Carrier's Case* was therefore part of a world in which there were two actions related to personal property, one of which could lead to criminal liability. The relationship between detinue and conversion was an issue in the 1470s, and it might be that some of the judges saw *The Carrier's Case* as part of the ongoing debate.[96] The different attitudes of Bryan CJ and Choke J in *The Carrier's Case* can also be seen in other cases in the 1470s. *Rilston v Holbek* began in 1472, both in detinue and as an action on the case for damage to goods by a sub-bailee, the claim being brought by the executors of the bailor. All of the judges, including Choke, are reported as being in favour of liability in the action on the case, except for Bryan CJ, and the case was undecided for three years.[97] Bryan CJ's remarks in the printed report about privity to the initial bailment suggest that he considered the appropriate remedy to be detinue on a bailment rather than an action on the case. In a 1479 claim, Bryan insisted on detinue, while Choke considered conversion to be available.[98]

---

[95] It is not clear from the report whether Bryan meant that detinue should be used against the carrier or against the Sheriff of London. Detinue would not have been available against the carrier, as the detinue writ required that the defendant detained the plaintiff's property. In *The Carrier's Case*, the property was not in the hands of the carrier, but those of the Sheriff of London, against whom detinue *sur trover* may have been available.

[96] See, generally, Simpson, 'Introduction' 366–70. There is a risk in assuming too much consistency in late fifteenth-century judges' views over time. David Seipp notes that the judges do not seem to have been consistent in their approaches to corporations (D Seipp, 'Formalism and Realism in Fifteenth-Century English Law: Bodies Corporate and Bodies Natural' in P Brand and J Getzler (eds), *Judges and Judging in the History of the Common Law and Civil Law* (Cambridge, Cambridge University Press, 2012) 49–50). However, there does seem to be a degree of consistency in relation to personal property matters.

[97] *Rilston v Holbek* (1472) YB Mich 12 Edw IV, fo 13, pl 9. The record is in JH Baker, *Baker and Milsom: Sources of English Legal History: Private Law to 1750*, 2nd edn (Oxford, Oxford University Press, 2010) 576–77.

[98] (1479) YB Hil 18 Edw IV, fo 23, pl 5. David Seipp has suggested that the remarks attributed to Choke J in the report are those of Catesby Sjt, and vice versa, presumably on the

Developments in conversion may also have blurred Bryan CJ's clear emphasis on trespass with force and arms. Bryan CJ sought to maintain a rigid distinction between two writs related to personal property—detinue and trespass with force and arms—but this model of personal property law was breaking down. The introduction of conversion meant that there were now three writs, with the place and role of conversion uncertain. Furthermore, conversion writs often looked similar to trespass with force and arms writs. *Rilston v Holbek*, although not about breaking bulk, included allegations of force. The defendant's denial of the 'force and wrong' in that case is the same as is seen in the records for cases begun using writs of trespass with force and arms, suggesting a blurring between actions on the case relating to goods and trespass with force and arms.[99] In the early sixteenth century, conversion claims for breaking bulk sometimes included an allegation of force and arms, despite the claims not using the traditional trespass writs.[100] Conversion writs which included an allegation of force and arms may have looked very similar to trespass with force and arms writs. They included a wrong (a trespass) and an allegation of force and arms, the aspects of the tort of trespass which were also elements in the crime of larceny. The foundation of Bryan's reasoning, a clear distinction between two writs, was being eroded by the existence and form of conversion writs.

Bringing these possibilities together, the issues and debates in *The Carrier's Case*, as well as elsewhere, suggest parallels between contemporary discussions in larceny and conversion. Such parallels may provide an explanation as to why many of the judges considered the facts in the case to amount to felony—the law had come to recognise breaking bulk as a wrong, one which was sometimes described as being committed in a manner which would allow criminal liability in larceny.

These developments in the private law of property would integrate well with an analysis of the facts in *The Carrier's Case* on the *Bracton* model discussed above. Changes in the private law remedies for infringements of personal property made it clear that interferences other than taking or retaining possession could be remedied by the common law, something which analysis of the case through the lens of *Bracton* encouraged on the criminal law side. Two unrelated developments pushed in the same direction—for the law of theft to encompass more than merely the wrongful taking of possession.

---

basis that Catesby's reported remarks refer to Catesby in the third person in a hypothetical case (www.bu.edu/phpbin/lawyearbooks/display.php?id=20619). However, the parallel in the disagreement between Choke and Bryan suggests that the remarks are accurately attributed to Choke.

[99] Baker, *Sources* 576–77. For an example in a trespass with force and arms writ, see the record of *Rattlesdene v Grunestone* (Baker, *Sources* 341).

[100] Baker, *OHLE* 802 fn 11 has examples from 1506 to 1530. The relevant work has not been completed in the fifteenth-century records.

## IV. CONCLUDING REMARKS

*The Carrier's Case* is a landmark case in the law of larceny, with all the significance that this holds for the modern law of theft. Like many landmarks, its significance is perhaps more evident from a distance; the references to the case in its immediate aftermath suggest that lawyers did not support the decision and that the alignment between private law and criminal law which existed in *The Carrier's Case* did not last. A focus on larceny as the taking away of goods rather than an interference with property reappeared in the eighteenth century.[101] From then on, the competing frameworks through which the facts of the case could be viewed continued to be in competition into the twentieth century. The tension between them was a source for dissatisfaction with the law of larceny, especially as the law developed more in line with the idea of theft, but within the form of larceny. It was only with the Theft Act 1968, and similar legislation elsewhere in the common law world, that the constraints of larceny were removed. More generally, and positively, *The Carrier's Case* shows that the common law of crime did not develop solely though 'shabby expedients', as Milsom has claimed, but was influenced by wider legal developments and legal scholarship.[102]

---

[101] 1 Hawk PC 89 and 4 Bl Comm 230. Hawkins expressly noted the contrast with the civil law in his discussion.

[102] SFC Milsom, *Historical Foundations of the Common Law*, 2nd edn (London, Butterworths, 1981) 403.

# 3

# R v Saunders and Archer (1573)

## JOHN BAKER

THE MEMORABLE FACTS in *R v Saunders and Archer* have been known to many generations of law students as a result of the full report in Plowden's *Commentaries*.[1] It was the case where an adulterous husband's attempt to kill his wife with a poisoned apple went tragically wrong. But facts, under the common law system of procedure, did not always appear on the record.

The case began at Warwick Assizes on 27 February 1573, before Sir James Dyer, Chief Justice of the Common Pleas, and Mr Serjeant Barham, as justices of assize on the Midland circuit. John Saunders of Greenborough (now Grandborough), Warwickshire, husbandman, was indicted that on 20 September 1572 at Greenborough, he gave his daughter Eleanor two pieces of a baked apple (*duas pecias unius pomi tosti*)[2] mixed with poison called arsenic and rosaker,[3] with the intention that Eleanor would die through the working of the poison; that Eleanor sickened until 22 September and then died of the poison; and that Saunders was therefore guilty of her murder. The indictment also alleged that Alexander Archer on 20 September 1572 procured and counselled Saunders to commit the murder. Both were convicted. There was thus no point of law on the face of the record. Poisoning someone to death with the intention of killing them was obviously murder, and someone who procured and counselled such a murder was obviously an accessory before the fact.[4] However, as we learn from Plowden, the record was partly fictional. No doubt it had been drawn in

---

[1] *R v Saunders and Archer* (1573–76) Plowd 473; translation in 75 ER 706. There are no surviving assize records for Warwickshire before the seventeenth century, but Plowden printed the full record in Latin as well as his report in French.

[2] The word 'tosti' in the Latin record, which is garbled as 'rostir' in the French, has been variously rendered as roasted and toasted. F Pulton, *De Pace Regis et Regni* (London, 1610) fo 121v, says 'roasted'. But it is the past participle of *torreo*, which also means to bake.

[3] Red arsenic, or realgar. 'Roseacre' was also alleged to have been used in the poisoning of Sir Thomas Overbury in 1613. The other poison was presumably white arsenic.

[4] The counselling and procuring was laid on the same day as principal fact, but Archer was not alleged to have been present aiding and abetting.

that way in the hope of warding off any subsequent challenge in the King's Bench. It was not, however, the unvarnished truth, and it did not succeed in preventing discussion.

The full story emerged, as of course it would, in evidence at the trial. Saunders had not intended to kill his daughter, but rather his wife, so that he would be free to marry his lover. He had asked Archer's advice how to go about this, and Archer had recommended poison, which he bought for him. Saunders put the poison into the baked apple and handed it to his wife while she was lying ill in bed. She took only one or two bites and passed it on to their three-year-old daughter. Saunders remonstrated that apples were not good for such children, but the wife replied that they were better for children than for her. The little girl then ate the apple, with Saunders watching, and became fatally ill. The report says that Saunders had no malice towards his daughter, but rather 'graunde amoure', and had desisted from intervening only to hide his guilt. Doubts were then aired as to whether these circumstances amounted to murder, in the absence of any malice towards the child. But the judges, who had received an opinion to the same effect from Saunders CB before the trial,[5] held that it was murder, and the jury accordingly proceeded to convict both defendants. Saunders was promptly sent to the gallows.

However, there was a lingering doubt concerning Archer, and the case was continued on the gaol-delivery roll until Hilary term 1576 so that it could be discussed by all the judges of the King's Bench and Common Pleas. The only counsel Archer had provided was to kill Mrs Saunders, not the little daughter, whom he cannot have had in contemplation. The opinion of the judges was that this could not make him an accessory to the girl's murder, '(tr) but nevertheless they reprieved him from one sessions to another, for an example, to the intent that he should purchase his pardon and be delivered in that way rather than otherwise'.[6]

Plowden added his own commentary on the decision relating to Archer. He thought it reasonable that someone who counselled or commanded an evil thing should be deemed an accessory to everything which followed from the evil act, but not for any distinct thing. For example, if A commands B to rob C, and when B attempts the robbery, C defends himself, and B kills him, A is accessory to the murder which follows from the command. The same is true if he commands B to beat C, and C dies from the beating.[7] But it is otherwise if a different crime is committed, as where A commands B to

---

[5] Sir Edward Saunders had conducted the pre-trial examination as a Warwickshire magistrate. He was well known to Plowden through the Middle Temple, and Plowden became one of his executors. Originally from Northamptonshire, he settled in Warwickshire, but his sharing a surname with the prisoner was probably no more than a coincidence.

[6] *Saunders and Archer* (n 1) 475.

[7] Anthony Gell reported Dyer CJ as saying in 1562 that this had been decided by all the justices of both benches in the time of Henry VIII: *R v Wright* (1562) 110 SS 435. *cf R v Newbolt* (1512) 116 SS 614, per Fyneux CJ.

steal a white horse and he steals a chestnut horse, or A commands B to rob a certain goldsmith as he is going to Sturbridge Fair,[8] and he breaks into his house in Cheapside and steals his plate there.[9] However, a mere divergence in the manner of committing the crime does not make it a different crime for this purpose. Thus, if A commands B to kill someone with poison and he uses a sword,[10] or to kill someone in the country and he kills him in the town, or to kill someone on a particular day and he kills him on another day, in all these cases A is liable as an accessory, because the instrument, time and place are not the substance of the offence. Plowden approved of the decision in the present case in favour of Archer because poisoning the little girl was a different crime from the one he had counselled.

The case has caught the imagination ever since Plowden's report of it was published, in the second part of his *Commentaries*, in June 1579.[11] It still features, in abridged form, in some current casebooks,[12] and Archer's case (at least) is still discussed in the textbooks. It retains a precarious foothold in *Archbold* and *Halsbury*.[13] It has even occasioned some imaginative speculation linking the apple with original sin.[14] The facts alone were memorable enough. History records all too many cases of husbands killing or attempting to kill their wives, or wives their husbands; it was a lamentable but predictable consequence of the Church's teaching that marriage was dissoluble only by death. On any view, Saunders' behaviour was abhorrent. But how could a father possibly stand by as his little girl took the poison intended for his wife? Plowden's assertion that he loved his daughter greatly seems humanly incomprehensible. He took no action, according to Plowden, for fear that he should be suspected. Perhaps he was too ignorant of the law to

---

[8] A large annual fair at Chesterton, on the outskirts of Cambridge.

[9] The distinction here being between robbery and burglary.

[10] This case was agreed at Serjeants' Inn in 1554: J Baker (ed), *The Reports of William Dalison*, Selden Society vol 124 (London, Selden Society, 2007) 82.

[11] It was printed as an undated continuation of *Les Comentaries, ou les Reports de dyvers Cases* (1571). The first edition of the *Short-Title Catalogue* and JH Beale, *A Bibliography of Early English Law Books* (Cambridge, MA, Harvard University Press, 1926) 109, no R487, both showed the first edition of Part Two as that dated 15 February 1584.

[12] eg, MT Molan (ed), *Criminal Law: 150 Leading Cases*, 2nd edn (London, Old Bailey Press, 2002) 341–42; J Dine, J Gobbert and W Wilson, *Cases and Materials on Criminal Law*, 5th edn (Oxford, Oxford University Press, 2006) 156–57; HM Keating, SR Cunningham, T Elliott and MA Walters, *Clarkson and Keating Criminal Law: Texts and Materials*, 8th edn (London, Sweet & Maxwell, 2014) 592–94. It is less familiar across the Atlantic, though it was included in FB Sayre, *A Selection of Cases on Criminal Law* (Rochester, NY, Lawyers Co-operative Publishing Co, 1927) 676–78.

[13] *Archbold: Criminal Pleading, Evidence and Practice* (London, Sweet & Maxwell, 2014) 1906, para 18–24; Lord Mackay of Clashfern, *Halsbury's Laws of England*, 5th edn, vol xxv (London, LexisNexis, 2010) 53 fns 9–10 (Archer), 94 fn 8 (Saunders).

[14] P Crofts, *Wickedness and Crime: Laws of Homicide and Malice* (Abingdon, Routledge, 2013) ch 3; P Crofts, 'The Poisoned Apple of Malice' (2013) 22 *Griffiths Law Review* 150. The chapter in Crofts was adversely reviewed, with respect to the supposed significance of apples in the law of homicide, by Findlay Stark in (2014) 73 *CLJ* 222, 225–26.

know that attempted murder was not a capital offence. Perhaps he preferred seeing an innocent child die to facing the rest of his life yoked to a woman who knew he had tried to murder her, or the contempt of a daughter who discovered he had attempted to take the life of her mother. But did he really suppose no one would suspect his apple? No doubt, he was not a very intelligent or pleasant specimen of the human race. It is, however, idle to speculate as to his state of mind or his character. The concern of the legal historian is not with the psychological aspect of the story or with the choice of a baked apple rather than a pear or a bowl of porridge, for it will never be possible to know more than the law report tells us. The case is interesting enough for what the report does tell us.

We know of the case only from Plowden's account of it. This prompts the preliminary question whether it was reported by Plowden because it was considered highly unusual at the time, or whether it was highly unusual only because Plowden chose to report it. It was indeed unprecedented in 1579 for criminal trials in the country to be reported in such detail. The general indifference of law reporters to criminal cases, apart from a brief experiment in the early fourteenth century,[15] is attributable to the denial of counsel to prisoners tried for murder or felony. The profession was involved only at the judicial level, except in appeals of felony, where counsel were allowed,[16] or in technical quibbles about the wording of indictments.[17] There was no special pleading in the criminal courts, and therefore all cases were left to the jury on the general issue (Not Guilty). The only legal input was in any direction the judge chose to give the jury before they considered their verdict. Since this mostly occurred at the assizes and quarter sessions, and there was no way of challenging a judicial direction in Westminster Hall, the finer points of criminal law did not receive concentrated legal attention in the central courts.

The principal forum for the discussion of criminal law in the fifteenth and sixteenth centuries was, by default, the lecture room. The inns of court, from the 1340s, provided lectures on statutes (called readings), glossing

---

[15] JH Baker, 'Some Early Newgate Reports 1315–1328' in *Collected Papers in English Legal History*, vol 2 (Cambridge, Cambridge University Press, 2013).

[16] Appeals of murder and felony were reported in banc, as in a case moved by Plowden himself in Michaelmas term 1573: Lincoln's Inn MS Maynard 77, fo 178 (which held that an accessory after the fact could not in an appeal take advantage of a pardon of the principal). This is the unrelated case added as an appendix to Plowden's report of *Archer*, though out of fairly transparent professional modesty he attributed the motion to a nameless apprentice of the Middle Temple.

[17] Such cases were very numerous by the end of the sixteenth century and were a result of removing cases into the King's Bench by certiorari. The court could only consider technical errors on the face of the indictment, since the evidence was not recorded. As to whether the procedure was in fact used to overturn unsafe convictions on the merits, see JH Baker, 'The Refinement of English Criminal Jurisprudence 1500–1848' in Baker, *Collected Papers* vol 2, 994–95.

the texts phrase by phrase, and at least 50 surviving readings before 1550 touched on criminal law, a preoccupation markedly disproportionate to the number of relevant statutory texts.[18] Lectures are not now considered a source of law, especially if they are preserved only in student notes, but the readings in the inns passed on and refined the accepted common learning, subject to challenge by the judges and benchers who attended, and were just as authoritative as most of what could be found in the medieval law reports, the year books. All superior judges, and many of the more active justices of the peace, had themselves been readers in their inns. Attendance at readings therefore equipped assize judges and leading magistrates with enough legal principle to know how to deal with elementary questions raised by the evidence in criminal cases. This common learning eventually found its way into the printed treatises on pleas of the Crown and the reported case law, though the readings themselves were not printed at the time. It is true that some of the readers' hypothetical cases seem rather academic and far-fetched, more reminiscent of wildly inventive examination questions than of real trials. Nothing, however, is too far-fetched to occur in real life. One example previously given of a seemingly artificial case was that of the man in Henry VIII's reign who shot at someone to test a suit of armour, which failed the test:[19] yet that very case was to occur in real life in 2015.[20]

Occasional rulings on circuit are to be found in sixteenth-century notebooks and textbooks,[21] and there was some general knowledge of notorious crimes. By a remarkable coincidence, there was another cause célèbre in 1573 concerning a different Mrs Saunders, whose lover had murdered her husband on Shooters Hill.[22] But Plowden was breaking new ground in terms of detail and sophistication, and if he had reported more in the same vein, the history of criminal law might have been different. It was not merely a matter of showing how new questions had been decided; it was also a means of crystallising in writing some of the older common learning of the inns of court. Plowden had already reported in some detail two

---

[18] JH Baker (ed), *The Reports of Sir John Spelman*, vol 2, Selden Society, vol 94 (London, Selden Society, 1978), 302–03, 347–50; JH Baker, *The Oxford History of the Laws of England, vol VI, 1483–1558* (Oxford, Oxford University Press, 2003) (hereinafter *OHLE*) 528–29; JH Baker, 'The Inns of Court and Legal Doctrine' in Baker, *Collected Papers* vol 1, 360–61; Baker, 'The Refinement of English Criminal Jurisprudence', 1001–02.

[19] Baker (ed), *Reports of Sir John Spelman*, 312.

[20] *R v Catley* (2015) Southwark Crown Court, reported as a news item in *The Times* (16 January 2015). The deceased had asked the defendant to test a supposedly bulletproof vest, which he had bought second-hand in Cambridge, by shooting at him. The vest failed.

[21] Baker, 'The Refinement of English Criminal Jurisprudence', 999–1000; JH Baker, 'Criminal Justice at Newgate 1616–1627' in Baker, *Collected Papers* vol 2, 1076.

[22] *R v Saunders and Browne* (1574) Dyer 332, translation in 73 ER 751; A Fitzherbert, *Loffice et Aucthoritie de Justices de Peace*, ed R Crompton (London, 1583) (hereinafter Crompton, *Justices*), fo 13v (dated 15 Eliz, 1573); it was the subject of a report from Catlyn CJ to Lord Burghley, dated 19 April 1573 (BL MS Harley 6991, fo 37) and is mentioned in Stow's *Annales*. Mrs Saunders was eventually hanged as an accessory.

criminal cases at the Shrewsbury quarter sessions in July 1553 from his own observation as a magistrate there,[23] but the printed *Commentaries* contain no indication that he kept up the practice. The publication of *Saunders and Archer* is all the more remarkable because Plowden did not report it at first hand. His home was in Shropshire, not Warwickshire, he was not present at the assizes and he was no longer a justice of the peace anywhere. He reported the evidence on the relation of the judges and the clerk of assize,[24] and after he had written his report he had it approved by Dyer CJ and Mr Serjeant Barham. It was not included in Dyer's own reports. It was Plowden alone who turned *Saunders and Archer* into a model for the future, though it was to be a distant future.[25]

The second question posed above is whether *Saunders and Archer* decided anything new. There were three principal points. The first was whether Saunders could be a principal murderer when he had not himself killed his daughter. The second was whether his malice towards his wife was sufficient to support a charge of murdering his daughter, to whom he bore no ill will. This is sometimes referred to as 'transferred malice', though the term had not then been invented.[26] The third was whether if transferred malice was sufficient to convict Saunders, it could also be extended to Archer, who had only counselled and procured the killing of his wife. This is connected with the concept now known as joint enterprise, though it was not an enterprise in which Archer was a present participant and the question was whether he could be an accessory to a crime which did not turn out as planned. Each of these points may be considered in turn.

### I. SAUNDERS' CASE: (1) INNOCENT AGENCY

The first point of note in Saunders' case arose from the indirectness of the killing. This was not a real difficulty, because the teaching in the inns of court had long been that homicide could be committed through an unwitting agent. This is not to speak of agency in the usual sense, but rather of instrumentality,[27] since the agent could be an animal, such as a vicious

---

[23] *R v Griffith ap David* (1553) Plowd 97, fos 97–100; translated in 75 ER 152-8; Baker, *OHLE* 576–77 (concerning principals in the first and second degree); *R v Salisbury* (1553) Plowd 100, fos 100–101v; translated in 75 ER 158–60 (concerning joint enterprise).

[24] As he put it, '(tr) as I credibly heard, for I was not present, but what I write here I did upon the report of the said justices of assize and the clerk of assize'.

[25] For the importance of Plowden's reports generally, see JH Baker, 'Case Law in Medieval England' in Baker, *Collected Papers* vol 3, 566–67; JH Baker, 'English Law and the Renaissance' in Baker, *Collected Papers* vol 3, 1475–76; Baker, *OHLE* 474–75.

[26] cf Pulton, *De Pace Regis*, fo 121v: 'so is his malicious mind and intention expounded to be transferred from the one to the other'.

[27] cf GL Williams, *Criminal Law: The General Part*, 2nd edn (London, Stevens, 1961) 352, where it is paraphrased as 'tool or instrumentality'. The expression 'innocent instrumentality' was adopted by the High Court of Australia in *Pinkstone v R* [2004] 206 ALR 84, 99. *R v Saunders* is mentioned in this case at 110.

dog,[28] a wild animal or bird of prey,[29] or an inanimate object, such as a trap set in a public place, or a child below the age of criminal capacity, or an insane person.[30] The agents could even be bacterial, as where someone with plague symptoms gave another person a fatal embrace; Anderson CJ in the 1590s held this to be murder by poisoning.[31] An agent of the usual kind—a knowing human agent—would be the principal offender, if he committed a crime to order, and the 'principal' (whose agent he was) would normally, in criminal terms, be his accessory. That is the only sense in which innocence was relevant. If the human agent was innocent, his 'principal' became the principal offender. Thus, where a man ordered an unwitting servant to shoot into a hedge, knowing that his enemy was hiding there, the master was the principal.[32] The same is true in the more esoteric example of a blind man ordered to hit what was said to be a dog in front of him, but was actually a sleeping man.[33] Thomas Frowyk in 1493 thought that the same principle applied in cases of duress, where a man ordered someone on pain of death to do the killing.[34] Although the person giving the command in these cases was counselling and procuring the person who did the deed rather than doing the deed himself, he could not be an accessory because there was

---

[28] John Baldwin's reading in Gray's Inn (*c* 1445/55) CUL MS Hh.2.6, fo 91: '(tr) If I have a dog which I make dangerous, and I command it to go and murder a man, and it kills the man, it is felony in me and for this I shall suffer death etc.'

[29] Crompton reported a case in 1562 at Chester Assizes where a woman hid her living illegitimate baby in an orchard, covered with leaves, and it was killed by a kite. She was convicted of murder, and executed, on the principle that the will is taken for the deed (*voluntas reputatur pro facto*): Crompton, *Justices* fo 16. This was really a case of murder by neglect, since the woman had not directed the kite at the child.

[30] Richard Littleton's reading in the Inner Temple (1493) CUL MS Hh.3.6, fo 3v: '(tr) Likewise of a caltrap which is made to lame [*halter*] a man, or coercing someone else to commit the felony, or causing a madman to commit the felony, which he does: in all these cases he is principal, even though he was not present at the time of the act done.' Thomas Marow's reading in the Inner Temple (1505), printed in BH Putnam (ed), *Early Treatises on the Practice of the Justices of the Peace in the Fifteenth and Sixteenth Centuries* (Oxford, Clarendon Press, 1924) 380: '(tr) if someone commands an infant or an insane man to kill a man, and they do it, in this case the commander is principal and the infant or insane person is excused'. Mountford's reading (1527) BL MS Hargrave 87(2) fo 177 (hereinafter *Mountford's Reading*): '(tr) If a man makes a trap or caltrap in a road with the intention of catching someone, and he is thereby killed, this is homicide and felony. But if someone robs my park and I have made a caltrap there, whereby he is killed, this is not felony.'

[31] The case arose on his circuit in Devon, where a woman and her six children died after being embraced by her brother. The man could not be found, but Anderson CJ said later '(tr) I was resolved—and I still continue to be of the same opinion—that he should be hanged, for I consider this to be plain poisoning and murder': *Mayor of Coventry's Case* (1596) BL MS Add 25211, fo 129v.

[32] *Mountford's Reading* fo 177: '(tr) If I see someone behind a bush and I command my servant or someone else to shoot an arrow [*sagitter*] at the bush, and he kills the person who is hiding under the bush, this is felony in me and not in my servant.'

[33] ibid.

[34] Argument at Richard Littleton's reading (1493) in SE Thorne and JH Baker (eds), *Readings and Moots at the Inns of Court in the Fifteenth Century*, vol 2, Selden Society vol 105 (London, Selden Society, 1990) 274.

no principal. He had therefore to be treated as the principal himself, on the footing that *Qui facit per alium, facit per se*.[35] Richard Littleton applied the same principle to a wife: if her husband merely commanded her knowingly to commit a felony, she was the principal and he was her accessory, whereas if he coerced her into doing it, he was the principal and she was no felon at all.[36]

In all these cases, the person employing the agency or instrumentality was deemed to be performing the principal act himself.[37] And the innocent 'agent' could just as well be the murder victim herself. Indeed, this was a common situation in poisoning cases, where poisoned food or drink was left for the victim to take, and this had been held in the fifteenth century to be a felonious killing and murder even though the defendant did not touch the deceased.[38] If Saunders' wife had continued eating the apple and died, she would have been an innocent agent causing her own death. Handing the apple to the child meant that there were two innocent agents involved, but that could have no bearing on causation. The child's death was the direct consequence of her father's poisoning the apple. The 'force and arms' normally required in an indictment for murder could be attached to the placing of the poison and its delivery, even though that did not constitute the killing.[39] But Coke thought it was unnecessary anyway in poisoning cases.[40] No one has ever doubted the causation aspect of the decision.[41]

---

[35] F Bacon, *Maxims of the Law* [1597] in J Spedding, RL Ellis and DD Heath (eds), *The Works of Francis Bacon*, vol xiv (London, 1860) 162, 237 (principal actor insane).

[36] Richard Littleton's reading in the Inner Temple (1493) CUL MS Hh.3.6, fo 3v. It should be noted that there was no presumption of marital coercion. The presumption was in being by 1597: Bacon, *Maxims of the Law* 214.

[37] Littleton's reading (1493) CUL MS Hh.3.6, fo 3v: '(tr) in the contemplation of the law he directs the blow'. cf *Southern v How* (1618) Cro Jac 468, 469: 'where one is party to a fraud, all which follows by reason of that fraud shall be said as done by him ... And to that purpose were cited Saunders' case of the poisoned apple'. The principle was applied at Hereford Assizes in 1666, where a wife had sent her innocent daughters with a poisoned posset for their father, which killed him: Kel 53; 84 ER 1079.

[38] Baldwin's reading (*c* 1445/55) CUL MS Hh.2.6, fo 90: '(tr) It may be murder and felony even if the man does not lay a hand on or strike anyone, as where someone poisons another, or makes an engine whereby the other dies; and there it is a good indictment to suppose "that he feloniously slew" (*quod felonice interfecit*), even though he did not lay a hand on anyone.' Richard Littleton's reading (1493) CUL MS Hh.3.6, fo 3v: '(tr) Observe that one may be a principal even though he is not present, as where he had malice to someone else and set poison etc. Likewise even if he has no malice towards him, or if someone other than the person for whom it is set is poisoned etc.'

[39] In *Archer*, the administration of the poison was said to be with force and arms. An indictment of 1562 for poisoning his wife's pottage (or soup) alleged that the husband with force and arms poisoned a dish of pottage (*ferculum potagii*) and gave it to.his wife, and the wife not knowing that it was poisoned gulped it down (*gustabat, sorbiebat, edebat et degluciebat*), from which poisoned pottage she instantly died: BL MS Harley 72, fo 130v.

[40] *R v Long* (1604) 5 Co Rep 120, 122–23; translated in 77 ER 243, 248 ('in all indictments of murder ... a stroke [ie, striking] ought to be alleged, unless in case of poisoning'). There was no such allegation in *R v Vaux*, below (nn 44–71).

[41] It is referred to in *Pinkstone v R* (n 27) 110.

### Further Poisoning Problems: Vaux's Case

One of the advantages of poison is that it enables murderers to be absent from the scene when the fatal consumption occurs, and perhaps at a great distance from the event in terms of time as well as space. This raised serious evidential difficulties and gave rise to suspicions. False accusations of poisoning were rife.[42] It was debated in the 1530s, albeit without a final conclusion, whether the year-and-a-day limitation period should be disapplied in poisoning cases.[43] For the same reason, innocent agency was often a critical factor in poisoning cases, the usual agent being the unwitting victim. But a more puzzling situation was presented in a case of 1590 in which *Saunders* was cited. The outcome of the case was reported by Coke, though (as will be shown) his version does not tell the whole story.[44]

William Vaux was indicted at Northumberland quarter sessions in July 1590 for murder by poisoning and pleaded a previous acquittal (Auterfoits Acquit), whereupon the case was removed into the King's Bench. The record of the acquittal showed that he had already been indicted for the same murder and tried at Newcastle Assizes on 12 August 1588; the jurors on that occasion had found a special verdict that Vaux had not been present when the poison was taken, referring it to the judgment of the court whether he was guilty; and the judgment was that he should be discharged because it appeared not to be wilful murder. The implication of the judgment, as entered of record, was that the prisoner's absence at the fatal moment prevented him from being convicted of murder. If that really was the reason, it would have been plainly wrong, since it would have put many if not most poisoners beyond the reach of the criminal law, and it was contrary to the well-settled doctrine about inanimate or unwitting instrumentalities. But the main question now was whether Vaux could be tried again.[45]

---

[42] The Star Chamber dealt with at least three such accusations in the 1590s: BL MS Harley 2143, fos 22 (1595), 51 (1592) and 64 (1596).

[43] *R v Bradshaw and Pyteous* (1532) 93 SS 48 and 97; *Anon* (after 1530) 93 SS 71 (as to an appeal); Baker, *OHLE* 524, 555. The 1532 indictment alleged a conspiracy to murder in 1522 and the death in 1530, but omitted to say when the poison was put in the soup. Maud Pyteous, the principal, was eventually found to be insane: *R v Petewuse* (1535) 93 SS 58.

[44] *R v Vaux* (1591) 4 Co Rep 44 (translated in 76 ER 992), where there is an abstract of the record; 2 Co Inst 183; 3 Co Inst 138. Coke's autograph notebook for this period is missing. This decision in Easter term 1591 was also reported by Clench J, BL MS Harley 4556, fo 41. Another note of the decision, in CUL MS Ff.5.16, fo 47, cites Mich 32 & 33 Eliz [1590], fos 42–43, in 'Liber B' (which is not Coke's missing notebook, though it covered the same period).

[45] The law was fresh in Coke's mind. In *R v Wallwin* (1588) BL MS Harley 1331, fo 50, Coke took exception to the wording of an indictment after the jury were sworn in the King's Bench. The defendant was charged with murder, but the indictment failed to assert that he was present comforting and abetting. The Attorney-General wanted to enter a *nolle prosequi*, but Coke argued that there was no such course. Coke was then pressed to consent to a juror being withdrawn, but he refused, saying he wanted the trial to proceed so that the defendant's life would not be put in jeopardy a second time. If the jury convicted, he would make his objection again in arrest of judgment. The court nevertheless discharged the prisoner, leaving his position uncertain.

Although Coke's report does not mention it, a manuscript report shows that this question had been raised in the King's Bench in 1589, before the second indictment was preferred. Coke had himself argued the case for Vaux. He conceded that it was not necessary for a principal to be present, citing Marow's reading, but argued that the verdict was defective because it did not allege knowledge (*sciens*) or an intention to kill the deceased at the time when Vaux persuaded him to drink the poison.[46] The judges agreed that the verdict was bad, but the question then arose whether Vaux could be indicted again. The problem was the conclusion of the special verdict, namely that if the judges thought the facts did not amount to murder, they acquitted Vaux. If this amounted to an acquittal, Vaux could not be tried again for the same offence. It was suggested that the conclusion was just a common-form phrase inserted by the clerk of assize, but this was not a convincing way of undermining a record.[47]

At the next hearing, the judges found another way out, by holding the original indictment bad for want of an allegation of knowledge at the appropriate moment, so that Vaux had never been in jeopardy of his life.[48] Vaux was thereupon indicted again at Newcastle. He then entered the plea of Auterfoits Acquit, the Attorney-General (Sir John Popham) demurred, and the matter was reargued in banc.[49] Serjeant Owen, on behalf of Vaux, cited *Saunders and Archer* as showing that it was unnecessary to allege knowledge that the poison was poisonous. Richard Hutton, on the same side, argued that *Saunders and Archer* 'differed not a jot from our case';[50] no particular words were sacrosanct, and if Vaux's indictment was taken as a whole, there was a clear implication of an intention to poison. Coke

---

[46] *cf R v Ap Thomas* (1605) BL MS Lansdowne 1075, fo 151; BL MS Lansdowne 1111, fo 136v; BL MS Add. 24846, fo 97. The defendant was convicted on an indictment for giving the deceased a drink mixed with poison from which he died, and the conviction was quashed because it did not say that she knew it was poison. It was also thought that the indictment should specify what poison it was, though the judges said they could not take judicial notice of what substances were poisonous.

[47] BL MS Harley 1633, fos 72 (Mich 1589) 83 (Pas 1590); CUL MS Ll.3.9, fo 31v (Mich 1589). The reporter noted that it was thought to be a 'haut [high] et horrible murder'.

[48] Another point, taken later, was that the judgment took the form merely that Vaux should go without day (*sine die*), not that he was found not guilty. According to the report in BL MS Add 35955, fo 153, Wray CJ advised Ive, the clerk of the Crown, to make the record say that, because of the insufficiency of the verdict, the judges would not proceed to judgment of death.

[49] ibid, fos 168–v (Mich 1590, Tanfield for the Crown, Serjeant Owen for the defendant), 175v–76 (same term, Hutton for the defendant), 184r–v (Hil 1591, Popham A-G for the Crown, Hutton for the defendant); CUL MS Ff.5.20, fos 44v–45 (Mich 1590, Coke), 49 (same term, Tanfield, Owen, Hutton and Coke); MS Ii.5.16, fos 45 (Mich 1590), 69v–72 (Hil 1591, Coke, Popham, Hutton); BL MS Add. 35946, fos 183–85v (Hil 1591, Popham, Hutton, Owen, Tanfield); BL MS Add 35955, ff 148–49 (Hil 1591, Popham, Hutton and Tanfield), 150v (Tanfield, Coke), 153 (Owen), 155v (Tanfield, Owen, Hutton and Coke). No final outcome is reported in these manuscripts. The decision, according to Coke, was reached in Easter term 1591.

[50] BL MS Harley 1633, fo 184v; BL MS Add 35955, fo 148v.

argued to the same effect. Indeed, the prosecution case seemed to rest on a pedantic quibble about the word order,[51] or the use of adverbs instead of direct assertions.[52] But the judges were determined to reject the defendant's argument. Indictments were to be taken strictly, in favour of life,[53] a rule with the paradoxical consequence that Vaux could now safely be hanged. Since the defect rendered his trial a nullity, there was no bar to his being tried again. He was evidently then tried and convicted.[54] This decision was highly dubious—Hale said it was 'the hardest I ever met with in criminal causes'[55]—but that is beside the present concern. The preliminary part of the King's Bench decision, that an absent poisoner could be convicted of murder as a principal in the first degree, had already been settled by *Saunders* and was never again doubted.[56] The main historical question arising from Coke's report is why the assize judges at Newcastle should have made so elementary a mistake.[57] The answer is that they did not. There was far more to the case than was disclosed by the special verdict.

The facts are revealed in a manuscript report of one of the motions in the King's Bench and can be supplemented from local histories.[58] The deceased, Nicholas Ridley of Willimoteswick in Haltwhistle, Northumberland, was the senior representative of a long-established family in those parts and was serving as sheriff of the county at the time of his death in December 1585.[59]

[51] According to the report, the words were '(tr) of his devilish malice aforethought persuaded him to take or receive [*accipere*] the cantharides'. Coke's abstract of the indictment, which was presumably more accurate, says '(tr) devilishly intending the death, poisoning and destruction of the selfsame Nicholas ... feloniously, wilfully and of his malice aforethought persuaded the same Nicholas to receive [*recipere*] and drink ... the cantharides'. According to the report in BL MS Add 35949, fo 148v, the indictment was held bad because it did not say that the deceased drank and took the *aforesaid* drink.

[52] Coke argued (BL MS Add 35955, fo 148v) that '(tr) although it does not say "he intended" but is put adverbially as "intending", the participle must always refer to the verb'.

[53] BL MS Harley 1633, fo 184, per Popham A-G: '(tr) without such knowledge in him it cannot be murder, and since it is not expressed, in favour of life you ought to presume that he was not [knowing]'. Hutton had made a similar point on the other side (fo 184v, tr): 'a verdict ought to be taken favourably, in safeguard of a man's life'. He meant that the special verdict here should be understood as an acquittal on the merits.

[54] TNA: PRO E 178/1748 (inquisition as to the possessions of William Vaux, attainted for the murder of Nicholas Ridley); TNA: PRO SP 46/38, fo 350 (reference to his attainder and forfeiture).

[55] Hale PC 2: 394.

[56] It is approved in Hale PC 1: 431.

[57] They may be identified as John Clench (of the King's Bench) and Francis Rodes (of the Common Pleas): JS Cockburn, *A History of English Assizes 1558–1714* (Cambridge, Cambridge University Press, 1972) 266.

[58] BL MS Add 35949, fo 118v. This is dated Trinity term 1590; this term would have been over before the Northumberland Sessions on 27 July. This argument is missing from the full series of reports in n 49 above, none of which mention this background information.

[59] *List of Sheriffs for England and Wales*. Public Record Office Lists and Indexes no IX (London, HMSO, 1898) 99 (appointed 22 November 1585); J Hodgson, *History of Northumberland* vol 2 (Newcastle upon Tyne, E Walker, 1832) 324. Hodgson says that he was the eldest son of Sir Nicholas Ridley (d 1573) and that the date of death was found by inquisition to be 6 January 1586. The record printed by Coke lays the death as having occurred on 20 December 1585.

He had been married for a long time to Margaret, daughter of Thomas Forster, but the marriage was childless. The defendant, William Vaux, a barrister of Gray's Inn[60] and a friend of Ridley's, recommended that Ridley take cantharides to increase his potency. This was a well-known but dangerous aphrodisiac, made from grinding the desiccated wing-cases of beetles of the Spanish fly.[61] There was a lewd rumour in the 1580s, doubtless apocryphal, that Sir Thomas More had once tried something answering to its description, with unexpected consequences.[62] It was a particularly unpleasant drug, with a nauseous smell and a burning taste, and acted as a powerful irritant, though it has continued to be prescribed in minute doses by the medical profession for many purposes up to the present day.[63] It is also highly toxic. Half a grain—around 30 milligrams—is considered a lethal dose. Although some still cautiously recommend it as an aphrodisiac,[64] deaths have been reported as recently as the 1990s as a result of using it for that purpose. Indeed, it is so effective that death has been known to result from apoplexy, caused by over-exertion, rather than from its toxic effects.[65] Its use was therefore ambiguous. Even in the nineteenth century, putting cantharides into a tart with injurious consequences was not necessarily proof of an intention to injure.[66] Suspicion had lit upon Vaux because he was a beneficiary under Ridley's will to the tune of £100 worth of land. But his first indictment did not make it entirely clear whether he was supposed to have supplied the fatal dose of cantharides; apart from the general common-form allegation of malice aforethought and intending Ridley's death, it only said that he persuaded Ridley to receive and drink a certain drink mixed with cantharides, affirming and averring that the drink was not poisonous and that it would procure him to have issue by his wife. This was no doubt calculated to give the impression that Vaux had supplied the poison,[67] but it carefully avoided saying so. It did not state that he prepared the drink, or even that he obtained and delivered the drug to Ridley, but only that he prescribed it.

[60] Admitted in 1573, called 1581. He is so identified in the manuscript report. His counsel, Richard Hutton, was a Cumbrian member of Gray's Inn (admitted 1570, called 1586), who presumably knew him.

[61] The reporter glosses it as 'Blew flye', though the beetle in its natural state is emerald green.

[62] J Evans, *Aphrodisiacs, Fertility and Medicine in Early Modern England* (Woodbridge, Boydell & Brewer, 2014) 99, citing R Scot, *Scot's Discovery of Witchcraft* (1584) 64.

[63] See Evans, *Aphrodisiacs, Fertility and Medicine* 98–99; L Moen et al, 'Cantharidin Revisited: A Blistering Defense of an Ancient Medicine' (2001) 137 *Archives of Dermatology* 1357.

[64] C Philby, 'The Ten Best Aphrodisiacs' *The Independent* (London, 18 September 2008).

[65] Evans, *Aphrodisiacs, Fertility and Medicine* 99, citing a seventeenth-century French physician.

[66] *R v Sharp* (19 August 1850) *Old Bailey Sessions Papers*, Tenth Session 1849–50, 538–40; see below (at 47) for further discussion.

[67] Pulton (*De Pace Regis et Regni* fo 122) assumed that Vaux 'brought' the drink, but was absent when it was taken.

It seems from the report that Vaux may have merely recommended cantharides by name, failing to point out its dangerous properties or the need
for caution.[68] Some ingenuity would be needed to present this as an act of
poisoning. Murder could not be committed by words.[69] Francis Mountford,
as reader of the Inner Temple in 1527, had given the examples of telling a
timorous person that he had been accused of treason and that his friends had
already been executed, or that he had contracted the plague, so that he died
of fright, or advising someone to go to Islington, knowing that his enemies
were on the road and would kill him; these were held not to be homicide of
any kind.[70] Even if Vaux actually supplied the fatal dose of powder, Ridley
knew that he was taking a substance called cantharides. And, according to
the unpublished report, that had been the reason for Vaux's acquittal. Ridley could have found out for himself what cantharides was and whether it
was safe to take it. This was not, therefore, a straightforward case of unwitting agency. Since Vaux was not a physician, it was arguably negligent of
Ridley to trust his advice without further enquiry.[71] Yet there was no offence
of self-manslaughter to which Vaux might have been an accessory; people
were entitled to take risks with themselves that it would not be permissible
to take with others. How to frame an effective indictment against Vaux
must therefore have been a matter requiring considerable ingenuity.

## II. SAUNDERS' CASE: (2) TRANSFERRED MALICE

*Saunders and Archer* was also a prime authority on the concept later known
as transferred malice. To understand better its significance in this connection, it is necessary to consider what was denoted by malice in the law of
homicide. Malice aforethought was a constituent element in the offence of
murder, but it was an artificial concept and did not mean the same thing as
an intention to kill the person slain. An intention to hurt the person was
sufficient.[72] However, the history of malice in murder is bedevilled by the

---

[68] *cf* Coke's argument in BL MS Add 35955, fo 155v: '(tr) here he does not give poison, but
persuades him to take it'.

[69] Baker (ed), *Reports of Sir John Spelman* 307.

[70] Reading on Westminster II, c 12, in BL MS Hargrave 87(2) fo 177.

[71] It was thought in the sixteenth century that if someone died from a potion supplied by
someone who was not medically qualified, the supplier was guilty of manslaughter or even
murder: see Robert Brooke's reading in the Middle Temple (1551) in JH Baker (ed), *Selected
Readings and Commentaries on Magna Carta 1400–1604*, Selden Society vol 132 (London,
Selden Society, 2015), 190, citing a case in the eyre of Nottingham. It is difficult to see how
malice could be presumed in such a case. Michael Dalton questioned whether it was even manslaughter: M Dalton, *The Countrey Justice* (London, 1630) 239. So did Sir Matthew Hale, on
the grounds that 'we should have many of the poorer sort of people, especially remote from
London, die for want of help, lest their intended helpers might miscarry': Hale PC 1: 429–30.

[72] *Note* (1496) YB Trin 11 Hen VII, fo 23, pl 14, per Fyneux CJ (explained on the ground
that the act was unlawful); *R v Newbolt* (1512) SS vol 110, 613 per Fyneux CJ (similar);

failure of many of the earlier sources to specify which kind of homicide was under consideration. For most purposes, it was unnecessary to do so, since both murder and manslaughter were clergiable capital offences until the sixteenth century. The early thirteenth-century treatise called *Bracton* taught that if A, intending to strike B, accidentally struck and killed C, this was culpable homicide, but the author did not explain why, or clarify whether it was murder or manslaughter.[73] The point was regularly discussed in the inns of court. One of the classic authorities cited by the readers was a case of 1348, where two people were fighting and a third party who intervened to try to separate them was killed in the fracas; this was held to be 'felony' in both the fighters.[74] This was not discussed in terms of malice, and it seems that 'felony' must here have meant manslaughter.[75] The same conclusion was drawn where A shot at B, but hit and killed C,[76] or where A raised a sword or staff to strike B, but his hand swerved and it struck and killed C.[77] One reader said it was because the felonious purpose 'continued' against the stranger,[78] and so presumably considered it murder.

The manslaughter analysis was not adopted by John Port of the Inner Temple, later a King's Bench judge, who wrote in 1498s that if a person threw a key at someone and it hit and killed another, this was murder by reason of

*R v Herbert* (1558) SS vol 124, 130, pl 8 (explained on the ground of malice); *Long v Danvers* (1597) BL MS Harley 4998, fo 237v ('(tr) Note that it was agreed by the court and by Coke A-G that if someone comes up to another, intending to beat him, or with the intent to commit some tort against him, and in doing it he kills him, this is murder, for there is an evil intent precedent'; however, Sir Walter Long's appeal of murder seems to have been unsuccessful, because he was later indicted: 5 Co Rep 120). *Saunders and Archer* (n 1) 474v called it evil intent (*male entent*).

[73] GE Woodbine and SE Thorne, *Bracton on the Laws and Customs of England* vol 2 (Cambridge, MA, Harvard University Press, 1968–77) 438.

[74] *Anon* (1348) Trin 22 Edw III, Fitz Abr, *Corone*, pl 180, 262.

[75] Port thought it felony, not murder: JH Baker (ed), *The Notebook of Sir John Port*, Selden Society vol 102 (London, Selden Society, 1987) 86. Kebell says only that he shall be hanged: JH Baker (ed), *Reports of Cases by John Caryll*, vol 1, Selden Society vol 115 (London, Selden Society, 1998) 5. Richard Littleton cited it in the Inner Temple in the 1490s (Baker, *Notebook of Sir John Port* 107). Mountford, in his reading, said it was felony (*Mountford's Reading* fo 177v). It was held to be manslaughter at the Old Bailey during the reign of Charles II: *R v Tomson* (undated) Kel 66; 84 ER 1085.

[76] Anonymous reading, CUL MS Ee.5.22, fo 212. The reader thought this came under the same principle as someone who fired arrows (randomly) in the street; in other words, that it was manslaughter,

[77] *Mountford's Reading* fo 177v: '(tr) If I strike someone, and my rod or sword swerves and strikes another and kills him, this is felony.' *cf* Marow's reading (1505), Putnam, *Early Treatises* 378: '(tr) And note that in homicide the intention of the person who causes the death does not make the felony ... for if someone intends to beat another person and in this battery he kills someone else, this is felony notwithstanding that his intent was not to kill him.' The same example is given in *Saunders and Archer* (n 1) 474v, but it had become murder.

[78] Anonymous reading in CUL MS Ee.5.22, fo 211v: '(tr) because the person who killed him was in purpose to kill another, which was felony, and this felony continues in the other person'.

the malice.[79] Here we may see the beginnings of a theory of transferred malice. Although Sir Robert Brooke in the 1550s still took the view that such an offence was manslaughter, his judicial contemporary Sir Edward Saunders thought that it was murder because of the malice towards someone else.[80] A more pertinent case, in the present context, was that where poison was set with the intention of killing a specific person, but it was taken by a stranger. The case actually occurred in 1533, where a woman sent a little boy with poisoned soup for her husband in prison, and another hungry prisoner stole it and paid the price, but there is no report of any legal discussion.[81]

The case had been considered in the inns of court. Thomas Frowyk (later Chief Justice of the Common Pleas) said in 1493 that the person who set the poison was a principal felon, even though he had no malice towards the person who died.[82] He did not address the question whether it was murder or manslaughter, but his reading was on *Quia multi per maliciam volentes* (Statute of Westminster II, c 12) concerning appeals, and the appeal of death lay only for murder. In 1493 it mattered little, since both murder and manslaughter were still clergiable, but the distinction became a matter of life and death in the sixteenth century after clergy was removed from murder of malice aforethought.[83] When a similar case was debated at an assembly of judges in 1556, five of them (three from the King's Bench) held it to be murder, though four (all but one from the Common Pleas) took the old view that it was only manslaughter.[84] It seems from this that the well-known sixteenth-century philosophical divisions between the innovatory King's Bench and the more conservative Common Pleas were not confined to the sphere of private law. Therefore, *Saunders* might well be seen to have settled one of these intercurial disputes some 30 years before *Slade's Case*.[85]

---

[79] Baker (ed), *Notebook of Sir John Port* 86. This seems to have been a garbled version of a bizarre mayhem case, or a different application of its ratio decidendi: see *Anon* (1498) YB Hil 13 Hen VII, fo 14, pl 5, where a parish clerk struck at someone with the church keys, which flew out of his hand, out of a window and hit a woman passer-by in the eye; this was held to be mayhem.

[80] Robert Brooke's reading: Baker (ed), *Selected Readings* 188; *R v Herbert* (1556) Dyer 128 (translation in 73 ER 279); SS vol 124, 127.

[81] Baker (ed), *Reports of Sir John Spelman* 308.

[82] Case put at Richard Littleton's reading (1493): Thorne and Baker (eds), *Readings and Moots* 274; CUL MS Hh.3.6, fo 3v.

[83] Temporarily in 1512–14 and then permanently in 1531: Baker, *OHLE* 537–40. The Church resisted this reform strenuously, taking the irrational view that the benefit of clergy ought to be available to laymen who committed murder. After 1536, even real clergy could be tried and punished for murder.

[84] *R v Herbert* (nn 72 and 80). The judges who held it to be murder were Saunders CJ, Heigham CB, Whiddon, Browne and Dalison JJ. Frowyk's example was of poison taken by chance, whereas the case put in 1556 was of a person sent with poison who administered it to the wrong person.

[85] For these disputes, see JH Baker, 'Judicial Conservatism in the Common Pleas 1500–1560' in Baker, *Collected Papers* vol 1, especially 467–69; JH Baker, 'New Light on *Slade's Case*' in Baker, *Collected Papers* vol 3, 1147–75.

It endorsed the King's Bench thinking that the murderer whose act killed the wrong person was just as deserving of death as the murderer whose design was carried out as intended.

There was no doubt after 1579 that malice towards one person could be transferred to the killing of someone else so as to constitute murder. It was confirmed in 1611 in a case similar to *Saunders*.[86] Agnes Gore's husband had fallen ill, and her father out of goodwill consulted a physician and obtained a prescription for some medicine to cure him. The medicine was made up by an apothecary called Martin and was sent to Agnes, who added some rat poison before administering it to her husband, with the intention of killing him. The poisoned medicine made her husband worse, but did not kill him. Seeing its ill effects, her father took it back to Martin and complained, and, in order to vindicate his reputation, Martin gave it a stir with his knife and ate part of it in the father's presence. This time the poison worked. It killed Martin, and Agnes was indicted for his murder at the assizes. The assize judges, Fleming CJ and Tanfield CB, reserved the case and stated it in writing to all the judges of England.[87] The reason for the doubt was that Martin might himself have made the electuary more lethal by stirring it before taking some, a circumstance which perhaps distinguished the case from *Saunders*.

The assembled judges agreed unanimously that it was murder because (as Coke put it) the law 'conjoined' the murderous intention with the event which followed the poisoning of the medicine.[88] The stirring of the medicine would not have caused Martin's death if Agnes had not put in the poison. The judges added that the law would be the same if A put poisoned wine in a place where he expected B to drink it, and by accident C (a stranger) drank it and died, 'for the law couples the event with the intention, and the end with the cause'. Coke, who took part in the conference as Chief Justice of the King's Bench, added a policy reason. Someone who prepares poison to kill a human being is as great an offender if someone unintended dies from it as where it kills the person intended: 'and if the law should be [otherwise], this horrible and heinous offence would be unpunished, which would be mischievous, and a great defect in the law'. In his *Third Institute*, Coke explained the decision in terms of transferred malice: 'This malice is so odious in law, as though it be intended against one, it shall be extended

---

[86] *R v Gore* (1611) 9 Co Rep 81 (translated in 77 ER 853); 3 Co Inst 51; Hale PC 1: 431.

[87] So said Coke. A copy of the case stated, in English, has survived in Sir Christopher Yelverton's notebook, BL MS Hargrave 430, fo 226. It may be the earliest surviving example of such a case. Coke and Yelverton were both among the signatories.

[88] The written opinion in MS Hargrave 430 (unless Yelverton abridged it) said only: 'This was thought to be murther, considering first the intent to murder, and then the event of the death that followed after, though it was not in the same man that was purposed to be poysoned, because there was an intent att the first to poyson one.'

towards another.'[89] It might be added, for the sake of completeness, that the same principle was later held to apply even if the person killed by accident was the offender himself.[90]

*Saunders* was hailed at the time as a prime example of 'equity' in the criminal law.[91] And it is still cited with approval by some modern authors, though the underlying rationale of transferred malice has proved elusive.[92] One recent writer, while noting that it has been followed by most American courts, described it as 'dogmatic and unexplained' and 'troubling'.[93] It has the ring of fiction, and Lord Mustill condemned it as out of date on that ground.[94] It might appear to partake of the same nature as constructive malice, which was abolished in 1957,[95] and, indeed, Hale and Blackstone both treated it as a species of 'implied' malice.[96] Blackstone went so far as to say that 'all homicide is presumed to be malicious, until the contrary appeareth upon evidence'.[97] That would no longer be accepted. However, in the case of transferred malice, it may be the label which is inappropriate rather than the doctrine itself.[98] The line between a fiction, which is a falsification of facts, and a legal doctrine, which is an abstract interpretation of facts, is not always easy to draw.[99] For example, the implied and constructive contracts which used to be deployed to prevent unjust enrichment are now regarded as offensive fictions, whereas implied and constructive trusts are regarded

---

[89] 3 Co Inst 51.

[90] EH East, *Pleas of the Crown* (London, 1803) 1: 230, says that if a man shoots at someone and the gun bursts so that he is killed himself, he is *felo de se*. This derives from Bacon, *Maxims of the Law* 92.

[91] E Hake, *Epieikeia: A Dialogue on Equity in Three Parts*, ed DEC Yale (New Haven, Yale University Press, 1953) 66–69. This late Elizabethan treatise was not about equity as administered in the Chancery, but an exploration of equitable interpretations of common law and statute law.

[92] It is enough to cite GL Williams, *Textbook of Criminal Law*, ed DJ Baker, 3rd edn (London, Sweet & Maxwell, 2012) para 11-023. It is there said to make no difference whether Saunders was present or not.

[93] L Katz, *Bad Acts and Guilty Minds: Conundrums of the Criminal Law* (Chicago, University of Chicago Press, 2012) 170, 174.

[94] *Attorney-General's Reference (No 3 of 1994)* [1998] AC 245 (HL), 259D. Lord Mustill accepted that the doctrine in *Saunders and Archer* still survived 'in some small degree'.

[95] Homicide Act 1957 s 1. Constructive malice was the malice presumed by law from the commission or attempted commission of any felony or from resisting a lawful arrest. It was said that if A shoots at B's hen and kills C, this would be murder provided that he intended to steal the hen, because that was a felony: 3 Co Inst 56; approved in *R v Plummer* (1701) Kel 109, 117; 84 ER 1103, 1107, per Holt CJ; East, *Pleas of the Crown* 1: 255. Stealing a hen was only petty larceny, not a felony.

[96] Hale PC 1: 465–66; Bl Comm 4: 200–01, 202. See also *R v Hollowaye* (1628) Palm 545, 547; 85 ER 1213, 1214, per Berkeley, Sjt, referring to *Gore*.

[97] Bl Comm 4: 201.

[98] *cf* M Jefferson, *Criminal Law*, 11th edn (Harlow, Pearson, 2013) 123: 'Perhaps a more modern name for the doctrine would make transferred malice more acceptable to Lord Mustill.'

[99] See JH Baker, *The Law's Two Bodies* (Oxford, Oxford University Press, 2001) 33–57. A rule of law can never be a fiction, even it is cast in metaphorical language: eg, the king never dies.

as perfectly respectable. Malice, like contract or trust, is a mixture of fact and law. It would avoid the fiction problem if cases of transferred malice were seen merely as immaterial variations in the way in which crimes may be committed,[100] or as falling within a broader definition of malice. General malice can be viewed in the same way. There is no fiction in treating as a murderer the terrorist who kills indiscriminately, because the victims are all within the scope of his enterprise.

A more serious objection was raised by Glanville Williams in criticising the theory, put forward by the Criminal Law Commissioners in 1833, that in cases of transferred malice the criminal intention, the injury and the loss to society are the same as they would have been if things had gone according to plan. As the Commissioners put it, 'whether, therefore, the crime be estimated by the intention or the result, its magnitude cannot be affected by the consideration that the mischief did not light where it was intended'.[101] This was essentially Coke's reasoning in *Agnes Gore's Case* in 1611. But, in Williams's words, 'unfulfilled intention does not elsewhere constitute a crime, except in some instances that are not here relevant; and ... an unintended result does not elsewhere constitute a crime where intention is required'. The explanation is also unduly wide, since it would extend to cases where there was no negligence or causal proximity.[102] It is generally accepted that transferred malice will not operate if there is no nexus between the death and the malicious enterprise. For instance, if A decides to kill B, gets into his car to drive to B's house, and drives so furiously that he accidentally kills C on the way, his malice towards B will not convert his crime—manslaughter or causing death by dangerous driving—into murder. Nor would there be a murder if, in the course of witnessing a crime of violence, a bystander with a weak constitution was frightened to death.[103]

Williams offered an alternative justification. Since in cases of transferred malice there is always a crime of some sort, namely an attempt, treating it as murder does not affect criminal responsibility, but serves only to increase the punishment. Indeed, at the time he was writing, it made the difference between life and death. Attempts are generally treated less seriously than completed crimes, even though the moral culpability is the same, but this indulgence does not extend to the typical case of transferred malice because

---

[100] AP Simester, JR Spencer, GR Sullivan and GJ Virgo, *Simester and Sullivan's Criminal Law: Theory and Doctrine*, 5th edn (Oxford, Hart Publishing, 2013) 165. It is there denied that transferred malice is a 'doctrine' at all.

[101] Williams, *General Part* 135.

[102] ibid 135–36. The matter is discussed very fully ibid 126–39. See also J Horder, 'Transferred Malice and the Remoteness of Unexpected Outcomes from Intentions' [2006] *Crim LR* 383.

[103] In *R v Hueton and others* (1340) TNA: PRO KB 29/9, m 28, KB 27/357, Rex m 3d, it was alleged that in the course of a ferocious attack by many people on a house, involving robbery and the abduction of Margery de Beche, her chaplain (who was ill) was frightened to death, but it was not laid as a malicious or felonious homicide.

'public opinion is aroused just as strongly as if the attempt had succeeded'.[104] This might not be intellectually satisfying, since it 'depends upon an emotional reaction', but it is 'an arbitrary exception to normal principles'.[105]

A more radical approach is to say that if Saunders' case were to recur today, the appropriate charge would be manslaughter in respect of little Eleanor and attempted murder in respect of Mrs Saunders.[106] The manslaughter approach would seem to reflect some medieval opinion. The law of attempts is more elusive. Suppose that in Saunders' case Eleanor had been made very sick, but had survived. Attempting to poison someone was not a felony,[107] and it is far from clear whether at this date it was even treated as a misdemeanour. Virtually no notice is taken of attempts in the books of criminal law before the nineteenth century.[108] It is generally supposed that the punishment of attempts began in the Star Chamber, and William Hudson wrote that attempts to poison or murder were an ordinary feature of its jurisdiction.[109] Even if an attempt was already a punishable offence, there would have been no need to apply the notion of transferred malice to the attempt in Saunders' case, since the attempt on his wife's life was already complete when he handed her the apple.

The matter was complicated by Lord Ellenborough's Act 1803,[110] whereby certain categories of serious attempts were turned into felonies. Whether transferred malice would operate in relation to such felonies was a question which arose at the Old Bailey in 1850.[111] A young woman had sent a twopenny jam tart impregnated with cantharides to a theatre as a present for the actor James Elphinstone, with whom she was obsessed. Elphinstone gave it to his dresser and it was eaten later by the dresser's wife Charlotte, who was made very ill. The woman was charged under the 1803 Act that she had feloniously administered cantharides with the intention of murdering Charlotte. It was necessary to mention Charlotte because the statute specifically required an intention to murder the person to whom the poison was administered, though of course the defendant had no prior knowledge

---

[104] Williams, *General Part* 137.

[105] ibid 134.

[106] For the attempt approach, see A Ashworth, 'Transferred Malice and Punishment for Unforeseen Consequences' in P Glazebrook (ed), *Reshaping the Criminal Law* (London, Stevens, 1978) 86–89. Dine, Gobbert and Wilson (*Cases and Materials* 196) suggest that Saunders should have been charged with attempted murder of the wife, presumably transposing the case to the present day.

[107] This is explicitly stated in T Smith, *De Republica Anglorum* (London, 1583) 85.

[108] See the discussion by K Smith in W Cornish et al, *The Oxford History of the Laws of England, Vol XIII, 1820–1914* (Oxford, Oxford University Press, 2010) 297–302.

[109] W Hudson, *A Treatise on the Court of Star Chamber*, c 1621, first printed in F Hargrave (ed), *Collectanea Juridica* vol 2 (London, 1792) 108.

[110] 43 Geo III c 58.

[111] *R v Sharp* (19 August 1850) in *Old Bailey Sessions Papers*, Tenth Session 1849–50, 538–40.

of her existence. Counsel said that if the intention was to injure A, and B was injured instead, this came within the decided cases—meaning, presumably, *Saunders*. Platt B thought this was incorrect because 'the intent was the essence of the charge' under the statute. In other words, the statute required a specific intention, and it was not proved. Nevertheless, the learned judge, inexplicably, left it to the jury whether the intent was to injure Elphinstone or merely to give effect to some misguided amorous design, and the jury thereupon found the defendant not guilty.

No doubt, in all cases where transferred malice traditionally operates, there is necessarily an attempted murder, and in a case like *Saunders and Archer* there is also a conspiracy. But opinions differ as to whether those are sufficiently serious charges to satisfy justice in the case where a death actually results from the attempt. There might also be practicable difficulties in charging an attempt before the facts are fully ascertained. It was on those grounds that the Law Commission agreed to stay the hand of abolition from transferred malice, which it misleadingly renamed 'transferred fault'.[112] No one questions that there is a crime which ought to be punished; the only question is the severity of its categorisation and punishment. Even Lord Mustill, who expressed doubts as to whether the doctrine had any intellectual basis, acknowledged that it is 'useful enough to yield rough justice, in particular cases, and it can sensibly be retained'—but not extended.[113]

### III. ARCHER'S CASE

Saunders' case and its progeny are interesting enough, but it was Archer's case which caused the chief difficulty at the time and has caused the most discussion since. Although the judges in 1576 were inclined to think that Archer was technically not guilty, they nevertheless thought it undesirable to make this too clear, and so they gave judgment against him, but reprieved him so he could obtain a pardon. Sir Michael Foster said this was 'a Measure Prudence will often suggest in Cases of a doubtful or delicate Nature'.[114] The judgment would not be a precedent, even for those with access to the gaol-delivery roll, since the troublesome facts were not recorded on the roll.

The law before 1576 as to the liability of an accessory for unexpected outcomes was not well developed. Staunford, in the 1550s, summed it up with two contrasting cases. If A commanded B to beat C, and B beat C to death, this was 'felony' in A because 'it is difficult to beat a man in such a

---

[112] Law Commission, *Legislating the Criminal Code: Offences against the Person and the General Principles* (Law Com No 218, 1993) 80. No transfer of fault seems to be required, since the fault is deemed to be the same wherever the 'malice' is directed.

[113] *Attorney-General's Reference (No 3 of 1994)* (n 94) 261.

[114] M Foster, *A Report of some Proceedings ... to which are added Discourses upon a Few Branches of the Crown Law* (Oxford, 1762) 371.

way that he can be sure he will not die of such battery'. On the other hand, if A commanded B to arrest C and he robbed him, this would not make A an accessory to robbery because his command could have been effected without robbery and so B had exceeded his command.[115] The same point had been made earlier in the inns of court.[116] Staunford's authority was a case in the eyre of Northamptonshire 1329, abridged by Fitzherbert, about which we now know a little more than he did.[117] Sir Warin de L'Isle ('del Idle') had taken his men on an expedition to beat someone. The men carried out their instructions so immoderately that the victim was slain, though Sir Warin himself hid out of the way.[118] Sir Warin was arraigned as a principal, and the judges held that 'when several men come in company with a common purpose, and an offence is committed, such as homicide or robbery or some other misdeed, each of them will be held to be a principal, even those who stood aside and did nothing wrong'. The report added that, in another case, a man was condemned because he had participated in a disseisin in which someone was killed, even though the jury said he did not go there to do wrong. Thus, the question was from the outset connected with what is now called the principle of joint (or common) enterprise. The chief concern originally was not whether an offence had actually been committed, but whether the instigator who stood on the sidelines was a principal or only an accessory.[119] If the principal was guilty only of manslaughter, there could be no accessory before the fact.[120]

The connection between common enterprise and transferred malice had been further explored in 1556.[121] Sir George Herbert of Swansea, elder

---

[115] W Staunford, *Les Plees del Coron* (London, 1574) 41D (tr).

[116] *Mountford's Reading* fo 179: '(tr) If I command someone to beat a man, and he kills him, I am an accessory. If I command someone to take a distress or to enter in certain lands unlawfully, and a rescue is made, and he kills a man, this is felony in him but I am not an accessory.' The same distinction is drawn in John Hutton's reading in Gray's Inn, CUL MS Hh.3.10, fo 28v.

[117] Fitz Abr, *Corone*, pl 314; *Sir Warin del Idle's Case* (1329–30) 97 SS 190. The editor, Sutherland, found the record of the proceedings against the men, but not that concerning Sir Warin. The record shows that the attack was made on the mansion house of William FitzWarin in Mears Ashby.

[118] Sutherland translated 'ungla de coste' as 'rode aside', whereas *ungler* more probably means to kneel or crouch: LW Stone and W Rothwell (eds), *Anglo-Norman Dictionary* (London, Modern Humanities Research Association, 1977–92) 479. It seems to be derived from *ungle* or *ongle*, the nail of a hand or foot.

[119] For more on this question, see *R v Lord Dacre of the South* and *R v Mauntell* (1541) Brooke Abr, *Corone*, pl 171 (misdated 34 Hen VIII); *R v Salisbury* (n 23); discussed in JM Kaye, 'The Early History of Murder and Manslaughter' (1967) 83 *LQR* 571, 584–86; and in Baker, *OHLE* 575–77.

[120] This was confirmed in *R v Anon* (1587) CUL MS Ii.5.38, fo 232v. It was, however, possible for an accessory to be convicted of manslaughter if the principal was convicted of murder: *R v Salisbury* (n 23).

[121] *R v Herbert* (n 72); discussed in Kaye, 'The Early History of Murder and Manslaughter' 577–84; and in Baker, *OHLE* 556 (both written before Dalison's report was edited for publication).

brother of the Earl of Pembroke, and vice-admiral in South Wales, was engaged in a feud with Sir Rhys Mansell over a claim to the cargo of a French vessel wrecked near Oxwich.[122] One day, Herbert went with a party of 40 or more men to Mansell's house 'with the purpose of having an affray and fight with the said Sir Rhys and his son, but with no intention of killing anyone'. While Mansell's unarmed sister was trying to restore peace, she was struck and killed by a rock or stone thrown over a wall by one of Herbert's servants. No one had any malice against the woman, but Saunders CJ thought it was nevertheless murder, citing the old case of the stranger killed while separating combatants.[123] It presumably followed that Herbert was party to that murder. But other judges thought it was only manslaughter, and so the case was referred to all the judges in Serjeants' Inn, an early instance of the informal procedure which would lead nearly three centuries later to the Court for Crown Cases Reserved. According to Serjeant Dalison's report, the judges were equally divided:

> Saunders CJ, Whiddon and Browne JJ, Heigham CB and Dalison [queen's serjeant] were agreed that this was wilful murder, because it commenced upon an unlawful act to be done to a man's person, in which act they had malice to do an evil thing against the law, and in that malice the woman's death occurred, and therefore it is murder. Similarly if someone commands another to carry poison to John Style to destroy him, and the man carries it to John [Dale][124] and poisons him, this is murder, for John [Dale] is poisoned in this malice that John Style would have been in, had the poison been given to him ... [and] they are both wilful murderers now by the statute of 1 Edw. VI, c 12.[125] Moreover, when someone does a wrong (*un torte*) he shall be adjudged by the law in the most extreme wrong; and here Herbert did a wrong in assembling the people, and therefore it shall be adjudged murder when someone died as a result, and not manslaughter, which is the [lesser] offence. Serjeants Browne and Catlyn [queen's serjeants], Griffith A-G and the

---

[122] For the circumstances, see TG Watkin, 'Oxwich Revisited: An Examination of the Background to Herbert's Case, 1557–58' (2001) 8 *Transactions of the Honourable Society of Cymmrodorion* (New Series) 94–118. For the investigations in the Star Chamber, see BL MS Lansdowne 639, ff 59v, 60.

[123] According to the Star Chamber investigation, the deceased was Anne Mansell, a widow, and the suspected culprit was Herbert's illegitimate son Watkin John ap Watkin, who had since absconded. Herbert was fined £40 for not using his best endeavours to apprehend him: MS Lansdowne 639, fo 60.

[124] The manuscript says 'J S' throughout, but it is seems from the sense that a different person was intended.

[125] 1 Edw VI c 12, s 13: 'that all wilful killing by poisoning of any person or persons, that at any time hereafter shall be done, perpetrated or committed, shall be adjudged, taken and deemed wilful murder of malice prepensed, and that the offenders therein, their aiders, abetters, procurers and counsellors shall suffer death and forfeit in every behalf as in other cases of wilful murder of malice prepensed'. Taken out of context, this appears to draw a distinction between wilful and malicious killing. But the only purpose of the statute was to repeal 22 Hen VIII, c 9, which had turned murder by poisoning into high treason and imposed a horrific new form of death penalty: Baker, *OHLE* 539. In 1633, in charging a grand jury in the King's Bench, Jones J said the statute was 'but declaratory of the common law': Kel 52; 84 ER 1078.

S-G [Weston] were of the same opinion. But Brooke CJ, of the Common Pleas, Staunford, Dyer, and Morgan JJ, and Prideaux, queen's serjeant, to the contrary: that it was not murder but manslaughter. For murder is killing a man with malice aforethought (*occisio hominis ex malicia praecogitata*), and they had no malice towards this woman; but they said that, if Mansell or any of his servants in his company had been so killed, that would clearly have been murder. But this woman did not come in aid of Mansell or Herbert, but was a peacemaker between them, to whom both parties bore good will

Brooke CJ later explained his position:

> In all cases where someone comes accompanied by a multitude of people to do an unlawful act, such as beating someone or disseising someone, or putting him out of his house, if this man is killed in the course of this entry or battery, by him or his companions, or any of them, it is murder. It is otherwise if a stranger is killed in this entry or battery: that is only manslaughter, for it comes by chance medley. In the first case, however, the malice and killing come to the same party.[126]

Brooke CJ's side also adhered to the medieval view that the killing of an intervener by people fighting was only manslaughter.[127] Dyer CJ's report says that the judges who thought Herbert guilty of murder did so on the footing that the woman 'came in defence of, or on behalf of, Mansell'. But this was factually unclear, and so, according to Dalison, the matter was adjourned for further enquiry as to whether the woman was 'in part taking with Mansell' or came as a stranger, or as a friend to both sides. It was thus agreed that the implied malice towards Mansell and his party was sufficient for murder, even if the killing which occurred was merely a result of negligence, and the principal question was whether this implied malice could be transferred to an uninvolved third party. It would have been much clearer if one of Herbert's party had deliberately killed the woman. That would not have been within the common purpose, which at most was to attack Mansell and his defenders, and to resist their defences with violence, but an independent collateral crime. Yet, where someone stirred up a violent mêlée or siege, it might be said that anyone who was killed by being caught up in it came within the indiscriminate general malice.[128] Herbert's case sat on the dividing line.

Another borderline case of a similar kind arose in the King's Bench after the notorious siege of Drayton Basset manor house in Staffordshire on 3 September 1578. This was the most serious incident of its kind within memory and it attracted the queen's personal attention, not least because

---

[126] *R v Herbert* SS vol 124, 131.

[127] *R v Herbert* Dyer 128; translation in 73 ER 279–80.

[128] *cf R v Stanley* (1663) Kel 86, 87; 84 ER 1094 ('when several men joyn in an unlawful act they are all guilty of whatever happens upon it'). The law as to common enterprise was further considered by all the judges and was explained by Holt CJ in *R v Plummer* (1701) Kel 109, 118; 84 ER 1103, 1107.

it involved the interests of her favourite, Robert Dudley, Earl of Leicester, in a complex property dispute.[129] A party of at least 70 men led by John Robinson gained entry to the house, where they were besieged by an even larger party led by Humphrey Ferrers (the earl's protégé) attempting to gain re-entry. One of the invading party, Thurstan Ward, was killed in the courtyard at 10 pm by a single shot from a calliver, or musket. There was a full investigation by the Privy Council, led by William Fleetwood, recorder of London, and one of the difficulties they faced was to determine what offences had been committed and by whom. There were two principal indictments. On 20 September, before the Staffordshire magistrates at Burton-on-Trent, Robinson and 24 others were indicted that they, together with 50 persons unknown, in warlike array and armed with callivers, shot and killed Ward with a single bullet from a single 'gunne'.[130] This physically impossible assertion was obviously a fiction intended to make it clear that they were all charged as principals; at that stage, perhaps, it was unclear who had fired the fatal shot. On the following 13 March, at Wolverhampton, a coroner's inquest found a more specific and realistic verdict, to the effect that the shot had been fired by John Perkyns and that Robinson and 27 others were present aiding, abetting, procuring, comforting, maintaining and aiding him. They were thus indicted of murder as principals in the first and second degree.[131] Others were indicted separately for riot and forcible entry.[132] There were also proceedings against the same parties in the Star Chamber in Easter term 1580 for riot, and for contempt both of the local magistrates and of the Council.[133] The indictments were all removed

---

[129] The background was unravelled by DC Peck, 'The Earl of Leicester and the Riot at Drayton Basset, 1578' (1980) 27 *Notes & Queries* (New Series) 131–35; and S Adams, *Leicester and the Court: Essays in Elizabethan Politics* (Manchester, Manchester University Press, 2002) 372 fn 240, 387–90. The King's Bench proceedings have not been discussed before. See also *Lady Leicester v Thomas Robinson* (1589) BL MS Lansdowne 62(53) (Exchequer suit concerning the same estate).

[130] *R v John Robynson and others* (Hil 1580) TNA: PRO KB 27/1272, Rex, m 5; KB 29/214, m 74. This entry ends with a *habeas corpora juratorum*, returnable in Easter term 1580. Many of the parties who did not appear in the King's Bench were pardoned in 1583: TNA: PRO KB 29/215, m 45d.

[131] *R v Perkyns and others* (Trin 1580) TNA: PRO KB 27/1274, Rex, m 5. The concept of principal in the second degree is first found in a judgment of Bromley CJ at Shrewsbury quarter sessions in 1553: *R v Griffith ap David* (n 23); Baker, *OHLE* 576–77.

[132] *R v Harecourt and others* (1580) TNA: PRO KB 27/1275, Rex, m 17 (forcible entry); *R v Thomas Robynson and others* (n 130) m 19 (riot). These entries end with imparlances. Most of these defendants were outlawed, but Thomas Robinson (John's brother) was pardoned: TNA: PRO KB 29/215, mm 80, 90 (annotations in the controlment roll).

[133] The account in BL MS Harley 2143 fo 37 gives a different version of events: '*Attornatus Regis et* Harecourt, Robinson *et alios* for a ryott att Drayton Bassett in Staffordshire, for which some weare convicted for that they did not departe after warning given by the justice of peace, and after a privie sessions for that purpose, and after proclamation made according to the statute, and after letters from the queen and Councell, and yet disobeying all untill they weare removed by *posse comitatus*. For which great and rebellious riott manie were sentenced and comitted during the queens pleasure, as by the severall orders appeareth.'

into the King's Bench, where Robinson and 12 others appeared and were granted bail.[134] After several challenges to two juries, both by the parties and by the Attorney-General, the trial took place in November 1580. All the defendants were acquitted of murder, but Robinson and three others were convicted of manslaughter.[135] This verdict was only permissible by virtue of their indictment as principals, since they could not be accessories before the fact to manslaughter,[136] and the concept of transferred malice was inapplicable. Richard Crompton, a Staffordshire magistrate and bencher of the Middle Temple, thought the case sufficiently interesting (or surprising) to include in his 1583 edition of Fitzherbert's book for justices of the peace in the section dealing with manslaughter, though he did not go into the reasoning.[137] *Herbert* was not yet in print, but it was almost certainly well known.[138] Only one law report relating to the Drayton case has been found. It suggests that the case was considered in banc and it shows that the main concern was to distinguish the principals from the accessories, on the footing that there was sufficient malice to support convictions for murder:[139]

> Note that it was held upon the same arraignment[140] that if several men take possession of a house with force, and then (being in possession) they conspire amongst themselves to maintain the possession of the same house, and to kill anyone who tries to put them out of possession, and then they divide themselves into separate rooms of the house in order the better to defend themselves in the house, and then one of them who is in one room kills one of the men who wish to put them out of possession: all those who are in the house, if they are within sight or hearing of the person who kills the man, are principals of this murder, but if they are not within the sight or hearing but are further off, so that they cannot see or hear what is done, they are only accessories, as in the Lord Dacre's case.

The jury were presumably informed of this opinion and therefore, assuming they were impartial, it must be supposed that they did not find it proved that there was a general conspiracy to kill any assailant. There is no suggestion

[134] One of Robinson's two bail was Lawrence Tanfield of the Inner Temple, later Chief Baron of the Exchequer.

[135] This is noted in the controlment roll of the clerk of the Crown, TNA: PRO KB 29/215, m 45 at m 45d. There is a marginal reference on m 45 to 'rotulo quinto', ie, KB 27/1272, Rex, m 5, where the indictment is set out verbatim, but not the outcome.

[136] See above, n 120.

[137] *Crompton* fo 17 (dated Mich 1580). He said that 'R' (now identifiable as Robinson) was convicted of manslaughter and that the others were arraigned as principals (ie, to murder), but he did not say that the others were convicted of manslaughter

[138] Dyer CJ was still living, though his reports were not published until 1586. Dalison's much fuller report of the case was not printed until 2007. *Crompton* fo 15v noted Catlyn CJ's opinion that it was murder, without referring to any dissent; on fo 16, he refers to the same case anonymously as contrasting with that of Drayton Basset.

[139] BL MS Add 36080, fo 122 (tr).

[140] This refers to the previous paragraph, where the case is said to be that of one Stanford and others. But the date is Michaelmas term 1580 and it presumably refers to the events at Drayton.

that Tristram Ward was an uninterested bystander or that Perkyns was acting on an independent whim; his gun can hardly have been concealed from the rest of his party. Nor would killing in self-defence have been justifiable, since the defendants had gained possession by force.[141] But the way in which juries decide cases on the facts does not affect the principles of law. The harder line taken by the judges was affirmed at Serjeants' Inn in 1585 after a park-keeper in Dorset was killed in a fight with a group of armed poachers; the unlawful assembling with weapons was enough to demonstrate 'malice in law'.[142]

In between these two causes célèbres, Archer's case also sat on the dividing line, though it was different in that Archer was not present aiding and abetting. Archer had counselled the use of poison as the best way of killing a wife and had bought some for Saunders. He was not said to have had any personal interest in the death of Mrs Saunders, as distinct from any other person, and so he could be regarded as having counselled the death of a human being whose identity was immaterial to him. Poison was notoriously deadly and might easily be taken by the wrong person. It is arguable that if Saunders had been absent when his wife took the apple and handed it to his daughter, Archer would have been guilty as an accessory since the death followed directly from Saunders' act. It would have been 'a clear case of unintended miscarriage of the common purpose'. On that footing, the only point in the case was whether Saunders' presence and his failure to intervene was tantamount to a change of plan, a new crime which took it outside the common venture that Archer had abetted.[143] If it had been Saunders himself who gave the apple to the daughter, Archer would clearly not have been guilty.[144] The court reluctantly took the view that his inaction had the same consequence,[145] but it is open to posterity to differ, and several later writers have done so. In any case, even if Archer is considered to be not guilty of murder, he would certainly in today's law be guilty of some lesser offence.[146]

---

[141] *Crompton* fo 17v mentions *R v Harecourt* (C 1563), another Staffordshire case, in which a tenant in peaceful possession of a house at Ranton had shot and killed a would-be intruder (who claimed title) with a crossbow, and the judges ruled it to be only manslaughter. But it was a criminal offence to hold with force lands into which entry had been made forcibly: 15 Ric II c 2; 8 Hen VI c 9.

[142] *Attorney-General's Question* (1585) Sav 67, translated in 123 ER 1016: 'the assembling to do an act unlawful, and coming with weapons, and the first assault offered by shooting an arrow, doth declare their intention to be malicious against such as should withstand them'.

[143] Williams, *General Part* 403; DJ Baker, *Textbook of Criminal Law*, 3rd edn (London, Sweet & Maxwell, 2012) para 14-083.

[144] Coke, commenting on the case, said that it made no difference if the means of killing were different from those counselled, whereas a change of victim, even if it resulted from a mistake by the principal, would exculpate the accessory: 3 Co Inst 51.

[145] Hake nevertheless thought it a 'righteous exposition of the law' and another example of 'equity' in the criminal law: Hake, *Epieikeia* 68.

[146] Ashworth ('Transferred Malice and Punishment' 81 fn 18) suggested incitement to murder. This offence has since been replaced under the Serious Crime Act 2007.

Some have drawn a distinction between the judges' decision on the facts in *Archer* and Plowden's commentary on it.[147] But Plowden only purported to be explaining the decision. His first statement of the principle was that the accessory's procurement and assent could not be stretched further than as he had given it, and he had not assented to the killing of the daughter. He then went on to say that it was reasonable to hold the accessory liable for everything which followed from the act to which he had assented, but not for another distinct thing. These formulations do not seem greatly different, especially since Plowden affirmed that he agreed with the decision, though it has been suggested that the latter version rested solely on the directness of the consequence, which was preferable to basing liability on the scope of the authority, and accorded with the majority view in *Herbert*.[148] Directness is the basis on which the principal's guilt rests, and the accessory does not deserve to be in a better position. Francis Bacon in 1597 rephrased the principle thus: 'any accessary before the fact is subject to all the contingencies pregnant of the fact, if they be pursuances of the same fact ... *quia in criminalibus praestantur accidentia*'.[149] The difficulty in *Archer*, however, was in deciding whether causal directness, or 'pursuance', could be interrupted for this purpose by the principal's failure to avert an unintended consequence when it was in his power to do so. Glanville Williams doubted whether the decision on the facts accorded with common sense, since the principal's dilemma over whether to intervene made the case more like an involuntary miscarriage of his plan than a deliberate change of victim.[150] The problem is not so much with the law as stated in Plowden's report, which has been described recently as 'a masterly analysis of accomplice liability',[151] but with its application in a borderline case. Sir Michael Foster, with his usual precision of thought, suggested the appropriate jury direction in 1762: 'Did the principal commit the felony he standeth charged with under the influence of the flagitious advice, and was the event in the ordinary course of things a probable consequence of that felony? Or did he, following the suggestions of his own wicked heart, wilfully and knowingly commit a felony of another kind or upon a different subject?'[152] It is difficult to imagine that a sensible jury, after receiving such a direction, would have acquitted Archer.

---

[147] Foster (*Crown Law* 370–72) referred to two different interpretations rather than to a difference between Plowden and the judges.

[148] D Lanham, 'Accomplices and Transferred Malice' (1980) 96 *LQR* 110, 114–17. The judges were in fact equally divided in *Herbert*, but there was a majority if the law officers are counted in.

[149] Bacon, *Maxims of the Law* 222. The text in Latin means that accidents in the commission of crimes must be answered for.

[150] Williams, *General Part* 403.

[151] Lanham, 'Accomplices and Transferred Malice' 124.

[152] Foster, *Crown Law* 372.

A remarkably similar case arose in South Africa in 1938.[153] A supplied poison to P for the purpose of poisoning P's wife. P put it into the drinking water in the hut which she usually occupied, but later discovered that the hut was now occupied by X. P did nothing to remove the poisoned water. X drank the water and died of the poison. It was held that A was not liable as an accessory—or, to use the Roman–Dutch term, *socius criminis*—because he could not have foreseen it as likely that P would leave the poison in place once he knew that the hut was occupied by someone else. The reference to foresight may have been unnecessary to the decision, since the liability of the accessory turned not on his own knowledge, but on that of the principal.[154] As with *Archer*, which was cited by counsel, it was the failure of the principal to intervene and prevent the death, when he could have done so, which broke the chain connecting the death with the common enterprise; the result would presumably have been different if P had not known about the change of occupancy. The accessory in such cases as these may not be guilty of murder, but he is certainly not free from moral blame. Today the solution might be a charge of conspiracy to murder, or aiding and abetting attempted murder.[155]

A final point in Plowden's commentary on *Archer*, though not related to the facts of the case, concerned the effect of a purported retreat by the accessory from his involvement in the crime. He suggested that an accessory should be allowed to repent, provided he communicated his change of mind to the principal before the deed was done.[156] This was not the first pronouncement on the subject,[157] but it has generally been accepted ever since.[158]

## IV. CONCLUSION

Very few cases from the sixteenth century are still under discussion by lawyers, other than legal historians, over four centuries later. It may be

---

[153] *R v Longone*, 1938 AD 532 (De Villiers JA dissenting).

[154] The foresight of the accessory has nevertheless been treated as the basis of liability in common enterprise cases: *Chan Wing-Siu v The Queen* [1985] AC 168 (PC); *Hui Chi-Ming v The Queen* [1992] 1 AC 34 (PC); *McAuliffe v The Queen* (1995) 69 AJLR 621; *R v Powell* [1999] 1 AC 1 (HL); *R v Rahman* [2008] UKHL 45, [2009] 1 AC 129; *R v Gnango* [2011] UKSC 59, [2012] 1 AC 827. *Saunders and Archer* (n 1) 474v spoke of foresight (*prevoyer*) only in relation to the principal, and in the different sense that it is incumbent on him to guard against any harm resulting from his actions.

[155] MJ Allen, *Textbook on Criminal Law* 12th edn (Oxford, Oxford University Press, 2013) 246. For accessories to attempts, see Williams, *General Part* 405.

[156] *Saunders and Archer* (n 1) 475v–476.

[157] *cf* Marow's reading (1505), cited in Putnam, *Early Treatises* 380; *Mountford's Reading* fo 179.

[158] 3 Co Inst 51; *R v Becerra* (1975) 62 Cr App R 212; KJM Smith, 'Withdrawal in Complicity: A Restatement of Principles' [2001] *Crim LR* 769.

true that criminal law is in essence more timeless than most other branches of law, which respond to transformations in the forms of wealth and commerce.[159] Leaving aside the evidential transformations brought about by modern science, the facts in cases of violent crime are generally no more complex today than they were in the past. What has changed is that lawyers are now involved in criminal law and have access to more case law and more analytical commentaries, from scholars as well as practitioners. The earlier treatises such as Staunford's, like the readings which preceded them, were heavily dependent on brief snippets of fourteenth-century cases found in the eyre reports of 1329–30 and the *Liber Assisarum*, because law reporters in general had thereafter lost interest in trials. Difficult criminal cases were being discussed by the assembled judges in Serjeants' Inn or the Exchequer Chamber from at least the 1480s,[160] but their deliberations were generally unknown to posterity and perhaps to the legal profession at the time. Even in the later eighteenth century, judgments in reserved criminal cases were still being given without reasons. Lest we be inclined to feelings of condescension, it might be recalled that the same ethos lived on much longer with respect to sentencing, which was similarly relegated to the world of practitioners until very recent times. Where now there are textbooks and reports of sentencing cases, only 50 years ago there was nothing to be studied beyond how to navigate *Archbold* and make pleas in mitigation. The change with respect to the substantive law of crimes began much earlier. And that is why Plowden's report of *Saunders and Archer* is a landmark. It marked the beginning of a new and more sophisticated approach to criminal law, at any rate in the printed sources which were coming to replace the more evanescent learning of the late medieval profession.

[159] *cf* SFC Milsom, *Historical Foundations of the Common Law* (London, Butterworths, 1969) 353 ('murder and theft stand as they always have, legal monoliths, because they are unalterable parts of the social landscape'). This passage is not in the second edition.
[160] Baker, *OHLE* 526–28.

# 4

# *R v Jones* (1703)

## SIMON STERN

A N 'OBJECTIVE' MEANS of assessment, in modern legal parlance, applies uniformly to all parties, regardless of their individual traits and capacities. Almost all rules, standards, lists and tests are objective, in this sense, but the term is usually applied to a small subset of these devices—the ones that are specified by reference to the reasonable person. Analyses of the reasonable person account for most of the scholarly attention bestowed on objective grounds of liability, and this tendency is significant because when an objective measure is rendered in a personified form, we are quickly plunged into debates about how generic the measure must be and whether (and how) to factor in certain personal traits, such as a party's age or mental capacity. That the reasonable person has, for most of its history, been cast as the reasonable man helps to show how readily the personification acquires specific features that may undermine its universal application. Though typically traced back to the 1837 case of *Vaughan v Menlove*,[1] this figure has various precursors in eighteenth-century law. Even before the eighteenth century, English law had occasionally borrowed personified standards from the civil law, such as the 'good father of the family' (*bonus paterfamilias*) who models a certain kind of diligence, and the 'firm man' (*constans vir*) who withstands duress. Those figures, however, had not yielded replicas or variants, but remained doctrinally confined, possibly because their personifications appear to specify a fixed level, appropriate to specific contexts, rather than embodying the flexibility now associated with the reasonable person. This latter figure, once introduced, would grow like kudzu in the garden of the common law.

A landmark precursor for the reasonable person appears in *R v Jones* (1703),[2] which addressed the question of criminal liability for fraud, using a personified standard in a different fashion from the civil law figures and from the modern versions: neither to exemplify a virtue nor to help in determining

---

[1] *Vaughan v Menlove* (1837) 3 Bing (NC) 468, 173 ER 232.
[2] *Anonymous* (1703) 6 Mod 105, 87 ER 464. Though styled as 'anonymous' here, the other reports call the case *Jones* (see nn 12 and 14), and I adopt that name for convenience.

the defendant's liability, but to draw the line between civil and criminal harms. In *Jones* and the jurisprudence that followed, we do not see a preview of the debates about adapting the standard with respect to personal characteristics, but we can discern the outlines of another contemporary debate associated with the personified standard, involving its ability to impose normative demands that are less easily communicated by non-personified standards. This chapter looks at how *Jones* introduced that question, how the standard was reframed when William Hawkins's treatise on criminal law catapulted it out of an obscure niche in one of the case reports, how the standard functioned in fraud jurisprudence and how it began to spread to other, more familiar, areas of criminal law.

*Jones* has a cryptic, almost fable-like quality that leaves the case open to various interpretations. A man borrows £20. A trickster appears, claiming that the lender sent him to collect the debt. The rube unhesitatingly pays up and discovers his error at leisure. The Queen's Bench refuses to convict, ruling that the deceit would be criminal only if it were 'such a Cheat as a Person of an ordinary Capacity can't discover'. In the court's disdainful summation, 'this is an Indictment to punish one Man because another is a Fool'.[3]

From this slender thread, various tales might be spun: a tale of contributory criminal fault, starring a boob who was so remarkably lax about protecting his own interests that in the court's view, he practically invited the harm; a tale about unreasonable reliance that strips the victim of any claim at all; a tale about the difference between civil and criminal liability, in which the malefactor's conduct does not threaten enough people, or is too mild, to be a crime; or a tale (which runs through several of the above) about the development of objective standards of liability. The focus here will be on the last two points. The use of a standard that is both objective and personified, to mark the threshold for criminal liability, is worthy of extensive discussion by itself.[4]

Preliminarily, it will help to contrast *Jones* with two contemporaneous cases, one involving commercial fraud and one involving a conspiracy to defraud. Jointly, these cases delineate the field that would define fraud jurisprudence over the next century and a half. In *Nehuff's Case* (1705), 'the Defendant borrowed 600l. of a Feme Covert, and promised to send her fine Cloth and gold-Dust as a Pledge, and sent no gold Dust, but some coarse Cloth worth little or nothing'. The Queen's Bench granted a certiorari to remove it from the Old Bailey, 'because the Fact was not a matter Criminal, but it was the Prosecutor's [victim's] fault to repose such a Confidence in

---

[3] *Jones* (n 2).

[4] As for the other possible interpretations, I discuss the question of contributory fault below (n 24), and while the case might belong to the pre-history of 'reasonable' reliance in the law of fraud (see n 26), this distinction did not figure in the eighteenth-century fraud jurisprudence.

the Defendant; And because it was an absurd Prosecution'.[5] The comments about the victim's credulity and the absurdity of the claim are reminiscent of *Jones*, and the importance of the victim's contributory fault—only a vague implication in *Jones*—comes to the fore. Because it featured parties in a commercial relationship, the dispute could be resolved on a different ground from *Jones*, by asking whether the defendant had breached a contract.

Taken together, *Jones* and *Nehuff* point up the distinction between civil and criminal fraud in two contexts: where the fraud arises as part of a contractual relationship and where it occurs among strangers. That the court in *Nehuff* did not apply *Jones*'s requirement of 'ordinary capacity' is hardly surprising; although both cases pitted the victim against the offender, breach of contract provided a ready doctrinal handle for addressing the problem, and its applicability helped to show why this was a private dispute, whereas in *Jones*, it was the lack of such an option that prompted the court to go further in explaining why the dispute was private. As we will see, disputes arising out of commercial relationships would typically yield the same result as in *Nehuff*, although courts usually cited *Jones* instead, ruling that the victim had been deceived by 'mere words' and had only a civil claim.

Conversely, in *R v Mackarty* (1705), the court held the defendants criminally liable, apparently because they had formed a conspiracy.[6] Posing as wine merchants, they offered to trade 'true new Lisbon wine for a quantity of hats', but what they exchanged was 'good for nothing' and 'non potabile nec salubre' (neither drinkable nor wholesome). The dispute turned in part on a question of mens rea: the need to specify, in the indictment, that the defendants knew their wine was worthless, because their claims about its quality might have been an innocent mistake. The court was clear that it could not 'presume the defendants knew wine better than the prosecutor [victim]'. The judgment does not address that issue directly, but says only that 'the fact as it appeared upon the evidence was criminal' and that the allegations in the indictment were sufficient: 'here enough was set out, to shew the defendants to be cheats'.[7]

The court could have treated this case, like *Nehuff*, as a breach of contract or (considering the remarks about the atrocious wine) might have likened it to *Jones* as another easily detectable deceit. The court cited neither one, but later courts would treat *Mackarty* as showing that conspiracies were, by

---

[5] *Nehuff's Case* (1705) 1 Salk 151, 91 ER 139. *Nehuff* has the distinction of appearing on the first page of Kenny's *A Selection of Cases Illustrative of English Criminal Law* (Cambridge, Cambridge University Press, 1901); Kenny presents it as a case of breach of contract and uses it to illustrate 'the distinction between civil and criminal wrongs'.

[6] *R v Mackarty* (1705) 2 Ld Raym 1179, 92 ER 280. See also *R v Orbell* (1703) 6 Mod 42, 87 ER 804, which involved a prosecution for conspiring to cheat by persuading the victim to bet on a fixed race. The court suggested that such a conspiracy is, by its very nature, criminal: 'being a Cheat, though it was private in the Particular, yet it was publick in its Consequences'.

[7] *Mackarty* (n 6) 1182, 1184.

their nature, too clever to be readily detectable and hence that *Jones* did not apply to those cases.[8] The question of mens rea, however, offers another way to make sense of *Mackarty*. Evidently, despite the professed concern about presuming the defendants' knowledge, the court was willing to infer, from their conspiratorial conduct, that they knew exactly what they were doing; conversely, in the cases involving one-on-one commercial transactions, like *Nehuff*, the courts were reluctant to assume that the defendants knowingly cheated their customers or bought goods without intending to pay.

Taken together, *Jones*, *Nehuff* and *Mackarty* suggest a few distinctions that would become clearer as the jurisprudence developed. The 'ordinary capacity' rationale would usually be invoked to explain why commercial transactions were generally not criminal, but the standard's effect, in those cases, was actually to solve a problem of mens rea: rather than asking juries to distinguish the cases of intentional fraud from the ones involving an inadvertent mistake, the courts took that question out of the juries' hands by removing this whole set of cases from the criminal docket. In conspiracy cases, where mens rea was easily inferred, the 'ordinary capacity' standard served largely the same function, allowing courts to treat conspiracies as too sophisticated to be easily detectable. The result, once again, was to avoid any inquiry into mens rea, this time by treating the defendants' stratagem as proof of intentional deception. When we line up the cases that followed *Jones*, we see that very few involve defendants who (on the facts mentioned in the judgment) were clearly out to cheat the victim. The vast majority were commercial cases, where it was possible, even if not likely, that the defendant had made an innocent mistake. Judges often remarked, when acquitting these defendants, that if misstating the quantity of grain (or the like) were criminal, every breach might be turned into a criminal case.[9] This conclusion does not follow, but its frequent repetition shows that applying the doctrine of *Jones* seemed preferable to the more involved process that would be required to separate civil and criminal cases—namely, tasking the jury with an inquiry into the defendant's intentions. In a few cases—all of them outside the context of ordinary commercial transactions—the facts strongly supported an inference of culpable intent, and the courts convicted, either under *Jones* or by modifying its doctrine. *Jones* itself is notable as the only case in the whole series in which the defendant was acquitted even though he was clearly a fraudster. By the nineteenth century, the courts would largely abandon the personified standard in fraud cases, opting instead for a rule that distinguished (culpable) lies from (permissible) statements about the future, but in the meantime, the standard had begun to acquire its modern significance in other legal contexts.

---

[8] The point was finally announced directly in *R v Wheatly* (1761) 2 Burr 1125, 1127, 1129, 97 ER 746.

[9] See below, n 31.

## I. THE CASE

*Jones* comes down to us in three versions. The one in the *Modern Reports*, quoted above, is the most important for present purposes. This version was first printed in 1713, in time for William Hawkins to use it in the first volume of his treatise on criminal law (1716), where he reformulated the holding in terms that would give the case much more impact.[10] In the *Modern Reports*, the case occupies two short paragraphs. After describing the defendant's ruse, the court repeats a view taken from earlier fraud cases (and from the statute of 38 Hen VIII c 1 (1547)), noting that the defendant's conduct would have been criminal if it had involved 'a false Token' such as false dice.[11] Next, the distinction between artless and artful types of chicanery is explained by reference to the 'Person of an ordinary Capacity'—a touch that is unique to this report of the case. The remark about the victim's heedlessness follows immediately afterwards.

Salkeld's report, printed in 1717, compresses the facts and holding into a single paragraph. However, he makes no mention of any standard, instead moving directly from the absence of any 'false Tokens' to the conclusion that the court would not 'indict one Man for making a Fool of another'.[12] This report adds that the victim may have a civil claim ('Let him bring his Action'), showing that the dispute exposes a distinction between criminal and civil liability, whereas the version in the *Modern Reports* seems to imply that the victim had no recourse at all.[13] Salkeld's second paragraph is devoted to a comparison with *Bainham's Case* (not otherwise reported), in which the court refused to make a pawnbroker criminally liable for refusing to return an item when the bailor came in with the money to redeem it. The third report of *Jones*, in Lord Raymond, closely follows Salkeld's, but attributes to Holt CJ the line about the defendant's foolishness (a detail that all the reporters evidently relished), whereas the other two versions wrap all of the reasons together as 'per curiam'.[14]

The version in the *Modern Reports* is significant because of the effort to explain what differentiates a mere lie, leading to civil liability for breach of

[10] W Hawkins, *A Treatise of the Pleas of the Crown* (London, 1716) 1:188 (citing *Jones* (n 2)). Hawkins may have also have had access to a manuscript report of the case.

[11] *Jones* (n 2).

[12] *R v Jones* (1703) 1 Salk 379, 91 ER 330; quotations are from the first edition of Salkeld's *Reports* (1717). The second edition of *Modern Cases*, which includes *Jones*, printed in 1719, is attributed to Salkeld on the title page, but that attribution has not generally been accepted.

[13] ibid 379. If the victim had sought to bring a civil claim, he could not have been a witness in the case, because parties were excluded from testifying on oath. See MRT Macnair, *The Law of Proof in Early Modern Equity* (Berlin, Duncker & Humblot, 1999) 206; W Holdsworth, *A History of English Law* (London, Methuen, 1938) 9:193–97; JH Wigmore, *A Treatise on the Anglo-American System of Evidence*, 3rd edn (Boston, MA, Little, Brown & Co, 1940) 2: §575.

[14] 2 Ld Raym 1013, 92 ER 174; quotations are from the first edition of Lord Raymond's *Reports* (1743).

contract, from contrivances such as false dice, which led to criminal liability. The distinction was long-standing in contract law. In the early seventeenth century, it was held that if a party 'buys an horse upon [the seller's] warranting him to have both his eyes, and he hath but one Eye, [the buyer] is remedyless ... But otherwise it is ... where the matter is secret ... and cannot be known to him who buyes'.[15] The question, the court explained, is whether the truth 'lies in [the buyer's] own Conusance'.[16] This explanation anticipates the one that Holt would give, but applies only to tangible property (and also leaves the buyer without any claim at all, whereas *Jones* suggests that civil liability remains available). The same distinction was applied in a criminal case from the later seventeenth century. In *R v Worrall*, the prosecution argued that selling improperly dyed cloth should be criminal, by analogy to 'playing with false Dice', because both involved hidden defects, whereas 'a Horse having but three Legs' has an 'open and manifest' defect.[17] *Jones* grounds the distinction on an entirely different basis. In these earlier cases, the court sets out a rule and suggests no standard that would help to resolve future disputes that the rule does not cover. *Jones* attempts to do just that, offering the discernment of someone with an 'ordinary Capacity' as a means of determining which kinds of deceit are crafty enough to be crimes.

This approach may have been inspired, in part, by the court's experience, about six months earlier, in *Coggs v Bernard*, a bailment case that has been discussed in connection with the formation of objective standards of liability in tort, but which also discussed fraud, and considered the use of personified standards in ways that *Jones* would echo.[18] The reference in *Jones* to *Bainham's Case* suggests that Holt saw bailment as a fruitful source of analogies for the question at hand. In *Coggs*, confronted with the question of how much care a bailee was required to take when transporting some brandy that he had agreed to carry for free, Holt considered various standards that might apply ('ordinary care', 'reasonable care', the same degree of care the bailee shows for 'his own' goods or 'the utmost diligence, such as the most diligent father of a family uses') and concluded that the bailee was 'oblige[d] ... to a diligent management'; failing that, his 'neglect [was] a deceipt' that amounted to 'fraud' (in the civil sense).[19] Some of these standards are personal and some are generic, but only one—the diligence of the *paterfamilias*—uses a frame that is at once personified and external to the perspectives of the parties. Notably, that example pitches the standard

---

[15] *Bayly v Merrel* (1616) Cro Jac 386, 387, 79 ER 331.
[16] ibid.
[17] *R v Worrall* (1683) Skin 108, 109, 90 ER 51.
[18] *Coggs v Barnard* (1702) 2 Ld Raym 909, 92 ER 107; D Ibbetson, *A Historical Introduction to the Law of Obligations* (Oxford, Oxford University Press, 1999) 164–67; M Lobban, 'Mapping the Common Law: Some Lessons from History' [2014] *New Zealand Law Review* 21.
[19] *Coggs* (n 18) 913, 916, 917, 918, 919.

at a high level, rather than using these features to approximate a minimally adequate level of competence. By contrast, this is exactly what the 'Person of ordinary Capacity' does, in identifying a generic viewpoint: it locates the standard in a human figure that establishes not a paragon, but a kind of least common denominator. Although none of the alternatives in *Coggs* serves quite that function, Holt's review of these various options may have planted the seed for the approach he proposed in *Jones*, which raised the question of fraud in a different guise.

## II. WILLIAMS HAWKINS, *JONES* AND THE OBJECTIVE STANDARD

William Hawkins's 1716 *Treatise of the Pleas of the Crown* recapitulated the decision in *Jones*, presenting it in a way that endowed it with a new significance. Hawkins's interpretation of the 'Person of ordinary capacity' standard, though doubtless meant simply to restate and clarify Holt's ruling, would set it on a new footing that made it much more adaptable. Indeed, Hawkins's treatise offers one of the earliest portrayals of the figure whose qualities would eventually become familiar as the traits of the 'reasonable person'.[20] In elaborating on the rationale of *Jones*, Hawkins explains that 'a false Pretense of having a Message' to collect a debt 'is not punishable by a criminal Prosecution, because it is accompanied with no manner of artful Contrivance, but wholly depends on a bare naked Lie, and it is said to be needless to provide severe Laws for such Mischiefs, against which common Prudence and Caution may be a sufficient Security'.[21] This account emphasises the victim's vigilance rather than capacity. Practically speaking, the two amount to the same thing here: someone lacking the cognitive ability to guard against such deceit would fare no better than one who could have taken steps to ascertain the truth, but did not. Taken literally, Holt's language suggests that someone without 'ordinary capacity' does not fall within the ambit of the criminal law's solicitude. However, that is not the question he was addressing: he probably assumed that anyone who could obtain a loan of £20 also had the capacity to inquire about an ostensible agent's authority. He evidently thought that the debtor deserved to be called a 'fool' because of his carelessness, not because of his intellectual aptitude.

Hawkins follows Holt in suggesting an objective means, involving a personified standard, for determining what kind of deception (and, by implication, what kind of harm more generally) warrants the attention of the criminal law. Despite what he says, 'bare naked lies' are not invariably transparent

---

[20] On the history of this figure, besides the sources cited in n 18, see M Lobban, 'Common Law Reasoning and the Foundations of Modern Private Law' (2007) 32 *Australian Journal of Legal Philosophy* 39; RKL Collins, 'Language, History and the Legal Process: A Profile of the Reasonable Man' (1976) 8 *Rutgers-Camden Law Journal* 311.

[21] Hawkins, *A Treatise of the Pleas of the Crown* 1:188.

or easily verified, but the more basic point is that common prudence creates a standard for gauging the kind of deception involved, assessed in terms of the effort required, or the means available, to detect it. In both Holt's and Hawkins's formulations, the standard is normative in application and probably also in intent. To call the victim a fool is to imply that the case was a waste of the court's time and that the victim should learn to be less gullible. Nevertheless, a significant difference, which probably helps to explain why Hawkins's formulation became more influential, is that his version openly signals its normative orientation. 'Ordinary capacity' sounds more descriptive: even if it escapes precise definition, it appears capable of empirical measurement in a way that prudence and caution are not. Moreover, no legal standard will encourage someone with a limited capacity to become more astute, whereas a standard of 'common prudence' may induce the imprudent to be more careful. Because prudence and caution are interactive qualities, they harmonise more readily with a standard that evaluates interpersonal conduct. Eventually this standard would come to serve, in tort, as a means of evaluating the defendant's conduct, thus aligning the normative function directly with the imposition of liability: the duty to pay damages results from failing to act as a 'reasonable person' would (and causing harm as a result). *Jones* presents the mirror image of this alignment, demanding a certain level of vigilance from the victim and declining to punish the fraudster if the victim failed to meet that requirement.

Although the traits of prudence and caution are already recognisable here as exercising the same kind of demand that the 'reasonable person' standard imposes (and these traits would themselves be subsumed into the term 'reasonable'), the descriptive force of the concept, as Holt and Hawkins express it, is evident in the adjectives they use—'ordinary' and 'common'. It would be a mistake to saddle these terms with a particular statistical meaning at a time when conceiving of populations in this way had barely begun.[22] Rather than designating an average, the idea is simply to indicate a usual, prevalent kind of conduct. Persons of common prudence and caution take measures that, by virtue of their ordinariness, obviate the need for criminal sanctions to prevent the harm. Someone who fails to take those measures ought to adopt them, instead of seeking to have the malefactor punished. A tension between the normative and descriptive functions of the standard (a tension that persists in contemporary uses)[23] is apparent from its inception.

Criminal law was an unlikely area for the incubation of this standard, given that it rarely looks to the victim's conduct.[24] Deceit is one of the few

---

[22] TM Porter, *The Rise of Statistical Thinking, 1820–1900* (Princeton, Princeton University Press, 1986).

[23] For a helpful overview and analysis in the context of tort, see AD Miller and R Perry, 'The Reasonable Person' (2012) 87 *New York University Law Review* 323.

[24] However, for arguments that criminal law does consider contributory fault and should do so more, see Aya Gruber, 'Victim Wrongs: The Case for a General Criminal Defense Based

criminal contexts where this consideration might arise, because it involves a criminal act that must somehow be distinguished from the voluntary transfer of property that it resembles. Just as this question would later make 'larceny by trick' a proving ground for the shift from 'manifest' to 'subjective' criminality,[25] here the question prompts the court to focus on the interaction between fraudster and dupe, and to adopt an approach that imposes certain demands on the latter, if the loss is to justify a criminal prosecution. Ultimately, as we will see, the same type of personified, objective standard would find a place in other areas where criminal law considers the interaction between the parties, as here, but uses the personification to examine the perspective of the defendant, whom it construes, in effect, as a kind of victim—namely, in the law of duress and provocation.

### III. FRAUD AFTER *JONES*

The option of civil liability, which the reports of Salkeld and Lord Raymond highlight, would be a persistent theme as the jurisprudence developed. The *Jones* standard—as articulated by Hawkins—was being used, in these cases, to mark the place where criminal law intervenes, rather than to mark the difference between reasonable and unreasonable reliance in fraud and misrepresentation generally. Today, that distinction serves to screen out the deceptions that should escape liability altogether, in various American jurisdictions that continue to require reasonable reliance as an element of fraud.[26] Thus, although we see the incubation of an objective standard here, it serves a different function from the one now performed by the 'reasonable person'.

In *Jones* and its successors, the deception is a public offence when it threatens enough people (everyone who takes care to look after their own interests) or poses a high enough degree of harm (because the usual practices of self-interest will not guard against it), whereas the feeble effort that would only deceive a fool does not require what Hawkins calls the 'severe' machinery of the criminal law. Given the elliptical language of Holt's judgment, these justifications remain implicit, although Hawkins's explanation

---

on Wrongful Victim Behavior in an Era of Victims' Rights' (2003) 76 *Temple Law Review* 45; A Harel, 'Efficiency and Fairness in Criminal Law: The Case for a Criminal Law Principle of Comparative Fault' (1994) 82 *California Law Review* 1181; *Forum on Comparative Liability in Criminal Law* (2005) 8 *Buffalo Criminal Law Review*.

[25] *Pear's Case* (1779) 2 East PC 685, 1 Leach 212, 168 ER 208; J Hall, *Theft, Law, and Society*, 2nd edn (Indianapolis, Bobbs-Merrill, 1952) 40; GP Fletcher, 'The Metamorphosis of Larceny' (1976) 89 *Harvard Law Review* 469, 504–07; G Ferris, 'The Origins of "Larceny by Trick" and "Constructive Possession"' [1998] *Crim LR* 175, 182–86.

[26] See CA Wright et al, *Federal Practice and Procedure: Civil* 5A: § 1297, 3rd edn (St Paul, Thomson West, 2002).

goes some way towards unpacking them. The logic seems to be that criminal sanctions are 'needless' because people should, and usually can, be expected to take at least that much care in protecting their own interests, and if they will not, they should have the burden of pursuing a civil claim instead of seeking criminal sanctions. In all likelihood, however, the very reason for bringing criminal charges was that the victim lacked any other recourse: because plaintiffs could not testify in civil disputes, the criminal fraud cases were presumably the ones in which the victim been driven to that route because there were no other witnesses to the transaction.[27] Practically speaking, then, by dismissing the criminal charges, the courts were probably terminating the litigation altogether.

As the doctrine of *Jones* was applied, many courts simply followed the holding without comment, but when they bothered to mention the rationale, they invariably opted for Hawkins's language rather than Holt's.[28] The phrase 'ordinary capacity' is nowhere to be found in the case law that followed. Commentators, similarly, echoed Hawkins rather than Holt.[29] Giles Jacob, in his *A New Law-Dictionary* (1729), copies Hawkins almost word for word.[30] Though lawyers would not have relied on Jacob, his recapitulation of Hawkins's treatment may have helped it reach a wider audience of non-professional readers. In any case, the transition from Holt's to Hawkins's version of the criterion marks a crucial development in the evolution of objective standards of liability. In expanding on Holt's rationale, Hawkins hit on a phrase that would slowly seep into the legal vernacular, spreading into various parts of criminal law and beyond it, and seeding the bed for the time when a more pronounced demand for a personified standard would arise. Treatises have performed a vitally important role in the history of the common law by highlighting easily overlooked points in the process of collecting, aligning and explaining decisions; one lesson from the fraud cases is that a fortuitously timed treatise can make a huge difference in the development of a line of jurisprudence.

In most of the eighteenth-century cases that drew on *Jones*, the holding was taken to provide a bright-line rule about fraud, and almost every

---

[27] See n 13. The court in *Wheatly* hinted at this conclusion, observing that the dispute was a 'private breach of contract' and if it were allowed to proceed as a criminal case, 'the injured person [could become] a witness upon the indictment, which he could not be (for himself) in an action' (*Wheatly* (n 8) 1128).

[28] See, eg, *Wheatly* (n 8) 1129, 1130; *R v Bower* (1775) 1 Cowp 323, 324, 98 ER 1110; *Pasley v Freeman* (1789) 3 TR 51, 64, 65, 100 ER 450; *Young v R* (1789) 3 TR 98, 99, 100, 100 ER 475; *R v Lara* (1795) 6 TR 565, 567, 568, 101 ER 706; *R v Bazeley* (1799) 2 Leach 835, 838, 168 ER 517; *R v Haynes* (1815) 4 M & S 214, 219, 105 ER 814; *R v Goodhall* (1821) Russ & Ry 461, 463, 168 ER 898; *R v Woolley* (1850) 3 Car & K 102, 104, 175 ER 479; *R v Hudson* (1860) Bell 263, 267, 169 ER 1254.

[29] See, eg, R Burn, *The Justice of the Peace* (London, 1755) 1:179; TW Williams, *The Whole Law Relative to the Duty and Office of a Justice of the Peace* (London, 1793–95) 2:584; *R v Grantham* (1709) 11 Mod 222, 88 ER 1002 (note b) (note added by Leach to the 1796 text).

[30] G Jacob, *A New Law-Dictionary* (London, 1729), sv 'counterfeits'. The same account appears in the nine later editions published between 1732 and 1797.

time the question arose, the doctrine saved the accused from criminal liability because there had been no false token. The usual setting involved a misstatement as to the quantity of goods, such as grain, coal or beer. The courts refused to treat these cases as criminal even if the defendant had falsely marked the container; in order to be liable for using a false token, the defendant had to go through the motions of weighing out the goods.[31] Often, the courts made a point of observing that the harm alleged was private in nature, sometimes because the victim had been a fool, sometimes because the lack of false tokens showed that it might have been an innocent mistake—and increasingly, as time went by, because otherwise every breach of contract would be converted into a crime.[32] These last two points explain the commercial cases most effectively and also help to explain the pattern that developed in these cases, by which even 'bare words' could be sufficient to support an indictment, but only when the defendant had impersonated someone else or had procured the fraud through a conspiracy.[33]

In a short-lived line of cases, the courts focused on the victim's failure to exercise common prudence, but instead of acquitting the defendants, as the criminal/civil distinction in *Jones* would require, the courts reduced the gravity of the offence. This was a judicial version of the 'pious perjury' that jurors sometimes used to undervalue stolen goods. If the victim's inattentiveness had created the opportunity for theft, the court ruled that the statutory (and non-clergyable) offence of 'felonious Taking of [property] from the Person of any other ... privily without his Knowledge'[34] could not apply, but the defendant could be convicted of stealing at common law. In *R v Trippet and Fannen*, tried at the Old Bailey in 1769, the victim became intoxicated and fell asleep late at night on a bench on Westminster Bridge. A printer's apprentice and a waiter from Vauxhall, 'walk[ing] about to pass the time away', stole his watch and shoe buckles, and then made the mistake of calling on an acquaintance at Tothill Fields Prison, where they were apprehended. The two were found guilty of 'stealing, but not privately from the person'.[35]

[31] See, eg, *R v Channel* (1728) 2 Stra 793, 93 ER 852; *R v Wilders* (1732) 11 Mod 309, 88 ER 1057; *R v Pinkney* (1733) Sess Cas 57, 93 ER 58; *R v Pickley* (1733) 2 Barn KB 244, 94 ER 477; *R v Combrune* (1751) 1 Wils KB 301, 95 ER 630; *R v Driffield* (1754) Sayer 146, 96 ER 844; *Wheatly* (n 8); *R v Dunnage* (1761) 2 Burr 1130, 97 ER 749; *R v Osborn* (1765) 3 Burr 1697, 97 ER 1052.

[32] See, eg, *Wheatly* (n 8) 1128; *Osborn* (n 31) 1697; *Bower* (n 28) 324; *R v Codrington* (1825) 1 Car & P 661, 663, 171 ER 1358.

[33] *Wheatly* (n 8) 1127 makes explicit the point about conspiracy; see also *Lara* (n 28) 567, 569. For impersonation, see, eg, *R v Govers* (1755) Sayer 206, 96 ER 854; *R v Story* (1805) Russ & Ry 81, 168 ER 695; *R v Douglass* (1808) 1 Camp 212, 170 ER 933; *R v Barnard* (1837) 7 Car & P 784, 173 ER 342.

[34] 8 Eliz 1 c 4, s 2.

[35] *R v Trippet & Fannen*, Old Bailey Sessions Papers (hereinafter OBSP), 28 June 1769. The case is cited in *R v Gribble* (1782) 1 Leach 240, 168 ER 222, which describes the facts without giving a name or citation. Indeed, one might think, from the account in *Gribble* that the case is apocryphal; however, *Trippet* perfectly matches the description.

More than half a dozen similar cases, featuring intoxicated or sleeping victims, were tried at the Old Bailey with similar results between the mid-1760s and the early 1780s.[36] Only in the last of these, *R v Gribble* (1782), did the court explain why the culprit could not be convicted of 'such a stealing privately as would oust the offender from the benefit of clergy': once again echoing Hawkins's language, the court observed that 'the statute was intended to protect the property which persons by proper vigilance and caution should not be enabled to secure'.[37] Perhaps the judge's effort to rationalise this approach was one of the factors that brought about its demise. The other prosecutions, at least as recounted in the *Old Bailey Sessions Papers*, included no reference to similarly decided cases, but in *Gribble*, Perryn B mentioned the facts of *Trippet*, showing that this way of handling the cases was becoming routine. Four years later, two cases tried at Newcastle Assizes marked the end of this line. In one case, the defendant and some associates had conspired to intoxicate and rob their victim; in the other, the accused was convicted stealing a watch from the master of a ship 'while he was asleep in his cabin ... and without his knowledge'.[38] Both were convicted at trial, and when reserved and sent up to the 12 judges, the convictions were affirmed.[39] The next such case to be tried at the Old Bailey, in 1788, produced the same result.[40]

At around the same time, some courts began to repudiate the suggestion that 'bare lies' could not support an indictment for fraud. At Chester Assizes in 1778, the Chevalier de Villeneuve was convicted and sentenced to three years' hard labour for obtaining 12 guineas from Sir Thomas Broughton.[41] Villeneuve had told a story about incurring unforeseen expenses while traveling on behalf of the Duke de Lauzun, but the latter disclaimed any knowledge of him. Villeneuve thus was convicted on the basis of mere

---

[36] *R v Hatch*, OBSP, 16 October 1765; *R v Jones*, OBSP, 15 July 1767; *R v Green*, OBSP, 24 October 1770; *R v Marshall*, OBSP, 3 July 1771; *R v Bodkin*, OBSP, 23 October 1771; *R v Richards*, OBSP, 9 December 1772; *R v Reading and Jones*, OBSP, 9 December 1778; *R v Gribble*, OBSP, 20 February 1782 (*cf* n 35).

[37] *Gribble* (n 35). As reported in the OBSP, the judge instructed the jury that Gribble could be found guilty of stealing, but 'it cannot be a capital offence'.

[38] *R v Branny* (1786) 1 Leach 240, 168 ER 222 (note); *R v Thompson* (1787) 1 Leach 443, 168 ER 323; see also EH East, *A Treatise of the Pleas of the Crown* (London, Strahan, 1803) 2:704–05; NH Tomlins, *A Digested Index to the Crown Law* (London, W Clarke, 1816) 115.

[39] On this procedure, see J Oldham, 'Informal Lawmaking in England by the Twelve Judges in the Late Eighteenth and Early Nineteenth Centuries' 29 (2011) *Law & History Review* 181; DR Bentley (ed), *Select Cases from the Twelve Judges' Notebooks* (London, J Rees, 1997).

[40] *R v Willan* (1788) 1 Leach 495, 496, 168 ER 349. The prisoner's counsel argued that 'the Act did not extend to protect the property of persons asleep' and the court responded that 'whatever notions might have formerly prevailed upon this subject, the contrary had lately been determined by all the Judges of England'.

[41] The case is unreported, except in Buller J's judgment in *R v Young* (1788) 1 Leach 505, 168 ER 354, but several newspapers covered the case; see *Morning Post* (London, 22 December 1777) 4; *St James's Chronicle* (London, 30 December 1777) 3; *Adams's Weekly Courant* (Chester, 28 April 1778) 3.

words unaccompanied by any false token. This case would provide helpful support 10 years later, in *R v Young* (1788), where the King's Bench explained that the statute of 30 Geo II c 24 (1757) had 'introduced another offence', distinct from fraud at common law and formulated in 'extremely general' terms that covered all kinds of frauds, including those achieved by words alone.[42] Unlike the cases of mismeasured commercial goods, *Young* featured a scheme with obviously malicious defendants. They had obtained 20 guineas from an army colonel through a complicated ruse involving a pretended bet with each other. According to Ashurst J: 'The Legislature saw that all men were not equally prudent, and this statute was passed to protect the weaker part of mankind.' Buller J agreed, observing that 'the ingredients of this offence are the obtaining money by false pretences, and with an intent to defraud', crisply specifying the actus reus and mens rea in a fashion that excluded any inquiry into the type of deception or the amount of vigilance required to detect it.[43] This language signals a departure from the approach taken in *Jones*, focusing on the effects of the fraudster's efforts rather than their nature and sophistication. If *Young* had been followed, references to 'common prudence and caution' probably would have been become much rarer, and might have vanished before the standard could drift into other areas of law and gain the foothold that allowed it to spread in the nineteenth century.

However, *Young* was quickly forgotten. Hardly any of the reported fraud cases tried over the following three decades involved recourse to the doctrine of *Jones* and, as a result, this reversal had faded from memory by the time the question of the defendant's guile arose again. Nevertheless, the arguments in *Young* were prescient in anticipating a view that would come to dominate in the nineteenth century. In *Young*, William Fielding (son of the novelist Henry Fielding), representing the defendants and attempting to apply the standard in *Jones*, insisted that it necessarily precluded criminal liability for statements about the future. If the defendant's statements referred to 'thing[s] past or present', Fielding contended, they might be prohibited by the statute of 30 Geo II, because they might be so cunning that 'caution cannot guard' against them, whereas statements about 'future transaction[s]' are always detectable: 'inquiries may be made' and consequently 'the party can only be imposed upon through his own negligence'. Fielding maintained that the defendants' bet, as a statement about the future, necessarily fell

---

[42] *Young* (n 41) 508. In specifying its subject matter and scope, the statute addressed: 'All persons who knowingly by false pretences shall obtain from any person money, goods, &c. with intent to cheat or defraud.'

[43] ibid. *Young* furnished the basis for a fictional case, presented as an extract from a volume of trial reports (*Meautyss's Elegant Collection of Trials*) in John Cordy Jeaffreson's novel *Live it Down* (London, 1863) 2:229–38. The defendant, a barrister, tries to exonerate himself by citing *Trippet* (n 35), but is convicted of fraud.

outside the statute.[44] The logic is dubious: the conspirators pretended they had already made a bet, not that they were going to make one; moreover, there was no one else to consult in order to verify the details, so any inquiry would have been pointless. However, instead of engaging with Fielding's logic, the court concluded that even the imprudent were entitled to protection under the statute. In the years following *Young*, the courts addressed various aspects of the doctrine—such as how to treat false impersonations and what details needed to be set out in the indictment—but none of these cases required resort to *Young*'s expansion of the scope of fraud.[45]

No more is heard about this treatment of future-oriented statements for more than 30 years, and then it was adopted with little explanation in *R v Goodhall* (1821). The defendant had ordered 250 pounds of meat (valued at £4 10s), but failed to pay on delivery. Indicted under the statute of 30 Geo II, he was convicted at trial, at Stafford Assizes, with a finding by the jury that 'at the time he applied for the meat ... he did not intend to return the money'. It was reserved and sent to the 12 judges, who reversed the decision, without inviting argument from counsel.[46] There is only one report of the case, which gives the justification in a single sentence: 'It was merely a promise for future conduct, and common prudence and caution would have prevented any injury arising from the breach of it.'[47] This explanation corresponds perfectly to Fielding's argument, yet there is no reference to *Young*. Indeed, as one commentator notes, under the procedures for considering reserved cases, the judges did not have the power to overrule the King's Bench, making it unlikely that they had consulted *Young*.[48] Nor was the idea likely borrowed from a treatise, because only a few mentioned the 'future promise' argument, and they noted that *Young* had rejected it.[49]

One might speculate that *Goodhall*'s holding reflected the same logic we have seen in the eighteenth-century jurisprudence, which preserved judicial control over the commercial cases by excluding them from the criminal docket, rather than trusting to the jury's ability to assess mens rea. That explanation has some force, given that this was an era of increasing distrust

---

[44] *Young* (n 41) 506.

[45] It was, however, noted in a few treatises. See R Burn (J King (ed)), *The Justice of the Peace*, 21st edn (London, 1810) 1:445–48; J Williams, *The Laws of Trade and Commerce* (London, 1812) 172; J Chitty, *A Practical Treatise on the Criminal Law* (London, AJ Valpy, 1816) 3:997.

[46] The defendant, Moses Goodhall, evidently did not mend his ways, because he was convicted of another offence at the Stafford Quarter Sessions in 1839 and was transported to New South Wales. The conviction was recorded under the name 'Moses Goodall'. Transportation Register, 10 October 1839, National Archives, HO 11/12/101.

[47] *Goodhall* (n 28).

[48] AR Pearce, 'Theft by False Promises' (1953) 101 *University of Pennsylvania Law Review* 967, 974. Pearce notes that if 'the King's men had marched up the hill' in *Young*, they 'marched down again' in *Goodhall*, and that given the change in personnel in the interim, 'it was not the same men; it appears they did not even know it was the same hill'. ibid 972.

[49] See n 45.

of juries in England, when questions of fact were being recharacterised as questions of law precisely to maintain judicial control.[50] Nevertheless, solving the mens rea problem is not the only possible explanation for the 'future promises' rule, as we may see from a trio of commercial fraud cases decided by the New York Court of General Session two years before *Goodhall*.

In the first of these cases, *People v Conger* (1819), New York City Mayor Cadwallader Colden acknowledged that he lacked the authority to 'settl[e] the law on any point', sitting as he was on a 'subordinate tribunal', but sought nevertheless to propose 'some general rules upon this subject' because 'indictments of this nature are becoming very frequent'. He referred to *Young* at several points and adopted Fielding's argument about future-oriented misrepresentations, but rejected Fielding's justification that a prudent person can always investigate them. Instead, he reasoned that such statements were neither true nor false. *Conger* was a prosecution for using false pretences to obtain more than 300 dollars' worth of fabrics. Colden acquitted the defendant, in part because '[a] false pretence must relate to an existing fact' and one who 'promises to pay for [goods] at a future time' has made 'false promises and not false pretences'.[51] This view was consistent with the holding of *Young*, according to Colden, because the conviction there had turned not on a false promise, but on a false pretence (the defendants' supposed bet).[52] At the same time, Colden showed no inclination to remove these cases from the jury. After referring to the received wisdom about 'mere naked lie[s]' that 'common sagacity or common precaution might detect', he rejected the 'bare words' rule and embraced the personified standard that had accompanied it. Deceptions were not criminal, he explained, if they would not deceive 'a person ... possessed of ordinary caution ... But what would or would not be ordinary caution, is a question for the jury, which may depend on a thousand circumstances to be considered on a trial'.[53] How to gauge ordinary caution and how to tell which 'bare lies' might baffle it were for the jury to decide in any given case. Colden applied this approach in two later jury trials during the same term, yielding another acquittal and a suspended sentence.[54]

*Conger* is a remarkable decision. It is more methodical, more carefully researched and more disciplined in its reasoning than any of the English judgments on the subject over the previous century. It is also one of the first

---

[50] For a relatively contemporaneous observation about this phenomenon, see [HP Brougham], 'Rossi on Criminal Law' (1831) 54 *Edinburgh Review* 183, 222. The pattern is usually associated with civil law, not criminal law; see P Handler, 'The Court for Crown Cases Reserved, 1848–1908' (2011) 29 *Law and History Review* 259, 283–84 and the sources cited there.

[51] *People v Conger* 4 NY City-Hall Recorder 65, 68–69 (Sess Ct 1819).

[52] ibid 69.

[53] ibid 72.

[54] *People v Collins* 4 NY City-Hall Recorder 143, 149 (Sess Ct 1819); *People v Stuyvesant* 4 NY City-Hall Recorder 156, 157 (Sess Ct 1819).

decisions in any common law jurisdiction that clearly adopted a standard akin to the 'reasonable person' as a question for the jury. If *Conger* had been more widely reported, it might have influenced the jurisprudence significantly. But unlike Holt Colden did not have a Hawkins to record and publicise the decision. *Conger* was printed in a short-lived reporter that was not gathered into a larger series until 1854.[55] In the interim, other American courts followed the holding in *Jones*. In *Commonwealth v Drew* (1837), the Supreme Judicial Court of Massachusetts signed on to the view that statements about the future 'afford an opportunity for inquiring into their truth', and *Drew* was treated as a leading authority in the first edition of Francis Wharton's influential treatise on American criminal law (1846).[56] *Conger* adopted the 'future promises' doctrine in a fashion that was consistent with giving juries more control over these cases, whereas the primary means by which the doctrine developed in England and the US depended on preserving the rule about 'bare promises' and giving judges the control.

Over the following decades, the present/future distinction became a basic tenet of the jurisprudence in both England and the US.[57] Predictably, the courts tied themselves up in knots trying to determine which statements related to existing facts, which ones related to future facts, which ones in either category were material in prompting the victim to pay the defendant, and in which instances the statements about the present and future were so hopelessly intermingled that the whole charge had to be rejected as defective for want of a clearly specifiable falsehood.[58] (The distinction also figured as a loophole in a mystery story, ostensibly aimed at legal reform.)[59] Little purpose would be served by detailing these cases; the complications they spawned have yielded various results. Some jurisdictions have maintained the distinction, while others have recognised that statements about the future may also be intended as lies (as the *Goodhall* jury itself had concluded). Some jurisdictions have gone further, eliminating 'reasonable' reliance

[55] JD Wheeler, *Reports of Criminal Law Cases Decided at the City-Hall of the City of New York* (Albany, Gould, 1854) 1:448.

[56] F Wharton, *A Treatise on the Criminal Law of the United States* (Philadelphia, Kay, 1846) 453; see also ED Pearl, 'Criminal Law: False Promises as False Pretenses' (1955) *California Law Review* 719, 723; I Ayres and G Klass, *Insincere Promises: The Law of Misrepresented Intent* (New Haven, Yale University Press, 2005) 172.

[57] *Commonwealth v Drew*, 36 Mass 179 (1837) is usually cited as the first US case to make such a distinction. *Drew* cites *Stuyvesant's Case*, which in turn repeats the doctrine of *Conger* (though without citing it).

[58] See, eg, *Codrington* (n 32); *R v Douglas* (1836) 1 Mood 462, 168 ER 1345; *R v Wickham* (1839) 10 Ad & E 34, 113 ER 14; *R v Johnston* (1842) 2 Mood 254, 169 ER 101; *R v Bates & Pugh* (1848) 3 Cox CC 201; *R v Woolley* (1850) 1 Den 559, 169 ER 372. The courts cast some doubt on this treatment of future promises, but did not actually repudiate it, in *R v Parker* (1837) 7 Car & P 825, 173 ER 360.

[59] MD Post, 'The Men of the Jimmy' in *The Strange Schemes of Randolph Mason* (New York, Putnam's, 1896) 169; *cf* S Stern, 'Detecting Doctrines: The Case Method and the Detective Story' (2011) 23 *Yale Journal of Law and the Humanities* 339, 346–47.

as an element of fraud, which also abolishes the temporal distinction, where it was adopted under Fielding's theory.[60] For present purposes, the significance of these changes—the treatment of future promises as categorically incapable of supporting reliance and the elimination of reliance as an element of fraud—is that both of them effectively remove the 'man of ordinary prudence' from the inquiry. This line of jurisprudence began by adopting a human measure to evaluate fraud, but ultimately gravitated towards solutions that make no reference to a personified standard.

## IV. CRIMINAL LAW PERSONIFIED

In the early nineteenth century, however, the standard began to find other outlets in the criminal law, which enabled it to spread further. In *R v Southerton* (1805), the court adopted this approach in evaluating an extortion threat. Southerton had demanded £10 from a pair of druggists, Richard and William Allen, saying that otherwise he would prosecute a trumped-up information against them for 'selling ... medicines without stamps'.[61] He was convicted of extortion at trial, but the King's Bench reversed the decision, ruling that he uttered 'a mere threat to bring an action which a man of ordinary firmness might have resisted'.[62] This standard was suggested by Attorney-General Spencer Perceval for the prosecution in an effort that backfired. Perceval evidently thought to propose this approach partly because of the 'constans vir' in the law of duress and partly by way of analogy to the fraud cases.[63] Drawing again on Hawkins's account of *Jones*, Perceval argued that even if Southerton's threat 'could be considered only as a fraud upon an individual, yet if it were such against which common prudence could not guard, nor common firmness resist, it would still be indictable' and that 'no prudence can guard against a false charge'.

Lord Ellenborough accepted the premise but not the conclusion. He mentioned the 'man of common firmness' and the 'man of ordinary firmness', as well as the 'ordinary free will of a firm man', and perhaps we should treat one of those qualifiers as implicit in his fullest statement of the rationale. Stating that 'the threat must be ... calculated to overcome a firm and prudent man', he concluded that the Allens had been too easily rattled by a threat that 'a firm and prudent man might ... and ought ... to have resisted'.

---

[60] Besides the sources cited in nn 48 and 56, see M Bedi, 'Contract Breaches and the Civil/Criminal Divide: An Inter-common Law Analysis' (2012) 28 *Georgia State University Law Review* 559.

[61] *R v Southerton* (1805) 6 East 126, 127, 136, 140, 142, 102 ER 1235. East's report summarises the facts very cursorily; for a fuller account, see 'Summer Assizes' *Morning Chronicle* (London, 20 August 1804) 3.

[62] *Southerton* (n 61) 141.

[63] ibid 132–33.

This language is even more openly normative than the language of the fraud cases: 'firmness' carries a strong moral charge and the 'ought' emphatically prescribes a norm. Lawrence J agreed, but hewed more consistently to the common and the ordinary: after citing *Jones*, he observed that extortion required 'means [that] common prudence and firmness cannot guard against' and that in this case, 'a man of ordinary firmness' would have left Southerton to 'prosecute ... at his peril'.[64]

Perceval's analogy, in fact, was very apt. The interpersonal dynamics of extortion mirror those of fraud. A avoids, or cannot manage to avoid, suffering a loss—in one case, depending on whether A can see through B's more or less wily fabrication and, in the other case, depending on whether A can withstand B's more or less severe threat. Insofar as criminal law now uses different means to calibrate the threshold for the two offences, then, that is not because of a difference in the relationship between victim and victimiser; it is because, according to contemporary social norms, a scam artist is more contemptible than even a highly gullible victim, whereas an extortionist is less contemptible than a fearful victim who will pay anything to avoid a minor physical harm. This difference in social norms explains why a personified standard might be apt for extortion, but not for fraud. In both instances, the attempt cannot become a completed offence without the would-be victim's participation, but we do not consider the fraud victim's perceptions as relevant to the analysis, nor (for the most part) do we use the law to establish a standard indicating the level of deceit that people can and should resist—even a blatant lie is good enough. It is therefore useless to adopt a device that asks the trier of fact to consider the fraud victim's perspective or to gauge a communal norm of reasonable vigilance, which are the functions that a personified standard would serve.

Conversely, this standard does have something to contribute to the analysis of extortion. That analysis takes the victim's perceptions into account, at least to the extent of asking whether someone in the victim's position would actually have perceived a threat. The analysis also asks, normatively, whether the victim should have perceived a threat under the circumstances. Lord Denman makes the latter point in an 1849 judgment that explains the holding of *Southerton*: 'Whether a threat be criminal or no, cannot be taken to depend on the nerves of the individual threatened, but on the general nature of the evil with which he is threatened.'[65] Formulated in this way, the exercise would not seem to demand a perspectival inquiry; however, assessing the gravity of the threat is a normative exercise in which a personified standard can assist. If 'the general nature of the evil' could be measured on a scale, yielding an objective and unchanging distinction akin to the 'bare

---

[64] ibid 142–43.
[65] *R v Smith* (1849) 1 Den 510, 514, 169 ER 350.

words' rule, a personified standard would serve no purpose; however, in the absence of that option, a plausible way to identify the applicable norm is to refer to an embodiment of the community that holds the norm and to bear in mind the descriptive considerations that pitch the requirement at an 'ordinary' or 'common' level. The personified standard does not tell us how to reconcile the tensions between normative and descriptive considerations— which is why Lord Ellenborough's different formulations are significant and why commentators continue to debate these issues—but by figuring the standard in a human form, we can at least indicate what kind of evaluation is to be undertaken.

From extortion to duress and provocation was only a short step conceptually (though hardly one that followed automatically) and, as these comments have implied, duress and provocation resemble extortion rather than fraud with respect to the kind of inquiry they prompt. Starkie, in the second edition of his treatise on evidence (1833), adds *Southerton* to the section on 'duress',[66] thus facilitating a move by which the court's analysis would be applied to the definition of a defence rather than being used to define an offence. In the following decades, in both criminal and civil contexts, the courts increasingly referred to the 'man of ordinary firmness' in duress cases.[67] Similarly, whereas Blackstone treats the standard categorically, listing various threats that will not amount to duress and quoting Bracton's requirement of a 'virum constantem', his nineteenth-century editors would recharacterise the standard as requiring 'common firmness'.[68] *Southerton*, and doubtless various other expressions of the personified standard as embodying 'common' or 'ordinary' traits, also led jurists to recraft the civil law standard of duress so as to partake of the same features as the 'reasonable' person.

Provocation developed in a similar fashion: whereas the defence had formerly operated categorically, covering a short list of triggers, the court in *R v Kirkham* (1837) introduced the idea of 'reasonable control', and some 30 years later, in *R v Welsh* (1869), the standard would be formulated as requiring 'the amount of provocation' sufficient to spark the passion of 'a reasonable

---

[66] T Starkie, *A Practical Treatise on the Law of Evidence* 2nd edn (London, J & WT Clarke, 1833) 2:288 (and later editions).

[67] See, eg, *R v Vincent* (1839) 9 Car & P 91, 109, 173 ER 754; *Skeate v Beale* (1841) 4 Jurist 766, 767; *R v Miard* (1844) 1 Cox CC 22, 24. The American courts, similarly, began to explain duress by reference to a man of 'ordinary', 'common' or 'reasonable' firmness; see, eg, *D'Arcy v Lyle* (Pa 1813) 5 Binn 441, 449; *Barrett v French* (1815) 1 Conn 354, 357; *Johnson v Ballew* (Ala 1835) 2 Port 29, 30.

[68] Compare William Blackstone, *Commentaries*, 9th edn (London, 1783) 1:131 (explaining that '[a] fear of battery, or being beaten ... [or] having one's house burned' would not constitute duress), with JF Hargrave (ed), ibid, 21st edn, (London, Sweet & Maxwell, Stevens & Norton, 1844) 1:130 (citing various authorities, including *Southerton*, in connection with the 'man of common firmness and prudence').

man'.[69] Historical research has suggested that *Welsh* inaugurated the modern approach to provocation in England;[70] the American courts started to use a personified standard around the time of *Kirkham*, and while those cases deserve more attention, an examination would take us beyond the scope of the present inquiry.[71]

Extortion, duress and provocation all turn on a person's ability to resist a certain amount of pressure, as well as on the person's perception of the pressure. A personified standard directs the trier of fact to the actor's perspective (when that is relevant) and provides a means of factoring in the normative and descriptive concerns that inform the analysis. Liability for fraud, even in the eighteenth century, did not depend on these questions; as we have seen, Holt proposed the standard for a different purpose, and Hawkins's reformulation, though it would prove tremendously productive in other contexts, functioned in fraud mainly as a redescription of the 'mere words' rule, serving to manage a question of mens rea and thereby removing it from the jury's control, rather than formulating an issue for the jury to consider.

Well into the nineteenth century, the modern uses of the 'common', 'ordinary' or 'reasonable' person were hardly self-evident. In *R v Wickham* (1839), Lord Denman queried *Jones*'s objective approach, doubting that it struck the right standard, but also doubting that any objective standard could be established. Told that a promissory note was a 'bare assertion' and not the kind of 'artful device as will impose on a man of ordinary caution', Denman asked: 'Suppose a man has just art enough to impose upon a very simple person, and defraud him, how is it to be determined whether the degree of fraud is such as shall amount to a misdemeanor? Who is to give the measure?' The answer he received—'The law prescribes it'—might worry a modern lawyer, insofar as it treads on the jury's discretion, but it evidently worried Denman for a different reason. He soon repeated the question: 'There are indeed cases where the pretence is so very foolish that it is difficult to say that an imposition is practiced; but still, who is to give the measure?'[72] 'The law prescribes it' would be a satisfactory answer to

---

[69] *R v Kirkham* (1837) 8 C & P 115, 173 ER 422; *R v Welsh* (1869) 11 Cox CC 336.

[70] R Singer, 'The Resurgence of Mens Rea: I—Provocation, Emotional Disturbance, and the Model Penal Code' (1985) 27 *Boston College Law Review* 243; B Brown, 'The "Ordinary Man" in Provocation: Anglo-Saxon Attitudes and "Unreasonable Non-Englishmen"' (1964) 13 *ICLQ* 203; M Wiener, *Men of Blood: Violence, Manliness, and Criminal Justice in Victorian England* (Cambridge, Cambridge University Press, 2004) 175–200.

[71] See *State v Hill* (NC 1839) 4 Dev & Bat 491, 496 ('men of ordinary tempers'); *State v McCants* (SC 1843) 1 Speers 384, 387 ('an ordinary reasonable man'); *People v Stonecifer* (1856) 6 Cal 405, 411 ('a reasonable person'); and particularly *Maher v People* (1862) 10 Mich 212, 220, which discusses the question at length, speaking of 'ordinary men, of fair average disposition' and 'reasonable, *ordinary human nature*, or the average of men recognised as men of fair average mind and disposition', while making allowance for 'some peculiar weakness of mind or infirmity of temper' if it does 'not aris[e] from wickedness of heart or cruelty of disposition'.

[72] *Wickham* (n 58) 36–37.

anyone who takes the standard to be normative—in this case, the law may have prescribed it incorrectly, but the law is competent to prescribe normative standards. Denman, however, seems to regard the standard as purely descriptive. He is not playing devil's advocate, but is denying that the law could prescribe a standard that makes an empirical claim about people's acuity and behaviour. His resistance does not reflect a doubt that the 'person of ordinary caution' can achieve the function it was designed to serve so much as a doubt about what that function is. That he could be uncertain about this function is, perhaps, not surprising. 'Common prudence and caution' had largely been a motto in the fraud cases, serving as a paraphrase of the rule that 'bare lies' did not constitute fraud, and in 1839 this standard had appeared only by fits and starts in other legal domains, such as tort. Denman's questions are significant precisely because they remind us that despite the landmark of *Jones* and the cases following it, in the 1830s, the idea of a personified objective standard could not yet be taken for granted.

# 5

# R v Bembridge (1783)

## JEREMY HORDER

### I. INTRODUCTION

> I have, as Paymaster, great sums in my hands which, not applicable to any
> present use, must either lie dead in the Bank or be employed
> by me ... I sell out and gain greatly.[1]

**B**ETWEEN 1693 AND 1815, England was at war on different fronts
for no less than 56 years. These wars were financed, in part, by a
36-fold increase in revenue extracted by what became a 'fiscal-military'
English state.[2] In that regard, by the late eighteenth century, some three-
quarters of government expenditure was being devoted to the Army, Navy,
Ordinance and war-related debts.

Until a payment actually needed to be made, the huge sums of money
required for this crucial task were commonly held in private hands, by
high-ranking Crown-appointed public officials. For our purposes, the most
important of these offices of state was the office of Paymaster General of the
Forces and the most important holder of that lucrative office was Henry Fox
(Lord Holland), whose attitude towards the £40 million or so that he held
as Paymaster General is expressed in the passage cited above. Outrageous as
his attitude to the use of public funds might now seem, it reflects a curious
eighteenth-century practice whereby, so long as they ultimately made good
any deficit (quite commonly years after leaving office), senior public officials
were free to use these great sums for the purposes of private enrichment.[3] To
that end, Paymasters commonly drew large sums before they were needed.

---

[1] Henry Fox, Lord Holland, 'Memoir' in Countess of Ilchester and Lord Stavordale, *Life and Letters of Sarah Lennox*, 2nd edn (London, John Murray, 1902) 72. Lord Holland is referring here to the commonly accepted practice whereby holders of high office invested public money not currently being used as they saw fit and kept the interest thereby earned for themselves.

[2] WJ Ashworth, 'Practical Objectivity: The Excise, State, and Production in Eighteenth Century England' (2004) 18 *Social Epistemology* 181, 182. The phrase 'fiscal-military' state is taken from J Brewer, *The Sinews of Power: War, Money and the English State, 1688–1783* (London, Unwin Hyman, 1989).

[3] For some of the possible implications, see VL Johnson, 'Internal Reform or External Taxation: Britain's Fiscal Choice, 1763' (1954) 98 *Proceedings of the American Philosophical Society* 31.

That is the part of the background against which I will take as my focus a criminal case bearing on this phenomenon, *R v Bembridge*.[4] The case was decided in 1783, at a watershed moment in British history, when the process of holding public officials to account for their use of public money began in earnest.[5] Central to the making of that moment, and to Bembridge's case, was politician and philosopher Edmund Burke (noted opponent of the American revolutionary war), whose importance will become clear in due course.

*R v Bembridge* is commonly acknowledged to be a common law foundation stone of the modern criminal law governing the offences of misconduct in a public office[6] and of cheating the public revenue.[7] Following the lead of the Court of Appeal in *R v Dytham*,[8] in *Attorney-General's Reference (No 3 of 2003)*, the Court of Appeal relied on a passage from the judgment of Lord Mansfield in *Bembridge* in seeking to define the scope of the misconduct offence. In setting out what he took to be the basic elements of the offence, Lord Mansfield laid down the following rule-like formula (drawing, as we will see, on the wording of the information laid against Bembridge),[9] which is now regarded as authoritative in the modern law:

> Here there are two principles applicable: first, that a man accepting an office of trust concerning the public, especially if attended with profit, is answerable criminally to the King for misbehaviour in his office; this is true by whomever and in whatever way the officer is appointed ... Secondly, where there is a breach of trust, fraud, or imposition, in a matter concerning the public ... as between the King and the subject it is indictable. That such should be the rule is essential to the existence of the country.[10]

---

[4] *R v Bembridge* (1783) 3 Doug 327 (hereinafter 'Doug'), 99 ER 679 (hereinafter 'ER'); (1783) XXII State Trials 1 (hereinafter 'ST'). The latter report, although little used or referred to now, should be relatively reliable, in that the reporter on whose shorthand notes that the report is based was a Mr Gurney, a barrister, who came from a family of noted shorthand writers.

[5] On which, see AS Foord, 'The Waning of the Influence of the Crown' (1947) 62 *English Historical Review* 484, 499–501; and P Harling and P Mandler, 'From "Fiscal-Military" State to "Laissez-Faire" State 1760–1850' (1993) 32 *Journal of British Studies* 44, 54.

[6] *Attorney-General's Reference (No 3 of 2003)* [2005] QB 73, [2004] EWCA Crim 868; *R v Dytham* [1979] 1 QB 723; C Nicholls et al, *Corruption and Misuse of a Public Office*, 2nd edn (Oxford, Oxford University Press, 2011) 154.

[7] See D Ormerod, 'Cheating the Public Revenue' [1998] *Crim LR* 627.

[8] *R v Dytham* [1979] 1 QB 723.

[9] See text at n 59 below.

[10] *Bembridge* (n 4) Doug 332; ER 681, cited in *Attorney-General's Reference* [2004] EWCA Crim 868 [35]. The reference to 'profit' is, as we will see, not so much a reference to a salary as to the receipt of specific fees in exchange for particular services on the part of a public official. Such practices were lawful and not uncommon at that time. An example was fee-charging by eighteenth-century Justices of the Peace for their otherwise unpaid services. Such systems of remuneration were, of course, as prone to corruption then as they are now: N Landau and J Beattie, *Law, Crime and English Society 1660–1830* (Cambridge, Cambridge University Press, 2002) 46. Upon conviction, Bembridge was fined the amount of the fee he had charged for attending to the accounts that were the subject matter of the charge.

A detailed historical analysis of the case is provided here. Such an analysis has considerable value: first, it casts light on the moral and political context in which legal analysis of public responsibilities was developed in the late eighteenth century; and, second, the discussion has some resonance in relation to integrity issues in modern parliamentary life (although it will only be possible to touch on these at the end).

## II. *R V BEMBRIDGE* (1): 'THE GREAT POWELL AND BEMBRIDGE SCANDAL'[11]

'I ... never knew a more industrious, capable officer any where than Mr Bembridge.'[12]

'A very honest, and a very able officer.'[13]

'A wild, precipitate senseless and ... desperate wretch.'[14]

On 21 April 1794, Charles Bembridge died at his home, 65 Berners Steet, Fitzrovia, London.[15] Bembridge had been for much of his life what we would now call a 'career civil servant'. He had been appointed Secretary at the Wine Licence Office in February 1752,[16] but most significantly, eight years later in November 1760, he entered the service of the Paymaster General of the Armed Forces as a Deputy Paymaster.[17] At that time, a small number of Deputy Paymasters were sent abroad to oversee finance and accounting matters on site for Britain's armed forces in the field. The early 1760s saw Bembridge serving as a Deputy Paymaster on various military expeditions, and then in Bellisle and Portugal.[18] However, by July 1767, he was back in London at the office of the Paymaster General of the Forces (adjoining

---

[11] In the words of DL Kier, 'Economical Reform, 1779–1787' (1934) 50 *LQR* 368, 372.

[12] The Rt Hon Richard Rigby, former Paymaster General, speaking at Bembridge's trial: *Bembridge* (n 4) ST 66.

[13] Lord North, former Prime Minister and Paymaster General, speaking at Bembridge's trial: ibid.

[14] The Rt Hon Edmund Burke's description of Bembridge on receiving a letter from Bembridge himself in October 1784 (following Bembridge's conviction and punishment for misconduct in a public office). Bembridge had implied that further scandal—this time relating to one of Burke's friends, Richard Champion—was in the offing and could add yet more political damage to Burke's reputation, following the calamitous effect on it of Bembridge's own saga: FP Locke, *Edmund Burke*, vol 2 (Oxford, Clarendon Press, 2006) 5.

[15] *Morning Post* (22 May 1794).

[16] *London Evening Post* (15–18 February 1752); *General Advertiser* (18 February 1752).

[17] *London Evening Post* (20–22 November 1760).

[18] *Lloyds Evening Post* (20 August 20 1762). While he was in Bellisle, Parliament voted Bembridge £89 'for the contingencies of his office' (12th Parliament of Great Britain, 3rd Session, 21 February 1764, 862), a procedure some aspects of which were to cause great controversy 20 years later, as we will see. Bellisle, in the Bay of Biscay, was captured after a siege by British forces in June 1761 during the Seven Years' War.

Horse Guards), serving as First Clerk, under joint Paymasters General Lord North and George Cooke.[19] In March 1776, he was promoted to the office of accountant by the then Paymaster General, the Rt Hon Richard Rigby.[20] Rigby had held office since 1768 and was succeeded by Edmund Burke in 1782, an event of great significance, which is taken up in detail below.[21] In that regard, Bembridge's duties as accountant were described at his trial as follows by a witness named Crawfurd who worked in the office:

> I consider the duty of the accountant of the pay-office is, to examine and state the accounts of the several garrisons at home and abroad, and to see that the proper deductions are made; to examine and state the claims of the several general and staff-officers, and officers of hospitals at home and abroad, and to see that the proper deductions are made therein; to examine and state the account of the army extraordinaries that annually occur; to settle the several remittances to be made to the paymasters abroad; to examine the accounts of the several deputy paymasters; to examine every memorial and report; to do the official correspondence in general; and he has the general superintendence and direction of the office.[22]

It was while working as an accountant in the Paymaster General's office some 15 years later that Bembridge was to commit what would now be regarded, under the Fraud Act 2006, as fraud by failing to disclose information (or by abuse of position) in relation to the accounts of a former Paymaster General: Henry Fox, Lord Holland. Bembridge, in league with one John Powell,[23] had fraudulently omitted to disclose to the Auditors of the Imprest over £48,000 of public money that should have formed part of these accounts, acting on behalf of the Exchequer.[24] At the end of the eighteenth

---

[19] Who had become joint Paymasters General in 1765, with Cooke continuing until his death in 1768. Cooke was a lawyer, chief Prothonotary in the Court of Common Pleas and MP for Middlesex. Under George II, he was a Tory, described by Horace Walpole as a 'pompous Jacobite', but by the late 1750s, he had become (and remained) a follower of Pitt.

[20] A Paymaster General automatically became a Privy Councillor upon taking up office as Paymaster General (hence 'Rt Hon') then, as now.

[21] When Burke succeeded Rigby as Paymaster General, he found the kitchens in the Pay Office in Whitehall far too large for his more modest needs. There were, moreover, no bookshelves: *Morning Herald* (20 April 1782), cited by Locke, *Edmund Burke* 508. This reflected the very different lifestyles and attitudes to office of these two sworn enemies.

[22] *Bembridge* (n 4) ST 63.

[23] Powell was Bembridge's predecessor as accountant, and at the time of the fraud the Paymaster's cashier working in the same office. Powell was described as Bembridge's 'friend, benefactor and patron': *Lloyds Evening Post* (18–21 July 1783). The paper goes on to report prosecuting counsel as describing Bembridge as 'having connived at a criminal concealment of the public money on the part of one of his associates simply because Bembridge felt bound not to betray his patron and benefactor'.

[24] The financial magnitude of this offence can be gauged by considering the fact that the financial difference between being of the 'middling sort' and being well-off in Bembridge's day was very roughly the difference between an income of £100 and £500 *a year*: www.oldbaileyonline.org/static/Coinage.jsp; R Porter, *English Society in the Eighteenth Century*, revised edn (London, Penguin, 1990) 70–72. On pay office salaries, see below.

century, the appropriate criminal charge was a charge of what has become commonly known as 'misconduct in a public office'.[25]

Sensationally,[26] in what was already a much-discussed case, Powell committed suicide just before the trial, having earlier resigned his post as cashier (notwithstanding the glaring conflict of interest involved, he had also been acting as the sole executor of Lord Holland's estate at the relevant time). As the *General Advertiser* reported (28 May 1783), relating to his death on 26 May 1783:

> John Powell, esq, at his house in Bennet Street, St James ... that morning had, through extreme depression of spirits and despondency, put an end to his unhappy life; when it appeared, upon the clearest evidence, given by Mr Rigby, Mr Burke ... and diverse other witnesses, that the deceased, since the time of his examination before the Lords of the Treasury, has been generally in a state of insanity. The jury unanimously brought in their verdict, lunacy.[27]

We will come back to the role played by these star witnesses, this time at Bembridge's trial. The suicide obviously left Bembridge to 'carry the can' for the fraudulent misconduct in which the two men had engaged. In replying to the defence, scorn was poured by prosecuting counsel on any notion that the evidence or the suicide indicated that it was Powell who was really to blame:

> Had he [the defence Counsel] forgot that the prosecutions against Mr Powell and Mr Bembridge had gone hand in hand together; that their names had on all occasions been coupled, and no mention made of the one, without an equal mention of the other?[28]

In what immediate context should we place the commission of the offence? That question can be answered at different levels, but let us focus first on office politics. In the eighteenth century, there was a history of engagement by state employees in financial misconduct, often encouraged or connived at by the employers to whom they were beholden. As Roy Porter memorably put it: 'The state at their disposal, grandees pioneered the art of political asset-stripping.'[29] For example, when Lord Chancellor Macclesfield was successfully impeached in 1725 for bribery, extortion and abuse of trust, he

---

[25] According to Lord Mansfield, Bembridge could not have been charged with fraud, as that offence was then understood, because at that time, 'a fraud of a pecuniary nature ... is a civil injury, and therefore not indictable': *Bembridge* (n 4) ST 155.

[26] See the account of the trial in, eg, *Whitehall Evening Post* (17–19 July 1783); *Lloyds Evening Post* (18–21 July 1783).

[27] Burke had said of Powell that the latter was 'incapable of acting rationally in any one concern of his life' and that Powell 'seemed very much declined in his Faculties ... and his discourse ... confused and contradictory' (cited in Locke, *Edmund Burke* 524).

[28] *Lloyds Evening Post* (18–21 July 1783). Powell and Bembridge had been indicted earlier in 1783, but, fatefully, when Edmund Burke came into office, he reinstated them, only for the prosecution to be re-started (this time ending in the conviction of Bembridge) later that year: see the text following n 100 below.

[29] Porter, *English Society* 61.

was found not only to have encouraged risky investments of court funds by his employees, but also to have assisted them in an attempt to cover up the practices of embezzlement into which the investment policy led.[30] Notably, Macclesfield sought to rob Peter to pay Paul, making up missing sums of money from the accounts of some masters in Chancery by switching funds from other masters' accounts.[31] In Bembridge's case, the background culture of financial abuse was similar, but, instead, visited upon Bembridge were the sins of his employers: some of the Paymasters General.

Notwithstanding periodic virulent criticism,[32] Paymasters General milked that most lucrative of sinecures for all it was worth[33] and, in doing so, drew the pay office's employees into the abuse. It is clear that the cashier and the accountant themselves had a great deal of freedom, in the words of Sutherland and Binney, 'to play with Pay Office money'.[34] Powell himself became very rich through his association with Lord Holland's affairs, Holland himself having been once described by no less a figure than the Lord Mayor as a 'Public Defaulter of Unaccounted Millions'.[35] For example, at Lord Holland's request, Powell[36]—described as Holland's 'chief man of business'[37]—lent Holland £73,000 to help him buy off some of the creditors of Charles James Fox (one of Lord Holland's sons).[38] Putting aside the ethics of an employee lending to an employer to assist a relative of the latter

---

[30] J Rudolph, 'Jurisdictional Controversy and the Credibility of Common Law' in D Coffman, A Leonard, L Neal (eds), *Questioning Credible Commitment: Perspectives on the Rise of Financial Capitalism* (Cambridge, Cambridge University Press, 2013) 104.

[31] Like so many impeachments, Macclesfield's impeachment was as much motivated by politics (embarrassing the Whigs, who were, in turn, happy enough to have found a scapegoat) as by a concern to bring an offender to book. Lord Macclesfield was found guilty of bribery and mishandling £100,000 and was fined £30,000. He was sent to the tower until the fine was paid off. See Porter, *English Society* 59.

[32] See, eg, PDG Thomas, 'A Mid-eighteenth Century Tory' (2008) 17 *Parliamentary History* 333, 353: 'Criticism of government as corrupt and inefficient remained the stock-in-trade of opposition speakers, exemplified in demands ... for Place Bills to reduce the number of officeholders in Parliament and thereby curb the influence of the King's ministers.'

[33] With the benefit of hindsight and a sea change in public opinion, John Wade's took the following view in his notorious (and often unreliable) 'black book': 'Sinecures are offices without employment! ... In the Departments of the Army, Navy, and Revenue, are numerous sinecures, which ought to have been long since extinguished. Such are the Paymaster of the Forces, £2,000': J Wade, *The Extraordinary Black Book: an Exposition of Abuses in Church and State, Courts of Law, Representation, Municipal and Corporate Bodies, with a Precis of the House of Commons, Past, Present, and to Come*, revised edn (London, Effingham Wilson, 1832) 398–99.

[34] L Sutherland and J Binney, 'Henry Fox as Paymaster General of the Forces' (1955) 70 *English Historical Review* 229, 253.

[35] The accusation against Lord Holland of the Lord Mayor of London in his address to the Sovereign on behalf of the Livery of the City, *Gentleman's Magazine* 1763, 290, 329 ff and 363.

[36] Who, let us remember, was to become Lord Holland's personal representative: see the text following 27.

[37] Sutherland and Binney, 'Henry Fox as Paymaster General' 243.

[38] ibid 253 fn 1.

financially, the questions are: how did Powell come to be in possession of such a huge sum and why was he willing to use it for such a purpose? The likelihood is that, in order to please one Paymaster, Powell simply decided to use the unspent balance of another Paymaster (either in or out of office),[39] knowing that the deficit could doubtless be made up further down the line in a like manner—a kind of Macclesfield-style, public sector 'Ponzi' scheme. If there had always been room for the exercise of such unchecked discretion by officers working for the Paymaster, Powell and Bembridge could count themselves as simply unlucky. They attempted to perpetrate their misconduct at what turned out to be turning of the tide, when—as we will see—the Accounts Commissioners and the Treasury Board had been constituted to enquire into just such conduct.

Bembridge was in effect paying the penalty for a dramatic change in public and political opinion. In the last quarter of the eighteenth century, the running of public finances was under fire and critical scrutiny as never before. To understand fully the notoriety of Bembridge's offence, it is not enough merely to point to the sum of money involved. Bembridge's counsel felt obliged to complain on his behalf (as so many have complained about newspaper publicity ever since) that:

> [C]lamour had prevailed unjustly against his client and the late Mr Powell, that their names had been bandied about in every common newspaper, and that misrepresentation and ignorance had attempted to fix a stigma where none was merited.[40]

This is really a criticism (not without at least some merit) of an element of scapegoating involved in Bembridge's trial and conviction. By 1783, the year of Bembridge's trial (and the year after the American War of Independence was formally ended by treaty), Britain's national debt had reached £230 million, having been only £72 million in 1755. George III had, of course, been behind the vigorous prosecution of the American war, at a total cost of £80 million.[41] The experience of having the Crown throw vast sums of good money into a losing cause inevitably led people to believe that the expenditure of the Crown, and its influence on public officers, was legitimately the subject of criticism and a high degree of scrutiny.[42] What is more,

---

[39] ibid 253.

[40] *Lloyds Evening Post* (18–21 July 1783).

[41] Famously, George III said that he was committed 'never to acknowledge the independence of the Americans, and to punish their contumacy by the indefinite prolongation of a war which promises to be eternal'. GO Trevelyan, *George the Third and Charles Fox: The Concluding Part of the American Revolution*, vol 1 (New York, Longmans Green, 1912) 4.

[42] Johnson, 'Internal Reform or External Taxation'; Foord, 'The Waning of the Influence of the Crown' 499–501. At 505, Foord says: 'Stemming from the Rockingham reform movement in 1780 was a steady flow of reforms which had a cumulative effect in reducing the King's interest.'

such scrutiny now had a firm empirical basis, in the widely publicised[43] and voluminous[44] Reports of the Accounts Commissioners, appointed in February 1780 under the Audit of Public Accounts Act (20 Geo 3 c 54), to look into the nation's finances.[45] In that regard, the Accounts Commissioners took a great interest in the workings of the office of the Paymaster General. Having examined on oath both Bembridge and Powell (on more than one occasion), amongst others, the 5th Report sarcastically remarked in relation to the accounting practices of Paymaster General's public officers:

> They are considered as incapable of improvement; the officers, educated in, and accustomed to the forms in use, are insensible of their defects, or, they feel them, have no leisure, often no ability, seldom any inclination, to correct them; alarmed at the idea of innovation, they resist the proposal of a regulation, because it is a change, though from a perplexed and intricate, to a more simple and intelligible system.[46]

It is important to note what a change in attitude and approach to the conduct of public officials such criticisms represented. At an earlier period, in the wake of great victories in war or the expansion of empire, national pride led many, albeit grudgingly, to accept or simply to ignore the sinecure status of the Paymastership. As Roy Porter says, of the grandees who held public office, 'the French revolutionary wars conveniently underscored their virility as the warrior champions of Church, State and Britannia'.[47] Anyone accepting that view might be disposed to overlook the fact that, for example, in 1765, Paymaster General Charles Townshend appointed as a ledger keeper in the office a man whose sight was so poor that he was unable to perform his duties. The man was still in post in 1783, his work being done by a deputy employed at yet further public expense.[48] By 1810, the cost, more generally, of such unreformed sinecures was £200,000 a year.[49]

It is worth making the point that such practices were not confined to the pay office. The sensitivity of the issues when the nation's public finances were under such scrutiny was underlined by the practice in other departments of government. In the Exchequer, for example, amongst a number

---

[43] Excerpts from the Reports of the Commissioners were usually printed verbatim in contemporary newspapers.

[44] There were no less than 15 Reports in all, compiled between 1780 and 1786.

[45] The appointment of the Commissioners came shortly after a devastating attack in Parliament on the excesses of Crown expenditure by soon-to-be Bembridge trial witness Edmund Burke: see Kier, 'Economical Reform' 374.

[46] 'The fifth Report of the Commissioners Appointed to Examine, Take, and State the Public Accounts of the Kingdom', *New Annual Register*, 1 August 1781, 19. See Johnson, 'Internal Reform or External Taxation' 34 and 37.

[47] Porter, *English Society* 66.

[48] *Sixth Report of the Commissioners of Public Accounts* (1782) at 10 and 64, cited by Johnson, 'Internal Reform or External Taxation' 36.

[49] P Harling, 'Rethinking "Old Corruption"' (1995) 147 *Past and Present* 127, 135–36. By 1810, it had been dramatically reduced to £17,000.

of sinecures revealed by the Accounts Commissioners in their 6th Report,[50] were the four positions of 'second clerk', each of whom received an annual salary of £1,000. According to one Deputy in the Tellers' offices, not a single second clerk had put in an appearance at the office for the preceding *36 years*.[51] Bembridge was no absentee sinecure-holder, but the lack of value for money that he provided, even when doing his job properly, simply highlighted another source of extravagance in the Office, one that cast Bembridge personally in a poor light as a participant in the 'monstrous abuse'[52] of the financing of public office.

The Paymaster General received from Parliament an allowance to pay office staff, which under Richard Rigby's long tenure of the office (1768–82) was £3,000, subject to further deductions for tax and other charges. As accountant, Bembridge received a salary of £150 a year, but his income was liable to be greatly enhanced by the custom of paying additional fees to the accountant (and to other officers involved) for the making up of the balances of individual former Paymasters General. He could expect to receive a sum many times the size of his salary in fees, depending on how many accounts he signed off. As noted below, upon his conviction, he was fined the large sum of £2,600, this being the sum he received for making up (in both senses of that term, as things turned out) Lord Holland's account. He testified to the Commissioners for Public Accounts that he was paid one guinea per thousand on remittances paid to the troops in North America and four guineas per regiment for settling their accounts, which, along with other fees, amounted to £1,358 in the year ending 1780. Powell, over the same period, received £6,715 on a similar basis. The eighteenth century saw no less than 28 Paymasters General take up and leave office, 22 of them having done so by 1783. At the time of Bembridge's trial, the accounts not only of Lord Holland but also of Richard Rigby were still to be made up. Such rich rewards for performing a function respecting which the officers in question already received a salary came in for understandable criticism. Jumping on the critical bandwagon, at the end of his judgment in *R v Bembridge*,[53] Willes J remarked of the cost of the Paymaster General's office:

> I cannot help lamenting the unhappy state of this country, that in these times of necessity and public distress, the passing the accounts [sic] of a paymaster should cost the state, in fees paid to its officers, the enormous sum of £14,900, as appears by the warrant read. The right to these extravagant fees ought to be, and I hope will be hereafter, a subject of parliamentary enquiry.[54]

[50] *Sixth Report of the Commissioners of Public Accounts* (1782) 13, 143 and 152.
[51] ibid 137 ff, cited in Johnson, 'Internal Reform or External Taxation' 35, who notes that, in addition, one of holders of an Exchequer sinecure was found to be underage (his father had been pocketing the fees). See further Harling 'Rethinking "Old Corruption"' 137–38.
[52] The term 'monstrous abuse' was that of Wade, *The Extraordinary Black Book* 487–88.
[53] *Bembridge* (n 4) ST.
[54] *Bembridge* (n 4) ST 160.

Willes J's comments are just one example of how, by the end of the American revolutionary war, the arguments for continued complacency in the face of such abuses were wearing thin.[55] Parliamentary criticism of government as corrupt and inefficient had long been a weapon of choice for opposition speakers,[56] but now 'aristocratic trusteeship'[57] was widely rejected outside Parliament as well. Such developments are relevant because they had adverse implications for a key defence argument at Bembridge's trial: the claim that Bembridge was accountable for his misdeeds only in private law to Lord Holland's estate because he did not hold a 'public office'.

## III.  *R V BEMBRIDGE* (2): TRIAL AND DEFENCE

Bembridge was tried at Westminster before Lord Mansfield and a special jury[58] on 22 November 1782. Count 1 of the information (the other two counts are not relevant here) read:

> The said Charles Bembridge ... wrongly, unjustly, and fraudulently contriving to conceal from the said Lewis, Lord Sondes, the said auditor of the imprest, to whom the said final account was delivered ... the said several sums of money which ought to have been charged as aforesaid, and to cheat and defraud our present Sovereign Lord the King, did not, at the several days and times when he was so requested as aforesaid, discover or make known to the said Lewis, Lord Sondes, the several sums of money ... but wickedly, wilfully, fraudulently and corruptly did refuse and neglect to discover to make known the same to the said Lewis, Lord Sondes, contrary to the duty of the said Charles Bembridge, as such accountant as aforesaid, to the evil example & c.[59]

In that regard, Bembridge's office as accountant is described in the information laid against Bembridge by Attorney-General James Wallace as 'a place

---

[55] In general, there was popular dislike of American independence, although politically this did not assist Burke and his allies when the war was lost, because they were distrusted as supporters of the rebels: Locke, *Edmund Burke* 432.

[56] See Thomas, 'A Mid-Eighteenth Century Tory'. Charles James Fox, Lord Holland's own son, himself attacked Lord North's tottering administration, branding government ministers 'either impotent or treacherous': speech of 27 November 1781, reprinted in J Wright (ed), *The Speeches of the Rt Hon CJ Fox in the House of Commons*, vol 1 (London, Longman, 1815) 429.

[57] The helpful phrase of J Brewer, 'Rockingham, Burke and Whig Political Argument' (1975) 18 *Historical Journal* 188, 197.

[58] A 'special' jury was a jury comprised of those living in homes with a higher rateable value that that required for ordinary juries. Either party could opt for trial by special jury, at a cost (12 guineas in 1949). Lord Mansfield had a liking for trial by special jury.

[59] *Bembridge* (n 4) Doug 328–29, ER 680, per Lord Mansfield. At that time, there was no understanding that the fault element in a crime should, in the interests of both trial fairness and trial efficiency, be limited to one or two appropriate forms that had to be proved beyond reasonable doubt (eg, 'intentionally or recklessly').

and employment of great public trust and confidence, touching the making up the accounts [sic] of the receiver and Paymaster general, and the adjusting and settling the same with the auditor of the imprest'.[60] Powell, when he was accountant before Bembridge, had originally made up Lord Holland's account on 11 January 1772,[61] and sent the account to the auditors for adjusting and settling. The account made no mention of some £48,709 contained in different accounts, having been received by various people under Lord Holland's authority and meant for the discharge of the latter's duties.[62] After the delivery of the accounts, but (crucially) before the final account had been adjusted and settled by the auditors, Bembridge became the Paymaster's accountant on 31 March 1776. The Holland account then remained open and unsettled for another six years. During that time, Bembridge failed to report the missing money to the Imprest, even though on 15 January 1782 he had admitted to a Treasury Board enquiry[63] (held shortly before the trial) that he knew of the relevant account's existence and that he should have reported the sums involved.[64]

When the auditors of the Imprest finally turned their attention to auditing the Holland account, the omission was discovered and queried, and the accounts were sent back to Bembridge. Bembridge duly returned the accounts to the Imprest, but with the missing sums now crudely pencilled in[65] (a practice that the Imprest said to the Treasury Board was unprecedented). In point of guilt or innocence, as opposed to mitigation, it cannot have helped Bembridge's cause greatly that on 22 February 1783, he offered to pay back the missing sums, and did so two weeks later. The information laid against Bembridge described his actions, in the usual terms, as 'to the evil example of all others in the like cases offending, to the great injury and

---

[60] *Bembridge* (n 4) Doug 327–28, ER 679.

[61] Holland left office as Paymaster in 1765.

[62] Subsequently, Powell explained his actions, in an attempt to shift the focus of blame to Bembridge, that he had not mentioned the missing money because this could not be done 'without injuring a friend' (Bembridge).

[63] The Treasury Board consisted of Pitt the Younger, William Grenville (Lord of the Treasury, 1780–82), Richard Jackson KC (another Lord of the Treasury, nicknamed 'omniscient Jackson'), with, amongst others, Lord Shelburne (as First Lord of the Treasury). The membership of the Board gives some indication of what a high-profile matter the accounting in the Paymaster General's office had become.

[64] *Whitehall Evening Post* (17–19 July 1783). Both Powell and Bembridge were dismissed, during the Treasury Board enquiry, in early March 1783. Given the damaging nature of Bembridge's admission to the Board, his counsel felt he had to launch a full-blooded attack on the Board's procedure: 'He [Bembridge] stood before something more like an inquisition than anything that has been seen in this country since the years before the flood. Party zeal, which, like Caesar's, in this case, will not be satiated even with blood, was pursuing it; they hunt him down': *Bembridge* (n 4) ST 94.

[65] Although subsequently copied over in ink by an office junior called Colbourne (probably under Bembridge's instructions), who was not charged with any offence.

deceit of our said Lord the present King, and against the peace of our said Lord the present King, his crown and dignity'.[66]

Against this background, Lord Mansfield said to the jury:

> The duty of the defendant is obvious; he was a trustee for the public and the paymaster, for making every charge and every allowance he knew of ... If the defendant knew of the omission, he must have applied to Powell for explanation; and if he concealed it, his motive must have been corrupt. That he did know was fully proved, and he was guilty therefore, not of an omission or neglect, but of a gross deceit. The object could only have been to defraud the public of the whole, or of part of the interest.[67]

Following such a direction, there was unlikely to be much doubt about the outcome. Bembridge was found guilty, following a five-hour trial, with the jury having retired to consider its verdict for a mere 20 minutes. He was sentenced to six months' imprisonment and a fine of £2,650, that sum being the fee that he had charged for 'settling' Lord Holland's account.[68]

Bembridge could certainly not complain that his conviction was attributable to a lack of adequate representation. He was represented by four counsel, including Edward Bearcroft KC[69] and Sir Thomas Erskine KC.[70] Nor did Bembridge lack for important or credible (or even both) witnesses. He was able to call in evidence both the Rt Hon Edmund Burke and Lord North, along with two other former Paymasters General, Lord Sydney and the Rt Hon Richard Rigby.[71] Amongst a variety of defence arguments that were ultimately rejected, the one worth commenting on is the claim that Bembridge did not occupy a 'public' office and thus fell outside the scope of the misconduct offence.

The main argument for the defence was that the Office of the Paymaster General was in certain crucial respects a private office, or at least that the duties owed by the accountant to the Paymaster were more like those of someone's personal accountant: a matter (at that time) for private remedy

---

[66] The wording of the information as a whole (see the text at n 59 above) is quite obviously in part the basis for the famous passage, still commonly cited (see n 10 above), in Lord Mansfield's judgment: *Bembridge* (n 4) Doug 332, ER 681.

[67] *Bembridge* (n 4) Doug 331, ER 681.

[68] On these fees, see the text at n 53 above.

[69] Subsequently MP for Hindon in 1784 (a seat formerly held both by Henry Fox, before he became Lord Holland, and by William Blackstone) and Chief Justice of Chester in 1788. In Cobbett's *Parliamentary History of England*, vol XXIX (London, TC Hansard, 1817), at 32 Geo III c 1411, he is described thus: 'Mr Bearcroft was not only a great lawyer, but was better, a friend to the constitution, and an honest man.'

[70] Erskine was a leading light in the treason and seditious libel trials of the late eighteenth century, when he was often to find Bearcroft acting for the prosecution. Erskine had, after some prompting from Lord Mansfield, taken silk in May 1783: J Hostettler, *Thomas Erskine and Trial by Jury* (Chichester: Barry Rose, 1996) 43. The Crown was represented by the Solicitor General, John Lee, and by Sir Thomas Davenport (a noted Nisi Prius leader).

[71] Lord Sidney had become Paymaster General, along with George Cooke, when Lord North demitted office.

rather than for criminal prosecution. Ironically, it had been one of Burke's criticisms of the Paymaster's Office, when he became Paymaster himself, that:

> It [fell] ... to my lot to do something for what I considered as the improvement and reformation of that office—the principal fault of which I considered to be, that it had been rather like a private office of account, than a public administration.[72]

Certainly, the Paymaster General himself was liable only in civil law for loss of funds or maladministration (a liability that would pass on his death to his heirs).[73] Mr Bearcroft KC, on Bembridge's behalf, had sought bolster this argument by pointing out that, before 1783, a Paymaster General going out of office (or, if dead, his representative):

> Had a right to take every book, and every scrap of paper that would serve to make up his account, away from the pay-office, to his own closet ... it is the means of his doing that which the law says he is bound to do.[74]

Had this argument been accepted, then the remedy against Bembridge would have been a private law matter in the hands of Lord Holland's representatives—who ironically included, at one point, Bembridge's alleged partner in crime, John Powell—rather than criminal proceedings. However, bearing in mind the conclusions of the very public and critical investigation of the Paymaster's office by the Accounts Commissioners, as well as the parlous state of public and political opinion concerning Crown expenditure,[75] the argument was never likely to succeed. In the end, there was no answer at Bembridge's trial to the prosecuting Solicitor General John Lee's[76] sardonic riposte before the jury:

> Why, gentlemen, I am told, that it is meant gravely to be contended, that Mr Bembridge is not a public officer, but a private clerk, appointed by the private gentleman who shall happen to be in the office of paymaster to the forces; then, I do not know what it is that constitutes a public officer ... he is appointed in consequence of a public situation, for public purposes, and paid by the public purse.[77]

Albeit somewhat faintly, the defence argument on the 'public' nature of Bembridge's office also raised issues that are perhaps still of some relevance today. If A is found to be holding public office, will there be sufficient certainty about the basis of A's liability such that B, C, D and so on, working in

---

[72] *Bembridge* (n 4) ST 66.

[73] J Norman, *Edmund Burke: Philosopher, Politician, Prophet* (London, William Collins, 2013) 94.

[74] *Bembridge* (n 4) ST 54–55.

[75] See the text at nn 55–57 above.

[76] Lee owed his appointment as Solicitor General to the Rockinghamite Whigs. He later became Attorney-General in 1783, following the death of James Wallace. Lee had a reputation for integrity, but also for coarse—even abusive—manners.

[77] *Bembridge* (n 4) ST 32–33.

other government offices, can tell if the misconduct offence will be applied to them?[78] How will the limits of public office-holding be determined? Mr Bearcroft KC asked rhetorically:

> [W]ill it be said to be this, that every man who is a clerk's clerk in office, where the head officer has a place under the great seal, is answerable by indictment, for every fault he commits?[79]

One weakness in this argument lies in the fact that by the late eighteenth century, of the 16,000 officers in Britain's fiscal-military state, 80 per cent were involved in the state's financial bureaucracy.[80] So, we may hypothesise that there would at that time have been clear and predictable analogies between Bembridge and other 'clerk's clerks' in government service.

More broadly, though, as indicated above, the public versus private argument had now tipped decisively in favour of the former. In the prevailing climate of opinion, as the Accounts Commissioners high-mindedly observed of the workings of the pay office: 'The public have a right to be informed how their money has been expended, and as speedily as possible after the expenditure.'[81] Ironically, Bearcroft's rhetorical question was turned against him. At a time of such public concern about the national debt—a debt that had risen to some 214 per cent of national income by 1784[82]—it must have seemed all too attractive to the jury to answer Bearcroft's question confidently in the affirmative, for the simple reason that this was a golden opportunity to declare where, publicly, the buck stopped.

## IV. FROM 'SECRET INFLUENCE' TO DOUBLE STANDARDS: BURKE AND REFORM

> If an arrangement could be made to stop men from using office as a means of private gain, it would provide a way—the only possible way—for combining democracy with aristocracy.[83]

Aristotle's claim still has contemporary relevance if one substitutes a concept such as 'middle class Government' in place of 'aristocracy', but how determined has Parliament ever been to eliminate the use of public office for private gain? In this section, I start by considering briefly the political and legal

---

[78] For the recent discussion of a related problem, see *R v Mitchell* [2014] WLR (D) 61 (CA).

[79] *Bembridge* (n 4) ST 146.

[80] Harling and Mandler, 'From "Fiscal-Military" State to "Laissez-Faire" State' 54.

[81] Commissioners of Public Accounts (5th Report), *New Annual Register*, 1 August 1781, 195. Note that in his address to the jury cited at n 77 above, the Solicitor General uses similar language, speaking of Bembridge as being 'accountable to the public'.

[82] P Vries, 'Public Finance in China and Britain in the Long Eighteenth Century', LSE Working Papers No 167/12, www.lse.ac.uk/economicHistory/workingPapers/2012/WP167.pdf.

[83] Ernest Barker (ed), Aristotle, *The Politics*, Book V (Oxford: Clarendon Press, 1946) Ch viii at 17.

role of Edmund Burke as an anti-corruption reformer, as well as providing further detail on his involvement in the *Bembridge* case. Burke's legal reforms certainly did something to introduce—for the first time—legal accountability and openness in the expenditure of public money. However, these reforms were not in any general sense aimed at 'cleaning up' politics. As we will see, Burke himself defended his right to use the privilege of public money for the purpose of patronage, so long as he was quite open about doing so.

Burke's attack on the traditional rights and privileges of unaccountable Crown-appointed placemen was two-pronged: first, there was to be a reduction of the sheer number of such placemen (and of the pensions granted to them when out of office); and, second, there was to be the introduction of greater openness and of financial accountability to Parliament in order to constrain the opportunities for the remaining Crown appointees to enrich themselves at the public expense. In itself, this was a radical and controversial approach. It had since the early eighteenth century been the very lack of accountability to Parliament of a Crown appointee such as Lord Holland—along with his deputies—that in part sustained the 'secret influence' of the Crown in British politics: influence described by no less a figure than Blackstone as 'most amazingly extensive'.[84] The only coercive check on the operation of Crown Offices was the haphazard threat of criminal trial for misconduct (as in Bembridge's case, but almost unthinkable in the case of a Member of Parliament or a Crown appointee), or of impeachment for an individual's culpable misconduct or failure to perform a public duty.[85] Other than that, there was only the paper tiger constituted by the Auditors of the Imprest and its ineffectual brand of accounting oversight.[86]

Significant changes came after Parliament reassembled on 25 November 1779, when the Rockinghamites (including Burke) introduced a new theme of 'economical reform' as part of their opposition to Lord North's now-troubled administration.[87] Burke was part of an administration that, as one contemporary put it: 'Had pledged themselves to many regulations and reforms, which they began to carry into execution as soon as the parliament met, with a degree of alacrity and liberality unknown in the parliamentary history of this country.'[88] There were a number of elements to 'economical reform', many eventually being watered down, frustrated or dropped completely. Be that as it may, alongside Burke's proposal for £200,000 worth of savings through the abolition of Crown appointments (which he considered

[84] 1 Bl Comm 336.
[85] Foord, 'The Waning of the Influence of the Crown' 488–91; B Silverman, *Cages of Reason: The Rise of the Rational State in France, Japan, the United States and Britain* (Chicago, University of Chicago Press, 1993) 316–17.
[86] Before 1714, there had been annual commissions to present public accounts, but the Hanoverian succession put paid to that practice.
[87] Locke, *Edmund Burke* 446.
[88] Anon, *The Beauties of the late Right Hon Edmund Burke: Selected Writings*, vol 1 (London, JW Myers, 1798) xcv.

equivalent to the influence of 50 MPs),[89] there was a proposal by Lord Shelburne for a check on the huge growth of 'extraordinary' (unplanned-for) payments for army contracts. These were payments for which the Paymaster General was responsible.[90] Burke's famous speech on 'economical reform' came on 11 February 1780,[91] and in it he set down 'seven fundamental rules' (which were in reality proposals for Bills), amongst which were:

1. Wasteful Offices of more expense than use to the state should be cut, as should those positions that prevent unified control of public expenditure;
2. Payments should be made in a particular order in accordance with due process, and not at the discretion of a minister;
3. Departmental expenditure should be better controlled, and 'subordinate treasuries' (separate sources of funds for expenditure of public money) should be abolished.[92]

In particular, under these headings, Burke's took aim at the Office of Paymaster General (at that point held by his mortal enemy, Richard Rigby). Lord North's response to this initiative was to appoint the independent Commissioners of Public Accounts (established by 20 Geo III c 54), whose work ultimately led to the prosecution of Bembridge.[93] Further, on 6 April 1780, the House of Commons passed John Dunning's famous Commons motion that 'the influence of the Crown has increased, is increasing, and ought to be diminished',[94] which led the House of Commons to resolve that:

[I]t is competent to this house to examine into and to correct abuses in the expenditure of the civil list revenues, as well as in every other branch of the public revenue, whenever it shall seem expedient to the wisdom of this house to do so.[95]

[89] Edmund Burke, in P Langford et al (eds), *Writings and Speeches*, vol iii (Oxford, Oxford University Press, 1981) 467–76. The Civil List and Secret Service Money Act 1782 was a watered-down version of Burke's proposals in this regard, and abolished 134 offices in the royal household and civil administration, along with the position of third Secretary of State and the Board of Trade. Pensions were also limited and regulated. The Act was projected to save a more modest £72,368 a year. In 1780, the House of Commons included around 50 government officials, 30 sinecurists, 25 court officials, 65 naval and military officers, 11 government contractors and 11 holders of secret service pensions—altogether just under 200 'placemen' who owed their position to Crown influence: IR Christie, *Myth and Reality in Late Eighteenth Century British Politics* (Berkeley, University of California Press, 1970) 296.

[90] Locke, *Edmund Burke* 448.

[91] Its title was: 'A plan for the better security of the Independence of Parliament and the economical reformation of civil and other establishments.'

[92] Locke, *Edmund Burke* 450; Norman, *Edmund Burke* 93.

[93] Public Accounts Commissioners becoming a permanent feature of checks on the executive from 1785 (25 Geo III c 52), the same year as the abolition of the Auditors of the Imprest.

[94] Compare the words of Charles James Fox in an impromptu election speech at the King's Arms Tavern, Palace Yard, London: 'I flatter myself you have seen, and know enough of yourselves, to be well afforded, that by maintaining the dignity of the House of Commons against the secret advisers and the influence of the Crown, I have maintained your cause.' Anon, *A History of the Westminster Election* (London, 1754) 62

[95] William Cobbett, *Cobbett's Parliamentary History of England: from the Norman Conquest to 1803* (London, Bagshaw, 1806), vol xxi, 367.

Lord North's administration came to an end two years later on 20 March 1782, all associated with it being condemned by Burke as 'erroneously and criminally negligent' for having stood by and done nothing about 'the system of corruption'.[96] However, Burke's zealotry (and a cooling of relations between the two men) saw him excluded from Rockingham's cabinet when the latter took power in 1782, with Dunning effectively taking his place.[97] It was thus at this point that Burke instead became Paymaster General of the Forces (replacing Richard Rigby), and hence a member of the Privy Council, with a brief to reform the Pay Office.

In his brief initial term of office as Paymaster General, helped (ironically) by inside information and advice provided by Bembridge and Powell, Burke saw into legislation the Paymaster General Act 1782, which effectively ended the post as a lucrative sinecure. Paymasters were now obliged to put the money they had requested to withdraw from the Treasury into the Bank of England, from where it was to be withdrawn only for specific purposes. The Treasury was to receive monthly statements of the Paymaster's balance at the Bank. This Act was shortly thereafter repealed by Shelburne's administration, but the Act that replaced it repeated verbatim almost the whole text of Burke's Act. Rockingham's unexpected death in July 1782, and his replacement as Prime Minister by Shelburne, put an end to Rockingham's administration after only a few months. Burke could have brazenly hung on to office as Paymaster, but a sense of honour compelled him to resign. He was replaced by Isaac Barré, whose proposal for a Commission of Public Accounts had upstaged Burke's own initiatives to that end.[98] It was during Barré's tenure in office that the investigations of the Commissioners of Public Accounts and of the Treasury Board (to whose members both Powell and Bembridge made highly damaging admissions) uncovered the role of Powell and Bembridge in concealing the large sum missing from Lord Holland's account. Barré dismissed them both in February 1783 and prosecutions were instigated against them.

However, when the Fox–North coalition came to power in April 1783, Burke was restored to the Office of Paymaster. It was at this point that he made what some have argued was perhaps the most serious misjudgement of his career. Perhaps grateful to them for the help that they had provided, and well known more generally as someone who could unexpectedly befriend another down on his luck,[99] Burke reinstated both Bembridge and Powell to their offices, pending prosecution, to put into practice the principle that someone is innocent until proven guilty. This decision was soon called into question in the House of Commons,[100] being described by a

---

[96] Cobbett, *Cobbett's Parliamentary History* vol xxii, 1130–33.
[97] For discussion, see, eg, D Jarrett, *Britain 1688–1815* (London, Longmans, 1965) Ch 14.
[98] Locke, *Edmund Burke* 460.
[99] ibid 492.
[100] 15th Parliament of Great Britain, 3rd Session 1783 (2 May) 578.

Mr Martin MP as a 'gross and daring insult to the public'.[101] On hearing this, Burke had to be restrained by Richard Sheridan, 'lest his [Burke's] heat should betray him into some intemperate expressions',[102] but criticism was taken up by others, Sir Edward Astley suggesting ('with much vehemence') that 'to restore persons charged with a crime amounting to public robbery, was a great slight for the opinion of the public, and a daring insult'.[103] Fatefully, Charles James Fox sought to come to Burke's aid by suggesting that: 'It was not to be presumed, that his honourable friend would have restored two persons to their offices, under him, of whose unimpeachable character he was not in his own mind perfectly convinced.'[104] The session ended with a complaint to the speaker that 'the whole conversation had been irregular and disorderly'.[105]

From there, things went from bad to worse. Powell committed suicide on 26 May 1783, leaving Bembridge to face the music and what—as we have seen—was a hostile press and public reaction when proceedings were recommenced.[106] Burke stuck loyally to the line he had taken in the House of Commons debate, testifying (reinforced by further testimony from Lord North and Richard Rigby) that:

> I had received from Mr Rigby the strongest recommendation of Mr Bembridge's diligence, fidelity, and ability; and in the time that I was in office, I had all the reason in the world to be persuaded that he perfectly answered that character and description, in every respect.[107]

Following Bembridge's conviction, it is small wonder, then, that the shorthand reporter of *R v Bembridge* allows himself the liberty of concluding that:

> The compassion which on these and all other occasions was manifested by Mr Burke for the suffering of these public delinquents, the zeal with which he advocated their cause, and the eagerness with which he endeavoured to extenuate their criminality, have received severe reprehension.[108]

However, putting aside the personal consequences for Burke of Bembridge's trial and conviction, Burke's conduct of his role as Paymaster General, and as prime mover in the pursuit of 'economical reform', are instructive.

---

[101] ibid 581; Locke, *Edmund Burke* 523.
[102] Debrett, ix, 678–83, cited by Locke, *Edmund Burke* 523. Burke had tried to rise to speak, but got no further than an initial riposte: 'It is a gross and daring...'
[103] 15th Parliament of Great Britain, 3rd Session 1783 (2 May) 581.
[104] ibid 581–82. It must be kept in mind that, of course, Powell was the sole executor of Charles James' father's (Lord Holland's) estate, as Charles James pointed out to the House.
[105] See n 101.
[106] See the text at n 40.
[107] *Bembridge* (n 4) ST 66.
[108] ibid 160. The damage that was done to Burke's reputation by the Bembridge case was only compounded by Burke's long drawn-out but unsuccessful attempt to impeach Warren Hastings (former Governor General of India) between 1788 and 1795 soon afterwards on misconduct charges relating to mismanagement and personal corruption.

On the one hand, Burke was a prime mover in seeking to introduce by law greater financial control, openness and accountability into public financing. These were reforms specifically aimed at reducing the opportunities for corruption amongst office-holders created by secrecy, reliance on personal discretion in decision-making and the lack of an obligation publicly to account. On the other hand, he saw no inconsistency between championing such reforms and using his own position as Paymaster to benefit members of his family through nepotism.

For example, upon appointment as Paymaster, Burke promptly appointed his son as a Deputy Paymaster in London at £500 per year, his cousin Will to a newly created post of Deputy Paymaster in India at £5 per day, as well as securing for his brother a position as Secretary to the Treasury at £3,000 per year.[109] Allegations against him of gross hypocrisy were met by his argument that he was opposed to the secret influence of the Crown in making appointments,[110] thereby undermining Parliament's influence on public policy. He was *not* opposed to the quite open use of high office as a means to reward relatives or favourites.[111] Nepotism was, of course, central to the working of many state and private institutions—the church being prominent amongst them—at that time and for years afterwards.[112] For example, whilst he was Prime Minister, Lord North saw to it that his half-brother, Brownlow, became Dean of Canterbury at 29 years of age, Bishop of Lichfield at 30, Bishop of Worcester at 33 and Bishop of Winchester at 40.[113] It has also been argued that, in fairness to Burke, anyone coming into public office at that time could expect to receive many requests for favours and, more significantly, could be expected to grant a fair proportion of them.[114] As Hans Stanley MP (an associate of the elder Pitt) remarked: 'Get into Parliament, make tiresome speeches; you will have great offers; do not accept them at first, then do; make great provision for yourself and family, and then call yourself an independent country gentleman.'[115] Nonetheless, we should not shrink from categorising such nepotism as misuse of public office, both then and now. Morally, how different really was Burke's conduct in principle from that of Lord Holland?

---

[109] Locke, *Edmund Burke* 508–09.

[110] The argument is set out in Edmund Burke, *Thoughts on the Cause of the Present Discontents* (London, J Dodsley, 1770).

[111] In a way, this was the very means by which Burke had himself been appointed Paymaster General, as a consolation prize from Rockingham to boost Burke's meagre income when Burke was not included in Rockingham's cabinet.

[112] W Gibson, 'Patterns of Nepotism and Kinship in the Eighteenth Century Church' (1987) XIV *Journal of Religious History* 382–89.

[113] Porter, *English Society* 59.

[114] Locke, *Edmund Burke* 509, who remarks: 'As soon as he was perceived to have influence, Burke was inundated with requests for favours.'

[115] L Namier and J Brooke, *The House of Commons 1754–1790* (London, Secker & Warburg, 1964) 471, cited by Norman, *Edmund Burke* 52.

### V. MISCONDUCT IN HIGH PLACES, PRESENT AND PAST

In Lord Holland's conduct and in Burke's attitude, there are some remind-
ers of the expenses scandal of the so-called 'rotten' Parliament of 2005–10.
First, there is the corrupt relationship between office-holder and staff. Compare Lord Holland's relationship with his office staff and that of modern
MPs with the now defunct Fees Office. The Fees Office—which was meant
to check that MPs' expenditure fell within the rules—behaved (ironically)
more like Lord Holland's Pay Office: as MPs' servants rather than as their
impartial advisers bound by the rule of law. As Sir Thomas Legg put it,
speaking of parliamentary practice in relation to expenses:

> The [Assisted Costs Allowance] system was deeply flawed, In particular, the rules
> were vague, and MPs were themselves self-certifying as to the propriety of their
> use of the allowance. Taken with the prevailing lack of transparency and the 'cul-
> ture of deference', this meant that the Fees Offices' decisions lacked legitimacy;
> and many of them were in fact mistaken.[116]

Second, there are the strong echoes of Burke's nepotism. There is now, of
course, a nominally independent body overseeing the use of such expenses:
the Independent Parliamentary Standards Authority (IPSA).[117] However,
what remains remarkable is the insouciance of IPSA when it comes to critical analysis of an official privilege that, however understandable it might
have been in the eighteenth century, surely has scant justification now.
This is the widespread use of office to engage in nepotism and favourit-
ism. This exploitation of office-holding takes place through the highly questionable use of the Staffing Expenditure budget (£140,000 to £147,000 in
2015, depending on the location of the MP's constituency). In 2008, the
House of Commons extended the scheme to cover the employment of up to
3.5 members of staff.[118] In 2009, the Committee on Standards in Public Life
remarked that 'MPs offices are not family businesses. They are supported by
public funds'[119] and in Recommendation 15, the Committee said:

> MPs should no longer be able to appoint members of their own families to their
> staff and pay them with public funds. Those currently employing family members
> should be able to continue to do so for the life of one further Parliament or five
> years, whichever is the longer.[120]

Since then, the recommendation has simply been ignored and quietly
dropped. MPs have certainly filled their boots—and their family incomes

---

[116] Sir Thomas Legg, *Review of Past ACA Payments: First Report of Session 2009–10*, HC
348 (2010), Executive Summary, para 2.
[117] See www.parliamentarystandards.org.uk/Pages/default.aspx.
[118] R Kelly, *Members' Pay and Allowances* (House of Commons Library SN/PC/05075,
2009) 12.
[119] Committee on Standards in Public Life, *MPs' Expenses and Allowances Supporting Parliament, Safeguarding the Taxpayer*, 12th Report Cm 7724 (London, HMSO, 2009) para 6.20.
[120] ibid 14.

in particular—through the use of this quite extraordinary privilege. Some £4,000,000 is currently spent by 155 (predominantly male) MPs in employing family members, using their staff allowance. The average salary paid is well over £25,000, higher on average than the salaries offered to non-family members doing the same or a similar job.[121]

One wonders how IPSA regards this systematic nepotism as consistent with the claim, in the current Green Book of parliamentary rules and standards, that amongst what it calls the 'fundamental principles' is the principle that: 'Members must ensure that claims do not give rise to, *or give the appearance of giving rise to*, an improper personal financial benefit to themselves or anyone else' (emphasis added).[122] MPs' willingness simply to ignore this injunction when it comes to the employment of family members shows that it is as true now as it was when James Madison said it in 1788 that:

> In framing a government which is to be administered by men over men, the great difficulty lies in this: you must first enable the government to control the governed; and in the next place oblige it to control itself.[123]

---

[121] www.labourlist.org/2013/09/labour-mps-are-almost-as-bad-as-tory-mps-when-it-comes-to-hiring-family-members-data-shows.

[122] www.publications.parliament.uk/pa/cm200809/cmselect/cmmemest/142/14204.htm. This repeats wording drawn from the *Code of Conduct for Members of Parliament*, agreed by the House of Commons in July 1995.

[123] J Madison, 'The Structure of the Government Must Furnish the Proper Checks and Balances between the Different Departments', Federalist Papers No 51, *Independent Journal*, 6 February 1788.

# 6

# *R v Shipley* (1784)

## The Dean of St Asaph's Case

### KEVIN CROSBY*

IN 1784, WILLIAM Shipley, the son of St Asaph's radical bishop Jonathan Shipley, and himself the Dean of St Asaph,[1] was prosecuted for republishing a controversial political pamphlet.[2] William Jones, the pamphlet's author and a recently appointed colonial judge, was surprised to find that a prosecution for the publication of an abstract work of political philosophy was even possible.[3] The Treasury refused to pay the costs of the prosecution.[4] While an English jury was eventually persuaded to convict Shipley 'of publishing' the pamphlet, he was subsequently discharged by the judges of the King's Bench, owing to the fact that under the prevailing doctrine of seditious libel, a guilty verdict was understood as a de facto special verdict, leaving legal questions (including whether a particular pamphlet was

* I am grateful to Arlie Loughnan and Colin Murray for comments on earlier drafts of this chapter. I am also grateful for the helpful feedback I received from the other contributors to this volume at the 'Landmark Cases in Criminal Law' workshop at the University of Cambridge, as well as the helpful comments from the editors of this volume on an earlier draft of this chapter.

[1] See, eg, N Sykes, *Church and State in England in the Eighteenth Century* (Cambridge, Cambridge University Press, 1934) 52, 64, 341.

[2] *R v Shipley* (1784) 21 St Tr 847 and *R v Shipley* (1784) 4 Doug KB 73; 99 ER 774. Citations throughout this chapter are to the State Trials report unless otherwise noted, due to the detail in the State Trials account.

[3] J Oldham, *English Common Law in the Age of* Mansfield (Chapel Hill, University of North Carolina Press, 2004) 228 fn 80.

[4] Erskine used this as a way of arguing at Shipley's trial that the publication was not seditious, as the government had no desire to have Shipley prosecuted: *R v Shipley* (1784) 21 St Tr 847, 901–02. The Treasury may have felt that Shipley's high-status prosecutor—the outgoing Prime Minister's brother—could afford the expense. Shipley himself hinted at this possibility when addressing Lord Kenyon at the Denbigh assizes: *R v Shipley* (n 2) 874 (on the strong inverse correlation between the social status of a prosecutor and their receipt of expenses in property crimes, see P King, *Crime, Justice and Discretion in England 1740–1820* (Oxford, Oxford University Press, 2000) 47–52).

actually seditious) to a later judicial determination.[5] This case is primarily famous because of the challenge it posed to this established doctrine, highlighting the fact that this strange form of verdict was, in Lobban's words, an 'unworkable stretching of the law'.[6] It ultimately led to the passage in 1792 of legislation condemning the practice as contrary to the common law.[7] And it is not only modern commentators who have considered Shipley's trial to be a landmark case in the criminal law. Two decades after it was decided, the Whig *Edinburgh Review*, praising Thomas Erskine's defence of Shipley as 'by far the most learned commentary on that inestimable mode of trial, which is anywhere to be found', argued that the Act of 1792 was 'merely declaratory of the principles, which were laid down in this argument with unrivalled clearness'.[8]

Shipley's trial is a 'landmark case' in its exploration of the relationship between judge and jury implicit in the general verdict. The Court of Appeal has, in recent years, repeatedly held that the alternative to a general verdict—a 'special' verdict, setting out the facts and leaving all legal questions to a subsequent judicial determination—should only be used in criminal cases very rarely,[9] but the European Court of Human Rights has held that a general verdict will only be acceptable if the jury's understanding of the law can be clearly inferred from other elements of the trial, including the details of the indictment and the directions the jurors received from the Bench.[10]

---

[5] See generally J Fitzjames Stephen, *A History of the Criminal Law of England*, vol 2 (London, Macmillan, 1883) 298–395, explicitly taking Mansfield's account of the law's development in *Shipley* 'as my guide' (ibid 316); and P Hamburger, 'The Development of the Law of Seditious Libel and the Control of the Press' (1985) 37 *Stanford Law Review* 661.

[6] Michael Lobban, 'From Seditious Libel to Unlawful Assembly: Peterloo and the Changing Face of Political Crime c 1770–1820' (1990) 10 *Oxford Journal of Legal Studies* 307, 317.

[7] Libel Act 1792, 32 Geo 3 c 60; subsequently repealed by the Coroners and Justice Act 2009, sch 23, pt 2.

[8] 'Review: *The Speeches of the Honourable Thomas Erskine (now Lord Erskine), when at the Bar, on Subjects connected with the Liberty of the Press, and against Constructive Treasons*' (1810) 16 *Edinburgh Review* 102, 104–05. See also Norgate's 'Preface to the Second edition' in W Jones, *The Principles of Government in a Dialogue between a Gentleman and a Farmer*, 2nd edn (TS Norgate ed, London, 1797).

[9] See, eg, *R v Hopkinson* [2013] EWCA Crim 795; [2014] 1 Cr App R 3. The major exception is the verdict of not guilty by reason of insanity, on which see A Loughnan, *Manifest Madness: Mental Incapacity in Criminal Law* (Oxford, Oxford University Press, 2012) particularly at 165–67, and her discussion of *R v M'Naghton* (1843) 10 Cl & Fin 200; 8 ER 718 in this volume. The courts have sometimes been keen to treat general verdicts as a kind of 'black box' for concealing legal uncertainty, as in *DPP v Shaw* [1962] AC 220 (HL), discussed by Henry Mares in this volume.

[10] *Taxquet v Belgium* (2012) 54 EHRR 26. See generally P Roberts, 'Does Article 6 of the European Convention on Human Rights Require Reasoned Verdicts in Criminal Trials?' (2011) 11 *Human Rights Law Review* 213; and M Coen, '"With Cat-Like Tread": Jury Trial and the European Court of Human Rights' (2014) 14 *Human Rights Law Review* 107. The English Court of Appeal swiftly ruled, in *R v Ali* [2011] EWCA Crim 1011, that *Taxquet* simply required general verdicts to be preceded by proper directions from the trial judge; see also *R v Lawless* [2011] EWCA Crim 59; (2011) 175 JP 93. And in *Judge v UK* (2011) 52 EHRR SE17, the ECtHR ruled that the broadly comparable Scottish system was Convention-compliant.

*Shipley* grapples with similar questions, with defence counsel Thomas Erskine arguing at length that criminal trial juries have a constitutional right to deliver general verdicts, and Lord Mansfield insisting that the general verdict's opaqueness is contrary to the rule of law. Erskine's argument ran contrary to the settled eighteenth-century law of seditious libel, but, while Mansfield ruled against him, Erskine's speech at the King's Bench is widely understood to have led to the passage of the Libel Act 1792, securing the jury's right to deliver a general verdict in all such cases. This case, while going against the jury's supposed right, is therefore of central importance to our understanding of the general verdict.

## I. THE BACKGROUND TO SHIPLEY'S TRIAL

Shipley was prosecuted for publishing a dialogue between a Gentleman and a Farmer,[11] in which the Gentleman insisted 'that every state or nation was only a great *club*'.[12] In other words, the gentleman sought to analogise government to a mutual insurance scheme of working men. Such schemes were well known at the time as an alternative to the support offered by the local church-state hybrid of the parish[13] and, a decade later, a social campaigner felt able to praise them as demonstrating 'one great and fundamental truth, of infinite national importance; viz. that, with very few exceptions, the people, in general of all characters, and under all circumstances, with good management, are perfectly competent to their own maintenance'.[14] One consequence of this analogy was that the Gentleman was able to persuade the Farmer that a nation's laws, just like the rules governing the local scheme, must all be made by mutual consent,[15] that political representation must be open to all men not reliant on parish relief[16] and that tyrants may be removed by force.[17] Membership of such clubs was limited, however, by the informal requirement for members to have income to spare and by the formal requirement imposed by some societies that members must

---

[11] Shipley's edition, under the title *The Principles of Government, in a Dialogue between a Gentleman and a Farmer*, was reprinted as an appendix to M Dawes, *England's Alarm! On the prevailing doctrine of libels, as laid down by the Earl of Mansfield* (London, John Stockdale, 1785). The original pamphlet had a slightly different title: [W Jones], *The Principles of Government, in a Dialogue between a Scholar and a Peasant* (Society for Constitutional Information, 1782).

[12] *Shipley* (n 2) 895.

[13] See D Eastwood, *Government and Community in the English Provinces, 1700–1870* (Basingstoke, Macmillan, 1997) 40–41; and PHJH Gosden, *Self-Help: Voluntary Associations in Nineteenth-Century Britain* (London, BT Batsford, 1973) 1–10.

[14] FM Eden, *The State of the Poor*, vol 1 (London, 1797) xxiv.

[15] *Shipley* (n 2) 896.

[16] ibid 896.

[17] ibid 897–98.

be drawn from a particular cultural or professional class.[18] We can also see echoes of this set of qualifications in the Gentleman's argument that political representation is no concern of those reliant on parish relief. The 'Farmer', then, should probably be understood as a member of the public rather than a penniless revolutionary—what contemporaries would have described as a member of a democratic 'mob'.[19] The Gentleman concluded by convincing this implicitly middle-class Farmer that the best way to protect against future tyranny was for gentlemen to provide their farmers with firearms, and for the farmers to 'spend an hour every morning ... in learning to prime and load expeditiously, and to fire and charge with bayonet firmly and regularly'.[20]

The pamphlet had not been written by the Dean, but was instead the work of his brother-in-law, the then barrister and philologist William Jones.[21] Shipley felt the pamphlet deserved a wide readership and secured the consent of 'a committee of gentlemen of Flintshire ... associated for the object of reform'[22] to have it re-published. In a short preface, Shipley argued that given Jones's work had been 'publicly branded with the most injurious epithets ... the sure way to vindicate this little tract from so unjust a character, will be as publicly to produce it'.[23] Unfortunately for Shipley, one of the more consistent features of the doctrine of seditious libel was a policing of public discourse: in *de Libellis Famosis*, for example, Coke had analogised libels to vigilantism publicly subverting the authority of those occupying governmental offices,[24] and in 1688, in the famous *Case of the Seven Bishops*, the bishops were prosecuted not so much for disagreeing privately with the king as for the reputational damage caused by the public airing of their

---

[18] Gosden notes, for example, that it was not until the 1850s that agricultural labourers seem to have joined the affiliated orders (ie, larger societies organised on a federal rather than purely local basis) in large numbers: PHJH Godsen, *The Friendly Societies in England 1815–1875* (Manchester, Manchester University Press, 1961) 81.

[19] On the difference between the 'public' and the 'mob', see H Barker and S Burrows, 'Introduction' in H Barker and S Burrows, *Press, Politics and the Public Sphere in Europe and North America 1760–1820* (Cambridge, Cambridge University Press, 2002); and H Barker, 'England, c 1760–1815' in ibid.

[20] *Shipley* (n 2) 898.

[21] Jones had married Shipley's sister Anna Maria in 1783: MJ Franklin, 'Jones, Sir William (1746–1794)' in *Oxford Dictionary of National Biography: Online Edition* (Oxford, Oxford University Press, 2011) www.oxforddnb.com/view/article/15105. For a sense of the breadth of Jones's work, see SS Pachori (ed), *Sir William Jones: A Reader* (Oxford, Oxford University Press, 1993). On the relationship between Jones's political thought, the pamphlet and Shipley's trial, see DJ Ibbetson, 'Sir William Jones (1746–1794)' (2001) 7 *Transactions of the Honourable Society of Cymmrodorion 66*, 71–74.

[22] 'Speech of the Honourable Thomas Erskine, at Shrewsbury, August the Sixth, AD 1784, for the Reverend William Davis Shipley, Dean of St Asaph, on His Trial for Publishing a Seditious Libel' in JL High (ed), *Speeches of Lord Erskine while at the Bar*, vol 1 (Chicago, Callaghan & Co, 1876) 156.

[23] *Shipley* (n 2) 892.

[24] *The Case de Libellis Famosis* (1605) 5 Co Rep 125a, 125b.

grievances.[25] By the early eighteenth century, Holt CJ had expanded the doctrine so that it no longer simply protected the king and particular officers from public criticism, but also protected government itself, with Holt holding that: 'If men should not be called to account for possessing the people with an ill opinion of Government, no Government can exist.'[26] Shipley sought to defend his re-publication of Jones's pamphlet through an early version of the 'marketplace of ideas' argument, but the problem for Shipley was precisely that he 'had chosen to give it a wider airing by exposing it to the poorer reader'.[27] And it was this that seems to have prompted local elites to pursue a prosecution.[28]

Social historians have noted the growing significance of written, as opposed to purely oral, libels at this time. Shoemaker argues that an eighteenth-century decline in public insult stemmed from a growing sense that the community no longer had a legitimate role in the enforcement of a single monolithic morality, and that the decline in prosecutions for oral slander was connected to a feeling that such slanders were usually committed in the heat of the moment and therefore lacked intent. Printed libels, he concludes, were particularly pernicious both because they could be expected to reach wider audiences than community-driven oral slander and because they took a relatively long time to produce suggested intention.[29] But while Shoemaker's argument suggests that printed libels were cleanly distinguishable from community morality, Olson has argued that the contest over juror power in seditious libel trials on both sides of the Atlantic demonstrates that these trials concerned the constitution of a community's shared political outlook.[30] As the 'seditious' aspect of 'seditious libel' concerned attacks on government (whether conceived narrowly as individual office-holders or broadly as government itself), what was at stake in the late eighteenth-century seditious libel trials was not simply a narrow question of doctrine, but, rather, the question of who should define the limits of critical comment regarding government: state insiders, as represented by the judge, or members of the public, as represented by the jury? For Mansfield, the lifelong supporter of political authority, the answer was clear, and yet this very clarity prevented

[25] *Case of the Seven Bishops* (1688) 12 St Tr 183. See generally S Sowerby, *Making Toleration: The Repealers and the Glorious Revolution* (Cambridge MA, Harvard University Press, 2013) 153–92.
[26] *R v Tutchin* (1704) 14 St Tr 1095, 1128. See generally Hamburger, 'Development of the Law of Seditious Libel' 734–43.
[27] Lobban, 'From Seditious Libel' 316.
[28] See A Page, 'The Dean of St Asaph's Trial: Libel and Politics in the 1780s' (2009) 32 *Journal for Eighteenth-Century Studies* 21, 25.
[29] RB Shoemaker, 'The Decline of Public Insult in London 1660–1800' (2000) 169 *Past & Present* 97.
[30] A Olson, 'The Zenger Case Revisited: Satire, Sedition and Political Debate in Eighteenth Century America' (2000) 35 *Early American Literature* 223.

him from seeing the central judicial role preserved under Erskine's model of the general verdict.

As we shall see below, the prosecutor in Shipley's trial eventually removed the case from its native Welsh context to an English town, and this certainly suggests that the prosecutor was aware of seditious libel's potential to bring community politics into the courtroom. It is possibly an awareness of these issues which led Shipley to translate Jones's original 'Peasant' to a 'Farmer',[31] and which convinced him to abandon his original plan to publish the pamphlet not only in Wales but, significantly for its proposed political audience, in Welsh.[32] While Welsh juries were at times difficult to control, the issue here was not simply the attempt to extend constitutional discourse from an English to a Welsh public.[33] While this was doubtless an important part of the political backdrop to Shipley's trial, the more significant issue seems to have been the concern among local Tory elites that the pamphlet implicitly extended the concept of the 'public' to a point where it included a lower-class 'mob'. It should also be noted that in rejecting the argument that the jury should have been permitted to return an inscrutable general verdict, both Buller J at first instance and Lord Mansfield on appeal emphasised the threat posed to the rule of law by any attempt to enlarge the jury's power in this area of the criminal law. This fear was revisited when Shipley was eventually discharged, with one supporter of the prosecution writing to Lord Kenyon to inform him that: 'The mob escorted [Shipley] to Ruthin ... All the lower part of the Vale met him there or beyond Denbigh, at which place the two-legged brutes seized the carriage and drew it to Llanerch, where they were received with bonfires, &c.'[34] Fears about the public circulation of such ideas and the constitution of a democratic mob clearly loomed large in the decision in *Shipley*.

A further problem for Shipley was that, under the doctrine developed over the preceding decades, the legality of the public airing he sought to achieve would not ultimately be judged by the public to whom he was appealing. Jurors in trials for seditious libel were restricted to two factual questions: whether the accused really did publish the allegedly seditious writings; and whether the innuendoes specified in the indictment accurately conveyed the meaning of the document under discussion.[35] It would then be for the judges at Westminster to determine whether the facts alleged in

---

[31] Franklin, 'Jones, Sir William'.

[32] *Shipley* (n 2) 920.

[33] R Ireland, 'Putting Oneself on Whose Country: Carmarthenshire Juries in the Mid-nineteenth Century' in TG Watkin (ed), *Legal Wales: Its Past, its Future* (Cardiff, Welsh Legal History Society, 2001).

[34] Thomas Pennant to Lloyd Kenyon, 29 December 1784, quoted in Page, 'The Dean of St Asaph's Trial' 28.

[35] On the legal and cultural development of the concept of an 'innuendo', see A Roper, '"Innuendo" in the Restoration' (2001) 100 *Journal of English and Germanic Philology* 22.

the indictment actually constituted sedition.[36] One particularly contentious point in Shipley's appeal to the King's Bench would be the origins of this doctrine, and therefore its conformity to the principles of the 1688 Revolution. The doctrine's effect, if it was allowed to go unchallenged, would be to remove from the jury significant questions of the common law's relationship to the constitution, and Erskine repeatedly argued—both before the jury and, later, before the King's Bench—that the political philosophy of the English constitution (not to mention the internal logic of the general verdict) required such questions to be settled by a jury. It was therefore important for Erskine to prove that the established doctrine was a post-revolutionary innovation and not an inherent part of the constitutional settlement.

One of the more significant problems Erskine faced in arguing that the settled doctrine was unconstitutional, and that juries should be permitted to return general verdicts encompassing both law and fact in trials for seditious libel, was that this proposition could easily be interpreted as a call for jury lawlessness. This was a particular problem when the case eventually reached the King's Bench, where Erskine had to reckon with Lord Mansfield. While Mansfield was, in some areas of his judicial practice, accused of acting more like an equitable chancellor than a common law judge[37] and while he was keen to use special juries of merchants to help develop commercial law in England,[38] he was also at times keen to avoid the vagaries of the jury system, treating certainty as the chief virtue of a properly functioning legal system.[39] One explanation for the difference in approach may be that in commercial law cases, Mansfield used particularly expert jurors, and it may have been that he found such jurors easier to trust than ordinary, non-special jurors. Oldham, on the other hand, has explained the difference between Mansfield's approach to commercial law and his approach to the law of seditious libel by reference to the judge's political philosophy, noting that:

> Had Mansfield approached the doctrine in the spirit of modernizing the law and making it procedurally effective—the spirit that animated his commercial law decisions—he could have agreed with defense counsel and instructed the jury to consider the 'whole matter' ... [But] Mansfield the royalist believed at bottom that political authority emanated from the King; documents advocating the contrary view, such as Junius's letters or even Jones's dialogue, were, to Mansfield, patently seditious. The position ... that ultimately prevailed [in the 1792 Act] ...

---

[36] On the development of this doctrine, see the sources referred to in n 5 above.

[37] See, in particular, the arguments of Junius to this effect: 'Letter XLI' in J Cannon (ed), *The Letters of Junius* (Oxford, Clarendon Press, 1978). Another letter by Junius was subject to Mansfield's interpretation of the law of seditious libel in *R v Almon* (1770) 20 St Tr 803.

[38] See JC Oldham, 'The Origins of the Special Jury' (1983) 50 *University of Chicago Law Review* 137, particularly at 140 fn 13; and more generally Oldham, *English Common Law* 79–205.

[39] See Oldham, *English Common Law* 211.

was not merely a differing view of the jury function; it was a differing vision of government.[40]

Oldham's argument from constitutional principle permits much greater nuance than Holdsworth's claim that the decision in *Shipley* should simply be read as a formalistic necessity,[41] but in seeking to draw a clear line between Mansfield's constitutional perspective and his 'view of the jury function', Oldham misses something of the relationship between these two points. As we shall see below, Erskine's argument was just as much about democratic self-governance as it was about procedural theory, and it seems Mansfield's fear of the politics of jury equity blinded him to the actual image of the judge–jury relationship which Erskine sought to establish. In this way, the crossover between constitutional politics and the judge–jury relationship played a crucial, if slightly out-of-focus, part in the decision at the King's Bench.

## II. SHIPLEY'S TRIAL

Shipley was initially indicted at the Welsh town of Denbigh in April 1783. At the start of his trial, the prosecution alleged that the Society for Constitutional Information, which was funding the Dean's defence, had, in advance of the assizes, circulated writings concerning the jury's function in trials for seditious libel.[42] Despite one of the jurors insisting that he was unaware of the material being circulated,[43] the distribution of a pamphlet specifically challenging the procedures followed in such cases was clearly problematic. However, Erskine, who had been retained on Shipley's behalf by the Society,[44] disagreed, urging that the relevant test was whether the documents circulated had been 'productive of undue influence' or would 'prevent the right administration of justice' in this particular case.[45] The fact

---

[40] ibid 235. See also Page, 'The Dean of St Asaph's Trial' 22. On Mansfield's ambivalent view of juries generally, see J Oldham, *The Mansfield Manuscripts and the Growth of English Law in the Eighteenth Century*, vol 1 (Chapel Hill, University of North Carolina Press, 1995) 82–99. Poser has recently argued that Mansfield's view of authority was necessarily more complex than this, given his close family ties to Jacobitism: NS Poser, *Lord Mansfield: Justice in the Age of Reason* (Montreal, McGill-Queen's University Press, 2013) 35, 100–11, 244.

[41] W Holdsworth, *A History of English Law*, vol 10 (London, Methuen, 1938) 680.

[42] The pamphlet contained extracts from 'The Life of John Lilburne' in J Towers (ed), *British Biography*, vol 6 (London, 1770) 63–67 fn r; and 'The Life of Sir George Jefferies' in J Towers, *British Biography*, vol 6 (London, 1770) 141–43. Towers was himself a member of the Society for Constitutional Information (FD Cartwright (ed), *The Life and Correspondence of Major Cartwright*, vol 1 (London, Henry Colburn, 1826) 135); the Society regularly used pre-trial publicity as a way of spreading its constitutional ideas: Page, 'The Dean of St Asaph's Trial' 29.

[43] *Shipley* (n 2) 849.

[44] ibid 862.

[45] ibid 863.

that materials regarding jury trial had been circulated could not, in itself, be sufficient to cause a trial to be postponed unless there was some more specific reason for supposing that the publications were likely to pervert the course of justice. Lord Kenyon, presiding at the Denbigh assizes, agreed with Erskine's abstract statement of the relevant legal principles, but sharply disagreed with him about their application to this trial, holding that the trial 'ought not to proceed' as the Society's pamphlet 'may affect some men's minds'.[46] When, the following April, the trial came to be heard anew, the prosecutor arrived with a writ of certiorari, removing the case to the King's Bench.

The King's Bench directed the trial to be heard at the next Shrewsbury assizes, Shrewsbury being the English assizes closest to Denbigh. This made Shipley's trial in effect the fact-finding phase of a King's Bench trial, with the result that the trial judge refused to give any indication of the legal question as to whether Shipley's pamphlet should actually be considered seditious (he thought that giving such directions would mean doing something which was not meant 'for me, a single judge sitting at *nisi prius*').[47] This later allowed Erskine to argue before the judges of the King's Bench that his client had not really received a trial at all and that it did not make any sense for a jury to find a person 'guilty' if the jurors had not been advised on the relevant law. The trial was eventually heard at Shrewsbury in August 1784, notwithstanding Shipley's appeal to Lord Kenyon in April the previous year: 'My lord, in God's name let me have a verdict one way or the other! don't let me be kept further in suspense!'[48] What Shipley perhaps failed to appreciate was that the unusual verdict used in seditious libel trials during the eighteenth century meant that even if his case had not been twice put off, a jury could not have given him 'a verdict one way or the other'—if a jury decided he had published the pamphlet and that he intended the innuendoes alleged,[49] he would still have to wait for a separate judicial determination regarding the publication's seditious nature or effects.[50]

Much of the debate at the Shrewsbury assizes between Bearcroft (for the prosecution) and Erskine (for the defence) concerned the context of the pamphlet's allegedly seditious tendencies.[51] Bearcroft, explaining that

---

[46] ibid 872.

[47] ibid 944–45.

[48] ibid 875. Erskine does not appear to have suspected the government of involvement in the change of venue, instead aiming his scorn at the local prosecutor.

[49] Which were here limited mainly to 'G' standing for 'Gentleman' and 'F' standing for 'Farmer'.

[50] The only exception to this being if the jury delivered a general verdict of not guilty; however, this would have required a finding that the Dean had not published the pamphlet, a fact which was not disputed at his trial.

[51] Bearcroft and Erskine appeared on the same side in *R v Bembridge* (1783) 3 Doug 327; 99 ER 679, discussed by Jeremy Horder elsewhere in this volume.

'the foundation of criminality in a libel' is 'to break the public peace',[52] focused on the pamphlet's objective meaning, arguing that its proposals regarding electoral reform could only be understood if set within the context of its discussion of the right to bear arms, implying a violent constitutional change.[53] Read in this way, the pamphlet as a whole was clearly aimed at breaking the public peace and was therefore criminal. Erskine, however, insisted the Farmer was asked not to overthrow the government, but to sign a petition for reform, noting that 'I do not sign my name with a gun'.[54] He also observed that the pamphlet actually described three figures against which violent revolutions might occur—a tyrannical monarch, a bad ministry and a corrupt aristocracy—and that the latter two scenarios were explicitly couched in terms of coming to the king's aid.[55] Erskine therefore sought to establish, by a close reading of the pamphlet's text, that it was not objectively seditious. Indeed, the origins of the pamphlet seem to support this interpretation. The *Oxford Dictionary of National Biography* notes that it 'began as an essay written at the Paris house of Benjamin Franklin to persuade Franklin that the mysteries of the state might be made intelligible to the working man'[56] and it could therefore be argued to have been written with an educational intent, albeit one set against the background of a revolutionary war.

The second half of Erskine's argument from context concerned the pamphlet's actual, practical consequences. He claimed to see in Bearcroft's argument an implicit question: even if we accept that parliamentary reform may be a debatable issue, 'why tell the people so?'[57] The main thrust of Erskine's argument here was against this kind of elitism, although he did briefly—but possibly sarcastically—praise Shipley's decision not to have the pamphlet translated into Welsh, lest 'the ignorant inhabitants of the mountains … collect from it, that it is time to take up arms'.[58] Putting any such anti-Welsh prejudices to one side, Erskine nonetheless argued that 'hewers of wood and drawers of water' should be made to understand 'that government is a trust proceeding from themselves'.[59] Drawing on the writings of both the Whig John Locke and the Tory Lord Bolingbroke in order to demonstrate political

---

[52] *Shipley* (n 2) 886.

[53] ibid 887–89.

[54] ibid 909. In fact, calls for a well-regulated militia and for constitutional education were often intertwined in the writings of the various political associations active during the 1780s: Page, 'The Dean of St Asaph's Trial' 23.

[55] *Shipley* (n 2) 911–12.

[56] Franklin, 'Jones, Sir William'.

[57] *Shipley* (n 2) 914.

[58] ibid 920. After the King's Bench concluded that the pamphlet was not seditious, it was translated into Welsh, becoming, as Ibbetson has noted, 'the first political tract in Welsh' (Ibbetson, 'Sir William Jones' 74).

[59] *Shipley* (n 2) 917.

consensus on this point,[60] he insisted that pursuing a programme of popular constitutional education was not sedition and that in order for it to be held as such, his opponent must 'show ... how this dialogue has disturbed the king's government'.[61] Before seditious libel can be established, actual disturbances must have occurred. And this, of course, must be a question of fact for the jurors.

But this was only one part of Erskine's attempt to undermine the settled doctrine. He insisted that by returning a general verdict of 'guilty' or 'not guilty', the jurors were implicitly being asked to pronounce on more than just the fact of publication (and, where relevant, the innuendoes alleged in the indictment). For if a jury was to accept that the question of seditious intent was to be decided by a judge after the verdict was in, a jury would also be required to bring someone in as 'guilty' if they were, for example, charged with publishing the Bible 'with a blasphemous intention',[62] even if the only evidence introduced at trial was that the defendant had actually published the book. The form of verdict adopted under the eighteenth-century law of seditious libel, while not a straightforward general verdict—in *Shipley*, for example, Buller J accepted a verdict of 'Guilty of publishing, but whether a libel or not the jury do not find'[63]—still meant the jury must find a defendant 'guilty' without any reference to the seditious nature of the impugned publication. For Buller J, this was simply a mechanism for guaranteeing judicial control of the law,[64] thereby upholding the maxim that 'ad quæstionem facti respondent juratores, ad quæstionem juris respondent judices'.[65] For Erskine, this was illogical: if the question whether the pamphlet was *actually* seditious is reserved for later judicial determination, then insisting on a verdict including the word 'guilty' meant 'call[ing] upon [the jurors] to pronounce that guilt, which [the judges] forbid [them] to examine into'.[66] This was therefore in substance a special verdict, a type of verdict in which jurors did not pronounce guilt or innocence, and Erskine believed the English constitution precluded judges from demanding verdicts of this type.

[60] ibid 914–17. Erskine quotes from 'The Second Treatise' in J Locke, *Two Treatises of Government and a Letter Concerning Toleration* (I Shapiro (ed), New Haven, Yale University Press, 2003) 189–90, 200–01; and from Bolingbroke in (1734) 430 *The Craftsman* 25, 30. Bolingbroke, it should be noted, had been a personal friend of Mansfield: Poser, *Lord Mansfield* 57–58. Erskine also preferred historical or philosophical perspectives in his later defence of Thomas Paine (M Crosby, 'The Voice of Flattery vs Sober Truth: William Godwin, Thomas Erskine and the 1792 Trial of Thomas Paine for Sedition' (2010) 62 *Review of English Studies* 90).

[61] *Shipley* (n 2) 927.

[62] ibid 928.

[63] ibid 955.

[64] ibid 944–45.

[65] Roughly, 'questions of fact are for the jury while questions of law are for the judge': ibid 947. For a detailed discussion of the maxim's meaning and history, see the argument of Welch, Erskine's junior counsel, at ibid 1023–32.

[66] ibid 906.

This was a common structural feature of Erskine's argument throughout *Shipley*: beyond simply appealing to recently decided cases (on which he clearly knew his position was fairly weak), he also peppered his argument with appeals to constitutional history[67] and the internal logic of the institutions he was critiquing.[68]

While Erskine's argument at the Shrewsbury assizes was quite basic (at least compared to the detailed form it would take at the King's Bench), he was careful to explain that none of this was meant as an incitement to juror licentiousness. He explained to Shipley's jurors that he simply desired 'that the judgment of the court should be a guide to yours in determining, whether or not this pamphlet should be a libel'[69] and insisted that, after *Bushell's Case*,[70] the courts had no power to compel special verdicts.[71] But rather than encouraging a tension between judges and jurors, he was clear that they should respect one another's true functions:

> The days I hope are now past, when judges and jurymen upon state trials, were constantly pulling in different directions; the Court endeavouring to annihilate altogether the province of the jury, and the jury in return listening with disgust, jealousy, and alienation, to the directions of the Court.—Now [defendants] may be expected to be tried with that harmony which is the beauty of our legal constitution:—the jury preserving their independence in judging of the intention, which is the essence of every crime ... listening to the opinion of the judge upon the evidence, and upon the law.[72]

Erskine, in emphasising harmony among institutions not only as 'the beauty of our legal constitution' but also as the essence of the jury system, was arguing that the settled law of seditious libel was a violation of constitutional (including revolutionary) principles and should therefore be abandoned in favour of a more harmonious separation of powers.

In fact, judicial directions were already a well-established part of the political tradition of jury independence: in the years between *Bushell's Case* and 1688, several pamphleteers had maintained that the juror's oath required him to reach a conscientious verdict and that this meant judicial directions must be considered as nothing more than advice.[73] This position was built on a presumption that those called to serve as jurors would already have a working knowledge of the law (and that it was therefore the citizen's

---

[67] See in particular ibid 923–28, 974–76.

[68] There are echoes here of the techniques Erskine later used in his defence of Paine, which are discussed in Crosby, 'The Voice of Flattery'.

[69] *Shipley* (n 2) 922.

[70] *Bushell's Case* (1670) Vaughan 135; 124 ER 1006.

[71] *Shipley* (n 2) 926.

[72] ibid 900.

[73] K Crosby, '*Bushell's Case* and the Juror's Soul' (2012) 33 *Journal of Legal History* 251, 280–88. On the political reception of *Bushell's Case* more generally, see S Stern, 'Between Local Knowledge and National Politics: Debating Rationales for Jury Nullification after *Bushell's Case*' (2002) 11 *Yale Law Journal* 1815.

duty to acquire such an understanding in anticipation of being called to serve). But Buller J, giving his directions to Shipley's jury, was evidently not convinced that jurors could be trusted to understand judicial directions on the law, asking 'are you possessed of [the relevant] cases in your own minds? Are you apprized of the distinctions on which those determinations are founded? Is it not a little extraordinary to require of a jury that they should carry all the legal determinations in their minds?'[74] Buller declined to provide any such guidance and stuck firmly to the settled doctrine, directing the jurors to return a verdict of 'guilty' if they were sure of the publication and the innuendoes.

Despite Erskine's earlier insistence that they should treat the settled doctrine as being no less ineffectual than King Canute's mock warning to the sea,[75] Shipley's jurors seem ultimately to have been perfectly happy to be restricted to a verdict on the facts, but not the law. They wished to make it clear that they found Shipley was the publisher and that the innuendoes alleged in the case had been proven, but that they did not find whether the pamphlet was seditious or not. This was precisely what Buller had asked them to do, but their refusal to find Shipley simply 'guilty' gave the judge a great deal of trouble, with several pages of the report devoted to his increasingly desperate attempts to contort their plain meaning into a judicially acceptable form.[76] These difficulties suggest that Erskine's arguments had been at least partially successful: while the jurors were willing to be restricted to a mere finding on the facts, they were unwilling to present their restricted response as a general verdict (ie, a verdict of 'guilty' or 'not guilty'). Perhaps spurred on by this partial success, when Erskine took this case to the King's Bench, his earlier argument regarding the technical structure and ontological preconditions of the general verdict became central to his overall position.

### III. ERSKINE'S MOTION FOR A NEW TRIAL

**A. Erskine's Argument**

Erskine brought a motion for a new trial on the ground that Buller J had acted improperly in his handling of Shipley's trial. His argument for a new trial was, ultimately, an argument about the difference between a general and a special verdict. While, as Oldham has observed, there was probably little chance of Erskine actually persuading Mansfield, who had decided many such cases in favour of the settled doctrine,[77] Erskine's argument at

---

[74] *Shipley* (n 2) 947.
[75] ibid 921.
[76] ibid 950–55.
[77] Oldham, *English Common Law* 228–229.

the King's Bench nonetheless provides a rich theoretical view of the general verdict. Given the well-known connection between *Shipley* and the Libel Act of 1792, which famously secured the jury's right to deliver general verdicts in trials for seditious libel, it will be important to understand what exactly Erskine meant by a 'general verdict'. Far from being the coded appeal to jury lawlessness which Lord Mansfield and Crown counsel understood it to be, Erskine's contention was that a general verdict was not possible in the absence of a strong working relationship between judge and jury, including, crucially, a judicial direction on the law.

The motion for a new trial was surprisingly lengthy, being reported across more than 100 pages. Given Lord Mansfield's well-known support for the existing doctrine of seditious libel, it is at first surprising to see the arguments recited at such great length.[78] The motion's great length is even more surprising when put in the context of Erskine's much shorter, and ultimately successful, motion in arrest of judgment.[79] As we shall see below, when Erskine introduced his second motion, he explained that he had never been worried about his client's case, as he always knew that his short, technical argument would be successful.[80] The question then becomes why did Erskine insist on a lengthy motion which he was reasonably certain would fail? The answer probably lies in the fact that his argument was quickly published as a standalone pamphlet.[81] Erskine seems to have believed that his argument, however unsuccessful it may have been in the short term, was going to genuinely add something to the ongoing debate about the meaning and purpose of jury trial. His argument, which sets out a theoretically robust view of the relationship between judge and jury implicit in the general verdict (albeit one which sat uncomfortably with the day's doctrine), is what makes Shipley's trial a landmark case.

Erskine based his motion for a new trial on five main propositions. First, when a defendant puts himself or herself on their country with a general plea of 'not guilty', the jury are charged with their general deliverance and not with a simple finding of facts,[82] and this is the primary difference between civil and criminal trials.[83] Second, guilt requires mens rea and 'the intention, even where it becomes a simple inference of reason from a fact or facts established, may, and ought to be, collected by the jury with the judge's

[78] *R v Shipley* (1784) 21 St Tr 847, 956–1041; *R v Shipley* (1784) 4 Doug KB 73; 99 ER 774, 784–829.
[79] *Shipley* (n 2) 1041–45. On the procedure for making a motion for a new trial or a motion in arrest of judgment at the King's Bench, see W Tidd, *The Practice of the Court of King's Bench in Personal Actions*, vol 2 (London, A Strahan and W Woodfall, 1794) 601–30.
[80] See below, at nn 116–17.
[81] W Blanchard (ed), *Never before Printed, the Rights of Juries Vindicated. In the speeches of the Dean of St Asaph's counsel, in the Court of King's Bench, Westminster, on the 15th November, 1784* (London, H Goldney, 1785).
[82] *Shipley* (n 2) 961.
[83] ibid 977–79.

assistance'.[84] The only exception he would permit here was where the jury voluntarily delivers a special verdict, making a detailed finding of facts and then leaving it to the court to apply the law to those facts; given the first proposition in his argument, it must always be the jurors who choose to deliver such a verdict. Third, trials for seditious libel are no different in this respect from ordinary criminal trials: criminal trial juries always have a right to deliver a general verdict.[85] Fourth, the likely seditious effect of a publication must be a question of fact for the jury.[86] Finally, if the defendant challenges the allegation in the indictment that he or she had a 'mischievous intention', the question of intent becomes a pure question of fact for the jury.[87] This five-pronged argument has, as its central concern, the legitimate relationship between judge and jury. Which questions are really factual and which are really legal? Which of these questions is the jury asked to adjudicate on? How do the two halves of the judicial task come to be combined in a single finding of guilt or innocence? Erskine's theory of the general verdict offers a clear answer to these questions.

Erskine had, at the Shrewsbury assizes, urged Vaughan CJ's decision in *Bushell's Case* as grounds for the legal protection of the jury's right to choose whether to deliver a general or a special verdict; Buller J instead focused on Vaughan's use of the *juratores non respondent* maxim as justification for the distribution of judicial functions in the eighteenth-century law of seditious libel. It should be noted that Erskine's argument does indeed diverge from the reasoning in *Bushell's Case*, but not in the way that Buller J had suggested. Vaughan had explained that one reason why a jury could not be punished for the exercise of its judicial function was that it was very difficult for a judge to assess the reasoning behind a general verdict. A major cause of this uncertainty was that judicial directions must always be hypothetical: 'If you find the following facts, the relevant law will be as follows.' The only circumstance in which it would be possible for a jury to be found to have disobeyed judicial directions would therefore be if the jurors had already made a conclusive finding of facts before the judge had directed them on the law.[88] Vaughan's judgment thus concludes that an extremely contrived set of circumstances would be needed before the precise impact that a judge's directions had on a particular verdict could be established. Erskine's argument shifts the emphasis in an important way. By insisting that jurors' inferences from the facts require 'the judge's assistance', judicial directions become a central part of the jury's task, even when the jury delivers a general verdict. Therefore, rather than sharply distinguishing between judge and jury as a way of demonstrating the absurdity of punishing a juror

---

[84] ibid 961.
[85] ibid 962–63.
[86] ibid 963–66.
[87] ibid 966–67.
[88] *Bushell's Case* (n 70) 144–45.

for delivering a verdict with which the trial judge disagreed, the general verdict here is a composite product of both judicial actors' work. This is a central (but easily overlooked) part of Erskine's argument.

Noting comments to the same effect by the King's Bench justices Foster and Raymond,[89] Erskine emphasised once again that his was not an argument for jury lawlessness, insisting that jurors 'have not a capricious discretion to make law at their pleasure, but are bound in conscience as well as judges are to find it truly'.[90] The solution to a perceived problem regarding jury nullification (which was, it must be recognised, a live issue at this time)[91] was not to invent a strange third type of verdict, somewhere between a special and a general verdict: what Erskine referred to as a 'monster in law, without precedent in former times, or root in the constitution'.[92] Rather, the solution was to be found in the judge's responsibility to adequately equip the jury with the legal understanding necessary to bring in a general verdict that would be both lawful and conscientious. In short, the general verdict (which the jury was constitutionally entitled to return at its discretion) required cooperation between the two parts of the judiciary in a criminal trial.

As Erskine's junior counsel, Welch, put it, the basic error in the settled doctrine of seditious libel was the presumption that 'the office of the judge, was an independent and separate one, from that of the jury'.[93] The judge's role, Welch insisted, was simply to advise the jury. But unlike the Restoration pamphleteers who used this argument to attempt to neuter the judge in the eyes of a conscientious jury, Welch was keen to emphasise that the judge, while strictly limited to advising the jury, must nonetheless act 'in a way … somewhat more than ministerial'.[94] What Welch is alluding to here is a distinction between 'ministerial' and 'judicial' functions, which played a key part in Vaughan's decision in *Bushell's Case*. 'Ministerial' functions are those that, unlike 'judicial' functions, are simply required by the holders of a particular office, without the use of discretion or judgement. A key reason why Vaughan would not permit a jury to be punished for bringing in a false verdict was that this would amount to an illegitimate review of a jury acting

---

[89] M Foster, *A Report of Some Proceedings on the Commission of Oyer and Terminer and Gaol Delivery for the Trial of the Rebels in the County of Surrey, and of Other Crown Cases, to Which are Added Discourses Upon a Few Branches of the Crown Law* (Oxford, Clarendon Press, 1762) 255–256; *R v Oneby* (1726) 17 St Tr 29, 49. Both Foster and Raymond were discussing homicide verdicts, not verdicts for seditious libel; however, Erskine's argument was that this distinction was irrelevant in principle, despite the fact Raymond himself had supported the eighteenth-century doctrine of seditious libel in *R v Franklin* (1731) 17 St Tr 625.

[90] *Shipley* (n 2) 982.

[91] See in particular TA Green, *Verdict According to Conscience: Perspectives on the English Criminal Trial Jury, 1200–1800* (Chicago, University of Chicago Press, 1985) 267–317; and JM Beattie, *Crime and the Courts in England 1660–1800* (Oxford, Oxford University Press, 1986) 419–30.

[92] *Shipley* (n 2) 996.

[93] ibid 1027.

[94] ibid 1030.

in its strictly judicial capacity.[95] Erskine, exploring at length the constitutional history of the general verdict, had argued that the task of medieval sheriffs had simply been 'to summon the jurors, to compel their attendance, ministerially to regulate their proceedings, and to enforce their decisions'.[96] And while judges may initially have been limited to an equally ministerial task, Welch is here arguing that their role is now 'more than ministerial'. Judges too must exercise judgement, but as part of a judicial task which is shared with the jury. Judicial directions on the law, then, become a necessary precondition of a properly constituted general verdict. However, the lawyers must have known that this argument was unlikely to work: a decade earlier, when the diarist and biographer James Boswell had asked Mansfield whether juries could be relied upon to follow judicial directions, he had replied: 'Yes. Except in political causes where they do not at all keep themselves to right and wrong.'[97] As Poser has recently noted, it seems likely that Mansfield had trials for seditious libel in mind when he made this remark.[98]

## B. Crown Counsel's Response

Crown counsel's argument did not respond directly to Erskine's five main propositions, referring instead to the two claims they were reduced to by Mansfield: 'viz. 1. That the jury not only have the power, but that where they choose, they ought to judge of the law; 2. That the defence was not sufficiently left to the jury as a justification'.[99] In response to the first broad issue, Crown counsel conceded that judges generally had a duty to direct their juries on the law and that juries had an equivalent duty to obey these instructions. Restrictions on juror punishment, however, meant that these duties were moral rather than legal.[100] In language neatly anticipating

[95] For a discussion of the ministerial-judicial distinction as a way of accounting for juror punishment in England between the 1825 abolition of the attaint and the 2015 creation of indictable offences involving independent juror research, see K Crosby, 'Before the Criminal Justice and Courts Act 2015: Juror Punishment in Nineteenth- and Twentieth-Century England' (2016) 36 *Legal Studies* 179.

[96] *Shipley* (n 2) 974.

[97] 'Journal Entry of 11 Apr 1773' in J Boswell, *Boswell for the Defence 1769–1774* (WK Wimsatt Jr and F Poddle eds, New York, McGraw-Hill, 1959) 173–79; cited in Poser, *Lord Mansfield* 120.

[98] Poser, *Lord Mansfield* 120.

[99] *R v Shipley* (1784) 4 Doug KB 73; 99 ER 774, 784.

[100] ibid 785–86. Crown counsel argued that 'corruption only can be a ground for an attaint, not mistake or ignorance': ibid 786. Modern scholarship suggests the attaint could actually be used for either of these purposes at various points in its history: JQ Whitman, *The Origins of Reasonable Doubt: Theological Roots of the Criminal Trial* (New Haven, Yale University Press, 2008) 154–56 and the sources cited therein. Nonetheless, by the late eighteenth century, attaint had fallen into desuetude, with no less a figure than Lord Mansfield dismissing it in 1757 as 'a mere sound, in every case', replaced in practice by 'opportunities of reconsidering the cause by a new trial'. *Bright v Enyon* (1757) 1 Burr 390; 97 ER 365, 366,

Mansfield's later judgment, they argued that allowing juries to decide the law for themselves would leave 'intricate and abstruse legal questions' to an inexpert body with a constantly changing membership, meaning that 'instead of that certainty which is so necessary for the regulation of men's conduct, the law would regularly fluctuate, and nobody would be able to discover what it is, or where to find it'.[101] The law of seditious libel escaped this difficulty by insisting that all legally relevant facts were recorded on the indictment. This meant that a jury could find simply on the facts without the need to deliver a detailed special verdict, leaving the law to a later judicial determination.[102] On this approach, the special verdict protected rule-of-law values, with the general verdict tending inevitably towards juror lawlessness.

The second of Mansfield's two issues can be dealt with fairly briefly. Crown counsel's argument here was that the mens rea in the crime of seditious libel was an intention to publish, not an intention to cause sedition. The question of intent, then, is indeed a question of pure fact for the jury (as Erskine had argued), provided that by 'intention' we mean the *express* intent to publish. 'But the words "intending to raise seditions", &c., which are what are used here, are ... words merely expressive of the *implied* intention, which the law infers, without proof, from the publication of the libel set forth' (emphasis added).[103] This argument rests heavily on Buller J's charge at the Shrewsbury assizes, which, in turn, drew heavily on the settled eighteenth-century doctrine. As with the settled doctrine more generally, this argument served to distinguish cleanly between the roles of judge and of jury, obscuring the possibility that the general verdict might be understood as the composite product of both judicial bodies in a criminal trial.

## C. The Judgments at the King's Bench

Having heard arguments from both sides, Mansfield decided there were actually four main issues in *Shipley* rather than the five Erskine had presented or the two Mansfield had instructed Crown counsel to explore. The first issue was that Buller J had not permitted the jury to consider any lawful excuse Shipley may have had for publishing Jones's pamphlet. Echoing Buller J's ruling at the Shrewsbury assizes, Mansfield held that lawful excuses were a sentencing consideration rather than forming any part of the initial question of guilt or innocence, and that it was therefore proper to exclude this question from the jury.[104] The second issue was that Buller J had failed to give

---

[101]  *R v Shipley* (1784) 4 Doug KB 73; 99 ER 774, 784.
[102]  ibid 784.
[103]  ibid 790.
[104]  *Shipley* (n 2) 1033.

an opinion on whether the pamphlet was actually seditious. Third, he had instructed the jury to 'leave that question upon record to the Court, if they had no doubt of the meaning and publication'. The final issue was that the jury was not left to consider Shipley's intent.[105] Taking these three points together, Mansfield held that the fact that seditious libel prosecutions put all relevant facts on record cleanly distinguished between factual questions (for the jury) and legal questions (for the judge). All this meant that 'a general verdict "that the defendant is guilty" is equivalent to a special verdict in other cases', with the general verdict simply an administratively easier solution than actually requiring special verdicts.[106] This conclusion, of course, fails to engage with Erskine's lengthy theoretical argument about the conditions necessary in order for a jury to find a person 'guilty'.

Mansfield was sceptical about the extent to which general theory was of value in legal adjudication. After exploring in detail the reported cases on seditious libel from the preceding century (as well as a few cases reported from his own memory),[107] he dismissed Erskine's motion for a new trial by noting that: 'Such a judicial practice in the precise point from the Revolution ... down to the present day, is not to be shaken by arguments of general theory, or popular declamation.'[108] But it was not simply change that Mansfield opposed; as Oldham has noted, the Chief Justice was happy enough to change the law in other areas. The specific problem here was not change per se, then, but rather a kind of change that replaced the stability of precise legal doctrine (subject to lawful review) with a general theory that called for a constantly shifting, never-ending plebiscite (subject to no meaningful legal constraints):

> [W]hat is claimed for? That the law shall be in every particular case what any twelve men, who shall happen to be the jury, shall be inclined to think, liable to no review, and subject to no control, under all the prejudices of the popular cry of the day, and under all the bias of interest in this town, where thousands, more or less, are concerned in the publication of newspapers, paragraphs, and pamphlets [Mansfield presumably meant London, not Denbigh or Shrewsbury]. Under such an administration of law, no man could tell, no counsel could advise, whether a paper was or was not punishable.[109]

This argument clearly misrepresents Erskine's position. Far from claiming that juries should be free to depart from core rule-of-law values, his whole argument had been built upon the claim that a general verdict was

---

[105] ibid 1034–35.
[106] ibid 1035.
[107] ibid 1036–39.
[108] ibid 1039.
[109] ibid 1040. Compare to the comments on the growing idea of the literate 'public' in Barker, 'England, c 1760–1815', particularly at 94–95, concerning the collapsing distinction between 'high' and 'low' politics.

the shared product of a judge and a jury. Mansfield, in his desire to avoid general theory and in his aversion to what he considered mob justice,[110] seems to have missed 'what was claimed for', relying heavily on an older model of jury equity dating to the Restoration rather than the model actually presented by Shipley's counsel.

While all three judges at the King's Bench agreed that the motion for a new trial should be dismissed,[111] there were differences between them. Willes J agreed in several important points of principle with Erskine, but did not think that many of these principles actually applied to Shipley's trial. He agreed, for example, that criminal trial juries had a right to deliver general verdicts, but did not think that Shipley's jury had been denied this right, interpreting the back-and-forth between Buller J and the jury as evidence of the jurors' willingness to return what amounted to a special verdict.[112] But while Willes was in broad agreement with Erskine on the jury's right to deliver a general verdict, he did not join him on the question of a judicial duty to direct on the law, conceding no more than that 'I think it is fit, it is meet and prudent, that the jury should receive the law of libels from the Court' and explicitly stating that the general verdict gave trial juries a power to escape the worst excesses of the criminal law.[113] While Willes J purported to be in agreement with Erskine on this point, he seems to have shared Mansfield's misunderstanding, treating the motion for a new trial as a coded argument for juror lawlessness. But while Willes J agreed with (what he took to be) Erskine's abstract argument, he did not agree that the jury had actually been denied their right to deliver a general verdict on this occasion. Equally, while the jury should have heard any evidence genuinely tending to excuse or justify the Dean's publication, he doubted the evidence presented at trial actually satisfied this requirement.[114]

Shipley, then, was not granted a new trial. But the immediate consequences of this decision were not particularly serious for the Dean: Mansfield had already had him released on bail (with Bearcroft's consent),[115] and Erskine followed his unsuccessful argument for a new trial with a successful motion in arrest of judgment. He once again argued that the jury's verdict had not really been either a general or a special verdict, but recognised that he was unlikely to persuade the court on this point. Nonetheless, he felt that

---

[110] Despite his well-known insistence that justice should be done, though the heavens fall, it should be remembered that Mansfield had recently lost his London home in the Gordon Riots: Poser, *Lord Mansfield* 254, 295, 360–75.

[111] Ashurst J only provided a separate judgment in order to make it clear that his vote rested on Mansfield's rather than Willes' reasoning: *R v Shipley* (1784) 4 Doug KB 73; 99 ER 774, 784, 827.

[112] ibid 826–27.

[113] ibid 824.

[114] ibid 827.

[115] *Shipley* (n 2) 987 n*.

'the warfare was safe for his client, because he knew he could put an end to the prosecution any hour he pleased, by the objection he would now at last submit to the Court'.[116] To this end, he complained that the indictment had been defective, failing to refer to the contextual questions at the heart of the prosecution's case. In the absence of such political context featuring on the record, the King's Bench justices could only assess the pamphlet's seditious tendencies as if it had been 'taken off the dusty shelves of a library, and looked at in the pure abstract'.[117] Mansfield agreed and invited the prosecution to identify the objective sedition in the pamphlet; however, they failed to convince the court and Shipley was accordingly discharged.

## IV. CONCLUSIONS

Erskine's primary argument, concerning the meaning of the general verdict and the respective roles of judge and jury, failed ultimately to persuade the court. However, this does not mean that the argument was not ultimately effective; the 1792 Libel Act provided that criminal trial juries have the right to return a general verdict[118] and, crucially, that such verdicts should be preceded by the judge's 'opinion and directions to the jury on the matter in issue … in like manner as in other criminal cases'.[119] While an examination of the legislative debates leading to the passage of the 1792 Act is well beyond the scope of this chapter, it seems clear enough that Erskine's argument in defence of the Dean of St Asaph was centred on what became the two key principles in the subsequent Act: that it is for juries to choose whether they deliver a special or a general verdict; and that a properly constituted general verdict requires adequate judicial directions. To the extent that the Libel Act seems to have reined in jury lawlessness in trials for seditious libel,[120] this should be understood as part of the move in Erskine's argument from a model of the general verdict predicated on a mutual antagonism between judge and jury towards one which sees the general verdict as the shared product of the two judicial actors.

In making this argument, Erskine was keen to establish that a general verdict was not, as Mansfield feared, an incitement to mob justice opposed to the rule of law. Rather, by emphasising that the judge's role was not simply to administer a trial, but also to participate fully in the jury's judicial task, Erskine sought to establish that the correct legal norms could always be pre-loaded into a general verdict by any sufficiently competent judge.

---

[116] ibid 1041–42.
[117] ibid 1043.
[118] Libel Act 1792, s 1.
[119] ibid s 2.
[120] See Stephen, *History of the Criminal Law* 363; and Lobban, 'From Seditious Libel' 321.

These are precisely the issues that the European Court of Human Rights's recent decision in *Taxquet* requires European jury systems to attend to, and so a proper understanding of Erskine's arguments in *The Dean of St Asaph's Case* will make an important contribution to the continued debate over the compatibility of unreasoned verdicts under the Article 6 guarantee of properly reasoned decisions. Shipley's trial remains a landmark case in the criminal law.

# 7

# M'Naghten's Case (1843)

ARLIE LOUGHNAN*

## I. INTRODUCTION

IN JANUARY 1843, Daniel M'Naghten drew a pistol and shot Edward Drummond, Private Secretary to Prime Minister Sir Robert Peel.[1] After Drummond's death, M'Naghten was tried for murder before the Queen's Bench. The trial, held at the Old Bailey, lasted two days and M'Naghten was acquitted on the basis of insanity. The enormous controversy that followed the verdict culminated in all of the common law judges being called to appear in the House of Lords to defend the decision. The outcome of this proceeding was what came to be known as the *M'Naghten Rules*, which continue to define the test for insanity in England and Wales (and elsewhere). The *Rules*, and the insanity defence more generally, by turns fascinate, confuse and frustrate students of law and procedure, and the various professionals and lay people—judges, lawyers, expert medical witnesses, jurors and defendants—involved in criminal cases in which insanity is raised.

By contrast with some other landmark criminal trials, *M'Naghten* is known beyond the confines of the academy and the profession. *M'Naghten's Case*—the trial, defence and verdict, and the development of the *M'Naghten Rules* in the aftermath of the decision—garnered popular attention right from start. An alchemy of politics, crime and 'madness', *M'Naghten's Case* was front-page news right across the UK in 1843, and occasioned intense and wide-ranging public debate in an era in which each one of the three ingredients of the case was the subject of popular interest. Investigative reports, court reports and opinion pieces pulled apart the details of

* This chapter was prepared while I held the HSF Visiting Fellowship at the Law Department of the University of Cambridge. I would like to thank my hosts, David Fox and Henry Mares, the editors of this collection, and Mikah Pajaczkowska-Russell for excellent research assistance.
[1] The spelling of M'Naghten is disputed (see BL Diamond 'On the Spelling of Daniel M'Naghten's Name' in DJ West and A Walk (eds), *Daniel McNaughton: His Trial and the Aftermath* (Ashford, Gaskell Books, 1977) 86–90). In this chapter, I adopt a common variant of the spelling of M'Naghten.

M'Naghten's offence, his treatment at the hands of the authorities, the hearing and his successful insanity defence, and the legislative response to the case. The notoriety of *M'Naghten* lives on. In the current era, it still enjoys an extra-legal life, invoked in news media coverage of high-profile insanity cases[2] and featuring in novels and other literary texts.[3]

*M'Naghten's Case* took place at a time of great tumult in British society. Multifaceted changes going under the labels of industrialisation, urbanisation and the rise of the middle classes profoundly affected political, social and cultural life. The early Victorian era was marked by major political change, with altered relations between church and state, the extension of suffrage and the development of 'parliamentary government'.[4] Politics— 'the public life of the community'—loomed large in the social organisation of life in the period, and fear of revolution fermented by 'Radicals', Chartists and the Anti-Corn Law League subsisted in the 1830s and 1840s.[5] In terms of criminal justice, the early Victorian era was marked by a generalised and diffused social concern about crime and disorder, and the so-called 'perishing' or 'dangerous classes'.[6]

In its examination of *M'Naghten's Case*, this chapter draws on the contemporaneous press coverage of the crime, trial and the formulation of the *M'Naghten Rules*.[7] Newspapers and other print media are a particularly useful source for the study of criminal case law of the Victorian era. Facilitated by changes in printing technology, periodicals, books and newspapers, published in London and all around the country, proliferated. In London alone, daily papers included *The Times* (with the largest circulation), the *Morning Post* and the *London Standard*. This period produced the 'first mass reading public', and the spread of newspapers in particular contributed to a growing sense of national identity.[8] Newspapers fell along party political lines and, via editors-cum-owners, wielded considerable influence (for instance, through its editor, *The Times* helped to install a new government

---

[2] eg, press treatment of the recent acquittal of Nicholas Salvador for murder on grounds of insanity: J Grierson, 'Family of Decapitated Woman Tell of Despair as Killer Cleared of Murder' *The Guardian* (London, 24 June 2015) (referencing '172 year old legislation'); see also JP Martin, 'The Insanity Defense: A Closer Look, *Washington Post* (Washington DC, 27 February 1998) (tracing the origins of US insanity law to a '19th century Scotsman').

[3] eg, S Busby, *McNaughten: A Novel* (Ann Arbour, Short Books, 2010).

[4] See A Hawkins, *Victorian Political Culture: 'Habits of Heart and Mind'* (Oxford, Oxford University Press, 2015) Ch 1.

[5] ibid 3 and, more generally, Ch 1.

[6] See M Wiener, *Reconstructing the Criminal: Culture, Law and Policy in England, 1830–1914* (Cambridge, Cambridge University Press, 1990).

[7] I relied on the British Newspaper Archive (www.britishnewspaperarchive.co.uk) for primary sources. My investigation of the contemporaneous print media yielded over 60 articles, letters to the editor, court reports and other pieces discussing M'Naghten and *M'Naghten's Case*.

[8] See M Rubery, 'Journalism' in F O'Gorman (ed), *The Cambridge Companion to Victorian Culture* (Cambridge, Cambridge University Press, 2010) 177; see also J Strachan, 'Satirical Print Culture' in the same volume.

under Robert Peel in 1834).[9] Politics was a staple of newspapers of the period. Newspapers provided reports of both parliamentary and court proceedings (they were able to provide reports of most trials without interference from the 1790s)[10] as well as commentary on political, legal and other topics. In keeping with general practice until the last decades of the nineteenth century, editorials-cum-articles (then incompletely distinguished from each other) were typically published anonymously to protect the identity of the writer. The gradual reduction of taxes on newspapers from 1833 reduced price and increased circulation, and, over time, newspapers established themselves as independent sources of news rather than political partisans.[11]

This chapter discusses the trial of Daniel M'Naghten and the creation of the *M'Naghten Rules* following his acquittal on the basis of insanity, and assesses the reasons for *M'Naghten*'s profound impact on criminal law. *M'Naghten's Case* generated extensive public and political debate in 1843. The contemporaneous debate reveals both the controversy surrounding the case, and the depth and relative sophistication of the discussion about the criminal law of insanity, process and punishment. *M'Naghten* is also notable for its long-lasting effect on the criminal law. This chapter suggests that the combination of three factors—the manner in which the *Rules* were created, the use of terms of art within the *Rules* and their dependency on the special verdict tying successful use of the insanity defence to disposition—together with a lack of political will to institute reform, account for the far-reaching and ongoing impact of *M'Naghten* on the criminal law, despite the well-recognised limitations of the *M'Naghten Rules*.

## II. OFFENCE AND TRIAL

The facts of the crime committed by Daniel M'Naghten are well known. On 20 January 1843, in Downing Street, London, M'Naghten, who had armed himself with two pistols, shot Edward Drummond, Sir Robert Peel's Private Secretary, perhaps in the belief that he was shooting Peel himself.[12] The shooting, which took place 'in the high street and in broad daylight',[13] was reported as an attempted assassination. M'Naghten was arrested immediately and detained in Newgate jail. Drummond was wounded and later died in hospital of his injuries.

---

[9] See A Hobbs, 'The Deleterious Dominance of *The Times* in Nineteenth Century Scholarship' (2013) 18(4) *Journal of Victorian Culture* 472, 473. *The Times* gained its nickname 'The Thunderer' from a leading article in support of the Reform Bill 1832.

[10] Rubery, 'Journalism' 186.

[11] ibid.

[12] HL Deb 13 March 1843, vol 67, cols 714–44 (Lord Brougham).

[13] 'Letter to the Editor' *Morning Post* (London, 23 January 1843) 4.

The high-profile offence captured public attention straight away and generated a rather alarmist and wide-ranging debate that encompassed various matters, such as policing practices and capital punishment.[14] The political overtones of the crime fed existing concerns about the stability of the political order and the safety of public figures. M'Naghten was a Scottish national who, at his appearance at the magistrates' court on 21 January, blamed 'the Tories in my native city' for his act of violence.[15] Initially, his 'violent and Radical politics'[16] gave rise to speculation that he was part of a 'sect of assassins' attempting to bring down the Tory government.[17] Even after those concerns were eclipsed by the realisation that he acted alone, the tragedy of the death of the 'amiable and unfortunate' Drummond continued to 'occupy the public mind to the exclusion of every other topic'.[18] Such was the public interest in M'Naghten's case that when he made appearances at Bow Street police court in the period leading up to his trial, crowds of persons gathered, 'anxious to catch a sight of the prisoner'.[19] He was committed to stand trial for murder on 2 February 1843.

The question of M'Naghten's insanity was raised in the press almost immediately after the shooting because of M'Naghten's belief that he was being persecuted by Tories—that he was 'incessantly watched and dogged by certain parties who had an ill-will to him'[20]—was widely reported. The public discussion of insanity in the wake of the offence is notable for both its heated nature and its relative sophistication. Newspapers focused on M'Naghten's 'morbid delusions' regarding persecution and canvassed issues such as the 'various species of insanity'.[21] Articles extracted letters from doctors found amongst M'Naghten's possessions that labelled his belief about persecution from the Tories a 'delusion of mind'.[22] Reflecting preoccupations of the time, discussion included the question of whether insanity was hereditary. M'Naghten's family history,[23] his employment and 'previous habits', both while living in Glasgow and since moving to London a few months earlier, were raked over, and the evidence of eccentricity and hypochondria

---

[14] eg, 'The Attempt to Assassinate Mr E Drummond' *Morning Post* (London, 23 January 1843) 4.

[15] ibid.

[16] 'The Assassin M'Naughten' *The Times* (London, 27 January 1843) 5.

[17] 'The Murder of Mr Drummond' *The Times* (London, 28 January 1843) 4 (editorial comment on letters to the editor received by the newspaper, dismissing these concerns as baseless and likely to prevent M'Naghten from receiving a fair trial if believed).

[18] 'The Character of Daniel M'Naughten When in Glasgow' *London Standard* (London, 1 February 1843) 3.

[19] 'Final Examination of the Assassin M'Naughten' *The Times* (London, 30 January 1843) 5.

[20] 'M'Naughten, the Assassin' *The Times* (London, 28 January 1843) 3.

[21] 'Insanity of Criminals' *Hampshire Advertiser* (Southampton, 4 February 1843) 4.

[22] 'The Assassin M'Naughten' *The Times* (London, 27 January 1843) 5.

[23] 'M'Naughten, the Assassin' *The Times* (London, 28 January 1843) 3: 'From evidence taken by the parties appointed to investigate the subject here, we are able to state that none of his family showed any indications of insanity.'

led some newspaper editors to conclude that there was 'no doubt' that he was insane.[24] Other newspapers reached opposite conclusions with equal confidence. Some held that he was sane at the time of the offence on the basis of evidence of his planning and preparation,[25] while others queried whether, even if he was insane, that properly excused his offence (whether he had 'the degree of privation that ought to prevent his being treated as a murderer')[26] or whether the insanity defence should be available to so serious an offence as murder.[27]

M'Naghten's trial for wilful murder took place at London's central criminal court, the Old Bailey, on Friday 3 and Saturday 4 March 1843, six weeks after the shooting.[28] Reflecting the immense public interest in the case, admission to the courtroom had to be restricted because so many people sought to observe the trial,[29] and full reports of the proceedings were printed in several daily newspapers at the time.[30] Lord Tindal CJ and Williams and Coleridge JJ heard the case together with a 12-man jury. As M'Naghten had admitted the shooting, the main issue at trial was his mental state. The Solicitor General, Sir William Follett, gave the opening address for the Crown. He turned quickly to the 'painful duty' of the jury to decide whether M'Naghten had to be acquitted on the basis of insanity—a question to be decided by 'fact and common sense'.[31] He acknowledged that M'Naghten did not claim a 'constant general insanity', but rather one that perhaps affected him at the time he committed the act, making him an 'irresponsible agent' and unable to tell right from wrong.[32] Follett reviewed the case law on insanity, and questioned police and people who had witnessed the crime or known M'Naghten, but did not call either of the two medical witnesses who had examined the prisoner for the Crown.[33]

Mr Alexander Cockburn was M'Naghten's defence counsel. As a result of the passage of the Prisoners' Counsel Act 1836, Cockburn was able to address the jury.[34] He was regarded as a great orator: it was reported that

[24] 'The Assassin M'Naughten' *The Times* (London, 27 January 1843) 5.

[25] 'Character of Daniel M'Naughten When in Glasgow' *London Standard* (London, 1 February 1843) 3.

[26] 'The Murder of Mr Drummond' *The Times* (London, 28 January 1843) 4.

[27] eg, 'Verdicts of Insanity' *Exeter and Plymouth Gazette* (Exeter, 11 February 1843) 3 (calling for a 'full inquiry' into the valid grounds of a plea of insanity).

[28] *M'Naghten's Case* (1843) 10 Cl & Fin 200, 8 ER 718. A full record of the trial is available via the Old Bailey Online database (www.oldbaileyonline.org): *OBPs Online*, version 7.2, Daniel M'Naughten, 27 February 1843, t18430227-874.

[29] 'The Trial of M'Naughten' *Morning Chronicle* (London, 3 March 1843) 4.

[30] The development of shorthand systems had improved the accuracy and speed of reporters sitting in court or observing parliament: see Rubery, 'Journalism' 186.

[31] 'Trial of Daniel McNaughten for the Assassination of Mr Drummond' *Morning Chronicle* (London, 4 March 1843) 7.

[32] ibid.

[33] HL Deb 13 March 1843, vol 67, cols 714–44 (the Lord Chancellor).

[34] *Prisoners' Counsel Act* 1836 (6 & 7 Will IV c 114) authorised defence counsel to address speeches to the jury directly in felony trials for the first time.

his 'eloquent' opening address, spoken in a low tone of voice, lasted four hours.[35] He was said to have referred to the 'deep sense of responsibility' he felt, given the character and position of the deceased, Mr Drummond, and the esteem in which he was held.[36] Perhaps to counter the conclusion that might have been drawn from the evidence of planning involved in procuring pistols and staking out the area where Drummond was shot, he pointed to the 'total absence of motive' (M'Naghten had 'no extravagant opinions on the subject of politics'), emphasising that the act was committed in 'the broad face of day', on a busy thoroughfare and in front of crowds of people, and concluding that the crime was 'an act of frenzy, committed under the influence of insanity'.[37] Given this, he argued, it would be an offence to God who had seen fit to make M'Naghten insane and would 'violate every principle of justice and humanity' to hold M'Naghten responsible and to punish him.[38]

In support of his claims, Cockburn relied on two types of evidence—lay and expert. In this respect, *M'Naghten's Case* was typical of the period as, at this time, lay people were regarded as competent to testify to insanity.[39] Lay evidence was adduced from acquaintances of the prisoner, those who knew M'Naghten's condition, because, as Cockburn stated, M'Naghten had applied to them 'from time to time, and again and again, for escape and safety from the fancied misery that he himself imagined'.[40] The second type of evidence was provided by various 'gentlemen of the medical profession', in whose opinion M'Naghten was mad ('that he was the creature of delusion and of ungoverned impulse that took away all responsibility from him').[41] Some of these medical witnesses were individuals who, controversially, had been called to give evidence only after observing the prisoner in court and hearing evidence given by others. With reference to what the 'mad doctors' of the time called 'monomania'—a condition of sanity in all respects but one—the medical witnesses testified to M'Naghten's delusion and his lack of self-control.[42] One medical witness was Mr McMurdo, the well-known surgeon of Newgate jail, who testified that M'Naghten was of 'unsound mind' on the charge on which he was indicted.[43]

At the close of the defence case, the Lord Chief Justice stated that he and his learned brothers had concluded that the 'strong evidence' from Cockburn

[35] 'Assassination of Mr Drummond' *The Era* (London, 5 March 1843) 8.
[36] 'Trial of M'Naughten for the Murder of Mr Drummond' *Morning Post* (London, 6 March 1843) 2.
[37] ibid.
[38] 'Assassination of Mr Drummond' *The Times* (London, 6 March 1843) 5.
[39] See for discussion A Loughnan, *Manifest Madness* (Oxford, Oxford University Press, 2012) Ch 6.
[40] 'Assassination of Mr Drummond' *The Era* (London, 5 March 1843) 8.
[41] ibid.
[42] ibid.
[43] ibid.

meant that the murder charge could not be sustained.[44] Lord Tindall CJ asked the Solicitor-General if he had evidence to combat the medical testimony adduced by the defence, and when Follett replied that he did not, the proceedings were stopped. The Solicitor-General was able to address the jury one last time (he did not sum up the evidence, but admitted that 'the whole of the medical evidence is on one side').[45] Lord Tindall CJ expressed the question to be determined as 'whether at the time the act in question was committed the prisoner had or had not the use of his understanding, so as to know that he was doing a wrong or wicked act'.[46] The members of the jury quickly returned a verdict that M'Naghten was not guilty, being insane at the time he committed the act.[47] This form of verdict, the special verdict—including the conclusion and the statement of fact on which it rested—was standard practice in insanity cases by this time.[48] Although he was acquitted, the provisions of the Criminal Lunatics Act 1800 meant that M'Naghten could be held in 'strict custody' ('detention during her Majesty's pleasure') and he was detained.

In addition to securing an acquittal for his client and sparing him the death penalty, Cockburn's chief achievement was to have brought delusion squarely within the bounds of the insanity defence. Although delusion had been an element of the successful insanity plea raised by James Hadfield in 1800,[49] its status as a ground for exculpation was unclear. Legal ambiguity about the significance of delusion reflected wider fluidity in expert knowledge about insanity. At this time, expert knowledge about 'madness', as yet still emergent, was marked by significant conflict and contestation. Just as a range of individuals claimed specialist knowledge of 'madness'—including surgeons, prison doctors, midwives and 'mad doctors'—a variety of ideas about 'madness' competed for dominance. Inchoate psychiatric and psychological knowledge emphasised disorders of the emotions and the will, as opposed to of the intellect (evident in then-current concepts such as 'moral insanity', 'lesion of the will' and 'monomania').[50] In *M'Naghten's Case*, Cockburn argued that, as a disease, madness operated 'on the mind' rather than the body and, in an apparent effort to sidestep the import of relevant case law authorities, claimed that 'the pathology of the disease, in its present scientific form, was a matter altogether of modern discovery'.[51] In effect, he

[44] ibid.
[45] 'Assassination of Mr Drummond' *The Times* (London, 6 March 1843) 5.
[46] *M'Naghten's Case* (n 28) 202.
[47] 'Assassination of Mr Drummond' *The Times* (London, 6 March 1843) 5.
[48] On the development of the special verdict, see R Moran, 'The Origin of Insanity as a Special Verdict: The Trial for Treason of James Hadfield' (1985) 19 *Law and Society Review* 487.
[49] *R v Hadfield* (1800) 27 St Tr 1281; see further Loughnan, *Manifest Madness* 109–10.
[50] Wiener, *Reconstructing the Criminal*; JP Eigen *Witnessing Insanity: Madness and Mad Doctors in the English Court* (New Haven, Yale University Press, 1995) 79.
[51] 'Trial of M'Naughten for the Murder of Mr Drummond' *Morning Post* (London, 6 March 1843) 2.

suggested that the criminal law needed to catch up to contemporary medical knowledge and include delusion within the scope of the insanity defence.

The consternation over M'Naghten's acquittal was immediate. Famously, Queen Victoria wrote to Sir Robert Peel to express her concern.[52] In the print media, reactions to the result fell loosely along party lines, reflecting the clear political allegiances of newspapers in this period.[53] Broadly, the Tory or conservative press condemned the outcome.[54] While some commentary focused on the 'abrupt termination' of the trial,[55] most discussion focused on the success of the insanity defence and the verdict of 'not guilty by reason of insanity'. Newspaper columns noted the 'astonishment and alarm' that the verdict had produced, while others claimed that the verdict represented an abuse of the plea of insanity.[56] Letters to the editors of the newspapers argued that the case had exposed a 'monstrous defect' in the criminal law,[57] with the result leaving members of the public vulnerable to murderous attacks.[58] The view was that, in acquitting M'Naghten on the grounds of insanity, he would be assured a 'comfortable and permanent abode in Bethlehem Hospital at the expense of the nation' as the consequence of his homicidal act.[59] Other papers—'the Whig and Radical press'[60]—expressed satisfaction with the verdict, claiming that 'British Justice', in the form of the jury, had not been able to disregard the medical evidence and suggesting that if M'Naghten had been hanged, it would have been an outrage as he would not have understood the punishment.[61]

In the fallout from the trial, the use of medical testimony by the defence drew the heaviest criticism. The outcome was seen to be the result of the 'great deal too much latitude [that] was allowed to the "mad doctors"',

[52] eg, J Dalby, 'The Case of Daniel McNaughton' (2006) 27(4) *American Journal of Forensic Psychiatry* 17, 28.

[53] The newspaper coverage of *M'Naghten* is notable for its inclusion of criticism of the line on the case adopted by other newspapers.

[54] This led one paper to express surprise that those newspapers seemed to have preferred that M'Naghten was 'a monster and not a madman': see 'M'Naughten's Trial' *Bristol Mercury* (Bristol, 11 March 1843) 5.

[55] eg, 'M'Naughten's Acquittal' *The Standard* (London, 14 March 1843) 1.

[56] See untitled article, *The Standard* (London, 7 March 1843) 2 and 'Methodical Madness' *North Wales Chronicle* (Bangor, 14 March 1843) 3, respectively.

[57] Letter to the Editor, *Morning Post* (London, 7 March 1843) 6.

[58] Letter to the Editor, *The Times* (London, 6 March 1843) 2; see also Letter to the Editor, *Morning Post* (London, 8 March 1843) 5; and 'Methodical Madness' *North Wales Chronicle* (Bangor, 14 March 1843) 3.

[59] 'Killing No Murder' *Morning Post* (London, 7 March 1843) 6.

[60] 'The Monomaniac Theories' *Statesman and Dublin Christian Record* (Dublin, 14 March 1843) 2.

[61] See untitled article, *The Caledonian Mercury* (Edinburgh, 16 March 1843) 3 and untitled article, *Morning Post* (London, 8 March 1843) 4, respectively; see also 'M'Naughten's Trial' *Bristol Mercury* (Bristol, 11 March 1843) 5 and Letter to the Editor, *Hertford Mercury and Reformer* (Hertford, 18 March 1843) 2.

who were permitted to 'dictate the law'.[62] While there was some criticism of the reliance of the defence on medical men who had merely observed the prisoner in court,[63] the main target of condemnation was the condition 'monomania', explained as a condition that meant a man 'might be perfectly sane in the general affairs of life, though laboring under a strange delusion upon one point'.[64] On this point, the 'mad doctors' were accused of merely producing 'a new sample of jargon', rendering society vulnerable to a 'neologically described class of murders'[65] and excusing individuals who were conscious of their criminality.[66] Some commentary boldly suggested that M'Naghten did not suffer from madness on the basis of delusions, but from 'self-idolatry'.[67] Equally strongly, it was suggested that, even admitting that M'Naghten suffered from a 'morbid delusion', he retained moral responsibility and should not have been excused for an act amounting to revenge.[68] Even those newspapers expressing approval of the outcome (a smaller number) queried whether, if M'Naghten was a monomaniac, this might be a 'middle state' between unsoundness of mind and soundness for the purposes of the criminal law.[69]

Like the public debate prior to trial, the post-trial assessment of the law of insanity points to the controversy surrounding the case, and the depth and relative sophistication of the discussion of criminal insanity and its relation to criminal process and punishment. In the aftermath of the trial, a number of concerns were expressed about the law of insanity: that medical evidence usurps the role of the jury,[70] that variation in medical fashions and differences of opinion between 'mad doctors' makes their evidence unhelpful,[71] and that madness should have mitigatory effect only (ie, act as a basis for a recommendation of mercy from the judges).[72] A concern familiar to readers from the current era—fear of fakery (that anyone who 'practices an eccentric line of conduct' will escape punishment for murder)[73]—also appeared. The concerns expressed about the law were not all on the conservative or

---

[62] *The Standard* (London, 7 March 1843) 2; see also 'The Plea of Insanity' *The Times* (London, 9 March 1843) 6 and 'Methodical Madness' *North Wales Chronicle* (Bangor, 14 March 1843) 3; 'The Plea of Monomania' *Exeter and Plymouth Gazette* (Exeter, 18 March 1843) 3.

[63] See, eg, untitled article, *The Standard* (London, 7 March 1843) 2 and untitled article, *The Standard* (London, 17 March 1843) 2.

[64] 'Assassination of Mr Drummond' *The Era* (London, 5 March 1843) 8.

[65] Untitled article, *The Standard* (London, 6 March 1843) 2

[66] 'M'Naughten's Acquittal' *The Standard* (London, 14 March 1843) 1.

[67] Untitled article, *The Standard* (London, 14 March 1843) 2; see also untitled article, *The Standard* (London, 17 March 1843) 2.

[68] 'The Plea of Insanity' *The Times* (London, 9 March 1843) 6; see also Letter to the Editor, *Morning Post* (London, 13 March 1843) 16.

[69] Untitled article, *Morning Post* (London, 7 March 1843) 4.

[70] 'The Plea of Monomania' *Exeter and Plymouth Gazette* (Exeter, 18 March 1843) 3.

[71] Untitled article, *Yorkshire Gazette* (York, 25 March 1843) 5.

[72] 'Mr Guthrie on M'Naughten's Insanity' *Leicestershire Mercury* (Leicester, 25 March 1843) 4.

[73] 'Insanity of Criminals' *Hampshire Advertiser* (Southampton, 4 February 1843) 4.

punitive side: some newspapers used the case to advocate for preventive rather than retributive punishment, cautioning that 'punishment out of all proportion with the offences, are [sic] as bad for society as they are unjust to the individual'.[74]

Public concern about reliance on medical evidence in *M'Naghten's Case* and the success of the insanity plea generated escalating calls from the press for reform of the criminal law.[75] Across the country, newspapers called on parliament to intervene.[76] I turn now to the period following the trial and the creation of the *M'Naghten Rules*.

## III. THE *M'NAGHTEN RULES*

Within days of M'Naghten's acquittal in March 1843, several members of the House of Lords and the Lord Chancellor, Lord Lyndhurst, were discussing whether 'anything could be done to remedy the evil' of the decision.[77] On 13 March 1843, the House of Lords held a debate on the law of insanity. In an effort to quiet the 'public mind' about whether there was 'some great defect in the laws of the country', the Lord Chancellor carefully reviewed *M'Naghten's Case*, stating that it was 'quite impossible beneficially to alter the law [of insanity], or render it better adapted than it is' and concluding that there was no need for a change in the 'mode of administering the law'.[78] Nonetheless, and somewhat ambiguously, he suggested that it might be possible to develop 'measures of precaution stronger than those now in existence' and recommended that, as a first step in possible reform, the House 'take the opinion of the judges' as to a correct statement of the law of insanity.[79]

In this March debate, some of the Lords expressed concern about the detention of insane acquittees after trial. The Lord Chancellor stated that there was no need for legislation on that matter because the law already provided Her Majesty with 'the power of confining them in such a manner as she might consider most advisable for the safety of the public'.[80] The Lord Chancellor was alluding to the provisions of the Criminal Lunatics

---

[74] 'The Plea of Insanity: Absurdities of the Newspaper Press' *Belfast News Letter* (Belfast, 24 March 1843) 1.

[75] eg, untitled article, *Caledonian Mercury* (Edinburgh, 16 March 1843) 3.

[76] eg, Letter to the Editor, *Morning Post* (London, 8 March 1843) 5 (calling on Parliament as 'guardians of public safety' to launch an inquiry into the law on insanity and public morals); see also 'M'Naughten's Trial' *Bristol Mercury* (Bristol, 11 March 1843) 5 (stating the legislature owes it to persons of 'rank and station' to 'legislate cooly but promptly').

[77] HL Deb 6 March 1843, vol 67, cols 288–90 (Lord Chancellor); see also untitled article, *The Standard* (London, 7 March 1843) 2.

[78] HL Deb 13 March 1843, vol 67, cols 714–44 (Lord Chancellor).

[79] ibid; see also untitled article, *Caledonian Mercury* (Edinburgh, 16 March 1843) 3.

[80] HL Deb 13 March 1843, vol 67, cols 714–44 (Lord Chancellor).

Act 1800, mentioned above. Following *Hadfield's Case* in 1800,[81] and amid uncertainty about the precise legal basis for detaining dangerous insane prisoners, the Criminal Lunatics Act 1800 was passed to ensure that insane prisoners were no longer able to walk free after trial. The 1800 Act provided that, where a 'person was insane at the time of the commission' of a felony offence, he was to be acquitted and 'the jury shall be required to find specially whether such person was insane at the time of the commission of such offence', after which the court 'shall order such person to be kept in strict custody'.[82] Thus, in what would become known as indefinite detention, after 1800, a prisoner raising insanity successfully (receiving a special verdict) would be detained although he or she had been acquitted. In the wake of *M'Naghten's Case*, the House of Lords debate on the law on insanity proceeded on the basis that, with a particular disposition tied to the successful use of the insanity defence, there was no concern that, in being acquitted, dangerous defendants would be placed beyond the law. As such, the special verdict and indefinite detention together formed what might be called a condition of the possibility of what we now know as the *M'Naghten Rules*.

All of the judges of the superior courts of common law were called to appear in the House of Lords on 26 May (when no questions were put to the judges) and again on 19 June 1843 (when debate took place). While the judges expressed some concern about discussing the law in the abstract and without the benefit of counsel,[83] they provided responses to all five questions put to them. The responses, given by Lord Tindal CJ on behalf of 14 of the 15 judges (Maule J spoke for himself), became known as the *M'Naghten Rules*. As this indicates, the *M'Naghten Rules* do not come from the *M'Naghten* case.[84] Indeed, it is one of the curious features of *M'Naghten* that the eponymous law that the decision generated did not arise from the trial itself.

The now famous response given by Lord Tindall CJ to the questions from the Lords provided in part:

[T]he jurors ought to be told in all cases that every man is to be presumed sane, and to possess a sufficient degree of reason to be responsible for his crimes, until the contrary be proved to their satisfaction; and that to establish a defence on the ground of insanity it must be clearly proved that at the time of the committing of the act, the party accused was labouring under such a defect of reason, from a

---

[81] *Hadfield* (n 49).
[82] Criminal Lunatics Act 1800 (39 & 40 Geo 3 c 94).
[83] HL Deb, 19 June 1843, vol 70, cited in *M'Naghten* (1843) 10 Cl & Fin 200, 204 (Maule J). It appears that these same concerns may have explained why there was no debate when the judges were first called to the House of Lords: see 'Law Intelligence: House of Lords' *Morning Post* (London, 26 May 1843) 6.
[84] The case report of the *M'Naghten* judgment obscures this feature by not distinguishing clearly between the court and parliamentary proceedings.

disease of the mind, as not to know the nature and quality of the act he was doing, or, if he did know it, that he did not know he was doing wrong.[85]

This statement forms the core of the *M'Naghten Rules*. Lord Tindall CJ also responded to some questions about the significance of delusions on the part of individuals claiming insanity (stating that individuals should be judged 'as if the facts, in respect to which the delusion exists, were real') and to one question about the role of medical evidence given by a 'medical man' who has only seen the defendant in court and heard the evidence given by witnesses (stating that reliance on this type of evidence on matters of science is admissible).[86] These parts of the judges' response to the Lords' questions were not the focus of judicial or other attention after they were drafted and are no longer regarded as authoritative.[87]

The *M'Naghten Rules* formalised the insanity defence for the first time in the development of the common law. The passage of the *Rules* marked the appearance of a more technical and juridical test for insanity. Prior to *M'Naghten*, insanity had been an informal plea, with evocative formulations, such as the 'wild beast' test, more like loose standards, partly descriptive and partly prescriptive of insanity, rather than strict tests.[88] Until the late eighteenth century, a capacious informal insanity law combined with informal criminal processes to provide a wide scope for exculpation on the basis of incapacity. At the time of *M'Naghten*, a loose and partially moralised idea of incapacity was gradually giving way to a narrower and more medicalised notion of disability as a basis for exculpatory insanity.[89] This change was ushered in by the emergence of a specialist medical knowledge and language of 'madness', evident from the last decades of the eighteenth century and increasingly prominent from the first decades of the nineteenth century, and reflected in the presence of 'mad doctors' in the *M'Naghten* courtroom.

As is well known, the *M'Naghten Rules* comprise three limbs: (1) that an individual suffer from a 'defect of reason', which is (2) caused by a 'disease of the mind', and, as a result, (3) he or she does not know the 'nature and quality' of the act or that it was wrong. In order to raise the insanity defence successfully, a defendant must satisfy the first and second limbs, and one or other part of the third limb. With no significant conceptual development of ideas of non-responsibility in the second half of the nineteenth century, these limbs were gradually subject to judicial elaboration over the twentieth century, when their limitations became apparent. I discuss each limb in turn.[90]

---

[85] *M'Naghten's Case* (n 28) 210.
[86] ibid 204–05, 206–07.
[87] See N Walker, *Crime and Insanity in England (Vol 1)* (Edinburgh, Edinburgh University Press, 1968) 100; T Ward, 'A Terrible Responsibility: Murder and the Insanity Defence in England 1908–1939' (2002) 25 *International Journal of Law and Psychiatry* 361, 374.
[88] On the 'wild beast' test, see Loughnan, *Manifest Madness* 106–07.
[89] See also ibid Ch 5.
[90] The discussion of the limbs of *M'Naghten* insanity draws on Loughnan, *Manifest Madness* 116–121.

The first limb of *M'Naghten* insanity, 'defect of reason', is both a cause and an effect: it must cause an individual not to know the 'nature and quality' of the act or, alternatively, not to know that it was 'wrong', and it must be an effect of a 'disease of the mind'. A 'defect of reason' need not be permanent, but a defendant must be 'deprived of the power of reasoning' at the time of his or her act: it is not sufficient that a defendant fail to use his or her reasoning capacity or be 'momentarily absentminded or confused'.[91] The requirement that a defendant seeking to make an insanity plea must suffer from a 'defect of reason' has been narrowly interpreted to include only cognitive defects.[92] This narrowness has been a chief source of complaint about the *M'Naghten* insanity. The effect of interpreting 'defect of reason' in the *M'Naghten Rules* to denote cognitive defects has been to exclude defects of conation, the psychological processes of desire and volition. Thus, *M'Naghten* insanity excludes what has been called 'irresistible impulse' or 'uncontrollable impulse'.[93] This means that a number of mental disorders will not be able to form the basis for a 'defect of reason' because they do not affect the defendant in the requisite way.

The 'disease of the mind' limb of *M'Naghten* insanity forms the core of the defence, providing what I have called elsewhere a 'discrete and ostensibly scientific basis for the exculpation that flows from a successful plea'.[94] By contrast with 'defect of reason', 'disease of the mind' has been interpreted broadly.[95] The first judicial discussion of this limb of *M'Naghten* took place in 1957 in the first instance decision of *Kemp*, in which Devlin J stated that the phrase refers to 'the mental faculties of memory, reason and understanding', and was intended to be a limitation on the scope of 'defect of reason'.[96] The broad approach to 'disease of the mind'—as a 'disease which affects the proper functioning of the mind'[97]—arising from an 'internal' as opposed to 'external' cause has meant a narrow scope for automatism (to which no particular disposal attaches).[98] In *Bratty v Attorney-General for Northern Ireland*, Lord Denning stated that 'disease of the mind' includes, but is

---

[91] *R v Clarke* (1972) 56 Cr App R 225, 228 (CA).

[92] *R v Kemp* [1957] 1 QB 399 (Bristol Assizes).

[93] *R v Kopsch* (1925) 19 Cr App Rep 50 (CCA), 51–52. 'Irresistible impulse' is now accommodated by the partial defence of diminished responsibility: see Homicide Act 1957, s 2(1); *R v Byrne* [1960] 2 QB 396 (CCA).

[94] Loughnan, *Manifest Madness* 117.

[95] Although, as the Law Commission points out, the narrow interpretation of the other limbs means that the *M'Naghten Rules* do not capture all defendants with a serious mental disorder: see Law Commission, *Criminal Liability Insanity and Automatism:* (Law Com DP, 2013) [1.47].

[96] *Kemp* (n 92) 407.

[97] *R v Hennessy* [1989] 1 WLR 287 (CA), 292.

[98] A broad approach to 'disease of the mind' has also meant that certain physical disorders, such as hyperglycaemia, sleepwalking and epilepsy, which impact on the brain, fall within the ambit of 'disease of the mind' and thus within the bounds of insanity for criminal law purposes: *R v Hennessy* (n 97) (hyperglycaemia); *R v Burgess* [1991] 2 QB 92 (CA) (sleepwalking); *R v Sullivan* [1984] 1 AC 156 (HL) (epilepsy).

not limited to, the major mental disorders as identified by psychiatrists and other medical professionals.[99] As this indicates, despite reference to clinical labels and conditions, what constitutes a 'disease of the mind' is a question of law for the judge.

In addition to consideration of the effect of a particular condition on an individual's 'mental faculties of memory, reason and understanding', whether mental disorder is prone to recur effects the categorisation of a particular condition as a 'disease of the mind'. In *Bratty*, Lord Denning stated that 'any mental disorder which has manifested itself in violence and is prone to recur is a disease of the mind'.[100] In *Burgess*, the Court of Appeal stated that although the low probability of recurrence does not mean a condition is *not* a 'disease of the mind', 'if there is a danger of recurrence that may be an added reason for categorising the condition as a disease of the mind'.[101] This feature of 'disease of the mind' exposes the preoccupation with dangerousness that underpins insanity jurisprudence. As several scholars suggest, this concern has animated the law since before *M'Naghten*.[102] Concern with dangerous individuals continues to drive the way in which the boundary of the insanity doctrine is drawn.

The third limb of *M'Naghten* insanity specifies two ways in which a 'defect of reason' must affect an individual if he or she is seeking to rely on the insanity defence: it must affect either his or her knowledge of the 'nature and quality' of the act, or his or her knowledge that it was 'wrong'. The phrase 'nature and quality' of the act has been interpreted narrowly to refer to the physical circumstances and consequences of the defendant's act.[103] Knowledge of 'wrongness' has also been interpreted narrowly; after some earlier contradictory authority, in *Windle* in 1952, the House of Lords concluded that this part of the *M'Naghten Rules* denotes knowledge of legal rather than moral wrongness.[104] Although this is a narrow interpretation, the wrongness limb is significant because it means that the insanity defence can exempt or excuse an individual even if they had the mens rea required for the offence.[105] Overall, the interpretation of the third limb of the *M'Naghten Rules* has been criticised on the basis that it overly restricts the exculpatory potential of insanity. As RD Mackay writes, the effect of the narrow approach to the third limb of *M'Naghten* is to exclude 'the vast

---

[99] *Bratty v Attorney-General for Northern Ireland* [1963] AC 386 (HL), 412.

[100] ibid.

[101] *Burgess* (n 98) 99.

[102] See, eg, RD Mackay, *Mental Condition Defences in the Criminal Law* (Oxford, Clarendon Press, 1995).

[103] *R v Codère* (1916) 12 Cr App R 21 (CCA), 26–27.

[104] *R v Windle* [1952] 2 QB 826 (CCA), 833.

[105] Insanity actually operates in two ways: it either negates an element of the offence (mens rea) or, via the knowledge of wrongness limb, it has a more fundamental impact, exculpating an individual although he or she performed the actus reus with the requisite mens rea.

majority of mentally disordered persons' from the realm of the insanity, as 'inevitably in most cases they will know what they are doing and that the offence they are committing is legally wrong'.[106]

Over and above their content—the test for insanity—the *M'Naghten Rules* are notable for the distinctive evidentiary and procedural frame they give the insanity defence. There are two aspects to this distinctive frame. The first is the requirement that the insanity defence must be left to the jury ('jurors ought to be told')—it is not open to the Crown to accept a plea of insanity.[107] At the time of the passage of the *Rules*, this was not notable and certainly did not constitute a restriction, because matters were routinely brought to trial. In the twentieth century, with the growth of the criminal justice system, the systematisation of prosecution practices, and the common use of psychological and psychiatric evidence, this feature of the *Rules* has come to mark insanity out from other mental incapacity defences (for example, diminished responsibility). While the practical significance of this aspect of the *M'Naghten Rules* has been queried (on the basis that juries may be directed to return a special verdict or presented with a situation where all the expert evidence supports the insanity defence),[108] viewed in light of the controversy surrounding the Queen's Bench judges' decision to stop M'Naghten's trial and the related concern about abdication in decision-making to 'mad doctors', this feature of the evidentiary and procedural frame for insanity established by the *M'Naghten Rules* takes on particular importance.

The second aspect of the distinctive evidentiary and procedural frame given to insanity by the *M'Naghten Rules* has two parts: the presumption of sanity and the burden of proof. The *Rules* provide that 'every man is presumed to be sane ... until the contrary be proved to their [the jurors'] satisfaction'. The standard of proof is the balance of probabilities.[109] Imposition of a substantive (as opposed to evidential) burden on the defendant is atypical; indeed, the law of insanity is the only part of the common law of crime in which a defendant bears a substantive burden of proof. This feature of the *M'Naghten Rules* caused a problem when the House of Lords considered the question of burdens of proof in *Woolmington v DPP*.[110] Famously, the *Woolmington* court held that the prosecution bears the burden of proving

---

[106] Mackay, *Mental Condition Defences* 100.

[107] *R v Crown Court at Maidstone ex p London Borough of Harrow* [2000] 1 Cr App R 117 (CA), 123.

[108] RD Mackay, BJ Mitchell and L Howe, 'Yet More Facts about the Insanity Defence' [2006] *Crim LR* 399, 404.

[109] *R v Soderman* (1935) AC 462; *R v Carr-Briant* [1943] KB 607. It is possible for the insanity to be raised by the prosecution and, if this occurs, the prosecution bears the burden of proving insanity beyond all reasonable doubt: *R v Podola* [1960] 1 QB 325 (CCA); *R v Grant* [1960] Crim LR 424 (CA).

[110] *Woolmington v DPP* [1935] All ER 1 (HL).

the guilt of the accused (rather than the defence bearing the burden of proving innocence); however, the court also stated that, in insanity cases, 'it is incumbent upon the accused to prove his innocence'.[111] The court's explanation for authorising an exception to the general principle about burdens of proof solely for insanity was simply that 'M'Naghten's case stands by itself ... It is quite exceptional and has nothing to do with the present circumstances'.[112] The readiness of the *Woolmington* court to treat insanity exceptionally is striking,[113] but seems to follow from the unusual status of the *M'Naghten Rules*, which I discuss below.

In recent decades, the evidentiary and procedural frame accorded to insanity by the *M'Naghten Rules* has been augmented (in effect) by the requirement that expert medical evidence be adduced in support of the plea. Since the passage of the Criminal Procedure (Insanity and Unfitness to Plead) Act 1991, no jury is entitled to find insanity without evidence from two or more registered medical practitioners.[114] The objective of this recent reform stands in marked contrast to the chief concern at the time of *M'Naghten*: that courts and juries should not rely too heavily on medical experts. The presence of 'mad doctors' in the courtroom in 1843 seemed to provoke anxiety about insanity exculpating too many offenders (although, as Joel P Eigen and others have argued, such experts would not have been able to enter the courtroom without the permission of the judges).[115] By the late twentieth century, when expert evidence was mandated, the particular knowledge mix governing evaluations and adjudications of insanity—lay and expert—had become a familiar feature of the criminal law on mental incapacity.[116]

It is generally acknowledged that, having been called to appear to defend the *M'Naghten* decision, the *M'Naghten Rules* themselves were in effect an admission from the judges that the case had been wrongly decided.[117] The process in the House of Lords was presented in a neutral way—as the judges simply providing information about what 'the law really is', should the House, in its legislative capacity, be called upon to change it.[118] But the questions themselves betrayed the critical tone of the process by focus-

---

[111] ibid 8.
[112] ibid 5.
[113] I consider explanations for the *Woolmington* decision on insanity elsewhere: see Loughnan, *Manifest Madness* 164–65.
[114] Criminal Procedure (Insanity and Unfitness to Plead) Act 1991, s 1(1).
[115] J Eigen and G Andoll, 'From Mad-Doctor to Forensic Witness: The Evolution of Early English Court Psychiatry' (1986) 9 *International Journal of Law and Psychiatry* 159, 169; see also J Eigen 'Delusion's Odyssey' (2004) 27 *International Journal of Law and Psychiatry* 395, 411; T Ward 'Observers, Advisors, or Authorities? Experts, Juries and Criminal Responsibility in Historical Perspective' (2001) 12 *Journal of Forensic Psychiatry* 105, 110.
[116] On the knowledge mix governing insanity, see Loughnan *Manifest Madness* Ch 6.
[117] eg, Walker, *Crime and Insanity* 102.
[118] HL Deb 19 June 1843 vol 70; *M'Naghten* (n 28) 213 (Lord Campbell).

ing on the most controversial issues of the trial—delusion as a basis for exculpatory insanity, and reliance on medical witnesses who merely saw the prisoner and heard the evidence in court. In 'accepting' the responses offered by the judges as to the state of the law on insanity—with the implication that the responses did not constitute a change in the law—the House of Lords was relieved of the need to pass legislation to clarify the scope of insanity. But the responses themselves arguably constituted a change in the law. Because he did not have a 'defect of reason' and understood the 'nature and quality' of his act, and that it was wrong, it is not clear that M'Naghten himself was entitled to an acquittal under the *Rules*; however, as Walker writes, no one in the House was 'tactless enough to point out that if the judges' answers represented the law M'Naghten should have been convicted'.[119] Thus, another of the curious features of *M'Naghten* is that Daniel M'Naghten may not have been successful in raising the insanity defence had the *Rules* that bear his name applied to him.

Despite the great notoriety of his trial and the development of the eponymous *M'Naghten Rules*, Daniel M'Naghten lived the remainder of his life in quiet obscurity. He spent 20 years in Bethlem Royal Hospital. While there was some initial public interest in his conduct in Bethlem,[120] he did not attract ongoing attention. In 1864, he was transferred to the newly opened Broadmoor Asylum, and he died there on 3 May 1865.[121]

## IV. THE LONGEVITY OF *M'NAGHTEN*

Providing the test for insanity, the *M'Naghten Rules* form the basis of the current law of insanity in England and Wales. While the *Rules* themselves have been of primary concern to legal scholars and their limitations are now well recognised, their durability is just as remarkable. Three factors together account for the long-lasting effect of the *Rules*: the manner in which they were created, the use of what quickly became terms of art within the *Rules*, and their dependency on the special verdict in tying disposition to the successful use of the insanity defence. Together with a lack of political will to institute reform, these factors help to explain the long-lasting effect of the *M'Naghten* decision on the criminal law. I now discuss each of these factors in turn.

The first of the three factors which account for the longevity of the *M'Naghten Rules* is the most significant: it is the way in which they were created. As mentioned above, the *Rules* were the result of a debate in the House of Lords (in its legislative capacity) regarding the law of insanity and

---

[119] Walker, *Crime and Insanity* 102.
[120] eg, 'The "Monomaniacs" in Bedlam' *Morning Post* (London, 10 April 1843) 7.
[121] Dalby, 'The Case of Daniel McNaughton' 28.

the outcome of M'Naghten's trial rather than the trial itself. The unique character of the *Rules*—a judicial formulation, developed independently of a specific trial and in a parliamentary context—has led Cairns to label them 'judicial legislation',[122] and they have been treated as exceptionally authoritative. The 'quasi-legislative status' of the *Rules*,[123] which presumably played into the comments made by the court in *Woolmington* about the exceptional position of insanity in relation to the burden of proof (referred to above), has meant they have been cemented in the criminal law and it has been assumed that they cannot be overturned in the usual way. The *Rules* were recognised by the House of Lords in *Bratty v Attorney-General for Northern Ireland* and *R v Sullivan* without any express reflection on their status.[124] In 2007, the Court of Appeal stated that 'it has always been recognised' that the genesis of the *Rules*—'answers given by the judges to a series of questions from the House of Lords which they dealt with without, it would appear, any argument by counsel'—means they have to be approached with 'some caution'.[125] The absence of change to the *Rules* in England and Wales (and amendments made to *M'Naghten* insanity in other common law jurisdictions) suggests that legislation is required to alter the *Rules*.

The second of the three factors that together account for the longevity of the *Rules* is their reliance on what quickly came to be regarded as terms of art: 'defect of reason' and 'disease of the mind'. While these terms were arguably sufficiently well known in 1843, such that they did not to require explanation in the *Rules* or in the subsequent case law of the nineteenth century, they strike the student or practitioner from the current era as odd or antiquated. These phrases, long orphaned by developments in expert medical knowledge and changes in psychiatric and psychological terms and concepts, now appear as terms of art. The sheer artistry of these terms has sheltered the insanity defence from the changing winds of clinical fashion, with *M'Naghten* insanity effectively floating above any particular diagnostic category or group of conditions. Indeed, set against expert medical knowledge of insanity in the current era—now constructed across distinctions between organic and functional disorders, and cognitive and affective conditions—the *Rules* seem to almost stand outside time.

While the artistry of terms such as 'disease of the mind' has enabled the *M'Naghten Rules* to accommodate developments in psychiatric and psychological knowledges and helped the *Rules* withstand the test of time, the 'mismatch between the legal test and modern psychiatry' is now regarded as

---

[122] DJA Cairns, *Advocacy and the Making of the Adversarial Criminal Trial, 1800–1865* (Oxford, Clarendon Press, 1998) 178.

[123] I Dennis, *The Law of Evidence*, 3rd edn (London, Sweet & Maxwell, 2007) 459.

[124] See *Bratty v Attorney-General for Northern Ireland* (n 99); and *Sullivan* (n 98).

[125] *R v Dean Johnson* [2007] EWCA Crim 1978 (CA) [14].

a cause for concern.[126] The inclusion of terms that do not relate to expert medical practice has meant that, in effect, an insane defendant receives a pseudo-diagnosis solely for the purposes of the criminal trial: labels of 'defect of reason' and 'disease of the mind' are superimposed onto operational clinical labels such as schizophrenia or psychosis. Indeed, these limbs of the *Rules* produce expert testimony in their own image, with psychiatrists and others who provide expert evidence in insanity cases giving life to the terms of the *Rules* in giving their evidence. The Law Commission has expressed concern that the antiquated terms used in the *Rules* may lead experts into error in applying the correct test for insanity, and repeated the concerns of experts that the *Rules* do not assist the witness in explaining the defendant's clinical situation to the court.[127] While this 'mismatch' between the law and psychiatry is not new, it seems to be coming to effect the legitimacy of the criminal law on mental incapacity.

The third of the three factors together accounting for the longevity of the *M'Naghten Rules* is the special verdict ('not guilty by reason of insanity') and its attendant powers of disposal, on which, as mentioned above, the *Rules* rest. By contrast with the first two factors accounting for the longevity of *M'Naghten*, this factor relates not to the *Rules* themselves, but to allied procedural provisions, which I suggested together constituted a condition of possibility of the creation of the *Rules*. The special verdict and its attendant powers of disposal have contributed to the longevity of the *Rules* because, together, they have discouraged the use of insanity and thus have circumscribed opportunities to develop jurisprudence around the defence or galvanise momentum for reform.

The special verdict—'not guilty by reason of insanity'—has the distinct procedural function of distinguishing an insane defendant from someone entitled to an ordinary acquittal. As discussed above, a long-standing concern with dangerousness lies behind the special verdict. The special verdict is regarded as a unique device by which the detention of insane defendants in the interests of social protection was brought within the bounds of the criminal law.[128] In serving this function, the special verdict both reflects and feeds into a wider issue about the stigma of the insanity plea. As the Law Commission notes, 'the label of "insane" is outdated as a description of those with mental illness, and simply wrong as regards those who have learning disabilities or learning difficulties, or those with epilepsy'.[129] Over and above concerns with accuracy, it is easy to see that, in some instances,

---

[126] Law Commission, *Insanity* [1.58].

[127] ibid [1.57], [1.58].

[128] eg, TH Jones, 'Insanity, Automatism and the Burden of Proof on the Accused' (1995) 111 *LQR* 475, 515; E Colvin, 'Exculpatory Defences in Criminal Law' (1990) 10 *OJLS* 381, 392; Mackay, *Mental Condition Defences* 73, 90–92.

[129] See Law Commission for England and Wales, current reference on 'Insanity and Automatism', www.lawcom.gov.uk/project/insanity-and-automatism.

another defence or even conviction (for a low-level crime) may be a more attractive option for an individual than the insanity defence.[130]

The discouraging effect of the special verdict is reinforced by the disposal powers that are attached to it. For most of the life of insanity since *M'Naghten*, there was only one disposal option, indefinite detention, which became indefinite hospitalisation in 1964.[131] Although the insanity defence is a general defence, in that it is available across the board of criminal offences,[132] the singular disposal option meant that, historically, there was little incentive to raise it except in relation to serious charges attracting significant penalties. It was only in the 1990s that a range of disposal options was made available to courts in England and Wales. The courts may now order an absolute discharge, a supervision order or an order that the person be detained in hospital, possibly with the restriction that he or she is not to be released until permission is given by the Secretary of State.[133] But the legacy of indefinite detention has placed an indelible mark on the jurisprudence around the defence (and also public perception of it).

These three factors together explaining the longevity of the *M'Naghten Rules* must be viewed against a backdrop marked by the absence of political will to change the law. The problems with the defence have long been well known. There have been numerous reviews of insanity in the twentieth and twenty-first centuries—from the Atkin Committee in the 1920s to the Criminal Law Revision Committee in the 1960s and the Butler Committee in the 1970s[134]—and, at the time of writing, the Law Commission for England and Wales is reviewing the law[135]—and the only changes that have been made to the insanity defence relate not to the law, but to procedure, diversifying disposal options and making expert evidence mandatory. The small number of insanity cases in any given year and the difficult political issues raised by the insanity defence—in relation to appearing to be 'soft on crime' or ignoring the concerns of victims of crime—militate against political action.

---

[130] This raises a fair labelling issue: see for discussion J Chalmers and F Leverick, 'Fair Labelling in Criminal Law' (2008) 71(2) *MLR* 217 (arguing that the principle should apply to defences as well as offences).

[131] Criminal Procedure (Insanity) Act 1964.

[132] In *DPP v H* [1997] 1 WLR 1406 (DC), the court determined that the insanity defence is available to all offences with a mens rea element, but this decision has been criticised, as the way in which the *M'Naghten Rules* are constructed (see n 105) means that insanity may be a defence to crimes of strict liability as well: see A Ashworth and J Horder, *Principles of Criminal Law*, 7th edn (Oxford, Oxford University Press, 2013) 143.

[133] See further Law Commission, *Insanity* [1.25].

[134] See *Report of the Committee on Insanity and Crime* ('Atkin Committee') (Cm 2005, 1923), the Criminal Law Revision Committee's *Third Report: Criminal Procedure (Insanity)* (Cmnd 2149, 1963) and the *Report of the Committee on Mentally Abnormal Offenders* (Cmnd 6244, 1975) ('Butler Committee'), respectively.

[135] See Law Commission, *Insanity*.

## V. CONCLUSION

*M'Naghten's Case*, and the subsequent debate in the House of Lords that gave rise to the *M'Naghten Rules*, has attracted controversy and consternation from 1843 onwards. Nonetheless, *M'Naghten* continues to determine the law on insanity in England and Wales (and elsewhere). As discussed in this chapter, the combination of three factors accounts for the far-reaching and ongoing impact of *M'Naghten* on the criminal law. These three factors have ensured the remarkable stability of a core part of the criminal law that deals with mental incapacity. When combined with a lack of political will to institute reform, an explanation for the stasis in this area becomes apparent. However, it is unlikely that this state of affairs will subsist much longer. Looking forward, it is likely that, in England and Wales, *M'Naghten* insanity will have to be amended in light of developments in international human rights law, in particular Article 12 of the United Nations Convention on the Rights of Persons with Disabilities, which guarantees equal protection before the law and problematises disability-specific criminal laws.[136] It is this area of law that will guide the future development of the law of insanity and determine the future life of *M'Naghten*.

---

[136] See P Bartlett, 'The United Nations Convention on the Rights of Persons with Disabilities and mental health law' (2012) 75 *MLR* 752, 775–77.

# 8

# *R v Flattery* (1877)

REBECCA WILLIAMS*

## I. INTRODUCTION

LAVINIA THOMPSON, THE prosecutrix, was 19 years of age and the daughter of 'labouring people in the neighbourhood of Halifax'. For a year prior to the events in the case, she had been in 'ill-health and subject to fits', including one in the presence of the defendant, John Flattery, and one wonders if today she would have been diagnosed as having epilepsy. On 4 November 1876 (which was apparently market-day in Halifax), she went with her mother to Halifax to consult the defendant, who kept an 'open stall' in the market, at which he gave medical and surgical advice in exchange for payment. Flattery took the two women into the neighbouring Peacock Inn, where he claimed that 'it was nature's string wanted breaking' and asked if he could break it. Mrs Thompson replied that 'she did not know what he meant but that she did not mind if it would do her daughter any good'. The defendant then took Miss Thompson into the next room, where he had sex with her, 'solely to gratify his passion', as Mellor J put it; there was no suggestion that Flattery thought he was undertaking medical treatment. Miss Thompson, on the other hand, made 'but feeble resistance', believing that she was undergoing a surgical operation to cure her of her fits. Flattery was thus indicted for rape, and was tried and convicted at the Winter Assizes at Leeds in December, 1876, but the learned judge postponed judgment until the next assizes in order to obtain the opinion of the Court for Crown Cases Reserved as to whether or not Flattery's conviction was warranted. The Court (Kelly CB, Mellor, Denman and Field JJ, and Huddleston B) unanimously held that it was.[1] In Mellor J's words, 'she consented to one thing, he did another materially different, on which she had been prevented by his fraud from exercising her judgment and will', or,

* I would like to record my thanks to the editors and other participants in the project for their very helpful comments on earlier drafts, as well as to Elizabeth Wells for her help with research into historical sources. Any remaining errors are, as always, mine alone.
[1] *R v Flattery* (1877) 2 QBD 410 (QBD), (1878) 13 Cox CC 388.

as Denman J put it: 'There must be consent to the act of sexual connection. I can see no evidence whatever of consent to that.'[2]

John Flattery therefore became the first reported person in England to be convicted of rape using deception rather than force, although in doing so, the Court relied on the decision in *R v Case*,[3] in which the defendant had been convicted of assault on very similar facts. Not only was the decision in *Flattery* therefore novel, it was also wide-ranging. In the Queen's Bench Report[4] of the case, Huddleston B notes that the case was different from that in *R v Barrow*,[5] in which 'the woman permitted intercourse, though under a mistake fraudulently induced as to the person', but Huddleston B nonetheless declined to distinguish the two cases, holding instead that he 'should like to have the point decided in [*Barrow*] reconsidered' too. This view was unanimously shared by the rest of the Court, Kelly CB going as far as to state that he was not 'prepared to say that if she did know the nature of sexual intercourse it would have been any evidence of consent', going on to 'lament that it has ever been decided to be the law of England that where a man obtains possession of a woman's person by fraud that it does not amount to rape'.[6]

Given the current state of the law relating to vitiation of consent to sex by misapprehension, the importance of the decision in *Flattery* cannot be over-estimated. Over the past eight years, the issue has been through the courts seven times, three of them in the last two years, suggesting an exponential growth in litigation on the topic.[7] The current significance of *Flattery's* land-mark is therefore clear, but 140 years later, and despite several statutory developments in the field, we have yet to determine the precise width and application of the rule it created. In that sense, then, *Flattery* is not so much a landmark as a doorway, with the potential to become a floodgate.

## II. WHAT HAPPENED NEXT: 1877 TO THE PRESENT DAY—THE HISTORY OF DECEPTIVE SEX IN ENGLISH CRIMINAL LAW

The statute to which the court refers in *Flattery* was the 1285 Statute of Westminster (13 Edw 1 c 34), which stated that rape occurs 'if a man ravish a married woman, maid, or other woman, when she neither assented before

---

[2] ibid (QB Report), 413–14.
[3] *R v Case* (1850) 169 ER 381 (Crown Cases).
[4] *Flattery* (n 1) (QB Report). Cox's Criminal Cases in general contains the more detailed report, but this particular point is more apparent in the QB Report.
[5] *R v Barrow* (1868) Law Rep 1 CC 156 (Crown Cases).
[6] *Flattery* (n 1) (Cox CC) 391.
[7] See section III below.

nor after'. Originally rape was a capital offence, but by the mid-1830s, executions for capital felonies other than murder had almost ceased, and by the time Flattery was convicted, the punishment had been formally reduced (in 1841) to penal servitude or hard labour.[8] However, as Smith notes, until well into the nineteenth century, this also meant that prosecutions for rape were rare, given the ease of false accusations and difficulties of proof.[9] Although reduction in the severity of punishment reduced juries' reluctance to convict,[10] these difficulties persisted and they remain to a significant extent today, even though the sentence has been further reduced.

In addition, there were two legally contentious issues causing controversy at the start of the nineteenth century: whether rape required emission as well as penetration and proof of consent or lack thereof.[11] Lord Landsdowne's Act of 1828[12] settled the former question by establishing that emission was not required. The latter question was to some extent resolved on a procedural level by refining the rules of evidence, in particular those relating to the victim's character.[13] Of course, these developments did not address the more substantive and fundamental question at the heart of *Flattery* and the subsequent case law—namely, the extent to which absence of consent would be sufficient on its own, as opposed to a positive requirement of force and resistance. This further emphasises how striking the decision in *Flattery* is, where Mellor J in particular regards the requirement of resistance to prove lack of consent as a 'fallacy'. For him, the point is that the victim has been 'disarmed' 'by fraud', 'acquiescing under a misrepresentation ... only'. In other words, she has been deprived of even the choice whether to resist or not, which means a fortiori that her consent has been vitiated.[14]

This fact takes on particular significance when it is noted that the first statutory mention of deception in the context of sexual offences had actually preceded *Flattery*. Section 1 of the 1849 Protection of Women Act[15] contained an offence of 'procuring the defilement of women'. This was replaced by section 49 of the Offences Against the Person Act 1861, which contained the offence of 'procuring, by false pretences, false representations or other fraud, a girl under 21 to have illicit carnal connexion with any man'.[16]

---

[8] K Smith, 'Criminal Law' in W Cornish et al, *The Oxford History of the Laws of England, Vol XIII: 1820–1914* (Oxford, Oxford University Press, 2010) 401.

[9] ibid.

[10] Along with other factors leading to increased levels of prosecution, such as changing moral attitudes in the Victorian era, the increased presence of professional police forces and an expanding availability of specialised medical witnesses: ibid 403.

[11] ibid 402.

[12] 9 Geo IV c 31.

[13] Smith, 'Criminal Law' 401–04.

[14] *Flattery* (n 1) (Cox CC) 392.

[15] 12 & 13 Vict c 76.

[16] 24 & 25 Vict c 100.

It would therefore presumably have been possible for *Flattery* to have been charged under this section rather than with rape, but there is no discussion of that issue whatsoever in the report of the case.[17] Thus, *Flattery* is a significant landmark both in establishing the possibility of rape by deception and in choosing to deal with the issue of deception through the 'ordinary' provisions rather than that specifically enacted to deal with deception. That *Flattery* sets such a dual precedent can be seen by the subsequent decision of *R v Williams*.[18] Section 49 of the 1861 Act was in turn repealed and replaced by section 3 of the Criminal Law Amendment Act 1885, which provided that 'any person who ... (2) By false pretences or false representations procures any woman or girl, not being a common prostitute or of known immoral character, to have any unlawful carnal connexion, either within or without the Queen's dominions, shall be guilty of a misdemeanour', for which the maximum sentence was two years, and for which corroboration would be required as a matter of law, unlike for rape. However, this enactment had no more impact on the courts than had its predecessors, since it was confirmed in *R v Williams* (a case very similar to *Flattery*, in which the defendant convinced the victim that she was undergoing an operation to create an 'air passage') that the defendant would still be guilty of rape in such circumstances. (The 1885 Act also clarified, at the end of section 4 (which otherwise deals with punishments rather than substantive offences), that 'whereas doubts have been entertained whether a man who induces a married woman to permit him to have connexion with her by personating her husband is or is not guilty of rape, it is hereby enacted and declared that every such offender shall be deemed to be guilty of rape.')

The 1885 Act remained in force until 1956, when it was repealed completely by the Sexual Offences Act 1956. The 1956 Act in turn incorporated the two references to deception from the 1885 Act, providing first in section 1(2) that 'a man who induces a married woman to have sexual intercourse with him by impersonating her husband commits rape' and in section 3

---

[17] The Act of 1885 which succeeded that of 1849 was very much focused on the issue of public health and the deterrence of prostitution, and it is interesting on that front that it contained in clause 2 an offence of procuring a woman to be a common prostitute or to enter a brothel. Against that background, the clause 3 offence could potentially have been seen as being designed to deal with those who induced girls to have sex with a third party rather than with the defendant himself, which might explain why it was not used in two-party situations. However, against this interpretation is the fact that in the discussion in Parliament, Horace Davey (the Solicitor General at the time) drew a distinction between clause 2 and clause 3, emphasising that it was clause 2 which was aimed at the trade of procuring (Hansard, HC Deb 30 July 1885, vol 300, cols 596–97), while the discussion of clause 3, dealing with fraud: (a) concerned an offence which, having been initially enacted in 1849, pre-dated the 1885 Bill; and (b) discussed the overlap between the clause 3 offence in its threat/pressure form and the offence of rape, making it clear that it did pertain to the two-party situation rather than the 'trade of procuring' (Hansard, HC Deb 30 July 1885, vol 300, cols 597 and 623).

[18] *R v Williams* [1923] 1 KB 340.

that: 'It is an offence for a person to procure a woman, by false pretences, or false representations, to have unlawful sexual intercourse in any part of the world.' The section 1(2) husband impersonation provision was extended by the 1994 decision in *R v Elbekkay*[19] to include 'boyfriend', and this took on a double significance when in 1994, section 142 of the Criminal Justice and Public Order Act replaced section 1 of the 1956 Act with a section which included for the first time reference to male victims of rape. Although what was now section 1(3) of the amended 1956 Act still referred to impersonation of a married woman's husband, the existence of *Elbekkay* presumably[20] meant that gay men could also be protected from impersonation of their partners.

The criminalisation of deceptive sex seems not to have received a great deal of attention in Parliament during the enactment of these various pieces of legislation. In introducing the first (1849) Act, the Bishop of Oxford, Samuel Wilberforce, was at great pains to spare the House 'the details of the painful subject which rendered the measure necessary', trusting that 'the great necessity' of such legislation would be accepted.[21] The 1861 and 1956 Acts were then seen as principally involving codification and then consolidation, and in relation to the 1885 Act, the principal focus of discussion on the section related to the procurement by threats[22] rather than by false pretences, and the desirability of making the offence a misdemeanour only rather than a felony.[23] The only discussion of the latter related to the undesirability of rendering criminally liable those who did not realise that marriage between a widower and his deceased wife's sister would be illegal in England,[24] and questions of territorial jurisdiction.[25] Perhaps unsurprisingly, given the focus in *Flattery* and *Williams* on rape, the specific provisions were apparently not much used either. In debating the replacement of section 49 of the Offences Against the Person Act 1861 by the 1885 Act, Charles Hopwood, MP for Stockport, asked rhetorically whether any success had attended this provision of the law and whether there had been a single prosecution under it.[26] And a search of cases decided under section 3 of the 1956 Act reveals only *R v Jheeta*[27] (discussed further below), in addition to comments in both

---

[19] *R v Elbekkay* [1995] Crim LR 163 (CA).
[20] There seem to be no reported cases on the issue.
[21] Hansard, HL Deb 25 May 1849, vol 105, col 972.
[22] See, for example, the arguments of Mr Edward Clarke, MP for Plymouth, Hansard, HC Deb 30 July 1885, vol 300, cols 626–27.
[23] See, for example, the arguments of Mr Charles Hopwood, MP for Stockport, Hansard, HC Deb 30 July 1885, vol 300, cols 624–25.
[24] See, for example, the arguments of Mr Cavendish Bentinck, MP for Whitehaven, Hansard, HC Deb 31 July 1885, vol 300, col 701.
[25] See, eg, Hopwood (n 23).
[26] Hopwood, Hansard, HC Deb 9 July 1885, vol 299, col 200.
[27] *R v Jheeta* [2007] EWCA Crim 1699, [2008] 1 WLR 2582.

*R v Linekar*[28] and *R v Dica*[29] noting the absence of a charge under section 3 in either *Linekar* itself or *R v Clarence*,[30] in which the defendant was not convicted of rape despite transmitting gonorrhoea to his wife through sexual intercourse. In other words, whether or not there has been a specific deception-based offence available as an alternative and lesser charge, the history of the law has, with the exception of *Jheeta*, continued as it began in *Flattery*: either the defendant has been guilty of rape or he has not been found guilty of anything at all.

## III. THE CURRENT LAW ON DECEPTIVE SEX

Perhaps as a result of this lack of use, section 3 of the 1956 Act was not replaced in the 2003 Sexual Offences Act which repealed the 1956 Act.[31] Instead, the 2003 Act makes a lack of consent (and a lack of reasonable belief in consent) central to all offences such as rape (section 1), assault by penetration (section 2), sexual assault (section 3) etc. Consent is then defined generally in section 74 so that 'a person consents if he agrees by choice, and has the freedom and capacity to make that choice'. However, section 76 adopts the relatively unusual drafting technique of listing two circumstances in which it is to be 'conclusively presumed' 'that the victim did not consent to the relevant act' (section 76(a)) and 'that 'the defendant did not believe that the victim consented to the relevant act' (section 76(b)). Effectively, then, section 76 provides that the relevant offence will have been committed in circumstances where either (section 76(2)(a)) 'the defendant intentionally deceived the victim as to the nature or purpose of the relevant act' or (section 76(2)(b)) 'the defendant intentionally induced the victim to consent to the relevant act by impersonating a person known personally to the victim'. It is this section which has given rise to the apparently exponential growth rate of litigation in recent years and the current lack of clarity in the law. Nonetheless, it does at least seem possible to distil the following rules.

---

[28] *R v Linekar* [1995] QB 250 (CA) 261.

[29] *R v Dica* [2004] EWCA Crim 1103, [2004] QB 1257 [36].

[30] *R v Clarence* (1888) 22 QBD 23 (QBD).

[31] The absence of a new provision is evident from the decision in *R v Jheeta* (n 27), in which the defendant was charged with two counts of procuring by false pretences under s 3 of the 1956 Act in relation to the events which took place before the replacement of the 1956 Act with that of 2003, but with four counts of rape contrary to s 1 of the 2003 Act in relation to the conduct which took place after the legislative change. As Sir Igor Judge P notes in giving the judgment of the court, 'the allegations of rape arose in identical circumstances to the allegations of procuring sexual intercourse by false pretences' (at [2]).

## A. Section 76

### i. If There is a Positive Deception as to Nature, Purpose or Identity, This Will Raise the Conclusive Presumption of Section 76

The question, of course, is what each of these three words mean.

### a. Identity (Section 76(2)(b))

Identity is relatively straightforward and is apparently interpreted fairly restrictively. In *Devonald*,[32] the defendant's 16-year-old daughter had been in a relationship with the victim, a 16-year-old boy. To the distress of the daughter, the relationship had broken down and in response, the defendant assumed the identity of a 20-year-old female, 'Cassey', and corresponded with the complainant through the internet. 'Cassey' quickly began to make sexual demands of the victim and twice persuaded him to expose himself and masturbate in front of a webcam. The victim alleged that he only did so to provide sexual gratification for 'Cassey' and that he would never have done so had he known that the person watching was instead the 37-year-old father of his ex-girlfriend. The defendant for his part stated that he felt his daughter had been mistreated and he had thus intended to embarrass the defendant and teach him a lesson. The Crown argued that both section 76(2)(a) and section 76(2)(b) were applicable because the defendant had deceived the victim as to nature, purpose and identity. However, Leveson LJ, giving the judgment of the Court of Appeal,[33] preferred to concentrate only on intentional deceit as to the *purpose* of the relevant act rather than either identity or nature. This suggests that in practice, the identity provision will only have a very limited bite. Essentially, it seems, in the light of *Devonald*, only to apply to situations such as *Elbekkay*[34] under the old law, which it was enacted to cover. But in fact, in such cases the victim is often asleep, which would in any case raise a rebuttable presumption under section 75(2)(d) of the 2003 Act.[35]

---

[32] *R v Devonald* [2008] EWCA Crim 527.
[33] Which also included Mr Justice Hedley and Sir Peter Cresswell.
[34] *Elbekkay* (n 19).
[35] Section 75(1): 'If in proceedings for an offence to which this section applies it is proved— (a) that the defendant did the relevant act, (b) that any of the circumstances specified in sub- section (2) existed, and (c) that the defendant knew that those circumstances existed, the complainant is to be taken not to have consented to the relevant act unless sufficient evidence is adduced to raise an issue as to whether he consented, and the defendant is to be taken not to have reasonably believed that the complainant consented unless sufficient evidence is adduced to raise an issue as to whether he reasonably believed it. (2) The circumstances are that—... (d) the complainant was asleep or unconscious at the time of the relevant act.'

## b. Nature (Section 76(2)(a))

This is plainly *Flattery*'s statutory successor, covering cases such as *Flattery* and *Williams*,[36] in which the victims did not even know they were having sex. The court in *Devonald* also thought that it might apply to cases such as *R v Green*,[37] in which young men agreed to masturbate while wired up to monitors for the purposes of a bogus medical experiment to ascertain potential for impotence, or *R v Tabassum*,[38] in which women consented to participate in a breast cancer research programme when in fact the defendant conducting their physical examinations was not medically qualified or trained or conducting any such research. This would have extended the rule beyond that established by *Flattery* to cover cases in which the victims understood the nature of the touching, but thought that it was for medical purposes rather than for sexual gratification. However, the courts in both *Jheeta* and *Bingham*[39] thought that such cases should be regarded as falling into the third type of case caught by section 76, as follows.

## c. Purpose (Section 76(2)(a))

As the court in *Bingham*[40] suggests, it is not clear what exactly the word 'purpose' covers in this context. Herring has argued that it can and should be given a relatively wide interpretation, so that, for example, sex for the purpose of consummating a marriage, as in *Papadimitropoulos*,[41] would constitute rape if the defendant had deceived the victim as to the validity of the marriage.[42] *Devonald* fitted with this interpretation, in that the deception in that case (that the sex was for the purposes of gratification when in fact it was for the purpose of humiliating the victim) was held to be a deception as to purpose, which raised section 76. However, this result is somewhat out of line with the decision in *Jheeta*.[43] In this case, the defendant and the victim had been involved in a sexual relationship for some time when the victim began to receive threatening text messages and telephone calls. These were in fact from the defendant, but the victim did not know this and so told the defendant about them and allowed him to contact the police on her behalf. The defendant, of course, did no such thing, and instead sent the

---

[36] *R v Williams* (n 18).
[37] *R v Green* [2002] EWCA Crim 1501.
[38] *R v Tabassum* [2000] 2 Cr App R 328 (CA).
[39] *R v Bingham* [2013] EWCA Crim 823, [2013] 2 Cr App R 29. Bingham was another case involving deception as to identity over the internet, but this time it also involved blackmail regarding the resulting topless pictures of the victim.
[40] ibid [19].
[41] *Papadimitropoulos v R* (1957) 98 CLR 249 (HCA).
[42] J Herring, 'Mistaken Sex' [2005] *Crim LR* 511. See also J Herring, 'Human Rights and Rape: A Reply to Hyman Gross' [2007] *Crim LR* 228.
[43] *Jheeta* (n 27).

victim a series of false text messages purporting to be from a succession of police officers dealing with the investigation. He also obtained £700 from the victim for security protection which he pretended to arrange. Eventually the victim wanted to break off the relationship, but on approximately 50 occasions over a four-year period, the defendant, posing as a police officer, sent text messages to the claimant telling her to have sex with him, that the defendant had tried to kill himself and she should do her duty and take care of him, and that she would be liable to a fine if she did not have sex with him. On each occasion, the victim complied with the instructions, solely as a result of the text messages, but therefore as a result of both deception and pressure. Eventually the defendant sent lurid letters to the victim's home asserting her sexual promiscuity. This caused considerable distress to her family and finally led the victim to contact the police, leading to the defendant's arrest. In relation to the events which took place prior to the coming into force of the Sexual Offences Act 2003 on 30 April 2004, the defendant was charged under section 3(1) of the Sexual Offences Act 1956, but in relation to the later offences, he became the first recorded defendant to be dealt with under the new law. Initially he was advised to plead guilty to all the counts, including rape, under the 2003 Act on the basis that his admitted behaviour fell within the ambit of section 76. However, when he appealed against the sentence imposed on him, the Court of Appeal had more extensive concerns about whether the substantive law of the 2003 Act had been applied correctly and gave leave to appeal against conviction of these counts as well. Sir Igor Judge, P, giving the judgment of the Court of Appeal,[44] held that:

> In our judgment the ambit of section 76 is limited to the 'act' to which it is said to apply. In rape cases the 'act' is vaginal, anal or oral intercourse [ie, cases such as *Flattery*]. Provided this consideration is constantly borne in mind, it will be seen that section 76(2)(a) is relevant only to the comparatively rare cases where the defendant deliberately deceives the complainant about the *nature or purpose* of one or other form of intercourse. No conclusive presumptions arise merely because the complainant was deceived in some way or other by disingenuous blandishments or common or garden lies by the defendant. These may well be deceptive and persuasive, but they will rarely go to the nature or purpose of intercourse. Beyond this limited type of case, and assuming that, as here, section 75 has no application, the issue of consent must be addressed in the context of section 74.[45]

The court held that Jheeta's guilty plea and conviction were perfectly safe, given that the victim had not had a free choice to consent.

*Jheeta* therefore answers one question, but creates another in its place. When the 2003 Act was first passed, it was not clear what exactly the

---

[44] Also including Simon J and Judge Goldsack QC.
[45] *Jheeta* (n 27) [24].

relationship would be between sections 76 and 74. If a situation fell outside the specific conclusive presumptions of section 76, could it still be dealt with using the general consent provision in section 74? Or did the existence of section 76 impliedly mean that unless a situation was prohibited under that section, it should not be caught by the Act at all? Different academics took different views on this: Miles had argued that section 76 did impliedly exclude mistakes from the scope of section 74,[46] but Rook and Ward disagreed,[47] as did I.[48] The Court of Appeal decision in *Jheeta*[49] seems to go some way towards confirming this latter view, in that a situation held not to fall into section 76 was in that case held to fall into section 74 instead. *Jheeta* itself was of course not a straightforward deception case, but the decision in *Assange*[50] now confirms *Jheeta* on this point,[51] so it does appear as if deceptions which fall outside section 76 can instead be considered under the general consent provision of section 74. Indeed, in *Bingham*,[52] the Court of Appeal held that 'where, as here, a statutory provision effectively removes from an accused his only line of defence to a serious criminal charge, it must be strictly constructed'. 'So it will be a rare case in which section 76 is applied.' The combination of *Bingham* and *Assange* thus suggest that because the issues in section 76 lead to a conclusive presumption, although that section was specifically created to deal with issues of deception, in fact, a deliberate effort will be made to bring issues of deception *outside* section 76 into section 74 so that the question of consent is open to proof in the usual way.

So much for the question answered by *Jheeta*. As for the issue raised in its place, this concerns the status of the decision in *Devonald*. After all, if *Devonald* contained a deception as to purpose because the sex was actually for the purposes of humiliation rather than sexual gratification, why should *Jheeta* not also contain a deception as to purpose on the basis that the sex was for Jheeta's gratification rather than for the purpose of preventing his suicide, as the victim believed? In *Bingham*, the Court of Appeal (Hallett LJ) held that 'if there is any conflict between *Jheeta* and *Devonald*', it would 'unhesitatingly follow *Jheeta*', while the court in *McNally* somewhat resignedly left open the question 'whether and if so how *Jheeta*, *Devonald* and *Bingham* fit together'.

---

[46] J Miles, 'Sexual Offences: Consent, Capacity and Children' (2008) 10 *Archbold News* 6.
[47] His Honour Judge Peter Rook and Robert Ward CBE, *Rook and Ward on Sexual Offences Law and Practice*, 4th edn (London, Sweet & Maxwell, 2014) para 1.99.
[48] R Williams, 'Deception, Mistake and Vitiation of the Victim's Consent' (2008) 124 *LQR* 132, 145.
[49] *Jheeta* (n 27).
[50] *Assange v Sweden* [2011] EWHC 2849 (Admin) [78]–[91], discussed in section III.B.ii.
[51] ibid [88]–[91].
[52] *Bingham* (n 39).

The conclusion therefore seems to be that *Flattery* situations now count as a deception as to the nature of the act under section 76(2)(a), because V does not know that the nature of the act is sexual at all. If V knows that (s)he is experiencing some (potentially) sexual conduct, but thinks that this is for medical rather than sexual purposes (as in *Tabassum*[53] and *Green*),[54] this will count as a deception as to purpose. But if this is so, then it is not clear why we need references to both nature *and* purpose. Certainly, the victims in *Flattery* and *Williams* were deceived as to the purpose of the act as well as to its nature.

In any case, all other deceptions now seem likely to fall outside section 76 altogether and into the general provision of section 74 where the question of consent is open to proof in the usual way.

## B. Section 74

Within this more general provision, the law is, if anything, even more entangled, but seems to operate as follows.

### i. If There is an Active Deception as to Subject Matter Which Does Not Fall within Section 76, it May Still be Caught by the Act under Section 74

This seems to be the implication of three cases, the first of which is *Jheeta*. The second case to give this impression is *Assange*,[55] a case which arose under the dual criminality provisions of the European Arrest Warrant.[56] Here the High Court held that if D deceived V into believing he was wearing a condom when in fact he was not, this should be caught by section 74 rather than section 76.[57] It might be argued, the court accepted, that sex with a condom was fundamentally different in nature from unprotected sex, but the conclusive presumption of section 76 meant that it should be given a 'stringent construction' and thus the case should be dealt with under section 74 instead.[58]

The third and most difficult of the three cases is that of *McNally*.[59] The defendant was born female and conducted an internet relationship with

---

[53] *Tabassum* (n 38).

[54] *Green* (n 37).

[55] *Assange* (n 50).

[56] These are the provisions which apply to the non-framework offences; see further ibid [59]. In such cases, the offence must be an offence in England and Wales as well as in the country issuing the warrant.

[57] Rook and Ward, *Sexual Offences Law* para 87.

[58] ibid.

[59] *R v McNally* [2013] EWCA Crim 1051, [2014] QB 593.

the female victim, the defendant purporting to be a boy called Scott. When
the defendant was 17 and the victim just 16, some three years after the start
of the relationship, the defendant, presenting herself as a boy, visited the
complainant. Over the following months, the defendant visited the victim
on four occasions. There was one allegation that the victim was penetrated
with a dildo, which was denied and not pursued, so that all the counts of
sexual contact which were found to have taken place involved oral and
digital penetration of the victim. On the fourth and final visit, the victim's
mother confronted the couple with the fact that she believed the defendant to be a girl, at which point the defendant admitted this. The victim
was described as feeling physically sick at the revelation and stated that she
considered herself heterosexual and had only consented to the sexual acts
on the basis that they were taking place with a boy called Scott, which was
consistent with evidence that the victim had bought condoms in anticipation
of their having full intercourse.

D was charged under section 2 of the Sexual Offences Act 2003 (assault by
penetration) and Leveson LJ, giving the judgment of the Court of Appeal,[60]
held that:

> [W]hile in a physical sense, the acts of assault by penetration of the vagina are the
> same whether perpetrated by a male or a female, the sexual nature of the acts is, in
> any common sense view, different where the complainant is deliberately deceived
> by a defendant into believing that the latter is a male. Assuming the facts to be
> proved as alleged, M chose to have sexual encounters with a boy and her prefer-
> ence (her freedom to choose whether or not to have a sexual encounter with a girl)
> was removed by the defendant's deception.[61]

'[D]eception as to gender', concluded the Court, 'can vitiate consent' and
therefore the defendant had not been wrongly advised when she chose to
plead guilty.

The decision in *McNally* has given rise to problems on two fronts. First,
Sharpe challenges the idea that such defendants are actually engaging in
deception at all, since they identify as male, and there is 'nothing fabricated
about their feelings or performance of masculinity, or at least none more
so than in the case of cisgender men'.[62] Second, although the decision in
*McNally* adds to *Flattery* by opening the door to instances of sexual assault
by fraud more widely, it does not regard the door as completely open. 'In
reality', says the Court, 'some deceptions (such as, for example, in relation
to wealth) will obviously not be sufficient to vitiate consent', suggesting
instead that 'the evidence relating to "choice" and the "freedom"' to make

[60] Which also included Kenneth Parker and Stewart JJ.
[61] *McNally* (n 59) [26].
[62] A Sharpe, 'Criminalising Sexual Intimacy: Transgender Defendants and the Legal
Construction of Non-consent', [2014] *Crim LR* 207, 215. Sharpe also discusses the case of
*R v Wilson (Christopher)* unreported, 6 March 2013, Scotland.

any particular choice must be approached in a broad, commonsense way'.[63] The difficulty with this approach is that it is not possible to predict with any certainty which 'active deceptions'[64] will count as vitiating V's consent under section 74 and which will not.

### ii. If V Positively Specifies a Condition, without Fulfilment of Which (S)he Will Not Consent to the Contact, Failure to Comply with this Condition Will Vitiate Consent under Section 74

In *Assange*, the court held that where the victim 'had made clear that she would only consent to sexual intercourse if Mr Assange used a condom', there was as a result 'no consent if, without her consent, he did not use a condom, or removed or tore the condom without her consent'.[65]

This appears to be confirmed by the decision in *R(F) v DPP*.[66] In this case, D deliberately ejaculated inside V knowing that she did not want him to do so because she did not want to become pregnant again. A decision was taken not to prosecute D and V was granted leave to bring a judicial review of that decision. The court held that V was deprived of choice relating to a crucial feature on which her original intent was based, thus negating her consent.

*Assange* and *F* may seem relatively straightforward, but in fact they too raise various questions. Their conclusions arose, at least in part, because in *R v B*,[67] the court had held (following earlier cases such as *Clarence*[68] and *Dica*)[69] that a failure to disclose one's HIV positive status would not vitiate consent to sex (though non-consensual transmission of the disease could, following *Dica*, amount to grievous bodily harm). The court in *Assange* needed to distinguish the decision in *B* if Assange were to be potentially liable for an offence in England as well as Sweden, and there may be other pragmatic reasons to support the rule,[70] but it is difficult to justify the rule from a more conceptual perspective.

It is not clear what authority the courts have for apparently creating this 'positive condition' rule from section 74, since nothing in that section suggests that a potential victim's ability to 'agree by choice with the freedom and capacity to make that choice' is infringed in circumstances where (s)he has specified a particular condition, but not in circumstances where (s)he has not, and neither court does anything to explain this in any detail.

---

[63] *McNally* (n 59) [25].
[64] ibid [21].
[65] *Assange* (n 50) [86].
[66] *R(F) v DPP and A* [2013] EWHC 945 (Admin), [2014] QB 581.
[67] *R v B* [2006] EWCA Crim 2495, [2007] 1 WLR 1567.
[68] *Clarence* (n 30).
[69] *Dica* (n 29).
[70] See further n 93 and surrounding text.

For example, the implication of this distinguishing of *B* is that if in *B* the victim had specifically told the defendant that she would only consent to sex on the basis that D was HIV negative, the case could have been one of rape after all.[71] This is also consistent with the reasoning in *B* itself, which specifically left open the question of positive deception. But it is not clear as a matter of policy whether this is desirable. Why should a defendant for the purposes of the Sexual Offences Act 2003 be permitted to assume that if a V cared about D's HIV status, V would have specified this as a condition on which agreement to sex would be based? This question is particularly pertinent when the law has adopted the opposite view in the context of the Offences Against the Person Act 1861.[72]

Second, the court in *Assange*[73] cited the case of *Linekar*,[74] decided under the 1956 Sexual Offences Act. In *Linekar*, the Court of Appeal quashed the conviction of a man who had never intended to pay a prostitute with whom he had had sexual intercourse after she had agreed to sexual intercourse for £25. The Court in *Assange* does not suggest that this case would be decided any differently under the new law and, indeed it was not referred to in either the arguments or the decision in *R(F) v DPP*. But what was the discussion about payment in *Linekar* if it was not an express condition precedent to sex imposed by the victim? *Linekar* could, of course, be distinguished from *Assange* on the basis that the *Linekar* condition was unlawful (which would perhaps be an unfortunate echo of the fact that the original 1885 section 3 deception offence had not been applicable to 'common prostitutes' or girls 'of known immoral character'). Alternatively, *Linekar* could be distinguished on the basis that the defendant actually only decided not to pay after the sex rather than before or during it. But given that such distinctions were not in fact drawn in *Assange*, as things now stand, Linekar would now commit rape on the basis of *Assange* and *F*. It is not at all clear from its citation of the case at paragraph [80] that the court in *Assange* was aware of this implication of its decision. Here again, then, we are left with uncertainty as to the width of the rule established by *Assange* and *F*. Will any positive specification of a condition suffice to vitiate consent if that condition is not fulfilled? Or will we, as with 'active deceptions' of the kind at issue in *McNally*, have to draw 'common sense' lines and, if so, where does common sense dictate that those lines should be drawn? Would *Linekar* be inside it or outside?

---

[71] Presumably the same would also hold true for an 'active deception'.
[72] *Dica* (n 29); and *R v Konzani* [2005] EWCA Crim 706, [2005] 2 Cr App R 14.
[73] *Assange* (n 50) [80].
[74] *Linekar* (n 28).

*iii. If, However, D Simply Fails to Disclose Something But for Which*
   *V Would Not Have Consented, This Does Not Vitiate Consent*

This appears to be the implication of *R v B* as analysed and distinguished in
*Assange*. It is not completely clear whether this is true for all mistakes, for
example, a failure by D to disclose identity, nature or purpose,[75] but since
in principle there would be no obvious way to distinguish such cases from
*B*, this tends to suggest that even these mistakes would not suffice to vitiate
consent.

## IV. THE CURRENT LAW: AN ASSESSMENT

What these cases demonstrate, therefore, is that this area of law continues to
be governed by haphazard and unprincipled reasoning, driven in part by the
Sexual Offences Act 2003 itself, but also by the lack of an overall guiding
principle in the case law. This does not leave the law in a particularly satisfactory or coherent state. The HIV status of the other party is perhaps the
one thing most people would prioritise above all others in deciding whether
or not to consent to sexual contact, and yet unless D positively deceives V
about it or V has expressly pointed this out to D (*Assange* interpreting *B*), V's
consent will not be deemed to have been vitiated for the purposes of section 74,
never mind the fact that it does not appear at all in section 76. Conversely,
there are those for whom the identity of their sexual partner is not even
a necessary condition of consent to contact, and yet if it does matter and
D deceives V about it, it is one of the selected matters which will raise the
section 76 conclusive presumption. Nor is it clear why a victim's consent
should be regarded as vitiated when that mistake was brought about by
deception or when V has expressly raised the relevant issue with D, but not
otherwise.

   Second, the law is, as a result also relatively unpredictable. In principle,
following the enactment of the 2003 Act, *Jheeta* could have been decided
on the basis of section 76 (as Herring argued)[76] or section 74, or neither, if
Miles had been correct that what did not fall into section 76 could not therefore fall into 74.[77] Once *Jheeta* had been decided as it was, it would then
have been difficult to predict the result in *Devonald*, given the discrepancy
between those two cases as noted above. And, indeed, doubt has now been

---

[75] This would apparently not count as a deception for the purposes of s 76, although it may
do in other contexts such as fraud. See, for example, the decision of *R v Rai* [2000] 1 Cr App
R 242 (CA) or *R v Barnard* (1837) 173 ER 342 (Assizes). These cases were decided prior to the
enactment of the Fraud Act 2006, but there is no reason to think that that statute narrowed
liability on this point, its more general impact being to widen liability.
[76] Herring, 'Mistaken Sex'.
[77] Miles, 'Sexual Offences'.

cast on *Devonald* by *Bingham*, meaning that we now cannot be completely sure of the validity of *Devonald*. And nothing in any of the decided cases, and in particular in *B* itself, could have led easily to the prediction that HIV status/condom use would count as long as the victim made this expressly clear, yet this was what the court decided in *Assange*. Indeed, the result in *Linekar*, confirmed in *Jheeta*, might well have suggested the complete opposite, and of course following *Assange*, the current status of *Linekar* is therefore uncertain too. Obviously it could be argued that this is not a huge problem; defendants in this area who turn out to fall foul of the law might be thought likely to fit within the so-called 'thin ice' principle.[78] But even if this is accepted,[79] certainty is still important so that defendants know how to plead, as several of the cases discussed here demonstrate.[80]

## V.   *R V FLATTERY*: A LANDMARK, A DOOR OR A FLOODGATE?

The reason for the lack of clarity and unpredictability in the current law is not hard to find: *Flattery* and subsequent developments raise a challenge which is easy to state, but much more difficult to solve. If the victim would not have consented to the sexual activity but for a particular condition, and that condition is absent, then the victim did not consent to the sexual activity. And if, as Field J puts it, for the purposes of rape, 'the question is one of consent, or not consent',[81] then *all* instances of sex-by-deception are by definition sex offences. The door opened by *Flattery* thus becomes a floodgate and there is no coherent analytical means by which its impact can be limited. Even in *Flattery* itself, as noted above, the court declined to distinguish the case of *R v Barrow*,[82] a case in which the victim had consented to sex, albeit with a different person.

The difficulties of limiting the impact of *Flattery* can be easily seen by examining the three cases discussed above in relation to *Flattery*'s statutory successor, section 76(2)(a) of the Sexual Offences Act 2003. We might take Huddleston B's suggestion that cases such as *Flattery*[83] can be distinguished from all other deceptions on the basis that *Flattery* concerns the most fundamental kind of 'fraud in the factum'.[84] But then we might wonder how *Tabassum*'s case should be categorised. After all, Tabassum's victims did know that their breasts were being examined, just as Lavinia Thompson must

---

[78] See Lord Morris in *Knuller v DPP* [1973] AC 435 (HL) 463.

[79] And for the counter-arguments, see AJ Ashworth, 'Interpreting Criminal Statutes: A Crisis of Legality?' (1991) 107 *LQR* 419, 428.

[80] See, eg, *McNally* (n 59); and *Jheeta* (n 27).

[81] *Flattery* (n 1) (QB Report) 414. For a contrasting view from the US, see R West, 'A Comment on Consent, Sex and Rape' (1996) 2 *Legal Theory* 233.

[82] *Barrow* (n 5).

[83] And, on similar facts, *Williams* (n 18).

[84] See further Williams, 'Deception, Mistake'.

have known which parts of her anatomy were being touched by Flattery; it is just that, like Lavinia Thompson, Tabassum's victims thought that the process was a medical examination rather than a sexual touching. And if we therefore group *Tabassum* under the same heading as *Flattery*, does this mean that all instances of touching for sexual gratification are therefore fundamentally different in nature from touching for medical purposes? And, if so, then do we not also have to bring *Green*'s case under the umbrella too? In *Green*'s case, the victims may have known that they were undertaking sexual activity, but they did so on the basis that it was for medical purposes rather than the defendant's sexual gratification, and so the basis for distinguishing them from Lavinia Thompson is more difficult than might at first be thought; indeed, section 76(2)(a) itself groups deceptions as to 'purpose' alongside deceptions as to 'nature'. But, of course, once we have then let in deceptions as to 'purpose', it is difficult to exclude, as Herring has argued, deceptions as to sex 'for the purpose of consummating a marriage'[85] and so on.

## A. Option 1: All 'But for' Misapprehensions Vitiate Consent

We could react to this 'floodgate' or 'slippery slope' effect in several different ways. One option (that advocated by Herring himself) is simply to leave the floodgates open, so that we do indeed conclude that any 'but for' misapprehension on the part of the victim vitiates consent for the purposes of criminal law.[86] Some jurisdictions apparently adopt precisely this approach.[87] However, as I have argued elsewhere,[88] it has two significant drawbacks.

First, there is no requirement that the victim's assumption be in any way reasonable or desirable. What if the victim is anti-Semitic and argues that (s)he would never have had sex with the defendant if (s)he had known that the defendant was Jewish?[89] Under the pure 'but for' approach, this is at least the actus reus of rape.

---

[85] See further Herring, 'Mistaken Sex'.

[86] See also J Herring, 'Consent in the Criminal Law: The Importance of Relationality and Responsibility' in A Reed and M Bohlander (eds), *General Defences in Criminal Law* (Farnham, Ashgate, 2014).

[87] Rubenfeld notes that in Tennessee, 'rape is already defined to include "sexual penetration ... accomplished by fraud"' (citing Tenn Code Ann § 39-13-503(a)(4)(2010), that in *State of Israel v Kashour* (Crim C (Jer) 561/08) 19 July 2010, the Supreme Court of Israel upheld the rape conviction of an Arab man who had posed as a Jewish bachelor interested in a serious romantic relationship with the victim, and that in Canada, L'Heureux-Dubé held in *R v Cuerrier* [1998] 2 SCR 371, 374 that rape is committed wherever sex is procured through 'dishonesty'. J Rubenfeld, 'The Riddle of Rape-by-Deception and the Myth of Sexual Autonomy' (2013) 122 *Yale Law Journal* 1375.

[88] Williams, 'Deception, Mistake'.

[89] Facts not hugely removed from those at issue in *State of Israel v Kashour* (n 87). Sharpe, 'Criminalising Sexual Intimacy' sees the decision in *McNally* as an instance of a similar kind of prejudice.

Second, and connectedly, it is worth noting that section 76, the developments under section 74 and the jurisdictions which have taken the wide approach that Herring advocates all focus principally on situations in which the defendant has 'actively deceived' the victim (as the Court of Appeal put it in *McNally*)[90] or, at least, like *Assange*, situations in which the victim has consented only on the basis of a condition made explicit to the defendant.[91] But, in fact, the source of the victim's misapprehension is completely irrelevant to his or her lack of consent. If V would not have consented had (s)he known the truth, then (s)he does not consent, regardless of whether the misapprehension arose from the defendant's deception, the deception of a third party, a spontaneous mistake or any other imaginable source. From a conceptual point of view, therefore, the current exclusion of 'failure to tell' cases such as *R v B*[92] from the scope of the law is both difficult to defend and, as noted above, undesirable from a policy perspective.

However, it is conversely very easy to understand from a pragmatic perspective once it is recalled that the victim's lack of consent to the activity is only half of the picture. In addition to this actus reus, the prosecution must also prove mens rea, currently defined by the Sexual Offences Act 2003 as a lack of reasonable belief in consent on the part of the victim.[93] If the defendant 'actively deceived' the victim or the victim expressly stated the condition on which (s)he was consenting to the activity, and the defendant knows that the condition is not satisfied, lack of reasonable belief will be easy to prove. If, however, the defendant simply failed to tell the victim about something which in fact the victim regarded as a sine qua non of consent, the court then has to decide whether this omission and the consequential assumption of consent was 'reasonable'. Even if we could, for example, agree that it may be unreasonable to fail to disclose one's HIV positive status,[94] it may be more difficult to agree on D's duty to tell V of his/her gender identity[95] or religion. At what point ought D to know that a feature of his or her physical person, history or identity would be of significance to V's consent to sexual contact, such that a failure to disclose it would negate a reasonable belief in consent? When, in contrast, is D entitled to privacy or to present the best image of him or herself that (s)he can to the victim?

---

[90] *McNally* (n 59).

[91] *Assange* (n 50); and *F* (n 66).

[92] *B* (n 67).

[93] See, eg, Sexual Offences Act 2003, s 1(1)(c) and 1(2). Section 1(2) specifies that whether a belief is reasonable is to be determined having regard to all the circumstances, including any steps A has taken to ascertain whether B consents.

[94] Which would be consistent with the line taken in the law of offences against the person by both *Dica* (n 29) and *Konzani* (n 72), but which is disputed in that context by M Weait, 'Criminal Law and the Sexual Transmission of HIV: *R v Dica*' (2005) 68 *MLR* 121.

[95] See further Sharpe, 'Criminalising Sexual Intimacy'.

The conclusion is therefore as follows. From the point of view of conceptual coherence, whenever V would not have consented but for a condition which is not fulfilled, V does not consent, and this is so regardless of the source of V's belief that the condition was fulfilled. This therefore establishes the actus reus element, so that the 'reasonableness' element of the mens rea must do all the work of drawing the line between criminal and non-criminal conduct. However, since this would involve the courts making difficult and controversial judgments of morality and policy, they have avoided this logical outcome and have instead drawn what might otherwise be regarded as arbitrary lines within the actus reus between 'active deception'/positive specification by the victim on the one hand and simple failure to tell on the other, thereby manipulating the actus reus in order to avoid difficult questions in the context of mens rea.

## B. Option 2: Draw a Pragmatic Line

If for these reasons it therefore becomes impossible to open the floodgates completely, an alternative might be simply to accept that pure intellectual coherence cannot be reconciled with a desirable outcome in terms of public policy, and thus a pragmatic compromise between the two must be struck instead. The courts could therefore simply create a series of clearly delineated, justifiable and predictable categories in which a misapprehension by the victim would vitiate his or her consent.[96] It would not be an intellectually perfect solution, but if it were clear what kinds of misapprehension would vitiate consent, how these situations could be distinguished from others which would not count and why they had been chosen, and it could be demonstrated that the policy implications of adopting them were not too problematic, this could at least provide a predictable and acceptable solution.

This is, in a sense, what the courts did under the Sexual Offences Act 1956, when the only issues which would vitiate consent were impersonation of the victim's husband (section 1(2) of the Sexual Offences Act 1956) and *Flattery/Tabassum* cases.[97] Rubenfeld argues that these exceptions make perfect sense against the historical context of rape as defilement, where rape was not so much unconsented to sex as '*nonmarital* sex with a woman who had not consented to *that*'.[98] As he puts it, regardless of how deceived she

---

[96] This was the suggestion I made in a previous piece: Williams, 'Deception, Mistake'.

[97] Rubenfeld, 'Riddle of Rape-by-Deception' 1395 refers to these as being 'the only generally recognized situations in which Anglo-American courts convict for rape-by-deception' for 'over a hundred years'.

[98] ibid 1401.

might have been about any *other* facts or circumstances, if V had willingly had sex with a man to whom she was not married, she would have consented to the very act that rape law was supposed to protect her against.[99] Only deceptions which affected the two key features of the act (sexual nature and wedlock) would therefore vitiate consent. This certainly fits with the fact that Huddleston B did not rule out extension of the ruling in *Flattery* to *Barrow*-type cases of husband impersonation, though it fits less well with the reasoning actually used in the case, which focuses simply on the vitiation of Lavinia Thompson's consent, meaning that in this sense, *Flattery* was ahead of its time.

The problem may thus simply be that, while historically these limits may have made sense, to modern eyes, limiting the law to these particular exceptions is bizarre: why should *Tabassum* not come in alongside *Flattery*? Why should boyfriends and partners not be included as in *Elbekkay*? And if we have broken the link with marriage so that we are only concerned with identity, why are we including those situations at all if they do not involve a mistake in the factum? If we are therefore going to extend to some mistakes in the inducement rather than in the factum, why stop here? Why in particular single out a feature which might not concern some sexual participants at all (identity), while ruling out those which are likely to be of concern to everyone (HIV status)?[100]

Perhaps, then, the solution is thus simply to outline a new series of (admittedly pragmatic) exceptions which better reflect current societal values.[101] If this is the approach the courts wish to adopt, there is, as is evident from the tangled state of the current law, still a great deal of work to be done, but such an approach would be consistent with Leveson LJ's idea of 'common sense' line drawing. However, a third approach must also be considered.

## C. Option 3: Undo *Flattery*

### i. *Undo* Flattery *Completely*

There are two versions of this view. The first, most radical form is suggested by Rubenfeld, who argues that 'good reasons underlie the intuition that sex-by-deception is not rape, or, generally a crime'.[102] This is connected to

---

[99] ibid.

[100] I have no formal empirical data for this, but I have taught this topic to cohorts of 20–40 students every year for 12 years. Each year I poll them on whether they would prefer to be mistaken about their sexual partner's identity or HIV status. No one has ever chosen identity.

[101] See further Williams, 'Deception, Mistake'.

[102] Rubenfeld, 'Riddle of Rape-by-Deception' fn 185. Interestingly, the example he gives is concealing a transmissible disease.

the fact that, in his view, 'the supposed right of sexual autonomy is a myth and should be rejected'.[103] However, even Rubenfeld hints that he might be prepared to accept a pragmatic compromise of the kind outlined above, which means that in fact he is only arguing against the full 'floodgates' position, which was also rejected here.

### ii. Remove Flattery *from the Law of Rape But Make Sex-by-Deception a Different and Lesser Offence*

In the light of the lack of clarity and unpredictability in the current law, various commentators[104] have suggested that the situation could be resolved by the addition of an equivalent to section 3 of the 1956 Sexual Offences Act, which made it 'an offence for a person to procure a woman, by false pretences, or false representations, to have unlawful sexual intercourse in any part of the world'. But as the law stands at present, the existence of such an offence would be difficult to justify. What exactly would be the wrong at the heart of the offence? We cannot answer that question by reference to V's lack of consent, because then we are back where we started: if V does not consent, then it is rape and we do not need a section 3 offence. But, conversely, if we are not to define the wrong by reference to V's lack of consent, then what precisely is it?

This in turn is connected to the fact that the section 3 offence is really akin to fraud offences in the property context, but there is a fundamental difference between the way in which property offences and sexual offences are currently structured. In the context of the core sex offences,[105] as *Flattery* itself makes clear, the law draws one binary distinction: consent or not. The offences are then subdivided by the kind of physical activity which takes place (penetration by a penis,[106] by any other object,[107] sexual touching[108] etc), but the key distinction centres on the presence or absence of consent. In the law of property offences, by contrast, as Green has written, there are at least 13 ways to steal a bicycle.[109] We do not, in the core offences, focus on the type of property affected, but conversely we do distinguish not just between the presence or absence of consent, but also the *way in which* that consent was avoided, vitiated or otherwise negated. We distinguish not only between theft and fraud, but also between blackmail and robbery and so

---

[103] ibid 1413.

[104] See, eg, JR Spencer, 'Sex by Deception' (2013) 9 *Archbold Review* 6; and K Laird, 'Rapist or Rogue? Deception, Consent and the Sexual Offences Act 2003' (2014) 7 *Crim LR* 492.

[105] ie, those which can be perpetrated by anyone against anyone, rather than being for the protection of a specific class of persons, such as children.

[106] Sexual Offences Act 2003, s 1, 'Rape'.

[107] ibid, s 2, 'Assault by Penetration'.

[108] ibid, s 3, 'Sexual Assault'.

[109] S Green, *Thirteen Ways to Steal a Bicycle: Theft Law in the Information Age* (Cambridge, MA, Harvard University Press 2012).

on. There is, of course, no immediate reason why the law of sexual offences could not be structured in the same way. Thus, we might regard *Elbekkay*[110] and *Barrow*[111] situations as the equivalent of theft, because in those cases the victims did not even know that their rights were being violated to begin with. Rape by force would become the equivalent of robbery, while coercion short of force[112] would align with blackmail (as indeed seemed to be envisaged by the aspects of section 3 of the 1885 Act that dealt with threats as opposed to fraud).[113] Sex by deception could then certainly be dealt with by a fraud offence equivalent to section 3 of the 1956 Act, and *Linekar*[114] could be charged with making off without payment.[115] Indeed, it may very well be that the best option for solving the sex-by-deception problem would be to move to such a disaggregated and subtle structure for the law of sexual offences in general. However, this cannot simply be done by parachuting one category from the property scheme into the completely different sex offence scheme any more than it would be possible to solve a fruit/vegetables classificatory problem by introducing a category of 'green things'. It is perhaps for this very reason that the history of deceptive sex and rape has been the same regardless of whether an alternative deception offence has been available, as was first established in *Flattery* itself.

Finally, it is worth noting that even if we did adopt not just a replacement for section 3, but also the whole change of classificatory system that it would necessitate, this would not remove the difficult questions raised by the current approach. In the context of fraud offences, even under the narrower precursors to the current Fraud Act 2006, we did not distinguish between different kinds of causative deceptions; as long as the deception had caused the property transfer, this was sufficient.[116] It is entirely possible, therefore, that even in the property context, the law might have to wrestle with the possibility that V transferred property to D on the basis of a false declaration of love by D,[117] or a false statement by D about his or her gender identity, religion and so on. It should also be noted that those who are in favour of an equivalent to section 3 often focus on the fact that it would only cover 'active deceptions', or possibly knowing breach of condition, but certainly not failures to tell.[118] But if the two kinds of offences were to be brought into line with each other, this would make it all the more difficult

---

[110] *Elbekkay* (n 19).

[111] *Barrow* (n 5).

[112] Such as occurs in cases like *R v Kirk* [2008] EWCA Crim 434 [85]–[92].

[113] See in particular the contributions of Mr Charles Hopwood to the debate, above n 26.

[114] *Linekar* (n 28).

[115] Subject to policy limits based on the underlying illegality of the transaction.

[116] See now Fraud Act 2006, ss 1–4. For the previous law, see s 15 of the 1968 Theft Act, 'Obtaining Property by Deception'.

[117] Facts not so very far removed from those of *R v Hinks* [2001] 2 AC 241 (HL).

[118] See, eg, Spencer, 'Sex by Deception'.

to explain why in the context of property rights, a failure to tell *would* in some circumstances be sufficient,[119] while in the context of protecting sexual autonomy or self-determination, it would not. The structure of a section 3-style offence and its moral import might be different,[120] but the floodgates would still be open.

## VI. CONCLUSION

There is no question, therefore, that by opening the door to rape-by-deception as well as by force, *Flattery* became an important landmark in the history of English criminal law. Its logic is impeccable; 'the question is one of consent, or not consent',[121] and there can be no consent where the victim 'had been prevented by [the defendant's] fraud from exercising her judgment and will'.[122] The difficulty is that if this premise is accepted, the floodgates are open to the potential for *any* causative misapprehension on the part of the victim to vitiate consent, and yet if all such misapprehensions were to create the actus reus of rape, we would be left with very difficult decisions both in mens rea and policy terms.

The courts have responded to this by attempting to draw sharp lines in the case law, and yet these lines are often unpredictable in advance, and in retrospect are difficult to justify in terms of either logic or policy. Deceptions as to identity of the kind found in *Elbekkay* will raise the conclusive presumption under section 76(2)(a), but any other deceptions as to identity such as that found in *Devonald* will not. And yet one wonders whether section 76(2)(a) will therefore do much work, since in many such cases the victim will be asleep, thereby raising a rebuttable presumption under section 75(2)(d) instead. Deceptions of the kind found in *Flattery* and *Williams* will raise the conclusive presumptions of section 76(2)(b) on the basis that there has been deception as to the nature of the act, and yet in such cases there will also have been a deception as to purpose as in *Green*, so that one wonders why nature and purpose are both included. There is then a further lack of clarity concerning the precise scope of deception as to purpose, given the uncomfortable precedential relationship between *Devonald*, *Jheeta* and *Bingham*. Any other situations not relating to *Elbekkay* or *Flattery/ Williams/Green*-type situations will fall outside the conclusive presumptions of section 76 into the general provision on consent found in section 74.

---

[119] See above n 75.
[120] By analogy with the property context, see further Green, *Thirteen Ways*.
[121] *Flattery* (n 1) (QB Report) 414 (Field J).
[122] ibid 413 (Mellor J).

But here the defendant will only be found to have committed an offence if (s)he has positively deceived the victim (*Bingham*) or where there has been a positive specification of a sine qua non condition by the victim (*Assange* and *F*). And yet even here, there may be some (as yet unspecified) limits to the kinds of deception or condition which will count (as the decisions in *Bingham* and *Linekar* suggest). Simple failures to disclose will not lead to criminal liability. This is completely comprehensible in pragmatic terms, given that if they were to be accepted, this would shift attention to questions of mens rea and the defendant's reasonable belief in consent or lack thereof. But such decisions are very difficult to justify in terms of logic, rationality or coherence with the context of property offences, to which some commentators have suggested we move, at least by creating a section 3 procuring by deception offence.

The significance of *Flattery* as a landmark is therefore clear, but so is the challenge it sets us, and even today we are clearly a long way away from being able to meet that challenge.

# 9

# *DPP v Beard* (1920)

PHILIP HANDLER

I N JULY 1919, Arthur Beard raped and killed 12-year-old Ivy Wood
in Hyde, Cheshire. He was tried and convicted of murder at the Chester Assizes in October and sentenced to death. Beard appealed on the
grounds that the judge had misdirected the jury on the effects of his intoxication and on the scope of the felony-murder rule. When his appeal was
upheld in the Court of Criminal Appeal, the Director of Public Prosecutions
(DPP) took the unprecedented step of appealing to the House of Lords.[1]
Invited to rule on questions of substantive law for the first time since its
establishment as the final appellate criminal court in 1907, the House of
Lords restored the murder conviction.[2] In the leading speech, Lord Birkenhead LC set out the felony-murder rule in strict terms that made any killing
committed during the course of a violent felony murder. He also indicated,
albeit in unclear terms, that drunkenness could only serve as an excuse to
a criminal charge when the offence required proof of a specific intent. The
case had long-lasting effects. It became a landmark for judges seeking to reconcile orthodox subjective principles of mens rea with constructive liability
and the practical need to criminalise drunken violence. Lord Birkenhead's
ambiguous speech offered footholds for a range of approaches to these
problems. In *Majewski*, the House of Lords used one of those footholds to
establish the current rules on intoxication.[3] These have been the subject of

[1] *DPP v Beard* [1920] AC 479 (HL). Transcripts of proceedings at the trial, in the Court of
Criminal Appeal and House of Lords are in the DPP files: TNA: DPP 1/51B. They are also held
at the Parliamentary Archives: HL/PO/JU/4/3/697.
[2] There were four previous cases, all of which concerned questions of evidence or procedure:
*R v Ball* [1911] AC 47 (HL); *Leach v R* [1912] AC 305 (HL); *Felstead v R* [1914] AC 534
(HL); *Thompson v R* [1918] AC 221 (HL). Prior to the Court of Criminal Appeals Act 1907,
the House of Lords had a very limited general criminal jurisdiction by way of writ of error, but
in practice this had become obsolete by the middle of the nineteenth century (R Stevens, *Law
and Politics the House of Lords as a Judicial Body* (London, Weidenfeld & Nicolson, 1979)
38 fn 3).
[3] *DPP v Majewski* [1977] AC 443 (HL).

considerable debate and extensive criticism, but, despite a number of reform proposals, they remain law.[4]

This chapter does not offer an interpretation of *Beard* that supports any single approach to the familiar challenges that constructive liability and intoxication present.[5] It draws on recently released case files to consider its historical context and addresses some of the key issues that subsequent debates have overshadowed or obscured.[6] The case was decided at a time when understandings of criminal responsibility for violence and its relation to drunkenness and insanity were in flux. The Victorian emphasis on strict individual moral accountability for drunkenness and its consequences had been modified. In the last three decades of the nineteenth century, as consumption of alcohol and recorded violent crime fell, an understanding of drunkenness as a disease emerged. Habitual drunkards, or inebriates as they came to be known, required treatment, and could not be held fully accountable for their actions. By the 1890s, the view as expressed by one commentator that '[i]ntoxication is insanity pure and simple' had become orthodox in medical circles and gained acceptance among policy-makers, with even the Home Secretary publicly equating the two conditions.[7]

This blurred the distinction between insanity and drunkenness in courtrooms in the late nineteenth and early twentieth centuries, and prompted an increased tendency to combine the pleas. These issues came into sharp focus in the immediate aftermath of the First World War. In addition to the fears about rising crime and social disorder that accompanied demobilisation, there was widespread concern about the war's general brutalising effects and the psychological injuries that it had inflicted on participants. Beard was a 'shell-shocked' ex-serviceman who combined his traumatic war experience and drunkenness in his defence and appeal. His case brought the relationship between insanity, intoxication and criminal responsibility for fatal violence into sharp focus in the highest court of a nation struggling to come to terms with the violence of its immediate past.

---

[4] The literature on intoxication is very extensive. For a recent discussion, see R Williams, 'Voluntary Intoxication—A Lost Cause?' (2013) 129 *LQR* 264.

[5] For interpretations of *Beard* that do, see A Gold, 'An Untrimmed "Beard": The Law of Intoxication as a Defence to a Criminal Charge' (1976) 19 *Criminal Law Quarterly* 34; T Quigley, 'A Shorn Beard' (1986–87) 10 *Dalhousie Law Journal* 167.

[6] The Home Office files were released in 2014; see TNA: HO 144/20991. For the DPP and Assize records (in which items of evidence from the trial are preserved), see TNA: DPP 1/51B; TNA: ASSI 65/24/1. The House of Lords files contain little that is not in the DPP files; see Parliamentary Archives: HL/PO/JU/4/3/697. For Beard's prison records, see TNA: PCOM 8/352.

[7] JF Sutherland, 'The Jurisprudence of Intoxication' (1898) 10 *Juridical Review* 309, 310; *The Times* (London, 6 December 1893) 3. The medical superintendent at Broadmoor expressed a similar view in 1924: W Sullivan, *Crime and Insanity* (London, Arnold, 1924) 60. See generally P Handler, 'Intoxication and Criminal Responsibility in England, 1819–1920' (2013) 33 *Oxford Journal of Legal Studies*, 243, 254–58.

## I. THE CRIME[8]

Beard served in the marines during the war. After his demobilisation in April 1919, he found work in his home town of Hyde as a night watchman at the Carr Field cotton mill. Ivy Wood lived very close to the mill with her parents at their hairdressing shop. She was well known in the locality for her fund-raising efforts for the Red Cross and her participation as a singer and dancer in local events for relatives of those in service.[9] On the evening of 25 July 1919, she was sent by her father on an errand to another local hairdresser. On her way home, at about 6.30 pm, she was seen entering the gate of the mill by a 14-year-old boy, Ernest Gosling, who knew her well.

Beard had spent the week drinking heavily. On the afternoon of 25 July, he had been drinking with Charles Jones, an engineer, also from Hyde. They parted at around 3 pm and agreed to meet later to attend a meeting of the Stockport and District Enginemen's and Firemen's Union. Beard purchased a bottle of whisky, part of which he consumed in the street before going to work at 5.30 pm. Beard's supervising officer, Albert Clegg, left him alone in the mill at around 6.15 pm and afterwards testified that at that point, he was fit to work and not drunk.[10]

In his first statement to the police, Beard claimed to have discovered Wood's body near the perimeter wall of the mill and carried her back to the lodge. This was viewed as implausible by the police and Beard was detained. The arrival of two officers from Scotland Yard the next day prompted a second statement in which Beard confessed. He admitted that he had gone out to look for Jones at around 6.30 pm, had seen Wood and had offered to show her round the mill. He had struggled with her and then taken her to the pump room where he 'got her down and she seemed to get unconscious'.[11] He left her there and returned to the lodge where he met with Jones about 6.40 pm. They had some whisky together before going to the Navigation hotel where Beard was admitted to the Union. After further drinking, Beard returned to the mill at around 10 pm, but had little recollection of what he did before 1.30 am, when he went on his rounds and found Wood lying dead in the pump room. His proffered excuse to the police neatly captured the legal basis for his defence and highlights the indistinct boundary between intoxication and insanity at the time: 'I should not have injured the girl in any way if I had not been sodden and mad with drink.'[12]

---

[8] The account of the crime presented here is based on the transcript of proceedings before the coroners and magistrates and at the trial. See *DPP v Beard Trial and Court of Criminal Appeal Transcript* (hereinafter *Trial and CCA Transcript*) TNA: DPP 1/51B 8–127.

[9] See *The Times* (London, 29 July 1919) 9; *North Cheshire Herald* (Hyde, 1 August 1919) 8–10.

[10] Beard claimed Clegg was lying because they had been drinking together the night before instead of working. See *Notice of Appeal*, TNA: HO 144/20991; *Trial and CCA Transcript* 130.

[11] *Trial and CCA Transcript* 122.

[12] ibid 123.

News of Beard's crime broke in a post-war nation that was 'haunted by the fear that violence had slipped its chains—by the fear that the ex-servicemen, the general public, the state or perhaps all three, had been irrevocably "brutalized" by the mass carnage' of the war.[13] The press carried regular reports of violence involving ex-soldiers in 1919. The weekend before Beard's crime, peace day celebrations in towns and cities across the country had been marred by violence and rioting.[14] In the preceding week, the *Daily Herald* reported an 'epidemic of violence and atrocious murder' throughout the country, which was the 'crop of the last four and a half years of slaughter'. The war, it contended, 'had altered the moral aspect of the country at large and sown such seeds of perversion and lust for violence that the crop will be heavy and bitter'.[15]

There was, in fact, no marked or unequivocal increase in violent crime generally or among those from the armed services.[16] The press sensationalised violent crime, but there was no consequent 'moral panic' focused on ex-servicemen. There was little appetite for newspaper campaigns vilifying veterans who had fought for four and a half years and emerged victorious.[17] The involvement of soldiers and ex-servicemen in crime or in civil unrest was a visible manifestation of more pervasive brutalising effects for which individuals could not be held wholly responsible. At the memorial service for Ivy Wood, the minister sermonised on the generally lowered moral standards consequent upon war and the fact that 'we had cultivated hatred and had sharpened passion to the point of destroying human life'.[18]

The term that captured this sense of collective trauma was 'shell-shock'. First diagnosed as a medical condition in the middle of the war, by 1919, the term had acquired a widespread cultural influence such that it became a 'metaphor for the nature of industrialised warfare'.[19] Action that would have been attributed to cowardice and lack of courage at the beginning of the war came to be recognised as a consequence of 'shell-shock'. Viscount Haldane, a member of the War Office Committee of Enquiry into 'Shell-shock'

[13] J Lawrence, 'Forging a Peaceable Kingdom: War, Violence, and Fear of Brutalization in Post-First World War Britain' (2003) 75 *Journal of Modern History* 557.

[14] See ibid 566–71. Beard's week of drinking in the run-up to his crime may well have begun with peace day celebrations in Hyde the previous weekend. See *North Cheshire Herald* (Hyde, 18 July 1919) 6.

[15] *Daily Herald* (London, 19 July 1919), as quoted in C Emsley, 'Violent Crime in England in 1919: Post-war Anxieties and Press Narratives' (2008) 23 *Continuity and Change* 173, 176.

[16] For the figures, see Emsley, 'Violent Crime' 176–82. A Metropolitan Police report in 1919 remarked upon the low incidence of violence despite the frequency of 'shell-shock'. See *Report of the Commissioner of the Police of the Metropolis for the Years 1918 and 1919* (Cmnd 543, 1920) 901, 11.

[17] See Emsley, 'Violent Crime' 173–76.

[18] 'Effect of War on Morals' *Manchester Guardian* (Manchester, 4 August 1919) 10; *North Cheshire Herald* (Hyde, 8 August 1919) 1.

[19] J Winter, 'Shell-Shock and the Cultural History of the Great War' (2000) 35 *Journal of Contemporary History* 7, 8.

(1920–22) and one of the Law Lords who heard Beard's appeal, admitted that military courts had done injustices in the early years of the war before shell-shock was understood.[20] The condition undermined pre-war beliefs about manliness, strength of character and willpower, and it unsettled contemporary views of insanity and mental illness. It 'was a legal, medical and moral half-way house in a society used to a clear division between the mad and the sane'.[21]

Shell-shock did not fit easily within the *M'Naghten Rules*, which marked the division between sanity and insanity in the criminal courts.[22] While it was not always a basis for an insanity plea, the condition became a standard trope in defences, offered as a means of excusing, explaining or mitigating conduct.[23] A Prison Commission report in 1920 noted one prison medical officer's evidence of the 'large use now made of "shell-shock" as an excuse for criminal acts'. He suggested that it was 'used as a catchword, and has taken the place of the "drink" excuse', but there was 'great difficulty' in identifying genuine cases and estimating the value of the excuse.[24] The proportion of those charged with murder who were found guilty but insane or unfit to plead by reason of insanity rose only modestly in 1919.[25] There was, nonetheless, a contemporary perception that the plea was being used far more frequently and that many were based on shell-shock. A 'medical correspondent' to *The Times* warned that 'no degree of caution in avoiding hostility to such pleas was excessive'.[26] Judges did not all share this view. One senior criminal law judge directed an Old Bailey jury: 'It was most necessary that it should be known what insanity in the legal sense was, and to uphold it, because there were no end of people now who were trying to trifle it away and allow persons in certain circumstances, particularly those in khaki, to kill others with little or no excuse.'[27]

Beard's case brought these tensions and themes sharply into focus. Biographical details began to emerge in the press soon after the crime was reported that reinforced anxieties about the brutalising effects of war. Beard

---

[20] 5 *Parliamentary Debates* 39, 1095 *House of Lords* 1105, as quoted in T Bogacz, 'War Neurosis and Cultural Change, 1914–1922: The Work of the War Office Committee of Enquiry into Shell-Shock' (1989) 24 *Journal of Contemporary History* 227, 228.

[21] Bogacz, 'War Neurosis' 229.

[22] *M'Naghten* (1843) 10 Cl & F 200, 210, 8 ER 718, 722. See the contribution by Loughnan in this volume.

[23] For the use of the shell-shock defence in trials, see C Emsley, *Soldier, Sailor, Beggarman, Thief: Crime and the British Armed Services since 1914* (Oxford, Oxford University Press, 2013) 148–59.

[24] *Report of the Commissioners of Prisons and the Directors of Convict Prisons* (Cmnd 972, 1920) 21.

[25] See *Report of the Committee on Insanity and Crime* (Cmnd 2005, 1923) 25.

[26] *The Times* (London, 15 October 1920) 7.

[27] *R v Pank*, *The Times* (London, 22 May 1919) 9 (Central Criminal Court), Darling J. For similar comments, see *R v Lucas*, *The Times* (London, 16 January 1920) 5 (CCC).

was from a good, stable family, which was well known in the locality.[28] He spent much of his time in service at sea, but in July 1917, he suffered a severe shock when HMS *Vanguard* exploded very near to his own ship, HMS *Warspite*, while both were moored at Scapa Flow. The explosion killed over 800 men, some of whom were flung into the water near to the *Warspite*.[29] According to Beard's own account, he was so affected by the experience that he sought land service. He served at the front in France from October 1917 until the end of the war, during which time he suffered trench fever and was gassed and rendered mute for a day.[30] On demobilisation, he was discharged with good character, but, although he found work at the mill, he had difficulty adjusting to civilian life and he increasingly turned to drink.

Here was a second feature of Beard's case that touched a controversial and sensitive contemporary issue. The war years witnessed what one historian has described as a 'national hysteria' on the issue of drink.[31] David Lloyd George, the Chancellor of the Exchequer, commented in 1915 that: 'We are fighting Germany, Austria and Drink; and, as far as I can see, the greatest of these three deadly foes is Drink.'[32] Fears centred upon the debilitating effects of alcohol on national efficiency and the war effort. This led to increased regulation of the drinks trade, accelerating a policy that had emerged in the nineteenth century and aimed at controlling the environment for drinking in order to minimise its effects. This contrasted with the dominant feature of policy in the first half of the Victorian period, which focused on individual moral discipline as the most effective safeguard against drink.[33] In the early decades of the twentieth century, the habitual drunkard was a weak figure, a victim of social circumstances and environment. Ex-servicemen like Beard were peculiarly vulnerable and it was therefore deemed particularly important to restrict their access to alcohol and to deal with drunkenness within the armed forces.[34] A report cited by the Prison Commission warned that it was not possible to overemphasise the 'menace to the community' of returning servicemen with shell-shock having access to drink.[35]

---

[28] The Chief Constable of Hyde gave evidence that his mother was 'one of the most respectable' women in the community; see *Trial and CCA Transcript* 90.

[29] The accident was one of the worst of the war; see W Schleihauf, 'Disaster in Harbour: The Loss of HMS Vanguard' (2000) 10 *Northern Mariner* 57.

[30] *North Cheshire Herald* (Hyde, 31 October 1919) 8; *Special Report to the Chief Constable of Hyde on Arthur Beard's Antecedents* (30 October 1919) TNA: HO 144/20991.

[31] J Greenaway, *Drink and British Politics since 1830: A Study in Policy Making* (Basingstoke, Palgrave Macmillan, 2003) 91.

[32] *The Times* (London, 30 March 1915) 11, quoted in Greenaway, *Drink and British Politics* 94–95.

[33] See Greenaway, *Drink and British Politics* 7–52; B Harrison, *Drink and the Victorians: The Temperance Question in England 1815–1872*, 2nd edn (Keele, Keele University Press, 1994).

[34] On drunkenness in the armed services, see Emsley, *Soldier, Sailor* 71–81.

[35] *Report of the Commissioners of Prisons and the Directors of Convict Prisons, with Appendices* (Cmnd 374, 1919) 16.

## II. TRIAL AND APPEAL

Beard was charged with murder and tried before Bailhache J on 25 October 1919 at the Chester Assizes. There was little dispute about the facts after Beard's counsel, Thomas Artemus Jones, failed in his attempt to exclude Beard's confession from evidence.[36] There were two principal lines of defence: Beard's war experience and his drunkenness at the time of the killing. Jones chose not to call any witnesses or put Beard on the stand in order to ensure that he, rather than the prosecuting lawyer, had the last word to the jury.[37] As a result, Beard's own claim that he was not a 'sane man' because he had drunk heavily throughout the day and in the preceding week was not put before the jury, and nor was the evidence of six witnesses Beard claimed could have supported his account.[38] Instead, the details and possible effects of Beard's war service and drunken state on his criminal responsibility were brought out indirectly in cross-examination. This evidence was mixed. One witness suggested that while Beard had been drinking, he was neither drunk nor sober, and the fact that so soon after the murder he had been admitted to the trade union, having responded 'fairly intelligently' to questions, also weighed against the defence.[39]

The defence trial strategy was unsuccessful. Its centrepiece, Jones' last word to the jury, was 'rather brief' and barely audible.[40] He urged a manslaughter conviction on the basis of drunkenness, but the judge virtually dismissed the notion in a summing up that very clearly favoured a conviction. The jury took only seven minutes to find Beard guilty of murder. Bailhache J passed the death sentence before warning the assembled crowd: 'You have just witnessed the trial of a man of good upbringing. You have seen to what a pass drink has brought this man. I want to beg you with all the force I can put into my words to take warning of this example, and for God's sake keep away from drink.'[41]

The message that Bailhache J sought to convey was directed against the evil of drink, but those who supported Beard focused on the crime as a product of war. The Hyde Comrades Club coordinated the campaign for a reprieve. It focused on Beard's war service, emphasising the injuries and traumas that he had sustained and the fact that, in his long service, he had

---

[36] The objection was that the Scotland Yard officers had obtained this confession improperly; see *Trial and CCA Transcript* 101–02.

[37] The prosecution had the right to reply if the defence called witnesses. For the procedural rules, see W Russell, R Ross and G McClure, *A Treatise on Crimes and Misdemeanors*, 8th edn, 2 vols (London, Stevens & Sons, 1923) II, 1834–39.

[38] He contested the trial evidence that he had not been drunk by pointing out that he had been accused of putting on a waiter's apron in a pub, thrown off a tram by an inspector and had gone to work in the wrong boots and cap. See *Notice of Appeal*, HO 144/20991.

[39] *Trial and CCA Transcript* 64, 65.

[40] *North Cheshire Herald* (Hyde, 31 October 1919) 8.

[41] *The Times* (London, 25 October 1919) 9.

'done his duty'.[42] It appealed directly to comrades and parents who had seen the changes that had come over their sons during the war and maintained that Beard had suddenly 'taken leave of his senses'. The petition was well supported by thousands of signatories, including the Mayor and Chief Constable of Hyde, and it generated considerable publicity.[43] Ivy Wood's parents felt obliged to write to the Home Office to refute claims that they had signed it.[44] When leave for appeal was granted, it was reported that the grounds of appeal were that Beard 'suffered from shell-shock in France'.[45]

The actual notice of appeal, written by Beard, focused on his state of drunkenness, which was not distinguished from insanity, and consequent irresponsibility. It was clear that he had not taken legal advice when preparing the statement, which was poorly written and made no attempt to set out the grounds of appeal.[46] Leave was granted and the case came on before the Earl of Reading LCJ, Coleridge and Sankey JJ in November. Jones appeared again and argued two grounds of appeal. First, the trial judge had misdirected the jury on the felony-murder rule. This long-established rule meant that any death resulting from a felony was treated as murder, regardless of whether the risk of death was foreseeable. The defendant's felonious intent supplied the 'malice aforethought' required for murder. The wide scope of the rule was subjected to sustained criticism during the nineteenth century, but judges made only very limited efforts to narrow it.[47] Jones suggested that the jury should have been directed to consider whether death had been caused 'accidentally'. This submission relied upon a fine distinction between the act of Beard putting his hand over the girl's mouth, which was intended to stop her screaming during the rape (not to cause suffocation) and the actual cause of death, which was the pressure on the girl's throat produced by his thumb. Jones contended that a correctly directed jury could have reached a manslaughter verdict by finding that the pressure on the throat was accidental. Here he relied on Stephen J's attempt, in the case of *Serné*, to restrict the scope of the felony-murder rule to cases in which the relevant act was 'known to be dangerous to life, and likely in itself to cause death'.[48] Jones argued that the jury should have been invited to consider whether Beard would, as a reasonable man, have contemplated that death would result from his actions.[49]

[42] See *North Cheshire Herald* (Hyde, 31 October 1919) 8.

[43] *Manchester Guardian* (15 November 1919) 6. The petition was not presented because the Court of Criminal Appeal quashed the murder conviction. See William Beard to Sir John Gilmour (Home Secretary), 8 August 1933, TNA: HO 144/20991.

[44] John Wood to Under Secretary of State for Home Office, 4 November 1919, TNA: HO 144/20991.

[45] *Manchester Guardian* (Manchester, 15 November 1919) 6.

[46] *Notice of Appeal*, HO 144/20991; *Trial and CCA Transcript* 129–30.

[47] See K Smith, 'Criminal Law' in W Cornish et al, *The Oxford History of the Laws of England, Vols XI–XIII* (Oxford, Oxford University Press, 2010) XIII, 412–16.

[48] *R v Serné* (1887) 16 Cox CC 311 (CCC).

[49] See *Trial and CCA Transcript* 131–51.

This ground of appeal generated considerable discussion in argument, but rather less in judgment, when the Earl of Reading dismissed it quickly as contrary to the evidence. He took no care to reflect on the limitations suggested by both Stephen J and commentators on the scope of the felony-murder rule. Instead, his statement that 'an act of violence done in the course or in the furtherance of a felony involving violence' was 'beyond all question' murder stated the doctrine in its widest terms.[50] When the case went up to the House of Lords, the ruling was affirmed without qualification or reasoning: 'No attempt has been made in your Lordships' House to displace this view of the law and there can be no doubt as to its soundness.'[51] In fact, the point had been argued in the hearing when neither side had contended against the limitation on the rule suggested by Stephen J.[52] The decision by the Lords to adopt a strict approach may therefore have been an informed and deliberate one, but the absence of supporting reasoning makes it difficult to be certain.

The second ground of appeal taken in the Court of Criminal Appeal and the one that provided the main focus for the hearing in the House of Lords was a possible misdirection on drunkenness. Jones argued that Bailhache J had wrongly used the test for insanity when he should have applied the test for drunkenness set out in *Meade*.[53] In that case, the Court of Criminal Appeal had decreed that the only circumstances in which drunkenness could rebut the presumption that a person intended the natural consequences of his act was where drink rendered him 'incapable of knowing what he was doing was dangerous i.e. likely to inflict serious injury'.[54] By telling the jury that it had to be satisfied that Beard was so drunk that he did not know what he was doing or that what he was doing was wrong, the judge had used the insanity test, which was to the defendant's disadvantage. This argument, which reflected the contemporary blurring between insanity and intoxication, had been peremptorily dismissed by Bailhache J in the trial, but was successful in the Court of Criminal Appeal, which ruled itself bound by *Meade*.[55] The Earl of Reading held that Bailhache J's direction effectively removed manslaughter from the jury's consideration and that it was impossible to say what the verdict would have been had the correct direction been given. The Court substituted a conviction for manslaughter and a sentence of 20 years of penal servitude.

The Court of Criminal Appeal's decision to quash the murder conviction was a cause of consternation at the Home Office. Its officers were highly

---

[50] *R v Beard* [1920] 14 Cr App R 110, 116 (CCA).

[51] *Beard* (n 1) 493.

[52] See *House of Lords Transcript* (16 December 1919) TNA: DPP 1/51B (hereinafter *HL Transcript*) 64–69.

[53] *R v Meade* [1909] 1 KB 895 (CCA).

[54] ibid 899.

[55] For the trial discussion of the point, see *Trial and CCA Transcript* 117.

sceptical of the evidential basis for the plea of drunkenness, suggesting that it was insufficient to warrant even a *Meade* direction. The decision in *Meade* itself was viewed as having 'gone very near making drunkenness an excuse for crime'.[56] In the three decades leading up to the war, the reduction in recorded violent crime and shifting medical understandings had encouraged the view that intoxication could be treated rather than punished. Immediately after the war, when the problems of violence, drunkenness and mental illness loomed large in public discourse, this approach seemed unduly lenient. So, although there were 'formidable' difficulties involved in an appeal to the Lords, the prospect of 'abolishing' *Meade* and resolving the uncertainty in the law prompted the decision to appeal.[57] The formal basis for an appeal to the Lords was a fiat from the Attorney-General certifying that the case raised an issue of exceptional public importance.[58] The fiat procedure operated very restrictively and few criminal cases reached the Lords throughout the period of its operation.[59] The object of the appeal, from the point of view of the Home Office and the DPP, was to 'to get an authoritative ruling as to the law with regard to drunkenness in relation to felonies of violence'.[60]

The Law Lords did not take the same view. They were quick to reject a suggestion in argument that they should lay down some general guidance for judges on drunkenness, as had been done in the *M'Naghten* case on insanity.[61] The early exchanges in the House of Lords betrayed considerable doubt about what process to follow. The judges were uncertain about the extent to which they were entitled to re-evaluate the evidence, the scope of their review and the effect that their decision would have on the conviction and sentence.[62] These uncertainties and reservations serve as a reminder of hostile judicial attitudes towards criminal appeals. Two of the key reasons for this hostility were manifested in Beard's case. It had been the judiciary's consistent view in the century before the Criminal Appeals Act 1907 that questions of criminal law were best resolved in trials and that final decisions on criminal responsibility were best left with juries.[63] They also feared that appellate remedies in criminal cases would cause delay and consequently

---

[56] *Home Office Minutes* (24 November 1919) TNA: HO 144/20991.

[57] ibid.

[58] Criminal Appeal Act 1907, s 1(6). For the certificate in Beard's case, see TNA: LO2/6.

[59] The total number of criminal cases heard in the House of Lords in the period during which the fiat operated (1908–60) was 23, of which only 12 raised issues of substantive law; see J Spencer, 'Criminal Law' in L Blom-Cooper, B Dickson and G Drewry (eds), *The Judicial House of Lords 1876–2009* (Oxford, Oxford University Press, 2009) 595.

[60] *Draft of Conditional Pardon* (18 March 1920) TNA: HO 144/20991. See also *Home Office Minutes* (24 November 1919) TNA: HO 144/20991.

[61] *HL Transcript* (18 December 1919) 23, Lord Birkenhead and Lord Sumner.

[62] *HL Transcript* (16 December 1919) 7–8.

[63] See P Handler, 'The Court for Crown Cases Reserved, 1848–1908' (2011) 29 *Law and History Review* 259.

undermine the deterrent and exemplary effects of punishment, particularly the death penalty. The Court of Criminal Appeal, by hearing cases within a few weeks of the trial and delivering unreserved judgments, could limit these effects, but they were particularly marked in an appeal to the Lords. The delay caused, and the fact that Beard had been in prison for so long with the uncertain prospect of execution, prompted the Home Office to decide that, whatever the outcome of the appeal to the Lords, the death penalty would not be carried out.[64] The wider considerations that had featured in the trial and engaged press interest, such as Beard's personal history and shell-shock, the death penalty and local context of the case, retreated into the background. Beard's attendance at the House of Lords emphasised the contrast. The press noted his incongruous and unacknowledged presence at the back of the grand chamber and his mute attempts to follow the complex legal arguments.[65] By the time that the case came before the House of Lords, he was a marginal figure in the proceedings.

The delay did allow for an unusually high level of legal expertise to be devoted to the case. The office of the DPP consulted with leading criminal lawyers, one of whom, Archibald Bodkin, prepared a very detailed opinion.[66] Gordon Hewart, the Attorney-General and future Lord Chief Justice, led for the Crown and had six leading criminal barristers in support.[67] Eight Law Lords, including the Earl of Reading, heard argument over three days and reserved judgment.[68] This contrasts with typical proceedings in the Court of Criminal Appeal, which usually gave an unreserved judgment following much shorter hearings.[69]

The prospect of an authoritative ruling from the most senior court also carried significant risks because of the issues involved. The absence of any legislation or ruling from the Court for Crown Cases Reserved on intoxication prior to 1907 was in part the result of fears of conveying the wrong

---

[64] *Home Office Minutes* (24 November 1919) HO 144/20991. Lord Birkenhead announced it publicly when reserving judgment; *HL Transcript* (19 December 1919) 35.

[65] See *Daily Mail* (London, 17, 19 December 1919) 7, 5; *Manchester Guardian* (Manchester, 17, 20 December 1919) 9, 6; *The Times* (London, 17, 19 December 1919) 5, 4.

[66] See A Bodkin, *R v Beard (Note)* TNA: DPP 1/51B. The actual DPP, Charles Matthews, does not appear to have taken a very active role in the case. He was suffering from ill health and when he died in office in 1920, Bodkin took his position. See A Lentin, 'Mathews, Sir Charles Willie, Baronet (1850–1920)', *Oxford Dictionary of National Biography*, online edn (Oxford, Oxford University Press, 2004), www.oxforddnb.com/view/article/34935; C Humphreys, 'Bodkin, Sir Archibald Henry (1862–1957)', revised by Mark Pottle, *Oxford Dictionary of National Biography*, online edn (Oxford, Oxford University Press, 2004), www.oxforddnb.com/view/article/31942.

[67] The DPP also instructed the Solicitor General (Sir Ernest Pollock KC), Sir Ellis Griffiths KC, Sir Richard Muir, GAH Branson and Ralph Sutton. Artemus Jones, Austin Jones and Dallas Walters appeared as counsel for Beard.

[68] Lord Birkenhead LC, Earl of Reading LCJ, Viscount Haldane, Lord Dunedin, Lord Atkinson, Lord Sumner, Lord Buckmaster and Lord Phillimore.

[69] See R Pattenden, *English Criminal Appeals 1844–1994* (Oxford, Clarendon Press, 1996) 27–34.

public message on an issue that featured in such a high proportion of violent crimes.[70] These fears overshadowed the deliberations in the Lords and help explain their reticence in argument to commit to offering any final and definitive guidance in the case. The judges seldom referred explicitly to the press coverage and wider issues raised, but they framed their deliberations. At the beginning of the second day of the hearing, the Earl of Reading felt obliged to make a short statement to refute suggestions in the press that he had, on the first day, indicated that drunkenness might be an excuse for crime.[71]

### III. THE HOUSE OF LORDS

The hearing and judgment in the House of Lords focused on two principal issues. The first was the applicable rules on intoxication and the second was the relationship between intoxication and insanity. On the first question, a considerable amount of the argument and judgment was devoted to the emergence of doctrine in the nineteenth century. As Lord Birkenhead noted, the law had developed in trials and, as a result, it was difficult to find any 'single or very intelligible principle' to which the course of development could be attributed.[72] The account presented in argument and Lord Birkenhead's speech established a narrative history of mitigation of the old, strict common law rule against drunkenness. This mitigation was only for crimes of specific intent, which were those where drunkenness could be admitted into evidence to rebut the presumption that a person intended the natural or probable consequences of their actions. This presumption was supposed to be one of evidence, but in practice operated as one of law for much of the nineteenth century because it was so difficult to rebut.[73]

Specific intent had not been discussed in the trial or the Court of Criminal Appeal, but it became a principal focus for investigation in the Lords. The uncertainty surrounding its meaning stemmed in part from misreading the nineteenth-century cases as being directed towards relaxing the law. Recent research has demonstrated that Victorian judges were primarily concerned to reduce the scope for drunkenness to operate as an excuse. During the era of the 'bloody code' in the long eighteenth century, the old rule against drunkenness, although strictly set out in institutional works, was not enforced in trials when judges and juries regularly allowed drunkenness to negate malice as a means of avoiding a death sentence.[74] Faced

[70] See Handler, 'Intoxication and Criminal Responsibility' 247–48.
[71] *HL Transcript* (18 December 1919) 2.
[72] ibid 495.
[73] See Smith, 'Criminal Law' 410–20.
[74] See D Rabin, 'Drunkenness and Responsibility for Crime in the Eighteenth Century' (2005) 44 *Journal of British Studies* 457, 470–73.

with rising levels of violent crime and widespread public concern with the problem of intemperance, Victorian trial judges made efforts to enforce the common law rule and hold individuals strictly responsible for their drunken actions.[75] There was no compunction about using the initial fault of getting drunk as the basis for responsibility for consequences subsequently caused. Trial judges faced the problem that juries sometimes took a lenient view of drunken violence. To overcome this, judges restricted its relevance to where a defendant was incapacitated by drink and to crimes that required proof of a 'specific intention'.[76] The term did not carry any technical or precise meaning. It emerged in the context of the new statutory non-fatal offences against the person, the most serious of which required proof of a specific intention to cause grievous bodily harm or death.[77] By restricting the excuse of drunkenness to serious felonies, judges sought to ensure that those who committed violence while drunk would at least be convicted of a lesser offence.

By the time of *Beard*, this strict approach to intoxication had been undermined and partially eclipsed by its increasingly confused relationship to insanity. In the first half of the Victorian period, judges were stringent in maintaining a distinction. Insanity was an illness, whereas voluntary drunkenness was understood as self-caused and a result of individual moral failing.[78] It was only in very rare circumstances, such as when the condition of delirium tremens was diagnosed, that extreme drunkenness might provide the basis for a defence of insanity. This strict approach was destabilised in the late nineteenth and early twentieth centuries by the emerging social and medical understanding of intoxication as a disease or form of insanity.[79] In the criminal courts, this understanding coexisted uneasily with the older moralistic view of strict individual culpability for drunkenness. The precedent-based system of common law crimes struggled to react to changing scientific and social norms. Expert evidence on the effects of drunkenness on mental capacity was not always accepted as the basis for an insanity plea, but the distinction became blurred.[80] In *Meade* and *Beard*, insanity was not pleaded and yet in both cases the trial judges imported the language of the

---

[75] M Wiener, 'Judges v Jurors: Courtroom Tensions in Murder Trials' (1999) 17 *Law and History Review* 467, 490–97; Handler, 'Intoxication and Criminal Responsibility' 248–54.

[76] See Handler, 'Intoxication and Criminal Responsibility' 248–54.

[77] These were established in a series of nineteenth-century statutes that were consolidated in 1861. See P Handler, 'The Law of Felonious Assault in England, 1803–1861' (2007) 28 *Journal of Legal History* 183.

[78] 'Drunkenness is not insanity … unless the derangement … becomes fixed … thereby rendering the party incapable of distinguishing between right and wrong.' *R v Rennie* (1825) 1 Lewin 76, 168 ER 965 (Assizes) Holroyd J.

[79] See above n 7.

[80] For an argument that judges and juries defined their own 'lay' knowledge of intoxication against expert medical knowledge, see A Loughnan, 'The Expertise of Non-experts: Knowledges of Intoxication in Criminal Law' in J Herring et al (eds), *Intoxication and Society: Problematic Pleasures of Drugs and Alcohol* (Basingstoke: Palgrave Macmillan, 2013).

*M'Naghten Rules* when directing the juries. The Court of Criminal Appeal's decisions sought to correct the tendency to merge the two tests, but, as a manuscript note on the DPP's transcript indicated, in doing so, it imposed a test for drunkenness that was more favourable to the defendant than the one for insanity.[81]

The judges in the House of Lords affirmed a clear distinction between drunkenness and insanity. They did so after hearing lengthy argument on the point. Viscount Haldane in particular found the distinction difficult to grasp, questioning whether in criminal law, as in civil law, drunkenness should be put substantially 'on the same footing as any other form of madness'.[82] These doubts ultimately gave way to the more pragmatic conclusion that there should be a clear distinction between those rare cases where excessive drinking caused insanity and cases in which 'the defence of drunkenness ... produces a condition such that the drunken man's mind becomes incapable of forming a specific intention'.[83] In the absence of any expert medical evidence of insanity, both *Beard* and *Meade* were cases of the latter type and, as a result, a direction based on *M'Naghten* was inappropriate. After expressing some doubt on the point in his speech, Lord Birkenhead felt able to conclude that Bailhache J's direction, although 'unhappily conceived', had not prejudiced the defendant and was not therefore a material misdirection.[84]

The House of Lords judgment aimed to make it much more difficult for defendants to combine the pleas in future and to end a course of development that had threatened to undermine the strict Victorian approach to the excuse of drunkenness. Yet once it had been disentangled from insanity, the circumstances in which drunkenness could supply such an excuse remained to be considered, and on this question, the House of Lords judgment was much less clear. The key question for interpretation was the effect of *Meade*. In the Attorney-General's submission, the decision in *Meade* had extended the scope for drunkenness to excuse well beyond previous limits. He maintained that nineteenth-century judges had only allowed drunkenness to operate as an excuse where the crime required proof of a 'major' or 'specific' intention. The Court of Appeal statement of the law in *Meade* had obscured this distinction and had led the courts subsequently to allow drunkenness as a possible excuse for any type of crime if it prevented the defendant from appreciating that what they were doing was dangerous.

Here the conflict between principle and pragmatism came into focus. In principle, drunkenness might render someone incapable of forming intention and, as a consequence, as Lord Phillimore put it, 'if intention is part of the crime I would respectfully submit that the drunken man goes free'.

[81] *Trial and CCA Transcript* 172.
[82] *HL Transcript* (16 December 1919) 98.
[83] *Beard* (n 1) 500.
[84] ibid 506–07.

In a revealing exchange in argument, Lord Birkenhead asked the Attorney-General whether they should be shocked by such a conclusion. Before he could reply, the Earl of Reading, who of all the judges seemed most mindful of the possible practical consequences of the decision, interrupted to say that he thought that would be shocking.[85] This fundamental tension was not resolved in Lord Birkenhead's speech. The first part of the speech appeared to favour the pragmatic approach of restricting the excuse of drunkenness to crimes requiring proof of specific intention, even if there was little guidance as to what the term meant. This was undermined later in the speech by the suggestion that this was 'on ultimate analysis, only in accordance with the ordinary law applicable to crime, for, speaking generally ... a person cannot be convicted of a crime unless the mens was rea'.[86]

It is not clear what, if anything, Lord Birkenhead meant by 'specific intention'. Murder required 'malice aforethought', but killings were presumed to be malicious. As Lord Atkinson put it in argument in *Beard*: 'All the prosecutor has to do in murder is to prove that the accused killed the man. Then the law presumes that he did it of malice aforethought.'[87] According to this analysis, murder was not a crime of specific intention, but in some instances nineteenth-century judges had allowed drunkenness to reduce murder to manslaughter. This followed from a narrowing of the definition of malice aforethought in some murder cases to require proof of intention to kill or cause grievous bodily harm. In such cases, judges allowed the presumption of that intention to be rebutted if the jury was satisfied that the defendant was incapacitated by drink.[88] *Meade* was such a case because it involved a brutal beating with a broomstick and the key question was whether it was done with intent to cause grievous bodily harm.[89]

The position was not the same where the felony-murder rule applied because that only required proof of mens rea in relation to the initial felony. Such was the case in *Beard* itself and this was the basis upon which the House of Lords distinguished it from *Meade*. It ruled that no proof of specific intention was required in relation to the death or even its dangerousness. Drunkenness 'could be no defence unless it could be established that Beard at the time of committing the rape was so drunk as to be incapable of forming the intent to commit it'.[90] The point could not be contended for on the evidence presented. This conclusion followed from the strict interpretation of the felony-murder rule that the courts adopted. The defence tried in vain

---

[85] *HL Transcript* (16 December 1919) 54–55.

[86] *Beard* (n 1) 504.

[87] *HL Transcript* (16 December 1919) 96.

[88] The clearest statement of this approach was Stephen J's in *R v Doherty*, *The Times* (London, 20 December 1887) 12 (CCC). See Handler, 'Intoxication and Criminal Responsibility' 253–54.

[89] *Meade* (n 53).

[90] *Beard* (n 1) 504–05.

to argue that the drunkenness may have prevented Beard from realising that the act of placing his hand over the girl's mouth could be dangerous. The argument was rejected because it was sufficient that death occurred during the course of the violent felony; the act of rape and suffocation could not be regarded as separate. It was on this basis that the murder conviction was restored. The case is not a good authority for the proposition that murder is a crime of specific intention.[91]

## IV. EFFECTS

The House of Lords judgment allowed the appeal, but initially there was uncertainty about precisely what this meant for Beard's conviction and sentence. An order was made to remit the case to the Court of Criminal Appeal, which restored the murder conviction.[92] However, it had no power to alter the sentence of death, and so a conditional pardon was needed to reduce the death sentence to penal servitude for life.[93] Officials at the Home Office were hardly pleased at the outcome. In a strongly worded memorandum a few weeks after the House of Lords judgment, the Permanent Under Secretary, Ernest Blackwell urged two points that had been 'somewhat obscured' by the trial and appeal proceedings. He maintained, first, that there was 'no evidence' that Beard was drunk at the time of the killing and, second, he rejected the contention that the suffocation may have been accidental by asserting his view that she had been killed to prevent his subsequent identification and detection.[94] Blackwell recorded these points in order to influence further consideration of the case and they did indeed inform subsequent deliberations on the possibility of Beard's release from prison in the 1930s.[95] If it had been left to the Home Office to exercise the prerogative of mercy or if the Court of Criminal Appeal had confirmed his murder conviction, Beard would have hanged.[96]

Beard began his life term at Parkhurst Prison in March 1920, but within two months, he had been certified as insane and committed to Broadmoor lunatic asylum. The precise reason for his committal is obscure.[97]

---

[91] It is often cited as such; see, for example, A Simester, J Spencer, F Stark, G Sullivan and G Virgo, *Simester and Sullivan's Criminal Law Theory and Doctrine*, 6th edn (Oxford, Hart Publishing, 2016) 715.

[92] *R v Beard* (1920) 14 Cr App R 200 (CCA).

[93] For the conditional pardon, see TNA: ASSI 65/24/1.

[94] *Home Office Minutes* 23 March 1920, TNA: HO 144/20991.

[95] See *Home Office Minutes* (29 June 1931) TNA: HO 144/20991. Beard was eventually released in 1937. For his prison records and related correspondence, see TNA: PCOM 8/352; HO 144/20991.

[96] See *Home Office Minutes* (23 March 1920) TNA: HO 144/20991.

[97] Some records relating to his committal were destroyed. Those that survived are in TNA: HO 144/20991.

The records make oblique reference to a 'bad habit', but the absence of further detail prompted uncertainty in subsequent prison and Home Office correspondence about whether and when it would be safe for him to be sent back to prison.[98] He was returned to Parkhurst two years later. This aspect of the case is a further illustration of the elision of the distinction between drunkenness and insanity, but it came at a stage in the criminal process when it may have been more acceptable to policy-makers and officials. Blackwell was kept informed of developments, but did not intervene. Beard's mental health had been monitored closely in the run-up to his trial, but prison doctors had found no evidence of insanity.[99] Once this had been established, the prospect of Beard being excused or exempted from responsibility by linking insanity and drunkenness in the trial and appellate process, with its attendant publicity, was unacceptable to the Home Office and, in the end, to the Law Lords.

The House of Lords judgment attracted positive coverage in the general press for restricting the scope of the excuse of drunkenness. The *Manchester Guardian*, for example, welcomed the decision as a timely one to prevent any lenient treatment of a vice that was the 'cause of almost all the violent crimes committed by soldiers'.[100] Much of the press comment focused on the fact that the murder conviction had been restored as the basis for the view that the law had been strengthened. Whether the case had such an effect in the courts is more difficult to gauge and would require a more detailed survey of the trial reports than can be offered here.[101] The 1920s and 1930s witnessed a sharp diminution in excess drinking and the drink question ceased to be such a prominent social issue.[102] This may help explain the scarcity of reported cases in which *Beard* was cited in those decades, although there is evidence that the Earl of Reading's successor as Lord Chief Justice, Lord Hewart (who had appeared in *Beard* when he was Attorney-General), pursued a characteristically uncompromising approach.[103]

The strict ruling on the scope of the felony-murder rule seems to have been applied despite strident academic criticism. In an influential article on mens rea, Turner complained that the decision had 'nullified all progress

---

[98] *Home Office Minutes* 11 June 1921, TNA: HO 144/20991.

[99] See statements of Dr East (Liverpool prison doctor) 18 October 1919 and Dr Pearson (Manchester prison doctor) (20 October 1919) TNA: HO 144/20991.

[100] *Manchester Guardian* (Manchester, 6 March 1920) 10. An editorial in *The Times* welcomed the decision (London, 6 March 1920, 15); see also *Daily Telegraph* (London, 6 March 1920).

[101] It was almost immediately adopted in Scotland, where the High Court interpreted the decision in its narrow sense so as only to allow drunkenness to prevent proof of a specific intention. See *HM Advocate v Campbell* 1921 JC 1 (High Court of Justiciary).

[102] Greenaway, *Drink and British Politics* 114.

[103] In one murder appeal, he dismissed an argument that the trial judge should have directed the jury on specific intent in an unreserved judgment that took no care to address any of the issues that preoccupied the House of Lords in *Beard*. See *R v Lincoln*, *The Times* (London, 16 February 1926) 5 (CCA).

in improving the law of murder which had been achieved over the past century'.[104] In *Stone*, the trial judge, Hewart LCJ, and the Court of Criminal Appeal were unequivocal in holding that a killing during the course of a rape was murder 'without the least intention to kill'.[105] In *Jarmain*, a defendant who shot and killed a cashier during the course of a robbery but claimed to have pulled the trigger inadvertently was convicted of murder. The Court of Criminal Appeal upheld the conviction on the basis that it was a violent felony and nothing further needed to be proven.[106] It took the intervention of the legislature in 1957 to overturn the rule.[107]

It was the conflicting dicta on the circumstances in which drunkenness could prevent proof of mens rea that caused most difficulty and debate subsequently. Commentators at the time anticipated some of these effects. In a case note in the *Law Quarterly Review*, Stroud commented that the implication that any form of mens rea might be negated was 'an extension of the defence of drunkenness far beyond the limits which have hitherto been assigned to it'.[108] Kenny adopted the same broad interpretation of the decision, noting only that the more complex the intent required, the more likely drunkenness was to be relevant.[109] In contrast, leading practitioner treatises took the more restrictive view that drunkenness was only relevant where a specific intention had to be proved, although none were clear on the meaning of the term.[110]

When subjectivist theory assumed prominence in the second half of the twentieth century, commentators and judges grappled with these conflicting and ambiguous aspects of Lord Birkenhead's speech in more detail.[111] The problem was partially resolved when the House of Lords in *Majewski* affirmed that the earlier part of the speech referring only to crimes of specific intent was to be preferred.[112] In doing so, it rejected arguments from subjectivists who wanted to rely on the part of the speech that indicated that it could negate any form of mens rea.[113] The nature of crimes of specific intention continues to be disputed. In *Majewski*, the misleading account

---

[104] J Turner, 'The Mental Element in Crimes at Common Law' (1936) 6 *Cambridge Law Journal* 64. For similar criticism, see J Hall, 'Intoxication and Criminal Responsibility' (1944) 57 *Harvard Law Review* 1045, 1069–71. *cf* D Stroud, 'Constructive Murder and Drunkenness' (1920) 36 *Law Quarterly Review* 268, 268–69.

[105] *R v Stone*, The Times (London, 30 June 1937) 4 (CCC), (London, 30 July 1937) 4 (CCA).

[106] *R v Jarmain* [1946] KB 74 (CCA). See also *R v Betts* [1931] 22 Cr App R 148 (CCA).

[107] Homicide Act 1957, s 1.

[108] Stroud, 'Constructive Murder' 270.

[109] See CS Kenny, *Outlines of Criminal Law*, 10th edn (Cambridge, Cambridge University Press, 1920) 61–62.

[110] See Russell, Ross and McClure, *Treatise on Crimes* I, 89; J Jervis, H Roome and R Ross, *Archbold's Pleading, Evidence & Practice in Criminal Cases*, 26th edn (London, Sweet & Maxwell, 1922) 19–20.

[111] For discussion, see the works cited above in n 5.

[112] *Majewski* (n 3) 473–74 (Lord Elwyn Jones LC).

[113] See, for example, J Smith and B Hogan, *Criminal Law*, 2nd edn (London, Butterworths, 1969) 133.

offered in *Beard* of the gradual relaxation of the strict common law rule in the nineteenth century was adopted and entrenched. This course of development, it was argued, ended with *Beard*, which set in place the foundation for the current distinction between basic and specific intention.[114] The judges in *Majewski* offered a number of ways of making this distinction, none of which has proved wholly satisfactory.[115] In the absence of an alternative, the current rules continue to offend against basic subjective principles of criminal liability.

It is not surprising that courts and commentators grappling with these problems since the middle of the twentieth century have found *Beard* 'a difficult case to understand'.[116] The questions did not arise in the same terms in 1919. Crimes of specific intention were those for which it was permissible for the defendant to use drunkenness to rebut a presumption that would otherwise operate to establish mens rea. For other crimes, the mens rea was presumed from the relevant act. This obscured any distinction between advertent and inadvertent wrongdoing. It also helps to explain the stated requirement in *Beard* that the drunkenness had to be such as to incapacitate the defendant. The proposition that if the defendant was capable, intent would be presumed in fact was difficult to defend after *Woolmington* (the next House of Lords criminal case after *Beard*) and could not survive the enactment of section 8 of the Criminal Justice Act 1967.[117] The subjectivist approach to criminal liability that has been entrenched in law since then is at odds with the approach in *Beard*. Lord Birkenhead and his colleagues operated within a framework in which constructive liability and an expansive notion of prior fault were accepted parts of the broad-based assessments of criminal responsibility that were made in trials. This allowed Lord Birkenhead to state with little compunction or justification that which has prompted much debate and controversy since: 'the cause of the punishment is the drunkenness which has led to the crime, rather than the crime itself'.[118]

---

[114] This was set out most fully in Lawton LJ's Court of Appeal judgment and by Lord Elwyn Jones LC in the House of Lords. See *Majewski* (n 3) 452–57, 471–72.

[115] See Williams, 'Voluntary Intoxication'.

[116] *Majewski* (n 3) 454 (Lawton LJ).

[117] *Woolmington v DPP* [1935] AC 462 (HL). See also *R v Sheehan* [1975] Crim LR 339 (CA).

[118] *Beard* (n 1) 500.

# 10

# *R v Jordan (1956)*

## DAVID IBBETSON

*R v JORDAN* is a well-known case on causation, described in the current edition of *Smith and Hogan's Criminal Law* as one of a triumvirate of cases, together with *Smith* and *Cheshire*, laying down the modern rules determining when the chain of causation between injury and death is broken by medical treatment.[1] It stands for the proposition that, while normal medical treatment of an injury will not break the chain of causation between injury and death, if the medical treatment is abnormal, then the chain of causation will be broken; though it was perhaps not until the decision in *Smith* in the Courts Martial Appeal Court that this interpretation crystallised, and even after that, there was considerable room for doubt as to its scope.[2]

Therefore, it is something of a leading case on causation, but if we approach it on its own terms, it takes on a rather different hue. Its facts are as interesting as the law, and it is the argument of this chapter that the law might have been formulated the way that it was in substantial measure because of the factual background. Much of the detail is found in the Director of Public Prosecutions' papers in the National Archives,[3] amplified by newspaper reports.

## I. THE COURT OF CRIMINAL APPEAL AND THE FACTS

It is simplest to begin with the case as it appears from the judgment of the Court of Criminal Appeal.[4] James Clinton Jordan, the defendant, stabbed

---

[1] *R v Jordan* (1956) 40 Cr App R 152 (CCA). See D Ormerod and K Laird (eds), *Smith and Hogan's Criminal Law*, 14th edn (Oxford, Oxford University Press, 2015) 103; *R v Smith* [1959] 2 QB 35 (CMAC); and *R v Cheshire* [1991] 3 All ER 670 (CA).

[2] JC Smith and B Hogan, *Criminal Law* (London, Butterworths, 1965) 169.

[3] TNA: PRO DPP 2/2531 (preserved as two files). These files are not paginated, so page references can only be given to the transcript of the trial, which is contained in file 1. Other relevant files in the National Archives are that of the Clerk of Assizes (TNA: PRO ASSI 45/264) containing the formal papers relating to the prosecution, and that of the Court of Criminal Appeal (TNA: PRO J 82/13), which contains nothing that is not in TNA: PRO DPP 2/2531, except a copy of the Court's judgment.

[4] *Jordan* (n 1).

Walter Beaumont in a brawl in the Blue Bird, a dockside cafe in Hull, one Friday night in May 1956. Beaumont was taken to hospital and operated on immediately, but a few days later, he died of bronchopneumonia as a result of post-operative complications. Jordan was prosecuted for murder, the trial taking place at Leeds Assizes, and he was duly convicted with a strong recommendation for mercy, but the formal sentence was death, as it had to be. He appealed to the Court of Criminal Appeal, where new evidence was presented to the effect that the treatment Beaumont had been given in hospital was 'palpably wrong'. First, he had been given a broad-spectrum antibiotic, terramycin. The terramycin had been stopped after he had demonstrated an intolerance, but very shortly afterwards it had been started again and continued for a day before it was again stopped; it was this administration of terramycin after the intolerance was known that was criticised. The effect of the terramycin was that he had developed acute diarrhoea. Two intravenous drips were fixed up to rehydrate him, and it was said that the amount of fluid he had received was inappropriate and had brought about the pneumonia from which he had died. The prosecution had been permitted to cross-examine the witnesses who had testified that the treatment was wrong, but they were not allowed to lead evidence of their own.[5] The Court of Criminal Appeal gave an unreserved judgment allowing the appeal on the basis that the jury 'would have felt precluded' from convicting the defendant if they had had the benefit of hearing the new evidence, whatever direction had been given by the judge.[6]

The case made something of a splash. Both the initial conviction and the appeal were widely reported as news in Britain.[7] There was particular interest in the US since Jordan was an American serviceman: both the *Washington Post* and the *New York Times* reported it.[8] Moreover, a letter sent by the Staff Judge Advocate of the US Air Force to the Director of Public Prosecutions (DPP) two days after the successful appeal, in which he asked the DPP to waive jurisdiction over any further charges of unlawful wounding, referred to the 'strong Congressional and national' interest in the

---

[5] The headnote to the Criminal Appeal Report is clear that prosecution counsel had alternative medical evidence and this was referred to by the Court (*Jordan* (n 1) 156), but there is no hint of this in the DPP's file (where we should surely have expected to find at least a reference to it).

[6] The rule was stated in *Archbold* that the Court should quash the conviction if they considered that there might have been reasonable doubt in the minds of the jury had the evidence been before them: TR Fitzwalter Butler and M de la Paz Garsia (eds), *Archbold's Pleading, Evidence and Practice in Criminal Cases*, 33rd edn (London, Sweet & Maxwell, 1954) 330.

[7] In England, see, in particular, *The Times* (London, 21 July 1956, 22 August 1956); *Manchester Guardian* (Manchester, 21 July 1956, 22 August 1956). It was the subject of a leader in *The Observer* (London, 26 August 1956).

[8] *New York Times* (New York, 21 July 1956); 'British Jury Dooms GI in Knife Murder' *Washington Post* (Washington, 21 July 1956). Interestingly, only the initial conviction and not the successful appeal was reported in either newspaper.

case.[9] Its legal ramifications were discussed in the *Criminal Law Review*,[10] it was criticised in the *British Medical Journal*[11] and a talk on the Third Programme by Glanville Williams was printed in *The Listener*.[12]

## II. LEGAL PROCESS: TRIAL AND APPEAL

The unfolding of the law in *Jordan* can only be understood in terms of the legal process. The bare bones appear in the judgment of the Court of Criminal Appeal, and it is as well to begin here before putting flesh on the bones. At the trial, it seems never to have been doubted that the cause of death was pneumonia brought about by the stabbing, but, within a couple of days of the original conviction, a doctor who had observed the victim in hospital contacted the US Air Force Base outside Hull where Jordan was stationed and said that, in his opinion, the real cause of death was not the stab wound, but the improper treatment Beaumont had been given in hospital. This was passed on to Jordan's solicitors and an appeal was lodged on the basis of the new light that this shed on the case. Reports were obtained from two very eminent medical men, Dr Keith Simpson and Mr Guy Blackburn. Simpson was one of the most eminent pathologists in the country,[13] one of the founders of the Association of Forensic Medicine and author of a standard textbook on the subject.[14] He had already achieved a degree of fame in identifying the remains of one of the victims of the 'Acid Bath Murderer' in 1949, and shortly after he appeared in *Jordan*, he was to be retained by the Medical Defence Union as one of the defence team in the trial of Dr John Bodkin Adams.[15] Guy Blackburn was less well known but hardly less eminent: a consultant surgeon at Guy's Hospital and sometime Hunterian Professor at the Royal College of Surgeons.[16] According to the headnote to the report in the Criminal Appeal Reports, the two men testified that in their opinion, death had been caused not by the stab wound, but by the administration of terramycin after the intolerance had been shown and by the excessive amounts of fluid which had been given.[17] As interpreted by Hallett J, giving the judgment of the Court, this was an interpretation

---

[9] TNA: PRO DPP 2/2531 file 1, letter dated 23 August 1956. Donal Barry, the Assistant DPP, had already consulted the Clerk of Assizes to verify that there were no outstanding charges on file: see below, n 41.

[10] GL Williams, 'Causation in Homicide' [1957] *Crim LR* 429, 510; F Camps and J Havard, 'Causation in Homicide—A Medical View' [1957] *Crim LR* 576.

[11] *British Medical Journal* (13 October 1956).

[12] GL Williams, 'Homicide and Medical Negligence' *The Listener* (11 July 1957) 63–65.

[13] R Odell, *Medical Detectives* (Stroud, History Press, 2013) 172–208.

[14] K Simpson, *Forensic Medicine* (London, Arnold, 1947).

[15] K Simpson, *Forty Years of Murder* (London, Harrap, 1978), 159–66, 207–18.

[16] *Who was Who*, www.ukwhoswho.com/view/article/oupww/whowaswho/U171173.

[17] *Jordan* (n 1) 153.

of the evidence 'from a medical point of view'; it did not foreclose the question whether there had been a break in the chain of causation from a legal point of view.[18] However, in the opinion of the court, if the jury had heard the evidence of 'two doctors of the standing of Dr Keith Simpson and Mr Blackburn', they could hardly have said that they were satisfied that the death had been caused by the stab wound.[19] In the light of this, the appeal was allowed.

The central feature in terms of the process in the case, clearly, was the admission of the new evidence.[20] A broad power to receive this was contained in section 9 of the Criminal Appeal Act 1907. In practice, this had been narrowly interpreted by the courts and, in particular, it had been stressed that the evidence should not have been available at the time of the trial. The power was wide enough to allow the consideration of new medical evidence, though the Court of Criminal Appeal hardly ever permitted this and stressed that it was only in very exceptional cases that the power would be exercised (though without saying what it was that made a case exceptional). It had been allowed in *Harding*,[21] where a mother had been prosecuted for killing her baby by throwing it into a canal. The medical evidence at the trial had been that the death—by shock rather than drowning—could in reality only have occurred if the child had been thrown into the canal, but subsequent to the trial, it was suggested that the condition of the body was consistent with the baby having rolled into the canal while the mother was dozing. There was no realistic sense in which it could be said that the evidence was not available at the time of the trial; it was not as if there had been some scientific breakthrough between the trial and the appeal, only that a doctor willing to express an alternative opinion had been found. *Harding* was relied upon by counsel for the appellant in *Jordan* and the argument was structured in very much the same way. In both cases, there was new expert evidence; in both cases, the jury had made a strong recommendation for mercy; in both cases, there was reason to believe that the jury had deliberated very carefully before returning their guilty verdict.[22] We might say, too, that in both cases, it was wholly unclear why the case was so exceptional that the new medical evidence should be admitted and relied upon. Looking at both *Harding* and *Jordan*, the lawyer feels a sense

[18] ibid 155.
[19] ibid 156.
[20] R Pattenden, *English Criminal Appeals 1844–1994* (Oxford, Oxford University Press, 1996) 131–33. It was mooted that the case should be retained as a precedent by the DPP for this reason, but the suggestion was rejected: TNA: PRO DPP 2531/2, file 1. These precedents are to be found in TNA: PRO DPP 5.
[21] *Harding* (1936) 25 Cr App R 190 (CCA).
[22] Although in *Harding* the jury were concerned about the way in which the child had met its death, in *Jordan* they were concerned about the collateral question of the defence of provocation.

of discomfort that the evidence was not tested by the jury; the doctors were cross-examined, it is true, but the normal safeguard against expert evidence being believed too easily—the presence of expert evidence on the other side—was wholly absent. The best solution, perhaps, might have been to hold a new trial before a new jury, but the power to award a new trial was only introduced in 1964.[23]

The approach of the Court of Criminal Appeal to the new medical evidence is very telling, revealing the extent to which the odds were stacked in favour of the appellant. The report of the hearing in the *Manchester Guardian* notes prosecuting counsel being asked by Donovan J: 'Are you saying that this opinion from Dr Simpson is palpably wrong and untenable?'[24] In other words, there was a very strong presumption that Simpson's judgement was correct. The effective consequence was, as prosecuting counsel observed, that 'as soon as further medical evidence was admitted before the court, the appeal had to be allowed'.[25] Ormerod J is reported as having retorted to this that it was only in extreme cases that new medical evidence would be admitted in the Court of Criminal Appeal. This was no doubt true, but it did not answer the point; it merely underlined the fact that it was the decision to admit new evidence that was of fundamental importance, not the nature or quality of that evidence, and there was, so far as we know, no reason given why Jordan's case was an exceptional one.

Leaving aside for the moment the issue of the quality of the new evidence, we should dispose of the question of the availability of the evidence at the trial. On the face of it, it might seem that there was no more than a blatant attempt by the defence to produce favourable medical opinion which could have been raised at the trial, but which was not produced for tactical reasons. The cynical critic might even think that the tactical reason was specifically to prevent its consideration by the jury, inevitably alongside evidence from expert witnesses for the prosecution testifying to the contrary. If it could be introduced on appeal, without contrary medical opinion being admitted, then it would be unchallenged. Such a suggestion would be unfair. The question had been adverted to early on when the decision to prosecute for murder was made in the DPP's office: 'Assuming the medical evidence associates the stab wound with the cause of death', a murder charge could be brought.[26] The focus of the trial, however, was on completely different matters.

[23] Criminal Appeal Act 1964.
[24] *Manchester Guardian* (Manchester, 22 August 1955) 2.
[25] ibid.
[26] TNA: PRO DPP 2/2531, file 2. Note also the clear statement of Jordan's counsel that it was not relevant that Beaumont had died of pneumonia: 'In this country, if you cause a death, directly or indirectly, you are guilty, according to the circumstances, of manslaughter or murder': TNA: PRO DPP 2/2531, file 1, trial transcript, fourth day, 52.

Jordan was not tried alone, but with three other airmen. The real questions, on which practically everything at the trial hinged, were which of the four accused had wielded the knife and whether his co-accused could be guilty as secondary parties. Almost nothing was said about anything that had happened after Beaumont's admission into hospital. It was recognised from the start that the factual issues were complex and that careful preparation was needed by all the defence lawyers.[27] In the event, there was considerable evidence that it was Jordan who had inflicted the stab wound, and it was assumed that it was the stab wound which 'ultimately, though perhaps rather indirectly'[28] had led to the death from bronchopneumonia. The evidence was strong that the other defendants had known that he had the knife (and one or more of the others may have been carrying a knife too), but Jordan had used it on the spur of the moment and they were not acting in concert. At the end of the prosecution's case, counsel for the other three defendants all submitted that there was no case to answer. It was only if there was a 'common design'—today we would probably say a 'joint enterprise'—that the others could be held guilty as secondary parties.[29] After legal argument, the judge agreed and the three co-defendants were acquitted on his direction. Jordan's own defence was either that he was acting in self-defence or under provocation. It was this that the jury were concentrating on: two hours after they had retired, they returned for further direction explicitly on the defence of provocation, and only after that did they bring in their verdict of murder.[30] In terms of the dynamics of the trial, therefore, it was excusable not to have dealt with the question of the causal link between the stabbing and the death: the post-mortem report, which was naturally available to both the defence and the prosecution,[31] contained very little to suggest that there was anything to break the chain of causation and there was a great deal of other complex evidence to be winnowed.

It was only after the trial that the treatment of Beaumont was questioned. A relatively junior surgeon who had been concerned in a minor way with the treatment,[32] one Mr Dadaczynski, claimed to have been party to a conversation in the doctors' sitting room, where the suggestion had been made that Beaumont's death had been caused by acute diarrhoea, seemingly caused by the administration of terramycin. He had contacted the American authorities and the Coroner's office almost immediately after the trial, the police

---

[27] TNA: PRO ASSI 45/264, noting that the case had been transferred from the York Assizes to the Sheffield Assizes, and thence to the Leeds Assizes because of the need to give the defence time to prepare.

[28] TNA: PRO DPP 2/2531, file 1, transcript of trial, fourth day, 9.

[29] *Davies v DPP* [1954] AC 378 (HL).

[30] TNA: PRO DPP 2/2531, file 1, transcript of trial, fifth day, 17–19.

[31] Camps and Havard, 'Causation in Homicide' 585.

[32] *Jordan* (n 1) 153 seemingly exaggerates his role, suggesting that he had been the doctor treating Beaumont. As House Surgeon, his job was to see that the instructions of the Surgical Registrar were carried out.

investigated the claims very promptly, the Chief Constable alerted the DPP and, five days after the original conviction, an appeal was lodged. None of the other doctors recollected the conversation in the same way as Dadaczynski, and only one recalled any conversation at all.[33] It was suggested by some of the doctors that Dadaczynski had some ulterior motive for pressing the point. He had fought for the Germans in the war, only deserting and coming over to the side of the Allies at a late stage; he was now seeking entry into the US, but had been told that he would have to wait three years, and his motive in informing the American authorities, it was suggested, was to ingratiate himself with them in order to accelerate this. Moreover, he was thought to have a grudge against the consultant surgeon responsible for treating Beaumont, who was said to have refused to give him a reference because of his inefficiency. Whether this is true or not it is impossible to say, but at the very least, there is substantial evidence that there was friction between Dadaczynski and other doctors in the hospital. The pathologist who had carried out the post mortem, Dr Shillitoe, was also interviewed in the light of Dadaczynski's allegations; he denied that there was any necessary relationship between the terramycin and Beaumont's diarrhoea, citing a very recent paper in the *Journal of Clinical Pathology*,[34] and said that in any event, the diarrhoea had cleared up before the death and was therefore irrelevant to it.

In reality, Dadaczynski's claims did not come to much. His statement consisted of nothing more than an opinion of a junior doctor: 'I consider the real cause of death to be his much weakened condition caused by acute diarrhoea which was the result of the use of terramycin.'[35] It was described as a 'hare' in the DPP's brief to counsel, but reports were sought and received from Keith Simpson and Guy Blackburn.[36] Each was based on a study of the notes, hospital records and the autopsy report. Each was to the effect that in the normal course of events, Beaumont would have been expected to have recovered given the prompt treatment that he received. That he did not recover required explanation, and the explanation was found in the administration of terramycin to a patient who had shown that he was intolerant to it. Blackburn said carefully in his statement that the renewed administration was 'not without risk', though in the Court of Criminal Appeal, he is reported as having gone further and described it as 'extremely hazardous';[37] Simpson that it was 'dangerous' and an 'error of judgement'. There was,

---

[33] The notes on the interviews with the doctors are in counsel's brief for the appeal: TNA: PRO DPP 2/2531, file 1.

[34] M Corridan, 'Antibiotic-Resistant Staphylococcal Pseudomembraneous Enteritis' (1956) 9 *Journal of Clinical Pathology* 131.

[35] TNA: PRO DPP 2/2531, file 1.

[36] ibid.

[37] *Manchester Guardian* (Manchester, 22 August 1956) 2.

said Simpson, 'a clear novus actus interveniens *from a medical point of view*' (emphasis added).

In response to the successful appeal, and the evidence of Simpson and Blackburn on which it was based, the Leeds Regional Hospital Board set up a committee of enquiry with three independent medical assessors: Professor John Biggart, Dean of the Medical Faculty at Queen's University, Belfast; Professor James Bruce, Regius Professor of Clinical Surgery at the University of Edinburgh; and Dr Frank Parsons, Assistant Director of the Medical Research Council's surgical research unit at the Leeds Infirmary and the pioneer of kidney dialysis. They reported on 13 September, little more than three weeks after the appeal had been heard. Their report, printed in the *British Medical Journal*,[38] exonerated the doctors entirely; it was based on all the notes used by Simpson and Blackburn, interviews with the doctors principally involved in the treatment of Beaumont, and examination of the histological preparations relating to the autopsy. They paid tribute to the care and devotion of the senior surgeons, especially to the Surgical Registrar who had moved into the hospital so as to be available immediately if he was needed. Disagreeing with Simpson and Blackburn, they reported that damage had occurred to Beaumont's organs very soon after the attack, damage which was in itself sufficient to have brought about his death. Moreover, he was already on the point of death on the fifth post-operative day,[39] being so ill that the consultant surgeon had advised the police to take a dying deposition and that a special magistrates' court had been convened at the bedside. The initial treatment with terramycin and its withdrawal were wholly proper, and although the renewed administration was 'possibly unwise', it was 'not unreasonable and certainly not blameworthy', and in any event by this time Beaumont's condition was irreversible.

It is impossible, of course, to attempt to resolve the conflict of medical judgement. There is perhaps a hint that the committee of enquiry's report leaned heavily in favour of exonerating the doctors, but that does not mean it was wrong any more than that their judgement meant that the opinion of Simpson and Blackburn was wrong. For our purposes, it does not matter. What was important was that there was a significant difference in medical opinion, but that the way in which the evidence was received in the Court of Criminal Appeal prevented this from being teased out. It is hard to gainsay the view of counsel for the prosecution that as soon as credible medical evidence was produced and could not be controverted, there was little choice but to allow the appeal.

A second aspect of the process should be noticed in passing, though it is less obvious than the receipt of new evidence. There was at the time a

---

[38] *British Medical Journal* (22 September 1956) 716–17.
[39] That is, before the renewed administration of terramycin.

rule that where a person was charged with murder, this should not be con-joined with any lesser charges.[40] The four defendants were initially charged with unlawful wounding, but when Beaumont died and the murder charge was brought, these original charges were therefore dropped. The jury's ver-dict, unaffected by the appeal, clearly implied that Jordan was guilty of the lesser offence, but once he had been acquitted of murder, there was no other charge to fall back on. The day after the appeal, the Assistant DPP wrote to the Clerk of Assizes to check as a matter of urgency whether there were any outstanding charges on file since the American authorities wanted to bring charges before a Court Martial, receiving an answer that there were none.[41] A decision was taken not to bring new charges of unlawful wounding.[42] Jordan was therefore handed over to the Americans and fur-ther British jurisdiction was waived. A few days later, it was reported that he had received a punishment of 30 days' imprisonment and a $50 fine for violating the military regulation prohibiting the carrying of a knife with a blade more than two inches long.[43]

## III. THE CASE AND ITS CONTEXTS

### A. Murder and the Abolition of the Death Penalty

The most immediate context into which the decision in *Jordan* must be fitted, though one hardly visible in the case itself, is the debate over the abolition of capital punishment for murder.[44] The law at the time was clear that a person convicted of murder should be sentenced to death by hanging, though the Home Secretary, in the exercise of the royal prerogative, then had the power to reprieve him or her. Home Secretaries, it was said, strained to find reasons not to order that the law should take its course. The reten-tion or abolition of the death penalty was a matter of acute controversy: a clause to abolish it in the Criminal Justice Bill 1948 had been passed by the House of Commons, but rejected by the House of Lords. A Royal Commis-sion had been set up under the chairmanship of Sir Ernest Gowers and, after four years, it had recommended changes, but the government had taken

---

[40] *Jones* [1918] 1 KB 416 (CCA); reversed by *Practice Direction (Homicide: Indictment)* [1964] 1 WLR 1244.
[41] TNA: PRO DPP 2/2531 file 1.
[42] ibid.
[43] *Manchester Guardian* (Manchester, 29 August 1956).
[44] The unfolding background is described in B Block and J Hostettler, *Hanging in the Bal-ance* (Winchester, Waterside Press, 1997) 170–85. The only hint of this in the trial transcript is the warning by Jordan's counsel that the jury should put out of their mind what they had read in the paper about this sort of case: DPP 2/2531, file 1, trial transcript, fourth day, 44. His statement, no doubt, was intended to have precisely the opposite effect.

no steps to implement any of the recommendations. The suggestion that it should be left in the hands of the jury to determine the appropriate penalty, subject to a final long-stop of the prerogative of mercy where the jury had imposed the death sentence,[45] had been very heavily criticised, and while a recommendation to mercy (as occurred in *Jordan*) might influence the Home Secretary, the Commission noted that there had been 112 cases in the previous 50 years where such a recommendation had been disregarded.[46]

Earlier in 1956, the House of Commons had resolved that legislation should be introduced to abolish or suspend the death penalty, though the view of the government as expressed by the Home Secretary was that it should be retained.[47] The Prime Minister assured the House that the government would give full weight to the Commons' decision,[48] but it was left to a private member's bill formally to propose abolition, which was opposed by the government. The bill was given a third reading in the House of Commons on 28 June,[49] but was rejected on the second reading in the House of Lords on 10 July.[50] By the time that Jordan's trial started on 16 July, the newspapers had been full of the whole debate for the better part of two weeks. Moreover, the government's position, and that of the Home Secretary, was very publicly known to be in favour of the death penalty. And although every murderer convicted since the middle of 1955 had been reprieved by the Home Secretary,[51] it could not be assumed that this did not simply represent a fortunate run,[52] or more likely a sensible practice while the bill was progressing through Parliament, but which would be brought to an end once it had been rejected in the House of Lords. The supposition that Jordan would almost certainly be reprieved, as expressed in the *New York Times*,[53] may have been optimistic. It was perhaps this that led Jordan's legal advisers to pursue an appeal on the basis of Mr Dadaczynski's very thin suggestion of medical negligence.

There is no reason to suspect that this influenced the Court of Criminal Appeal. Whilst the views of the three judges in the court are not known, the judiciary was generally as much in favour of the retention of the death penalty as was the government, subject always to the Home Secretary's

[45] Home Office, *Report of the Royal Commission on Capital Punishment* (Cmd 8932, 1953) 194–208.

[46] ibid, 203, para 579.

[47] Hansard HC 16 February 1956, cols 2536–655.

[48] ibid, col 2656.

[49] Hansard HC 28 June 1956, cols 713–839.

[50] Hansard HL 9 July 1956, cols 564–676, 10 July 1956, cols 679–843.

[51] *The Times* (London, 11 July 1956). The last execution had taken place on 12 August 1955.

[52] See the remarks of former Home Secretary Chuter Ede, Hansard HC 16 February 1956, col 2561.

[53] *New York Times* (New York, 21 July 1956).

power to reprieve, and in the absence of very clear evidence it is impossible to suppose that three judges would have acted cynically to undermine the decision as to whether to exercise the prerogative. But were it not for this background, it might never have reached them at all.

## B. Expert Medical Evidence

So far as the Court of Criminal Appeal's decision is concerned, the most visible context into which *Jordan* fits is that of the relationship between the law and the medical profession in the mid-1950s. Central to the way in which the appeal unfolded was the deference shown by the Court to Simpson and Blackburn. So far as we can tell from the report of the argument, it was only if their opinions were shown by the prosecution to be 'palpably wrong' that the appeal would have failed.[54] In this, it reflects what was a potentially serious problem: the inability of the courts to assess medical treatment or medical evidence.

This was not a new problem. It can easily be traced back to the first quarter of the twentieth century as medical treatment became increasingly dependent on complex technology and new drugs, but it was probably only in the 1950s that it was coming to be recognised. Its best-known instantiation is the jury direction of Macnair J in *Bolam v Friern Hospital Management Committee* in 1957[55] that a doctor would not be liable in negligence if he or she had followed a recognised line of medical opinion, whether or not the court thought that opinion was right. While this is commonly seen as affecting the standard of care demanded of doctors, its real effect was to relieve the jury of the necessity of having to weigh up conflicting evidence from different experts without having any proper criteria for doing so.[56]

Related to this in the 1940s and 1950s was the problem of expert evidence from pathologists. After the death of Sir Bernard Spilsbury in 1947, whose evidence was for better or worse largely unchallenged, there emerged a trio of very able pathologists: Keith Simpson, Francis Camps and John Glaister.[57] There was a degree of rivalry among them, and between Simpson and Camps in particular the rivalry descended at times into downright unpleasantness.[58] Commonly these pathologists would be pitched against each other—one for the prosecution and one for the defence—and their evidence would inevitably be framed in such a way as to support the side that had called them. Medical experts could be undermined in cross-examination

---

[54] Above, n 24.
[55] *Bolam v Friern Hospital Management Committee* [1957] 1 WLR 582 (QB).
[56] J Bell and D Ibbetson, *European Legal Development: The Case of Tort* (Cambridge, Cambridge University Press, 2012) 99.
[57] Odell, *Medical Detectives* 110–208.
[58] ibid 170.

if they had expressed themselves incautiously,[59] but Simpson, Camps and Glaister were good witnesses as well as experts in their field. All too frequently, the jury was left with a simple choice as to which of them to believe and, by the late 1950s, this was coming to be seen as a real problem.[60] Insofar as the system of parties' expert witnesses depends on a degree of cooperation between the witnesses, the relationship between Camps and Simpson in particular was putting it under stress. Moreover, the scholarship in the field was advancing rapidly, as witnessed by the successive editions of Simpson's *Forensic Medicine* and the appearance of Camps' *Practical Forensic Medicine* in 1956, together with the foundation of the Association of Forensic Medicine by Simpson and others in 1950, and of Camps' rival British Academy of Forensic Sciences in 1958.

The evidentiary context casts some light on the way in which the appeal progressed, but it does no more than that. It hardly explains the willingness of the judges to hear the new evidence *in this case*, what it was that made the case exceptional. Clearly, it is not enough to say that there was a strongly expressed medical opinion from two eminent doctors, for if this was sufficient, it would too easily open the way for the defence to suppress medical evidence at the trial stage and to introduce it by way of appeal, uncontroverted, with a strong presumption that the appeal would succeed unless the expert witness broke down under cross-examination. We need to look more closely at the background context of the case to see why *Jordan* might have been thought of as exceptional.

## C. The US Air Force and the Cold War

Jordan was a US airman, serving at Holme-on-Spalding Moor a few miles outside Hull. A wartime RAF base, this had been used by the US Air Force since 1952 as a base for training aircrew and subsequently as a base for those who were rebuilding the runway at nearby RAF Elvington. There can be little doubt that this was intended to be a forward operating base from which the US could launch a nuclear attack on the Soviet Union or China.[61] The Cold War was very much a reality in 1956. While there is no evidence of resentment towards the US Air Force on the part of the residents of

---

[59] Most memorable was the destruction of the evidence of Dr Arthur Douthwaite, the prosecution's expert, by Geoffrey Lawrence QC in the trial of John Bodkin Adams: S Bedford, *The Best We Can Do* (London, Collins, 1958).

[60] Glanville Williams alluded to this in 'Homicide and Medical Negligence' at 65, saying that it would be better if there was a medical assessor, since only an expert could judge between experts.

[61] W Cocroft and R Thomas, *Cold War: Building for Nuclear Confrontation 1946–1989* (Swindon, English Heritage, 2003), 54.

Holme-on-Spalding Moor—and perhaps even the reverse[62]—friction had occurred elsewhere in England[63] and in his closing speech at the trial, Jordan's counsel alluded to a degree of prejudice which was thought to be widespread:

> Do you doubt but that there is not considerable feeling about airmen ... whom some people seem to think have a lot too much money?[64]

There was also serious political concern about the use of a base in England to launch U2 planes on reconnaissance missions behind the Iron Curtain and, in June 1956, just as *Jordan* was unfolding, the American U2 base was moved from Lakenheath in Suffolk to Wiesbaden in Germany.[65] This was probably not generally known in 1956, but the sensitivity of relations with the US Air Force was clear.

## D. Race Relations in Britain

Jordan was not merely an airman—he was a 'coloured' airman, as were his co-accused. The judgment of the Court of Criminal Appeal refers to his colour, as do all of the English newspaper reports; the papers in the DPP's file and the transcript of the trial both bring out a strong racial undercurrent in the case.[66]

The events leading up to Beaumont's stabbing fitted neatly into a stereotype. The Blue Bird cafe was in the docklands area of Hull, and it was in the areas round docks that the marginalised and indigent members of society had long congregated. In particular, since the early years of the twentieth century, it was around docks that foreign communities had come together. The Chief Constable, in a letter to the DPP, had described the cafe as a place 'frequented by coloured men, seamen and prostitutes',[67] and in the course of the trial, a police sergeant admitted that he was not surprised that 'that coloured men should go into that part of Hull where they may think they will be tolerated better and where coloured men are seen regularly'.[68] In truth there seems to have been very little suspicion of tension based on the

---

[62] *Yorkshire Post* (Leeds, 26 August 1954), referring to the popularity of the American troops in the area.

[63] R Jackson, *United States Air Force in Britain* (Shrewsbury, Airlife, 2000) 51.

[64] TNA: PRO DPP 2/2531, file 1, trial transcript, fourth day, 46.

[65] GW Pedlow and DE Welzenbach, *The Central Intelligence Agency and Overhead Reconnaissance: The U-2 and OXCART Programs, 1954–1974* (Washington DC, Central Intelligence Agency, 1992) 95–96, available at www.foia.cia.gov/sites/default/files/document_conversions/18/1992-04-01.pdf.

[66] For a contemporary analysis of the issue, see M Banton, *White and Coloured* (London, Jonathan Cape, 1959), which is substantially based on research done in 1956.

[67] TNA: PRO DPP 2/2531, file 2.

[68] TNA: PRO DPP 2/2531, file 1, trial transcript, third day, 72.

airmen's colour rather than their nationality: the owner of the cafe, Jama, was from the Caribbean, and all the evidence points to his having been fully integrated as a member of the community. That the airmen were Americans may perhaps have been a source of friction: it may have been a customer's calling them 'Damn Yanks' that was one of the events precipitating the brawl.[69]

Yet if there was in fact no colour-based friction behind the fight, a narrative of racial tension could easily be constructed. Race relations in England in the mid- and late 1950s were increasingly tense, culminating in the so-called Notting Hill Riots of 1958. The judge had warned the jury that they should not be prejudiced by Jordan's colour,[70] though making no mention here of his nationality or status as a member of the US forces. Jordan's counsel clearly entered into such a narrative too. In the context of arguing that the fight had been started by Ernest Milnes, Beaumont's friend with whom he had been in the cafe, he suggested that witnesses might have misremembered what they had seen:

> Is there a sort of unconscious prejudice by which people say: 'Oh, black men, black men. It is their fault one of them had a knife and look what happened.' So, possibly quite unconsciously, it all builds up.[71]

As a serviceman, Jordan did not trigger two of the common fears which led to racial prejudice: competition for jobs and competition for housing. But he could be seen as triggering a third fear: competition for girls. The principal witnesses in the case were the young women with whom the airmen had been spending time earlier in the evening and who had gone to the cafe with them. Presumably in an attempt to paint a picture of Milnes having started the fight, defence counsel asked him 'Do you approve of coloured American airmen going out with white girls?', and in his closing address he dropped in that: 'Some white people do not approve of coloured men going out with white women.'[72]

There may have been a legal point to counsel's raising issues of race. On the law at the time—and now—provocation would reduce a conviction from murder to manslaughter only if it would have provoked a reasonable man to lose his self-control. Counsel's argument was that, in the circumstances, Jordan's response to the alleged provocation was reasonable. As a stranger, and a coloured stranger to boot—'There are not so many of his colour about'[73]—he should be seen as particularly vulnerable. The judge had ignored this aspect in his summing-up, directing the jury that the question for them was whether the words 'damn yanks' were enough to make

[69] TNA: PRO DPP 2/2531, file 1, trial transcript, fourth day, 55–56
[70] ibid 55.
[71] ibid 49.
[72] TNA: PRO DPP 2/2531, file 1, trial transcript, second day, 50.
[73] TNA: PRO DPP 2/2531, file 1, trial transcript, fourth day, 46.

a reasonable man lose his self-control and making no reference to special sensitivities.[74] But however much this formed part of the background to the case, there was nothing there that justified an appeal. If anything, the judge's direction had been too favourable to Jordan, assuming that words could constitute provocation a year before this was to be made clear in the Homicide Act. And although the context would not have escaped the judges in the Court of Criminal Appeal, we cannot think that it would have affected their judgement.

## E. The Legal Status of Foreign Servicemen

More significant, perhaps, was the legal status of American servicemen in England. Under the North Atlantic Treaty Organization's Status of Forces Agreement of 1951, the primary right to exercise jurisdiction over offences allegedly committed by members of the forces of one state committed in another lay with the civil authorities of the receiving state, other than where the offence related to the property or security of the sending state or arose in the performance of official duty.[75] Jordan did not fall within any of the exceptions, so on the face of it, he fell within the jurisdiction of the English courts. The receiving state might waive jurisdiction, and the Agreement provided that a request that jurisdiction be waived should be treated sympathetically,[76] but it was not obliged to accede to any request. This was a matter of considerable sensitivity in the US. In July 1956, very shortly after Jordan's conviction, Representative Thomas J Dodds of Connecticut had protested against this 'outrageous agreement' in the House of Representatives, saying that its consequence was to deprive US servicemen—'men we send abroad to defend this nation and the entire free world from the aggressive designs of Communist imperialism'—of normal constitutional protections.[77]

The day after Beaumont's death, a request had been made to the British authorities that jurisdiction over Jordan and his co-defendants should be waived, but it was politely declined (using the precise language of 'sympathetic consideration' found in the Status of Forces Agreement).[78] Before this, the British and American authorities had followed the normal procedure applicable where there was to be a trial in the civilian court: Lieutenant Shapiro, of the US base at Holme-on-Spalding Moor, had been appointed US investigative officer and had interviewed the four airmen under oath the

[74] ibid 55–56.
[75] NATO Status of Forces Agreement 1951, art 3(b).
[76] ibid, art 3(c).
[77] Congressional Record, 27 July 1956, 15763.
[78] TNA: PRO DPP 2/2531, file 2, letters of 14 and 15 May 1956. The opening sheets of DPP 2/2531, file 2 show that the matter had received serious consideration.

day after the stabbing had occurred.[79] It requires little imagination to see that the real concern was not simply that the men would be tried in the English courts, but that they would be tried on a capital charge in the English courts. There is also reason to believe that the American authorities had not fully cooperated with the court, refusing to supply documentation relating to Jordan's character.[80] This context was clearly alluded to in the *New York Times*'s report of the conviction, which stated that Jordan was the first American serviceman to be sentenced to death in a British court since jurisdiction had been granted to the British courts.[81] While Jordan's case was not explicitly mentioned in Dodds's speech in the House of Representatives, it was probably not coincidental that his criticism of the Status of Forces Agreement was made less than a week after the conviction was reported in the American newspapers.

We cannot know that this was something which, consciously or subconsciously, affected the minds of the judges in the Court of Criminal Appeal. At the least, we can say that the new medical evidence provided grounds for allowing the appeal—perhaps—and the immediate context of British relations with the US made it very convenient that the appeal should be allowed.

## IV. CAUSATION AND THE LAW

*Jordan* had an intellectual context too. Criminal law was becoming academically respectable, with new editions of *Russell on Crime* and Kenny's *Outlines of Criminal Law*, both from the hand of Cambridge's JWC Turner, in 1950 and 1952, respectively. Glanville Williams's magisterial *Criminal Law: The General Part* had appeared in 1953. The *Criminal Law Review* had begun in 1954 with an intended audience of academics as well as those involved in the practice of the law, and although the contents of the 1956 volume contained pieces of journalistic interest (and also light fiction) and instructional pieces on the bringing of prosecutions under the new Road Traffic Act and the like, there were also articles by academic criminal lawyers such as JC Smith, Glanville Williams and JWC Turner.

The whole issue of causation in criminal law before *Jordan* was rather unsophisticated, and it was probably the decision in *Jordan* and the subsequent discussion of it that began to put it on a new footing. The topic was not mentioned in the first edition of *Criminal Law: The General Part*.[82] Turner's edition of Kenny's *Outlines* said little more than that the accused's act had to be a but-for cause of the injury; it recognised that an intervening

---

[79] TNA: PRO DPP 2/2531, file 2.

[80] TNA: PRO DPP 2/2531, file 1, trial transcript, third day, 71.

[81] *New York Times* (New York, 21 July 1956).

[82] Williams, *Criminal Law*. It was hardly remedied in the second edition of 1961.

act might break the chain of causation, but said no more than that it was necessary to be careful since the earlier and later acts might both have contributed to the injury.[83] Only *Russell on Crime*, also edited by Turner, was more forthcoming. Recognising that difficult questions might arise where there was an intervening act of a third person, it identified a trio of nineteenth-century cases where it had been held that the bona fide treatment of an injury by a regular medical practitioner which then brought about death would not break the chain of causation, even if the initial injury was not mortal.[84] This was reflected in section 197 of the Canadian Criminal Code, reproducing in substance section 258 of the Criminal Code of 1927:

> Where a person causes to a human being a bodily injury that is of itself of a dangerous nature and from which death results, he causes the death of that human being notwithstanding that the immediate cause of death is proper or improper treatment that is applied in good faith.[85]

The judgment of the Court of Criminal Appeal fits into this pattern of emerging law. The cases cited by *Russell on Crime* were not mentioned and there was just a hint of the brief analysis of the law given there:

> We are disposed to accept it as the law that death resulting from any normal treatment employed to deal with a felonious injury may be regarded as caused by the felonious injury, but we do not think it necessary to examine the cases in detail or to formulate for the assistance of those who have to deal with such matters in the future the correct test which ought to be laid down with regard to what is necessary to be proved in order to establish causal connection between the death and the felonious injury.[86]

The *Journal of Criminal Law* simply picked up this distinction: the earlier cases were dealing with normal treatment, whereas *Jordan* was concerned with treatment that was not normal.[87] There was no recognition that the earlier cases (as digested in *Russell on Crime*) had been concerned with bona fide treatment by a regular practitioner, not with normal treatment. The comment on the case in the *Criminal Law Review* said no more than that the case was following well-established authority, but at the same time noting that it was more generous to the accused than were the earlier cases.[88]

It was only in 1957 that the serious discussion of causation in the light of *Jordan* began. The principal contribution was that of Glanville Williams in

---

[83] JWC Turner, *Kenny's Outlines of Criminal Law: an Entirely New Edition*, 16th edn (Cambridge, Cambridge University Press, 1952) 20–21.

[84] JWC Turner (ed), *Russell on Crime: A Treatise on Felonies and Misdemeanours*, 10th edn (London, Stevens, 1950), citing *Pym* (1846) 1 Cox CC 339; *McIntyre* (1847) 2 Cox CC 379; and *Davis* (1883) 15 Cox CC 174.

[85] 'Letter to the Editor' [1957] *Crim LR* 760.

[86] *Jordan* (n 1) 157.

[87] (1956) 20 *Journal of Criminal Law* 357.

[88] Citing *Holland* (1841) 2 M & Rob 351, 174 ER 313; *Davis* (1883) 15 Cox 174; and *Mabila* 1956 (1) SA 31 (noted [1956] *Crim LR* 513).

his two-part article in the *Criminal Law Review*,[89] complemented by a piece written from the medical standpoint by Francis Camps and John Havard.[90] Williams's article was a wide-ranging piece which attempted to reconstruct, or construct, the role of causation in murder and manslaughter, while that of Camps and Havard was more narrowly focused on the decision in *Jordan* itself. Camps, it will be remembered, was Keith Simpson's rival as a pathologist; Havard, the principal author, was a young doctor who had qualified at the bar in his spare time and who later became General Secretary of the British Medical Association.[91] The articles brought out three questions stemming from *Jordan*: whether it was right for doctors to say what was the legal, as opposed to the medical, cause of death; what would be the effect of the decision on the medical profession; and what was the correct rule for determining whether the chain of causation was broken.

There was agreement that it was not for the doctors to say whether or not the wound was the cause of death.[92] They could properly give evidence as to what had happened medically, but the legal interpretation was for the court. Smith and Hogan, in the first edition of their textbook, referred to this criticism approvingly, but added that 'perhaps all the witnesses intended to say was that the treatment alone was the medical cause of death'.[93] The critics were surely right to say that it was not for the doctors to say whether or not the wound was a cause, but were wrong to criticise them for doing so. It is only in the headnote that it is noted that they had said that in their opinion, death had not been caused by the stab wound.[94] In the judgment itself, Hallett J was quite unequivocal that they were only speaking about medical causation:

> [B]oth the doctors called are of opinion that, from the medical point of view, it cannot be described as caused by the wound at all. Whether from the legal point of view it could be described as caused by the wound is a more doubtful question.[95]

That this is what they had indeed said is borne out by their witness statements, where they clearly spoke only of medical causation.[96]

So far as the second question was concerned, there was general acceptance that the decision might cause difficulties for doctors. Camps and Havard,

---

[89] G Williams, 'Causation in Homicide' [1957] *Crim LR* 429, 510. See also Williams, 'Homicide and Medical Negligence' 63.

[90] Camps and Havard, 'Causation in Homicide'.

[91] For Camps, see Odell, *Medical Detectives* 144–70; for Havard, see *British Medical Journal* (19 June 2010) 1361. Havard's responsibility as the main author is described by Camps in a letter to the DPP, sending the unfootnoted typescript to him: DPP 2/2531, file 2.

[92] Williams, 'Causation in Homicide' 431; Camps and Havard, 'Causation in Homicide' 582.

[93] Smith and Hogan, *Criminal Law* 169.

[94] *Jordan* (n 1) 153.

[95] ibid 155.

[96] Above, text after n 37.

giving the medical view, pointed to the undesirability of doctors and surgeons being deterred from acting in an emergency for fear that they would be criticised subsequently for having done something which was 'not normal', and they raised the spectre of the courts in similar cases being swamped with investigations of the medical response to homicidal assaults.[97] Williams recognised that it was unfortunate that the competence of doctors should be impeached in a homicide trial, where a jury might be inclined to accept the evidence of negligence in order to acquit the defendant: 'On the other hand, to exclude such evidence ... would inevitably create a sense of injustice in the convicted person.'[98] He was more concerned with the procedural problem of witnesses critical of medical treatment being produced at trial unexpectedly when it was impractical to adjourn to hear the evidence of the doctors themselves: the solution, he suggested, was to require the accused to give advance notice of the defence; and the problem of the jury's assessing expert medical evidence could be dealt with by having medical assessors to interpret and evaluate the evidence.[99] Until changes of this sort were introduced, however, the admission of evidence aiming to criticise the treatment given to the victim of an assault would necessarily create difficulties, albeit difficulties he considered warranted in order to avoid injustice to the accused.

The third question was far more problematic. The Court of Criminal Appeal had said no more than that the treatment which Beaumont had received was 'palpably wrong' and 'not normal'.[100] Furthermore, they expressly disclaimed any intention of laying down a rule of law which would be a guide in future cases.[101] While perhaps alluding elliptically to the law as stated in *Russell on Crime*, they appear to have treated the previous cases as very substantially fact-dependent.[102] Still, though, the case had to stand as authority for the proposition that medical treatment that was not normal would break the chain of causation. This was accepted with some regret by Camps and Havard, recognising that this was a departure from the previous authorities which had held that treatment which was administered in good faith by a regular medical practitioner would not break the causal link between the initial injury and the death.[103] At the same time, they rightly pointed out that the court had nowhere explained what it meant by 'normal treatment'.

---

[97] Camps and Havard, 'Causation in Homicide' 583, 585
[98] Williams, 'Causation in Homicide' 513; Williams, 'Homicide and Medical Negligence' 65.
[99] Williams, 'Homicide and Medical Negligence' 65.
[100] *Jordan* (n 1) 157.
[101] ibid 157.
[102] Above, n 84.
[103] Camps and Havard, 'Causation in Homicide' 583

Glanville Williams's approach was rather different. He examined a far wider range of nineteenth-century cases on both murder and manslaughter, as well as American cases illustrating the issues,[104] and attempted to draw out some general principles. He recognised that the decision in *Jordan* marked a significant departure from the earlier cases[105] and attempted to construct a coherent picture of the law. Behind this, no doubt, lay his own opinion, which was openly stated in his article in *The Listener*: the decision in the case accorded with what he described as the plain man's opinion.[106] Although the judgment in *Jordan* itself provided no warrant for it, he characterised the medical treatment as negligent, generating a rule that the chain of causation would be broken whenever negligence intervened; while accepting that a test of gross negligence would be consistent with *Jordan*, it was the 'clear and simple' test of negligence that he preferred.[107] Yet for all that his approach was clear, there was an undoubted instability in his language. His description of the judgment in *Jordan* used the precise language of the court,[108] so that the interpretation of the treatment as negligent represents his own superstructure erected on top of this; it is not that he simply misread the case. In addition, when dealing with the conduct that would not break the chain of causation, it was 'proper' medical treatment that he was concerned with, not non-negligent medical treatment.[109] However, as Camps and Havard pointed out, criticising the article in *The Listener*, 'treatment which is "not normal" is not necessarily negligent'.[110] Williams admitted that mistaken advice (and therefore treatment) was not negligent simply because with hindsight it turned out to be wrong, provided that it 'appeared reasonable at the time when it was given',[111] and it may be that the word 'appeared' is significant if it indicates that it was the belief of the doctor giving the treatment that mattered rather than that of a reasonable outsider assessing the doctor's conduct. If so, it would bridge the gap between 'negligent' and 'proper' treatment, on the assumption that it would not be proper for a doctor to give treatment which he or she believed was unreasonable. But the use of the word 'negligent' almost inevitably raised the connotation of the objective approach of the law of tort.

Although Glanville Williams had put forward a coherent test, the fact remained that it was some way from being justified by the Court of Criminal

---

[104] Note his citation of the comment in (1933) 31 *Michigan Law Review* 659: Williams, 'Causation in Homicide' 517.

[105] Williams, 'Causation in Homicide' 429, 516.

[106] Williams, 'Homicide and Medical Negligence' 63.

[107] Williams, 'Causation in Homicide' 513.

[108] Williams, 'Causation in Homicide' 429, 430.

[109] The contrast is stark in Williams, 'Causation in Homicide' 516, 517; and in Williams, 'Homicide and Medical Negligence' 63–65.

[110] Camps and Havard, 'Causation in Homicide' 583 fn 20. Williams' article in the *Criminal Law Review* would have appeared too late for Camps and Havard to take account of it.

[111] Williams, 'Causation in Homicide' 516.

Appeal's judgment. Hence, Turner, in the 1958 edition of Kenny's *Outlines of Criminal Law*, could lament that 'even at the present time it is unfortunate that the principles to be applied in deciding what chain of causation will in law be sufficient to establish criminal liability are far from clear'.[112] The subject became yet more confused by the judgment of the Courts Martial Appeal Court in *Smith*[113] a year later, where *Jordan* was treated as 'a very particular case depending on its exact facts'.[114] There the medical treatment of a stab wound was described as 'thoroughly bad', but not so bad that it was 'so overwhelming as to make the original wound merely part of the history'.[115] The matter was further confused by the fact that the treatment in *Smith* was to do (almost) nothing, so that the wound itself was medically the cause of death; it could be described as still being a 'substantial and operating cause'. *Smith* itself might be marginalised as a case depending on its exact facts. It did not solve the problems raised by *Jordan*, and both subsequent editions of Kenny's *Outline* and Smith and Hogan's *Criminal Law* continued to point to the ambiguous state of the law. If anything, the final case in Smith and Hogan's triumvirate, *Cheshire*,[116] added to the confusion: negligent treatment would only break the chain of causation if it was 'so independent' of the accused's acts and 'in itself so potent in causing death as to make the contribution of the original deed to the death insignificant'.[117] Neither independence nor potency was clarified.

## V. CONCLUSION

It cannot be said that the development of the law from *Jordan* onwards reflects well on criminal law as a subject of scientific study, notwithstanding Glanville Williams's attempts to move the problem of causation in this direction. That may or may not be a bad thing. The close study of *Jordan* reveals the importance of context to the decision reached in any case, with findings of fact being made, and legal language and legal rules being manipulated in order to justify the result being reached. It is only when scholars, or later courts, attempt to reduce complex fact situations to clear and simple rules that problems arise, and here the common law is robust enough to allow previous decisions to be distinguished almost out of existence where that is thought necessary or desirable. Law is not, and cannot be, simply a matter

---

[112] JWC Turner (ed), *Kenny's Outlines of Criminal Law*, 17th edn (Cambridge, Cambridge University Press, 1958) 20–21.
[113] *Smith* (n 1).
[114] ibid 43.
[115] ibid.
[116] *R v Cheshire* [1991] 1 WLR 844.
[117] ibid 852.

of mechanically identifying and applying rules and principles to bloodless sets of facts ripped out of their contexts. Criminal law in particular, dealing with the punishment of seriously egregious conduct, must be able to adjust itself to precise sets of facts.

That said, the way in which a rule is formulated does have some effect. Canonical formulations of rules, especially when appearing in textbooks which are ostensibly descriptive of the law, can—and commonly do—function as the starting point of arguments in later cases. This became particularly evident in the civil law, where the publication of Blackstone's *Commentaries* in particular largely spawned the treatise tradition.[118] However objective the statements of law in these treatises appeared, with normative propositions neatly justified by authoritative cases in footnotes, the way in which the rules were described was the result of an exercise of construction by the treatise's author. Hence, in the law of contract, for example, Pothier's will theory became embedded in English law largely as a result of Chitty's work, and the developed doctrine of privity looks to have been shaped by successive editions of Addison's *Law of Contract*.[119]

As criminal law became more scientific in the 1950s and beyond, decisions, especially those in appellate cases, shaped the way in which the law was formulated in textbooks and treatises, and that in its turn shaped the way in which evidence was produced and arguments were presented. *Jordan* was one such decision, framed by reference to the earlier case law, but at the same time reorienting it along lines flowing from the need or desire to reach a particular result. In its turn, the formulation of the law in *Jordan* influenced the way in which *Smith* was argued, and this in its turn influenced the argument in *Cheshire*, though in neither case was the result necessitated by the previous decisions. The understanding of law as a dynamic system, progressing through a sequence of decisions in which the desired result is reached by the application and moulding of the existing rules, requires that we see individual cases in terms of the interrelationship between formal law and context, not just in terms of one or the other.[120]

---

[118] AWB Simpson, 'The Rise of the Legal Treatise: Legal Principles and the Forms of Legal Literature' (1981) 48 *University of Chicago Law Review* 632.

[119] AWB Simpson, 'Innovation in Nineteenth Century Contract Law' (1975) 91 *Law Quarterly Review* 247; D Ibbetson and W Swain, 'Third Party Beneficiaries in English Law: From *Dutton v. Poole* to *Tweddle v. Atkinson*' in EJH Schrage (ed), *Ius Quaesitum Tertio* (Berlin: Duncker & Humblot, 3008) 191, 209–10. See generally W Swain, *The Law of Contract 1670–1870* (Cambridge: Cambridge University Press, 2015).

[120] I have attempted to argue this at greater length in 'Comparative Legal History: A Methodology' in A Musson and C Stebbings (eds), *Making Legal History* (Cambridge, Cambridge University Press, 2012) 131.

# 11

# Shaw v DPP (1961)

## HENRY MARES[*]

### I. INTRODUCTION

O  N 18 MARCH 1961, halfway through the hearing in the House of Lords of *Shaw v DPP*,[1] Viscount Simonds wrote to Sir Owen Dixon, Chief Justice of the High Court of Australia:

> At this very hour we are engaged in considering whether a man can be said to 'live wholly or in part upon the earnings of prostitution' if he published a so-called 'Ladies Directory' giving the names, addresses, telephone numbers & sometimes photographs of prostitutes ... He is also charged with conspiring with other persons to corrupt the morals of the public. And that is a pretty good one too. For what after all did Lord Mansfield mean when he said that the Court of King's Bench was now 'custos morum'? On this matter much ink has been spilt![2]

It is safe to say, of course, that much more ink was still to be spilt; the case was reported extensively in *The Times*,[3] noted with interest in leading

---

[*] Very many thanks are due to many people, but in particular to Sir John Baker, Simon Bronitt, the workshop participants, and to the other editors of this volume. All errors are entirely the author's own.
[1] *Shaw v DPP* [1962] AC 220 (HL).
[2] A collection of Simonds's letters to Dixon is in the National Library of Australia, MS Acc09.166.
[3] Initial motions were reported in '"Ladies Directory" Summonses' *The Times* (London, 27 July 1960) 8; the trial was reported in 'Advertising by Prostitutes: Trial of Publisher on Three Charges' *The Times* (London, 17 September 1960) 10; 'Unofficial Advice Query to Police: "Ladies Directory" Trial' *The Times* (London, 20 September 1960) 4; 'Rebuke for Man in "Directory" Case: Half an Hour Late Arriving at Court' *The Times* (London, 21 September 1960) 5; the verdict and sentence were reported in '"Ladies Directory" Man Sentenced' *The Times* (London, 22 September 1960) 6. The Court of Criminal Appeal hearings were reported in 'Ladies Directory Appeal' *The Times* (London, 13 December 1960) 3; 'Conspiracy to Corrupt Public Morals' *The Times* (London, 14 December 1960) 3; 'Ladies' Directory: Convictions and Sentence Stand' *The Times* (London, 15 December 1960) 13; and 'Ladies Directory Appeal Dismissed: Leave to Appeal Granted' *The Times* (London, 22 December 1960) 3. The House of Lords hearings were reported in '"Ladies' Directory" Appeal' *The Times* (London, 14 March 1961) 21; 'The Queen's Peace and Public Law and Order' *The Times* (London, 16 March 1961) 9; 'Solicitor General's Submissions' *The Times* (London, 17 March 1961) 22; 'From 1663' *The Times* (London, 21 March 1961) 19; 'Crown's Case Concluded' *The Times*

English and American law journals,[4] formed part of the continuing debate between HLA Hart and Lord Devlin,[5] and was the basis for a BBC Radio 4 afternoon play.[6] It is still discussed in the most recent edition of *Smith and Hogan*.[7] *Shaw* was, and remains, a landmark case: for Viscount Simonds's assertion of an apparently creative 'residual power to superintend those offences which are prejudicial to the public welfare';[8] for the conclusion of the Court of Criminal Appeal, expressly left open by Lord Tucker, that corrupting public morals itself was a substantive offence; and for the clear finding by the majority in the House of Lords that conspiracy to corrupt public morals, in all its vagueness, was also an offence.

This chapter considers the background to the case, before moving on to consider the trial, and Shaw's subsequent appeals. It examines the reasoning in the House of Lords—not only through the usual law reports, but also as revealed in Viscount Simonds' letters—and the context of the decision in mid-twentieth-century jurisprudence. Focusing then on the corruption of public morals point, the chapter discusses the antecedents to the decision in *Shaw*, while briefly exploring also aspects of the surrounding issues of legal certainty.

## II. THE CASE

### A. The Background

Not much is discernible of the background of Frederick Charles Shaw. The main sources for his life, and for the process followed against him, are the law reports, the trial transcript in the House of Lords archive[9] and two files in the National Archives.[10] He had been convicted in December 1947 of receiving stolen property; he was divorced from his wife in 1959 and

---

(London, 22 March 1961) 9; 'Opinions Reserved' *The Times* (London, 23 March 1961) 5; and the decision in 'Ladies' Directory Appeal Dismissed' *The Times* (London, 5 May 1961) 21.

[4] AL Goodhart, 'The Shaw Case: The Law and Public Morals' [1961] *LQR* 560; 'Criminal Law. In General. Courts Have Power as *Custodes Morum* to Punish Conspiracy to Do Acts Newly Defined as Corruptive of Public Morals. *Shaw v. Director of Public Prosecutions* (H.L. 1961)' (1962) 75(8) *Harvard Law Review* 1652.

[5] See, for example, HLA Hart, *Law, Liberty, and Morality* (Stanford, Stanford University Press, 1963) 9–11, 25 and 44; P Devlin, *The Enforcement of Morals* (Oxford, Oxford University Press, 1965) 88 and 100.

[6] On 24 July 1998; see (1998) 3884 *Radio Times* 117.

[7] D Ormerod and K Laird, *Smith and Hogan's Criminal Law*, 14th edn (Oxford, Oxford University Press, 2015) 522–23.

[8] *Shaw* (n 1) 268.

[9] HL/PO/JU/4/3/1089.

[10] TNA: PRO MEPO 2/10559 and TNA: PRO Crim 1/3467. Another file, TNA: PRO DPP 2/3390, is closed until 2042.

was in arrears on child support for his five children.[11] He was a former lab assistant at the Royal Arsenal, Woolwich. After this he had several small business ideas, but no regular employment.[12] Then, in October 1959, he took over a small office at 11 Greek Street in Soho to start production of the Directory.[13]

The 1957 Wolfenden Report,[14] famous also for its conclusions about homosexuality, had concluded about prostitution that:

[T]here is no doubt that the aspect of prostitution which causes the greatest public concern at the present time is the presence, and the visible and obvious presence, of prostitutes in considerable numbers in the public streets of some parts of London and of a few provincial towns.[15]

The problem with the law relating to street prostitution at the time of the Report was that it had to be demonstrated that the prostitute had caused annoyance through her solicitation, and it was difficult to get the clients to give evidence that they had been annoyed; the Wolfenden Report concluded that this requirement should be removed. This was effected by the Street Offences Act 1959, section 1(1) of which provided merely that it would 'be an offence for a common prostitute … to loiter or solicit in a street or public place for the purpose of prostitution' and which consequently made it much harder for prostitutes to attract business.

There was thus a gap in the market for prostitutes to appeal directly to their clients, apparently spotted by Shaw. As Police Inspector Shrubsole recalled, in a 1959 witness statement, of a conversation he had had with Shaw:

Shaw said: 'Till two months ago I rarely came into the West End except to go to the Pictures. I was up here a few weeks ago just before the law was changed.' I interrupted and said, 'What law?' He said 'The law that stops prostitutes from getting the men by soliciting them in the street.' He went on, 'I thought then they would need some other way of getting in touch with their clients so I got the idea of this book.'[16]

---

[11] His former wife, Pamela, wrote to Marcus Lipton MP to offer to provide information against Shaw: TNA: PRO MEPO 2/10559/16A-F.
[12] These biographical facts come from a document entitled 'Antecedents of Frederick Charles Shaw' by Detective Inspector Charles Monahan in the unpaginated folder TNA: PRO Crim 1/3467.
[13] *Ladies Directory* (London, Shaw Publishing Company, 1959–60). Issues 7, 7 revised, 8, 9 and 10 were printed, along with a 'Special Supplement'. It appears that the first issue was 7 (see HL/PO/JU/4/3/1089 at 66); it is unclear why. Copies are in the British Library, Cup.1001.d.5; and in TNA: PRO MEPO 2/10559 and Crim 1/3467.
[14] Home Office, Report of the Committee on Homosexual Offences and Prostitution (Cmnd 247, 1957).
[15] ibid, para 229.
[16] TNA: PRO Crim 1/3467.

The idea was apparently a successful one. As the police noted: 'all the prostitutes who subscribed to it considered it a heaven-sent alternative to the street patrolling methods of obtaining clients to which they had hitherto been used, and most of them had become far better off financially as a result of the advertisements in the publication'.[17] A representative from Shaw would find details for the prostitutes through their cards on the London Underground or in shops, would telephone or call on them, and agree the advertisement.[18]

For Shaw also, the venture was reportedly successful.[19] The Directory was funded both by payment by the women themselves and also by the cost of purchasing the booklet, which was sold by some news vendors on Denman Street,[20] about 80 copies a week per kiosk, and by resellers on trains into London.[21] The 'Special Supplement' to the Directory also offered a subscription option.[22]

The Directory itself was small, about 18 cm by 13 cm, and under 30 pages. Each issue contained several pages of advertisements; one typical advertisement might give the pseudonym, the specialism and the contact details for an advertiser. For example, '*Miss Wyplash*, ex-governess, strict disciplinarian, telephone: Bayswater 5473' was the entire text of a whole-page advertisement appearing in both Issues 8 and 9.[23] Others advertised 'rubberwear' or 'full corr.'[24] Some advertisements also contained addresses and hours of availability. Others contained nude or semi-nude photographs; other nude photographs were less clearly related to the advertisements. Most of the advertisers were in London, but there were some exceptions: 'When in Nottingham why not visit a delightful model, Jean...' began one advertisement, before going on to give a Nottingham phone number. Yet other advertisements were for book exchanges and for 'sealed collections of photographs'.

Shaw, in his questioning by police, was inconsistent in his description of the advertisers: he said once that the advertisers were all prostitutes,[25] then

---

[17] Because of that, it was difficult to obtain evidence against Shaw, and the police who did, including Charles Monahan (who was also involved in the Lady Chatterley trial), received commendations as a result: TNA: PRO MEPO 2/10559/30A.

[18] TNA: PRO MEPO 2/10559/12A at 5.

[19] TNA: PRO MEPO 2/10559/12A.

[20] TNA: PRO MEPO 2/10559/14B1.

[21] For the attempted sale on the train to London to an off-duty policeman, see TNA: PRO MEPO 2/10559/36D.

[22] Copies of the Special Supplement, a less polished typescript insert, are in both TNA: PRO Crim 1/3467 and TNA: PRO MEPO 2/10559.

[23] This particular advertisement was in addition noted in the House of Lords debate of the Criminal Justice Bill by the Lord Chancellor. Ms Wyplash, the police noted after interviewing her, 'does not have intercourse with her customers but as her name suggests specialises in flagellation' (TNA: PRO MEPO 2/10559/12A at 3).

[24] The latter is explained in trial testimony: HL/PO/JU/4/3/1089 at 22.

[25] According to the deposition of DI Charles Monohan, TNA: PRO Crim 1/3467.

that all were prostitutes except one[26] and then that 'I advertise them as models, what they do in their spare time is no business of mine'.[27] And indeed, when questioned by police, a few of the advertisers maintained to the end that they were models.[28] Although it was not raised at trial, the police files also indicate that at least one advertiser, Yoland, was 'a known homo-sexual and transvestist who lives as a female'.[29]

The Directory had come to the notice of the police in several ways, and Shaw's interactions with the various branches of the police were complicated. Shaw himself had come into New Scotland Yard in October 1959 and asked for advice from the police on whether the publication would be legal; the police and Shaw each sent a copy to the DPP,[30] who requested a report from the police on the publication.[31]

But even independently of the consequences of that request for advice, the Directory came to the attention of the police and other authorities: its publication provoked questions in the House of Commons;[32] a concerned wife wrote to the police after she found a copy of the Directory in her husband's coat pocket;[33] and a seller on a train tried to sell a copy to an off-duty policeman.[34] Various sellers had also been arrested for using insulting behaviour on the street.[35] In at least one of these cases, a magistrate suggested further inquiry into the booklet.[36] Inspector Shrubsole had held his conversation with Shaw when Shaw materialised in court to stand surety for a seller of the Directory, Kranas, who had been arrested for importuning.[37] Shaw had asked for Shrubsole's advice at that meeting too; in his witness statement, Shrubsole noted that Shaw 'conveyed he wanted to stay within the law'.[38]

## B. The Charges

All of this attention resulted in a conference in the chambers of JH Buzzard, Treasury Counsel, to discuss with the DPP and the Metropolitan Police

---

[26] According to the deposition of DC Derek Clissold: 'He [Shaw] said "They are all prostitutes except the first one, I should make a bomb out of this".' TNA: PRO Crim 1/3467.

[27] TNA: PRO Crim 1/3467.

[28] TNA: PRO MEPO 2/10559/26D, 26E and 26F. And see n 23 above.

[29] TNA: PRO MEPO 2/10559/19B at paras 78–86.

[30] TNA: PRO Crim 1/3467, in particular the statement of Chief Inspector Leslie Jones.

[31] GR No 210/59/307 in TNA: PRO MEPO 2/10559.

[32] The Home Office requested a copy of the police reports to prepare the Home Secretary for questions: TNA: PRO MEPO 2/10559/3A.

[33] TNA: PRO MEPO 2/10559/9C.

[34] TNA: PRO MEPO 2/10559/36E.

[35] Under the Metropolitan Police Act 1839, s 54(13).

[36] TNA: PRO MEPO 2/10559.

[37] Under the Sexual Offences Act 1956, s 32.

[38] TNA: PRO Crim 1/3467.

what should happen.[39] Shaw was indicted on three counts, the first of which was conspiracy to corrupt public morals. To be more precise, the first charge was:

> On divers days between the 1st day of October 1959 and the 23rd day of July 1960 within the jurisdiction of the Central Criminal Court, conspired with certain persons who inserted advertisements in issues of a magazine entitled 'Ladies Directory' numbered 7, 7 revised, 8, 9, 10 and a supplement thereto, and with certain other persons whose names are unknown, by means of the said magazine and the said advertisements to induce readers thereof to resort to the said advertisers for the purposes of fornication and of taking part in or witnessing other disgusting and immoral acts and exhibitions, with intent thereby to debauch and corrupt the morals as well of youth as of divers other liege subjects of Our Lady the Queen and to raise and create in their minds inordinate and lustful desires.

The second count was living on the earnings of prostitution contrary to section 30 of the Sexual Offences Act 1956. This section provided in subsection (1) that it was 'an offence for a man knowingly to live wholly or in part on the earnings of prostitution'.

The third count was publishing an obscene article contrary to section 2 of the Obscene Publications Act 1959. This section provided in subsections (1) and (4) that:

> (1)   Subject as hereinafter provided, any person who, whether for gain or not, publishes an obscene article shall be liable—
>
> ...
>
> (b)   on conviction on indictment to a fine or to imprisonment for a term not exceeding three years or both.
>
> ...
>
> (4)   A person publishing an article shall not be proceeded against for an offence at common law consisting of the publication of any matter contained or embodied in the article where it is of the essence of the offence that the matter is obscene.

It was Buzzard, later a circuit judge, who was responsible for the decision to draft the charge of conspiracy to corrupt public morals. As it was reported in *The Times* during the House of Lords hearing:

> [Buzzard] was entirely responsible for the initiation and conduct of this prosecution, and if anybody had been wrong in including the conspiracy count in the indictment it was he. It had been done because this was the first prosecution under the Obscene Publications Act of 1959 and though the Crown would have been prepared to submit that this magazine was an obscene publication within the Act, it was very different from the ordinary case of obscene libel, for on its face it did not immediately conjure up impure thoughts in the mind. It might have been dif-

---

[39] TNA: PRO MEPO 2/10559/12A.

ficult to persuade a Judge and even more difficult to persuade a jury that this was an obscene libel. Further … on this much graver charge of conspiracy the punishment would be at large and not limited to the two years under the Act. For those reasons the conspiracy count had been put in the indictment.[40]

The conspiracy count served to demonstrate the inadequacy of section 2(4) of the Obscene Publications Act 1959, and a few years later became part of the debate in Parliament about the reform of that Act.[41]

It seems possible that the nature of the services offered by the advertisers might have had some impact on the popular perception of the matters perpetrated. Shaw and his counsel were provided with the deposition of Dr Francis Brisby, 'Principal Medical Officer H.M. Prison, Brixton', who was prepared at trial to say that:

> The corruptive influence in advertising those deviations associated with the infliction of or suffering of pain or degradation is recognized as leading to the most violent outrages against human nature or to the most fantastic humiliations of human nature. It is, in the adult, essentially atavistic.[42]

However, even the prosecution appeared dubious about the utility of this analysis. The file note on this point has pencil annotations: 'for jury not for expert', 'issue: morals, not health', and '?Brisby expert on corruption of morals? of any value'.

## C. The Trial

The case was heard on 16, 19 and 20 September 1960 at the Central Criminal Court. A transcript of the trial is in the records in the House of Lords archive.[43] Counsel for the prosecution were Buzzard and Michael Corkrey. Shaw was defended at trial by a publicly funded lawyer, Anthony Babington,[44] under the Poor Prisoner's Defence Act 1930.[45]

Evidence was led by the prosecution from various advertisers that they had paid Shaw, or a canvasser for Shaw, for their advertisements to be placed. Then, before he led any evidence, submissions were made by Babington for the defence, arguing that Shaw had no case to answer, and replies were made by Buzzard.[46] The police report of the trial notes:

[40] 'Crown's Case Concluded' *The Times* (London, 22 March 1961) 9.

[41] In which the expertise of WR Rees-Davies, the Conservative MP for Thanet, and Shaw's counsel in the Court of Criminal Appeal and the House of Lords, was called upon in the House of Commons: HC Deb 3 June 1964, vol 695, col 1175.

[42] TNA: PRO Crim 1/3467.

[43] HL/PO/JU/4/3/1089 at 13.

[44] The slip indicating this is in TNA: PRO Crim 1/3467.

[45] For the operation of the Act, see RM Jackson, *The Machinery of Justice in England*, 4th edn (Cambridge, Cambridge University Press, 1964) 140.

[46] HL/PO/JU/4/3/1089 at 46.

[E]xtensive legal submissions were made by the defence that there was no case to answer by Shaw concerning counts (2) and (3) of the indictment. The conspiracy charge was particularly criticised on the basis that no charge could exist in law. However, in support of that charge Mr Buzzard quoted several previous cases, the oldest being dated 1434 and the most recent being dated 1875.[47]

The defence then decided to call no evidence; it is not clear why.[48] This decision, especially as it applied to the obscenity point, can be contrasted with the trial a month later of Penguin Books for *Lady Chatterley's Lover*. Penguin, much better resourced, contacted over 300 'writers, scholars, and public commentators' for their support, and many testified at the trial; Penguin was acquitted.[49]

On 20 September, the jury retired to consider their verdict. In the National Archives is a note from the jury to the clerk of the court:

> Sir, I have a feeling that there will be a long deliberation on this case. If his lordship's summing up ends after 3pm, are we expected to stay well into the evening, or can we use tomorrow to reach our verdict?[50]

As it happens, after an absence of only one and a half hours, the jury returned verdicts of guilty on all three charges.[51] Shaw was sentenced to nine months in prison, at least some of which he spent in Wormwood Scrubs.

## D. In the Court of Criminal Appeal

Shaw appealed on all three points, represented by William Rees-Davies, but the Court of Criminal Appeal upheld the conviction on all grounds. The appeal on the obscenity ground was dealt with swiftly; arguments about intention were dispatched, and any misuse of evidence introduced for the other counts had not led to a substantial miscarriage of justice. The living on the earnings of prostitution point likewise did not require lengthy exegesis.

More difficult was the conspiracy to corrupt public morals point. Buzzard had argued in the first place that the kind of conspiracy alleged was a conspiracy to do an unlawful act, and had argued that the corruption of public morals itself was a substantive common law misdemeanour. The main issue on appeal was whether this was correct, as, if it was, then the conspiracy would exist as a crime. Buzzard had also reserved the back-up position that

---

[47] TNA: PRO MEPO 2/10559 at 27A.

[48] HL/PO/JU/4/3/1089 at 63; 'Rebuke for Man in "Directory" Case: Half an Hour Late Arriving at Court' *The Times* (London, 21 September 1960) 5.

[49] P Carter, 'Lady Chatterley's Lover trial (*act*. 1960)' *Oxford Dictionary of National Biography*, www.oxforddnb.com/view/theme/101234. Inspector Charles Monahan, also involved in the Shaw investigation, was the only prosecution witness in the Penguin trial (ibid).

[50] TNA: PRO MEPO 2/10559 at 27A.

[51] TNA: PRO Crim 1/3467.

even if no such substantive offence existed, the conspiracy itself was a crime, following the eighteenth-century case of *Delaval*.[52]

The judgment was read by Ashworth J, who held, after referring to *Sedley*,[53] *Curl*[54] and other cases, that:

> In our opinion, having regard to the long line of cases to which we have been referred, it is an established principle of common law that conduct calculated or intended to corrupt public morals (as opposed to the morals of a particular individual) is an indictable misdemeanour.[55]

Thus, a substantive crime existed even without the conspiracy; having come to that conclusion, it was clear too that 'it must follow that a conspiracy of the type alleged is an indictable offence'.

The Court of Criminal Appeal certified that points of law of 'general public importance' were involved in the conspiracy to corrupt morals count and the living on the earnings of prostitution point, and granted leave to appeal to the House of Lords on those points. No leave to appeal was granted on the obscene publications point.[56]

## E. In the House of Lords

### i. Argument

Argument in the House of Lords took almost seven days, and the Solicitor General, Sir Jocelyn 'Jack' Simon, himself appeared with Buzzard to argue for the DPP.[57] Shaw was again represented by William Rees-Davies, as he had been in the Court of Criminal Appeal, and by PS Lewis.[58] On the first count, Rees-Davies argued, contrary to the findings of the Court of Criminal Appeal, that there was no offence of corrupting public morals and no offence of conspiracy to corrupt, and that the courts should not create one.[59] For the DPP, on the other hand, it was argued that there was a line of authority from *Sedley* demonstrating the existence of the offence,[60] and that *Sedley* was important as its later use in other, distinct, factual scenarios showed that it set out not merely a specific offence, but also a principle of wider application.

---

[52] *Rex v Delaval* (1763) 3 Burr 1434, 97 ER 913, discussed below at n 74.

[53] *Le Roy v Sr Charles Sidley* (1664) 1 Sid 168, 82 ER 1036; *Sir Charles Sydlyes Case* (1664) 1 Keble 620, 83 ER 1146; discussed below at nn 158–77.

[54] *Dominus Rex v Curl* (1727) 2 Strange 788, 93 ER 849; discussed below at nn 173–76.

[55] *Shaw* (n 1) 233.

[56] ibid 236.

[57] The future Baron Simon of Glaisdale: SM Cretney, 'Simon, Jocelyn Edward Salis, Baron Simon of Glaisdale (1911–2006)' in L Goldman (ed), *Oxford Dictionary of National Biography 2005–2008* (Oxford, Oxford University Press, 2013) 1045.

[58] *Shaw* (n 1) 237.

[59] ibid 241.

[60] ibid 249.

On the second count, it was argued by Rees-Davies that Shaw lived on his earnings as a publisher, not on the earnings of prostitution, and that living on the earnings of prostitution required something akin to 'preying on' prostitutes,[61] for example, asking for protection money.[62] The counter-argument was that 'lives on' should take its ordinary meaning:[63] if a service provided was unrelated to the prostitution, then the offence would not be made out, but if it was 'rendered in such a way that it promoted the prostitution', then the defendant would be within the terms of the section.[64]

### ii. Judgment: Living on the Earnings of Prostitution

Shaw's conviction was upheld by all the Law Lords on the living on the earnings of prostitution point.[65] In the leading speech, Viscount Simonds concluded that the test was whether a defendant was 'paid by prostitutes for goods or services supplied by him to them for the purpose of their prostitution which he would not supply but for the fact that they were prostitutes'.[66] Lord Reid expressed himself as agreeing on the conclusion, but disagreeing with Viscount Simonds's reasoning.[67] For Lord Reid, the test appeared to be whether the occupation of the defendant was parasitic: whether 'it would not exist if the women were not prostitutes'.[68]

Although the tests may at first glance seem similar, and both led to the same conclusion with respect to Frederick Shaw, Viscount Simonds's test was wider: it would encompass a tradesman providing something he knew was for the purposes of prostitution. Lord Reid left open the possibility of liability for a tradesman who 'used his trade as a means to become a joint adventurer with prostitutes', but, setting such cases to one side, to supply 'to a prostitute in the ordinary course of things' was not sufficient to attract liability.[69]

### iii. Judgment: Conspiracy to Corrupt Public Morals

On the conspiracy to corrupt public morals point, the court divided in its conclusion, upholding the conviction by a majority. The leading speech for the majority on this point was ostensibly by Lord Tucker, with whom Lord

---

[61] ibid 240.
[62] ibid 258.
[63] ibid 256.
[64] ibid 247.
[65] ibid 264 and 269 (Viscount Simonds); agreeing with Viscount Simonds at 282 (Lord Tucker), 291 (Lord Morris) and 292 (Lord Hodson).
[66] ibid 264.
[67] ibid 269.
[68] ibid 270.
[69] ibid 272.

Morris and Lord Hodson agreed.[70] Viscount Simonds also expressed himself as agreeing with Lord Tucker,[71] adding almost three pages of gloss on Lord Tucker's decision on this point.[72] Lord Reid disagreed with Lord Tucker.[73] The judgments feature two interrelated issues, with differing emphases in the speeches: whether, and on what basis, the offence of conspiracy to corrupt public morals could exist; and concern about legal certainty if the offence did exist. Considerably more effort was spent on the former questions.

Lord Tucker's judgment was on the basis that there are some conspiracies which are criminal even though the acts agreed to be done are not themselves criminal, or even tortious, if done by individuals; the presence of the conspiracy itself sufficed to render the conduct criminal. Thus, for example, liability resulted where the agreement was to do something 'outrageously immoral'. But Lord Tucker also found liability on the basis that a conspiracy to corrupt public morals was an instance of conspiracy to effect a public mischief, and that that was a crime itself.

Lord Tucker thus did not need to rely on cases where individuals were committing common law misdemeanours, such as *Sedley* or *Curl*, but rather conspiracy cases such as *Delaval*.[74] In that case, Lord Mansfield had held that a conspiracy to deliver a young girl to Delaval was within the jurisdiction of the King's Bench for two reasons: first, because the Court was the *custos morum* of the people; and, second, because of the element of conspiracy. Lord Tucker hence based his decision in *Shaw* on the facts presenting a conspiracy to commit a wrongful act calculated to cause public injury, but he insisted that he did not want to be taken to be rejecting the ground of the Court of Criminal Appeal that conduct calculated to corrupt public morals was a substantive offence itself without the conspiracy.

Lord Tucker cited the relatively recent prosecutions of *Berg* in 1927[75] and *Dale* in 1960[76] for authority for the existence of the crime of conspiracy to corrupt morals. Lord Tucker noted the lack of other modern precedent, skirting around this by quoting Parke J in *Mirehouse v Rennell*.[77] But other precedents did exist: the prosecutions of the publishers of the

---

[70] Lord Morris agreed with both Simonds and Tucker: *Shaw* (n 1) 291, as did Lord Hodson: ibid 292. Lord Morris reiterated his agreement with Lord Tucker when the issue arose again in *Knuller (Publishing, Printing and Promotions) Ltd v DPP* [1973] AC 435 (HL), 466.

[71] *Shaw* (n 1) 261.

[72] ibid 266–69.

[73] ibid 272.

[74] See below nn 158–77.

[75] (1927) 20 Cr App R 38 (CCA).

[76] Unreported, TNA: PRO PRO Crim 1/387. A copy of the indictment in the case was in looseleaf in the notebook for *Shaw* in the files of Lord Reid, albeit that he did not discuss it in his speech.

[77] (1833) 1 Cl & F 527.

'personals' magazine *The Link*[78] was for conspiracy to corrupt;[79] the prosecution of Billie Joice for her nightclub in Little Denmark Street [80] was for
the substantive offence of corruption itself. But though *The Link* case in
particular seemed directly germane, neither prosecution had been mainly
concerned with heterosexual conduct. Whether that kept them in an apparently distinct category, or whether Lord Tucker was just unaware of them, is
unclear.

In his speech for the majority, Viscount Simonds left detailed examination
of the authorities to Lord Tucker. Simonds held that conspiracy to corrupt
public morals was an offence known to the common law. He repeated that
he was not an 'advocate of the right of the judges to create new criminal
offences', but he thought that such a conspiracy was a known crime, and
that it applied here. He thought it was fallacious to argue that this could not
be a conspiracy to corrupt public morals merely because such a set of facts
had not been held to be such a conspiracy before. That was not the way of
common law argument.[81]

More generally, Simonds also agreed with Lord Mansfield in *Delaval*,
who, he thought, had asserted that the King's Bench was the *custos morum*
of the people and that there was in the court a:

[R]esidual power, where no statute has yet intervened to supersede the common
law, to superintend those offences which are prejudicial to the public welfare.[82]

As for the argument that this offence was too uncertain, for Simonds, just
as in the civil law of negligence some concepts would fall to the jury, so it
was here:

[T]he uncertainty that necessarily arises from the vagueness of general words can
only be resolved by the opinion of twelve chosen men and women.[83]

Lord Reid, dissenting on this ground of appeal, thought that there was no
such general offence as conspiracy to corrupt public morals.[84] Although
it could be conceived to be an instance of conspiracy to commit a public mischief, it would be a new instance of such a conspiracy. Even if
there were such a 'vestigial' power to extend the grounds of conspiracy,
it should not be exercised except when there was 'general agreement that

[78] See HG Cocks, '"Sporty" Girls and "Artistic" Boys: Friendship, Illicit Sex, and the
British "Companionship" Advertisement, 1913–1928' (2002) 11(3) *Journal of the History of
Sexuality* 457.

[79] TNA: PRO MEPO 3/283.

[80] TNA: PRO DPP 2/355; TNA: PRO Crim 1/903. See M Houlbrook, *Queer London:
Perils and Pleasures in the Sexual Metropolis 1918–1957* (Chicago, University of Chicago
Press, 2005) 72 and 82.

[81] *Shaw* (n 1) 267.

[82] ibid 268.

[83] ibid 269.

[84] ibid 272.

the offence to which it is applied ought to be criminal if committed by an individual'.[85]

As Lord Reid wrote in his notebook for the case, in what appears to be a note to himself in the only line on page 32: 'Wrong general principle—censor morum.'[86] In looseleaf pages inserted into the notebook, he expanded:

Censor morum

No limit but what jury refuses to accept

Not principle—high sounding words to justify

limited number of offences—if real

principle many more cases wld have arisen

as little principle as Christianity part of law

negatived in *Bowman*

Real principle—public order disturbed.[87]

Lord Reid suggested that the conviction might have been maintained on the basis that 'a public invitation to indulge in sexual perversion does so outrage public decency as to be a punishable offence'.[88] But the jury had not been properly directed on this and, in any case, this would not apply to 'ordinary prostitution'.

## iv. The Judgment in Light of Hart, Devlin and Radcliffe

The decision of the majority in the House of Lords meant, as Lord Hodson put it, that in 'the field of public morals it will thus be the morality of the man in the jury-box that will determine the fate of the accused'.[89] Although Devlin was not cited in the judgments, and Lord Devlin's low estimation of Lord Hodson has been noted elsewhere in this series,[90] in Lord Hodson's contentedness to rely on the jury, one might trace some influence of Lord Devlin in his Maccabean Lecture to the British Academy of 1959. The standard of morality to be enforced, Devlin had said, should be 'that of the reasonable man ... the man in the street ... the man in the Clapham omnibus ... the man in the jury box'.[91] As 'law exists for the protection

---

[85]  ibid 276.

[86]  House of Lords Archive, Rei/4, *Shaw v DPP*, 32.

[87]  House of Lords Archive, Rei/4, *Shaw v DPP*, looseleaf, 40. The underlined sections are as in the original.

[88]  *Shaw* (n 1) 281.

[89]  ibid 294.

[90]  P Mitchell, '*Hedley Byrne & Co Ltd v Heller & Partners Ltd* (1963)' in C Mitchell and P Mitchell (eds), *Landmark Cases in the Law of Tort* (Oxford, Hart Publishing, 2010) 183.

[91]  P Devlin, *The Enforcement of Morals* (Oxford, Oxford University Press, 1965) 15.

of society' and society 'cannot exist without morals', this objective moral standard served a crucial instrumental purpose.[92] Devlin discussed *Shaw* itself throughout his late 1961 lecture at the University of Pennsylvania,[93] interpreting it in line with his own theses about societal self-protection,[94] and to some extent welcoming it for its recognition of the role of the jurors' morality in reducing questions of morals to questions of fact:

> Shaw's case settles for the purposes of the law that morality in England means what twelve men and women think it means—in other words it is to be ascertained as a question of fact. I am not repelled by that phrase nor do I resent in such a matter submission to the mentality of the common man.[95]

However, Devlin made less clear the extent to which he was content with the role the jury now played in determining which immoralities to suppress,[96] and he was even less happy with another possible interpretation of *Shaw*, or at least of Viscount Simonds's judgment: a reading of it endorsing moral perfectionism. Devlin thought that it potentially destroyed freedom of conscience and was 'the paved road to tyranny'.[97]

*Shaw* was also not welcomed by Devlin's jurisprudential sparring partner, HLA Hart. The multifaceted debate between Hart and Devlin is relatively well known[98] and pre-dated *Shaw*; indeed, like *Shaw*, it had arisen in part out of the Wolfenden Report, in particular the recommendation that homosexual conduct in private be decriminalised. One decisive ground of the recommendation was that part of the private realm should remain 'not the law's business'.[99] Hart's position in the debate was, in comparison to Devlin's, a relatively liberal one; on the point of *Shaw*, Hart set out his view in his lectures at Stanford published as *Law, Liberty, and Morality*. Predictably, he was critical of the wide-ranging jurisdiction apparently claimed by Viscount Simonds. Hart distinguished two grounds for the enforcement of morals: the 'moderate', as in Devlin, for the protection of society; and the 'extreme', for its own sake, which he attributed to Sir James Fitzjames Stephen.[100] But a subtler and more influential version of the extreme thesis had been espoused more recently by another of the law lords, Lord Radcliffe.[101] Radcliffe had

---

[92] ibid 22 and 24.

[93] ibid 86–101.

[94] ibid 89.

[95] ibid 100.

[96] ibid 99.

[97] ibid 88–89. See also R George, *Making Men Moral* (Oxford, Oxford University Press, 1993) 75.

[98] For a discussion, see N Lacey, *A Life of H.L.A. Hart: The Nightmare and the Noble Dream* (Oxford, Oxford University Press, 2006) 221 and 256–61.

[99] Home Office, *Report* para 61.

[100] HLA Hart, *Law, Liberty, and Morality* (Stanford, Stanford University Press, 1963) 48.

[101] See generally N Duxbury, 'Lord Radcliffe out of Time' (2010) 69(1) *Cambridge Law Journal* 41.

a major influence on *Shaw* itself, and his work is crucial in making sense of Viscount Simonds's otherwise disjointed remarks in his judgment.

One source for confirming Lord Radcliffe's influence is the correspondence, quoted at the start of this chapter, between Simonds and Owen Dixon. A few months earlier, before the House of Lords hearing, in 1961, Simonds had written to Dixon:

> Cyril Radcliffe has given me a little volume of 3 lectures which he gave at the University of Chicago last year. They are outstandingly good and I am trying to get a copy for you. If I can't I must send you mine for I wouldn't like you to miss anything so good. As a colleague he is a joy to me—I believe I am in danger of following him blindly![102]

The reference here is to the volume of lectures by Lord Radcliffe that came out as *The Law and its Compass.*[103] In these lectures, Radcliffe was engaged in a reflexive contemplation of English law and of his own austere conception of liberalism, and had been concerned in these speeches to explore what it would have meant for English law if there had been a 'reception' of natural law. The lectures are subtle and hard to pin down; in them and in his other lectures, Radcliffe was engaged in the development of a theory of authority that would explain and justify allegiance to law.

A few days later, Simonds wrote another note to Dixon:

> I have managed to get another copy of those lectures of which I wrote in my last letter. In fact Cyril Radcliffe gave it to me to give to you. I hope you may find time to read them.[104]

After the judgment was handed down, Simonds wrote again:

> Do tell me too what you thought of Radcliffe's lectures which I sent you—I hope they arrived. I borrowed from one of them in a judgment I wrote in Shaw v the Director which has aroused an equal amount of enthusiastic support & hostile criticism. I have not been moved by the latter.[105]

And after some time off for ill health, Simonds wrote to Dixon once more:

> I find on my return that I have been fiercely, almost scurrilously, attacked by some of the academic lawyers for my judgment in the 'Ladies Directory' case. So be it: I will fight to the death for a 'residual power' in the Queen's Bench to deal with such cases: in Cyril Radcliffe's picturesque phrase one of the 'unravished remnants of the common law'. I think the L.Q.R. has not yet dealt with it, but shall be surprised and disappointed if Arthur Goodhart does not take a better view.[106]

---

[102] National Library of Australia, MS Acc09.166, 16 January 1961.
[103] C Radcliffe, *The Law and its Compass* (London, Faber & Faber, 1960). The lectures were the Rosenthal Lectures given at Northwestern University in Chicago, and not at the University of Chicago.
[104] National Library of Australia, MS Acc09.166, 25 January 1961.
[105] National Library of Australia, MS Acc09.166, 3 August 1961.
[106] National Library of Australia, MS Acc09.166, 28 October 1961.

Amusingly, given the concern evidenced from Simonds about the *LQR*'s view of his judgment, it is worth parenthetically noting that about a month before that letter, and indeed hence before the *LQR* had published its casenote on *Shaw*, Simonds had directly written to Arthur Goodhart, the *LQR* editor:

> I shall be interested to see what you say about *Shaw*. I missed G. Williams. There has been much misunderstanding, but I'll fight to the death for the principle of the decision.[107]

Removed from its context this lobbying seems now remarkable; nonetheless, given the practices described by Neil Duxbury,[108] it may not be atypical for its time.

The influence of Radcliffe, demonstrable via Simonds's correspondence, was visible in the finished judgment in *Shaw*, as Simonds quoted Radcliffe in *Shaw* explicitly, albeit when he did so, it was not in a very meaningful way. In Simonds's conclusion in *Shaw* that, in conspiracy to corrupt public morals cases, it sufficed for the jury to decide, he had quoted Lord Radcliffe's lectures to the effect that there are still 'unravished remnants of the common law'.[109] In the initial version of the report of *Shaw* in the *Weekly Law Reports* and the *All England Reports*,[110] there was no footnote for that quote, as John Finnis noted in the *Adelaide Law Review* shortly afterwards,[111] but Finnis was able to attribute it correctly to Radcliffe's lectures and, indeed, by the time of the Appeal Cases report, an asterisked footnote had been added into *The Law and its Compass*.[112]

More interesting perhaps are the sections based on Lord Radcliffe's lectures, but not demarcated by quotation marks, one of which Finnis also noted at the time. For example, Viscount Simonds wrote in his judgment that:

> The law must be related to the changing standards of life, not yielding to every shifting impulse of the popular will but having regard to fundamental assessments of human values and the purposes of society.[113]

This is very similar indeed to Radcliffe:

> Unless the law is to equate itself in the eyes of society with the varying impulses of popular feeling, as interpreted by these assemblies or the political parties which

---

[107] September 5 1961; Bod. MS Eng C 2890.

[108] N Duxbury, *Jurists and Judges* (Oxford, Hart Publishing, 2001) 91. The *LQR* casenote is discussed below at n 129.

[109] *Shaw* (n 1) 269, quoting Radcliffe, *The Law and its Compass* 53.

[110] *Shaw v DPP* [1961] 2 WLR 897, 918; [1961] 2 All ER 446, 453F.

[111] J Finnis, 'Developments in Judicial Jurisprudence' (1962) 1(3) *Adelaide Law Review* 317, 318.

[112] *Shaw* (n 1) 269.

[113] ibid 268.

dominate them, its conception of the public interest must be related to some more fundamental assessment of human values and of the purposes of society.[114]

Soon after *Shaw* was handed down, Glanville Williams in *The Listener* made the point that while on the one hand, Viscount Simonds in *Shaw* held that any vagueness of general words will be resolved by the jury, on the other hand, he wanted the law not to 'yield to every shifting impulse of the popular will', but to have regard to the 'fundamental assessments of human values and the purposes of society'.[115] There is a tension here; this may be because Simonds has unhappily combined Devlin with Radcliffe. As Stevens points out:

> The two basic Devlin themes appear to be first, that there is no private realm of morality into which the law cannot enter and second, that the morality that the law enforces must be popular morality. On the first, Devlin might have had Radcliffe's support; on the second he would not, for Radcliffe was not primarily interested in the beliefs held by the ordinary reasonable man or the 'man in the jury box'.[116]

Radcliffe was not as interested in maintaining popular morality in order to maintain society as Devlin was; he verged more towards what he might consider right than popular. What we see in *Shaw* on this point is less a reflection of the 'liberal against popular moralist' aspect of the Hart–Devlin debate and more an attempt by Simonds to weld together moderate and extreme natural law theories.

The influence of Lord Radcliffe also makes sense of an otherwise confused section of Viscount Simonds' judgment discussing public policy. When Simonds held that 'there remains in the courts of law a residual power to enforce the supreme and fundamental purpose of the law, to conserve not only the safety and order but also the moral welfare of the State'[117] in 'safety and order' and 'moral welfare', he was borrowing from Radcliffe's description of public policy. By 'public policy', admittedly something which he felt was a bad label, Radcliffe had essentially meant that 'that there are some things that the law will not stand for'[118] and he had subdivided this along French lines into public order and public decency.[119] Ultimately, he thought: 'It is ... the dignity of the individual, that, I believe, affords the true basis for a doctrine of public interest to be applied by the courts as a substantive part of law.'[120]

---

[114] Radcliffe, The Law and its Compass 53.
[115] G Williams, 'Conspiring to Corrupt' [1961] *The Listener* 275, 280.
[116] R Stevens, Law and Politics: The House of Lords as a Judicial Body, 1800–1976 (London, Weidenfeld & Nicolson, 1979) 459.
[117] *Shaw* (n 1) 267.
[118] Radcliffe, The Law and its Compass 37.
[119] ibid 44.
[120] ibid 57.

Simonds had stressed that:

> We are perhaps more accustomed to hear this matter discussed upon the question whether such and such a transaction is contrary to public policy. At once the controversy arises. On the one hand it is said that it is not possible in the twentieth century for the court to create a new head of public policy, on the other it is said that this is but a new example of a well-established head.[121]

Radcliffe, just like Simonds, had denied that the heads of 'public policy' had been finally determined and were closed. And he argued that:

> I doubt whether it will matter very much whether judges do or do not regard themselves as at liberty to 'invent' new heads of public policy. To some extent it is a question of words. Heads of this kind are inevitably a question of categorisation after the event. The instances come first and the classification follows.[122]

This then is at least one explanation for Simonds's otherwise apparently somewhat cavalier claim that:

> It matters little what label is given to the offending act. To one of your Lordships it may appear an affront to public decency, to another considering that it may succeed in its obvious intention of provoking libidinous desires it will seem a corruption of public morals. Yet others may deem it aptly described as the creation of a public mischief or the undermining of moral conduct.[123]

Of course, it would not be surprising to find a confluence of mid-century thought amongst these judges, and there are many possible causes. But reliance on Lord Radcliffe was marked, and made the case more complicated for Viscount Simonds.

## III. THE AFTERMATH

One consequence of *Shaw* was a now-relatively obscure string of cases of conspiracy to corrupt public morals in the following few years.[124] In addition, the charge was laid in more high-profile cases, including the *Oz Magazine* prosecution.[125] The real challenge, however, came in *Knuller*,[126] where, although the House of Lords upheld the existence of conspiracy to corrupt public morals as a crime, this was without, as Lord

---

[121] *Shaw* (n 1) 267.
[122] Radcliffe, *The Law and its Compass* 55.
[123] *Shaw* (n 1) 267–68.
[124] *Keenan* (1962) TNA: PRO Crim 1/3864; *Kelly* (1963) TNA: PRO Crim 1/4102; *Fitzgerald* (1964–65) TNA: PRO Crim 1/4281; *Douglas* (1964–65) TNA: PRO Crim 1/4328; *Murray* (1965–66) TNA: PRO Crim 1/4360; *Lennon* (1965–66) TNA: PRO Crim 1/4425; *Davis, Michael* (1965–66) TNA: PRO Crim 1/4465; *Davis, Francis* (1965–66) TNA: PRO Crim 1/4478; *Hart* (1966) TNA: PRO Assi 26/371; *Kent* (1966–67) TNA: PRO Crim 1/4536; *Lomax* (1966–70) TNA: PRO Crim 1/4610.
[125] TNA: PRO Crim 1/5453.
[126] *Knuller* (n 70); DPP 2/4668, 4669 and 4670.

Reid, now of the majority, put it, 'affirming or lending support to the doctrine that the courts still have some general or residual power ... to create new offences'.[127] However, Lord Simon, formerly Solicitor General Sir Jocelyn Simon and counsel in the House of Lords in *Shaw*, left open the 'applicability of established offences to new circumstances to which they are relevant'.[128]

The immediate reaction of academics to *Shaw* was not entirely enthusiastic. Arthur Goodhart was perhaps the most welcoming, hailing the decision's contributions to the criminal law.[129] Even he, however, had some criticism for the breadth of the doctrine of public mischief as espoused by Viscount Simonds. The future Lord Wedderburn, at the time a Fellow of Clare College, Cambridge, wrote to *The Times* suggesting that the offence could be used to prosecute those who 'conspire to promote racial hatred'.[130] Glanville Williams and Colin Turpin also both had some deep concerns. Turpin wrote in the *Cambridge Law Journal*:

> A principle of considerable importance but disquieting possibilities was established by the House of Lords in *Shaw* ... It is difficult not to regard the decision in *Shaw's* case as a serious blow to the principle *nullum crimen sine lege*, 'one of the oldest and most enduring of all the ideas of Western civilisation'.[131]

That might have been overstating the case. The better view was that of Glanville Williams in *The Listener* and of Alan Rodger many years later: the principle, not one of the oldest ideas of Western civilisation, dated chiefly from the French Revolution and had been classicised by von Feuerbach in the early nineteenth century.[132]

## IV. THE ISSUES OF PRINCIPLE

Both of the two key issues in *Shaw* — the existence and justification of a broad crime of conspiring to corrupt public morals, and balancing that scope against professed concerns for legal certainty — were and are linked to the past. Critics of *Shaw* such as Turpin saw the case as undermining long-standing historical principle, while the House of Lords relied heavily on seventeenth- and eighteenth-century cases to justify their decision. But both of those understandings of the past are open to question.

---

[127] *Knuller* (n 70) 457–58.
[128] ibid 490. Lord Kilbrandon expressed himself as agreeing with Lord Simon (at 495). Lord Morris interpreted *Shaw* as not claiming any jurisdiction to create new crimes (at 464–65). See also *DPP v Withers* [1975] AC 842 (HL).
[129] Goodhart, 'The Shaw Case' 567.
[130] KW Wedderburn, 'Conspiring to Corrupt' *The Times* (London, 10 May 1961) 13.
[131] CC Turpin, 'Criminal Law—Conspiracy to Corrupt Morals' (1961) 19(2) *CLJ* 144, 144 and 146.
[132] Williams, 'Conspiring to Corrupt' 275; A Rodger, 'A Time for Everything under the Law: Some Reflections on Retrospectivity' (2005) 121 *LQR* 57, 65–66.

## A. Legal Certainty

*Shaw*, with its assertion of a flexible and creative jurisdiction, brings to the fore the vexing issue of how to balance stability and predictability, a key attribute of the rule of law, against the potential for 'attacks which may be the more insidious because they are novel and unprepared for'.[133] As Alan Rodger wrote:

> [T]he rule expressed in these maxims is not self-evidently an unqualified good. Take *nullum crimen sine lege* (no crime without a law). It is clear, not least from the Nuremberg trials, that there are acts which are so unspeakably bad that they must be regarded as criminal even if there is no specific text making them so. The damage to the public interest if they were to go unpunished is obvious.

The countervailing issue of certainty of course remains, now partly determined by human rights obligations, but still arising in cases for the superior courts. In his unpublished memoir, written only a few years later in 1964, even Viscount Simonds reiterated his desire for certainty in the law,[134] and for reform to come from Parliament.[135]

The background to the history of the principle of legal certainty is not all that well understood. In his 2005 judgment in the leading House of Lords case of *Rimmington*, Lord Bingham approved and adopted in full a set of paragraphs on legal certainty from the Court of Appeal judgment in the 2004 manslaughter case of *Misra*.[136] The judgment in *Misra*, by Judge LJ, quoted Francis Bacon, sometime Lord Chancellor, dealing with the history of concerns about legal certainty in the criminal law, in the following terms:

> [T]here is nothing novel about them in our jurisprudence. Historic as well as modern examples abound. In the 17th century Bacon proclaimed the essential link between justice and legal certainty:
>
> > For if the trumpet give an uncertain sound, who shall prepare himself to the battle? So if the law give an uncertain sound, who shall prepare to obey it? It ought therefore to warn before it strikes ... Let there be no authority to shed blood; nor let sentence be pronounced in any court upon cases, except according to a known and certain law ... Nor should a man be deprived of his life, who did not first know that he was risking it.[137]

As a description of Bacon's position, and the position of the criminal law at the time and even much later, this is quite misleading, albeit that one might

---

[133] *Shaw* (n 1) 267, per Viscount Simonds.
[134] G Simonds, 'Random Recollections of an Idle Old Man' New College, Oxford, Archives PA/SIM 2, 144.
[135] ibid 145.
[136] *R v Rimmington* [2005] UKHL 63 [33].
[137] *R v Misra* [2004] EWCA Crim 2375 [32], citing for the quotation 'Coquillette, *Francis Bacon* pp. 244 and 248, from Aphorism 8 and Aphorism 39—A Treatise on Universal Justice'. See below at nn 150–56 for discussion. A similar reference to Bacon was made in the High Court of Australia in Heydon J's dissent in the recent *PGA v The Queen* [2012] HCA 21.

trace some concerns for certainty back to the mid-seventeenth century and, indeed, to *Leviathan*.[138]

### *i. Legal Certainty and the Star Chamber*

The criminal law system in the first half of the seventeenth century was a complex network of courts operating at the local and national levels. One of the most important courts in that network was the court of Star Chamber.[139] Despite later being viewed with some scepticism, this was a court which Sir Edward Coke, protector of the common law and common liberty, at the time described as:

> [T]he most honourable Court (our Parliament excepted) that is in the Christian world, both in respect of the Judges of the Court, and of their honourable proceeding according to their just jurisdiction, and the ancient and just orders of the Court.[140]

It is clear that Star Chamber and its jurisdiction were firmly entrenched in the constitutional establishment at the time Bacon was writing. Star Chamber's jurisdiction was wide indeed and little concerned with legal certainty. Here is how Coke described the jurisdiction of the court:

> And seeing the proceeding according to the laws and customs of this Realm cannot by one rule of law suffice to punish in every case the exorbitancy and enormity of some great horrible crimes and offences ... this Court dealeth with them, to the end that the medicine may be according to the disease.[141]

As the clerk of the court, the learned William Hudson, put it:

> I come to express the great and high jurisdiction of this court, which, by the arm of sovereignty, punisheth errors creeping into the Commonwealth, which otherwise might prove dangerous and infectious diseases, or giveth life to the execution of laws, or the performance of such things as are necessary in the Commonwealth, yea although no positive law or continued custom of common law giveth warrant to it.[142]

After providing examples, Hudson continued:

> Infinite more are the causes usually punished in this court, for which the law provideth no remedy in any sort or ordinary course, whereby the necessary use of this court to the state appeareth.[143]

---

[138] A Ristroph, 'Criminal Law for Humans' in D Dyzenahus and T Poole (eds), *Hobbes and the Law* (Cambridge, Cambridge University Press, 2012) 100.
[139] TG Barnes, 'Star Chamber Mythology' (1961) 5 *American Journal of Legal History* 1.
[140] 4 Co Inst 65.
[141] 4 Co Inst 63.
[142] W Hudson, 'A Treatise of the Court of Star Chamber' in F Hargrave, *Collectanea Juridica*, vol 2 (London, E and R Brooke, 1792) 107.
[143] ibid 112.

William Lambarde in his *Archion* similarly noted Star Chamber's criminal jurisdiction to penalise conduct not penalised before, 'where the evil and crime itself is either new in device' or where the harm is extraordinary, and noted that the offences punished 'be variable, and infinite in their sundry sorts'.[144] It is not necessary to go on. The great court of Star Chamber, 'most honourable' and central to the criminal law at the time Bacon was writing, was taken to have a broad jurisdiction to punish new crimes.

It is true, of course, that there was argument about precedent in the Star Chamber, albeit more perhaps as one policy consideration among many,[145] and not as binding precedent in the style of the nineteenth century. But demands for legal certainty, or refusal of jurisdiction, in Star Chamber were a rarity. True, in his report of *Ann Hungate*, a Star Chamber case to do with procuring the acknowledgement of a fine by an underage heir, Coke wrote:

> [I]t was resolved by the two Chief Justices, and the Chief Baron, that there was not any crime punishable by the law in this case: for the Judges of law and of this Court may punish such offences and crimes as are determinable in this Court: but the Judges cannot create offences, nor do as Hannibal did, to make his way over the Alps when he could find none, for *judicandum est legibus; et ubi non est lex, nec est transgressio*.[146]

Similarly, although our reports are uncertain, it appears that Star Chamber refused to hear a prosecution of Coke's daughter, the unfortunate Lady Purbeck. Our sources for this are incomplete, but in 1708 in the Queen's Bench, Read was prosecuted for printing *The Fifteen Plagues of a Maidenhead*. The report of *Read* in Fortescue's reports contains some discussion of 'Lady Purbeck's Case' in Star Chamber. Fortescue reported that Powell J remarked in *Read*: 'There was Lady Purbeck's Case, which was in the Star-Chamber, they quashed the indictment because it was for matters of bawdry.'[147] In the yet later case of *Curl*, Fortescue was by then one of the

---

[144] W Lambarde, *Archion, or, a Discourse upon the High Courts of Justice in England* (London, Printed for Daniel Frere, 1635) 91–93.

[145] TG Barnes, 'A Cheshire Seductress, Precedent, and a "Sore Blow" to Star Chamber' in MS Arnold, TA Green, SA Scully and SD White (eds), *On the Laws and Customs of England: Essays in Honor of Samuel E. Thorne* (Chapel Hill, University of North Carolina Press, 1981) 359.

[146] *Ann Hungate* 12 Co Rep 122, 122, 77 ER 1397, 1398. Translated, the Latin reads: judgment should be by law, and where there is no law, there is no transgression. This case does not appear to be in Coke's notebook: BL MS Add 35956. The comment does not appear in Rolle's report (*Sir Henry Day v Hungat*, 1 Rolle 113) or in the report of the case in Francis Moore's report in Folger MS V.a.133.

[147] *The Queen v Read* (1708) Fort 98, 100, 92 ER 777, per Powell J. This is presumably a reference to Frances, Viscountess Purbeck. She was a daughter of Sir Edward Coke from his marriage with Lady Elizabeth Hatton, and had been married, apparently against her will, to Buckingham's elder brother. When he developed signs of mental infirmity, she left him, and had a child, whom she baptised Robert Wright, later called Danvers, presumably with Sir Robert

judges, and Strange reports his comment in *Curl* that: 'Lady Purbeck's case was for procuring men and women to meet at her house, and held not indictable, unless there had been particular facts to make it a bawdy-house.'[148] But even when Star Chamber did not claim jurisdiction, there were yet other courts to do so: Frances Purbeck was instead prosecuted in the ecclesiastical court of High Commission.[149] In any case, far more frequent than the court resiling from claiming jurisdiction were assertions of almost unlimited jurisdiction over non-felonious wrongful acts.

## ii. Bacon and De Augmentis

It is in this context that we need to interpret what Bacon had to say. In *De Augmentis*, the work from which Judge LJ quotes in *Misra*, Bacon set out an initial section of a Treatise containing aphorisms that discussed aspects of an idealised system of government and jurisprudence. The Treatise was written not as an account of the English legal system, but, as Coquillette put it, 'for a universal, cosmopolitan audience',[150] and as more of a normative than descriptive project. However, the connections Bacon drew between the Star Chamber and his 'Censorian' courts seem clear.[151]

Howard. There is a record of their prosecution in the High Commission for this behaviour, and while there is no apparent record of a prosecution of Frances in the Star Chamber reports, there is a hint that a prosecution of Howard in Star Chamber was contemplated: see the potentially unreliable Anon, *The Curious Case of Lady Purbeck: A Scandal of the XVIIth Century* (London, Longmans, Green & Co, 1909) 83–105 and 114–18, although no evidence is provided for the claim by the anonymous author. It is possible, although unlikely, that the reference in *Read* is to the earlier dispute in Star Chamber between Coke and Lady Elizabeth Hatton over the marriage of Frances to Sir John Villiers, later Viscount Purbeck.

[148] *Dominus Rex v Curl* (n 54) 791. It is not clear why there is a reference to an indictment, which was not the procedure for prosecution in the Star Chamber; see, for example, the useful procedural detail set out in TG Barnes, 'Due Process and Slow Process in the Late Elizabethan-Early Stuart Star Chamber' (1962) 6 *American Journal of Legal History* 221, 227.

[149] RL Greaves, 'Danvers, Robert, Styled Second Viscount Purbeck (1624–1674)' in HCG Matthew and B Harrison (eds), *Oxford Dictionary of National Biography* (Oxford, Oxford University Press, 2004), vol 15, 103. Dates for Frances and Sir Robert's High Commission appearances include: March 1625 and 19 November 1627 (Greaves); see also the statement 'Buckingham had the pair [Frances and Robert Howard] cited before the court of high commission on 19 February 1625' in HM Chichester, 'Howard, Sir Robert (1584/5–1653)' revised by S Kelsey, in HCG Matthew and B Harrison (eds), *Oxford Dictionary of National Biography* (Oxford, Oxford University Press, 2004) vol 28, 412. See also HR Williamson, *George Villiers: First Duke of Buckingham* (London, Duckworth, 1940) 165–69; L Nosworthy, *The Lady of Bleeding Heart Yard: Lady Elizabeth Hatton 1578–1646* (London, John Murray, 1935) 8–52.

[150] DR Coquillette, *Francis Bacon* (Edinburgh, Edinburgh University Press, 1992) 237.

[151] ibid 247. See also JS Spedding, RL Ellis and DD Heath (eds), *The Works of Francis Bacon* (London, Longman & Co, 1858) vol I, 810 fn 1: 'to everyone who is acquainted with the history of English law, it is manifest that Bacon's intention was to give an idealised description of the Court of Star Chamber'.

Aphorisms 32–47 dealt with 'Courts Praetorian and Censorian' and were not a cry for certainty:[152]

Aphorism 32

Let there be courts and jurisdictions to determine ... when the rule of the law is deficient. For the law ... cannot provide for all cases ... And time ... daily creates and invents new cases.

Aphorism 33

Fresh cases happen both in criminal causes which require punishment, and in civil causes which require relief. The courts which take cognizance of the former I call Censorian, those which respect the latter, Praetorian.

Aphorism 34

Let the Censorian Courts have power and jurisdiction, not only to punish new offences, but also to increase the punishments appointed by law for old ones...[153]

Bacon was clearly calling for the power of the courts to punish new offences and, in what is not a reception but perhaps a 'classicising',[154] likened Star Chamber to the censors of Rome, who had been thought to have a broad jurisdiction to punish or shame offenders for their immoral acts.[155] This is a proclamation of a link between justice and flexibility in the criminal law, not certainty. Of course, as Nicola Lacey has noted:

We can, surely, acknowledge that the eighteenth-century conception of the rule of law in England was different to that in the twelfth century without concluding that no such conception existed: indeed, it existed in part as a critical conception which informed some of the political conflicts that shaped modern constitutional structures.[156]

The same is true here. To understand that the rule of law in the seventeenth century, the period of both Star Chamber's zenith and of its abolition, was conceptualised as it was provides the necessary context for understanding the precedents that were later understood to have emerged from it.

---

[152] Spedding, Ellis and Heath, *The Works of Francis Bacon* vol V, 94; and Coquillette, *Francis Bacon* 245–50.

[153] Spedding, Ellis, and Heath, *The Works of Francis Bacon* vol V, 94.

[154] To borrow Ian Williams' term from another context: I Williams, 'A Medieval Book and Early-Modern Law: *Bracton*'s Authority and Application in the Common Law c. 1550–1640' (2011) 79 *Tijdschrift voor Rechtsgeschiedenis* 47, 77.

[155] J Suolahti, 'The Roman Censors: A Study on Social Structure' (1963) B(117) *Annales Academiae Scientiarum Fennicae* (especially at 49–52), AE Astin, '*Regimen Morum*' (1988) 78 *Journal of Roman Studies* 14.

[156] N Lacey, 'Institutionalising Responsibility: Implications for Jurisprudence' (2013) 4(1) *Jurisprudence* 1, 15.

## B. Corrupting Morals as a Crime

There have been, David Ibbetson writes, 'situations where new law has been made by resurrecting very old decisions and applying them far in excess of their original ambit'.[157] To what extent then was the Court of Criminal Appeal, with whom Lord Tucker expressly did not disagree, correct to hold that corrupting morals had been and was a crime, even when done without conspiracy or combination?

There was some authority for it, but perhaps of doubtful rigour. In 1663, the Restoration wit and minor poet Sir Charles Sedley,[158] despite, as Pepys put it, 'there being no law against him' for his actions,[159] pleaded guilty in the Court of King's Bench after hearing the information presented for his outrageous acts in Covent Garden.[160]

There are two reports of *Sedley*, one of which—Siderfin's—makes the claim that the King's Bench held in the case:

[A]lthough there was not at that time the Star Chamber yet they will make him know that this court is the *custos morum* of all the subjects of the King, and it is now high time to punish profanities such as this against all modesty which are so frequent, just as not solely Christianity, but also morality, has been set aside.

This appears to be the basis of the doctrine in *Curl* and was consequently espoused by Lord Mansfield in *Delaval*:[161] an implication that the King's Bench exercised this jurisdiction at least in part because it claimed to be the *custos morum* of all of the king's subjects since there was no longer a Star

---

[157] DJ Ibbetson, 'Ghosts of the Past and the English Common Law' in A Wijffels (ed), *History in Court: Historical Expertise and Methods in a Forensic Context* (Leiden, Ius Deco Publications, 2001) 118. In the footnote to this statement, he writes that the 'best-known examples' are *Rylands v Fletcher* (1866) LR 1 Ex 265 and *Shaw* (n 1).

[158] On Sedley's life see: JH Wilson, *The Court Wits of the Restoration: An Introduction* (Princeton, Princeton University Press, 1948; reprinted New York, Octagon Books, 1967); V de Sola Pinto, *Sir Charles Sedley 1639–1701: A Study in the Life and Literature of the Restoration* (London, Constable & Company Ltd, 1927); H Love, 'Sedley, Sir Charles, Fifth Baronet (bap. 1639, d. 1701)', in HCG Matthew and B Harrison (eds), *Oxford Dictionary of National Biography* (Oxford, Oxford University Press, 2004) vol 49, 657. The spelling of his surname varies.

[159] R Latham and W Matthews (eds), *The Diary of Samuel Pepys* (London, G Bells & Sons, 1971) vol IV, 210 (1 July 1663).

[160] For approximately contemporary accounts of his actions see: Latham and Matthews, *The Diary of Samuel Pepys* vol IV, 210 (1 July 1663). See also R Hutton, *The Restoration: A Political and Religious History of England and Wales 1658–1667* (Oxford, Oxford University Press, 1986) 186 and 344, endorsing the cautious approach in Wilson, *The Court Wits*. For reports of the case, see: *Le Roy v Sr Charles Sidley* (1664) 1 Sid 168, 82 ER 1036; *Sir Charles Sydlyes Case* (1664) 1 Keble 620, 83 ER 1146; Siderfin's report is also in translation in 17 State Trials at col 155, and the case is cited in 4 Bl Comm 64. The controlment roll entry is at TNA: PRO KB 29/313; the Rex roll entry is at TNA: PRO KB 27/1856. The information itself is missing from the National Archives, but is replicated in the Rex roll entry.

[161] See *Dominus Rex v Curl* (n 54); *Rex v Delaval* (1763) 3 Burr 1434, 97 ER 913. See also Hawk PC (6th edn) book II at 8.

Chamber to do it.[162] Certainly, on the abolition of Star Chamber, cases that it was thought might have been heard there were heard in King's Bench,[163] as the Statute abolishing Star Chamber had anticipated.[164]

However, it is unclear how, if at all, this jurisdiction had been exercised by Star Chamber before it was abolished in 1641 and how had it been passed on to the King's Bench. One theory was that the power had been in the King's Bench all along and was now merely being restored to it.[165] (It is unclear to what extent this claim of restoration of an authentic past is more than an example of the usual revolutionary rhetoric.[166]) That was, at any rate, much the same story as that told by Blackstone,[167] Stephen[168] and Holdsworth.[169] This was the story largely accepted by the Court of Criminal Appeal, and by Lord Tucker and Viscount Simonds in *Shaw*, who relied on Lord Mansfield in *Delaval*,[170] which in turn relied for authority on *Sedley* and *Curl*.

Keble's report of *Sedley*, on the other hand, does not deal with the *custos morum* point, saying merely that:

> He was fined 2000 mark, committed without bail for a week, and bound to his good behaviour for a year, on his confession of information against him, for shewing himself naked in a balcony, and throwing down bottles (pist in) vi & armis among the people in Covent Garden, contra pacem, and to the scandal of the Government.[171]

According to Keble, the case would appear to be merely a relatively clear, if outrageous, trespass. Not that long after *Sedley* was decided, there was reported doubt about the precise basis of the decision. According to Fortescue's report of *Read* (1708), Powell J in *Read* claimed that it had been the *vi et armis* element of Sedley's conduct that gave the King's Bench jurisdiction in *Sedley*.[172] Read, it was felt, should have been prosecuted in the ecclesiatical courts, and the indictment against him was quashed.

---

[162] *Le Roy v Sr Charles Sidley* (1664) 1 Sid 168, 168, 82 ER 1036, 1036. It appears that other bodies also exercised the jurisdiction of 'guardian of the public morals': see *Gethin v Gethin* (1862) 2 SW & TR 560, 562–63 on the Queen's Proctor. See also the comments of Munby J in *Singh v Entry Clearance Officer New Delhi* [2004] EWCA Civ 1075 [64]: 'The Court of King's Bench, or its modern incarnation the Administrative Court, is no longer *custos morum* of the people. And a judge, although it may be that on occasions he can legitimately exercise the functions of an aedile, is no censor.' These comments echo Munby J's comments in *Smeaton v Secretary of State for Health* [2002] EWHC 610 [48].
[163] *R v Edgerley* (1642) March NR 131, 133, 82 ER 443, 444. See also the notes of Roger North in 8 State Trials at col 165.
[164] 16 Charles I c 10, II.
[165] See *Rex v Johnson* (1687) Comb 36, 90 ER 328, 4 Bl Comm 306.
[166] Consider HJ Berman, *Law and Revolution: The Formation of the Western Legal Tradition* (Cambridge, MA, Harvard University Press, 1983) 15.
[167] 4 Bl Comm 263 and 306.
[168] JF Stephen, *A History of the Criminal Law of England*, vol 2 (London, Macmillan & Co, 1883) 470.
[169] WS Holdsworth, *A History of English Law*, vol 8 (London, Methuen & Co, 1925) 407.
[170] But see the comment in Lord Reid's notebook on this point (n 87).
[171] (1664) 1 Keble 620, 83 ER 1146.
[172] *The Queen v Read* (1708) Fort 98, 99, 92 ER 777.

But in *Curl* (1727),[173] a prosecution by information for publishing *Venus in the Cloister, or, The Nun in Her Smock*, it was decided unanimously in the King's Bench that publication of obscene writings even without force and arms was a temporal offence. Fortescue J, who had reported *Read*, argued against this in *Curl* initially,[174] and was replaced, on the accession of George II,[175] by Page J, 'often been branded one of the most brutal judges of the Walpolean era',[176] who assented with the majority. It is thus unsurprising that *Curl* does not provide an optimally reasoned interpretation of the prior cases.

An examination of the Rex roll shows that Keble's report is the more helpful.[177] The entry replicates the information against Sedley and unsurprisingly does not say anything about the court being the keeper of the public morals, but it does note that the matter was a *vi et armis* trespass against those in the crowd on whom Sedley threw bottles and urinated. All that said, at the time, people such as Pepys and Siderfin clearly thought something else was involved, and that perception held in *Curl*, and later in *Deleval*, and then later again in *Shaw*.

## V. CONCLUSION

Nicola Lacey has correctly noted that 'law's institutional quality makes a historical perspective an essential component of any satisfactory approach to legal theory'.[178] Indeed, to the extent that problems such as those that arose in *Shaw* remain persistent with respect to legality—on some accounts 'the distinctive modality of law'[179]—it is helpful to be reminded of the contingent nature of both the balancing we have reached and the concepts we use. *Shaw*, with its broad assertions of jurisdiction based on dubious authority from over 350 years ago, is the landmark from which we can attempt to steer ourselves towards a better understanding.

---

[173] *Dominus Rex v Curl* (1727) 2 Strange 788, 791, 93 ER 849, 851. See generally P Baines and P Rogers, *Edmund Curll, Bookseller* (Oxford, Clarendon Press, 2007) 155–69. The authors refer to the informations as indictments at 157, and helpfully note at 351 that they are in TNA: PRO KB 10/19.

[174] See the end of his report of *Read* (1708) Fort 98, 99, 92 ER 777; and *Dominus Rex v Curl* (1727) 2 Strange 788, 791, 93 ER 849, 851.

[175] D Lemmings, 'Aland, John Fortescue, First Baron Fortescue of Credan (1670–1746)' in HCG Matthew and B Harrison (eds), *Oxford Dictionary of National Biography* (Oxford, Oxford University Press, 2004) vol 1, 558.

[176] AA Hanham, 'Page, Sir Francis (1660/61?–1741)' in HCG Matthew and B Harrison (eds), *Oxford Dictionary of National Biography* (Oxford, Oxford University Press, 2004) vol 42, 324.

[177] TNA: PRO KB 27/1856.

[178] N Lacey, 'Jurisprudence, History, and the Institutional Quality of Law' (2015) 101 *Virginia Law Review* 919, 922.

[179] ibid 932.

# 12

# *DPP v Morgan* (1975)

## I. INTRODUCTION

D *PP V MORGAN* (1975) is a curious kind of landmark case.[1] It is
notorious, branded the 'rapists' charter', for establishing the rule
that any man who honestly believed a woman was consenting, however unreasonable his grounds for doing so, could not be convicted of rape.
In spite of this controversy, the decision was upheld and was even restated
in section 1 of the Sexual Offences (Amendment) Act 1976. However, when
the law of sexual offences was reformed in the Sexual Offences Act 2003,
the rule in *Morgan* was a prime target for reformers and was replaced with
a new test based on reasonable belief.[2] The case was central to a range of
debates, in the UK and beyond, about the criminal law in the last quarter of
the twentieth century, from rape law to the adoption of a subjective test of
mens rea to defences. However, its lasting significance may be best understood in terms of how it prompted change and reform rather than for having
established any lasting legal principle.

The facts of the case are well known. Morgan was an RAF sergeant.
Following a night of drinking in Wolverhampton, he invited three younger
colleagues to his home to have sexual intercourse with his wife, Daphne.
She still lived in the family home with their children, but there was a suggestion that the marriage was breaking up, and she certainly did not share a
bedroom with him. He allegedly told his colleagues that although she might
appear not to be consenting, she would in fact be consenting, and that she
was 'kinky' and this was sexually exciting for her. The younger men agreed
to accompany him and he distributed condoms to each of them. On arriving
at his house, she was woken where she was sleeping in a single bed, in a
room she shared with one of their two young children. She was dragged
from the room, screaming for the children to call the police, and taken to

---

* My thanks to James Chalmers for his comments on an earlier draft of this chapter.
[1] *DPP v Morgan* [1976] AC 182 (HL).
[2] Sexual Offences Act 2003, s 1.

another room where she was held down by the men as they each (including her husband) raped her. At the conclusion of this incident, she fled from the house to the nearest hospital, where she complained of having been raped.

The three younger men were charged with rape; Morgan could not be charged with rape because of the doctrine of marital immunity which was in force at the time, but was charged with aiding and abetting the rape. The three younger men had initially admitted their role in statements to the police, but at the trial they repudiated these statements and instead claimed that while Daphne Morgan had initially resisted, she had later shown signs of enjoyment and in fact had actively participated in the sex. Their defence was accordingly that she had consented and that, even if she had not, they had believed that she did. The trial judge directed the jury that the men could only be acquitted if their belief in consent was based on reasonable grounds. Moreover, he was at pains to point out that if the jury believed Daphne Morgan was not in fact consenting, they were in effect rejecting the evidence of the defendants and that it would stretch credibility to then give any particular weight to their claims about a genuine belief in consent. All four men were convicted. They appealed on the grounds that the trial judge had misdirected the jury on the question of whether they knew Daphne Morgan was consenting or not and on the relevance of that knowledge for a conviction of rape. The conviction was upheld in the Court of Appeal, which permitted an appeal to the House of Lords. The question of general public importance certified for appeal to the House of Lords was: 'Whether in rape the defendant can properly be convicted, notwithstanding that he in fact believed that the woman consented, if such belief was not based on reasonable grounds.'[3] The court famously decided that this question should be answered in the negative—that a man who honestly believed that the woman was consenting, even if this was based on unreasonable grounds, could not be convicted as he did not possess the necessary mens rea for the crime.

The decision was hugely controversial. It led to uproar in the media and questions being asked in the House of Commons. A private member's bill was introduced by Jack Ashley MP to impose a requirement of reasonableness where a mistaken belief in consent was alleged.[4] The government established a committee to look into the law, the Advisory Group on the Law of Rape, chaired by Mrs Justice Heilbron.[5] This body recommended 'declaratory' legislation to restate the decision in *Morgan*, in order to foreclose the possibility of future appeals on the grounds that the decision in *Morgan* was obiter dicta.[6] This became section 1 of the Sexual Offences (Amendment)

[3] *Morgan* (n 1) 199 and 205.
[4] For a full account of the aftermath, see J Temkin, *Rape and the Legal Process*, 2nd edn (Oxford, Oxford University Press, 2002) 119–22.
[5] Heilbron Committee, *Report of the Advisory Group on the Law of Rape* (Cmnd 6352, 1975).
[6] ibid, paras 81–84.

Act 1976. The Committee also recommended further changes to the conduct of rape trials around sexual history and character evidence and anonymity for complainants. But in spite of these efforts to explain and limit the impact of the decision, the controversy barely receded. The case was a lightning rod for critical accounts of the criminal law throughout the 1980s and 1990s. It was attacked as one of the high watermarks of subjective approaches to mens rea and as a symbol of outdated attitudes towards the protection of female victims of sexual assault. Ultimately the assumptions on which *Morgan* was built unravelled rapidly with the passing of the Sexual Offences Act 2003 (and 2009 in Scotland) and the case is now primarily of historical interest. In this chapter, I shall reassess the significance of *Morgan*, in particular by placing the decision and its aftermath in the context of mid-twentieth-century debates about mens rea and responsibility, and changing understandings of sexual offences.

## II. THE 'INEXORABLE LOGIC' OF SUBJECTIVISM

While the rule established in *Morgan* is well known, the process by which the court arrived at this outcome is not easy to follow—notwithstanding that it was described by Lord Hailsham as a matter of 'inexorable logic'.[7] All of the judges held that the men had been properly convicted, on the grounds that the jury had plainly not believed their claim that Daphne Morgan had consented—and thus that it could hardly be described as an honest belief in the circumstances. Lord Hailsham, for example, argued that there had been two completely incompatible stories before the court and that the jury had chosen between them.[8] Since they apparently believed Daphne Morgan's story, then the question of belief should not have arisen because consent was not at issue at all; it would only have been an issue if they had given credence to the defendants' account. However, he argued that, notwithstanding this, the appellants' contention that they believed she was consenting gave rise to a 'substantial question of principle'. In addressing this point of principle, each of the five judges on the court delivered a lengthy judgment.[9] The majority, Lords Hailsham, Cross and Fraser, argued for a test of honest belief; Lord Edmund-Davies agreed with the majority in

---

[7] *Morgan* (n 1) 214F. See also 213F–G, where he refers to the logical acceptability of certain positions and his unwillingness to sanction a principle that he regarded as a 'logical impossibility'. Similarly, Lord Fraser expressed relief that there was no authority which would have compelled him to answer the question in 'an illogical way' (at 239C–D).

[8] Because 'if there was reasonable doubt about belief, the same material must have given rise to reasonable doubt about consent, and vice versa': *Morgan* (n 1) 207G. See also Lord Cross at 204B–E.

[9] It was, in part, for this reason that the Heilbron Committee recommended declaratory legislation (*Report* (n 5) para 81).

principle, while arguing that the trial judge had directed the jury properly on the law as it stood; and Lord Simon dissented.

There were, broadly speaking, three issues which were addressed by the court in disposing of this question of principle. First, there was the question of whether or not belief in consent was a 'defence' to rape or was part of the mens rea of the crime: was the mens rea of rape to have sexual intercourse with a woman who was not in fact consenting or was it to have non-consensual sexual intercourse with a woman?[10] In the first case, it was argued that mens rea would extend only to the intention to have sexual intercourse, but in the second, it was argued that the mens rea was the intention to have non-consensual sexual intercourse.[11] One of the problems here was the absence of a clear definition of the crime of rape. Sir Edward Coke had defined the crime as 'when a man hath carnal knowledge of a woman by force and against her will', and this was seen as the foundation of the modern law.[12] Although section 1 of the Sexual Offences Act 1956 had replaced the term 'carnal knowledge' with the more modern 'sexual intercourse', the definition of the crime otherwise remained a matter of common law. The problem, as Lord Fraser pointed out, was that: 'Most offences, whether at common law or under statute, include some mental element, but the description of the offence normally refers only to the prohibited act, leaving the mental element to be implied.'[13]

The issue facing the court, then, was to formulate a more explicit definition of the mental element of the crime of rape. Lord Cross cited ordinary language or usage of the term 'rape' to suggest that the ordinary man would not regard as rape the situation where a man had sexual intercourse with a woman believing that she was consenting, though this was not in fact the case.[14] Lords Hailsham and Edmund-Davies cited the definition in Archbold's *Criminal Pleading*, which itself merely cited Hale and East.[15] This was not particularly clear one way or the other, as it did not distinguish between the elements of actus reus and mens rea, and there was a slippage between the older definitions in terms of consent being negated by force, fear or fraud and the idea that mens rea required either intent or knowledge of lack of consent. A number of nineteenth-century cases and Australian cases were cited before the court, but these again were inconclusive as there were authorities in support of both views. However, notwithstanding these

---

[10] See, eg, *Morgan* (n 1) 209C–G (Lord Hailsham) and 203D–204A (Lord Cross).

[11] In the first case, the crime would be regarded as analogous to bigamy, where the courts had recognised that a reasonable belief in a certain state of affairs (that one's spouse was dead, that the woman was consenting) could be a defence: *R v Tolson* (1889) 23 QBD 168 (CCR).

[12] 2 Co Inst 180, 3 Co Inst 60. *cf* Hale PC 627: 'Rape is the carnal knowledge of any woman above the age of ten years against her will'; EH East, *A Treatise of the Pleas of the Crown* (London, Butterworths, 1803) vol I, 434, citing Coke's definition almost word for word.

[13] *Morgan* (n 1) 236H.

[14] ibid 203D–G.

[15] ibid 210G and 225B.

uncertainties, all the judges came to the conclusion that the definition of the mens rea of rape should be the intention to engage in non-consensual sexual intercourse. It was then argued that a further consequence of this was that the crime could be committed either intentionally or recklessly, not caring whether or not the victim was consenting—as recklessness was seen as 'equivalent on ordinary principles to an intent to do the prohibited act without the consent of the victim'.[16] This, as was recognised by the Heilbron Committee, was significant as it was the first clear and unequivocal recognition that rape could be committed recklessly[17]—though this was also memorably described by Jennifer Temkin as the 'consolation prize' for those who opposed the decision in *Morgan*.[18]

Second, there was the question of where the burden of proof lay in cases such as this. This issue turned on the distinction between probative and evidential burdens of proof.[19] If awareness of the absence of consent was part of the mens rea of the crime, then it was necessary for the prosecution to prove this awareness. If, by contrast, it was a 'defence', the Crown would discharge its burden of proof by establishing that the accused had acted intentionally and the evidential burden then lay on the accused to raise the question of their belief.[20] This part of the decision is best understood in the context of the dismantling of presumptions around mens rea, a process in which the case of *DPP v Woolmington* was central.[21] While best known for the grand statement of Viscount Sankey affirming the centrality of the presumption of innocence in English law, *Woolmington* was in fact addressing the narrower question of what was to be presumed about mental state from proof of the facts. The traditional position in English law was that proof of the facts established a prima facie presumption of 'malice', unless the defendant raised evidence that could displace this. In place of this, the House of Lords in *Woolmington* held that the burden of proof always rested

---

[16] ibid 209H (Lord Hailsham). See also at 215C–D, where he describes recklessness as 'the equivalent intention of having intercourse willy-nilly not caring whether the victim consents or no', and Lord Edmund-Davies at 226F.

[17] Heilbron, *Report* para 77. However, this was then subject to further controversy over the issue of what constituted recklessness in the wake of the decision in *R v Caldwell* [1982] AC 341. See, eg, RA Duff, 'Recklessness and Rape' (1981) 3 *Liverpool Law Review* 49; G Williams, 'Recklessness Redefined' (1981) 40 *CLJ* 252; RA Duff, 'Professor Williams and Conditional Subjectivism' (1982) 41 *CLJ* 273.

[18] J Temkin, 'Limits of Reckless Rape' [1983] *Crim LR* 5, 5.

[19] See, eg, *Morgan* (n 1) 217E–F per Lord Simon, citing Lord Denning, 'Presumptions and Burdens' (1945) 41 *LQR* 379.

[20] This was the view of Bridge J in the Court of Appeal (*Morgan* (n 1) 191C–E) and of Lord Simon in the House of Lords (at 218G–H). See also Lord Edmund-Davies: 'In the absence of contrary evidence, the accused may be presumed to have appreciated the significance of circumstances which must have come to his notice' (at 226C).

[21] *DPP v Woolmington* [1935] AC 462 (HL). See the discussion in L Farmer, *Making the Modern Criminal Law: Criminalization and Civil Order* (Oxford, Oxford University Press, 2016) 181–88.

on the prosecution—even in cases of accidental killing or where excuse was claimed—and that it was necessary to prove both the fact of killing and the intention of the accused. If the defence wished to rely on other evidence which was not before the court, then they bore the evidential burden of raising it. The proof of an act was thus distinct from the proof of an intention and, while conduct might provide evidence of an intention, this was a matter of proof rather than presumption.[22] The burden of proof was thus on the Crown to establish not only the conduct but also the necessary mental state. A further consequence of this was thus that where crime definitions had previously not necessarily specified the mens rea element—as Lord Fraser had already pointed out—it was now necessary to specify this in order to be able to judge whether or not the burden of proof had been discharged. If knowledge of the circumstances (lack of consent) was part of the mens rea of the crime and not a 'defence', then a man ought not to be convicted of rape unless the prosecution proved that he intended to do what the law forbids.

The third issue was that of whether a belief needed to be held on reasonable grounds or whether an honest but unreasonable belief in consent would negate mens rea. While the Crown contended that this should be determined by a line of authorities from *Tolson*[23] onwards which had established that a mistake of fact would have to be based on reasonable grounds, the majority of the court viewed this as a matter of logic, which followed directly from the first two points. If the mens rea of rape was the intention to engage in non-consensual sexual intercourse and if the prosecution had to prove this mens rea, then an honest belief in consent would clearly negative intent and 'the reasonableness or otherwise of that belief can only be evidence for or against the view that the belief and therefore the intent was actually held'.[24] The existence of a belief in consent was thus, on this view, inconsistent with the burden of proof on the prosecution in a rape case.[25] This was argued by Lord Hailsham:

> To insist that a belief must be reasonable ... is to insist that either the accused is to be found guilty of intending to do that which in truth he did not intend to do,

---

[22] See, eg, G Williams, *Criminal Law. The General Part* (London, Stevens & Sons, 1953) 77–81 and 703–06. See also JWC Turner, 'The Mental Element in Crimes at Common Law' in L Radzinowicz and JWC Turner (eds), *The Modern Approach to Criminal Law* (London, Macmillan, 1948).

[23] *Tolson* (n 11).

[24] *Morgan* (n 1) 214G. However, Lord Edmund-Davies, who had agreed with the majority on the first two points, considered that the established law was that mistakes of fact should be based on reasonable grounds and that any change in this should be made by the legislature (at 235A).

[25] *cf* Lord Simon (dissenting on this point), who argued for a test of reasonableness on the grounds that the law should, as a matter of policy, 'hold a fair balance between victim and accused' and that this would protect the 'respectable woman' who was the victim of an attacker holding an absurd belief in consent (ibid 221B).

or that his state of mind, though innocent of evil intent, can convict him if it be honest but not rational.[26]

He went on to argue that:

[I]t seems to me to follow as a matter of *inexorable logic* that there is no room either for a 'defence' of honest belief or mistake, or of a defence of honest and reasonable belief or mistake. Either the prosecution proves that the accused had the requisite intent, or it does not ... Since honest belief clearly negatives intent, the reasonableness or otherwise of that belief can only be evidence for or against the view that the belief and therefore the intent was actually held. (Emphasis added)[27]

This was also viewed as an extension of the principle in section 8 of the Criminal Justice Act 1967, which had abolished the presumption that a person intended the natural consequences of their action, such that it was necessary to prove not only knowledge of consequences but also knowledge of circumstances.[28]

I want to note three further features of the decision. The first is that that the question was understood as one of principle, a matter of the 'academic' structure of the criminal law. Indeed, Lord Hailsham introduced his judgment by stating that the question before the court was one of 'great academic importance in the theory of the English criminal law'.[29] By this he did not mean that the point was irrelevant to the disposal of the appeal (though in a sense it was), but rather that it was central to the development of law and to the role of the House of Lords in the development of the criminal law. Although the House of Lords had formally been the court of final appeal since 1907, in practice, few cases came before the court before 1960 because of the need to obtain the fiat of the Attorney-General and the requirement that the appeal raised a point of 'exceptional' legal importance.[30] The Administration of Justice Act 1960 had relaxed this, allowing the Court of Appeal to grant leave to appeal where there was a point of law of *general* public importance. This not only had the effect of allowing a greater number of criminal appeals to come before the House of Lords, but also gave the Court a responsibility to develop the criminal law through consideration of these points of general public importance.[31] And given that this

---

[26] ibid 210B–C. See also Lord Edmund-Davies: 'Honest belief, however foolishly formed, that the woman was willing seems to me incompatible with an intention to rape her' (at 226E).

[27] ibid 214F–G.

[28] ibid 226F–G (Lord Edmund-Davies), citing JC Smith and B Hogan, *Criminal Law*, 3rd edn (London, Butterworths, 1973) 150 on precisely this point. This was also a point that had been made by JC Smith in his critical commentary on *Morgan* in the Court of Appeal: [1975] *Crim LR* 42.

[29] *Morgan* (n 1) 204G. He was not, of course, using the term in an ironic sense.

[30] DGT Williams, 'The Administration of Justice Act 1960' [1961] *Crim LR* 87; R Stevens, *Law and Politics: The House of Lords as a Judicial Body 1850–1976* (London, Weidenfeld & Nicolson, 1979) 415–20 notes that legal aid was extended to appeals to the House of Lords the following year. See also Anon, 'Appeals to the House of Lords' [1957] *Crim LR* 566.

[31] DGT Williams, 'The Administration of Justice Act 1960' [1961] *Crim LR* 87.

authority was, after 1966, more or less unconstrained by precedent, as the court could overrule its own previous decisions, it could in effect operate as a kind of law reform body.[32] However, the House did not get off to a good start in its new role. In *DPP v Smith*, the House applied an objective test of foresight of consequences in upholding Smith's murder conviction.[33] Then in *Shaw v DPP* (the 'Ladies' Directory' case), the House asserted its right to act as guardian of public morals in upholding the conviction of Shaw for a conspiracy to corrupt public morals.[34] In both cases, there was extensive criticism of the decisions. The decision in *Smith* was criticised by academics for the failure to apply a subjective test of mens rea, a move which led eventually to the Criminal Justice Act 1967 removing the inference that natural consequences were intended and replacing it with a test of actual intent or foresight.[35] *Shaw* was criticised for its wide interpretation of the crime of conspiracy, for the upholding of 'morals' offences and for usurping the role of Parliament in creating criminal offences.[36] As a result of these and other cases, a strained relationship developed between the House of Lords and leading academic lawyers.[37] By the early 1980s, prompted by the decision in *R v Caldwell* (1981), influential commentators, such as JC Smith and Glanville Williams, were publicly questioning the wisdom of the House of Lords in the area of criminal law.[38]

It was clear that the court in *Morgan* was acutely aware of this context, with Lord Hailsham, for example, referring to the 'unhappy experience' of the court after the decision in *Smith*.[39] This, however, points to the second feature of the decision, which was the substantial engagement by the court

---

[32] See Practice Statement (Judicial Precedent) [1966] 1 WLR 1234. See also A Paterson, *The Law Lords* (London, Macmillan, 1982) 146–53. On the House of Lords as a reform body, see generally ATH Smith, 'Criminal Appeals in the House of Lords' (1984) 47 *MLR* 133, esp 142–43.

[33] *DPP v Smith* [1961] AC 290 (HL).

[34] *Shaw v DPP* [1962] AC 220 (HL), on which see Henry Mares's chapter in this volume. See also *R v Manley* [1933] 1 KB 529 (CA). The case was later distinguished by the House of Lords in *Knuller v DPP* [1973] AC 435 (HL).

[35] Criminal Justice Act 1967, s 8. See also Criminal Law Revision Committee, *Seventh Report. Felonies and Misdemeanours* (Cmnd 2659, 1965). For criticism of the decision in *Smith*, see G Williams, 'Constructive Malice Revived' (1960) 23 *MLR* 626; G Williams, *The Mental Element in Crime* (Jerusalem, Magnes Press, 1965); R Cross, 'The Need for a Redefinition of Murder' [1960] *Crim LR* 728; R Buxton, 'The Retreat from Smith' [1966] *Crim LR* 195.

[36] HLA Hart, *Law, Liberty and Morality* (Oxford, Oxford University Press, 1963) 1–24; AL Goodhart, 'The *Shaw* Case: The Law and Public Morals' (1961) 77 *LQR* 560; D Seaborne-Davies, 'The House of Lords and Criminal Law' (1961) 6 *Journal of the Society of Public Teachers of Law* 104; G Williams, 'Conspiring to Corrupt' *The Listener* (London, 24 August 1961) 275.

[37] For a review, see Smith, 'Criminal Appeals' (n 32).

[38] *Caldwell* (n 17). See JC Smith [1981] *Crim LR* 392: 'The House of Lords has a dismal record in criminal cases'; G Williams [1981] *Crim LR* 580.

[39] *Morgan* (n 1) 210C, also referring to his discussion in *R v Hyam* [1975] AC 55, which had itself been criticised.

with academic commentary. The point here is less the conflict between the House of Lords and academics over the appropriate means of law reform than that there was a kind of extended dialogue going on. The courts were aware of academic commentary on their own decisions and responded to this: the law was being developed through this dialogue. The court thus referred approvingly to an article by JC Smith which was critical of the decision in the Court of Appeal.[40] More generally, the judges framed their discussion in terms of a new kind of academic language. Lord Simon, for example, began by arguing that it was essential to determine whether or not rape was a crime of basic or ulterior intent (following a distinction made by Smith and Hogan).[41] There was also considerable discussion of academic treatises, particularly those which had developed an account of subjective mens rea.[42]

What is significant about this is that although the court might have disagreed with academics on particular points, they had accepted the basic conceptual structure that was being developed in academic treatises.[43] This is clearly illustrated by the discussion of the distinction between actus reus and mens rea.[44] The point is less about the substantive claim (that serious crimes carry an implicit definition of mental element) than that the concepts of actus reus and mens rea were seen as the appropriate analytical tools for developing the criminal law. In other words, the question was not that of whether or not the crime of rape always required fault (about which there was no disagreement), but that it was seen as necessary to break the definition down into distinct elements of actus reus and mens rea. This understanding that malice could be separated into distinct elements—the voluntary act and the more specific question of intention—and that the prosecution had to prove both beyond reasonable doubt was a precondition for the restatement of the presumption of innocence.[45] This further helped to identify the point of principle that was at issue in the case as one relating to the moral blameworthiness of the accused and the 'liberty of the subject'.[46]

The third point that I want to make is that, for all that the case concerned a particularly shocking incident of multiple rape, there was remarkably little

---

[40] [1975] *Crim LR* 42.

[41] *Morgan* (n 1) 216–17.

[42] See, eg, ibid 226 and 230–31 (Lord Edmund Davies). The works discussed included Glanville Williams, *Criminal Law: The General Part*, 2nd edn (London, Stevens, 1961); Smith and Hogan, *Criminal Law*, 3rd edn ( London: Butterworths); JWC Turner, *Russell on Crime*, 12th edn (London, Stevens, 1964); J Hall, *General Principles of Criminal Law*, 2nd edn (Indianapolis, Bobbs-Merrill, 1960).

[43] For more discussion of this point, see Farmer, *Making the Modern Criminal Law* (n 4) 149–53.

[44] See, eg, *Morgan* (n 1) 210G (Lord Hailsham), 216–17 (Lord Simon) and 236H (Lord Fraser).

[45] See G Fletcher, *Rethinking Criminal Law* (Boston, MA, Little, Brown & Co, 1978) 537–38.

[46] Heilbron, *Report* para 54.

direct discussion or analysis of the law of rape; the question was instead approached by the majority as a matter of logic that did not engage with the substantive issues of rape law.[47] The decision was almost entirely framed in terms of questions of burdens of proof and the relationship between mens rea and defences. The court, indeed, were at pains to stress the extraordinary or exceptional nature of the facts, allowing them to argue that its exceptional nature justified the point of principle as it was unlikely that cases would arise where a defendant could claim an honest belief of this sort.[48] However, the feminist critique was not only that cases such as this were not unusual, but that such cases would only be viewed as unusual from within a particular view of rape and sexual assault. It was argued that the problem with *Morgan* was precisely that the law of rape was structured around a number of problematic beliefs about consent: that in the context of 'seduction', a woman saying no might mean yes; that sexually active women were more likely to consent; or that compliance through fear might be understood as an indication of consent.[49] These kinds of beliefs, it was argued, were further institutionalised in a criminal justice system where, in the investigation of rape, victims were routinely met with an attitude of suspicion and disbelief.[50] The problem with *Morgan* was not that it was exceptional, but that it exemplified a certain understanding of rape and sexual offences. Understanding the contrast between these two different views of *Morgan* requires that we place it in the context of the rapid transformation of understandings of sexual offences between the Sexual Offences Act 1956 and the passing of the Sexual Offences Act 2003.

## III. THE TRANSFORMATION OF SEXUAL OFFENCES

There was a massive transformation in social and scientific understandings of sex, beginning in the early part of the twentieth century.[51] A key development was the emergence of a new interest in, or science of,

---

[47] See also Temkin, *Rape and the Legal Process* 116–19.

[48] Though Lord Cross did suggest that the defendants might properly have been acquitted had they presented their defence in a more subtle way (*Morgan* (n 1) 204). See also Heilbron, *Report* (n 5) para 27. The facts were not so exceptional that they did not arise in other cases and in other jurisdictions; see, eg, *R v Cogan and Leak* [1976] QB 217; *Meek and others v HM Advocate* 1982 SCCR 613; *Jamieson v HM Advocate* 1994 JC 88.

[49] For examples of widely cited contemporary commentary, see, eg, S Brownmiller, *Against Our Will: Men, Women and Rape* (London, Penguin, 1976); C Smart and B Smart, 'Accounting for Rape' in *Women, Sexuality and Social Control* (London, Routledge & Kegan Paul, 1978); L Clark and D Lewis, *Rape: The Price of Coercive Sexuality* (Toronto, Women's Press, 1977).

[50] RE Hall, *Ask Any Woman: A London Inquiry into Rape and Sexual Assault* (Bristol, Falling Wall Press, 1985); Z Adler, 'Rape—The Intention of Parliament and the Practice of the Courts' (1982) 45 *MLR* 664. See generally Temkin, *Rape and the Legal Process* Ch 1; S Lees, *Carnal Knowledge. Rape on Trial*, revised edn (London, Women's Press, 2002).

[51] This section is based on the argument in Farmer, *Making the Modern Criminal Law* (n 21) Ch 9.

sex at the end of the nineteenth century, connecting an account of sexual acts to an inner psychology—the recognition of which in its turn allowed for the possibility of acts being characterised as 'sexual' depending on their motivation. Foucault, in one of the most important analyses of this development, viewed the science of sex as crystallising around four themes: the hystericisation of women's bodies; the supervision of children's sexual conduct; the stress on the importance of procreative sex for the social body; and the psychiatrisation of perverse pleasure.[52] The new science of sexology stressed the importance and normality of sexual pleasure for both men and women, expressed in the Edwardian belief that intimate relations should be a free and equal partnership between men and women.[53] However, it also recognised and sought to regulate or control forms of sexual perversion. Sexual conduct was categorised into normal and pathological forms, with an increased interest in, and regulation of, sexual deviancy. Sexual violence was distinguished from normal heterosexual behaviour by its inappropriate object choice, where children were the victims, or by the resort to extreme physical violence. In the area of criminal law, this was reflected in developments in three different areas: the efforts to measure the incidence of sex offences; the idea of the sex offender and their treatment; and the understandings of the impact of sexual crimes on victims.

Although criminal statistics had been systematically collected since the 1840s, sexual offences had not been singled out as a distinct category. Rape was recorded as a crime against the person, but information about other crimes involving sex was not disaggregated. Information was not routinely collected about the age or sex of victims, where this was not apparent from the crime definition, and few details were recorded for minor or summary offences. Beginning in the 1920s, there were moves to collect more, and more specific, information. The *Report of the Departmental Committee on Sexual Offences against Young Persons* (1925) contained a thorough discussion of these problems and recommended changes to the collection of criminal statistics to record the age and sex of victims and sentences imposed on offenders.[54] The 1957 *Cambridge Report on Sexual Offences*

[52] M Foucault, *The History of Sexuality. I The Will to Pleasure* (Harmondsworth, Penguin, 1978) 104–05. There is a huge literature on this. See, eg, J Weeks, *Sex, Politics and Society: The Regulation of Sexuality since 1800*, 3rd edn (London, Routledge, 2012); A Clark, *Desire: A History of European Sexuality* (London, Routledge, 2008) esp Chs 8 and 9; S Toulalan and K Fisher (eds), *The Routledge History of Sex and the Body, 1500 to the Present* (London, Routledge, 2013). There is a useful discussion in H Cocks, 'Modernity and the Self in the History of Sexuality' (2006) 49 *Historical Journal* 1211.

[53] See, eg, discussions in L Bland, *Banishing the Beast: Feminism, Sex and Morality* (London, IB Tauris, 2002).

[54] *Report of the Departmental Committee on Sexual Offences against Young Persons* (Cmd 2561, 1925) Ch 2 (Prevalence of Offences)—although many of these recommendations were not implemented. It also recommended changes to the trial of sexual offences against children. Many of these procedural changes were made in the Children and Young Persons Act 1933.

was the first systematic attempt to bring together the statistical evidence on different types of sexual offence, on the ways that they were committed and on sexual offenders.[55] Both studies noted rises in the incidence of sexual offences: the *Cambridge Report* finding an increase of 252 per cent in the number of indictable offences known to the police between 1937 and 1954, and noting that the actual number of offences was certainly higher.[56] These studies developed a distinct aetiology of the sex offender, assessing the seriousness of different types of crime in terms of the motivation of offenders, and linked this to the development of treatment regimes targeted at particular groups of offenders.[57] They also began to recognise the impact of sex offences, particularly on children, in terms of the trauma that it could cause and its interference with normal sexual development.[58] This awareness of the growing incidence of sexual offences, and of the idea that they represented a special sort of problem, shaped a new understanding of the criminal law, in which sexual offences began to be seen as a discrete area within, or even separated from, the law of offences against the person, which could be organised around its own set of principles.

The term 'sexual offences' was rarely used before 1956. The Sexual Offences Act 1956 was the first statute to use this term to describe this area of the law.[59] It was a consolidation measure, bringing together into a single statute diverse provisions from a range of nineteenth-century statutes with some minor amendments. It was not a complete codification of the field, since the common law was left largely untouched, particularly with respect to the crime of rape: as was noted above, the Act did not for this reason contain a definition of the crime of rape. The term 'carnal knowledge' was replaced by the more modern 'sexual intercourse', though in substance this

---

[55] L Radzinowicz, *Sexual Offences: A Report of the Cambridge Department of Criminal Science* (London, Macmillan, 1957). See also W Norwood East, *Society and the Criminal* (London, HMSO, 1949) Ch 7; W Norwood East, *Sexual Offenders* (London, Delisle, 1955); H Mannheim, *Social Aspects of Crime in England between Two Wars* (London, George Allen & Unwin, 1940) 121; H Mannheim, 'Two Reports on Sex Offences' (1949) 12 *MLR* 488; JE Hall Williams, 'Sex Offenses: The British Experience' (1960) 25 *Law and Contemporary Problems* 334.

[56] Radzinowicz, *Sexual Offences* (n 55) 5 and Part I generally. See F Mort, *Capital Affairs: London and the Making of the Permissive Society* (New Haven, Yale University Press, 2010) 43–44.

[57] See, eg, East, who notes that the medical conception of sexual offences, based on the motivation of the offender, might be wider than the legal one and that different crimes might be attended by different motivations: see East, *Society and the Criminal* (n 55) 94 and 107–21 for a typology (including the homosexual or invert, the sadist, fetishism and transvestism); and Radzinowicz, *Sexual Offences* (n 55) Part II (on offenders and their victims).

[58] *Report of the Departmental Committee on Sexual Offences* 23 and 66ff. See L Jackson, *Child Sexual Abuse in Victorian England* (London, Routledge, 2000) Conclusion.

[59] A Sexual Offences Bill was introduced in the House of Lords in 1920, although it was considerably narrower in scope, as part of the discussions that led to the Criminal Law Amendment Act 1922.

merely reflected the existing case law on 'carnal knowledge'.[60] The remainder of the Act was a restatement of a range of crimes: intercourse with minors, defectives, buggery and gross indecency, abduction, prostitution (with an emphasis on procuring) and living off the earnings of prostitutes. There was no indication of the meaning of 'sexual' and its usage was largely descriptive, denoting crimes that had a sexual element or that raised issues of sexual morality.

However, after 1956, the usage 'sexual offences' started to become more commonplace in treatises and academic works. The first book to have a separate chapter on sexual offences was the first edition of Smith and Hogan's *Criminal Law* (1965), though the authors apparently regarded the usage of the term as so worthy of remark that an asterisk after the title indicated that they had taken the term from the Cambridge study of sexual offences published in 1957.[61] In substance, though, the coverage of the chapter broadly corresponded to the content of the 1956 Act with little further comment or discussion.[62] Glanville Williams' slightly later *Textbook of Criminal Law* more self-consciously modernised both the classification and treatment of the law.[63] Sexual offences were dealt with in Part II of the book on the protection of the person (following assault and preceding murder), but in a striking departure from conventional legal usage, the chapter was called 'Sexual Aggression'. Williams began by distinguishing between different types of sexual offence: 'To speak of sexual offences as a class is somewhat misleading, since there are important differences of types. The two main groups are sexual aggression and breaches of sexual taboo.'[64] The distinction, in his view, was primarily founded in consent, with crimes in the first group consisting of 'injuries and affronts to a non-consenting victim'.[65] The chapter was concerned only with these crimes, thus leading him to exclude homosexual offences, forms of public indecency and 'morals' offences. His understanding of sexual aggression was informed by psychological literature on sex offenders, which was discussed extensively, considering the

---

[60] Sexual intercourse was defined in s 44 of the Sexual Offences Act 1956 as penetration, not requiring emission of semen.

[61] JC Smith and B Hogan, *Criminal Law* (London, Butterworths, 1965) ch 12, citing Radzinowicz, *Sexual Offences*.

[62] With the addition of public indecency. This corresponded to the understanding of 'sex crimes' in Radzinowicz, *Sexual Offenses*. For other books, see DW Elliott and JC Wood, *A Casebook on Criminal Law* (London, Sweet & Maxwell, 1963) Ch 10, 'Non-fatal Offences against the Person', including a section on sexual offences. *cf* PJ Fitzgerald, *Criminal Law and Punishment* (Oxford, Clarendon Press, 1962) Ch 2.6, 'Immorality' (including rape, unnatural offences and miscellaneous offences).

[63] G Williams, *Textbook on Criminal Law*, 2nd edn (London, Steven & Sons, 1983) Ch 10. *cf* T Honoré, *Sex Law* (London, Duckworth, 1976) for a comparable contemporary attempt to rethink legal categories in terms of a broader understanding of the meaning of sex.

[64] ibid 227.

[65] ibid. Abduction, which had hitherto been classed as a sexual offence, was dealt with in the preceding chapter on non-sexual injuries and threats.

sexual motivation that might lie behind various forms of criminal conduct (from murder to insulting conduct) to argue that it was essential that 'sexual deviationists [sic]' receive special treatment at the sentencing stage. He also discussed psychoanalytical beliefs about women's rape fantasies in the context of a discussion on consent.[66] What is significant here is less his specific views, which were much criticised, than the adoption of an understanding of sexual motivation as the defining characteristic of the offences in this area of the law and the attempt to reshape the category in the light of this understanding.

The recognition of sexual offences as a distinct area of the criminal law was shaped by one further development, which was the articulation of more liberal ideas around sex and sexual morality. Of central importance here was the Report of the Committee on Homosexual Offences and Prostitution in 1957 (the Wolfenden Committee), which articulated principles that were to be central to the development of the law in this area. The Committee's view was that the function of the law was 'to preserve public order and decency, to protect the citizen from what is offensive or injurious, and to provide sufficient safeguards against exploitation and corruption of others'.[67] This meant that 'it was not the function of the law to intervene in the private lives of citizens' and the Committee accordingly recommended the decriminalisation of homosexual conduct between consenting adults in private.[68] The recommendation was controversial, but led eventually in 1967 to the decriminalisation of sex in private between men over the age of 21.[69] Prostitution, by contrast, was seen in terms of public order or nuisance, and the Committee recommended changes to the law to remove the necessity of proving annoyance to individuals by solicitation.[70] The significance of the Committee's approach was that it translated an abstract distinction between the public domain of legally controlled activity and the private domain of personal morality into the physical terms of public and private spaces. Public sexual display or conduct was to be regulated by the criminal law, but conduct in private, including forms of private commercial sex which did not cause a nuisance, were viewed as being beyond the law. This thus

---

[66] ibid 238–39, citing the work of Helen Deutsch and Paul Gebhard. This is further discussed by J Forrester, 'Rape, Seduction and Psychoanalysis' in R Porter and S Tomaselli (eds), *Rape. An Historical and Cultural Enquiry* (Oxford, Blackwell, 1986) esp 64–66. Forrester criticises Williams for sliding from recognising the existence of rape fantasies to concluding that it is then possible to infer a woman's conscious consent in certain circumstances. For a discussion of Deutsch, see also J Bourke, *Rape: A History* (London, Virago, 2008).

[67] Wolfenden Committee, *Report of the Committee on Homosexual Offences and Prostitution* (Cmnd 247, 1957) 9–10.

[68] ibid 10 and 25.

[69] Sexual Offences Act 1967, s 1, subject to qualifications of privacy in s 1(2) (where more than two persons were present or in a public lavatory).

[70] Street Offences Act 1959, s 1(1): 'It shall be an offence for a common prostitute to loiter or solicit in a street or public place for the purpose of prostitution.'

institutionalised a view of private morality that corresponded to under-standings of middle-class domesticity. 'Normal' sex which took place in pri-vate, or private commercial sex, was not the concern of the law, but forms of sexual conduct which did not fit this model were subjected to ongoing regulation. Indeed, the recognition of diversity in the sphere of private free-dom came at the cost of a more intense policing of age of consent, public indecency and prostitution.[71]

It was against this backdrop that leading criminal lawyers began to make calls for the modernisation of the law of sexual offences in the 1970s.[72] These were largely framed as, on the one hand, calls to update and mod-ernise the law in accordance with changing social attitudes towards sexual morality and, on the other hand, as calls for liberalisation of the law, in accordance with Wolfenden, where conduct happened in private and did not injure others. This project was taken up by the Criminal Law Revision Committee (CLRC) in the late 1970s as part of its work on the codification project.[73] It produced a consultation paper on sexual offences in 1980 and a final report in 1984.[74] Simultaneously with the reference to the CLRC, the Home Secretary established the Home Office Policy Advisory Com-mittee on Sexual Offences which reported on the age of consent in sexual offences in 1981 and provided information to the CLRC on the incidence of sexual offences, which was a foundation for some of the CLRC's recom-mendations.[75] The CLRC took its lead from the position of the Wolfenden Committee that the criminal law should not intervene in the private lives of citizens or enforce any particular pattern of sexual conduct.[76] However, in its discussion of potential reforms of the law of rape, we see how its understanding of a modern law of sexual offences was consistent with the understanding of crime articulated by the House of Lords in *Morgan*.[77]

---

[71] Cocks, 'Modernity and the Self' (n 52) 1224; J Scoular and V Munro, 'Harm, Vulner-ability and Citizenship: Constitutional Concerns in the Criminalization of Contemporary Sex Work' in RA Duff et al (eds), *The Constitution of the Criminal Law* (Oxford, Oxford Univer-sity Press, 2012) 34–35.

[72] See B Hogan, 'On Modernising the Law of Sexual Offences' in P Glazebrook (ed), *Reshaping the Criminal Law* (London, Stevens & Sons, 1978); DJ West, 'Thoughts on Sex Law Reform' in R Hood (ed), *Crime, Criminology and Public Policy* (London, Heinemann, 1974); R Brazier, 'The Reform of Sexual Offences' [1975] *Crim LR* 421.

[73] Their first report was on *Indecency with Children* (Cmnd 835, 1959). The Indecency with Children Act 1960 criminalised any person committing an act of 'gross indecency' with a child, broadening the law of indecent assault.

[74] CLRC, *Working Paper on Sexual Offences* (London, HMSO, 1980); CLRC, *Fifteenth Report. Sexual Offences* (Cmnd 9213, 1984). See also Howard League Working Party, *Unlaw-ful Sex. Offences, Victims and Offenders in the Criminal Justice System of England and Wales* (London, Waterlow Publishing, 1985).

[75] See also Howard League Working Party, *Unlawful Sex.*

[76] CLRC, *Fifteenth Report* (n 74) para 1.5.

[77] For critical reviews, see C Wells, 'Law Reform, Rape and Ideology' (1985) 12 *Journal of Law & Society* 63; R Leng, 'The Scope of Rape' [1985] *Crim LR* 416; J Temkin, 'Towards a Modern Law of Rape' (1982) 45 *MLR* 399.

The CLRC considered a number of features of the law of rape. While it showed an increased awareness of the position of the victim, and of some of the criticisms that had been made by feminist campaigners of the conduct of rape trials and of lenient sentencing of those convicted of sexual assaults, it generally adhered to a traditional understanding of the ambit of the crime.[78] It opposed, for example, extending the definition of rape beyond vaginal penetration (and thus also to recognising male rape), on the grounds that rape was a distinct and serious wrong and that to broaden the definition would be to dilute its seriousness. The majority of the CLRC argued against the removal of the marital rape immunity on similar grounds, suggesting that rape was a 'unique and grave' offence and that, as forced intercourse between spouses was a less serious wrong, this might lead to rape as a whole being regarded as a less serious offence.[79] It was further argued that there would be insurmountable difficulties of proof in cases of interspousal rape and that it was necessary to protect, so far as possible, the institution of the family.[80] It adhered to the idea that rape should be organised around the concept of consent, but that the law should not attempt to define it.[81] And it upheld the test of honest but unreasonable belief in consent estab-lished in *Morgan*—notwithstanding the criticism that this could give rise to situations where there was no criminal liability even where a victim could be proven not to have consented.[82] And in the wake of the decision in *R v Caldwell*,[83] which adopted an objective test of recklessness and which would have limited the impact of *Morgan*, it argued that it was necessary to retain a subjective test of recklessness—a position subsequently affirmed by the Court of Appeal.[84] Finally, it approved the reforms made to the trial of rape and sexual offences made in the wake of the Heilbron Report, though its satisfaction about the operation of the 'rape shield' introduced by the 1976 Act seemed to have had little foundation.[85]

---

[78] CLRC, *Fifteenth Report* (n 74) paras 2.45–2.47.

[79] ibid, paras 2.64–2.70. Its earlier working paper had recommended the removal of the immunity.

[80] It was suggested that it was possible to distinguish between assault and unwanted sexual intercourse: the former could be prosecuted if there was evidence of harm, but the latter should not.

[81] There were limits to its understanding of consent, particularly in relation to homosex-ual conduct in locations which did not correspond to a narrow definition of private (CLRC, *Fifteenth Report*, Part X). This was ostensibly gender neutral, directed at sex clubs and shows, but the discussion in this part is focused on homosexual sex and also singles out sex in public toilets.

[82] On *Morgan* and the mens rea of rape, see ibid, paras 2.31–2.41.

[83] *Caldwell* (n 17).

[84] *R v Satnam and Kewal* (1984) 78 Cr App R 149 (CA).

[85] See also JC Smith, 'The Heilbron Report' [1976] *Crim LR* 97, 98, commending this as 'the rational development of the criminal law'. The influential research of Adler ('Rape—The Intention of Parliament') on rape trials was not discussed in the Report.

Overall, while the general approach was to understand sexual offences as a field of law capable of being organised around principles of consent and protection of the vulnerable, the report did not recommend any major changes to the law. Rape was understood as sex by means of violence, rather than seeing unwanted sex as wrong in itself, which reinforced the CLRC's conservatism on issues like marital rape. The report paid lip service to the idea of sexual freedom and consent supposedly articulated in the Wolfenden Report, but the general principle of non-intervention in private life under-pinned the CLRC's position that marital rape should not be criminalised.

This vision of sexual offences gained little purchase, being undercut vir-tually from the moment that it was articulated by a new understanding of sexual offences that placed much greater emphasis on sexual freedom and consent, on equality between the sexes and on the recognition of the victim. This alternative understanding can be seen in the quantity of legislation on sexual offences between 1976 and 2003, much of which disregarded the rec-ommendations of the CLRC.[86] There were further changes to the definition of rape to include non-consensual anal intercourse of a man or a woman and to lower the age of consent for homosexual intercourse.[87] In addition, meas-ures were taken to improve police investigation and prosecution procedures so as to improve reporting of the crime and reduce attrition rates, as well as to strengthen the 'rape shield' legislation or provisions for anonymity of victims or measures to protect vulnerable witnesses.[88] The courts were also sensitive to changing social attitudes, recognising marital rape in 1992.[89]

This process culminated in the Sexual Offences Act 2003 in England and Wales, which abolished much of the pre-existing common law, redefined the core offences and created a number of new offences—and notably replaced the rule in *Morgan* with a new requirement that there should be a reasona-ble belief in consent. These developments are significant because they reveal a completely changed understanding of sexual offences. The Act takes a gender neutral approach to the law and includes not only a greater range of conduct within the ambit of the basic offences but also a number of new offences. Crucially, the Act is organised around consent understood as an interior state that expresses sexual desire or rejection. Consent is framed in positive terms, as not merely submission or acquiescence to the desires of

---

[86] There were Sexual Offences Acts in 1985, 1992, 1993 and 2000 in addition to changes in the other legislation mentioned below.

[87] Criminal Justice and Public Order Act 1994, s 145 and Criminal law Consolidation (Scotland) Act 1995, s 13, reducing the age of consent to 18.

[88] Sexual Offences Act 1976; Youth Justice and Criminal Evidence Act 1999, s 41. For a review, see L Kelly, *Routes to Injustice: A Research Review on the Reporting, Investigation and Prosecution of Rape Cases* (London, CPSI, 2001); S Walklate, 'What is to Be Done about Violence against Women?' (2008) 48 *British Journal of Criminology* 39, 44–47.

[89] *R v R* [1992] 1 AC 599 (HL), following the Law Commission paper on marital rape (Law Commission, *Rape within Marriage* (Law Com WP No 116, 1990). *cf Stallard v HM Advocate* 1989 SCCR 248.

another, but a negotiated interaction or agreement in which the needs and desires of both parties are expressed and respected. This is articulated in terms of an ideal sexual relationship as a 'rich and fulfilling part of life', where consent is a means to the end of mutual pleasure.[90] Sex, it is argued, is a valued human activity such that the criminal law ought to protect our interest or right to pursue that end as we choose.[91] It thus follows that where a person has capacity to consent, but that consent to the conduct charged is absent, then a criminal wrong has been committed. This is strikingly framed in terms of human rights, as a principle of non-discrimination (supporting the decriminalisation of homosexual conduct) and as a right to private life (as a right to a more general sexual freedom).[92] This establishes sexual autonomy as a sphere in which women and men have the right to pursue a range of sexual options, free from fear or unwanted sexual encounters. From this perspective, the wrong of rape has come to be understood as the interference with sexual autonomy understood as, on the one hand, the protection of a sphere of intimacy and, on the other hand, the right to choose with whom and when to have sexual intercourse.[93] This is a departure from Wolfenden in that the sphere of autonomy, or the private, that the law should protect is understood in conceptual rather than spatial terms.

## IV. CONCLUSION

The story of *Morgan* can be seen as the triumph of subjectivism, the recognition of the liberties of the subject in the criminal law. This account stresses the importance of the logic of subjective mens rea and is represented by the views of those such as Hogan, who defended the 'essential good sense' of the decision and maintained that critics could be made to see the light of reason.[94] Alternatively, it can be presented as a major misstep, the moment that revealed the unreflective misogyny of the common law and provided a catalyst for the reform of the common law of rape around a new model of positive consent. On both these accounts, the case of *Morgan* is a landmark, a symbolic moment in the development of the law. However, these accounts have also established a tendency to see the case in terms of a conflict between two views of the criminal law—one based on the protection of the accused

---

[90] Home Office, *Setting the Boundaries. Reforming the Law on Sex Offences* (London, HMSO, 2000) para 1.1.3. See P Haag, *Consent: Sexual Rights and the Transformation of American Liberalism* (Ithaca, NY, Cornell University Press, 1999).
[91] Scottish Law Commission, *Report on Rape and Other Sexual Offences* (No 209) (Edinburgh, Stationery Office, 2007) para 1.25: 'a person freely choosing to engage in sexual activity'; see also Home Office, *Setting the Boundaries* (n 90) paras 0.7 and 1.3.2.
[92] Home Office, *Setting the Boundaries*, (n 90) sections 1.1 and 1.2.
[93] See the influential paper by J Gardner and S Shute, 'The Wrongness of Rape' in J Horder (ed), *Oxford Essays in Jurisprudence. Fourth Series* (Oxford, Oxford University Press, 2000). This was discussed in Scottish Law Commission, *Report* para 1.26.
[94] Hogan, 'On Modernising the Law of Sexual Offences' (n 72) 174.

and the other on the protection of the victim—where advances in one area are matched by losses in the other. The retreat from *Morgan* is seen as a retreat from subjectivism and to be either celebrated or mourned depending on one's understanding of the criminal law.[95] In this chapter, I have tried to present a different, and slightly more nuanced, understanding of the developments in this area by placing them within the context of the development of sexual offences more generally. This can explain something of the context in which the decision made sense, but also how it was undercut as the field of sexual offences was transformed. This is an approach which allows us better to understand the logic of *Morgan* and why it did not endure—as well as possibly opening up a critical understanding of the organisation of the category of sexual offences.

On my analysis, the competing conceptual approaches in question are thus different understandings of sexual offences. The logic of *Morgan* fits with a very different understanding of sexual offences. On this view, sexual offences were offences of violence or, as Williams argued, of 'sexual aggression' where actual physical violence was used, and the aim of the law was to punish this kind of violence.[96] The crime was framed in terms of lack of consent, and it was recognised that consent might be vitiated by force, fraud or fear, but otherwise violence was the defining characteristic of the crime. Sexual contacts outside heterosexual marriage were tolerated by law, but it did not seek to encourage sexual freedom. Subjectivism was defended in rape law because it fit with an understanding of the law which distrusted female complainants, aimed to protect a defendant against false complaints and defended only a limited view of sexual freedom. This view of subjective liability could be departed from in other areas, such as criminal damage (not without complaint), because it was seen as damaging to the aims of the law in these areas—for example, the protection of property. In its place we now have a very different view of sexual offences where the law is aiming to protect the right to sexual freedom and to criminalise conduct which interferes with the exercise of this sexual autonomy. Mens rea is no less central to this view of the law, but it is organised around awareness and respect for others, or taking responsibility for one's own conduct in relation to others. On this understanding of the law, there is no logic to *Morgan*, let alone an inexorable one, precisely because it would fail to recognise the concept of sexual autonomy that is central to this new understanding of the sexual offences.

---

[95] Contrast, for example, D Cowley, 'The Retreat from Morgan' [1982] *Crim LR* 198 and C Wells, 'Swatting the Subjectivist Bug' [1982] *Crim LR* 209.
[96] Williams, *Textbook on Criminal Law* (n 63).

# 13

# *Whitehouse v Lemon, Whitehouse v Gay News Ltd* (1979)

## J R SPENCER

A T FIRST SIGHT, the last prosecution for blasphemy in England and Wales might seem to be a historical curiosity and nothing more: like the attempt in *Ashford v Thornton* to revive trial by battle[1] or (more recently, at the other end of the scale) the obscenity prosecution, at Lincoln Quarter Sessions in 1954, of Donald McGill for his comic seaside postcards.[2] But on closer examination, it illustrates a number of issues that continue to be significant in English criminal law: the persistence into the present age of two ancient institutions (private prosecutions and common law offences) and the periodic problems they give rise to; the absence from English criminal law of any generally accepted rules for resolving doubts about the scope of criminal offences; and the distressing failure, at least in past years, of the final court of appeal to give criminal law the attention it deserves.

## I. THE CASE

*Gay News* was a fortnightly magazine founded in 1972 by Denis Lemon, a gay rights activist, to be the 'organ' (as *Private Eye* would say) of the burgeoning gay liberation movement. In June 1976, it published a poem by the minor poet James Kirkup[3] which consisted of the imaginary musings of a fictitious Roman centurion present at the Crucifixion, in which he fantasised

---

[1] *Ashford v Thornton* (1818) 1 B & Ald 405, 106 ER 405.
[2] Denis Gifford, 'McGill, Donald Fraser Gould' *Oxford Dictionary of National Biography*, online edn (Oxford, Oxford University Press, 2011) www.oxforddnb.com/view/article/55528.
[3] Kirkup was also a linguist and translated classical works from a wide range of languages. David Burnett records that Kirkup was 'exceptionally independent-minded, a conscious objector and pacifist, a vegetarian, and a founder member of the Campaign for Nuclear Disarmament and of Amnesty International' (David Burnett, 'Kirkup, James Harold', *Oxford Dictionary of National Biography*).

about, or possibly purported to describe, various sexual acts that he had carried out with Christ's body, and suggested that Christ had homosexual relations with other people too. The poem and how it was presented in issue no 96 of the magazine was described in the following terms by the Court of Appeal in its later judgment:

> Page 26 of that issue contained a poem by Professor James Kirkup entitled 'The Love That Dares to Speak its Name'. Printed alongside that poem and parallel with the entirety of its text was a drawing. We do not propose in this judgment either to read the poem or describe the drawing beyond saying that the poem purports to describe in explicit detail acts of sodomy and fellatio with the body of Christ immediately after the moment of his death.

As older readers will remember, Mary Whitehouse was a schoolteacher who became a public figure during the 1960s and 1970s through launching a 'Clean up TV' campaign, which led to the formation of a body called the National Viewers' and Listeners' Association (NVLA). The aim of this body was to stop to the BBC broadcasting material that she and her fellow workers perceived to be morally corrupting. While Mrs Whitehouse was its driving force, this pressure group attracted considerable public attention, though after her active involvement ceased, it largely sank from public view.[4] An evangelical Christian, with views shaped by the Oxford Group and Moral Re-Armament, it is hardly to be expected that she was among the regular readers of *Gay News*. However, a copy of the issue with the Kirkup poem in it reached her when one of her supporters who had seen it posted it to her in outrage. Equally outraged herself, she decided to launch a private prosecution against its publisher, Gay News Ltd, and its editor Denis Lemon, accusing them of the common law offence of blasphemous libel.[5] By statute, a prosecution brought against a newspaper for any offence of libel required a High Court Judge to give leave for a voluntary bill of indictment, which, to the surprise of some, one of the High Court judges obligingly granted her. This led, in June 1977, to the first successful prosecution for this offence for 50 years—a prosecution which, as already mentioned, also proved to be the last.

While Mrs Whitehouse and her supporters held prayer meetings in the corridors, the trial of the defendants took place before a judge and jury in a courtroom at the Old Bailey. The judge was Alan King-Hamilton QC—whose obituary in the *Daily Telegraph* described him as 'a robust and outspoken Old Bailey judge who cultivated an eccentric image and seemed to relish the publicity that attended his more provocative obiter dicta'.[6] At the

---

[4] It still exists, as Mediawatch-uk: www.mediawatchuk.com.

[5] There were two common law offences: blasphemy, which was oral; and blasphemous libel, which was written. Both were commonly referred to as 'blasphemy' and in this chapter I have sometimes done this.

[6] 'His Honour Alan King-Hamilton' *Daily Telegraph* (London, 24 March 2010).

time, the judge believed—as did many others, and probably correctly—that the case was purposely listed before him because he was a Jew:[7] the expectation being that, because of this, he would be less offended by the publication than a Christian might be (or, at any rate, less open to accusations of bias on account of his beliefs). However, if the plan had been to ensure that the trial would be presided over by someone whose stance was firmly neutral, it did not succeed. Reminiscing about the case in his autobiography, King-Hamilton describes himself as 'shocked and horrified' by the poem, adding that 'one did not have to be Christian to be revolted by it',[8] and he modestly goes on to describe his summing-up as 'the best, by far, that I have ever given. I can say this confidently without blushing because, throughout its preparation, and also when delivering it, I was half-conscious of being guided by some divine inspiration'.[9] Guided by the judge's summing-up and aided or unaided by supernatural intervention, the jury convicted by a majority of 10 to 2. Having commended the jury for their 'moral courage' in convicting and expressing his hope that 'by this verdict the pendulum of public opinion is beginning to swing back to a more healthy climate', he then sentenced Lemon to nine months' imprisonment, suspended for 18 months, plus a fine of £500, and imposed a fine of £1,000 on the company.

Lemon and Gay News Ltd appealed against their convictions and their sentences. In the first round of their appeal, before the Criminal Division of the Court of Appeal, they did not seek to argue that the judge was biased. (Nor did they complain of his eccentric behaviour on the bench; as was his usual practice, he had interrupted the trial at intervals to give the jury the latest Test Match scores!) Nor did they seek to argue, as they had done valiantly but hopelessly at trial, that blasphemous libel was no longer a criminal offence, the crime having died of old age and desuetude. Instead, they appealed on the ground that the judge, in his summing-up, had misdirected the jury as to the legal ingredients of the offence. The scope of the common law offence of blasphemous libel (and of blasphemy, its oral counterpart) had fluctuated widely over the centuries of its existence—as is explained in greater detail later in this chapter. At the time of the *Gay News* trial, *Archbold's Criminal Pleading, Evidence and Practice* said: 'The gist of the offence of blasphemy is the use of language having a tendency to vilify the Christian religion or the Bible.'[10] But if this laconic definition gave the general idea, it left a lot unsaid. In terms of actus reus, was the offence limited to *attacks* on Christianity, in the sense of statements asserting that it is false? And in terms of mens rea, was it necessary that the person publishing

---

[7] Alan King-Hamilton, *And Nothing But the Truth* (London, Weidenfeld & Nicolson, 1982), 172 ff.

[8] ibid.

[9] ibid.

[10] TR Fitzwalter Butler and S Mitchell, *Archbold's Criminal Pleading, Evidence and Practice*, 38th edn (London, Sweet & Maxwell, 1973) §3405.

the statement intended to vilify the Christian religion or the Bible—or was it enough that the statement, as interpreted by the jury, had the effect of doing so?

At trial, Judge King-Hamilton had dealt with both these questions and answered them in the negative. Dealing with the 'attack' point, he said:

> The Crown does not have to prove that the poem is an attack. For blasphemy it has got to be about Christianity or Christ or some aspect of the religion, not necessarily an attack at all. It has got to be about it, but about it in such terms as are likely to arouse resentment and so on.

On the mens rea point, as the Court of Appeal said paraphrasing his ruling, the judge had ruled that:

> [N]o evidence from Mr Lemon or from Professor Kirkup as to their respective intentions in publishing the poem and the drawing, or in writing the poem ... would have been relevant and therefore admissible.

Denis Lemon did not give evidence at trial, and so the court did not hear from his own mouth what his intention was. However, he later said that he had published the poem because he thought 'the message and intention of the poem was to celebrate the absolute universality of God's love'.[11] Furthermore, he was Christian—and a devout one, at least in his later life.[12] He would presumably have known that evangelical Christians who shared Mary Whitehouse's approach would be offended by the poem if they read it, and it is at least possible that he foresaw that some of them would do so. But even if he did, it hardly follows that his intention in publishing the poem was to vilify Christianity or Christ. So if the judge had directed the jury that intention to vilify Christianity was an ingredient in the offence and the jury had followed the direction, the defendants would have been acquitted—as they also would, presumably, if he had told them that the offence was limited to attacks upon Christianity, as against publishing material that causes Christians anger or resentment.

In the Court of Appeal, the defendants failed in their attempt to overturn the conviction. For three days in February 1978, the case was argued before a Court of Appeal comprising Roskill and Eveleigh LJJ and Stocker J, after which—unusually in criminal cases—judgment was reserved. A month later, in March 1978, Roskill LJ delivered a lengthy written judgment dismissing the appeals against conviction.[13] After examining the pronouncements of a range of judges and legal writers, some of them dating back to the beginning of the nineteenth century, they concluded that Judge King-Hamilton's directions on the law had been correct. To constitute a blasphemous libel, it was sufficient that the defendant's words were found by the jury to be 'insulting'

---

[11] Peter Burton, 'Lemon, Denis Edward' *Oxford Dictionary of National Biography*.
[12] ibid.
[13] *R v Lemon* [1979] QB 10 (CA).

or 'vilifying' in respect of Christ or Christianity, and if they were, the defendant's intention was irrelevant. However, the defendants were more successful in their appeal against sentence. Despite upholding the fines, the Court of Appeal quashed the suspended prison sentence which Judge King-Hamilton had imposed on Denis Lemon.

The defendants, wishing to appeal further, asked the Court of Appeal to certify a point of general public importance for the House of Lords, and it did so in the following terms:

> Was the learned trial judge correct (as the Court of Appeal held) first in ruling and then in directing the jury that in order to secure the conviction of the appellants for publishing a blasphemous libel: (1) it was sufficient if the jury took the view that the publication complained of vilified Christ in his life and crucifixion; and (2) it was not necessary for the Crown to establish any further intention on the part of the appellants beyond an intention to publish that which in the jury's view was a blasphemous libel?[14]

Though certifying a point of law of general importance, the Court, following its usual practice, refused leave to appeal.[15] In May 1978, the Appeal Committee of the House of Lords granted leave, and in November of that year the case was argued before a panel consisting of Lord Diplock, Viscount Dilhorne, Lord Edmund-Davies, Lord Russell of Killowen and Lord Scarman. The Crown was represented by John Smyth and Jeremy Maurice, and the appellants by Louis Blom-Cooper QC[16] and Geoffrey Robertson. In the House of Lords, the case was argued for five days—as against the three days taken in the court below—and the same historical terrain was traversed again, only this time at greater length and with the examination of more authorities.

When looking back on the arguments after an interval of nearly 40 years[17] and rereading the Law Lords' speeches that resulted from it, it is difficult not feel that the whole exercise was rather futile, because none of the material examined in such patient detail was conclusive of the point of law that the House of Lords had to decide. For example, in his *History of the Criminal Law*, Stephen describes how during the eighteenth century, the law relating to blasphemous libel developed alongside the law of seditious libel. In the course of this, he explains how one of the popular complaints against prosecutions for both offences was the fact that the judges used to instruct juries that the defendant's intention was irrelevant, and tells us that Fox's Libel Act of 1792 was intended, among other things, to cure this perceived ill,

---

[14] *Whitehouse v Lemon* [1979] AC 617 (HL), 620.

[15] A practice adopted after the House of Lords rebuked the Court of Appeal in *Lawrence v Metropolitan Police Commissioner* [1972] AC 626 (HL) for wasting its time by granting leave on points the Law Lords considered trivial, after which it left the Law Lords to decide for themselves what points of criminal law were worthy of their august attention.

[16] Replacing John Mortimer QC, who had led Geoffrey Robertson at the trial.

[17] The defence solicitors engaged me as a consultant and I then attended parts of the hearing.

adding that the Act tacitly assumes that the defendant's intentions are relevant and concluding that 'the law has ever since been administered on the supposition that they are'.[18] But as against this, judges in later cases usually coupled any direction to the jury to consider the defendant's intention with the remark that he was presumed to intend the natural and probable consequences of his act. And, similarly, the courts continued to hold booksellers criminally liable for any libels which, unknown to them, were contained in the books and journals which they sold—and continued to do this until the Libel Act of 1843 put a stop to it. In truth, the historical material was sufficiently ambiguous to justify a decision either way.

When judgment was delivered three months later, in February 1979, the House was divided. The result, translated into football terms, was a 2–2 draw, with the match decided in favour of the Crown (meaning in reality Mrs Whitehouse) by a goal scored in a penalty shoot-out by an unexpected striker for that side, Lord Scarman.[19]

Lords Diplock and Edmund-Davies delivered speeches in favour of allowing the appeal. In reaching this conclusion, both were guided by what they saw as the evolving principle of English law that defendants are not to be convicted of grave offences in the absence of mens rea. 'There are those who dislike this tendency', said Lord Edmund-Davies, 'but to treat as irrelevant the state of mind of a person charged with blasphemy would be to take a backward step in the evolution of a humane code.'[20]

On the other side, Viscount Dilhorne and Lord Russell delivered speeches in favour of dismissing the appeal. Viscount Dilhorne reached the conclusion that he did after analysing the case law at great length and interpreting it as leading to that conclusion. Lord Russell, by contrast, reached the same conclusion in a brief dismissive speech in which neither a single case nor a single writer was cited and of which the key passage was the following:

> When then should this House, faced with a deliberate publication of that which a jury with every justification has held to be a blasphemous libel, consider that it should be for the prosecution to prove, presumably beyond reasonable doubt, that the accused recognised and intended it to be such or regarded it as immaterial that it was? I see no ground for that. It does not to my mind make sense: and I consider that sense should retain a function in our criminal law.[21]

Lord Scarman, unlike Lord Russell, had clearly put some work into his speech, and the tone was lofty and didactic. At the outset, he accepted that the authorities were obscure and said that as a consequence, the courts were called upon to make a policy decision. In a preamble, he said that modern

---

[18] JF Stephen, *A History of the Criminal Law of England*, vol 2 (London, Macmillan, 1883) 359.
[19] *Whitehouse v Lemon* (n 14).
[20] ibid 656.
[21] ibid 657.

Britain was 'an increasingly plural society', where all religions ought to be protected from attack. Demonstrating that 'attacks' were central to his thinking, he quoted from Lord Macaulay: 'If I were a judge in India, I should have no scruple about punishing a Christian who should pollute a mosque.' 'My criticism of the common law offence of blasphemy', he went on to say, 'is not that it exists but that it is not sufficiently comprehensive. It is shackled by the chains of history.' In saying this, he made approving reference to Macaulay's criminal code for India, which had the foresight to create offences of blasphemy that protect all religions equally. All that, he said, pointed to the proper way forward for this country as it is today: 'In those days India was a plural society: today the United Kingdom is also.'[22]

From that premise, Lord Scarman then went on to reason that the defendants in the present case must be held guilty of the present crime of blasphemy, which protects only Christianity, whether or not they intended to attack it. This was an obvious non sequitur—and one all the more surprising because the relevant articles of the Indian Penal Code, which he praised as pointing the way forward, are to the opposite effect. Article 298, which is one of the relevant provisions, begins as follows: 'Whoever, *with the deliberate intention of wounding the religious feelings of any person*'; Article 295A, which is the other relevant provision, opens with a similar restriction. So if relevant to the case in hand, the Indian Penal Code suggested that the defendants' argument was right and the judge had indeed misdirected the jury when he told them that the defendants' intention was irrelevant. Thus, although he praised these provisions, he had clearly never looked at them.

As 'the movement of the law is illustrated by recent statutes', he went on, the courts should also look for guidance at a series of twentieth-century UK statutes—including the Race Relations Act 1976, which made it a statutory offence to utter words likely to cause racial hatred, even if racial hatred was not intended. His reasoning was once again distinctly odd, because the propriety of using twentieth-century legislation as an aid to the construction of seventeenth-century common law offences that deal with different issues is not immediately obvious. But 'All this makes sense', he explained:

> [I]n a plural society which recognises the human rights and fundamental freedoms of the European Convention. Article 9 provides that everyone has the right to freedom of religion, and the right to manifest his religion in worship, teaching, practice and observance. By necessary implication the article imposes a duty on all of us to refrain from insulting or outraging the religious feelings of others.[23]

This passage contains a further non sequitur. If religious freedom means the right to practise your religion and to preach it, it does not 'necessarily imply' the further right to have other people prosecuted in the criminal courts for saying things about it that offend you, much less the right to do so whether

---

[22] ibid 658.
[23] ibid 665.

or not they intended to offend you or even realised that you might take offence. This move is a major step that needs a solid justification. Furthermore, an obvious objection to interpreting the right to religious freedom in that extensive way is that it collides with the right of right of free expression, as protected by Article 10 of the European Convention on Human Rights.

Lord Scarman conceded that Article 10 of the Convention might appear to be an obstacle, but did not accept that it was a serious one. It was obvious, he said, that Article 10 could not be read so as to enable a person to 'evade the penalties of the law even though his words were blasphemous in the sense of constituting an outrage on the religious feelings of his fellow citizens'. To do that, he said, would be 'no way forward for a plural society'.[24]

For good measure, though not relevant to the issue before him, Lord Scarman added that it was not, as some had previously thought, an ingredient in the criminal offence of blasphemy that the words complained of should carry with them the risk of provoking a breach of the peace.[25] This again was curious, as earlier in his speech he had classified blasphemy as belonging 'to a group of criminal offences designed to safeguard the internal tranquillity of the kingdom'.[26]

This speech was, to put it bluntly, a bizarre performance. It was strange, in the first place, to see a senior and respected judge adopting such an incoherent chain of reasoning. And it was even odder, surely, that Lord Scarman, the first Chairman of the Law Commission, with a reputation as a law reformer, civil libertarian and occasional defender of the oppressed, should adopt a position so authoritarian and repressive.

The key to this paradox presumably lies in Lord Scarman's recurrent references to 'a plural society'. A thoughtful man, he was deeply concerned about race relations and worried about the social consequences likely to result if they were not sensitively handled. These were issues with which he had already been confronted when, a few years before, he had chaired the official inquiry into the Red Lion Square disorders—a riot that broke out when the National Front demonstrated against an amnesty for illegal immigrants, provoking a counter-demonstration,[27] and issues which he confronted again a few years later when he chaired a second official inquiry, this time into the Brixton riots—of which he identified racial disadvantage as one of the main causes.[28] And when reading his speech in the *Gay News* case, it is difficult to escape the conclusion that he had become so carried away with his own preoccupations about race relations and 'plural societies' that he simply lost sight of what the case in front of him was all about. It

[24] ibid.
[25] ibid 662.
[26] ibid 658.
[27] *The Red Lion Square Disorders of 15 June 1974: Report of Inquiry by the Rt. Hon. Lord Justice Scarman*, Cmnd 5919 (London, HMSO, 1975).
[28] *The Brixton Disorders 10–12 April 1981: Report of an Inquiry* (London, HMSO, 1981)

brings to mind the progressive prison governor in Evelyn Waugh's *Decline and Fall*, who was so absorbed in his own theories on the causes of and cures for crime that he ignored the obvious signs that the prisoner before him was a madman and had him issued, as a former carpenter, with a hammer and a saw, which he used to decapitate the prison chaplain.[29]

After this second reverse, the defendants tried to take the case to Strasbourg, where they failed again because their application was rejected there as inadmissible.[30] For Denis Lemon and Gay News Ltd, this series of forensic failures left them liable to pay, in addition to their fines, a large amount in costs. Fortunately for them, the Gay News Fighting Fund set up by their supporters collected more than enough money to save them from financial ruin. As a consequence, *Gay News* survived, though not for long, as in 1982 Denis Lemon sold the company because he wanted to retreat from public life and the paper lasted only briefly after his departure. He was not, it seems, the only member of the *dramatis personae* on whom the proceedings in the *Gay News* case exercised a lasting influence. After his retirement, Judge King-Hamilton went on to become the chairman of the Pornography and Violence Research Trust, formerly the Mary Whitehouse Research and Education Trust.[31]

If some found the outcome of the *Gay News* prosecution to their taste, many people were outraged by it and began pressing for the offence of blasphemous libel (and blasphemy, its oral counterpart) to be abolished. But the arguments of those who wished to see the crime(s) of blasphemy abolished were met by those who took their line from Lord Scarman and said that the existing offences served a useful purpose in protecting Christians from vilification and attack, and that far from being abolished, they should be extended to protect other religions too—in particular, minority ones, which as such were more vulnerable and in greater need of protection than Christians and Christianity.

In retrospect, it seems odd that anyone should take that positive view of the crime of blasphemy in light of what had happened in the *Gay News* itself. Who exactly, in that case, was persecuting whom? And which side, prosecutor of defendant, stood for the oppressed minority? A positive view of the merits of the offence becomes even harder to accept if one looks at the history of the offence and how it had been used in the past—as we shall do

---

[29] More unkindly, it might be thought that hubris also played a part. Scarman was sometimes criticised for a tendency to parade his progressive and socially inclusive views. When at the bar, his insistence, contrary to bar etiquette, of treating solicitors as equals once provoked his head of chambers, Melford Stevenson, to say 'Leslie helps solicitors on with their coats like Father D'Arcy elevating the host' (Stephen Sedley, 'Scarman, Leslie George' *Oxford Dictionary of National Biography*).

[30] Application 8110/78; Communiqué B (82) 21, 2.

[31] James Morton, 'Hamilton, (Myer) Alan Barry King' *Oxford Dictionary of National Biography*.

in the second section of this chapter. But many influential people at the time did take this line, following the lead given in a series of official pronouncements on the subject emanating from the Church of England.[32]

Faced with this division of opinion, the government referred the matter to the Law Commission, which issued a Working Paper on the topic in 1981[33] and four years later a Report.[34] But this, like the public debate which had led to the matter being referred to the Commission, was inconclusive, because (unusually) the Law Commissioners were divided. In their Report, a majority of the Commissioners recommended that the crime of blasphemy should be abolished without replacement, while a dissenting minority recommended its replacement by a new offence designed 'to penalise anyone who published grossly abusive or insulting material relating to [any] religion with the purpose of outraging religious feelings'.[35] Equally inconclusive on the future of the crime of blasphemy was the Report of a House of Lords Committee which appeared a few years later.[36] In the face of this, it is hardly surprising that, for 30 years after the *Gay News* prosecution, nothing happened. Members of Parliament introduced bills to abolish the offence from time to time, but without government support, none of them progressed. So the common law offences of blasphemy and blasphemous libel continued to exist in the form in which they had emerged from the majority judgments of House of Lords in the *Gay News* case. But there were no further prosecutions—not even when, in 2002, a group of gay rights protestors issued a public challenge to the law by reading the offending poem aloud on the steps of St Martin in the Fields in central London.[37]

The abolition of the crime of blasphemy eventually took place in 2008. In that year, the Prime Minister, Gordon Brown, announced that the government would not oppose an amendment to its Criminal Justice and Immigration Bill—then before Parliament—to abolish the crime of blasphemy. Shortly after, a government amendment to this effect was moved in the House of Lords—with the support of various influential people, including Lord Lester of Herne Hill. This attracted some discussion in the House, but no serious opposition, and in due course it became law as section 79 of

---

[32] In the Church of England's official response to the Law Commission's Working Paper (mentioned in the Law Commission's report, *Criminal Law: Offences against Religion and Public Worship* (Law Com No 145, 1981) 6 fn 15); and the report of a Church of England working party entitled *Offences against Religion and Worship*, sent to the Lord Chancellor in 1988.

[33] Law Commission, *Offences against Religion and Public Worship* (Law Com WP No 79, 1981).

[34] Law Commission, *Criminal Law, Offences against Religion and Public Worship* (Law Com No 145, 1985).

[35] ibid, §5.3.

[36] First Report of the Select Committee on Religious Offences in England and Wales, HL Paper 95-I, 2002–03 Session.

[37] 'Erotic Poem Challenges Blasphemy law' *Daily Telegraph* (London, 11 July 2002).

the Criminal Justice and Immigration Act 2008.[38] So at that late point in legal history, the common law offences of blasphemy and blasphemous libel finally disappeared.

The abolition of the crime of blasphemy, when it finally happened, took place with very little fuss, and this was possible because, in the years immediately before, a significant shift of opinion had taken place. By 2008, influential people were no longer claiming, as Lord Scarman had done in his judgment the *Gay News* case, that a crime of blasphemy was necessary to protect the religious from persecution and attack.

One reason for this was that Parliament, in 2006, had added to the long-standing offence of incitement to racial hatred a new offence of inciting religious hatred—a change which obviously cut much of the ground from under the feet of those who argued that the crime of blasphemy should be retained, or extended, to protect believers from conduct of this sort. Another equally important reason, I believe, was the controversy over Salman Rushdie's book *The Satanic Verses*. Passages in this book offended many Muslims and in 1989, a *fatwa* was uttered against the author by the Ayatollah Khomeini in Iran, condemning him to death for blasphemy. This led to public burnings of his book by groups of enthusiastic Muslims and death threats against Rushdie himself, which drove him into hiding. And in a more peaceful parallel to this, there were also calls from sections of the Muslim community for the law of blasphemy to be changed, so that Rushdie could be prosecuted and his book suppressed, as would have been theoretically possible if the offensive parts of it had been perceived as directed against Christianity. At this point, it became clear what the ultra-religious really wanted when they said a crime of blasphemy was needed to 'protect' their faith. Like many fervent Christians in the past, they were not looking for a criminal offence that would protect them against persecution, but one which made it possible for them to stop unbelievers saying things which the tenets of their faith decreed should not be said.

## II. BLASPHEMY BEFORE *GAY NEWS*[39]

Blasphemy as a crime in English law began in the Middle Ages, at a time when it would have been universally accepted as an obvious truth that anything which Christianity teaches to be sinful must be capable of redress on

---

[38] See Lucinda Maer, *The Abolition of the Blasphemy Offences*, Standard Note SN/PC/04597, 9 May 2009. For a summary of the discussion, see Francis Bennion, 'Farewell to the Blasphemy Laws' (2008) 172 *Justice of the Peace* 448.

[39] Much has been written on the history of the crime of blasphemy. The classic scholarly account, written from a legal perspective, is GD Nokes, *A History of the Crime of Blasphemy* (London, Sweet & Maxwell, 1928). An earlier and shorter account, also by a lawyer, is Courtney Kenny, 'The Evolution of the Law of Blasphemy' (1922) 1 *CLJ* 127. An excellent modern account, written by a historian, is David Nash, *Blasphemy in Modern Britain: 1789 to the*

earth—and, in essence, that is how the law operated at the time. The king's courts punished the more dramatic sins which threatened the peace of the community or royal authority, and beyond the royal courts lay the ecclesiastical courts, a network which extended to all corners of the realm and had the power to punish every other sort of sin, including blasphemy. Anyone could be summoned by these courts, compelled to answer questions on oath and, if found guilty, made to do penance. In the revolution against Charles I in the seventeenth century, these courts were abolished, and though reinstated at the Restoration, they no longer enjoyed the powers they had before. As a result, many things condemned by Christianity as sinful now began to go unpunished. Against this background, Parliament intervened to make a number of them criminal offences punishable in the ordinary courts.[40] And, in parallel, the Court of King's Bench declared itself 'custos morum of the people',[41] and in that capacity began to punish some of the acts which were formerly a matter for the now-moribund ecclesiastical courts: notably obscene publications, indecent behaviour in public—and blasphemy.

The decision that blasphemy was an indictable offence at common law was taken in the case of *Taylor* in 1676.[42] Taylor, who appears to have suffered from mental problems, was accused of 'uttering of divers blasphemous expressions, horrible to hear, (viz) that Jesus Christ was a bastard, a whoremaster, religion was a cheat; and that he neither feared God, the devil, or man'.[43] After an initial unsuccessful attempt to deal with him by sending him to Bedlam, the King's Bench fined him, ordered him to stand in the pillory and required him to find sureties for his future good behaviour.

In those days, most people would probably have thought imposing criminal liability for blasphemy was fully justified by the fact that the Christian religion condemned it as a grave sin. And some would have also thought it justified by another reason even further removed from modern ideas about the principles of criminalisation. Blasphemy, it was then widely said, was liable to provoke God's anger, with the risk that He would vent His wrath upon the country by inflicting some terrible disaster. In their propaganda, the Societies for the Reformation of Manners[44] interpreted the Great Plague, and the Fire of London, as God's punishment for blasphemy and other sins,

---

*Present* (Aldershot, Ashgate, 1999). Another modern account, which also deals with the position in the US, is Leonard W Levy, *Blasphemy* (New York, Knopf, 1993). A brief popular account, in which the most famous English trials for the offence are described, is Nicholas Walter, *Blasphemy Ancient and Modern* (London, Rationalist Press Association, 1990).

[40] eg, the Sunday Observance Act 1677 (29 Car 2 c 7) and the Act Against Profane Swearing and Cursing 1694 (6 & 7 Will & Mar c 11).

[41] *R v Sedley* (1663) 1 Sid 168, 82 ER 1036 (KB), 17 St Tr 155n (KB).

[42] *Taylor's Case* 1 Vent 293, 86 ER 189 (KB), 3 Keb 607, 84 ER 906 (KB) (where the case is reported as *R v Tayler*); Nokes, *A History* 46 ff.

[43] As quoted in the report in Ventris; further bizarre utterings are reported in Keble.

[44] For an account of these, see Edward J Bristow, *Vice and Vigilance: Purity Movements in Britain since 1700* (Dublin, Gill & Macmillan, 1977) Ch 1.

and the great Jamaican earthquake and the big storm of 1703 were later put to similar service.[45]

However, it was justifications different from these, but no less strange to modern ears, that were given by the King's Bench when holding blasphemy to be criminally punishable in *Taylor*. As reported by Ventris, the court's reasoning was this:

> And Hale said, that such kind of wicked blasphemous words were not only an offence to God and religion, but a crime against the laws, State and Government, and therefore punishable in this Court. For to say, religion is a cheat, is to dissolve all those obligations whereby the civil societies are preserved, and that Christianity is parcel of the laws of England; therefore to reproach the Christian religion is to speak in subversion of the law.[46]

In these words, two separate rationales for the crime of blasphemy can be discerned.[47]

The first rationale is the notion that the Church and State are one, and it is therefore right that public utterances that undermine the authority of either of them should be equally punishable. In those days, public utterances that undermined the authority of the king or of his ministers were criminally punishable as sedition or seditious libel, and so too, the court appears to say, should public utterances which undermine the authority of the Church be punishable as blasphemy or blasphemous libel. On that basis, it was then construed as blasphemy to publish anything which contradicted any central tenets of the teaching of the Church of England. And so it was that in 1729, Thomas Woolston (Fellow of Sidney Sussex College, Cambridge) was convicted of blasphemous libel for publishing a book in which he questioned the literal truth of the Miracles.[48] The second rationale, no less strange to modern eyes, is the notion that if Christianity could be publicly doubted,

---

[45] *An Account of the Societies for the Reformation of Manners*, 3rd edn (London, 1700); Society for the Reformation, *Proposals for a National Reformation of Manners* (London, 1694); *A Representation of the Impiety and Immorality of the English Stage* (London, 1704).

[46] *Taylor* (n 42), as reported by Ventris. In Keble's report, the court is reported as saying: 'These words though of ecclesiastical cognisance, yet that religion is a cheat, tends to the dissolution of all government, and therefore punishable here, and so of contumelious reproaches of God, or the religion establisht; which the Court agreed and adjudged. An indictment lay for saying the Protestant religion was a fiction for taking away religion, all obligation to government by oaths, &c. ceaseth, and Christian religion is a part of the law itself, therefore injuries to God are as punishable as to the King, or any common person.'

[47] DS Manning, who examines the case in the context of contemporary religious and social thought, thinks the court felt no need to give a secular justification for holding Taylor criminally liable. He suggests 'that the criminalisation of Taylor's words was an act based on a devout piety ... The gravity of the perceived offence of blasphemy cannot be overstated: blasphemy was to be sought out and punished on the basis that it was an act of spiritual treason' (DS Manning, 'Blasphemy in England, c.1660–1730' (PhD thesis, Cambridge University 2009) 37–38).

[48] *R v Woolston* (1728) Fitz-Gibbon 64, 94 ER 655 (KB): 'Christianity in general is parcel of the common law of England, and therefore to be protected by it; now whatever strikes at the very root of Christianity, tends manifestly to a dissolution of the civil government, and so

unbelief would spread—and from the spread of unbelief, social anarchy would inevitably follow.

As the eighteenth century progressed, religious scepticism grew and many religious and philosophical books were published which were clearly blasphemous under the law as stated in the early cases. But though some unlucky writers were prosecuted and convicted,[49] most of them were not. Most books of this sort were expensive and written with a narrow readership in mind. And provided this was so, neither the government nor any private citizens had much desire to prosecute.

It was different when Tom Paine's deistical work *The Age of Reason* appeared in 1795. This book, by contrast, was aimed at the common man and, as a consequence, its appearance was greeted by a flood of prosecutions for blasphemous libel. These were initially the work of an Evangelical action group, the Society for the Suppression of Vice—popularly known as the 'Vice Society'—of which the leading light was William Wilberforce, other prominent members being Charles Simeon and Thomas Bowdler, the editor who 'bowdlerised' Shakespeare. Although privately begun, the government of the day eventually took the campaign of prosecutions over with the aim of bringing it to a successful conclusion.

By this date, judges were no longer prepared to say, as their predecessors would have said, that Christianity is so important to society that any public utterance expressing doubt about its central tenets constitutes the crime of blasphemy. They did, however, accept the argument that Christianity is essential for the poor, and hence for public peace, because it helps them to endure their unhappy lot in life. And with that in mind, they redefined the crime of blasphemy as (in effect) anti-Christian propaganda which is likely to influence the minds of the poor. This is how Best J explained the law when directing the jury in one of the trials arising from *The Age of Reason*:

> Gentlemen, I put it to you, whether that is fair reasoning, whether that is temperate discussion, upon the subject of that book upon which our faith rests? If you think it is, give the defendant the advantage of that opinion; but if you think this not the way in which the Holy Scriptures should be treated, that this is not fair argument, then I am bound to say this is a libel, and having a tendency to vilify and to produce in the minds of the lower orders prejudice. Books of this description may do no mischief in minds enlighted, as yours are.[50]

was the opinion of my Lord Hale in *Taylor's case:* so that to say, an attempt to subvert the establish'd religion is not punishable by those laws upon which it is establish'd, is an absurdity' (per Raymond LCJ). Woolston's case is the subject of a lengthy chapter in Manning's thesis (see n 47), in which it is examined in detail from a theological and historical perspective.

[49] Including Jacob Ilive in 1756 and Peter Annet in 1762. Further details of these cases can be found in their entries in the *Oxford Dictionary of National Biography* (James A Herrick, 'Ilive, Jacob' and 'Annet, Peter').

[50] *Trial of Mary Ann Carlile* (1821) 1 St Tr NS 1033, 1047–48. Similarly, the need for a crime of blasphemy to keep material of this sort from corrupting the minds of the poor was regularly stressed by prosecuting counsel in these cases. An eloquent example can be found in Erskine's speech at the trial of *Thomas Williams* (1817) 26 *Howell's State Trials* 654, 664.

The campaign to suppress *The Age of Reason* ultimately failed, because the blasphemy prosecutions stimulated demand for the book, and because radical booksellers, led by Richard Carlile and his family, were prepared, in spite of repeated prosecutions and convictions, to defy the law by selling it.[51]

Despite this failure,[52] however, prosecutions for blasphemy still took place occasionally during the following decades. Unsurprisingly, given the new judicial slant upon the definition of the offence which *The Age of Reason* cases seemed to have given it, these later prosecutions were almost invariably brought against people of left-wing views whom the authorities suspected of seeking to stir up agitation among the poor. A prominent example was the case of the early socialist and secularist GJ Holyoake in 1842. At a political meeting, he said, in response to a question about the place of religion in society, that he had no room for religion and that if he had his way, the country would 'put the Deity on half-pay, as the government of the country does with subaltern officers'.[53] For this flippant remark he was prosecuted, at the instance of the Cheltenham magistrates, for blasphemy—and on conviction was sentenced to six months' imprisonment, during which, to his great grief, his little daughter died. Similar in spirit was the prosecution for blasphemous libel, brought by the government in 1840, against the radical journalist and publisher Henry Hetherington for publishing a book attacking the Old Testament.[54] To make a public point about the politically selective way in which the law was used, Hetherington responded to this by bringing a private prosecution against the 'respectable' publisher Edward Moxon for publishing Shelley's poem *Queen Mab* and secured a conviction.[55] But the political point duly made, he dropped the case and Moxon was not brought up for judgment.

The Hetherington case was the last blasphemy prosecution in which the Attorney-General was involved, and in the 40 years that followed, private prosecutors showed little appetite for them either.[56] In the 1880s, however, the position changed abruptly. On the one hand, there was a

---

[51] See Philip W Martin, 'Carlile, Richard' *Oxford Dictionary of National Biography*; and Nash, *Blasphemy in Modern Britain* Ch 3.

[52] And the even more dramatic failure of the government's attempt in 1817 to prosecute for blasphemy the radical pamphleteer William Hone for publishing parodies of well-known passages from the Book of Common Prayer in order to make fun of the ministers of the Crown and their supporters. The proceedings are described in Nash, *Blasphemy in Modern Britain* 80 ff. For a verbatim account of the trials, with commentary by the defendant, see William Hone, *The Three Trials of William Hone* (London, 1818).

[53] A full account of the proceedings was later published by Holyoake (GJ Holyoake, *The History of the Last Trial by Jury for Atheism in England* (London, J Watson, 1850)).

[54] *R v Hetherington* (1840) 4 State Trials (New Series) 563. The book was CJ Haslam's *Letters to the Clergy of All Denominations*.

[55] *R v Moxon* (1841) 4 State Trials (New Series) 693.

[56] An isolated exception was the case of Thomas Pooley, a Cornish well-sinker with mental problems, prosecuted for blasphemy in 1857 at the instance of the parish priest for utterances reminiscent of those in *Taylor* (n 42). His conviction and heavy sentence (of one year and nine months' imprisonment) led to something of a public outcry. For the details, see Nash, *Blasphemy in Modern Britain* 97–99.

religious revival, one of the manifestations of which was the appearance of the National Vigilance Association, which took over the surviving assets of the now-moribund Vice Society and waged an enthusiastic war against obscene publications and other publications which they thought immoral.[57] And, in parallel, there was a sudden upsurge of the Secularist Movement, under the charismatic direction of the radical politician Charles Bradlaugh. The war of words between the revivalists and the secularists escalated into a war of lawsuits when their opponents, later joined by the authorities of the City of London, launched a series of blasphemy prosecutions over the secularists' anti-religious propaganda.

These prosecutions included two that were brought against the publishers and editor of a secularist magazine, *The Freethinker*, in 1883.[58] Under their direction, this newspaper specialised in poking fun at religion, and they first found themselves prosecuted over a number which had carried a ribald cartoon, featuring an enormous bottom in the sky, clad in a pair of checked trousers, and inspired by the words of God to Moses, 'thou shalt see my back parts, but my face shall not be seen'.[59] For this they were tried before North J, a devout Roman Catholic, who made his disapproval of the publication plain and, on conviction, sentenced them to 12 months' imprisonment. This led to a huge public outcry and an immediate campaign to abolish the crime of blasphemy.

In the middle of this, Ramsey and Foote were taken from prison to face a second trial over another issue of *The Freethinker*. This time, however, the case came before the Chief Justice, Lord Coleridge, a liberal Anglican, and in his direction to the jury, he radically redefined the offence of blasphemy. He took the word 'vilification', which (as we saw) had been used earlier to indicate blasphemy that was likely to reach the poor, and gave it a new slant. He said that to deny the truth of Christianity was lawful as long as 'the decencies of controversy' were observed; what was not permitted, he said, was the 'vilification' of Christianity, by which was meant the publication of matter about it which believers find particularly offensive.[60] On this direction, the jury in this second trial failed to convict. This did not get the defendants out of prison, because as the law then stood, they had no right of appeal against their conviction in the first trial, where the jury had convicted after a direction based on the older definition of the offence.[61]

This narrowing of the offence did not satisfy all the critics of the crime of blasphemy. Sir James Fitzjames Stephen—by then a judge, but writing

---

[57] Bristow, *Vice and Vigilance* 207–08.
[58] For further details of both the prosecutions, see Nokes, *A History* 93 ff; and Nash, *Blasphemy in Modern Britain* Ch 4.
[59] Exodus 33:23. The title of the cartoon was 'Moses gets a back view'.
[60] The case is reported in 15 Cox CC 231 and 48 *Law Times* 733.
[61] North J's directions are summarised in 15 Cox CC 225n.

extra-judicially—argued for the complete abolition of the offence and dismissed Coleridge's attempt to limit it as follows:

> If you allow coarse and vulgar people to discuss these subjects freely, they must and will discuss them coarsely. You cannot really distinguish between substance and style. You must either forbid or permit all attacks on Christianity. You cannot in practice send a man to gaol for not writing like a scholar and a gentleman when he is neither one nor the other, and when he is writing on a subject that excites him strongly ... The truth is that effective discussion of these subjects in which masses of men are really interested is impossible unless appeals to their passions are allowed. To say that you may discuss the truth of religion, but that you may not hold its doctrines to contempt, ridicule, or indignation, is either to take away with one hand what you concede with the other, or to confine its discussion to a small and in many ways uninfluential class of persons.[62]

It did, however, bring the current wave of prosecutions to an end, and this took the sting out of the campaign for abolition. For some years, blasphemy and blasphemous libel retreated into the legal limbo which they had occupied for most of the previous 40 years.

The offences came back to life again in the early years of the twentieth century when they were deployed in another 'war of attrition'[63] between a new group of militant secularists and their opponents. The leading figure in this group of recurrent defendants was John William Gott, a man who attracted hostility by being, in addition to a secularist, an advanced socialist and an advocate of birth control. He found himself repeatedly prosecuted for offences of blasphemy for distributing a ribald pamphlet called *Rib Ticklers, or Questions for Parsons*. Written as a satire on a tract published by the Christian Evidence Society entitled *Questions for Unbelievers*, this consisted of two pages of rather feeble anti-religious jokes, of which the following are typical examples:

> Is it true –
>
> that parsons imitate Jesus in one respect, he rode upon donkeys and so do they?
>
> that much of the Bible reads as if it had been written in a pub under the influence of spirits?

For his *Rib Ticklers* and similar pamphlets, Gott was prosecuted four times in all, and since on two occasions the jury disagreed, he underwent a total of six trials. He was eventually convicted in all four prosecutions, and on each occasion a prison sentence was imposed. On the last occasion, he was tried at the Old Bailey, where the first jury disagreed and the second, despite convicting him, recommended him to mercy. But the judge, informed by a

---

[62] JF Stephen, 'Blasphemy and Blasphemous Libel' (1884) 37 *Fortnightly Review* (NS) 289, 315 and 317.

[63] Edward Royle, 'Gott, John William' *Oxford Dictionary of National Biography*.

police inspector that Gott was 'an atheist of the worst type',[64] sentenced him to six months' imprisonment with hard labour—a sentence which, together with the conviction, was upheld by the Court of Criminal Appeal.[65] Though this case led one distinguished commentator to express approval of the law as it had now evolved,[66] many people thought the prosecutions of Gott over his *Rib Ticklers* were grotesquely oppressive and a new campaign to abolish the crime of blasphemy was the result. But a bill to secure its abolition failed for lack of parliamentary time, Gott died shortly after his release from prison, no further prosecutions followed and, once again, the campaign for abolition ran out of steam.

It is hard to see how anyone who was aware of the history of the offence of blasphemy could seriously imagine, as Lord Scarman did in the *Gay News* case, that it existed to 'protect' anyone. If blasphemy was now limited to material that 'vilified' Christianity, it was not—and never had been— a requirement of the offence that anyone should be unwillingly exposed to it. So it 'protected' believers only in the sense that it saved them from being distressed by the thought that the material in question might be read or heard by other people; in other words, in the same convoluted sense in which a ban on homosexual acts between consenting adults in private could be said to 'protect' the feelings of those who are disgusted by the thought that this sort of behaviour might be taking place. In practice, as the history of the offence clearly shows, blasphemy prosecutions had almost invariably been used as a sword, not a shield—and in many cases, the result had been to make those prosecuted suffer for their beliefs or, at any rate, for their willingness to express them.

In reality, prosecutions for blasphemy were never common, and latterly they were extremely rare. As a consequence, most of those who published anti-Christian or anti-clerical propaganda were in practice left untouched by it and, for that reason, it could be said that the law was not seriously oppressive. But if it was not widely used, this was because it was employed selectively, and those singled out for prosecution for blasphemy were often people who were distrusted or disliked for other reasons—like Hone, Holyoake, Hetherington or Gott. So if criminal liability for blasphemy was not objectionable because it was oppressive, it was certainly open to objection because of the arbitrary way in which it was used.

---

[64] According to the report in the *Manchester Guardian* (Manchester, 10 December 1921). According to Nicholas Walter (*Blasphemy Ancient and Modern* 59), the police officer described him as a '*socialist and atheist* of the worst type'.

[65] *R v John William Gott* (1922) 16 Cr App R 87 (CA).

[66] Kenny, 'The Evolution of the Law of Blasphemy', which was praised as a 'brilliant article' by Lord Scarman in his speech in the *Gay News* case (*Whitehouse v Lemon* (n 14) 658).

## III. REFLECTIONS

The *Gay News* case prompts a number of general reflections about the state of criminal law as it was then—and, indeed, as it still is today. As all these points have been made elsewhere before, in this final section of this chapter they will be discussed briefly and not developed at great length.

The first general reflection is about private prosecutions and their survival in this country into modern times when most legal systems (including the one north of the border) tend to view the right to institute criminal proceedings as something which should be a function of the state rather than of the private citizen. In 1981, the Philips Commission, whose Report led to a major restructuring of the criminal process with the Police and Criminal Evidence Act 1984 and the Prosecution of Offences Act 1985 (which created the Crown Prosecution Service), thought that private prosecutions should be, in effect, abolished.[67] But Mrs Thatcher's government, enthusiastic about private enterprise in criminal justice as in other areas of public life, thought otherwise and, as a consequence, section 6 of the Prosecution of Offences Act 1985 explicitly retains them. Since then, the debate as to whether they are Good Thing or a Bad Thing has continued, even the Law Lords being divided on the issue in the leading case.[68] The history of the crime of blasphemy, it is suggested, shows up their negative rather than their positive side. Of the relatively few prosecutions that there were, a significant proportion were the work of vigilante groups, which were selective in their targets. Furthermore, some of the prosecutions were brought by private prosecutors who were using the criminal law as an instrument to other ends. Thus, the real target of the first prosecution brought against *The Freethinker* in the 1880s were not Ramsey and Foote, the publisher and editor, but the radical politician Charles Bradlaugh—who was originally prosecuted together with them, but who managed to extricate himself from the proceedings at an early stage. The original prosecutor was the financier and Conservative MP Sir Henry Tyler, who was one of Bradlaugh's political opponents and who instituted the prosecution as part of a wider campaign against him.[69] It was this case, presumably, that Stephen had in mind when, in his article calling for crime of blasphemy to be abolished, he wrote that this would:

[P]revent the recurrence at irregular intervals of scandalous prosecutions, which have never in any one instance benefited anyone, least of all the cause which they were intended to serve, and which sometime afford a channel for the gratification of private malice under the cloak of religion.[70]

---

[67] *Report of the Royal Commission on Criminal Procedure* (Cmd 8092, 1981).
[68] *Jones v Whalley* [2006] UKHL 41, [2007] 1 AC 63.
[69] See *R v Bradlaugh* (1883) 15 Cox 156, 217. Sir Henry Tyler's prosecution, though the first to be instituted, was the second of the two to reach the stage of trial—and it was in this second case that Coleridge LJC restated the ingredients of the offence. See n 60 above.
[70] Stephen, 'Blasphemy and Blasphemous Libel' 318.

The second is the survival into the twentieth century—and now into the twenty-first century—of common law offences. As modern writers on the criminal law unanimously agree, their continued presence in the criminal law is unsatisfactory, for many reasons. At a philosophical level, there is the issue of 'democratic legitimacy', because they were created by the judges rather than by a legislature democratically elected, and even though modern judges no longer claim to be able create new common law offences, the malleable nature of common law offences still enables them to be bent in the direction that judges dealing with them—like Lord Scarman in the *Gay News* case—feel that public policy, as understood by them, requires. (Though, that said, the speed and ease with which in modern times the government is able to steamroller through Parliament any change in the criminal law, however foolish and however needless, is surely just as worrying as the expansive role of judges in relation to common law offences.)

At a lower and more practical level, there is the problem of uncertainty, because the definition of common law offences has to be derived from the case law, and different judges interpret them as covering different things at different times. This happened with the crime of blasphemy, as we saw in the last section of this chapter. With blasphemy, a series of decisions in the nineteenth century narrowed the offence, but this was unusual, because the general tendency has been for successive generations of judges to widen the scope of common law offences rather than to narrow them. In this respect, the House of Lords was for many years conspicuously active—as will be further mentioned later in this chapter.

The third reflection concerns the surprising absence in English criminal law of any generally accepted principle or set of principles regulating the way in which the courts are expected to approach a disputed question about the limits of a criminal offence. In many other parts of the civilised world—and certainly in all or most of continental Europe—in a situation where either of two interpretations is equally plausible, the rule is that court should normally adopt the narrower of the two. In the French Criminal Code, for example, this principle of interpretation is expressly stated in Article 111-4, which is one of a series of articles at the beginning of the Code in which the general rules about the scope of the law are set out. According to this article, 'la loi pénale est d'interprétation stricte': criminal legislation is to be strictly construed.

In English law, by contrast, the position is doubtful. The 'strict construction' principle is recognised by the writers. But in the case law, it is sometimes invoked—and then in other judgments in which it would equally relevant, it is completely overlooked. In *DPP v Goodchild*, the House of Lords refused to give a broad reading of certain sections of the Misuse of Drugs Act 1981 which were ambiguous because, as Lord Diplock put it: 'A man should not be gaoled upon an ambiguity.'[71] And in this spirit, the House of Lords in

---

[71] *DPP v Goodchild* [1978] 1 WLR 578 (HL).

*Bentham* refused to read section 17(2) of the Firearms Act 1968 extensively so as to render guilty of possessing an imitation firearm a defendant who had put his hand into his pocket with his fingers extended and shouted 'Stick' em up!'.[72] Other examples can be given.[73] But more famously, no mention was made of the principle of strict construction (alias *in dubio pro reo*) in a series of cases in which the House of Lords extensively construed the definition of the offence of theft, as set out in sections 1 and 3 of the Theft Act 1968.[74]

If the courts have failed to apply the principle of strict interpretation consistently when dealing with statutory offences, in relation to common law offences they saw it, until recently, as having no relevance at all. Indeed, in a long series of decisions during the 1960s and 1970s, the House of Lords showed a great willingness to expand the reach of common law offences, both by confirming the existence of some which were in doubt and by expanding the outer limits of others of which the existence, if nothing else, was certain,[75] and the decision of the House of Lords giving an extensive reading to the offence of blasphemy in the *Gay News* case can be seen as part of this general pattern. In 2004, the pattern changed when, confronted with the quintessentially fluid common law offence of public nuisance, a very different House of Lords, invoking Article 7 of the European Convention on Human Rights,[76] said that common law offences should be restrictively construed[77]—a radical departure from the expansionist approach its predecessors had taken.

The final point for reflection is the general quality of House of Lords decisions when dealing with the criminal law. The dominant view of those who have commented upon this is that the quality was, on balance, rather poor. For example, Professor RM Jackson wrote: 'It cannot be said that the House of Lords have made adequate contributions to the criminal law.'[78]

---

[72] *R v Bentham (Peter)* [2005] UKHL 18, [2005] 1 WLR 1057.

[73] In *Milne v MPC: Boundford v MPC* (1939) 2 Cr App R 90 (CA), for example, Lord Wright said: 'The Act must be construed according to the natural meaning of the language used, all the more so since it is an Act creating a criminal offence.'

[74] *Lawrence v MPC* [1972] AC 626 (HL); *DPP v Gomez* [1993] AC 442 (HL); *R v Hinks* [2001] 2 AC 241 (HL).

[75] I analysed these decisions in L Blom-Cooper and G Drewery (eds), *The Judicial House of Lords: 1876–2009* (Oxford, Oxford University Press, 2009) 599 ff.

[76] 'No punishment without law: 1 No one shall be held guilty of any criminal offence on account of any act or omission which did not constitute a criminal offence under national or international law at the time when it was committed. Nor shall a heavier penalty be imposed than the one that was applicable at the time the criminal offence was committed. 2 This article shall not prejudice the trial and punishment of any person for any act or omission which, at the time when it was committed, was criminal according to the general principles of law recognised by civilised nations.'

[77] *R v Rimmington and Goldstein* [2005] UKHL 63, [2006] 1 AC 459.

[78] RM Jackson, *The Machinery of Justice in England*, 5th edn (Cambridge, Cambridge University Press, 1972) 152. In later editions his comments became harsher.

His words have been echoed by others.[79] And sadly the decision in *Gay News* case seems to fit this disappointing pattern.

A satisfactory decision from a final appeal court in a criminal case should, at the very least, see the point at issue and, if the point is an important one, show an understanding of its importance. The central issue in the *Gay News* case was whether blasphemy was a crime of which one of the ingredients was mens rea; in other words, whether the defendant, in order to be guilty, must have intended to perform the act the law forbids—or at least have been subjectively reckless as to whether he was doing so. By the 1970s, the general view in this country was that mens rea in this sense is normally a necessary legal ingredient of any serious criminal offence, and this is so, because it is, generally speaking, felt to be inhumane to impose criminal liability for grave offences on those who did not act with mens rea in the legal sense in which it was explained above. One would therefore have expected the Law Lords in the *Gay News* case to deliver judgments which recognised the existence of this principle and why it was usually thought to be important—and if they thought the normal rule should not apply to the crime of blasphemy, that they would give some solid reasons why. The mens rea issue was central to the speeches of the two dissenting judges, Lords Diplock and Edmund-Davies. But the speeches of the three majority judges contain no principled discussion of the mens rea issue at all, which is as astonishing as it is disappointing.[80] And as the three majority speeches contain no common thread, they leave us with a bare conclusion, for which no clear or cogent reason can be given. To put it bluntly, of weak decisions by the House of Lords, the *Gay News* case is a strong example.

Fortunately, from the 1990s onwards, the standard of judgments in criminal cases in the House of Lords was consistently better and, despite occasional exceptions, the Supreme Court has so far managed to maintain the higher standard. So it could be said, perhaps, that the unhappy story recounted in this chapter has a happy sequel, even if it did not have a happy ending.

---

[79] eg, David Robertson, *Judicial Discretion in the House of Lords* (Oxford, Oxford University Press, 1998) Ch 4; AH Manchester, *Modern Legal History of England and Wales 1750–1950* (London, Butterworths, 1980) 200.

[80] Within the broader issue of mens rea in this case, there was another and more subtle issue that nobody discussed. Absence of mens rea normally means ignorance of what are usually called the *primary facts*: for example, of the fact that V was in the room when D fired his gun across the room and shot him. By contrast, when it comes to *secondary facts*—evaluative decisions about the nature of the primary facts—defendants are normally held to disagree with the court's assessment at their peril. The majority Law Lords could perhaps have squared this with the existence of a mens rea requirement by saying that whether the poem was offensive enough to satisfy the actus reus requirement of the crime of blasphemy was a matter of secondary fact.

# 14

# *R v Hancock and Shankland* (1986)

MATTHEW DYSON*

## I. INTRODUCTION

DURING THE MINERS' strike of 1984–85, two miners dropped concrete objects onto the path of an incoming convoy bearing a strike-breaking miner.[1] There, on Heads of the Valleys Road, under Rhymney Bridge, events were set in motion to force English law to redefine what it means to intend death on a charge of murder.

English law only sought technical doctrinal precision in its fault, or mens rea, from the middle of the twentieth century. Before then, a person was *presumed* to intend the *natural and probable consequences* of his actions and, until 1898, there were significant limits on what evidence the defendant could give about his or her mental state.[2] Thereafter, English law needed a test for juries to use. Normally, a jury would be directed to use its 'common sense' understanding of 'intention'. However, there were some exceptional situations where the defendant's purpose was not death or grievous bodily harm; such situations required a special direction to the jury. This direction had been attempted by the House of Lords prior to *Hancock and Shankland*[3]—indeed, only a year before, in *R v Moloney*.[4] The direction in *Moloney* asked the jury to look for intention by considering whether the outcome alleged to be intended was a 'natural' consequence of the defendant's acts and if the defendant knew that. If the defendant had known that the outcome was in fact probable, the jury might *infer* that the defendant

* With thanks to Hannah Sears, David Ibbetson and Findlay Stark.
[1] Other than the published law reports, reference will be made to two other sources. The National Archives at Kew contains material on the Crown Court case, in file J 299/60, with subfolders 1 and 2 currently open, but subfolder 3 closed due to its personal contents. This file will be cited as 'Kew'. The other files, for the House of Lords hearing, are held at the Parliamentary Archives, in file HL/PO/JU/4/3/1558, which will be referred to hereinafter as 'HL' (further copies of basic materials are also held there under HL/PO/JO/10/11/2358 case 138).
[2] Criminal Evidence Act 1898.
[3] *R v Hancock and Shankland* [1986] AC 455 (HL).
[4] *R v Moloney* [1985] AC 905 (HL).

intended the outcome. This model direction was *too* simple; it left too much ambiguity in what constituted 'natural' consequences.

In *Hancock and Shankland*, the Court of Appeal had certified as a question of public importance whether this direction required amplification; the House of Lords replied affirmatively, but did not provide a direction containing it. Instead, they wiped away the earlier encrustations of vocabulary such as 'natural' and 'probable', temporarily removing any specific jury direction on intention. The space so created was immediately filled by the Court of Appeal in *Nedrick* in 1986 through a model direction,[5] confirmed by the House of Lords in *Woollin* in 1998:[6] the jury may find that the defendant intended the relevant consequence where he or she foresaw it as a virtual certainty and, in fact, it was a virtual certainty. In short, *Hancock and Shankland* made the modern law possible, though itself failed to achieve it.

This chapter will first set out (section II) how the events in *Hancock and Shankland* came to be determined by the House of Lords. It will (section III) analyse the central issue, the jury direction for intention and how the jury decided the case. It will then (section IV) assess the political context of the miners' strike and whether this had a role on the decision in the House of Lords; it is suggested that the law would have been the same even without the strike context. Finally, (section V) the role of *Hancock and Shankland* in English law moving towards more fully defined fault standards will be explored, followed by (section VI) a conclusion.

## II. PROCEDURAL OVERVIEW

Shortly before 5 am on 30 November 1984, Reginald Dean Hancock and Russell Shankland placed a concrete block and a concrete post on the parapet rail of Rhymney Bridge in South Wales. Both were 21-year-old miners on strike from nearby collieries[7] and the bridge sat over the A465, the route by which a convoy of police vehicles and a taxi would take David Williams, a strike-breaking miner, to work. Half an hour later, Hancock pushed the concrete block weighing 20 kg over the parapet. It struck the taxi's windscreen and killed David Wilkie the driver. At almost the same time, Shankland 'flipped' the concrete post, weighing some 30 kg, from the bridge. It fell onto the inside lane of the carriageway and gave the taxi a glancing blow. A third person, Anthony Glyndwr Williams, was on or near the bridge at the time.

---

[5] *R v Nedrick* [1986] 1 WLR 1025 (CA).
[6] *R v Woollin* [1999] 1 AC 82 (HL).
[7] Hancock was on strike from Oakdale Colliery in Blackwood, Caerphilly, a few miles from where Williams was working at Merthyr Vale Colliery: Kew, 88.

Hancock and Shankland accepted that they were guilty of manslaughter. The Crown preferred murder charges, including against Anthony Williams.[8] They were tried on 16 May 1985 at Cardiff Crown Court, before Mann J. The central issue was the test for intention in murder. The case for the Crown was that the appellants had agreed that they would together perform acts, each having the intention either to kill or cause serious injury,[9] that they did act in concert and that the acts in fact carried out caused the death of Wilkie. The appellants' case was that their intention was not to kill or harm anyone, only to scare and/or prevent passage; they positioned the concrete over the middle lane, thinking the convoy was on the nearside lane.

The jury returned guilty verdicts the same day and Mann J sentenced Hancock and Shankland to life in prison, the mandatory sentence for murder. Anthony Williams was found not guilty.

The Court of Appeal heard the defendants' appeal on 21 October 1985, handing down judgment 10 days later: Lord Lane CJ, Leonard and Rose JJ overturned the convictions for murder and substituted convictions for manslaughter with eight years' imprisonment. The Crown appealed, under section 33 of the Criminal Appeal Act 1968. The House of Lords heard the case on 11 and 12 December 1985 and gave judgment on 27 February 1986. The miners' strike had ended on 3 March 1985, before all of the court hearings.

## III. THE CENTRAL ISSUE

The central issue in the case was what direction the judge should have give the jury for deciding whether the defendants had a sufficient mental state for murder and what impact that direction had on the jury.

## A. Jury Directions on Intention

The judge's directions to the jury are the vital junction between the law and the fact-finding role of the jury. Directions must be given carefully, particularly because juries do not give reasons for their decisions, so an erroneous direction is one of the most significant grounds for appeal.[10] A model direction particularly helps to ensure that all juries' decisions on the same question are made in similar ways. The House of Lords had just provided

---

[8] They were also charged with conspiracy to damage proper property intending to endanger the life of another and conspiring to damage property being reckless as to whether the life of another would be endangered. Mann J discharged the jury from returning verdicts on these charges.

[9] *R v Vickers* [1957] 2 QB 664 (CA); *R v Cunningham* [1982] AC 566 (HL).

[10] Another being where the decision is manifestly unreasonable.

a model direction for a murder charge in *Moloney*. *Moloney* concerned a drunken game between a stepfather and stepson about who could load a shotgun first, and it was unclear whether, when he was dared to pull the trigger, the stepson knew the gun was pointing at his stepfather. The trial judge had failed to make this clear to the jury, so their verdict was unsafe. Accordingly, the murder conviction was quashed and a verdict of manslaughter was substituted. For the sake of future cases, the House of Lords went further, setting out what might be thought of as a four-stage approach to the direction on murder, an approach which Mann J applied in *Hancock and Shankland*.

First, the jury should apply their own common sense understanding of the idea of intention rather receive detailed judicial guidance. That even technical terms should be given their common meaning has long been the starting point in the criminal law. Lord Bridge thought a direction on intent would be 'extremely rare':[11]

> The golden rule should be that, when directing a jury on the mental element necessary in a crime of specific intent, the judge should avoid any elaboration or paraphrase of what is meant by intent, and leave it to the jury's good sense to decide whether the accused acted with the necessary intent, unless the judge is convinced that, on the facts and having regard to the way the case has been presented to the jury in evidence and argument, some further explanation or elaboration is strictly necessary to avoid misunderstanding.[12]

The reasoning appears to be that the law should use language within the common understanding of the jury; where the law does use such language, judges should not complicate the jury's work with explanations or elaborations.[13] The risk, it seems, is that a judge might confuse the jury or their 'good sense'; it does not appear that the other risk, of failing to give a detailed direction when one should, worried Lord Bridge. There was little risk of a successful appeal if a judge failed to give the detailed direction. However, it is open to doubt that the criminal law only uses words with such a common understanding. In addition, there is almost no way of knowing whether juries understand general directions like this. The only real test is where the jury's conduct or questions suggest that they do or do not or by reaching a perverse verdict.

Second, there was little guidance on exactly when a more detailed direction should be given. The threshold depended on the complexity of the facts and on the available evidence. It was likely met when there was doubt

---

[11] *Moloney* (n 4) 926.

[12] ibid.

[13] It might be argued that there is also a constitutional advantage in any ambiguity in the law being determined by a jury, but even if it exists, this is difficult to justify and is clearly not applied evenly across the criminal law. When applied in *Hancock and Shankland*, JC Smith criticised this jury façade as meaningless: JC Smith, 'Case Comment: Intention—Murder—Model Direction Laid Down in Moloney Unsafe and Misleading' [1986] *Crim LR* 400, 403. Note too I Dennis, 'Intention and Complicity: A Reply' [1988] *Crim LR* 649.

that there was an intention to kill, but the conduct was very dangerous in some objective sense. For example, the truth of the events in *Hancock and Shankland* was difficult to ascertain, and the defendants' explanation of the events, precluding an intention to cause any harm, was at least plausible. In those circumstances, Mann J was correct to give a more detailed direction, as the Court of Appeal noted[14] and as perhaps further validated when the jury needed clarification even after the initial direction.

Third, when given, the detailed direction should make clear that the jury were looking for *intention*; foresight was only ever *evidence* of intention, something from which a jury might infer intention if they wished. As Lord Hailsham put it in *Moloney*:

> [F]oresight and foreseeability ... should remain, what they always should have been, part of the law of evidence and inference to be left to the jury after a proper direction as to their weight, and not part of the substantive law.[15]

Fourth, the detailed direction should be clear on the law and the standard of proof: they should acquit if there was any doubt about intent remaining.[16] Lord Bridge's model detailed direction was:

> In the rare cases in which it is necessary to direct a jury by reference to fore-sight of consequences, I do not believe it is necessary for the judge to do more than invite the jury to consider two questions. First, was death or really serious injury in a murder case (or whatever relevant consequence must be proved to have been intended in any other case) a natural consequence of the defendant's voluntary act? Secondly, did the defendant foresee that consequence as being a natural consequence of his act? The jury should then be told that if they answer yes to both questions it is a proper inference for them to draw that he intended that consequence.[17]

This model direction was technically an obiter dictum. In *Moloney*, there was no evidence that the drunken son knew the gun was pointed at his beloved stepfather's head, so a direction on what he foresaw from how he pointed it was not required to resolve the case. Nonetheless, the model direction was clearly made with the intention of setting down the law and was followed as such. Mann J's resulting direction, described as 'admirably clear and succinct' by Lord Lane CJ in the Court of Appeal,[18] was:

> You may think that critical to the resolution of this case is the question of intent. In determining whether a person intended to kill or to cause really serious injury, you must have regard to all of the evidence which has been put before you, and draw from it such inferences as to you seem proper and appropriate. You may or may not, for the purpose of considering what inferences to draw, find it helpful to

---

[14]  *Hancock and Shankland* (n 3) 459.
[15]  *Moloney* (n 4) 913.
[16]  ibid 929, citing *R v Steane* [1947] KB 997 (CA).
[17]  *Moloney* (n 4) 929.
[18]  *Hancock and Shankland* (n 3) 458.

ask: Was death or serious injury a natural consequence of what was done? Did a defendant foresee that consequence as a natural consequence? That is a possible question which you may care to ask yourselves.[19]

The problem is that neither the Bridge nor Mann directions defined the key term 'natural consequence'. Lord Bridge, perhaps seeking to retain as much simplicity as possible, had only done so elsewhere in his speech in *Moloney*:

> I think we should now no longer speak of presumptions in this context but rather of inferences. In the old presumption that a man intends the natural and probable consequences of his acts the important word is 'natural'. This word conveys the idea that *in the ordinary course of events a certain act will lead to a certain consequence unless something unexpected supervenes to prevent it*. One might almost say that, if a consequence is natural, it is really otiose to speak of it as also being probable. (Emphasis added)[20]

Earlier in his speech, Lord Bridge had noted that 'the probability of the consequence taken to have been foreseen must *be little short of overwhelming* before it will suffice to establish the necessary intent' (emphasis added).[21]

Mann J followed Lord Bridge's model direction without the further explanations on probability, so the Court of Appeal overturned the convictions for murder: Mann J 'was unwittingly led into misdirecting the Jury by reason of the way in which the guidelines in Moloney were expressed'.[22] The Court of Appeal preferred the extended direction to require the jury to be sure that the defendant foresaw death or serious injury as 'highly likely', the term used in a full paragraph of model directions.[23]

The House of Lords agreed with the decision of the Court of Appeal that the model directions in *Moloney* were insufficient. Lord Scarman 'very much doubt[ed] whether a jury without further explanation would think that "probable" added nothing to "natural"', which he thought was a serious failing.[24] In his view:

> [T]he Moloney guidelines as they stand are unsafe and misleading. They require a reference to probability. They also require an explanation that the greater the probability of a consequence the more likely it is that the consequence was foreseen and that if that consequence was foreseen the greater the probability is that that consequence was also intended. But juries also require to be reminded that the decision is theirs to be reached upon a consideration of all the evidence.[25]

This issue of 'probability' would later return, as discussed below. Yet, for the moment, it was the key point which made the *Moloney* direction insufficient.

[19] ibid 458–59.
[20] *Moloney* (n 4) 929.
[21] ibid 925.
[22] *Hancock and Shankland* (n 3) 461.
[23] ibid 461.
[24] ibid 473.
[25] ibid.

However, while this sliding scale of probability should be left to the jury, the House of Lords disagreed with the Court of Appeal putting it into a model direction. According to Lord Scarman, the best course was to 'follow the traditional course of a summing up'[26] and not to rely on a model direction to guide juries. References to the 'probable' and 'natural' in *Moloney*'s model direction and the 'highly likely' in the Court of Appeal's model were wiped away, leaving only Lord Bridge's 'little short of overwhelming' hanging as a guideline.

It is not clear why the House of Lords did not give a new model direction. *Moloney* had recognised a real need for one. Indeed, so had the Court of Appeal in *Hancock and Shankland*, when it gave a model direction precisely in compliance with the full judgment in *Moloney*,[27] yet the House of Lords rejected it. First, perhaps this slightly later and differently configured House of Lords no longer thought a model direction was necessary, though it is hard to see why. Perhaps they now trusted a jury's common sense to resolve the issue without a direction. One way in which this would be the case was if the House of Lords' discussion of *Moloney* enabled trial judges to highlight the key parts of Lord Bridge's speech themselves with a sufficient level of fidelity even absent a model direction. It is hard to see this as convincing. Second, perhaps the decision not to give a model direction is better expressed as a relative statement: the House of Lords thought there was greater risk in a model direction itself being wrong, or appearing to be, than from bad decisions made in the absence of a model direction. They might have been particularly hesitant after being stung by the still recent attempt in *Moloney*. Third, the English system of adjudication can sometimes push towards narrower answers. Lord Scarman concluded his speech with a general order for the Court of Appeal to lay down guidelines for directing juries sparingly, leaving the trial judge to fulfil his duty to direct on the law.[28] Perhaps more generally, even in the highest courts there can be a tendency to only solve those facts rather than care more about the wider cases.

Another possibility is that it would have been embarrassing for the House of Lords to hand down another model direction, essentially correcting Lord Bridge while he was still serving, albeit he did not sit in *Hancock and Shankland* itself. It was well known that Lord Bridge was perhaps prone to more infelicities in criminal law than would have been desirable. In the same period, he had given an unimpressive speech in *Anderton v Ryan* (9 May 1985)[29] on the law of impossible attempts, a speech which was lambasted

---

[26] ibid 474.
[27] As noted by, eg, Smith, 'Case Comment' 403. See also B Mitchell, '*Hancock and Shankland* in the House of Lords: A Lost Opportunity and Only Further Confusion' (1986) 50(3) *Journal of Criminal Law* 267, 270.
[28] *Hancock and Shankland* (n 3) 474.
[29] *Anderton v Ryan* [1985] AC 560 (HL).

by Glanville Williams in the *Cambridge Law Journal*.[30] Lord Bridge himself recanted a year later on 15 May 1986 in *Shivpuri*.[31] Lord Bridge may have been recognised as sometimes going too far with his ideas about the law, but he was still sitting in the House of Lords and even indirect criticism may have been thought inappropriate. Avoiding that criticism might have been harder for the House of Lords, his peers, than the Court of Appeal. In addition, it should not be forgotten that many murder appeals were reaching the Court of Appeal and could apply for leave to reach the House of Lords, so perhaps their Lordships thought another less loaded opportunity would be available soon if it turned out to be needed.

So much for the law—what about the outcome? On the facts, did Mann J's use of Lord Bridge's model direction really make the convictions unsafe?

## B. The Jury's Decision

The prosecution case was that Hancock and Shankland had agreed together to kill or cause serious harm to Wilkie. The Crown's case pushed in two related ways to support a finding of intention:[32] (1) the targeting of the convoy; and (2) the targeting of Williams personally.

On the first, the targeting of the convoy, Mann J's summing up shows five key points. First, there was no credible eyewitness evidence of targeting the convoy: the two police officers in the Land Rover alleged that they saw two bodies appear on the bridge and throw an object down.[33] However, both also said that it was a cloudless and moonlit night with good visibility, while in fact Mann J pointed out it was cloudy and difficult to see, according to the police in the accompanying van and motorcyclist, and there was no moonlight.[34]

Second, the photographic evidence does not appear to have given the jury a clear and realistic way to decide where the defendants thought the block would land; even the likely position of the block on the bridge is unclear, uncertainty to which Mann J appeared to refer in the summing up.[35]

Third, in the defendants' evidence, Hancock admitted he pushed the block over the bridge, thinking the block was in the middle of the road, and from a position on the bridge so that he could have seen them coming.

---

[30] G Williams, 'The Lords and Impossible Attempts, or *Quis Custodiet Ipsos Custodes?*' [1986] *CLJ* 33.

[31] *R v Shivpuri* [1987] AC 1 (HL).

[32] There was further evidence from Hancock's girlfriend about his initial attempts to obtain an alibi, which suggested that in fact they had realised they had likely killed someone.

[33] Kew, 29–30. *cf* 44–46, 51, 58–63, 68, 72.

[34] HL, transcript, 13–14. The bypass road was illuminated, but the Heads of the Valleys Road was not: ibid 15.

[35] ibid 18.

In fact, when the convoy came, driving on the nearside lane,[36] Hancock's evidence was that he pushed the block over without raising his body over the parapet and that he 'didn't mean to do anyone damage—just to frighten him more than anything'.[37] Shankland admitted that he had added a push to an object in its motion off the bridge.[38] Mann J asked the jury to consider how two relatively small objects could really block a 33ft (10m) carriageway and why they should be tipped only after the police Land Rover had gone under the bridge. In evidence that did not form part of the summing up, Shankland had said there had been no specific plan to do what happened: 'It just happened.'[39]

Fourth, when indicating that Shankland had not known where the convoy would drive,[40] Mann J was in fact alluding to a fuller story that the jury had already heard. On 29 November, Hancock and possibly others had sawn off a lamp post and barred the A469 over the bridge to stop Williams getting to work.[41] That route, *on* the bridge, not *under* it, was indeed the more natural route.[42] The materials brought to the bridge could have been used on it or dropped from it. It would not explain why the concrete should be dropped only after the Land Rover escort had passed. The convoy also varied when it went through the area, between 5 am and 6.45 am each day.[43]

Fifth, the jury were reminded that expert evidence had shown that if the taxi had been travelling 2 mph faster, it would probably not have been hit by the block.[44] The judge noted that 'you may think that if one wishes to hit a moving object with another object, it is a matter of intuitive judgment of relative motions, based upon acquired experience rather than a matter of calculation'.[45] The concrete must have been pushed hard.[46]

In sum, the evidence did not prove conclusively that the block was positioned or thrown to kill or cause serious harm, but it did raise questions about the defendants' explanation of their actions.[47]

The Crown's second main argument, that the defendants targeted Williams personally, was less substantiated. On the one hand, it appears that Williams had been reported in a local newspaper as breaking the strike, though he 'didn't do it for the money', yet Hancock claimed not to be bitter

---

[36] ibid 12.
[37] ibid 15–17.
[38] ibid 16.
[39] Kew, 282.
[40] HL, transcript, 18.
[41] Kew, 291–93.
[42] ibid 52–53.
[43] ibid 74.
[44] HL, transcript, 19–20.
[45] ibid 20.
[46] HL, Cardiff Crown Court evidence, 5, Alexander Grant suggested from the lack of markings on the underhanging bridge structure that at least 1.5 feet per second of velocity needed to have been applied to move the block, and 5.9 feet per second for the pillar.
[47] *cf* MC Kaveny, 'Inferring Intention from Foresight' [2004] *Crim LR* 81, esp 95–97.

about Williams not giving anything approaching an acceptable reason.[48] What the jury was not told was that Williams himself said he had not received personal threats, though from 23 November, he wore a helmet as he approached the colliery.[49] On the other hand, there had been two earlier incidents. The judge's summing up had briefly alluded to earlier conduct by Hancock.[50] First, late on 24 November, Hancock had been arrested for besetting Williams' home by throwing a bottle at the house.[51] This altercation included reference to 'getting the fucking bastard', meaning Williams.[52] Second, there was the evidence of the lamp post obstruction *on* the bridge. This is not strong evidence of animus against Williams or of the defendants intending him at least serious harm. Mann J had not proposed to direct the jury on either event, describing the first as 'drunken behaviour' and the second as playing a part 'in the severance of the lamp post' (the post removed and then placed as an obstruction on the bridge); Mann J did not appear to treat this as any particular evidence of personal animus against Williams.[53] It is not possible to say how the jury interpreted this evidence, having been told simply to: 'Attach to them such significant as you think appropriate.'[54] It was also evidently against any striking miner's interests that a strike-breaker should be killed, and perhaps even seriously injured, given the terrible publicity against the strike itself that this would cause: as miners pointed out the day after the death, 'it's just plain stupid'.[55]

So, what did the jury make of these two prosecution angles? Crucially, the jury felt able to reach a decision on the facts, but were uncertain on the law. After immediately and unanimously finding Anthony Williams not guilty, the jury deliberated for five hours before being given permission to deliver a majority verdict on Hancock and Shankland.[56] They then returned a note shortly thereafter, indicating that while they were confident of the facts, there was uncertainty and dissent 'with regard to intent and foreseeable consequences.'[57] Mann J then confirmed with counsel that he would repeat the *Moloney* direction, and there was no disagreement over its form in respect of murder.[58] Mann J began by complimenting the jury, saying:

[48] Kew, 187, 220.
[49] ibid, evidence not tendered, 17.
[50] HL, transcript, 17.
[51] Kew, 7–11.
[52] ibid 13 (PC Evans).
[53] HL, transcript, 17.
[54] ibid.
[55] Michael Getler, 'Violence Escalates in Coal Strike' *Washington Post* (Washington DC, 1 December 1984) A13.
[56] HL, transcript, 23–24.
[57] ibid, transcript 25; the House of Lords added a further fragment of the note—*Hancock and Shankland* (n 3) 471: 'the jury has discussed at great length the factual aspects of this case and feel, under the circumstances, confident in dealing with this matter'.
[58] Counsel agreeing specifically with reference to *DPP v Newbury* [1977] AC 500 (HL); *Church* [1966] 1 QB 59 (CA); *R v Larkin* [1943] 1 All ER 217 (CA) on manslaughter and murder.

'If I may say so, [the question of intent and foreseeable consequences] shows a precise perception of a point which has troubled lawyers.'[59] He repeated his earlier direction,[60] though this was the *Moloney*-derived direction that had already proved insufficient.

In short, it is a plausible reading of this difficult case that the jury were misled by the *Moloney* direction and that they convicted on a test of 'natural' consequences, but would have acquitted on a test of 'very likely' or 'little short of overwhelming' consequences. In the Court of Appeal, counsel for Hancock suggested 'a workable possibility' that the verdict would have been different and the court agreed, albeit with some hesitation.[61]

## IV. DID THE SOCIAL AND POLITICAL CONTEXT AFFECT THE DECISION?

The events in *Hancock and Shankland* were tried two months after the miners' strike itself had ended, but that context may have played a role in the jury's decision. The first step will be to introduce the strike and then to use what evidence we have, largely Mann J's summing up, to see what we can learn about the jury's decision-making. After that, we can ask whether the appellate courts would have been affected by this context.

### A. The Miners' Strike

The miners' strike was a significant event in the political and social history of the second half of the twentieth century. Conservative governments from the early 1970s had pushed free market economics against the grain of the loss-making and government-owned National Coal Board (NCB). In the short term, this meant reduced government subsidies; in the medium term, it meant showdowns with the National Union of Mineworkers (NUM). Strikes in 1972 and 1974 had been successful in changing government policy, but the Conservatives under Margaret Thatcher had learnt new lessons by the 1980s. New tactics were developed, such as advanced surveillance, police deployment and the use of escorted convoys like that involving Williams.[62] Some of these measures were contentious in principle and highly difficult in practice.[63]

---

[59] HL, transcript, 25; noted by the Court of Appeal in *Hancock and Shankland* (n 3) 462.

[60] HL, transcript, 25–26.

[61] *Hancock and Shankland* (n 3) 462.

[62] See generally Jonathan Winterton and Ruth Winterton, *Coal, Crisis and Conflict: The 1984–1985 Miners' Strike in Yorkshire* (Manchester, Manchester University Press, 1989) Ch 5.

[63] See, eg, Independent Police Complaints Commission decisions on matters relating to the policing of events at Orgreave coking plant in 1984, 12 June 2015: www.ipcc.gov.uk/investigations/orgreave-coking-plant-referrals-south-yorkshire-police.

After a narrowly averted further strike in 1981, pit closures combined with pay restraint led to a series of strike ballots and unofficial strikes. The 1984–85 strike began on 6 March 1984 with a walkout at Cortonwood Colliery in Brampton Bierlow, South Yorkshire, which led the Yorkshire Area of the NUM to call an official strike. Miners supported the strike in South Wales: 99.6 per cent in November 1984, 98 per cent on February 1985 and 93 per cent on 1 March 1985, the most consistently high rates across the country (only Kent coming close, but it had only a seventh of the number of miners, at 3,000).[64] Nonetheless, the strike was disputed, even internally. On 28 September 1984, two cases reached the Chancery Division, where members of the NUM in Derbyshire[65] and Yorkshire[66] who did not heed the call to strike were subject to disciplinary actions which were found to be unlawful. Nicholls J found in both cases that there was no legal authority for the strike, there having been no motion ballot passed (50.1 per cent against in Derbyshire and no vote in Yorkshire). Without the authority of a ballot, when the National Executive Committee did in fact call for a strike and up to 85 per cent of miners responded across the country,[67] it was an illegal strike.

Ultimately, the strike ended in defeat for the striking miners. On 3 March 1985, the NUM voted to return to work. It was a defining moment in British industrial relations and the NUM's defeat significantly weakened the British trade union movement. The story in South Wales was particularly hard and the difficulty of economic recovery can be seen in person even today. The events on 30 November 1984 were particularly bleak. The NCB had offered a £650 Christmas bonus to any miners who had returned to work by 19 November, but even so, Williams had been one of only two strike-breakers at the Merthyr Vale Colliery.[68]

Strong picketing and national political manoeuvring were the miners' focus; violence off the picket line did happen, but was rarely fatal. For instance, just a week before the events at Rhymney, two Wakefield miners committed grievous bodily harm against a strike-breaker in his own home, but four others were acquitted of public order offences there; similar acquittals for threats to kill were handed down around the same time.[69] However, violence had been feared. As Anthony Williams left the court

[64] Andrew John Richards, *Miners on Strike: Class Solidarity and Division in Britain* (Oxford, Berg, 1996) 109.
[65] *Taylor v National Union of Mineworkers (Derbyshire Area)* [1984] IRLR 440.
[66] *Taylor v National Union of Mineworkers (Yorkshire Area)* [1984] IRLR 445.
[67] See also *Taylor v National Union of Mineworkers (Derbyshire Area)* [1985] BCLC 237, 256; and *Taylor v National Union of Mineworkers (Yorkshire Area)* (unreported) 14 November 1985 Nunnery Transcript (Lexis) (ChD).
[68] Mick Harvey, Martin Jenkinson and Mark Metcalf, *The Miners' Strike* (Barnsley, Pen and Sword History, 2014) 162.
[69] Winterton and Winterton, *Coal, Crisis and Conflict* 164.

after being acquitted, he told journalists: 'It was an accident. Those two boys wouldn't hurt anyone, they are not those sort of boys.'[70] The Chief Constable of South Wales, Mr David East, later told a press conference at Merthyr police station: 'This is not industrial action. This is not picketing. This is murder. Whoever threw those things down must have known the likely consequences.' He went further, recalling that in September, the Assistant Chief Constable, Mr Viv Brook, had warned that someone would be killed if pickets continued throwing pieces of concrete from motorway bridges. In that instance, striking miners had then been attempting to stop convoys of lorries taking coal to Llanwern steelworks.[71] According to Winterton and Winterton: 'Even NUM leaders were forced to criticize the killing of the taxi driver, yet Yorkshire activists had long feared a lorry driver or policeman would be killed because police operations prevented normal picketing.'[72]

It appears that, by the time of Wilkie's death, there had been more deaths amongst striking miners than amongst strike-breakers, one striking miner being hit by a brick and another hit by a truck, as well as two suicides. In fact, there had been more deaths than this—a total of five—from people scavenging for waste coal on slag heaps.[73]

## B. The Cardiff Crown Court Trial

The trial at Cardiff Crown Court was a significant event in the region, one which appears to be still remembered there and, indeed, around the UK.[74] The jury would have known about the strike, but it was their task to find facts independently of that knowledge. The jury were almost certainly taken from Mid Glamorgan,[75] a geographically small region close to Merthyr Vale. After an eight-day trial, Mann J made three intriguing remarks about the jury's task. He began his directions:[76]

> If you have sat upon a jury before, as I suspect some of you may, you will be familiar with the process of summing up and with some of the matters, at least, of which I shall speak to you about.

---

[70] ibid.

[71] Sarah Boseley, 'Two Men Charged after Taxi Driver Dies in Bridge Ambush' *The Guardian* (London, 1 December 1984)

[72] Winterton and Winterton, *Coal, Crisis and Conflict* 164.

[73] Special and Associated Press, 'Concrete Post Hurled at Cab 2 Men Charged in UK Mine Strike Slaying' *Globe and Mail* (Toronto, 1 December 1984).

[74] Anecdotally, locals from around England and Wales certainly remember the killing at least, and it is still described as a pivotal moment in the strike: eg, Anon, 'Shocking Killing is Now a Local Legend' *South Wales Echo* (Cardiff, 22 May 2004) 14.

[75] The county, under the Local Government Act 1972 from which the register was taken. This changed with the Local Government (Wales) Act 1994.

[76] HL, transcript 7–8.

He then makes clear that the onus is on them to decide all the questions of fact, while they must accept what he says the law to be. This instruction expressly included a reference to not being:

> [M]oved by any view which you may have as to the rights or wrongs of the strike in the coal industry ... Nor ... by any view which you might entertain about the part which violence played in that dispute, by whomsoever committed it.

The jury were also told that they must feel 'satisfied' by the prosecution that the defendant's guilt on a charge was established.

First, it is unclear what Mann J meant about suspecting that the jury had served before. The most likely explanation was that there was a strong chance, he thought, that some members of this panel had recently heard another case while serving that period of jury duty, rather than that the pool of jurors was so small that each might be called up multiple times.[77] Jury panel members were to be randomly selected from across the electoral roll across a whole county.[78]

Second, as for the direction on ignoring the political context of the strike, Mann J was on well-trodden ground and gave a clear instruction to the jury. Judges often cautioned juries on the importance of their independence, but in practice proving failures in independence or effectiveness were difficult.[79] In *R v Pennington*, the Court of Appeal had only just that year had to deal with a question of the independence of a jury member.[80] A striking miner had been convicted of criminal damage for turning over a car being driven to work by a Coal Board electrician in July 1984 in Lancashire; two other striking miners who had allegedly helped Pennington were acquitted. After the trial, Pennington discovered that a jury member had been a working miner. Pennington's application for leave to appeal, on the grounds of material irregularity, was unanimously rejected by the Court of Appeal. Skinner J, giving the ex tempore judgment of the Court of Appeal (with Lord Lane, LCJ and Simon Brown J), refused leave to appeal, finding that:

> It is no ground for disqualification of a juror that a juror might have personal reasons for some bias towards prosecution or defence. Even if it had been a ground for disqualification, that in itself is no ground for setting aside the verdict of a jury, provided that the juror's name was on the jury panel. That reasoning is the stronger where there is no disqualification but merely a suspicion of bias, as is the case here.[81]

---

[77] Juries hearing multiple cases in one period of service had been known to happen, though the Morris Report had recommended against hearing a long series of cases: Home Office, *Report of the Departmental Committee on Jury Service* (Cmnd 2627, 1965) [335]; the Committee was chaired by Lord Morris of Borth-y-Gest and is commonly known as the Morris Committee.

[78] ibid [235]; Juries Act 1974, s 3.

[79] eg, a jury member having been secretly deaf did not render a conviction unsafe: *R v Chapman* (1976) 63 Cr App R 75 (CA).

[80] *R v Pennington* (1985) 81 Cr App R 217 (CA).

[81] ibid 219.

It was apparently common practice in some courts for the trial judge to ask the jury panel members to withdraw if they had an interest in the strike and might have any difficulty in adhering to their oaths. However, whether to pose this question was entirely at the discretion of the judge.[82]

Yet, as DJ Birch pointed out in the *Criminal Law Review*, it was not illogical for the defendant to challenge a potential juror because the juror was perceived to be on the opposite side of a trade dispute.[83] The trouble was that a juror's occupation no longer appeared on the jury list, so this information might have been hard to glean.

Third, it is somewhat unclear why the standard of proof suggested by the judge was expressed in terms of 'satisfaction' and, in particular, that the jury were satisfied that the defendant's guilt was established, a potentially unhelpful way of phrasing the case. It might be imagined that a direction on satisfaction 'beyond reasonable doubt' or being 'sure' was simply otiose in the context.

With this direction, the jury would have known not to let their decision-making be affected by the strike and that they had to be certain of the defendants' guilt before convicting.

## C. The Strike's Uncertain Impact

Even if the strike affected the jury's decision-making, it is certainly not clear whether that context would have encouraged jury members to convict or acquit. Some may have sympathised with the miners, while others may have regarded Wilkie's death as too extreme to avoid a murder conviction for the defendants. Mann J acknowledged the miners' strike had 'engendered a climate of violence'; after the verdicts, one of Shankland's counsel, John Prosser QC,[84] said that his clients were victims in 'a nation at war'.[85] By contrast, for the victim's mother, it was not a question of fault and wrong-doing as much as the fact of his death in this way: 'Only a murder verdict

---

[82] ibid.

[83] DJ Birch, 'Trial: *R. v. Pennington*' [1985] *Crim LR* 394, 395.

[84] Many of the counsel involved in the case have gone on to have very significant legal and political careers. Counsel for Hancock included Gareth Williams, later Lord Williams of Mostyn, a Labour politician and Leader of the House of Lords. But for his untimely death, Williams would quite possibly have become Lord Chancellor: Chris Mullin, *A View from the Foot-hills: The Diaries of Chris Mullin* (London, Profile Books, 2009) 248, 'Wednesday 9 January 2002'. Hancock's other counsel was Christopher Pitchford, now Pitchford LJ. Counsel for Shankland were John Prosser QC, later a circuit judge, and Lord Elystan-Morgan, recently Labour MP for Ceredigion, then a recorder and soon after a circuit judge. At trial, the junior had been Gregg Taylor, then a relatively junior Cardiff barrister and later a QC. For the Crown, appeared Martin Thomas QC, OBE, later Baron Thomas of Geresford, already a recorder of the Crown Court, later a Deputy High Court Judge and ultimately a Liberal Democrat member of the House of Lords; his junior was Philip Rees, a successful junior barrister in Cardiff who did a mix of civil and criminal work, often involving labour issues.

[85] http://news.bbc.co.uk/onthisday/hi/dates/stories/may/16/newsid_2512000/2512469.stm.

would have been just after what happened to my son.'[86] The Plaid Cymru MP for Caenarfon, Dafydd Wigley, wrote to Lord Hailsham on 22 May 1985 to express his and some constituents' dismay at the convictions and sentences, particularly because the defendants 'clearly did not set out with the intention of killing the person who died' and were only 'reckless and no doubt criminally dangerous' enough for something less than murder.[87]

The appellate courts' approach of formally ignoring the context of the strike in deciding whether the conviction was unsafe was the only viable approach to this difficulty. While the strike was over, the dispute and the reasons for it were still alive and the Court of Appeal would almost certainly have known this. On hearing of the pair's convictions, 700 miners at the by then working plant walked out because they believed the death of Wilkie was not a deliberate act.[88] Perhaps replacing a murder conviction with manslaughter would have eased some of this residual tension. Yet it does not seem that either the Court of Appeal or the House of Lords reasoned that way, nor did they need to since there was an error of law in *Moloney*. Rather, Mann J had applied the test he was bound to apply—it was simply that that test had been wrong. The Court of Appeal felt confident enough in that error to refuse to apply a model direction from the House of Lords, a confidence that the House of Lords later agreed with when it heard the case. Their Lordships' reasoning was entirely textual and logical, building on the earlier cases to show the error in Lord Bridge's model direction. At the same time, it was this political context which made the decision so memorable for the public even today. The assumption that it must have played a role in the jury's decision to convict or the appellate decisions to quash the murder conviction and substitute one of manslaughter is understandable, but unsubstantiated. The political context was also most likely not why the case went to the House of Lords. The Crown's appeal was predictable, given the more restrictive test proposed by the Court of Appeal. The decision to hear the appeal was also not surprising, given how recent *Moloney* had been and the potential to correct an erroneous model direction. At the very least, the context of the strike served as a reminder of how human beings can behave and what legal rules need to be applied to and by whom.

## V. THE FAULTS IN HOMICIDE

We turn now from assessing the social context of *Hancock and Shankland* to assessing its wider legal historical setting; that is, how much the case

---

[86] Mark Oliver, 'Minister's Secret Role in Miners' Strike Death Inquiry' *The Guardian* (London, 26 January 2004).

[87] Kew, evidence not tendered, ref PC/A/86.

[88] Harvey, Jenkinson and Metcalf, *The Miners' Strike* 162.

moved English law closer to developing a precise and coherent collection of fault concepts. It is worth recalling that prior to trial, the defendants had pleaded guilty to manslaughter, but the Crown had laid charges of murder. As English law moved from (1) undifferentiated and amorphous notions of fault, it had to decide how to channel *deliberate risk-taking*. Such risk-taking could be pushed into the nascent concepts of (2) 'recklessness', (3) 'negligence' or (4) 'intention'. *Hancock and Shankland* was a key step towards closing off the last of these three, intention, and thereby (5) solidifying the fault element in different degrees of homicide.

## A. Undifferentiated Fault

The homicide cases that were tried prior to the twentieth century tell a very complex story that is open to different interpretations. What is clear is that one of the most significant substantive fault rules was that a man was taken to intend the natural and probable consequences of his actions, and this applied until well into the twentieth century.[89] Even in 1935, it was affirmed by the House of Lords in *Woolmington v DPP* that the presumption resolved the case unless the defendant proved 'excuse, justification, or extenuation'.[90] This wide liability for *intention* usually avoided the courts needing to give directions to the jury on *foresight*.[91] Indeed, finding out exactly what the defendant had intended or foreseen would have been difficult. It was only with the Criminal Evidence Act 1898 that a defendant was competent and, in practice, compellable to give evidence; a full defence by counsel was permissible from 1836 where counsel could be afforded, which was more likely in the generally more serious cases of felonies.[92]

The nineteenth-century notions of mens rea had been dominated by this broad and presumptive intention together with morally loaded terms like 'wickedness'[93] and 'malice'.[94] According to the Criminal Law Commissioners

[89] 4 Bl Comm 200; *R v Dixon* (1814) 3 Maule and Selwyn 11, 105 ER 516.

[90] *Woolmington v DPP* [1935] AC 462 (HL), 472–73. In practice, the appeal was allowed because Swift J had failed at trial to direct properly on the burden of proof. One of the last clear cases was decided in 1947 and was cited in *Moloney* (n 4) for other reasons: *Steane* (n 16) 1006.

[91] KJM Smith, *Lawyers, Legislators and Theorists: Developments in English Criminal Jurisprudence 1800–1957* (Oxford, Clarendon Press, 1998), 162–66 on the early history, esp 166. See, eg, *R v Pembliton* (1874) LR 2 CCR 119 (CCR), 122, per Blackburn J.

[92] See generally C Allen, *The Law of Evidence in Victorian England* (Cambridge, Cambridge University Press, 1997) Ch 5; KJM Smith, 'Criminal Law' in W Cornish et al, *Oxford History of the Laws of England, Vol XIII: 1820–1914* (Oxford, Oxford University Press, 2010) 71–115, esp 100–07.

[93] eg, JF Stephen, *A History of the Criminal Law of England* (London, Macmillan & Co, 1883) 120: 'wicked pleasure in giving pain'.

[94] See generally G Williams, *The Mental Element in Crime* (Oxford, Oxford University Press, 1965) 61–73.

of 1843, mens rea covered both those who act intending a result and those who act 'knowing or believing that the acts which they do are likely to occasion an injurious result, or that hurt or damage will probably result, wilfully incur the risk of causing the injurious consequences'.[95] In other words, the Commissioners were aiming to criminalise only 'wilfully incurring' risks,[96] though in an earlier report, they had at times referred to 'conscious risk-taking' to distinguish this conduct from the lower level of negligence.[97] Commentators saw much overlap here: for instance, Austin described malice as simply denoting intention in the context of murder.[98] Intention was sometimes even described as covering both the *desired* and the *foreseen as probable*: Jeremy Bentham famously did so in his *Introduction to the Principles of Morals and Legislation*,[99] but he was not alone.[100] The courts themselves began to refer to recklessness towards the end of the nineteenth century, though its use was 'impressionistic and unanalysed'.[101]

## B. Recklessness

It was only at the end of the nineteenth century that *recklessness* developed as a separate fault element in criminal law: foreseeing and taking a risk started to solidify as a separate form of wrong, with 'recklessness' as its name. The first time a court used subjective recklessness to mean 'foresight' was in a civil case, *Derry v Peek*, in 1889. There the House of Lords held that in order to be liable in deceit, a defendant needed to make a false statement, knowing it was false or 'recklessly, or without care whether it is true or false', implying that the defendant must have foreseen the risk that it was false.[102] They rejected the claimant's argument that gross negligence, or perhaps even a failure to have a reasonable belief, sufficed for recklessness.[103]

---

[95] Royal Commission on Criminal Law, 7th Rep (1843) Parl Pap, xix, 22.

[96] ibid 26.

[97] Royal Commission on Criminal Law, 4th Rep (1839) Parl Pap, xix, xxiv, xxv.

[98] John Austin, *Lectures on Jurisprudence*, vol I, Robert Campbell (ed) (London, John Murray, 1869) 355; and see generally Smith, *Lawyers, Legislators and Theorists* 122–27. See also EC Clark, *An Analysis of Criminal Liability* (Cambridge, Cambridge University Press, 1880) 81–82; RS Wright, *Draft of a Criminal Code and Code of Criminal Procedure for the Island of Jamaica* (London, HMSO, 1877) 3 and 98.

[99] Jeremy Bentham, *Introduction to the Principles of Morals and Legislation*, JH Burns and HLA Hart (eds) (Oxford, Oxford University Press, 1970) 84–87.

[100] eg, Clark, *An Analysis* 96–100; DA Stroud, *Mens Rea or Imputability under the law of England* (London, Sweet & Maxwell, 1914) 120.

[101] Edward Griew, 'Consistency, Communication and Codification: Reflections on Two Mens Rea Words' in Peter Glazebrook (ed), *Reshaping the Criminal Law: Essays in Honour of Glanville Williams* (London, Stevens & Sons, 1978) 62. See also, Smith, 'Criminal Law', 224–29 and also 219–24.

[102] *Derry v Peek* (1889) 14 App Cas 337 (HL), 350, 360.

[103] ibid.

It is worth pausing to consider this early link between recklessness and *indifference*. Indifference was a more obvious fault standard since it is clearly unjustifiable to run risks without caring about their likelihood or the reasons for running them. Indeed, to some subjectivists, the unjustifiable nature of the risk was a source of fault *because* the defendant had shown that he did not care enough about it.[104] Against this obvious standard, the criminal law was slow to develop focus on foreseen risks, as seen in *Derry v Peek*. Kenny, in his *Outlines of the Criminal Law* first published in 1902,[105] included within intention the desire to produce a result 'or only recklessness as to whether they ensue or not'.[106] It seems that he was referring to subjective foresight, as he had a lower (but still sufficient) class of mens rea for merely being able to foresee, but not actually foreseeing.[107] This was indicative of a kind of equivalence between indifference, recklessness and intention in the early twentieth century.[108]

It was the House of Lords in *DPP v Andrews* in 1937 that settled on something like the current use of the term recklessness in the criminal law, without referring to *Derry v Peek*:

> '[R]eckless' suggests an indifference to risk whereas the accused may have appreciated the risk and intended to avoid it and yet shown such a high degree of negligence in the means adopted to avoid the risk as would justify a conviction.[109]

The next key shift was in 1952, when JWC Turner had taken over the editorship of *Kenny* (16th edn) and rephrased 'malice'—that is, intention *and* recklessness—around foresight of risk:

> [I]n any statutory definition of a crime 'malice' must be taken not in the old vague sense of 'wickedness' in general, but as requiring either (i) an actual intention to do the particular *kind* of harm that in fact was done, or (ii) recklessness as to whether such harm should occur or not (i.e. the accused has foreseen that the particular kind of harm might be done, and yet has gone on to take the risk of it).[110]

---

[104] E Fruchtman, 'Recklessness and the Limits of Mens Rea: Beyond Orthodox Subjectivism Part I' (1986–87) 29 *Criminal Law Quarterly* 315, 319–320; E Fruchtman, 'Recklessness and the Limits of Mens Rea: Beyond Orthodox Subjectivism Part II' (1986–87) 29 *Criminal Law Quarterly* 435, 437–38.

[105] CS Kenny, *Outlines of Criminal law* (Cambridge, Cambridge University Press, 1902).

[106] Ibid 148; see also 147.

[107] ibid 39–44; note that he cited *R v Welch* (1875) 1 QBD 23 (CCR) for support where no attempt to foresee was made.

[108] Nothing significant had happened by Kenny's last sole edition in 1929: CS Kenny, *Outlines of Criminal Law* 13th edn (Cambridge, Cambridge University Press, 1929) 149.

[109] *DPP v Andrews* [1937] AC 576 (HL), 583, perhaps influenced by JWC Turner, 'The Mental Element in Crimes at Common Law' (1936–38) 6 *CLJ* 31, 38; expanded in L Radzinowicz and JWC Turner (eds), *The Modern Approach to Criminal Law* (London, Macmillan & Co, 1945) 207. His claim that all of mens rea at common law was intention or recklessness is almost certainly incorrect: JWC Turner 'Mens Rea and Motorists: A Memorandum for Students' (1933–35) 5 *CLJ* 61, 62–65.

[110] JWC Turner, *Kenny's Outlines of Criminal Law*, 16th edn (Cambridge, Cambridge University Press, 1952) 186, though in fact, this was not precisely what Kenny had written: *Outlines of Criminal Law* (1902) 43, 47, 48.

Ultimately, partly as a byproduct of discussing negligence and intention, recklessness developed objective and subjective limbs. A defining moment was the Law Commission's working paper on general principles of criminal law in 1970:

A person is reckless if,

  (a)  knowing that there is a risk that an event may result from his conduct or that a circumstance may exist, he takes that risk, and
  (b)  it is unreasonable for him to take it having regard to the degree and nature of the risk which he knows to be present.[111]

This definition was not without its critics,[112] but nonetheless was retained in the full report of 1985[113] and the Draft Criminal Code in 1989.[114] It was affirmed as axiomatic by the Court of Appeal in *R v Stephenson* in 1979.[115] Even *Archbold*, somewhat lagging behind legal developments, adopted this two-stage definition in 1976, albeit with a lingering presumption that a person is taken to foresee the probable consequences of his or her actions.[116]

This greater consensus in the debates came about just as recklessness was to bifurcate because of *Caldwell*.[117] A fire in a hotel had been started by a drunk defendant and the House of Lords responded by creating a fully objective form of recklessness in criminal damage and under the Road Traffic Acts, leaving the traditional subjective form elsewhere. Under the objective test, a person was liable for subjectively taking a risk or for taking a risk that would have been obvious to a reasonable person. This objective version had even been presaged in *Moloney*. Lord Bridge had suggested that the claim that the appellant never considered that he might even injure his stepfather by pulling the trigger was 'undoubtedly' a 'high degree of recklessness'[118] but it must, a priori, have been objective recklessness. In any case, in *R v G* in 2003, the Law Commission's original definition of recklessness has been reinstated for offences under the Criminal Damage Act 1971: the defendant must foresee the risk and go on, unjustifiably, to take it.[119]

---

[111] Law Commission, *Codification of the Criminal Law: General Principles. The Mental Element in Crime* (Law Com WP No 31, 1970) 47.
[112] See, eg, RA Duff, 'Recklessness' [1980] *Crim LR* 282, 282, 290–91. Duff's article is particularly interesting, foreshadowing the rise in objective recklessness, esp at 291–92.
[113] Law Commission, *Codification of the Criminal Law* (Law Com No 143, 1985).
[114] Law Commission, *Draft Criminal Code for England and Wales* (Law Com No 177, 1989) cll 18(c) and [41]; see also Appendix B, 18(iii)–(v).
[115] *R v Stephenson* [1979] QB 695 (CA), 703, per Geoffrey Lane LJ.
[116] SG Mitchell, *Archbold's Criminal Pleadings Evidence and Practice*, 39th edn (London, Sweet & Maxwell, 1967) [1443C]. For a critique of the preceding edition, see PR Glazebrook, 'Book Review: Archbold Pleading, Evidence and Practice in Criminal Cases' (1975) 34 *CLJ* 151.
[117] *R v Caldwell* [1982] AC 341 (HL).
[118] *Moloney* (n 4) 920.
[119] *R v G* [2004] 1 AC 1034 (HL) [41], per Lord Bingham.

## C. Negligence

Also in the early 1950s, Glanville Williams was at work on the relationship between negligence and recklessness, and his work helped to establish that advertent risk-taking was a possible but not a necessary part of negligence. Liability for negligence is rare in the criminal law, particularly once that term was clearly being used unambiguously from the early twentieth century and perhaps a little earlier. According to Williams:

> Recklessness is a branch of the law of negligence; it is that kind of negligence where there is a foresight of consequences … one must look into the mind of the accused in order to determine whether he foresaw the consequence … One must [then] ask whether in the circumstances a reasonable man having such foresight would have proceeded with his conduct notwithstanding the risk.[120]

This was the first 'double-barrelled', subjective and objective, definition.[121] Williams sustained the same position in the second edition in 1961[122] and 1965 in his *Mental Element in Crime*.[123]

However, most importantly, Williams later separated recklessness from negligence, while retaining the need in recklessness for the risk to be objectively unjustified.[124] In other words, once negligence and recklessness had been yoked together, recklessness thereafter carried an objective component. Other authors in the 1960s were starting to refer to the objective limb of recklessness as well,[125] though some were still slow to do so, including some leading texts.[126] Ultimately, negligence does not require subjective advertence to risk, though the defendant must exercise reasonable care, and that level of care will be informed by what risks were foreseeable and what precautions were reasonable.

---

[120] G Williams, *Criminal Law: The General Part* (London, Stevens & Sons, 1953) 52. His approach to social utility in negligence preceded one of the classic expositions of it by Lord Denning: *Watt v Hertfordshire County Council* [1954] 2 All ER 368 (CA), 371.

[121] Williams, *Criminal Law* 49–59.

[122] G Williams, *Criminal Law: The General Part*, 2nd edn (London, Stevens & Sons, 1961) 59–62.

[123] See also the following spritely exchange: AR White, 'Carelessness, Indifference and Recklessness' (1961) 24 *MLR* 592; PJ Fitzgerald and G Williams, 'Carelessness, Indifference and Recklessness: Two Replies' (1962) 25 *MLR* 49 and 55; AR White, 'Carelessness and Recklessness—Rejoinder' (1962) 25 *MLR* 437.

[124] G Williams, *Textbook of Criminal Law* (London, Stevens & Sons, 1978) 73. See also the second edition (London, Stevens & Sons, 1983) 97–99; and G Williams, 'The Unresolved Problem of Recklessness' (1988) 8 *Legal Studies* 74, 76–77.

[125] D Stuart, 'Mens Rea, Negligence and Attempts' [1968] *Crim LR* 647, 652–53.

[126] JC Smith and B Hogan, *Criminal Law* (London, Butterworths, 1965) 37.

## D. Intention

From this complex picture in the 1960s,[127] the definition of intention was surprisingly returned to its roots in the presumption that a man intended the natural and probable consequences of his act by *DPP v Smith*.[128] A policeman stopped Smith and sought legally to search Smith's car. Smith drove off, but the policeman held on to the bonnet until, having been knocked by other vehicles, he was thrown into the road and killed. The House of Lords decided that an accused was guilty of murder if a reasonable person would have foreseen the possibility of death resulting from his actions and death resulted.[129]

The extensive criticism of *DPP v Smith* led to section 8 of the Criminal Justice Act 1967. While labelled 'proof of criminal intent', it really separated out the two forms of fault:

A court or jury, in determining whether a person has committed an offence—

(a)   shall not be bound in law to infer that he intended or foresaw a result of his actions by reason only of its being a natural and probable consequence of those actions.

Instead, all the evidence available would be appropriate to such a determination. The first significant case after section 8 came into force was *Hyam v DPP* in 1974.[130] There, a disgruntled former girlfriend poured petrol through the letterbox of the home of her ex-partner's new fiancée at night and, without warning; the fiancée escaped, but her two daughters died in the fire. Hyam claimed she only wished to frighten the fiancée into leaving the neighbourhood. The case is similar to *Hancock and Shankland*. A majority of the House of Lords rejected the appeal and affirmed the conviction, holding that 'malice aforethought' was satisfied where the defendant knew that it was probable that at least serious bodily harm would be caused. The majority managed little more agreement than that on the meaning of intention. Lord Hailsham LC thought that intention was different from 'desire' and from foresight of probable consequences, being instead about seeking to bring about a state of affairs;[131] Viscount Dilhorne agreed with Ackner J at first instance that 'highly probable' was sufficient foresight for intention; Lord Cross thought deaths caused by a terrorist's bomb might be sufficiently

---

[127] See generally L Blom-Cooper and T Morris, *With Malice Aforethought* (Oxford, Hart Publishing, 2004) Chs 2–3. The leading case after the Homicide Act 1957 was *R v Vickers* [1957] 2 QB 664 (CA).

[128] *DPP v Smith* [1961] AC 290 (HL).

[129] For an extreme example of how far this presumption could be taken, see *Hardy v Motor Insurers' Bureau* [1964] 2 QB 745 (CA), 763–64, per Pearson LJ (a civil case): every person was presumed to be reasonable, absent other evidence of a condition affecting capacity.

[130] *Hyam v DPP* [1975] AC 55 (HL).

[131] ibid 73–74, citing *Cunliffe v Goodman* [1950] 2 KB 237 (CA), 253, per Asquith LJ.

'intended' even though the terrorist did not know or care if potential victims had evacuated in time;[132] Lord Diplock, who would have allowed the appeal for another reason, saw no difference once the defendant desired or was willing to run the risk of serious harm.[133] A slightly later Court of Appeal decision, *R v Mohan*, hedged its bets, suggesting that foresight of likely consequences could be sufficient for intention, but this would be up to the jury's good sense to decide.[134] After *Hyam* and *Mohan* came *Moloney*, which focused on 'natural' consequences and attempted a model direction.

After *Hancock and Shankland* cleared away *Moloney*'s model direction on 27 February 1986, it was barely four months before the Court of Appeal had to decide another murder case, *R v Nedrick*.[135] *Nedrick* had almost identical facts to *Hyam*, save that here the male defendant has poured paraffin through the letterbox. The trial judge directed that the jury could convict if they found that Nedrick had known that it was highly probable that his actions would cause serious injury. The direction was based on *Archbold's Criminal Pleading, Evidence and Practice*, which erroneously treated *Moloney* and *Hancock and Shankland* as setting a rule of law: that this degree of foresight *was* intention. This was clearly incorrect. The *Moloney* direction had been removed, but nothing had replaced it. Perceiving this gap, Lord Lane CJ set out a model direction for such exceptional cases:

> Where the charge is murder and in the rare cases where the simple direction is not enough, the Jury should be directed that they are not entitled to infer the necessary intention, unless they feel sure that death or serious bodily harm was a virtual certainty (barring some unforeseen intervention) as a result of the defendant's actions and that the defendant appreciated that such was the case.[136]

This decision was widely welcomed by academics, subject to some qualifications.[137] Some of those qualifications were then given effect in *Woollin*, 13 years later.[138] In particular, first, while Lord Lane had still thought Lord Bridge's two initial questions on probability were helpful, *Woollin* rejected them.[139] Second, 'infer' in the second clause was simplified to 'find', in that the jury *may find* intention, but did not have to.[140] Third, the House of Lords also deprecated the suggestion of the Court of Appeal in *Woollin* that

---

[132] *Hyam v DPP* (n 130) 96.

[133] ibid 86.

[134] *R v Mohan* [1976] QB 1, 10–11 (CA).

[135] *R v Nedrick* [1986] 1 WLR 1025 (CA). See, eg, RA Duff, 'The Obscure Intentions of the House of Lords' [1986] *Crim LR* 771.

[136] *Nedrick* (n 135) 1028. A direction requiring a 'very high probability' was not a material misdirection in *R v Walker and Hayles* (1990) 90 Cr App R 226 (CA).

[137] See JC Smith's commentary on Nedrick [1986] *Crim LR* 742, 743–44; G Williams, 'The Mens Rea for Murder: Leave it Alone' (1989) 105 *LQR* 387; JR Spencer, 'Murder in the Dark: A Glimmer of Light?' [1986] *CLJ* 366–67.

[138] *Woollin* (n 6). See, eg, AW Norrie, 'After Woollin' [1999] *Crim LR* 532.

[139] *Woollin* (n 6) 87, 96.

[140] Confirmed in *R v Matthews and Alleyn* [2003] 2 Cr App R 30 (CA).

the 'virtual certainty' direction should only be given where the evidence is solely of the admitted actions of the accused; such a distinction was vague and unhelpful in an area of law clearly in need of certainty.[141]

*Hancock and Shankland* was the groundwork for the modern law in *Nedrick* and *Woollin*. Yet the House of Lords failed to fully define intention. Ultimately, *Nedrick* and *Woollin* put the law where it should have been if *Hancock and Shankland* had simply gone as far as it should have done. All that was needed was 'little short of overwhelming' from *Moloney* to be transformed into the slightly more manageable 'virtual certainty', as *Nedrick* did.[142]

## E. Manslaughter?

When a man was taken to intend the natural consequences of his actions, only 'unnatural' consequences might be pushed into manslaughter charges. However, once precision in the fault element for murder was desired but not yet attained, manslaughter would have been a simpler alternative for prosecutors and juries.[143] It was relatively well established from the nineteenth century onwards that neither of the two most significant forms of involuntary manslaughter (gross negligence manslaughter and unlawful act manslaughter) required the defendant to advert to the risk of death.[144] Nonetheless, in *DPP v Newbury*,[145] the DPP supported an application to the House of Lords to settle the question of whether any foresight of death was required for manslaughter. The irony is that within 30 miles of Rhymney, another bridge and another slab had, only in 1976, been the trigger for another House of Lords decision on homicide, this time manslaughter. Two 15-year-old boys had pushed a loose paving slab off a bridge and onto the path of an oncoming train. The slab went through a glass window and killed the guard. The boys were convicted of manslaughter and sentenced to five years in prison. The boys appealed, ultimately to the House of Lords, arguing that manslaughter required the defendants to foresee a risk of death. The House rejected the appeal without even calling on the Crown as respondents.[146]

---

[141] *Woollin* (n 6) 95.

[142] After *Nedrick*, Lord Goff suggested, extra-judicially, that consciously taking a lethal risk should be a sufficient fault element for murder: Lord Goff, 'The Mental Element in the Crime of Murder' (1988) 104 *LQR* 30, to which Glanville Williams responded with trenchant criticism: Williams, 'The Mens Rea for Murder'.

[143] Spencer, 'Murder in the Dark' 162.

[144] eg, *R v Fenton* (1830) 1 Lew CC 179, 168 ER 100; and *R v Larkin* (1944) 29 Cr App R 18 (CA), 23 (which does not appear in the shorter report in the Official Reports: [1943] KB 174).

[145] *Newbury* (n 58).

[146] Including, as junior counsel, John Prosser, later counsel for Shankland.

## VI. CONCLUSION

*Hancock and Shankland* is a leading case in the development of the modern law of fault in homicide. It played a significant role in pushing deliberate risk-taking almost completely out of *intention*, being instead diverted into recklessness and, to some extent, negligence. Its political context is a reason for its notoriety, but probably not for its legal outcome.

However, *Hancock and Shankland* was an incomplete step, as it did not move fully away from general references to 'probability', nor did it settle on a precise model direction for juries. In *Woollin*, the House of Lords thought it unhelpful *not* to give a detailed direction to a jury on intention, especially by 'deflect[ing] such questions by the statement that "intention" is an ordinary word in the English language'.[147] The House of Lords had clearly changed in the 13 years since *Hancock and Shankland*, where they had thought no detailed direction necessary, forcing Lord Lane CJ to give one just six months later in the Court of Appeal in *Nedrick*.

In addition, some further problems remain. One is on the moral difference between foresight and intention. Another is what juries really do when they 'may' find intention under the *Woollin* test. Finally, questions remain about the role of the defendant's purpose: whether the defendant must, having a desire or belief in an outcome, act because of that desire or belief. This is a difficult question which has so far been pushed out of doctrinal legal work and court decisions. Yet if the defendant foresees an outcome, but that outcome plays no role in the choice to act, then even if that outcome was independently welcomed by the defendant, did the defendant intend that outcome? For these questions, we do not yet have answers in substantive law. Legislative answers are not forthcoming, even though there are plenty of Criminal Justice Bills. If these situations do arise for courts, lower courts are likely to continue to leave the question to the good sense, albeit not literal interpretation, of the jury. As to what the Supreme Court would make of it, we can only wait for a landmark like *Hancock and Shankland*. It would be better if we did not require a death to make our law clearer.[148]

---

[147] *Woollin* (n 6) 92.

[148] A point made forcefully even at the time: JR Spencer, 'Murder in the Dark' 164–65; similarly in calling for a criminal code: ATH Smith, 'Codification of the Criminal Law—Part 1: The Case for a Code' [1986] *Crim LR* 285, 287 fn 5. *cf* Celia Wells, 'Codification of the Criminal Law—Part 4: Restatement or Reform' [1986] *Crim LR* 314, 321 fn 37.

# 15

# R v Howe (1987)

## FINDLAY STARK*

IN *R v Howe*,[1] the House of Lords held that duress is no defence to murder.[2] The Lords relied upon three main arguments: (1) the Heroism Argument—citizens can legitimately be expected to sacrifice their own lives heroically rather than take an innocent third party's on the orders of a duressor; (2) the Terrorism Argument—duress must be unavailable lest terrorists or organised criminals cajole innocent citizens into carrying out murders; and (3) the Competence Argument—courts should defer to the legislature when developing the common law in an area where doctrine is relatively clear and the issues raised are viewed properly as controversial.

Textbooks tend to focus on Lord Hailsham's endorsement of the Heroism Argument, and its reliance on upholding the sanctity of life.[3] The Lords have been chastised for endorsing a 'blueprint for saintliness'.[4] This chapter seeks to rehabilitate the decision in *Howe* by arguing that it should be identified more with the Competence Argument. Given the relatively stable nature of the law on duress and murder before *Howe*, the inherent epistemic and deliberative limitations placed on criminal courts, and the fraught

* Thanks are due to Kathy Young for assistance in locating some sources, and to Ross Carrick, James Chalmers, Philip Handler, Henry Mares and the participants at the Landmark Cases in Criminal Law workshop for their comments on earlier versions. Sources marked 'TNA' are located in the National Archives at Kew. TNA files relating to the cases are: J287/262 (information concerning Howe and Bannister's trial), J82/4304 (Court of Appeal files relating to *Howe and Bannister*) and J82/4282 (Court of Appeal files relating to *Burke and Clarkson*). The Parliamentary Archives hold limited records relating to the appeal to the House of Lords, under references HL/PO/JO10/11/2358, HL/PO/JU/4/3/1596 and HL/PO/JU/4/3/1597.

[1] *R v Howe* [1987] AC 417 (HL).

[2] Other issues before the Lords will not be considered here.

[3] See, eg, AP Simester et al, *Simester and Sullivan's Criminal Law: Theory and Doctrine*, 6th edn (Oxford, Hart Publishing, 2016) 765 (*cf* 853–57); J Horder, Ashworth's *Principles of Criminal Law*, 8th edn (Oxford, Oxford University Press, 2016) 235–36; W Wilson, *Criminal Law*, 5th edn (Harlow, Pearson, 2014) 257; J Herring, *Criminal Law: Text, Cases and Materials* (Oxford, Oxford University Press, 2014) 654–55. *cf* D Ormerod and K Laird, *Smith and Hogan's Criminal Law* (Oxford, Oxford University Press, 2015) 407–08.

[4] JC Smith, *Justification and Excuse in the Criminal Law* (London, Stevens & Sons, 1989) 93.

issues of morality and politics involved in decisions about when killing is not criminal, the Lords' decision is defensible.

Section I presents the facts of the conjoined appeals at issue in *Howe*. Section II then outlines the development of the law on duress and murder beforehand. Section III moves to consider the trial and appellate proceedings in *Howe*. Section IV concludes by considering the aftermath of the Lords' decision.

## I. TWO 'TRULY HORRIBLE CASES'[5]

*Howe* involved two conjoined appeals. In the first, *Howe and Bannister*, Howe (19) and Bannister (20) became associated with Bailey (19) and Murray (35). As well as being significantly older, Murray's 25 previous court appearances for offences including actual bodily harm and robbery dwarfed the others' convictions for road traffic and property offences.

The group's first victim, Elgar (17), was lured to a public lavatory. There, Murray revealed Elgar to be a 'grass' and ordered him to be killed. Howe and Bannister assaulted Elgar, before Bailey strangled him to death. Howe, Bannister and Murray were charged as accomplices to murder, given their encouragement of Bailey. Similar events unfolded the next day. Howe and Bannister strangled the second victim, Pollitt (19), each pulling on the end of one of Bannister's shoelaces that had been tied around Pollitt's neck.[6] Howe and Bannister were charged with murder as principals, and Murray and Bailey were alleged accessories. The next day, the third intended victim, Redfern (22), escaped. The defendants were charged with conspiring to murder him.[7]

When interviewed, Howe, Bannister and Bailey claimed to have been coerced by Murray: 'I was told it was me or him so I killed him';[8] 'I had to take part or else it would have been me next'.[9] They refused to be near Murray at the police station, citing their fear of him.[10] Murray claimed that Bailey was the violent member of the group.[11]

The second case, *Burke and Clarkson*, similarly involved an older, violent man influencing someone much younger.[12] ('Kid') Burke (18) had an

---

[5] *Howe* (n 1) 423.

[6] There was a suggestion that Pollitt was a 'sacrifice' to allow Howe and Bannister to join a gang: 'Beauty Spot Victim a "Sacrifice"' *The Times* (London, 24 January 1985) 2.

[7] The defendants had, before being apprehended, also engaged in some handbag thefts and an attempted robbery: TNA: PRO J 82/4303, 765/R/85 (advice on appeal for Michael Antony Howe) 1.

[8] TNA: PRO J 287/262/1, S.18.A.74 (statement by DC Bowler, 17 October 1983) 3.

[9] TNA: PRO J 287/262/1, S.32.A.7 (statement by DCI Short, 15 October 1983) 2.

[10] TNA: PRO J 287/262/2, SS3.A126 (statement by DS Flaherty, 17 October 1983) 3.

[11] TNA: PRO J 287/262/3, A.243 S31B (statement by DS Hall, 10 November 1983) 5.

[12] Most of the details in this paragraph are taken from TNA: PRO J 82/4282 (letter from David Tudor Price, Common Serjeant of London, to Leon Brittan MP, Secretary of State for Home Affairs) 1–2.

'unhappy and disturbed background'.[13] He eventually came to live with ('Billy') Clarkson (37). Clarkson began to school Burke in crimes of dishonesty. Botton (63), 'a "general dealer" with a long criminal record who was associated in the 1960s with the Kray and Richardson gangs',[14] was to give evidence against Clarkson in a trial relating to a conspiracy to steal videos. Clarkson ordered Burke to kill Botton and supplied him with a shotgun. Dressed in his brother's security guard uniform (so as to look like a policeman), Burke approached Botton's house and shot him. He claimed that the gun went off by accident, but also that he was acting out of fear of Clarkson.

The defendants' stories will be left here for now. The next section charts the development of the law on duress and murder up until their trials. This context will explain the courses taken by the trial judges and the arguments utilised in the appellate proceedings.

## II. THE LAW BEFORE *HOWE*

### A. Principals

In a 1493 debate in the Inns of Court, it was suggested that 'if someone by my command, on pain of his life, kills someone else, I am the felon and the principal, and the other is no felon, because I am the person who has directed the blow'.[15] Spain reads this remark to suggest that duress was a defence to murder.[16] The statement appears following an explanation of how the law attributes the consequences of the operation of traps to the person who set them intending to cause harm. Just as the 'acts' of the trap are attributed to the person who set it, the perpetrator's act is attributed to the duressor. Rather than recognising a positive defence, then, the law simply disregards the perpetrator's agency.

If the 1493 debate recognised that a coerced killer would not be guilty of murder, by Hale's time, the legal position had changed. For Hale, the coerced citizen 'ought rather to die himself, than kill an innocent'.[17] This is an example of the Heroism Argument, but Hale also appeals to something like the Terrorism Argument: in peacetime, citizens should seek the law's protection rather than be used by the duressor to commit murder.[18] Later

---

[13] ibid 1.

[14] '"Billy and the Kid" Killers Get Life' *The Times* (London, 17 October 1984) 4.

[15] SE Thorne and JH Baker (eds), *Readings and Moots at the Inns of Court*, vol 105 (London, Selden Society, 1990) 274.

[16] E Spain, *The Role of Emotions in Criminal Law Defences: Duress, Necessity and Lesser Evils* (Cambridge, Cambridge University Press, 2011) 231.

[17] M Hale, *Historia Placitorum Coronæ: The History of Pleas of the Crown* (London, E&R Nutt, 1736) 51.

[18] ibid 49.

authors repeated Hale's view of the law, without much discussion of its rationale.[19] An exception is Stephen, who justified the exclusion of duress in murder with the Terrorism Argument: the law must 'speak most clearly and emphatically' to citizens who might be tempted by threats to act as agents for 'associations of malefactors'.[20]

It is worth noting in passing that a similar rule regarding 'necessity' and murder was recognised in *Dudley and Stephens*,[21] largely on the basis of the Heroism Argument.[22] The employment of the Heroism Argument explains why *Dudley and Stephens* was mentioned in *Howe*,[23] but the case need not be discussed further here.

The position with regard to principals was thus largely consistent by the end of the nineteenth century: duress was no defence to murder. The position of accessories proved more controversial.

## B.  Accessories (1838–1975)

Early cases involving accessories attempting to plead duress in relation to murder must be treated with caution because they all involved defendants who had voluntarily associated with the duressor. The 1838 decision in *Tyler and Price*[24] made clear that 'no man, from a fear of consequence to himself, has the right to make himself a party to committing mischief on mankind'.[25] The defendants in that case had no defence to murder because they had originally *voluntarily* become associated with their duressor when it was foreseeable that violent coercion could follow.[26] This voluntary association rule was stated as a general proposition, not simply a rule about murder.

The voluntary association rule was not always relied on expressly in duress and murder cases. In *Sephakela*,[27] there was evidence that the defendant remained present during the planning and performance of a ritualistic killing, passing up opportunities to escape in the intervening week. Had this evidence been accepted, the voluntary association rule could have been

---

[19] *cf* W Blackstone, *Commentaries on the Laws of England in Four Books*, vol 2, bk IV (Oxford, Clarendon Press, 1765–69) 30.

[20] JF Stephen, *A History of the Criminal Law of England* (London, Macmillan, 1883) 107.

[21] *R v Dudley and Stephens* (1884) 14 QBD 273 (QB).

[22] ibid 287–88.

[23] *Howe* (n 1) 429, 454.

[24] *R v Tyler and Price* (1838) 8 C&P 616 (QB).

[25] ibid 620.

[26] G Williams, *Criminal Law: The General Part*, 2nd edn (London, Stephens, 1961) 759–60. See, further, *R v Hasan* [2005] UKHL 22, [2005] 2 AC 467.

[27] Two useful accounts of the facts are 'Reasons for Dismissing Ritual Murder Appeal' *The Times* (London, 13 July 1954) 1 and *Sephakela* (1954) HCTLR 60 (PC), 60. See also *Sephakela* [1954] Crim LR 723 (PC).

applied.[28] The Privy Council nevertheless had misgivings about whether the defendant had been present during the planning of the killing.[29] It concluded that 'the evidence fell far short of' establishing duress,[30] on the alternative basis that there was no evidence of a specific threat to the defendant.[31] It is illogical to consider whether evidence exists of a defence that the law does not recognise.[32] *Sephakela* thus appears to be the first—implicit—recognition of the defence of duress for secondary parties to murder. The decision is nevertheless barely mentioned in later cases.[33]

*Rossides*[34] is a similarly overlooked decision. The defendant shot a British soldier, who was then hit with a spade. It was unclear whether the bullet or the spade killed the soldier. Rossides argued that the defence of duress should have been available if the spade was found to have caused death, as he was then a mere accessory. Section 16 of the Cyprus Criminal Code excluded duress in murder cases, but said nothing about the principal/accessory distinction. The Cyprus Court of Appeal rejected the defendant's argument because of a lack of evidence *and* his voluntary association with a Cypriot terrorist group.[35] The Privy Council dismissed his application for leave to appeal without giving reasons. It is thus difficult to discern the Privy Council's attitude towards his duress argument:[36] was it simply that voluntary association rendered duress unavailable? Like *Sephakela*, *Rossides* has been virtually ignored in later cases.[37]

The next developments occurred closer to home. In *Kray*,[38] a man named Barry had aided a murder by providing a gun to the killer. On appeal, Widgery LCJ described Barry's duress defence, which had succeeded at trial, as 'viable'.[39] Widgery LCJ's comment is nevertheless dubious, perhaps explaining why *Kray* generated little contemporary comment.[40] First, the Crown conceded that duress was available. Second, Barry associated voluntarily with his duressors, and the *Tyler and Price* rule should presumably have

[28] The rule was applied by the trial judge: *Sephakela* (1954) HCTLR 60 (PC) (n 27) 60.

[29] ibid 61.

[30] *Sephakela v R* [1954] Crim LR 723, 723.

[31] *Sephakela* (n 28) 63–64.

[32] *R v Brown and Morley* [1968] SASR 467 (Supreme Court of South Australia), 495–496.

[33] In *DPP for Northern Ireland v Lynch* [1975] AC 654 (HL), Lords Morris and Edmund-Davies viewed *Sephakela* as inconclusive regarding duress and murder (at 676 and 714). Lord Wilberforce thought the decision assumed that duress was available to accessories (683). *Sephakela* is cited, but not discussed, in *Howe* (n 1) 451.

[34] *Rossides v R* [1957] Crim LR 813 (PC).

[35] *Rossides* (1957) 22 Cyprus Law Reports 137 (Cyprus CA), 143.

[36] The argument certainly was discussed by counsel: see 'Soldier's Body Found Buried in a Field; Cypriot Murderer Refused Special Leave to Appeal' *The Times* (London, 3 October 1957) 6.

[37] *Rossides* was merely cited in *Lynch* (n 33) 683 and mentioned by counsel in *R v Howe* [1986] QB 626 (CA), 634. It was not mentioned in *Howe* (n 1).

[38] *R v Kray* (1969) 53 Cr App R 569 (CA). The Law Reports version ([1970] 1 QB 125) does not include discussion of duress.

[39] ibid 578.

[40] *cf* JC Smith, 'A Note on Duress' [1974] *Crim LR* 349.

applied, rendering his duress defence incompetent.[41] Third, Barry also argued that he lacked mens rea: thinking the gun defective, he did not intend to assist the murder.

Support later emerged for going further than *Kray*, though, and making duress available to all parties to murder. Opinions differed on whether duress should result in a complete acquittal[42] or a conviction for manslaughter,[43] demonstrating the difficult tensions raised by this topic (a theme to which we will return below). In 1974, the Law Commission's Working Party rejected the Heroism Argument and proposed making duress a full defence to murder for principals and accessories.[44] Voluntary association would continue to result in the forfeiture of the defence if the defendant had been *aware* of the risk of compulsion.[45] The Working Party's proposals were not taken forward before the next relevant decisions.

## C. Accessories (1975–87)

### i. Lynch

In *DPP for Northern Ireland v Lynch*,[46] the defendant claimed to have been instructed by the IRA to act as a driver. Lynch feared that he and his family would be harmed if he refused.[47] Lynch drove the terrorists to a garage, where they killed a policeman.

On the version of the facts given by the appellate courts, *Lynch* is the first secondary party murder case involving a defendant who was not at fault for voluntarily associating with his duressor. Although duress had been left to the jury in the similar *attempted* murder case of *Fagan*,[48] the trial judge refused to allow Lynch to rely on it. A majority of the Court of Appeal in Northern Ireland upheld this decision, distinguishing *Kray* on the basis that Barry was an 'accessory before the fact', not a 'principal in the second degree'.[49] Before its abolition in 1968,[50] this distinction turned on whether assistance or encouragement was given at the scene of a felony or beforehand—an absurdly technical basis upon which to distinguish *Kray*.

---

[41] *Howe* (n 1) 441.

[42] CC Turpin, 'Duress and Murder' (1972) 30 *CLJ* 202.

[43] R Miers, 'Duress as a Defence to Murder' (1974) 25 *Northern Ireland Legal Quarterly* 464, 477; RS O'Regan, 'Duress and Murder' (1972) 35 *MLR* 596, 605.

[44] Law Commission, *Defences of General Application* (Law Com Working Paper No 55, 1974) para 25.

[45] ibid, para 26.

[46] *Lynch* (n 33).

[47] Threatening citizens in this way was apparently a common IRA strategy: RAG O'Brien, 'Compelled to Abet Murder' (1975) 48–49 *Law & Justice—The Christian Law Review* 86, 86.

[48] *Fagan* (Belfast City Commission, 20 September 1974).

[49] *Lynch* [1975] NI 35 (CANI), 50.

[50] Criminal Law Act 1967, s 1.

On appeal, a majority of the House of Lords decided that duress *should* have been left to the jury. Lords Morris, Wilberforce and Edmund-Davies questioned the realism of the Heroism Argument, recognising the impact of the 'miserable, agonising'[51] circumstances in which the IRA could place ordinary citizens. In January 1972, when the murder had been committed, the IRA had conducted a spree of shootings and nail-bombings, and thus it was plausible that death or serious injury might be visited upon uncoopera-tive citizens.[52] If the defendant had shown a reasonable level of restraint in the light of this threat, then the majority thought convicting him would be unfair.[53] The context of Northern Irish terrorism meant, for the majority, that the law should be *relaxed*. The Terrorism Argument was, in essence, turned on its head.

For the minority (Lords Kilbrandon and Simon), the Competence Argu-ment stood in the way of allowing duress in murder cases.[54] Weighing in favour of the majority's decision were suspicious sources such as *Sephakela*, *Kray*[55] and—by extension—the trial judge's decision regarding attempted murder in *Fagan*. Against the majority's view were the clear statements by the early writers (who did not distinguish between different levels of partici-pation in murder) and *Dudley and Stephens*.[56] In such circumstances, the extension of the duress defence to explicitly cover secondary parties would be to overstep the legitimate boundaries of the judicial role.

The minority considered the possibility of duress reducing murder to manslaughter under the defence of diminished responsibility. However, the stumbling block was diminished responsibility's requirement of an 'abnor-mality of mind'.[57] If duress were to fit under diminished responsibility, this requirement would need to be altered, and only Parliament could make that alteration.[58] Given the significance of the change that this extension of diminished responsibility would have represented, the strength of the posi-tion on principals, and the thin authority supporting the majority's view on accessories, the minority's conclusion is defensible. A useful analogy could be drawn here with *Myers v DPP*,[59] where it was held that the exceptions to the exclusionary hearsay rule were closed at common law by the 1960s. The majority of the Lords in *Myers* decried modern 'judicial legislation', in favour of parliamentary intervention, particularly where judicial intervention

---

[51] *Lynch* (n 33) 670

[52] R English, *Armed Struggle: The History of the IRA* (London, Macmillan, 2012) 148.

[53] *Lynch* (n 33) 670, 685, 715–16.

[54] ibid 695–96.

[55] See also *R v Hudson and Taylor* [1971] 2 QB 202 (CA), 206 (another obiter statement by Widgery LCJ).

[56] *Lynch* (n 33) 692.

[57] Homicide Act 1957, s 2(1) (diminished responsibility was redefined, but not in ways relevant to this chapter, by s 52 of the Coroners and Justice Act 2009).

[58] *Lynch* (n 33) 697, 703–04.

[59] *Myers v DPP* [1965] AC 1001 (HL).

would produce uncertainty.[60] Uncertainty was the inevitable result of the majority's decision in *Lynch*, given the slim authority for it and the inconsistent treatment of principals and accessories. The majority did little to meet the Competence Argument.

The minority also took a different view from the majority on the Terrorism Argument. The fact that violence was likely to be threatened against ordinary citizens was, for them, a reason for the law's view to be *stricter* in order to avoid it becoming a 'charter for terrorists, gang-leaders and kidnappers'.[61]

Lynch was retried and convicted of murder. This result demonstrated that the requirements of duress, and jury scepticism, would be impediments to the development of a 'charter for terrorists, gang-leaders and kidnappers'. This point, together with the existence of the voluntary association rule, went some way towards meeting the Terrorism Argument, but left the Competence Argument unscathed.

### ii. Abbott

The distinction between principals and accessories caused by *Lynch* was criticised, and the Lords were urged to go further and allow duress to function as a defence to all parties to murder.[62] The opportunity to consider doing so arose soon.

In *Abbott*,[63] the defendant helped kill a woman by burying her alive. At trial, the defendant was not allowed to argue that he acted out of fear of the leader of the commune where he lived. When *Abbott* came before the Privy Council, a collision course with *Lynch* could have been avoided. Abbott had voluntarily associated with the violent leader. Furthermore, in *Lynch*, both Lords Morris and Wilberforce left open the question of how principals should be treated.[64] Only Lord Edmund-Davies suggested (hesitantly) that principals should be able to plead duress in murder cases.[65] The majority in *Abbott* (Lord Hailsham LC and Lords Kilbrandon and Salmon) nevertheless took the opportunity to signal their view that the majority's decision in *Lynch* was wrong.[66]

The majority was clearly influenced by the Terrorism Argument:

> We are not living in a dream world in which the mounting wave of violence and terrorism can be contained by strict logic and intellectual niceties alone. Common

---

[60] ibid 1021.

[61] *Lynch* (n 33) 688.

[62] L Walters, 'Duress—Precedent, Principle and the House of Lords' (1986) 136 *New Law Journal* 959, 959. *cf* PR Glazebrook, 'Committing Murder under Duress' (1975) 34 *CLJ* 185.

[63] *Abbott v R* [1977] AC 755 (PC).

[64] *Lynch* (n 33) 669, 671, 685.

[65] ibid 715.

[66] See, further, JW Harris, 'The Privy Council and the Common Law' (1990) 106 *LQR* 574, 577–78.

sense surely reveals the added dangers to which in this modern world the public would be exposed, if the change in the law proposed on behalf of the appellant were effected.[67]

There are also hints of the Competence Argument in the majority's opinion:

> Judges have no power to create new criminal offences; nor ... have they the power to invent a new defence to murder which is entirely contrary to fundamental legal doctrine accepted for hundreds of years ... If a policy change of such a fundamental nature were to be made it could, in their Lordships' view, be made only by Parliament.[68]

The dissentients in *Abbott* had been members of the majority in *Lynch*. Lords Wilberforce (who left open the question of what to do with principals) and Edmund-Davies (who had suggested that principals should have access to duress) emphasised that there was no time to wait for parliamentary intervention; Abbott's was a capital case.[69] This points to an unwelcome side-effect of the Competence Argument, insofar as it can be insensitive to the circumstances of an individual case.

Even without the context of capital punishment, the minority saw no reason to distinguish between principals and accessories, viewing the balance of authority only *just* pointing against the defence's availability.[70] Perhaps sensing the weakness of this argument in relation to *principals*, the minority added that the balance of 'sound ... law and better ethics' pointed towards making the defence available to all parties to murder.[71] Ultimately, juries would reject the defence in unmeritorious cases,[72] as they had done at Lynch's retrial. This reply also does nothing to meet the Competence Argument.

As the 1970s progressed, the voluntary association rule rendered *Lynch* of narrow application. Duress was withheld in cases where an accessory to a murder had joined a violent organisation voluntarily.[73] The concerns voiced by the minority in *Lynch* and the majority in *Abbott* regarding an increase in problematic acquittals/non-prosecutions (which motivated the Terrorism Argument) did not materialise.

Following *Abbott*, criticisms of the 'absurd and illogical'[74] principal/accessory distinction were repeated with added gusto: the distinction was

---

[67] *Abbott* (n 63) 766–67. The majority's separate comments regarding war crimes might also be read to endorse the Heroism Argument.
[68] ibid 767. See also 768.
[69] ibid 769.
[70] ibid 772.
[71] ibid.
[72] ibid 773.
[73] *R v Fitzpatrick* [1977] NI 20 (CANI); *R v Calderwood and Moore* [1983] NIJB 10 (CCNI).
[74] I Dennis, 'Duress, Murder and Criminal Responsibility' (1980) 96 *LQR* 208, 218.

apparently now endorsed by the Privy Council.[75] Confusion followed. In the aftermath of *Abbott*, there were Crown concessions allowing principals to plead duress[76] and aberrant trial judge decisions to the same effect.[77] There was little consensus about what the legal position should be, again hinting at the tensions raised by the topic of duress and murder (tensions that ought to have strengthened the Competence Argument). The first proposed option was to withhold duress in all murder cases.[78] The second option was to allow duress to 'reduce' murder to manslaughter.[79] The third option was to allow duress to be a defence to all parties to a murder.[80] No reforms took place before the proceedings in *Howe* were under way.

## III. THE PROCEEDINGS IN *HOWE*

### A. The Trials

Bailey and Murray pleaded guilty. Following *Lynch*, the trial judge allowed Howe and Bannister to rely on duress in relation to the killing of Elgar and the conspiracy to kill Redfern. The trial judge refused, following *Abbott*, to leave the defence of duress in relation to the killing of Pollitt, on the basis that the defendants were principals. He explained to the jury that 'No reasonable man would kill under duress'[81] and adverted to the voluntary association rule.[82] The jury convicted the defendants on all three counts after 80 minutes of deliberation.[83]

The trial judge in Burke's case similarly directed the jury that 'No threat, however grave, would excuse the gunman who deliberately shoots his victim dead'[84] and mentioned voluntary association.[85] The trial judge allowed Burke to plead duress in relation only to manslaughter *if* the jury reasonably doubted that the shooting was a voluntary act. Burke and Clarkson were convicted of murder.[86] The trial judge, the Common Serjeant of London,

---

[75] PR Glazebrook, 'Committing Murder under Duress—Again' (1976) 35 *CLJ* 206; JC Smith and B Hogan, *Criminal Law*, 4th edn (London: Butterworths, 1978) 201–02.

[76] *R v Graham* [1982] 1 WLR 294 (CA).

[77] *R v Gillard and King* (Exeter Crown Court, 28 July 1983).

[78] A Kenny, 'Duress *Per Minas* as a Defence to Crime: II' (1982) 1 *Law & Philosophy* 197.

[79] Lord Kilbrandon, 'Duress *Per Minas* as a Defence to Crime: I' (1982) 1 *Law & Philosophy* 185, 194–95. Lord Kilbrandon was a member of the minority in *Lynch*.

[80] Law Commission, *Defences of General Application* (Law Com No 83, 1977) paras 2.39–2.44.

[81] TNA J82/4304, 765/R/85 (transcript of judge's ruling re duress and summing up) 35.

[82] ibid 40.

[83] 'Teenagers' Killers Get Life' *The Times* (London, 29 Jan 1985) 5.

[84] TNA J82/4282, 6193/R/84 (transcript of submissions and summing up) 29.

[85] ibid 43–45.

[86] Clarkson received a (comparatively) long minimum term (25 years): '"Billy and the Kid" Killers Get Life' *The Times* (London, 17 October 1984) 4.

clearly had reservations about Burke's blameworthiness, explaining in a letter to the Home Secretary that 'Burke was completely under the evil influence and domination of Clarkson. It was something like immature hero worship', but accepting that: 'There should be punishment and retribution for [Burke's] wicked and deliberate act.'[87]

## B. The Court of Appeal

The Terrorism Argument motivated the Court of Appeal's rejection of a defence of duress for principals. Expanding the reach of duress was seen as 'highly dangerous', given the difficulties of proving beyond reasonable doubt that a defence was a fabrication, and the threat from terrorists.[88] Indeed, it was suggested that terrorist attacks might *increase* if duress were available—the same citizen could be used multiple times by terrorists, gaining skills with each murder. The court concluded that: 'Either the law should be left as it is or the defence of duress should be denied to anyone charged with murder.'[89]

The Court of Appeal's decision was poorly received. *Abbott*'s distinction between principals and accessories was 'alarming', but denying the defence to all defendants charged with murder was seen as worse.[90] The court's reliance on the Terrorism Argument was deemed 'naïve instrumentalism'.[91] Indeed, it might be thought that the threat of immediate death or serious injury from terrorists or organised criminals is likely to trump the threat of possible life imprisonment.[92]

## C. The House of Lords

When the conjoined cases reached the House of Lords, it was noted (in agreement with contemporary academic opinion) that the principal/accessory distinction resulting from *Lynch* and *Abbott* was 'vacuous'.[93] As Lord Griffiths noted, accessories might even be more culpable than principals[94]—Murray

---

[87] Letter (n 12) 3. I am grateful to Peter Glazebrook for explaining that such letters were written to assist the Home Secretary in setting the tariff.

[88] *Howe* (n 37) 641.

[89] ibid.

[90] HP Milgate, 'Murder and the Killer Who Acts under Duress' (1986) 45 *CLJ* 183, 184.

[91] SJ Bone and LA Rutherford, 'Murder under Duress—Awaiting the Final Word' (1986) 50 *Journal of Criminal Law* 257, 262.

[92] R Mullender, 'Murder, Attempted Murder, and the Defence of Duress: Some Objections to the Present State of the Law' (1993) 25 *Bracton Law Journal* 15, 15.

[93] R Campbell, 'Duress and Responsibility for Action' (1984) 1 *Journal of Applied Philosophy* 133, 138; *Howe* (n 1) 437.

[94] *Howe* (n 1) 445.

and Clarkson are good examples. The question was, then, what the House should do to bring more consistency to the law, whilst remaining within constitutional bounds. In deciding that *Lynch* should be departed from, the Lords relied on the Heroism, Terrorism and Competence Arguments. The next subsections analyse their treatment of each argument.

### i. The Heroism Argument

Lord Hailsham endorsed the Heroism Argument. His opinion is dogged by his failure to note the distinction, which was recognised by English academics and judges by the late 1980s,[95] between justifications and excuses. The justificatory aspects of Lord Hailsham's opinion arise from his conceptualisation of duress as a 'lesser evils' defence.[96] If a person chooses the 'lesser' of two evils, then presumably he does not do wrong; he is justified. Given that the defendant in the standard duress case would be choosing his life over another person's, Lord Hailsham held that he could not plausibly be choosing the lesser evil; he could only be choosing an equal evil and would thus lack a justification.

This example can, however, be complicated in two ways, neither of which was discussed convincingly by Lord Hailsham. First, the numbers of people involved can be changed. At some stage, what is referred to as the 'deontological threshold' might be met, where a net saving of life becomes permissible or at least not blameworthy.[97] A terrorist could threaten to explode a bomb in a busy shopping centre unless a citizen kills an innocent third party. If the bomb puts the lives of 400 other innocent third parties at risk, then perhaps committing one murder *is* the 'lesser evil'. In other legal systems, this might be where the defence of 'necessity' would come to the rescue, but it probably cannot in England and Wales because of *Dudley and Stephens*.

Second, the relationship between the parties involved can be altered. A citizen's entire family is threatened unless he participates in one murder.[98] Is it truly the 'lesser evil' to allow his (innocent) family of four to be slaughtered in order to save the life of an innocent stranger identified by the duressor as the target? It is not clear that the defendant is engaging in 'greater' evil even where he kills an equal number of strangers (in this example, four).[99]

Until now, consideration has turned simply on the equal sanctity and number of lives involved in an example. Can the 'innocence' of the third party that the defendant is ordered to kill help? No—in the absence of prior

[95] See, eg, *Lynch* (n 33) 673.
[96] *Howe* (n 1) 433. See also Williams, *Criminal Law* 760.
[97] See L Alexander, 'Deontology at the Threshold' (2000) 37 *San Diego Law Review* 893.
[98] H Milgate, 'Duress and the Criminal Law: Another About Turn by the House of Lords' (1988) 47 *CLJ* 61, 68.
[99] C Gearty, '*Howe* to Be a Hero' (1987) 46 *CLJ* 203, 205.

fault in being threatened by a duressor, the defendant is just as 'innocent' as the targeted third party.[100] It is not clear what, other than luck, renders the defendant, rather than the innocent third party, liable to die. An impasse appears to be reached. Contrast this with a case where the defendant is *at fault* for being in a situation where he is threatened with death if he does not commit murder. Here, the defendant lacks total 'innocence', and the lesser evil might well be his laying down his life.[101] But such cases are typically dealt with by the voluntary association rule.[102] No additional rule regarding murder is required.

The above-mentioned points address the matter of whether a *justification* should be given to the coerced defendant accused of murder. Even if someone does engage in wrongdoing, it is not necessarily a fait accompli that she is to be blamed—this is the function of excuses,[103] and duress is typically recognised as an excuse.[104] The idea underlying duress is that *reasonable* wrongdoing, in response to a threat of death or serious injury, should not be punished because the defendant's wrongdoing reflects nothing meaningful about her general motivational structure,[105] removing the firm foundation of blame that should be required for a criminal conviction.

Lord Hailsham's answer to this point leads to his invocation of the Heroism Argument:

> In general, I must say that I do not at all accept in relation to the defence of [duress in] murder it is either good morals, good policy or good law to suggest, as did the majority in *Lynch* and the minority in *Abbott* that the ordinary man of reasonable fortitude is not to be supposed to be capable of heroism if he is asked to take an innocent life rather than sacrifice his own. I have known in my own lifetime of too many acts of heroism by ordinary human beings of no more than ordinary fortitude to regard a law as either 'just or humane' which withdraws the protection of the criminal law from the innocent victim and casts the cloak of its protection upon the coward and the poltroon in the name of a 'concession to human frailty'.[106]

In short, it *is* reasonable to act like a hero when coerced into committing murder. Any citizen who fails to act heroically in such circumstances cannot

---

[100]  CL Carr, 'Duress and Criminal Responsibility' (1991) 10 *Law & Philosophy* 161, 173.

[101]  H Wechsler and A Michael, 'A Rationale of the Law of Homicide: I' (1937) 37 *Columbia Law Review* 701, 737–38.

[102]  A Reed, 'The Need for a New Anglo-American Approach to Duress' (1997) 61 *Journal of Criminal Law* 209, 218; A Reed, 'Duress and Provocation as Excuses to Murder: Salutatory Lessons from Recent Anglo-American Jurisprudence' (1996–97) 6 *Journal of Transnational Law and Policy* 51, 63.

[103]  J Dressler, 'Exegesis of the Law of Duress: Justifying the Excuse and Searching for its Proper Limits' (1988–1989) 62 *Southern California Law Review* 1331, 1372.

[104]  *cf* P Westen and J Mangiafico, "The Criminal Defense of Duress: A Justification, Not an Excuse—and Why it Matters' (2003) 6 *Buffalo Criminal Law Review* 833.

[105]  See H Frankfurt, *The Importance of What We Care About* (Cambridge, Cambridge University Press, 1988) ch 3.

[106]  *Howe* (n 1) 432.

satisfy the reasonableness requirement of duress. There is thus no need to recognise the defence of duress in murder cases.

Lord Hailsham's version of the Heroism Argument overstates what the criminal law can legitimately require of citizens. As Antony Duff explains, the criminal law cannot require 'heroic or saintly standards for us, and [can] condemn us only if we display a vice which involves the lack of the modest kind of virtue of courage or moral strength, of concern for legally protected interests that meeting those standards requires'.[107] Heroism is not the stuff of modesty, but reasonableness is.[108] To claim otherwise is to do abuse to the idea of 'reasonableness', whilst holding ordinary citizens up to standards that very few will reach. Such an approach is anathema to the general project of the criminal law in setting out to set basic norms that only *serious, culpable* wrongdoers will fail to meet.[109]

It is vital to bear in mind that Lord Hailsham was invoking the requirement of heroism for ordinary citizens in the context of their daily affairs during peacetime. Perhaps ordinary citizens *can* reasonably be expected to display heroism in other contexts, such as wartime.[110] Four of the five Law Lords who decided *Howe* had served in the Second World War.[111] Intriguingly, it is possible to discern different attitudes towards the Heroism Argument from different Lords with heroic incidents in their military histories. In his memoirs, Lord Hailsham describes an incident where, during his deployment to the Western Desert, he ran to a machine gun to defend his camp from three Messerschmitts. Lord Hailsham was injured by a bullet from one of the planes and was removed from front-line duties for the remainder of the war.[112] As described, this action sounds heroic, but perhaps it was viewed as being the only reasonable thing to do, in line with *wartime* duties.

Lord Brandon was awarded the Military Cross for his efforts directing Allied forces from behind Vichy French lines in Madagascar in 1942.[113] Again, this might have been a perfectly 'reasonable' activity to expect him to perform in the circumstances. Lord Brandon was nevertheless worried about requiring ordinary citizens during *peacetime* to lay down their lives to avoid a murder conviction.[114] He rejected the Heroism Argument in favour of the Competence Argument (which is returned to below).

---

[107] RA Duff, 'Virtue, Vice and Criminal Liability: Do We Want an Aristotelian Criminal Law?' (2002–03) 6 *Buffalo Criminal Law Review* 147, 177. See also Smith, *Justification and Excuse* 94.

[108] Milgate, 'Duress and the Criminal Law' 67; NM Padfield, 'Duress, Necessity and the Law Commission' [1992] *Crim LR* 778, 784

[109] G Williams, 'A Commentary on *Dudley and Stephens*' (1977) 8 *Cambrian Law Review* 94, 95.

[110] G Williams, *Textbook of Criminal Law*, 2nd edn (London, Stephens, 1981) 627.

[111] Lord Hailsham LC, Lord Griffiths, Lord Brandon and Lord Bridge.

[112] Lord Hailsham, *A Sparrow's Flight: Memoirs* (London, Collins, 1990) 172–73.

[113] 'Obituary: Lord Brandon of Oakbrook' *The Independent* (London, 29 March 1999), available at www.independent.co.uk/arts-entertainment/obituary-lord-brandon-of-oakbrook-1083781.html.

[114] *Howe* (n 1) 438.

It is submitted that Lord Brandon's approach is to be preferred. However violent the atrocities associated with the Troubles, and organised crime in the 1980s, the Lords were not setting standards for soldiers in a warzone; they were setting standards for ordinary citizens in peacetime. Furthermore, because of the voluntary association rule, these citizens would have no prior voluntary association with violent duressors. Lord Hailsham's requirement to 'take the Bowie line'[115] was rightly viewed as outmoded, demonstrating 'a breath-taking gulf between judicial expectations and human experience'.[116] The Heroism Argument should be rejected.

## ii. The Terrorism Argument

The Terrorism Argument was endorsed by Lords Hailsham and Griffiths.[117] For them, times had not moved on massively since the 'bad old days'[118] of Hale and Blackstone:[119]

> We live in the age of the holocaust of the Jews, of international terrorism on the scale of massacre, of the explosion of aircraft in mid air, and murder sometimes at least as obscene as anything experienced in Blackstone's day.[120]

As already noted, the Terrorism Argument trades on huge assumptions about the ability of the law to reach and move those placed under life-threatening pressure.[121] However real the threat of terrorism and organised crime was in the late 1980s, it was not clear that the rule in *Howe* could help remedy the situation. The voluntary association rule would have been sufficient to identify those who did not deserve a defence of duress. Like the Heroism Argument, the Terrorism Argument should be rejected as a basis for withholding duress in murder cases. This leaves the Competence Argument for consideration.

## iii. The Competence Argument

The Competence Argument was deployed in relation to a range of proposals presented to the Lords. The first one was to allow duress to result in a

---

[115] A reference to David Bowie's 'Heroes'—Gearty, *'Howe* to Be a Hero' 203.
[116] L Walters, 'Murder under Duress and Judicial Decision-Making in the House of Lords' (1988) 8 *Legal Studies* 61, 73.
[117] *Howe* (n 1) 443–44.
[118] ibid 433.
[119] ibid 434.
[120] It is noteworthy that Lord Hailsham referenced a case, decided after the hearing, where a man had sent his pregnant mistress aboard a plane with a suitcase filled with explosives: *R v Hindawi* (Central Criminal Court, 25 October 1986). The mistress was, however, apparently ignorant of the bag's contents, rather than acting under duress.
[121] P Alldridge, 'Duress, Murder and the House of Lords' (1988) 52 *Journal of Criminal Law* 186, 189; *R v Aravena* [2015] ONCA 250 [77]. *cf* G McFarlane, 'Murder: The Duress Defence' (1987) 131 *Solicitors' Journal* 383, 384.

conviction for manslaughter instead of murder. For Lord Hailsham, duress was not similar enough to provocation or diminished responsibility to, by analogy, invent a new partial defence of duress.[122] Added to this might be the fact that provocation had been recognised as a partial defence for a long time at common law, and diminished responsibility was a creature of statute. It is defensible, in such circumstances, to view the *common law* categories of partial defences as closed, and follow the Competence Argument.[123] A useful analogy can again be drawn with the decision in *Myers*.[124]

The second alternative model, whereby duress could be left to the jury in appropriate cases, was also rejected.[125] A similar discretionary model, which had by then found favour in relation to accessories in South African law,[126] was considered too uncertain to be defensible.[127] It is unfortunate that the Competence Argument was not invoked here expressly: if it would be too much to allow duress to reduce murder to manslaughter, it is not clear how a more radical, discretionary model could have been created permissibly.

The influence of the Competence Argument is plainer when consideration turns to the most severe option of allowing duress to be available generally in murder. *Lynch* was castigated as an 'excessive and perhaps improvident' example of 'judicial legislation',[128] which took a 'fundamental reform' option that was 'never open' to the Lords.[129]

Elements of the treatment of the Competence Argument, as explained in *Howe*, are unconvincing. For instance, the Lords made much of the failure of Parliament to implement the Law Commission's proposals to make duress a general defence to murder.[130] Lord Griffiths used Parliament's inaction as 'some indication that the community at large are not pressing for a change in the law to remedy a perceived injustice'.[131] This thesis is at least questionable.[132] Perhaps Parliament failed to act on the Commission's proposals *because* it was assumed that the defence *would* apply to accessories. Parliament had, after all, omitted to reverse *Lynch* in the decade before *Howe* was heard, which might constitute implicit assent.[133] Ultimately, finding 'Parliamentary intention in a blank statute book is ridiculous'.[134] Parliament

---

[122] *Howe* (n 1) 435. Further, duress is a full to defence to other crimes: ibid 445.
[123] ibid 456.
[124] See ibid 449.
[125] ibid 452–53.
[126] *S v Goliath* 1972 (3) SA 1. See J Burchell, 'Duress and Intentional Killing' (1977) 94 *South African Law Journal* 282, 285–86.
[127] *Howe* (n 1) 455–56.
[128] ibid 430.
[129] ibid 437.
[130] ibid 437, 455.
[131] ibid 443.
[132] See, further, PS Atiyah, 'Common Law and Statute Law' (1985) 48 *MLR* 1, 26.
[133] Milgate, 'Duress and the Criminal Law' 70; JC Smith and B Hogan, *Criminal Law*, 6th edn (London, Butterworths, 1988) 233.
[134] Alldridge, 'Duress, Murder and the House of Lords' 196. See, also, Walters, 'Murder under Duress' 66–67; *R v Clegg* [1995] 1 AC 482 (HL), 500.

may well have been blind to the controversy over duress and murder rather than mulling it over silently and refusing to act.[135]

The better version of the Competence Argument does not divine messages from Parliament's inaction, but rather looks at how substantial and controversial the change the court is being encouraged to make would be. This would bring into consideration the doctrinal situation before *Lynch* and the proper constitutional role of courts in developing the criminal law by the late 1980s. On the doctrinal front, it was demonstrated above that the authorities supporting the move in *Lynch* were weak, particularly given the large role that voluntary association played in earlier cases involving accessories. In this context, *Lynch* seems remarkably revolutionary, and an extension to cover principals even more so. These would not be modest developments in the gradual developing story of duress and murder, but would tear up much that had gone before.[136]

The question is whether the courts can make such revolutionary moves legitimately. On one view, judicial conservatism can be defended on epistemic grounds. The question of whether duress should be a defence to murder—and for whom—is a vexed one involving difficult issues of morality and policy.[137] Given the limits placed on the ability of even the highest appellate courts to canvas and appraise different views on such issues, it is epistemically more appropriate for Parliament to do so. However, there is also a point of principle here: where an issue is particularly controversial, it is fitting for elected representatives, rather than unelected judges, to resolve it.

A potential objection to the version of the Competence Argument sketched out above is as follows. If defendants would be disadvantaged by the judicial extension of a common law offence[138] or the removal of a defence (or similar argument),[139] then of course the court should defer to Parliament. But if the defendant is to be advantaged, for instance, by the recognition of a new defence, then existing doctrine can be disregarded and no parliamentary deference is required.[140] It is submitted that this distinction is unsustainable. It would allow the courts to disregard the general structure of the common law defences, however settled that structure was, and to

---

[135] Lord Walker, 'How Far Should Judges Develop the Common Law?' (2014) 3 *Cambridge Journal of International and Comparative Law* 124, 132. *cf Knuller v DPP* [1973] AC 435, 455–56 (a case cited in argument, but not discussed by the House of Lords in *Howe*: see HL/PO/JU/4/3/1596, 53).

[136] *cf* R Dworkin, *Law's Empire* (London, Fontana, 1986) 228–38; R Dworkin, *A Matter of Principle* (Oxford, Clarendon Press, 1985) Ch 6.

[137] *cf C (A Minor) v DPP* [1996] AC 1 (HL), 28 (distinguishing 'social policy' issues from 'purely legal' issues).

[138] eg, *R v Dica* [2004] EWCA Crim 1103, [2004] QB 1257.

[139] eg, *C (A Minor) v DPP* [1994] 3 WLR 888 (QBD).

[140] See, eg, Simester et al, *Simester and Sullivan's Criminal Law* 854; ATH Smith, 'Judicial Law-Making in the Criminal Law' (1984) 100 *LQR* 46, 63–67.

decide controversial social, moral and political questions it is ill-equipped to deal with.

The better view is that the Competence Argument is less compelling when there is genuine doctrinal uncertainty—to a much greater extent than existed before *Howe*—that must urgently be resolved in practice.[141] It is submitted that, even then, the solutions adopted for such controversies should be conservative (even if they are decisive) and viewed as imperfect solutions. Opportunities should, naturally, be taken to expose the need for legislative discussion. Lord Brandon's short opinion in *Howe* is a good example of such encouragement.

*Howe* should be viewed as an endorsement of the Competence Argument sketched out above rather than the weaker Heroism and Terrorism Arguments. Indeed, this is how the case has been viewed in some later decisions. In *C (A Minor) v DPP*, a case concerning the presumption of doli incapax (another controversial area), *Howe* was cited as an example of appropriate judicial restraint over developing the common law.[142] In *Clegg*, by contrast, *Lynch* was cited, pejoratively, as a source of 'encouragement' for deciding that excessive self-defence could lead to a manslaughter conviction rather than murder.[143] The implication was that *Lynch* was a misstep and *Howe* was an appropriate corrective measure.

Admittedly, this account of the Competence Argument sits rather uneasily with the decision in *R*,[144] where the 'marital rape' exemption was swept away by the House of Lords (including Lords Brandon and Griffiths). If the Competence Argument is right, then *R* is something of an aberration.[145] The rule was, like that regarding principals, duress and murder, clear from Hale's writings.[146] Change involved delicate questions of policy (though, to modern eyes, not *difficult* ones). Parliament had intervened in the area of sexual offences relatively recently and had not removed the exemption.[147] Such involvement (rather than the *omission* to be involved) might be a ground for exercising even greater restraint judicially, but is not relevant to *Howe*.

Nothing in this section is meant to suggest that the *result* in *Howe* is viewed as desirable or that the *result* in *R* is undesirable. The argument here is one about process, not substance. The decision in *Howe* should be seen in that light, rather than being identified with the weaker Heroism and Terrorism Arguments.

---

[141] *cf C (A Minor)* (n 137) 28.

[142] ibid 27–28.

[143] *Clegg* (n 134) 499.

[144] *R v R* [1992] 1 AC 599 (HL). See, further, A Kewley, 'Murder and the Availability of the Defence of Duress in the Criminal Law' (1993) 57 *Journal of Criminal Law* 298, 302

[145] See, further, M Giles, 'Judicial Law-Making in the Criminal Courts: The Case of Marital Rape' [1992] *Crim LR* 907; N Padfield and M Giles, 'Judicial Law-Making' [1992] *Crim LR* 680.

[146] Hale, *Historia Placitorum Coronæ* 629.

[147] Sexual Offences (Amendment) Act 1976, s 1

*iv. Taking the Consequences?*

On the basis of the Heroism, Terrorism and Competence Arguments, the earlier decision in *Lynch* was departed from. At that point, the *Practice Statement*[148] had been used in only one criminal case, *Shivpuri*,[149] on attempts. Lord Hailsham LC and Lords Mackay and Bridge had also heard *Shivpuri*. Lord Mackay remarked that the reasoning lying behind the use of the statement in that case was relevant to *Howe*.[150] Presumably, the relevant analogy concerns reliance: in *Shivpuri*, Lord Bridge thought that nobody could have relied on *Anderton v Ryan*[151] and now found themselves to be a criminal.[152] Similar thinking can be applied to duress, on the assumption that rational planning of conduct in the light of the criminal law's prohibitions is inconsistent with the unexpected, pressurised situation in duress cases.[153]

What is surprising about *Howe* is how open the Lords were to the harsh or illogical *results* of the rule they endorsed. For instance, the defendant who intends to cause serious harm to his victim (and manages to do so) may claim duress in relation to a charge under section 18 of the Offences Against the Person Act 1861. If the attack causes death, the defendant is a murderer and the defence of duress evaporates. This was viewed by Lord Hailsham as a problem with the mens rea of murder rather than as an aspect of duress.[154] Lord Griffiths was less impressed by the section 18 example, viewing the law as recognising the sanctity of life.[155] The 'lucky' attacker, who does not cause death, has not violated the sanctity of life in the manner that the 'unlucky' attacker has. This is true and is a reason to recognise in terms of criminal labelling and sentencing a distinction between the 'lucky' and 'unlucky' attacker. It nevertheless is an unsatisfactory ground for denying recognition of the fact that the defendant can be equally *blameless* in both cases. Neither the Heroism Argument nor the Terrorism Argument changes this fact.

Furthermore, refuge was taken in prosecutorial discretion and the parole board.[156] Those who were utterly blameless would not be prosecuted or would be released on licence.[157] It is odd that the tone of the Heroism and

---

[148] *Practice Statement (Judicial Precedent)* [1966] 1 WLR 1234.

[149] *R v Shivpuri* [1987] AC 1 (HL).

[150] *Howe* (n 1) 456–57.

[151] *Anderton v Ryan* [1985] AC 560 (HL).

[152] *Shivpuri* (n 149) 23.

[153] See P Alldridge, 'Rules for Courts and Rules for Citizens' (1990) 10 *OJLS* 487, 500. This is one reason why excuses apparently do not alter the 'rules of conduct' that some authors argue should form the mainstay of the published criminal code: see GP Fletcher, *Rethinking Criminal Law* (Boston, MA, Little & Brown, 1978) 457.

[154] *Howe* (n 1) 430, 432.

[155] ibid 445.

[156] ibid 433, 446.

[157] ibid 445.

Terrorism Arguments changes:[158] 'You don't deserve a defence, you coward/tool of terrorism, but we hope you aren't prosecuted!' If citizens are expected to be heroes or to fight the temptation to act as agents of terrorists, then surely they should be prosecuted for their failures.[159] If blamelessness can be recognised by prosecutors or the parole board, why not at the intermediary settings of trial, through the defence of duress?[160]

Despite the fears of some academics,[161] it appears that prosecutorial restraint was exercised in the aftermath of *Howe*. 'Proxy bombers' (members of the public instructed to drive cars laden with explosives into checkpoints or have their families killed by terrorists) were rarely prosecuted, even though technically they were murderers.[162] A voluntary association rule would have caught those who really *did* deserve the label of murderer (because of their voluntary association with their duressor), whilst recognising formally the innocence of those taken advantage of unsuspectingly. Consider the facts of *Howe and Bannister*—the defendants could have escaped, surely, after the first killing. Their continued association with violent Murray after the first murder points strongly towards the denial of a defence of duress. It is not clear, from the available public records, that Burke was similarly at fault in associating with Clarkson (their association appears to have involved offences of dishonesty, and it is not clear whether Clarkson had a reputation for *violence*), but he did have opportunities to go to the police before the shooting. Once again, what is required is a means of recognising undeserving candidates for a defence of duress, and the voluntary association rule appears to be sufficient.

### IV. AFTER *HOWE*

In the light of the analysis above, it is slightly unfair to decry the decision in *Howe* as being *entirely* 'bad ... unsupported by adequate reasons'[163] and 'unconvincing'.[164] That was, however, the overwhelming contemporary reaction to the case,[165] which did 'nothing to improve the House of Lords'

---

[158] Alldridge, 'Duress, Murder and the House of Lords' 200.

[159] GJ Bennett and B Hogan, '"Criminal Law, Criminal Procedure and Sentencing' [1987] *All England Reports Annual Review* 74, 75.

[160] One answer might be that the criminal law should recognise 'acoustic separation', but that is too large a matter to get into here. See M Dan-Cohen, 'Decision Rules and Conduct Rules: On Acoustic Separation in Criminal Law' (1983) 97 *Harvard Law Review* 625.

[161] Milgate, 'Duress and the Criminal Law' 71.

[162] S Gardner, 'Duress in Attempted Murder' (1991) 107 *LQR* 389, 392–93; S Gardner, 'Duress in the House of Lords' (1992) 108 *LQR* 349, 350.

[163] Alldridge, 'Duress, Murder and the House of Lords' 200.

[164] JC Smith, 'Murder—Defence of Duress Not Available to Person Charged with Murder' [1987] *Crim LR* 480, 481.

[165] *cf* JN Spencer, '*R v Howe*: Duress, Aiding and Abetting, Cannibalism and Morality' (1987) 151 *Justice of the Peace* 373, 376 (describing the decision as 'reasonable').

disappointing record in the field of criminal law in recent years',[166] and provided 'further potent evidence of the failure of the ... Lords to provide sound, well-reasoned decisions in the field of criminal law'.[167] The decision in *Howe* came five years after the much-maligned decision on recklessness in *Caldwell*[168] and two years after *Anderton v Ryan*. The Lords' card was already marked.

This did not stop the courts from following the logic of *Howe* in later cases, which continued to mix the unconvincing Heroism and Terrorism Arguments with the more defensible Competence Argument. In *Gotts*, it was confirmed that duress was no defence to attempted murder. Concern about the Terrorism Argument and bogus defences is clear throughout the Court of Appeal's decision (delivered by Lord Lane CJ, who had handed down the Court of Appeal's judgment in *Howe*).[169] Once again, the substantive law was to be unmoving: duress was no defence and sentencing could, in attempted murder at least, take full account of the circumstances in which the defendant found herself.[170] This is a slightly more honest line than that taken in *Howe*—at least the Court of Appeal envisaged the *prosecution* of coerced attempted murderers.

The Law Lords, once more by a majority (including Lord Lowry, who had decided *Lynch* in the Court of Appeal in Northern Ireland), upheld the Court of Appeal's decision.[171] The Heroism Argument, bolstered by the sanctity of life, was as instrumental and as unconvincing as it had been in *Howe*.[172] There was also a point of logic. A defendant who attempts murder must intend to *kill*, whilst a murderer need intend only to cause grievous bodily harm.[173] It is implausible that the former, whose intent is more 'evil',[174] should be able to profit from a defence of duress, whilst the latter could not.[175] In the light of this point, it was viewed as being unjustified judicial legislation to recognise a defence of duress to attempted murder, even though there was precious little authority on duress and attempted murder.[176] Again, then, matters turned to an extent on the Competence Argument.

It is not entirely clear what the Law Lords would have had Parliament do. Lord Lowry questioned the potential deterrent value of the murder rule

---

[166] Milgate, 'Duress and the Criminal Law' 75.
[167] Walters, 'Murder under Duress' 61–62.
[168] *R v Caldwell* [1982] AC 341 (HL).
[169] *R v Gotts* [1991] 1 QB 660 (CA), 667.
[170] ibid 668.
[171] *R v Gotts* [1992] 2 AC 412 (HL).
[172] ibid 426.
[173] *R v Whybrow* (1951) 35 Cr App R 141 (CA).
[174] *Gotts* (n 171) 419.
[175] ibid 426.
[176] ibid 438.

(casting doubt on the Terrorism Argument) and noted that logic would dictate a defence of duress that is available in relation to all crimes, or no crimes.[177] Lord Jauncey, by contrast, noted that Parliament had 'advisedly' not accepted the Commission's proposals to make duress a defence to all crimes, whatever the extent of the defendant's participation.[178] Lord Browne-Wilkinson similarly viewed duress as at most a ground for mitigation of sentence.[179]

In other cases, the clear ruling in *Howe* has not exerted as strong a gravitational pull. In *Ness*,[180] the trial judge decided that duress could be a defence to conspiracy to murder. This decision can perhaps be justified on the basis that conspiracy is further removed from the killing than an attempt is,[181] but such a line is necessarily arbitrary. It would be sensible for the rules regarding duress to be the same in all cases, and if parliamentary intervention was required in murder and attempted murder, the same conclusion should perhaps have been reached in *Ness* if the Competence Argument is accepted.

*Howe* was distinguished again, yet more convincingly, in *Re A (Children)*, the 'conjoined twins case', on the basis that it did not envisage a case involving such peculiar circumstances.[182] This ground of distinction speaks to the general usefulness of *Re A (Children)* as an authority: the Court of Appeal clearly meant its decision to be limited to the facts, and to avoid unsettling the architecture built by cases such as *Dudley and Stephens* and *Howe*.[183]

However, *Howe* could not be avoided in the unsettling case of *Wilson*,[184] where a 13-year-old boy fetched his father an axe, which was used to kill a neighbour. The boy was charged as an accessory to murder and argued that he acted out of fear of his father. This was recognised as being a putative case of duress, and the trial judge withheld this defence from the jury. Phillips LCJ recognised the 'grounds for criticising a principle of law that does not afford a 13-year-old boy any defence to a charge of murder on the ground that he was complying with his father's instruction, which he was too frightened to refuse'.[185] The law was, however, clear. Again, any change would be for Parliament. *Wilson* fits the general model of viewing

---

[177] ibid 441.
[178] ibid 424. *cf Hasan* (n 26) 490, where Lord Bingham described the *logic* of the Commission's argument as 'irresistible', but noted that they it not been acted upon 'no doubt because it is felt that in the case of the gravest crimes, no threat to the defendant, however extreme, should excuse'.
[179] *Gotts* (n 171) 442.
[180] *R v Ness* [2011] Crim LR 645.
[181] Simester et al, *Simester and Sullivan's Criminal Law* 765.
[182] *Re A (Children)* [2001] Fam 147 (CA), 225, 254.
[183] See F Stark, 'Necessity and *Nicklinson*' [2013] *Crim LR* 949, 958–61.
[184] *R v Wilson* [2007] EWCA Crim 1251, [2007] 2 Cr App R 31.
[185] ibid [18].

this potentially very controversial area of the law as being settled to the extent that it would be inappropriate for the courts to change it.

It is worth noting that a similar deference to Parliament was shown in the more recent case of *R (Nicklinson and Lamb) v Ministry of Justice*,[186] where the question of whether 'necessity' was a defence to voluntary euthanasia was considered. Although *Howe* was not mentioned in the High Court, the argument of Toulson LJ about the competence of the courts to recognise new defences regarding the taking of life is similar to the preferred reading of *Howe*: whatever the merits of legalising voluntary euthanasia, this is not a decision that judges can take, constitutionally, in modern times.[187]

The rectitude of the decision in *Howe* and related cases, if understood as being about the competence of the courts to change a potentially controversial area of the law in a significant fashion, has not been doubted. However, this does not prevent the resulting legal position from being unsatisfactory. The calls for parliamentary action in a number of cases, including *Howe*, and from commentators have not come to anything.

Such change would presumably be motivated by a Law Commission proposal. The Commission has continued to recommend the removal of the barrier to using duress in murder. Although duress was not included as a defence to murder or attempted murder in the Commission's 1989 Draft Criminal Code,[188] the commentary makes clear the Commission's preference for duress to be a defence to all crimes,[189] as does a 1992 report on general principles of criminal law.[190] In its 2006 report on homicide, the Law Commission pushed this view once more, having toyed briefly with the idea of a partial defence to murder.[191] The idea of duress reducing murder to manslaughter was seen as anomalous (duress functioning as a full defence to other crimes), and the fairness of convicting a defendant of *anything* if she satisfied the requirements of the duress defence was questioned.

It is not clear whether the Law Commission's proposals enjoy popular support. Respondents to the Law Commission's consultation on homicide were split on the issue of whether duress should completely excuse murder

---

[186] *R (Nicklinson and Lamb) v Ministry of Justice* [2012] EWHC 2381 (Admin), [2012] 3 FCR 233.

[187] Affirmed in *R (Nicklinson and Lamb) v Ministry of Justice* [2013] EWCA Civ 961, [2014] 2 All ER 32 (CA) (where *Howe* was cited, but not discussed).

[188] Law Commission, *A Criminal Code for England and Wales* (Law Com No 177, 1989) vol 1, cl 42.

[189] Law Commission, *A Criminal Code for England and Wales* (Law Com No 177, 1989) vol 2, para 12.13.

[190] Law Commission, *Offences against the Person and General Principles* (Law Com CP No 122, 1992) paras 18.14–18.20. The second-best solution was a partial defence to murder. See J Horder, 'Occupying the Moral High Ground? The Law Commission on Duress' [1994] *Crim LR* 334, 339–40.

[191] Law Commission, *Murder, Manslaughter and Infanticide* (Law Com No 304, 2006), pt 6.

or simply reduce it to second-degree murder or manslaughter.[192] This disagreement speaks to the need for proper, extended democratic debate rather than judicial trailblazing.

The Commission's proposals have, regrettably, never been taken forward to the stage of parliamentary debate. In contrast to the context of voluntary euthanasia, it seems unlikely that a human rights argument could lead to more pressure being exerted on Parliament. This is a disappointing conclusion (though injustice is no doubt avoided, as was suspected in *Howe*, by prosecutorial discretion), but it is one that is necessitated through accepting the Competence Argument sketched out above. *Howe* should be viewed as a landmark in the development of this constitutionally appropriate level of judicial restraint in developing the modern common law in potentially controversial areas, not as an unconvincing endorsement of weak arguments regarding heroism and terrorism.

It is worth noting, in closing, that recognising the decision in *Howe* as being explicable on the basis of the Competence Argument has implications for how persuasive the case should be viewed around the common law world. For instance, the Ontario Court of Appeal recognised the weakness of the Heroism and Terrorism Arguments recently in *Aravena*,[193] and held that the common law defence of duress was available to secondary parties to murder, even if the statutory version of the defence in the Criminal Code[194] makes duress unavailable to principals charged with murder. The compatibility of the exception for principals with the Canadian Charter of Rights and Freedoms was not directly at issue, but the Court concluded that 'subject to any argument the Crown might advance justifying the exception as it applies to perpetrators under s 1 of the Charter, the exception must be found unconstitutional'.[195] In a different constitutional structure, such as Canada's, the Competence Argument can be far less compelling or even inapplicable when deciding whether duress should be capable of excusing murder.[196]

---

[192] ibid, para 6.17.

[193] *Aravena* (n 121).

[194] Criminal Code of Canada (RSC 1985, c C-46), s 17.

[195] *Aravena* (n 121) [86].

[196] The Supreme Court of Canada dismissed Aravena's application for leave to appeal on 7 April 2016.

# 16

# *R v Brown* (1993)

## JONATHAN HERRING

## I. INTRODUCTION

IT'S THE CASE students of law love to hate. *R v Brown* fits the stereotype of judges being out-of-touch dinosaurs, whose judgments are motivated more by personal prejudice than respect for legal principle.[1] Students can proudly display their liberal credentials in their eloquent critique of the decision. And so they should. There is no doubt the voluminous criticisms of *Brown* are justified and well made.[2] It will be accepted in this chapter that the arguments used by the majority in *Brown* are very weak. Despite its reputation as a poor decision, this chapter will argue it does not follow that the legal precedent it set was completely wrong and that we should remove all criminal prohibitions on BDSM.[3] Most commentators suggest that the case law following *Brown* indicates its lacks of sound basis.[4] However, most commentators when discussing the issue focus on male-on-male BDSM and tie in their criticisms of the case with broader concerns about legal attitudes towards homosexuality and masculinity. I will suggest that while these criticisms are valid, it is important to consider the issues raised by BDSM in relation to women. I will argue that the subsequent case law reveals why some restrictions on BDSM are necessary. While many commentators see *Brown* as a case which should be consigned to the history books of judicial freaks and aberrations, I suggest a trimming and a better rationalisation is a preferable solution.

---

[1] *R v Brown* [1994] 1 AC 212 (HL).

[2] There is a summary in J Herring, *Criminal Law*, 6th edn (Oxford, Oxford University Press, 2014) Ch 4.

[3] The acronym is designed to convey practice including bondage and discipline (BD), dominance and submission (DS), and sadism and masochism (SM).

[4] eg, P Murphy, 'Flogging Live Complainants and Dead Horses: We May No Longer Need to Be in Bondage to *Brown*' [2011] *Crim LR* 758.

## II. THE FACTS

Brown, Laskey, Jaggard, Lucas, Carter and Cadman were all convicted in December 1990 for a series of offences connected with consensual sadomasochistic practices. These included assault occasioning actual bodily harm, unlawful wounding and keeping a disorderly house. Their sentences ranged from four years six months for Laskey to two years for Carter. The defendants belonged a group of men who 'willingly and enthusiastically participated in the commission of acts of violence against each other for the sexual pleasure which it engendered in the giving and receiving of pain'.[5] The activities took place in private rooms 'equipped as torture chambers'.[6] The group of some 44 men had been meeting from 1978 to 1988. Video cameras were used to record the activities. The recordings were sent to members of the group who were unable to make a particular meeting. A copy of the video was obtained by the police and formed the basis of the prosecution. It is thought the police at first believed they were viewing a 'snuff movie' and that the recorded acts were non-consensual. On discovering that it was consensual, the police, having used considerable resources in the investigation, felt they should still prosecute 16 of the men who had used 'violence'.[7] The recipients of the 'violence' were not prosecuted. Three counts give a flavour of the activities:

*Count 5* alleged an assault occasioning actual bodily harm. Laskey, together with Grindley and Wilkinson, both of whom have abandoned their appeals, aided and abetted by Brown and Carter, branded a man, A, with Laskey's initials using a wire heated by a blow lamp. Scarring from those injuries remains. Matches were taped to the victim's nipples and the navel and, having been set alight, were then doused.

*Count 14* alleged that Jaggard had committed an assault occasioning actual bodily harm. The victim had hot wax dripped into the urethra of his penis. The penis was burned with a candle flame and then a syringe needle was inserted.

*Count 17* alleged unlawful wounding against Lucas and Jaggard. Atkinson, a co-defendant, had his penis nailed to a bench. He was caned, hit and rubbed with a spiked strap, then cut with a scalpel by Lucas. There were five lateral cuts together with further cuts to Atkinson's scrotum. There was a free flow of blood.

All of the men prosecuted lost their jobs. Mr Jaggard required extensive psychiatric treatment as a result of the trial. The proceedings received

---

[5] *R v Brown* [1992] QB 491 (CA), 496 (Lord Lane).
[6] ibid.
[7] It was rumoured that around £4 million was spent on the investigation. The Spanner Trust, 'The History of the Spanner Case', www.spannertrust.org/documents/spannerhistory.asp.

widespread press coverage. Perhaps surprisingly, most of the press attention given to the case was favourable to the defendants. The tenor of much of the coverage was that judges should 'keep out of the people's bedrooms'.[8] That said, there was inevitably coverage which revealed prejudicial attitudes, such as the headline 'Leaders of Vicious and Perverted Sex Gang Jailed; Pornography Ring'.[9] Notably, it was the Law Commission's proposal to partially reverse the decision in *Brown* in 1992 which generated headlines most openly revealing an aversion to BDSM, with the *Daily Mail* leading with 'Law Chiefs Propose "Licence" for Sex Perverts' being a choice example.[10]

### III. THE COURT OF APPEAL

The basis of the application before the Court of Appeal was straightforward. The 'victims' had consented to the injuries and this should be accepted as a defence. Further:

> There was no permanent injury; no infection of the wounds; no evidence of any medical attention being sought. There was no complaint to the police. The facts came to light by chance during investigation of other matters. The actions were carried out in private.[11]

Lord Lane CJ took a straightforward approach and argued from the established case law that if there was an assault occasioning actual bodily harm or a more serious injury, then consent could not be a defence unless there was 'good reason' for the activity. He quickly concluded:

> What may be 'good reason' it is not necessary for us to decide. It is sufficient to say, so far as the instant case is concerned, that we agree with the trial judge that the satisfying of sado-masochistic libido does not come within the category of good reason nor can the injuries be described as merely transient or trifling.[12]

Interestingly, he did not even attempt to provide an explanation for why the satisfying of libido was not a sufficient reason to allow an exception. Presumably he thought the conclusion so obvious that it did not require any justification.

---

[8] Nick Cohen, 'Controversy over Court Ruling on Sado-masochism' *The Independent* (London, 20 February 1992); Robert Story, 'Love Hurts' *The Guardian* (London, 23 November 1992).

[9] David Young, 'Leaders of Vicious and Perverted Sex Gang Jailed; Pornography Ring' *The Times* (London, 20 December 1990).

[10] Quoted in Stephen Cretney, 'The Law Commission: True Dawns and False Dawns' (1996) 59 *MLR* 631.

[11] *Brown* (n 5) 498.

[12] ibid 501.

IV. THE HOUSE OF LORDS

Before the House of Lords, the focus was on the certified point of law:

> Where A wounds or assaults B occasioning him actual bodily harm in the course of a sado-masochistic encounter, does the prosecution have to prove lack of consent on the part of B before they can establish A's guilt under section 20 and section 47 of the 1861 Offences Against the Person Act?

Notoriously, their Lordships answered 'no' to that question by a majority of three to two. The consent of a victim to actions resulting in actual bodily harm or a more serious injury was no defence unless the case fell within an 'exceptional category'. Sadomasochism was not currently an exceptional category and the majority were not persuaded to create a new one to cover it. It is worth exploring the five judgments separately, starting with the three in the majority.

### A. Lord Templeman

Lord Templeman took the view that violence was generally punishable. However:

> Even when violence is intentionally inflicted and results in actual bodily harm, wounding or serious bodily harm the accused is entitled to be acquitted if the injury was a foreseeable incident of a lawful activity in which the person injured was participating.[13]

He went on to give examples of what would fall within the category of 'lawful activity': surgery, ritual circumcision, tattooing, ear piercing and violent sports (including boxing). Notably, he accepted that this list was not closed and was subject to changing social attitudes. Whether there should be additions or removals all turned on whether society regarded the behaviour as in the public interest. He noted that duelling and fighting were tolerated in the nineteenth century, but no longer. At this point in his judgment, the reader may be forgiven for believing that Lord Templeman was about to allow the appeal by adding sadomasochism to the list of exceptions, for he emphasised that: 'The attitude of the public towards homosexual practices changed in the second half of this century.'[14] This he noted was reflected in the decriminalisation of homosexual behaviour. However, he did not think that attitudes had similarly changed in relation to sadomasochism. If sadomasochism should be permitted in law, that should be a question for Parliament.[15]

---

[13] ibid 232.
[14] ibid 234.
[15] ibid 235.

Having reached that conclusion, Lord Templeman would have been well advised to end his speech at that point. He has been justly criticised for what he went on to say, but it should not be overlooked that his subsequent comments were, given the first part of his speech, obiter and unnecessary.

His speech went on to make an argument that the behaviour was not in the public interest. His arguments included:

(a)   'Sado-masochistic participants have no way of foretelling the degree of bodily harm which will result from their encounters.'[16] They were 'unpredictably dangerous'.[17]

(b)   Consent is not generally allowed as a defence in the criminal law and so a special case needs to be made if it is to be allowed in a particular circumstance.[18]

(c)   He rejected the argument that 'the sexual appetites of sadists and masochists can only be satisfied by the infliction of bodily harm and that the law should not punish the consensual achievement of sexual satisfaction'.[19] He stated that there was no evidence to support such a claim.

(d)   The practices of the appellant were immoral. He described them as 'degrading to body and mind', 'degraded and humiliated' and involving 'the indulgence of cruelty by sadists and the degradation of victims'.[20] He explained: 'Society is entitled and bound to protect itself against a cult of violence. Pleasure derived from the infliction of pain is an evil thing. Cruelty is uncivilised.'[21]

(e)   The practices were taught to 'persons whose consents were dubious or worthless'. He explained this remark by noting that the appellants, who were the ones inflicting the injuries, were 'middle-aged men' and the victims 'were youths some of whom were introduced to sado-masochism before they attained the age of 21'.[22] He referred to Lord Lane's judgment, which noted that Cadman and Laskey 'were responsible in part for the corruption of a youth K'.[23] Cadman had met K when he was 15 at a cafeteria and encouraged him in bondage affairs. Lord Templeman also noted that 'drink and drugs were employed to obtain consent and increase enthusiasm'.[24]

(f)   Reference was made to the dangers of infection (especially HIV) from the appellants' behaviour.[25]

---

[16]  ibid 236.
[17]  ibid 237.
[18]  ibid 236.
[19]  ibid 240.
[20]  ibid 237.
[21]  ibid 240.
[22]  ibid 238.
[23]  His prejudice against homosexuality is apparent in his added comment: 'It is some comfort at least to be told, as we were, that K has now it seems settled into a normal heterosexual relationship' (ibid 236).
[24]  ibid 236.
[25]  ibid 237.

(g)  Sadomasochism could be linked to other forms of dangerous behaviour. In particular, he noted: 'Cruelty to human beings was on occasions supplemented by cruelty to animals in the form of bestiality.'[26]

## B.  Lord Jauncey

Agreeing with Lord Templeman, Lord Jauncey concluded: 'I would therefore dispose of these appeals on the basis that the infliction of actual or more serious bodily harm is an unlawful activity to which consent is no answer.'[27] Like Lord Templeman, he went further than he needed to for disposing of the appeal. He emphasised that although the group before their Lordships were well disciplined, other groups may not be as 'controlled or responsible as the appellants are claimed to be'.[28] Further, although no serious injuries were caused by the appellants' activities, that was 'good luck rather than good judgement'.[29] He emphasised the dangers of septicaemia and HIV. Also, 'an inflicter who is carried away by sexual excitement or by drink or drugs could very easily inflict pain and injury beyond the level to which the receiver had consented'.[30]

To be fair to Lord Jauncey, he was quick to note that there was no evidence that these dangers had occurred in the case at hand, and he was simply highlighting the risks of the activities.[31] A generous reading of his speech is that in much of it, he was highlighting dangers on which Parliament would need reassurance before deciding that the practices should be permitted rather than expressing a concluded view.

## C.  Lord Lowry

Lord Lowry agreed with the 'reasoning and conclusions' of Lord Templeman and Lord Jauncey. His starting point was this principle:

> [I]t is not in the public interest that people should try to cause, or should cause, each other actual bodily harm for no good reason and that it is an assault if actual bodily harm is caused (except for good reason).[32]

Applying this general approach to the facts before him, he concluded that sadomasochistic activity was not 'conducive to the enhancement or enjoyment

[26] ibid.
[27] ibid 246.
[28] ibid 245.
[29] ibid 247.
[30] ibid.
[31] ibid.
[32] ibid 256.

of family life or conducive to the welfare of society'.[33] Like the others in the majority, he argued that the activities involve dangers—in particular, that 'under the powerful influence of the sexual instinct', serious harms, unforeseen by the parties, may occur.[34]

## D. Lord Mustill

Lord Mustill's dissenting speech opens: 'This is a case about the criminal law of violence. In my opinion it should be a case about the criminal law of private sexual relations, if about anything at all.'[35] Noting that the title of the relevant statute—the Offences Against the Person Act 1861—indicates that the violence in question should be *against* a person, he argued:

> Typically it involves brutality, aggression and violence, of a kind far removed from the appellants' behaviour which, however worthy of censure, involved no animosity, no aggression, no personal rancour on the part of the person inflicting the hurt towards the recipient and no protest by the recipient. In fact, quite the reverse.[36]

In deciding whether in a particular case consent should be a defence, he emphasised the distinction between law and morality:

> [T]hese are questions of private morality; that the standards by which they fall to be judged are not those of the criminal law; and that if these standards are to be upheld the individual must enforce them upon himself according to his own moral standards, or have them enforced against him by moral pressures exerted by whatever religious or other community to whose ethical ideals he responds.[37]

He referred to the right to respect for private life which is protected by Article 8 of the European Convention on Human Rights. This led him to conclude that the criminalisation of private sexual acts had to be justified. Then, echoing the arguments of the majority, he concluded that the issue is best resolved by Parliament, after a careful consideration of all the issues. As he explained, he differed from the majority in that his starting point is that the conduct should be lawful unless Parliament decides it should be illegal, while the majority believed the conduct should be illegal unless Parliament decides it should be legal.

## E. Lord Slynn

Lord Slynn, also dissenting, started by referring to his 'revulsion and bewilderment' that anyone would wish to be involved in the activities.[38] He went

[33] ibid.
[34] ibid.
[35] ibid 257.
[36] ibid 259.
[37] ibid 274.
[38] ibid 277.

on to emphasise that his finding that the acts were lawful did not indicate they were approved of or encouraged. At the heart of his reasoning was a view that the current law did not clearly prohibit sadomasochism and that it was not for the courts to decide to render the activities unlawful.[39] His judgment was therefore primarily based on a point about the separation of powers[40] and who should determine whether an activity was illegal, rather than one based on rights of privacy.

## V. THE EUROPEAN COURT OF HUMAN RIGHTS

The case went on to the European Court of Human Rights, which accepted, in a sparse judgment, that the conduct of the appellants fell within the scope of Article 8 of the Convention protecting the right to respect for private and family life.[41] The key question was whether an interference with that right could be justified under the second paragraph of that provision. This included interfering with Article 8 rights if it was proscribed by law and was necessary to protect the health of others.[42] In this case, given the severity of the injuries and acknowledging the margin of appreciation to which the UK government was entitled, the interference in the rights of the applicants was justified in order to protect health.

## VI. LATER CASES

The discussion in the House of Lords in *Brown* was notably marked by the masculine and same-sex nature of the behaviour. There was no discussion of BDSM in the opposite-sex context. It is notable that the subsequent case law involve opposite-sex couples. Indeed, those who suggest that the *Brown* decision was no more than reactionary bigotry often find support in the subsequent decision of *Wilson*, where the Court of Appeal allowed the appeal of a husband who had branded his initials on his wife's buttocks.[43] The Court of Appeal explained: 'Consensual activity between husband and wife, in the privacy of the matrimonial home, is not, in our judgment, normally a proper matter for criminal investigation, let alone criminal prosecution.'[44]

The decision offers no explanation as to why consensual harm is permissible between a heterosexual married couple, but not between homosexual

---

[39] ibid 283.
[40] This was similarly a concern of Lord Templeman, even though he was writing for the majority.
[41] *Laskey v UK* (1997) 24 EHRR 39.
[42] ibid [47].
[43] *R v Wilson* [1997] QB 47.
[44] ibid 50.

groups. It is interesting to note that while in *Brown* the immorality and many potential dangers were emphasised, the language of civility and privacy were used to describe Mr and Mrs Wilson's behaviour.[45] A comparison of *Wilson* and *Brown* at first sight seems to provide a conclusive case of the law in this area being driven by irrational prejudice rather than sound reasoning.

However, it is important to read *Wilson* in the light of the subsequent case of *Emmett*,[46] where the Court of Appeal retreated from the quoted statement in *Wilson*, with the court holding that 'we can see no reason in principle, and none was contended for, to draw any distinction between sadomasochistic activity on a heterosexual basis and that which is conducted in a homosexual context'. Nor could the marital status of the parties be relevant. The Court of Appeal went on to explain that the decision in *Wilson* could only be supported on the alternative basis referred to in *Wilson* itself—that the case was analogous to tattooing. In *Emmett*, which will be discussed further later on in this chapter, the consent of the defendant's female partner to serious injuries caused in a sadomasochistic encounter could not constitute a defence.

That explanation of *Wilson* sounds questionable and it was not until *Dica*, a case concerning the reckless transmission of HIV, that we had a more detailed and sophisticated rethinking of the issue.[47] Judge LJ, in a detailed discussion of *Brown* and the subsequent law, held a distinction could be drawn between *Brown* and *Emmett*, where the participants wanted to cause pain as a vehicle to sexual pleasure, and cases like *Wilson* and *Dica*, where there was a risk that the harm would be caused, but it was not desired.[48]

So we have, at last, in *Dica* a more plausible explanation of the case law as it relates to BDSM. The argument is that what the law objects to is the deliberate infliction of pain—that is, cases where a person is causing pain for the *purpose* of causing pain or where their purpose can only be achieved if there is pain. Hence, in *Wilson*, the point was that the aim of the husband was to put his initials on his wife's buttocks. He could have done this without causing pain and (presumably) would have been pleased if he had done so. By contrast, in *Brown* and *Emmett*, the pain was essential to the defendants' aims. No pain, no gain. Without the pain, the enterprise would have been a flop. Indeed, this provides a reasonably coherent explanation for the

---

[45] D Gurnham, 'Legal Authority and Savagery in Judicial Rhetoric: Sexual Violence and the Criminal Courts' (2011) 7 *International Journal of Law in Context* 117.

[46] *R v Emmett* [1999] All ER (D) 641. This quote is in the Smith Bernal report of the case, available at www.lexisnexis.com/uk/legal/results/enhdocview.do?docLinkInd=true&ersKey=23_T22927717574&format=GNBFULL&startDocNo=0&resultsUrlKey=0_T22927717577&backKey=20_T22927717578&csi=274662&docNo=9&scrollToPosition=798.

[47] *R v Dica* [2004] EWCA Crim 1103, [2004] QB 1257.

[48] ibid [51].

list of exceptions. Those engaging in sports, body piercing, surgery and the like all realise that pain may arise by their activities, but the infliction of pain is not an essential part of their aim;[49] they can succeed without the pain arising. Sadomasochism is different because the pain is an essential part of the activity. Whether there is a moral basis for this distinction will be discussed shortly. What, I suggest, cannot be claimed is that the current law as it has developed from *Brown* lacks any rational basis.

This chapter will now focus on considering whether there is any moral justification for the decision in *Brown*. There has been strong academic criticism of the case.[50] This chapter will be more sympathetic to the conclusions in *Brown*, but not for the reasons mentioned in the judgment, and I accept that my arguments will only have impact on certain kinds of BDSM.

## VII.  WHAT IS BDSM?

A wide range of practises falls under the heading 'BDSM'. One poll of practitioners found flagellation, verbal humiliation, gagging, electric shocks, the use of a straitjacket, wrestling and leather outfits all being mentioned as an aspect of it.[51] Often the activities use different role play scenarios to provide colour and background. The survey found the most common included 'guard and prisoner, cop and suspect, Nazi and Jew, White and Black, straight man and queer, parent and child, priest and penitent, teacher and student, whore and client'.[52]

Monica Pa[53] suggests that there are four main categories of sadomaso-chist behaviour:

(1) infliction of physical pain, usually by means of whipping, spanking, slapping or the application of heat and cold;
(2) verbal or psychological stimulation, such as threats and insults;
(3) dominance and submission, for example, where one individual orders the other to do his or her bidding;
(4) bondage and discipline, involving restraints such as rope and chains and/or punishment for real or fabricated transgressions.

---

[49] The one exceptional category that is not obviously so explained is religious mortification. It may be argued that if, somehow, penance was produced without the pain arising, the process would be a success.

[50] C Clarkson, H Keating and S Cunningham, *Clarkson and Keating Criminal Law*, 7th edn (London, Sweet & Maxwell, 2014) 299.

[51] N Nordling, N Sandnabba and P Santtila, 'Differences and Similarities between Gay and Straight Individuals Involved in the Sadomasochistic Subculture' in P Kleinplatz and C Moser (eds), *Sadomasochism: Powerful Pleasures* (Binghamton, NY, Harrington Park Press, 2006).

[52] P Califia, *The Lesbian S/M Safety Manual* (Boston, MA, Alyson Publications, 1988) 32.

[53] M Pa, 'Beyond the Pleasure Principle: The Criminalization of Consensual Sadomasochistic Sex' (2001) 11 *Texas Journal of Women and the Law* 51.

Pa goes on to add that there are other less popular activities which include 'include fetishistic, exhibitionistic and voyeuristic components, intense and/ or frustrated genital stimulation, age-play (infantilism, diapering), body mutilation (piercing, scarring, corsetting, tattooing), role reversal (cross-dressing) and defecation (urination, enemas, fecal play)'.[54]

Practitioners of BDSM emphasise the importance of three themes of their conduct. The first is that there is consent. Pa explains that consent is the 'first law' of SM. The parties will discuss carefully in advance what will be done and the safe word means that consent can be withdrawn. The second is that the behaviour must be safe. Although injuries may be inevitable, the treatment of these is arranged in advance. Long-lasting injuries are not seen as acceptable. The third is that the parties appreciate they are assuming roles and play acting. There must be a clear distinction in the parties' minds between reality and role play.[55]

BDSM relationships can be relatively casual or longer term. Katherine Guidoz[56] explains that some SM relationships are '24/7' relationship involving consensual ownership or 'slavery'. It then becomes a 'lifestyle' experience involving 'total power transfer'.[57] Other BDSM relationships are more casual encounters and are not part of an ongoing relationship.

The extent to which BDSM is practised is unclear. One study estimated that up to 10 per cent of the adult US population participates in some type of sadomasochistic activity.[58] Certainly, the book and film *Fifty Shades of Grey*[59] has made BDSM more 'mainstream' and BDSM paraphernalia is available in high street shops, suggesting some kind of market. The influential *Diagnostic and Statistical Manual of Mental Disorders* no longer lists sadism and masochism as necessarily indicative of mental disorders, indicating that BDSM is receiving acceptance even within the medical profession.[60] However, it is worth emphasising that at the time of *Brown* itself, sadomasochism was listed as a disorder under the *Manual* and as a Paraphilia by the World Health Organization.[61] It was not until 2013 that these designations were changed.

While there is some dispute in the literature,[62] most studies suggest that participants tended to identify as either dominant or submissive.[63] These

---

[54] ibid 51.
[55] ibid.
[56] K Guidroz, '"Are You Top or Bottom?": Social Science Answers for Everyday Questions about Sadomasochism' (2008) 2 *Sociology Compass* 1766.
[57] P Dancer, P Kleinplatz and C Moser, '24/7 SM Slavery' in P Kleinplatz and C Moser (eds), *Sadomasochism: Powerful Pleasures* (Binghamton, NY, Harrington Park Press, 2006).
[58] Guidroz, '"Are You Top or Bottom?"'
[59] E James, *Fifty Shades of Grey* (London, Random House, 2012).
[60] T Bennett, 'Sadomasochism under the Human Rights (Sexual Conduct) Act 1994' (2013) 35 *Sydney Law Review* 541.
[61] World Health Organization, *International Statistical Classification of Diseases and Related Health Problems, Tenth Revision* (Geneva, World Health Organization, 1992).
[62] K Guidroz, '"Are You Top or Bottom?"'
[63] A Hébert and A Weaver, 'Perks, Problems and the People Who Play' (2015) 24 *Canadian Journal of Human Sexuality* 49.

tend to reflect people's personality traits. One major study suggests that men preferred 'themes related to hyper masculinity'[64] and that 'by far the most common service paid for by men in heterosexual S/M is the extravagant display of submission'.[65] There is therefore evidence that in heterosexual BDSM, most men adopt the dominant role, although, of course, plenty of men prefer the submissive role.

## VIII. JUSTIFICATIONS FOR RESTRICTING CONSENT IN BDSM CASES

I will now turn to three arguments, none of which was raised specifically in the House of Lords judgment, but which might be used to support the conclusion reached.

### A. The Intent of the Actor

As mentioned earlier, in *Dica*, the Court of Appeal suggested that the explanation of the current law lies on the fact that the law criminalises those who cause pain for the purpose of causing pain or where the pain is a necessary part of their goal. But why might that make a difference?

The common commonly provided reason is that those acting in order to cause pain are showing a lack of respect for the dignity of the other party. Antony Duff has argued that BDSM participants are:

> [T]rying precisely to degrade and humiliate each other. They were enacting rituals of torture, which treat the person tortured as, or try to reduce him to, a humiliated and degraded animal. The conduct was, no doubt, set in a larger context in which they treated and respected each other as human equals, and they degraded each other in this way only because each freely consented to it. Nonetheless, what they consented to and sought was treatment that, in itself, denied their humanity.[66]

In Duff's analysis, there is an important distinction between a case where a person is doing an act which coincidentally runs a risk of causing pain or injury (eg, playing a sport) and an act which is done for the purpose of causing pain to another (even if it is hoped that as a result of the pain, sexual pleasure will result).[67] Only in the latter case is the person treating the other as lacking humanity. This argument is put in slightly different by Dennis

---

[64] A Laurence, P Santtila, N Sandnabba and N Nordling, 'Sadomasochistically Oriented Behavior: Diversity in Practice and Meaning' (2001) 30 *Archives in Sexual Behavior* 1.
[65] A McClintock, 'Maid to Order: Commercial Fetishism and Gender Power' (1993) 37 *Social Text* 87.
[66] A Duff, 'Harms and Wrongs' (2001) 5 *Buffalo Criminal Law Review* 13, 39.
[67] See further M Madden Dempsey, 'Victimless Conduct and the Volenti Maxim: How Consent Works' (2013) 7 *Criminal Law and Philosophy* 11.

Baker,[68] who argues that a person cannot forfeit their dignity by exercising their autonomy by agreeing to an act designed to cause pain.

There are difficulties with the argument as it is presented. The argument that what the inflicter wanted 'denied their humanity' needs justification. Margo Kaplan has argued that the purpose is not to inflict harm, but to cause sexual pleasure, and that should be regarded as good and life enhancing rather than bad and humanity denying.[69] In consensual BDSM, the parties themselves would not regard the acts as undignified.[70] As Nicholas Bamforth puts it:

> While sado-masochism necessarily *involves* the commission of violence towards, or the humiliation of the party assuming a masochist role, this is as a necessary element in the participants' *sexual* experience. Such behaviour might, to the outsider, appear to be no different from casual or malevolent violence; but the crucial point is that for sado-masochists, it is a meaningful part of sexual activity.

Margo Kaplan[71] is critical of a reliance on dignity. She describes dignity as a 'slippery concept' and 'nearly impossible to define'.[72] But, she states:

> [E]nduring pain or injury because you enjoy it is no more harmful to your dignity than enduring pain or injury because it is part of a contact sport that you are paid to participate in and because the harmful contact is considered intrinsic to the enjoyment of the game and the entertainment of its spectators. Indeed, the latter seems more harmful to dignity than the former.[73]

Kaplan argues that we need to recognise the value of sexual pleasure and respect sexual autonomy. She is willing to agree that there are limits to be drawn and:

> [E]ven sex-positive lawmakers may determine that sexual activities with a significant risk of physical trauma or death are not justified by the benefits of sexual pleasure, but such a determination requires us to turn a similarly critical eye to dangerous sports and elective surgery.[74]

The *Dica* argument may be better put not in terms of the infringement of the dignity of the victim, but by exploring the issue from the perspective of the defendant. The most sophisticated version of this argument has been presented by Michelle Madden Dempsey.[75] Her argument is based on a particular understanding of the role of consent. She explains that consent is

---

[68] D Baker, 'The Moral Limits of Consent as a Defense in the Criminal Law' (2009) 12 *New Criminal Law Review* 93.

[69] M Kaplan, 'Sex-Positive Law' (2014) 87 *New York University Law Review* 89.

[70] N Bamforth, 'Sado-masochism and Consent' [1994] *Criminal Law Review* 661.

[71] Kaplan, 'Sex-Positive Law'.

[72] ibid 130.

[73] ibid.

[74] ibid 156.

[75] Madden Dempsey, 'Victimless Conduct'.

required for an act when that act is a prima facie wrong. Such an act calls for a justification, and a consideration of all the facts may lead to an assessment that, all things considered, the act is justified. Where B consents, then the consent allows (but does not require) A to exclude some of the reasons against acting in that way based on the prima facie assumption that the act is contrary to B's well-being. This may lead the act to becoming justified. In colloquial terms, consent allows A to say: 'Well, B has considered the issue and decided that they want the act. I am willing to accept their assessment of what is good for them all things considered. After all B has capacity and has weighed all the evidence and I am willing to accept their assessment of what is in their best interests.'

I find that a very attractive way of accounting for consent, but a full explanation is beyond the scope of this chapter.[76] Let us assume that it is a correct understanding. Madden Dempsey highlights two consequences of this. The first is that it only operates insofar as the reasons against acting in the particular rest in B's well-being. B's consent cannot negate reasons against acting which are based on C's well-being. The fact that you consent to me uttering a racial insult to you does not provide a reason for me uttering the insult if others who hear it are distressed. These arguments are significant for the arguments raised under the heading 'Cultures of Repression' raised later in this chapter.

The second point (and the one relevant in this section of the chapter) is that it provides A with a justification only insofar as A acts *for* those reasons; in other words, A can rely on B's consent only if A is seeking to promote B's well-being (ie, is adopting the kind of reasoning summarised colloquially above). She argues that for a sadist, this is a problem:

> Despite B's consent, A keeps in play on his rational horizons (that is, A does not exclude) reasons he has not to punch B that are grounded in B's well-being, and A punches B, at least in part *for* reasons that are grounded in B's well-being. (That is, A's explanatory reasons include the fact that his conduct will cause B pain, injury, etc.) In such cases, despite B's consent, A's conduct nonetheless takes B as its victim; for, in virtue of A's sadistic explanatory reasons, B's consent failed to bear transformative normative force on the moral quality of A's conduct.[77]

In other words, because A is acting (in part) to cause B pain, A is acting in part against B's well-being. A has not properly used consent as completely taking over their assessment. I am not entirely convinced that this analysis applies in all BDSM cases, and Madden Dempsey is clear that she is not suggesting it does. First, where a defendant acts for mixed motives, it is not clear whether this defeats the justifying reason. Is a doctor who performs

---

[76] J Herring, 'Consent in the Criminal Law: The Importance of Relationality and Responsibility' in A Reed and M Bohlander (eds), *General Defences in Criminal Law* (Aldershot, Ashgate, 2014).

[77] Madden Dempsey, 'Victimless Conduct' 24.

an operation partly to help the patient, but also because they want to write about it in a journal doing anything very wrong as long as we believe that there was a justificatory reason? Second, we cannot assume that pain is contrary to a person's well-being. There are plenty of sensations which are somewhat complex. A tickle or the hot feeling caused by eating a curry seem pleasant to some and unpleasant to others. Other sensations contain elements of both pain and pleasure. In BDSM, it seems reasonable for A to say he is acting to give B an experience which will be both painful and pleasurable, and this is desired by B.

What Madden Dempsey has correctly highlighted is that there may be some cases where the consent should not operate as a defence in a BDSM (or, indeed, any consent case). There is where the defendant is motivated solely by his own desire for sexual gratification.[78] The model proposed requires A to be acting, at least in part, because B has consented and it is what B has assessed as in their best interests. One can imagine cases of BDSM involving prostituted people or a reluctant partner where this might not be so, or something like the *Emmett* case, where the defendant's sexual excitement meant that he failed to notice how his partner was responding because (presumably) he was overcome with the intensity of his own feelings. Indeed, this may be the best way of understanding what Lord Templeman was concerned about with his references to the defendant's actions being cruel.[79]

## B. Domestic Abuse

Perhaps the strongest argument against BDSM is that permitting it allows domestic abuse to take place without prosecution. It is not possible here to give a full account of domestic abuse and its nature.[80] I will, however, draw out two aspects which are particularly important. The first is that there is a growing understanding that 'coercive control' is at the heart of domestic abuse.[81] This is now recognised in statute. The new domestic abuse offence in section 76 of the Serious Crime Act 2015 states:

(1) A person (A) commits an offence if—

    (a)  A repeatedly or continuously engages in behaviour towards another person (B) that is controlling or coercive,

    (b)  at the time of the behaviour, A and B are personally connected,

---

[78] K Egan, 'Morality-Based Legislation is Alive and Well: Why the Law Permits Consent to Body Modification But Not Sadomasochistic Sex' (2007) 70 *Albany Law Review* 1615.

[79] *Brown* (n 1) 237.

[80] J Herring, 'The Meaning of Domestic Violence' (2011) 33 *Journal of Social Welfare and Family Law* 297.

[81] E Stark, *Coercive Control* (Oxford, Oxford University Press, 2007) 363.

(c)   the behaviour has a serious effect on B, and

(d)   A knows or ought to know that the behaviour will have a serious effect on B.

This approach to domestic abuse recognises that the behaviour should best be understood as a course of behaviour designed to control the other party. Psychologist Mary Ann Dutton explains:

> Abusive behaviour does not occur as a series of discrete events. Although a set of discrete abusive incidents can typically be identified within an abusive relationship, an understanding of the dynamic of power and control within an intimate relationship goes beyond these discrete incidents. To negate the impact of the time period between discrete episodes of serious violence—a time period during which the woman may never know when the next incident will occur, and may continue to live with on-going psychological abuse—is to fail to recognize what some battered woman experience as a continuing 'state of siege'.[82]

The second aspect of significance is that one of the features of domestic abuse is that the victim comes to believe that they deserve to be treated the way they do.[83] Their treatment is the proper punishment for their failure to satisfy their partners. They come to understand that violence is just punishment for the failure to obey their partner in all the minutiae of his commands.[84] With this understanding of domestic abuse in mind, let us recall again some of the English cases.

In *Emmett*, the defendant poured lighter fuel on his partner's breasts and set them alight, causing severe third-degree burns in a 24 cm squared area. He also put a plastic bag over her head and tightened it to the point that she could no long endure the pain and was unable to communicate with him. Pouring lighter fuel on someone's chest and setting it alight is not standard BDSM practise, nor is preventing the partner from using the safe word. Note that in this case, the victim went to see her doctor, who informed the police. She refused to give evidence in his defence.[85] The only person who knew her side of the story was the doctor and it is revealing that they decided to breach the duty of confidentiality that normally applies to doctor/patient communications and inform the police.[86] While we cannot know the truth, there must be a strong suspicion that this was simply a case of domestic violence to which the defendant gave the only defence he could: she wanted it. In cases where a domestic abuser is charged with assaulting their partner where there are proven injuries, explaining the injuries as the results of consensual sadomasochism is one of the few defences available to them and

---

[82] M Dutton, 'Understanding Women's Response to Domestic Violence' (2003) 21 *Hofstra Law Review* 1191, 1204.

[83] Stark, *Coercive Control* 363.

[84] ibid.

[85] *Emmett* (n 46).

[86] General Medical Council, *Confidentiality* (London, General Medical Council, 2009).

if the victim is too scared to give evidence, then it will be a hard defence for the prosecution to rebut. With that in mind, there is a strong case for saying that the defence of sadomasochism should not be available or, at the very least, that it must be proved by evidence from the victim.

In *Wilson*, Mr Wilson had branded his initials, W and A, on his wife's buttocks with a hot knife. She went to see the doctor and showed him what had happened. Again, the doctor notified the police, breaching patient confidentiality, and again the woman refused to give evidence in her husband's defence. Remarkably again, the court accepted the defendant's account. This time the court allowed the defence, as discussed earlier.[87] However, the branding of one's name on one's partner seems like the nadir for an abuser seeking the ultimate control over his spouse. It has all the hallmarks of coercive control referred to above.

In *Meachen*, the victim had been given a 'date rape drug' and had then been anally penetrated by a very large object, causing a serious injury requiring the permanent use of a colostomy bag. He claimed that she consented to this, although yet again the victim gave no evidence to support this. The court accepted that had she consented to this, he would have had a defence.[88] The case demonstrates the ease with which an abuser can rely on sadomasochism as a defence. In this case, the use of the drug appears to undermine the claim the case was one of consensual sex.

In *Lock*, also portrayed as a BDSM case, the woman had the words 'Property of Steven Lock' tattooed around her genitals. Lock chained the women 'like a dog' to his bedroom floor and whipped her repeatedly with a rope.[89] This case has all the hallmarks of the coercive control model of domestic abuse mentioned earlier.

Even if we look at *Brown* itself, there must be concerns over whether the relationship between the defendant and the victims was abusive. Lord Templeman asserted that the consents of the victims were 'dubious or worthless'.[90] He pointed out that the appellants were 'middle-aged men' and the victims were 'youths'.[91] They were recruited to join the activities through payment and it was said 'drink or drugs were employed to obtain consent'.[92] Again, we do not know where the truth lies for sure. Even if these suspicions are unfounded in *Brown* itself, there are certainly other cases where vulnerable people have manipulated into participating into sadomasochism without their consent.[93]

---

[87] *Wilson* (n 43).

[88] *R v Meachen* [2006] EWCA Crim 2414.

[89] B Kendall, 'Gardener Cleared of Assault after *Fifty Shades of Grey*-Inspired Sadomasochistic Sex Session' *The Independent* (London, 22 January 2013).

[90] *Brown* (n 1) 235.

[91] ibid 235.

[92] ibid 236.

[93] See, eg, *R v Keeble* [2001] EWCA Crim 1764.

With the understanding of domestic abuse mentioned earlier, these cases take on a very chilling aspect. Marianne Apostolides suggests that:

> [S]adomasochism involves a highly unbalanced power relationship established through role-playing, bondage, and/or the infliction of pain. The essential component is not the pain or bondage itself, but rather the knowledge that one person has complete control over the other, deciding what that person will hear, do, taste, touch, smell, and feel.[94]

This is precisely the kind of control the domestic abuser seeks to have over his victim. Frances Chapman in her study of sadism argues:

> [T]he essence of sadism lies in the ability 'to have complete mastery over another person, to make him-her [sic] a helpless object of our will, to become her God, to do with her as one pleases. To humiliate her, to enslave her are means to this end, and the most important radical aid is to make her suffer since there is no greater power over another person than that of inflicting pain on her to force her to undergo suffering without her being able to defend herself. The pleasure in the complete domination over another person is the very essence of the sadistic drive'.[95]

This kind concern becomes all the stronger in the cases mentioned earlier of lifestyle BDSM, where the whole relationship is characterised as a master/slave relationship.

So is there a way we can separate out 'consensual BDSM' and domestic abuse? Cheryl Hanna states that:

> If consent were allowed as a defense in the S/M context, defense attorneys would have carte blanche to raise it in every sexual assault case where the victim is injured. This would essentially gut rape law jurisprudence as it now stands. So too could defense attorneys raise the S/M defense in many cases of domestic violence, undermining the slow and steady strides the law has made in sanctioning male violence.[96]

Pa argues that the victim must testify at trial to corroborate a claim. An expert could give evidence on what good standard BDSM involves, such as the need for negotiations and revocable consent.[97]

Many of the writers on BDSM fail to put BDSM in the context of domestic violence. There are uncomfortable links between the cases where an abuser has sought to control his victim and every aspect of her life, and cases

[94] M Apostolides, 'The Pleasure of the Pain: Why Some People Need S & M' (1999) 32(5) *Psychology Today* 60, 61.

[95] F Chapman, 'Intangible Captivity: The Potential for A New Canadian Criminal Defense of Brainwashing and its Implications for the Battered Woman' (2013) 28 *Berkeley Journal of Gender, Law & Justice* 30, 59, quoting R Hazelwood et al, 'Compliant Victims of the Sexual Sadist' (1993) 22 *Australian Family Physician* 474, 478.

[96] C Hanna, 'Sex is Not a Sport: Consent and Violence in Criminal Law' (2001) 42 *Boston College Law Review* 239, 286.

[97] Pa, 'Beyond the Pleasure Principle' 78.

where a BDSM master has sought control of his slave. A fine example of the difficulties here is the novel *Fifty Shades of Grey*.[98] This has done more than anything to bring BDSM to the public attention. Yet many BDSM practitioners are very concerned at the portrayal, seeing it as 'the tale of an abusive relationship in which a reluctant, inexperienced and infatuated young girl is controlled and beaten by a rich sadist'.[99] Professor Amy Bonomi has condemned the novel as a 'glaring glamorization of violence against women'.[100] The story does not appear to include the hallmarks of negotiated consent that is seen as key to a good BDSM encounter, although not all practitioners agree. Yet here is the problem. Is *Fifty Shades* a tale of sexual experimental BDSM or a description of an abusive relationship? It is not clear. And that is revealing.

The argument I would made is that a straight reversal of *Brown* would completely fail to protect the rights of victims of domestic violence. It would breach our human rights obligations to protect victims of domestic abuse.[101] We need to make sure that domestic violence abusers cannot escape being held to account by claiming that their actions were consensual BDSM, which I suspect happens too often at the moment. It may require a reversal of burden of proof so that those claiming that BDSM was consensual must prove that by producing evidence from the alleged victim and demonstrating that their activities were in the context of a mutually respecting, autonomy-enhancing relationship.

## C. Cultures of Repression

In *Brown*, the House of Lords' analysis of sadomasochism was focused on a particularly masculine form of BDSM and did not consider the relationship between women and BDSM. Radical feminists have long argued that BDSM reflects and reinforces patriarchy and racism.[102] The claim is most convincing in relation to certain forms of BDSM where, for example, the sadist role is performed by the man and the masochist role is performed by the woman. In such a case, assuming there is genuine consent, there is an argument that

---

[98] J Horn, 'Fifty Shades of Oppression: Sadomasochism, Feminism, and the Law' (2015) 4 *Journal of Women, Gender and the Law* 1.

[99] Emer O'Toole, 'This Murder in Ireland Has Made Me Rethink My Sexual Practices' *The Guardian* (London, 31 March 2015).

[100] Quoted in R Berl, 'What's Wrong with "50 Shades of Grey"', http://health.usnews.com/health-news/health-wellness/articles/2013/08/12/whats-wrong-with-50-shades-of-grey-and-what-you-should-know-about-bdsm.

[101] J Herring and S Choudhry, 'Righting Domestic Violence' (2006) 20 *International Journal of Law Policy and the Family* 95.

[102] M Deckha, 'Pain, Pleasure, and Consenting Women: Exploring Feminist Responses to S/M and its Legal Regulation in Canada through Jelinek's *The Piano Teacher*' (2007) 30 *Harvard Journal of Law and Gender* 425.

the couple are re-enacting rape and/or sexual torture for sexual pleasure. Similar kinds of concerns might arise in respect to race or religion when slave or Nazi themes are used, which reflect racial torturing for other sexual pleasure. While many people would feel concern about these instances of BDSM, is there any basis for rendering them illegal?

One argument might be that the consent in such cases must be questioned. Does the woman who enacts finding pleasure being 'raped' or the black woman who agrees to being abused as a 'slave' consent or are these individuals simply reflecting a desire deformed by 'sexual regime fundamentally marked by male sexual coercion'.[103] As Deckha puts the argument:

> Because of their enculturation into a general overarching sadomasochistic patriarchal culture, women are unable to conceptualize their femininity, sexuality, and desirability to a man in a relationship of equals. Instead, they rely on a relationship of dominance and subservience both to be aroused and make themselves desirable to men. The contention is not that women who prefer the masochist role sublimate their sexual desires to those of their male partners, but rather that practices and discourses of gendering have socialized them to eroticize violence and have constrained their ability to formulate sexual desire outside of traditional patterns of male dominance.[104]

Catherine Mackinnon writes that: 'Dominance, principally by men, and submission, principally by women, [is currently] the ruling code through which sexual pleasure is experienced.'[105] In such a society, can we know the extent to which there is genuine consent?

The difficulty with this argument is that it might claim too much. Arguably, any sexual encounter, whether marked by BDSM or not, can be the product of 'distorted' desires. However, where oppressed groups declare that they enjoy acting out activities which mimic the tools of their oppression, questions acutely arise as to the extent to which these are values taken on by the individual as their own,[106] particularly where those tools (eg, rape or torture) are commonly justified on the basis that the victims 'wanted it really'. BDSM appears to reinforce the rape myths that 'women say no when they mean yes' and 'women will "consent" if some pressure is used' and even 'women enjoy being raped'. The difficulty is that in BDSM, these myths might appear to be reinforced, in which case we have what John Stoltenberg has called the 'eroticization of violence'.[107]

---

[103] ibid 432.

[104] ibid 433.

[105] Catharine A Mackinnon, *Feminism Unmodified* (Cambridge MA, Harvard University Press, 1987) 7.

[106] Anon, 'Nonbinding Bondage' (2014) 128 *Harvard Law Review* 713.

[107] J Stoltenberg, 'Sadomasochism: Eroticized Violence, Eroticized Powerlessness' in R Linden, D Pagano, D Russell and S Star (eds), *Against Sadomasochism: A Radical Feminist Analysis* (Palo Alto, CA, Frog in the Well Publishers) 126.

We could look at the behaviour as a form of hate speech. As Cheryl Hanna puts it:

The language of S/M—slave, master, bondage, domination—may have a particular meaning within consensual sexual activities, but it derives from a history of legal racism and slavery. It is important to understand the multiple and complex meaning of these concepts and why, for some at least, the whole notion of S/M could be considered dehumanizing when examined within a larger cultural context.[108]

This may tie into the arguments mentioned previously under the heading 'Intent of the Actor'. Where the intent is not focused on meeting the desires of the victim, but rather expressing hatred, the justifications for BDSM become much weaker. Not only that, but, as already mentioned, it appears to reinforce the rape myths that apparently non-consenting women are enjoying the experience of rape. The difficulty is this. BDSM practitioners accept that they 'play' with the values of objectification, domination and power within society. Can they reach out beyond these? Is it possible to re-enact and play with the values without adopting those values?[109]

BDSM practitioners reject such questions. They argue that there is no violence where the behaviour is consensual. Critics, they say, fail to appreciate that their acts are fantasies that bear no relation to real events.[110] Their actions are better understood as similar to drama exploring themes surrounding sexual domination or slavery. No one watching or participating in the film *Schindler's List* would be said to be encouraging or reproducing Nazism.[111] Nor would a person watching or participating in a drama in which a rape was portrayed understand the activity to be supporting rape.[112] Hopkins argues that sadomasochism should be conceptualised 'as a performance, as a staging, a production, a simulation in which participants are writers, producers, directors, actors, and audience' and that the objectionable essence of the behaviours (harm, oppression and violation) 'are absent'.[113] He suggests that the sadomasochist would detest real violence or sexism just as a rider on a rollercoaster would hate really hurtling to the ground.[114]

---

[108] C Hanna, 'Sex is Not a Sport' 287.

[109] T Bennett, 'Persecution or Play? Law and the Ethical Significance of Sadomasochism' (2014) *Social and Legal Studies* 914.

[110] J Butler, 'Lesbian S&M: The Politics of Dis-illusion' in Linden et al, *Against Sadomasochism* 172.

[111] N-H Stear, 'Sadomasochism as Make-Believe' (2009) 24 *Hypatia* 1.

[112] Pa, 'Beyond the Pleasure Principle' 78.

[113] P Hopkins, 'Rethinking Sadomasochism: Feminism, Interpretation and Simulation' (1994) 9 *Hypatia* 116, 123.

[114] Stear, 'Sadomasochism as Make-Believe' 29 argues that 'role-play SM is a means by which individuals enter into make-believe games' and therefore sadomasochism should not be compared 'to theatre, but to the engagement with or enjoyment of theatre, from the point of view of the audience'.

There are some difficulties with this explanation. First, unlike a play, real people are being hurt. BDSM is not like actors in a Shakespearean play acting out a duel or actors performing a rape.[115] There is real blood being spilled.[116] If BDSM were just play acting, why not re-enact as actors do without any injury being caused?

Second, while a drama like *Schindler's List* is designed to engender horror and a determination to prevent the acts occurring again, for BDSM participants, the acts are designed to give them pleasure. It is not obviously calling for the behaviour to stop or being critical of it. This is significant because of the impact of the re-enactment of those who have been affected. As Hein puts it:

> To treat with levity a self-chosen condition of humiliation which is a hated oppression to multitudes of other people is to reduce their suffering to a mockery. Every joyous torturer and willing torture negates and denies the real agony of six million Jews, countless Blacks and untold numbers of others whose victimization remains substantial and involuntary.[117]

Third, consider further Hopkin's point that the rollercoaster can be enjoyed without any enjoyment of hitting the ground. The problem is that riding the rollercoaster would be enjoyable even if hitting the ground were impossible (or was not a danger). But the 'fantasies' of slave abuse, Nazi concentration camps and rape depend for their pleasure on the fact that these events occurred. Why else choose Nazi re-enactment, other than for the fact that it was a real event? As Vadas emphasises, 'to take pleasure in SM is to make one's pleasure contingent on the actual occurrence and meanings of rape, racist enslavement, and so on'.[118] She goes on to say:

> The context that gives the meaning of rape to rape is the context of sexualized dominance and submission-of dominance and submission as sex itself-and it is this context that is purposely and seamlessly reproduced by SM practitioners in their simulations of rape and other unjust acts.[119]

But, even at their strongest, do these concerns raise a matter for the criminal law? Is it any different from a person who watches a rape scene in a film and finds it sexually exciting? That might be in bad taste and inappropriate, but not for the intervention of the criminal law.[120] Yet the description of 'bad taste' is not strong enough.[121] For the victim of sexual torture, their ordeal

---

[115] Hopkins, 'Rethinking Sadomasochism'.

[116] T Hoople, 'Conflicting Visions: SM, Feminism, and the Law: A Problem of Representation' (1996) 11 *Canadian Journal of Law & Society* 177, 206.

[117] H Hein, 'Sadomasochism and the Liberal Tradition' in Linden et al, *Against Sadomasochism* 87.

[118] M Vadas, 'Reply to Patrick Hopkins' (1995) 10 *Hypatia* 159.

[119] ibid 160–61.

[120] C Stychin, *Law's Desire* (New York, Routledge, 1995).

[121] S Hawthorne, 'Ancient Hatred and its Contemporary Manifestation: The Torture of Lesbians' (2006) 4 *Journal of Hate Studies* 33, 40.

is re-enacted by the parties for the sexual pleasure. It is not done to inform or educate on the horrors of the act. Not only does it not do that, it repeats those rape myths mentioned earlier that, despite the appearances, women enjoy rape.[122] Hence, Susan Hawthlorne argues that BDSM practitioners are 'appropriating the experiences of oppressed peoples'.[123] She explains:

> The practitioners of S/M turn an uncontrollable experience of torture into a game that can be stopped (but people undergoing real torture do not have the option of saying no) ... It is expropriation of experience. It is ultimately full of contempt for others.

> In a society in which torture can be described as 'performative' or as 'direct communication with Iraqi prisoners' and BDSM can be presented as a series of classes to those interested in 'healing themselves' or simply interested in the experience of powerfulness, these are central questions of social health.[124]

BDSM practitioners cannot escape so easily from the social practice they reflect, or from the impact of their activities on cultural perceptions about sex and violence.[125] As the European Convention on Human Rights acknowledges, the state is under a positive duty to take steps to prevent sexual violence and domestic abuse against women. Restrictions on BDSM can be justified on that basis.

## IX. CONCLUSION

This chapter has explored the decision in *Brown*. Quite rightly, it has been subject to considerable criticism. The reasoning used, especially as developed in some subsequent case law, is as prejudiced and illogical as many have argued. However, this chapter has argued that it would be wrong to think that *Brown* should simply be reversed. This chapter has raised issues which were not expressly considered by their Lordships, yet provide far stronger concerns about BDSM than were raised in the judgments. William Wilson questions whether the decision in *Brown* can be justified as necessary in the public interest. He writes: 'As things now stand, no threat to society's moral integrity is likely to result from the esoteric practices of a group of homosexuals, beyond the bursting of the odd blood vessel suffered by "Outraged of Tunbridge Wells".'[126]

---

[122] J Warren and R Hazelwood, 'Relational Patterns Associated with Sexual Sadism: A Study of 20 Wives and Girlfriends' (2002) 17 *Journal of Family Violence* 75.

[123] Hawthorne, 'Ancient Hatred and its Contemporary Manifestation' 43.

[124] ibid 40.

[125] K Miriam, 'From Rage to all the Rage: Lesbian-Feminism, Sadomasochism and the Politics of Memory' in I Reti (ed), *Unleashing Feminism: Critiquing Lesbian Sadomasochism in the Gay Nineties* (Santa Cruz, Herbooks, 1993) 36.

[126] W Wilson, 'Is Hurting People Wrong?' (1992) *Journal of Social Welfare and Family Law* 388, 392.

Yet this chapter has suggested that this overlooks three categories of case where criminalisation is justified. The first is where the defendant is acting for his own pleasure and is not motivated by the consent of the victim. Second, we need to be aware of the international obligations to protect women from domestic abuse and the way in which BDSM has been used (hijacked maybe) by those perpetrating domestic abuse. Third, it has also been argued that the activities mimic slavery, rape and torture against oppressed groups for the pleasure of the members of the group, which in a way reinforces negative messages about them.

So, what is the way ahead? First, I would recommend that invoking consensual BDSM as a defence should only succeed in cases where the participants prove positive consent to the activities as part of a relationship not marked by inequality. Contracts, signed in advance, are becoming increasingly common in BDSM circles and could be used to provide evidence of consent. Second, I would keep illegal BDSM activities which involve using the themes of rape, racist violence or other forms of torture.

*Brown* provides a fascinating insight into the judicial insight. An issue underpinning this chapter is what it says about masculinity, remembering that the judges hearing the case were all male. The disgust at the physical acts done, the fear of the homosexuality and the discomfort at the hyper-masculinity of the violent gay may are all apparent in the judgment. But what I have claimed in this chapter is that a preoccupation with the 'masculine' concerns led to an oversight of the real dangers in BDSM for women and racially disadvantaged groups, the invisibility of domestic violence and the implied perpetuation of rape myths.

# Index

Lightning Source UK Ltd.
Milton Keynes UK
UKHW021536131219
355331UK00002B/43/P